BERLITZ PHRASE BOOKS

World's bestselling phrase books feature not only expressions and vocabulary you'll need, but also travel tips, useful facts and pronunciation throughout. The handiest and most readable conversation aid available.

Arabic	French	Portuguese
Chinese	German	Russian
Danish	Greek	Serbo-Croatian
Dutch	Hebrew	Spanish
European (14 languages)	Hungarian	Latin-American Spanish
	Italian	
European Menu Reader	Japanese	Swahili
	Norwegian	Swedish
Finnish	Polish	Turkish

BERLITZ CASSETTEPAKS

Most of the above-mentioned titles are also available combined with a cassette to help you improve your accent. A helpful 32-page script is included containing the complete text of the dual language hi-fi recording.

Berlitz Dictionaries

Dansk	Engelsk, Fransk, Italiensk, Spansk, Tysk
Deutsch	Dänisch, Englisch, Finnisch, Französisch, Italienisch, Niederländisch, Norwegisch, Portugiesisch, Schwedisch, Spanisch
English	Danish, Dutch, Finnish, French, German, Italian, Norwegian, Portuguese, Spanish, Swedish
Espãnol	Alemán, Danés, Finlandés, Francés, Holandés, Inglés, Noruego, Sueco
Français	Allemand, Anglais, Danois, Espagnol, Finnois, Italien, Néerlandais, Norvégien, Portugais, Suédois
Italiano	Danese, Finlandese, Francese, Inglese, Norvegese, Olandese, Svedese, Tedesco
Nederlands	Duits, Engels, Frans, Italiaans, Portugees, Spaans
Norsk	Engelsk, Fransk, Italiensk, Spansk, Tysk
Português	Alemão, Francês, Holandês, Inglês, Sueco
Suomi	Englanti, Espanja, Italia, Ranska, Ruotsi, Saksa
Svenska	Engelska, Finska, Franska, Italienska, Portugisiska, Spanska, Tyska

BERLITZ®

italian-english english-italian dictionary

dizionario italiano-inglese inglese-italiano

By the Staff of Editions Berlitz

Revised edition 1979
Library of Congress Catalog Card Number: 78-78081

7th printing 1985
Printed in Switzerland

Contents

Indice

Preface

In selecting the 12.500 word-concepts in each language for this dictionary, the editors have had the traveller's needs foremost in mind. This book will prove invaluable to all the millions of travellers, tourists and business people who appreciate the reassurance a small and practical dictionary can provide. It offers them—as it does beginners and students—all the basic vocabulary they are going to encounter and to have to use, giving the key words and expressions to allow them to cope in everyday situations.

Like our successful phrase books and travel guides, these dictionaries—created with the help of a computer data bank—are designed to slip into pocket or purse, and thus have a role as handy companions at all times.

Besides just about everything you normally find in dictionaries, there are these Berlitz bonuses:

- imitated pronunciation next to each foreign-word entry, making it easy to read and enunciate words whose spelling may look forbidding
- a unique, practical glossary to simplify reading a foreign restaurant menu and to take the mystery out of complicated dishes and indecipherable names on bills of fare
- useful information on how to tell the time and how to count, on conjugating irregular verbs, commonly seen abbreviations and converting to the metric system, in addition to basic phrases.

While no dictionary of this size can pretend to completeness, we expect the user of this book will feel well armed to affront foreign travel with confidence. We should, however, be very pleased to receive comments, criticism and suggestions that you think may be of help in preparing future editions.

Prefazione

Selezionando le 12.500 parole-concetti in ogni lingua di questo dizionario, i nostri redattori hanno tenuto conto innanzitutto delle necessità di chi viaggia. Questo libro si rivelerà prezioso per i milioni di turisti, viaggiatori, uomini d'affari che apprezzano il contributo che può dare un dizionario pratico e di formato ridotto. Di grande utilità sarà anche per i principianti e gli studenti, perchè contiene tutti i vocaboli di base che sentiranno e dovranno usare, oltre a parole-chiave ed espressioni che permettono di affrontare situazioni correnti.

Come i nostri manuali di conversazione e le nostre guide turistiche, già molto apprezzate, questi dizionari – realizzati grazie a una banca dei dati su ordinatore – hanno la dimensione giusta per scivolare in una tasca o in una borsetta, diventando così i compagni indispensabili di ogni momento.

Oltre a tutto quanto si trova normalmente in un dizionario, i nostri volumetti contengono:

- una trascrizione fonetica accanto a ogni lemma, al fine di facilitarne la lettura; ciò si rivela particolarmente utile per quelle parole che sembrano impronunciabili
- un pratico lessico gastronomico, inteso a semplificare la lettura del menù in un ristorante straniero e a svelare i misteri di pietanze complicate e di nomi indecifrabili sui conti
- preziose informazioni sul modo di esprimere il tempo, di contare, sui verbi irregolari, sulle abbreviazioni e le conversioni nel sistema metrico, oltre alle espressioni più correnti.

Nessun dizionario di questo formato può pretendere di essere completo, ma il suo scopo è di permettere a chi lo usa di affrontare con fiducia un viaggio all'estero. Naturalmente saremo lieti di ricevere commenti, critiche e suggerimenti che potrebbero essere di aiuto nella preparazione di future edizioni.

italian-english

italiano-inglese

Introduction

The dictionary has been designed to take account of your practical needs. Unnecessary linguistic information has been avoided. The entries are listed in alphabetical order, regardless of whether the entry word is printed in a single word or in two or more separate words. As the only exception to this rule, a few idiomatic expressions are listed alphabetically as main entries, by order of the most significant word in the expression. When an entry is followed by sub-entries such as expressions and locutions, these, too, have been listed in alphabetical order.

Each main-entry word is followed by a phonetic transcription (see Guide to pronunciation). Following the transcription is the part of speech of the entry word, whenever applicable. When an entry word may be used as more than one part of speech, the translations are grouped together after the respective part of speech.

Irregular plurals of nouns are shown in brackets after the part of speech.

Whenever an entry word is repeated in irregular plurals or in sub-entries, a tilde (~) is used to represent the full entry word.

An asterisk (*) in front of a verb indicates that the verb is irregular. For details, refer to the lists or irregular verbs.

Abbreviations

adj	adjective	*num*	numeral
adv	adverb	*p*	past tense
Am	American	*pl*	plural
art	article	*plAm*	plural (American)
conj	conjunction	*pp*	past participle
f	feminine	*pr*	present tense
fpl	feminine plural	*pref*	prefix
m	masculine	*prep*	preposition
mpl	masculine plural	*pron*	pronoun
n	noun	*v*	verb
nAm	noun (American)	*vAm*	verb (American)

Guide to Pronunciation

Each main entry in this part of the dictionary is followed by a phonetic transcription which shows you how to pronounce the words. This transcription should be read as if it were English. It is based on Standard British pronunciation, though we have tried to take account of General American pronunciation also. Below, only those letters and symbols are explained which we consider likely to be ambiguous or not immediately understood.

The syllables are separated by hyphens, and stressed syllables are printed in *italics*.

Of course, the sounds of any two languages are never exactly the same, but if you follow carefully our indications, you should be able to pronounce the foreign words in such a way that you'll be understood. To make your task easier, our transcriptions occasionally simplify slightly the sound system of the language while still reflecting the essential sound differences.

Consonants

g always hard, as in **g**o
l^{y} like **lli** in mi**lli**on
ñ as in Spanish se**ñ**or, or like **ni** in o**ni**on
r slightly rolled in the front of the mouth
s always hard, as in **s**o
y always as in **y**et, not as in eas**y**

Vowels and Diphthongs

aa long **a**, as in c**a**r
ah a short version of **aa**; between **a** in c**a**t and **u** in c**u**t
ai like **air**, without any **r**-sound
eh like **e** in g**e**t
igh as in s**igh**
o always as in h**o**t (British pronunciation)
ou as in l**ou**d

1) A bar over a vowel symbol (e.g. $\overline{\mathbf{oo}}$) shows that this sound is long.

2) Raised letters (e.g. **ah**$^{\mathbf{ay}}$, **eh**$^{\mathbf{oo}}$) should be pronounced only fleetingly.

3) Italian vowels (i.e. not diphthongs) are pure. Therefore, you should try to read a transcription like **oa** without moving tongue or lips while pronouncing the sound.

4) A few Italian words borrowed from French contain nasal vowels, which we transcribe with a vowel symbol plus **~~ng~~** (e.g. **o~~ng~~**). This **~~ng~~** should *not* be pronounced, and serves solely to indicate nasal quality of the preceding vowel. A nasal vowel is pronounced simultaneously through the mouth and the nose.

A

a (ah) *prep* at; to; on
abbagliante (ahb-bah-*lyahn*-tay) *adj* glaring
abbagliare (ahb-bah-*lyaa*-ray) *v* blind
abbaiare (ahb-bah-*yaa*-ray) *v* bark
abbandonare (ahb-bahn-doa-*naa*-ray) *v* abandon
abbassare (ahb-bahss-*saa*-ray) *v* lower
abbastanza (ahb-bah-*stahn*-tsah) *adv* enough; fairly, rather, pretty, quite
abbattere (ahb-*baht*-tay-ray) *v* knock down, fell; dishearten
abbattuto (ahb-bah-*too*-toa) *adj* low, down
abbigliamento sportivo (ahb-bee-lyah-*mayn*-toa spoar-*tee*-voa) sportswear
abbigliare (ahb-bee-*lyaa*-ray) *v* dress
abbonamento (ahb-boa-nah-*mayn*-toa) *m* subscription; season-ticket
abbonato (ahb-boa-*naa*-toa) *m* subscriber
abbondante (ahb-boan-*dahn*-tay) *adj* plentiful, abundant
abbondanza (ahb-boan-*dahn*-tsah) *f* plenty, abundance
abbottonare (ahb-boat-toa-*naa*-ray) *v* button
abbozzare (ahb-boat-*tsaa*-ray) *v* sketch
abbracciare (ahb-braht-*chaa*-ray) *v* embrace, hug
abbraccio (ahb-*braht*-choa) *m* embrace, hug
abbreviazione (ahb-bray-vyah-*tsyoa*-nay) *f* abbreviation
abbronzato (ahb-broan-*dzaa*-toa) *adj* tanned
abbronzatura (ahb-broan-dzah-*too*-rah) *f* sunburn
aberrazione (ah-bayr-rah-*tsyoa*-nay) *f* aberration
abete (ah-*bay*-tay) *m* fir-tree
abile (*aa*-bee-lay) *adj* able; skilled, skilful
abilità (ah-bee-lee-*tah*) *f* capacity, ability; art, skill
abilitare (ah-bee-lee-*taa*-ray) *v* enable
abisso (ah-*beess*-soa) *m* abyss
abitabile (ah-bee-*taa*-bee-lay) *adj* inhabitable, habitable
abitante (ah-bee-*tahn*-tay) *m* inhabitant
abitare (ah-bee-*taa*-ray) *v* live; inhabit; reside
abitazione (ah-bee-tah-*tsyoa*-nay) *f* house; home
abito (*aa*-bee-toa) *m* frock; suit; **abiti** clothes *pl*; ~ **da sera** evening dress; ~ **femminile** robe, dress
abituale (ah-bee-*twaa*-lay) *adj* common, customary
abitualmente (ah-bee-twahl-*mayn*-tay) *adv* usually

abituare (ah-bee-*twaa*-ray) *v* accustom
abitudine (ah-bee-*tōō*-dee-nay) *f* habit; custom; routine
abolire (ah-boa-*lee*-ray) *v* abolish
aborto (ah-*bor*-toa) *m* miscarriage; abortion
abramide (ah-brah-*mee*-day) *m* bream
abuso (ah-*bōō*-zoa) *m* misuse, abuse
accademia (ahk-kah-*dai*-myah) *f* academy; ~ **di belle arti** art school
***accadere** (ahk-kah-*dāy*-ray) *v* occur, happen
accamparsi (ahk-kahm-*pahr*-see) *v* camp
accanto (ahk-*kahn*-toa) *adv* next-door; ~ **a** beside
accappatoio (ahk-kahp-pah-*tōā*-yoa) *m* bathrobe
accelerare (aht-chay-lay-*raa*-ray) *v* accelerate
accelerato (aht-chay-lay-*raa*-toa) *m* stopping train
acceleratore (aht-chay-lay-rah-*tōā*-ray) *m* accelerator
***accendere** (aht-*chehn*-day-ray) *v* *light; turn on, switch on
accendino (aht-chayn-*dee*-noa) *m* cigarette-lighter, lighter
accennare (aht-chayn-*naa*-ray) *v* beckon; ~ **a** allude to
accensione (aht-chayn-*syōā*-nay) *f* ignition; contact; **bobina di** ~ ignition coil
accento (aht-*chehn*-toa) *m* accent; stress
accerchiare (aht-chayr-*kyaa*-ray) *v* circle, encircle
accertare (aht-chayr-*taa*-ray) *v* ascertain
accessibile (aht-chayss-*see*-bee-lay) *adj* accessible
accesso (aht-*chehss*-soa) *m* access; approach, entrance
accessori (aht-chayss-*sōā*-ree) *mpl* accessories *pl*
accessorio (aht-chayss-*sōā*-ryoa) *adj* additional
accettare (aht-chayt-*taa*-ray) *v* accept
acchiappare (ahk-kyahp-*paa*-ray) *v* *catch
acciaio (aht-*chaa*-yoa) *m* steel; ~ **inossidabile** stainless steel
accidentato (aht-chee-dayn-*taa*-toa) *adj* bumpy
acciuga (aht-*chōō*-gah) *f* anchovy
acclamare (ahk-klah-*maa*-ray) *v* cheer
***accludere** (ahk-*klōō*-day-ray) *v* enclose
accoglienza (ahk-koa-*lʸehn*-tsah) *f* reception, welcome
***accogliere** (ahk-*kaw*-lʸay-ray) *v* welcome; accept
accomodamento (ahk-koa-moa-dah-*mayn*-toa) *m* arrangement, settlement
accompagnare (ahk-koam-pah-*ñaa*-ray) *v* accompany; *take
acconciatura (ahk-koan-chah-*tōō*-rah) *f* hair-do
acconsentire (ahk-koan-sayn-*tee*-ray) *v* consent
accontentato (ahk-koan-tayn-*taa*-toa) *adj* satisfied
acconto (ahk-*koan*-toa) *m* down payment
accordare (ahk-koar-*daa*-ray) *v* grant, extend; **accordarsi** *v* agree
accordo (ahk-*kor*-doa) *m* agreement, settlement; approval; deal; **d'accordo**! okay!
***accorgersi di** (ahk-*kor*-jayr-see) notice
***accorrere** (ahk-*koar*-ray-ray) *v* rush
accreditare (ahk-kray-dee-*taa*-ray) *v* credit
***accrescersi** (ahk-kraysh-*shayr*-see) *v* increase
accudire a (ahk-koo-*dee*-ray) attend to

accumulatore (ahk-koo-moo-lah-*tōā*-ray) *m* battery
accurato (ahk-koo-*raa*-toa) *adj* careful, accurate; thorough
accusa (ahk-*kōō*-zah) *f* charge
accusare (ahk-koo-*zaa*-ray) *v* accuse; charge
accusato (ahk-koo-*zaa*-toa) *m* accused
acero (*ah*-chay-roa) *m* maple
aceto (ah-*chāy*-toa) *m* vinegar
acido (ah-*chee*-doa) *m* acid
acne (*ahk*-nay) *f* acne
acqua (*ahk*-kwah) *f* water; ~ **corrente** running water; ~ **dentifricia** mouthwash; ~ **di mare** sea-water; ~ **di seltz** soda-water; ~ **dolce** fresh water; ~ **ghiacciata** iced water; ~ **minerale** mineral water; ~ **ossigenata** *m* peroxide; ~ **potabile** drinking-water
acquaforte (ahk-kwah-*for*-tay) *f* etching
acquazzone (ahk-kwaht-*tsōā*-nay) *m* shower, downpour
acquerello (ahk-kway-*rehl*-loa) *m* water-colour
acquisizione (ahk-kwee-zee-*tsyōā*-nay) *f* acquisition
acquistare (ahk-kwee-*staa*-ray) *v* *buy
acquisto (ahk-*kwee*-stoa) *m* purchase
acuto (ah-*kōō*-toa) *adj* acute
adattare (ah-daht-*taa*-ray) *v* adapt; adjust, suit
adatto (ah-*daht*-toa) *adj* proper, suitable, fit; appropriate
addestramento (ahd-day-strah-*mayn*-toa) *m* training
addestrare (ahd-day-*straa*-ray) *v* train, drill
addio (ahd-*dee*-oa) *m* parting
* **addirsi** (ahd-*deer*-see) *v* *become, suit; qualify
additare (ahd-dee-*taa*-ray) *v* point
addizionare (ahd-dee-tsyoa-*naa*-ray) *v* add, count
addizionatrice (ahd-dee-tsyoa-nah-*tree*-chay) *f* adding-machine
addizione (ahd-dee-*tsyōā*-nay) *f* addition
addolcitore (ahd-doal-chee-*tōā*-ray) *m* water-softener
addomesticare (ahd-doa-may-stee-*kaa*-ray) *v* tame; **addomesticato** tame
addormentato (ahd-doar-mayn-*taa*-toa) *adj* asleep
adeguato (ah-day-*gwaa*-toa) *adj* adequate; suitable
adempiere (ah-*dehm*-pyay-ray) *v* accomplish
adempimento (ah-daym-pee-*mayn*-toa) *m* achievement
adesso (ah-*dehss*-soa) *adv* now
adiacente (ah-dyah-*chehn*-tay) *adj* neighbouring
adolescente (ah-doa-laysh-*shehn*-tay) *m* teenager
adoperare (ah-doa-pay-*raa*-ray) *v* use
adorabile (ah-doa-*raa*-bee-lay) *adj* adorable
adottare (ah-doat-*taa*-ray) *v* adopt; borrow
adulto (ah-*dool*-toa) *adj* grown-up, adult; *m* grown-up, adult
aerare (ah^{ay}-*raa*-ray) *v* ventilate
aerazione (ah^{ay}-rah-*tsyōā*-nay) *f* ventilation
aereo (ah-*ai*-ray-oa) *m* plane, aircraft; ~ **a reazione** turbojet
aerodromo (ah^{ay}-*ro*-dro-moa) *m* airfield
aeroplano (ah^{ay}-roa-*plaa*-noa) *m* aeroplane; airplane *nAm*
aeroporto (ah^{ay}-roa-*por*-toa) *m* airport
affabile (ahf-*faa*-bee-lay) *adj* friendly
affacciarsi (ahf-faht-*chahr*-see) *v* appear
affamato (ahf-fah-*maa*-toa) *adj* hungry
affare (ahf-*faa*-ray) *m* matter, affair,

business; bargain; deal; **affari** business; ***fare affari con** *deal with; **per affari** on business
affascinante (ahf-fahsh-shee-*nahn*-tay) *adj* glamorous, enchanting, charming
affascinare (ahf-fahsh-shee-*naa*-ray) *v* fascinate
affastellare (ahf-fah-stayl-*laa*-ray) *v* bundle
affaticato (ahf-fah-tee-*kaa*-toa) *adj* weary, tired
affatto (ahf-*faht*-toa) *adv* at all
affermare (ahf-fayr-*maa*-ray) *v* state
affermativo (ahf-fayr-mah-*tee*-voa) *adj* affirmative
afferrare (ahf-fayr-*raa*-ray) *v* grasp, *catch, seize; *take
affettato (ahf-fayt-*taa*-toa) *adj* affected
affetto (ahf-*feht*-toa) *m* affection
affettuoso (ahf-fayt-*twōā*-soa) *adj* affectionate
affezionato a (ahf-fay-tsyoa-*naa*-toa ah) attached to
affezione (ahf-fay-*tsyōā*-nay) *f* affection, ailment
affidare (ahf-fee-*daa*-ray) *v* commit
affilare (ahf-fee-*laa*-ray) *v* sharpen
affilato (ahf-fee-*laa*-toa) *adj* sharp
affinché (ahf-feeng-*kay*) *conj* so that
affisso (ahf-*feess*-soa) *m* placard
affittacamere (ahf-feet-tah-*kaa*-may-ray) *m* landlord; *f* landlady
affittare (ahf-feet-*taa*-ray) *v* *let; rent
affitto (ahf-*feet*-toa) *m* rent; ***dare in** ~ lease; ***prendere in** ~ lease
***affliggersi** (ahf-fleed-*jayr*-see) *v* grieve
afflitto (ahf-*fleet*-toa) *adj* sad
afflizione (ahf-flee-*tsyōā*-nay) *f* affliction; grief
affogare (ahf-foa-*gaa*-ray) *v* drown; **affogarsi** *v* *be drowned
affollato (ahf-foal-*laa*-toa) *adj* crowded
affondare (ahf-foan-*daa*-ray) *v* *sink
affrancare (ahf-frahng-*kaa*-ray) *v* stamp
affrancatura (ahf-frahng-kah-*tōō*-rah) *f* postage
affrettarsi (ahf-frayt-*tahr*-see) *v* rush, hasten, hurry
affrontare (ahf-froan-*taa*-ray) *v* tackle, face
Africa (*aa*-free-kah) *f* Africa; **Africa del Sud** South Africa
africano (ah-free-*kaa*-noa) *adj* African; *m* African
agenda (ah-*jehn*-dah) *f* diary; agenda
agente (ah-*jehn*-tay) *m* policeman; agent; ~ **di viaggio** travel agent; ~ **immobiliare** house agent
agenzia (ah-jayn-*tsee*-ah) *f* agency; ~ **viaggi** travel agency
agevolazione (ah-jay-voa-lah-*tsyōā*-nay) *f* facility
aggeggio (ahd-*jayd*-joa) *m* gadget
aggettivo (ahd-jayt-*tee*-voa) *m* adjective
aggiudicare (ahd-joo-dee-*kaa*-ray) *v* award
***aggiungere** (ahd-*joon*-jay-ray) *v* add
aggiunta (ahd-*joon*-tah) *f* addition; **in ~ a** beyond
aggiustamento (ahd-joo-stah-*mayn*-toa) *m* settlement
aggredire (ahg-gray-*dee*-ray) *v* assault
aggressivo (ahg-grayss-*see*-voa) *adj* aggressive
agiato (ah-*jaa*-toa) *adj* well-to-do
agile (*ah*-jee-lay) *adj* supple
agio (*aa*-joa) *m* comfort, ease
agire (ah-*jee*-ray) *v* act; operate
agitare (ah-jee-*taa*-ray) *v* *shake
agitazione (ah-jee-tah-*tsyōā*-nay) *f* excitement, unrest
aglio (*aa*-lʸoa) *m* garlic
agnello (ah-*ñehl*-loa) *m* lamb
ago (*aa*-goa) *m* needle

agosto (ah-*goa*-stoa) August
agricolo (ah-*gree*-koa-loa) *adj* agrarian
agricoltura (ah-gree-koal-*tōō*-rah) *f* agriculture
agro (*aa*-groa) *adj* sour
aguzzo (ah-*goot*-tsoa) *adj* keen
aiola (igh-*aw*-lah) *f* flowerbed
airone (igh-*rōā*-nay) *m* heron
aiutante (ah-yoo-*tahn*-tay) *m* helper
aiutare (ah-yoo-*taa*-ray) *v* aid, help
aiuto (ah-*yōō*-toa) *m* assistance, help; relief
ala (*aa*-lah) *f* wing
alba (*ahl*-bah) *f* dawn
albergatore (ahl-bayr-gah-*tōā*-ray) *m* inn-keeper
albergo (ahl-*behr*-goa) *m* hotel
albero (*ahl*-bay-roa) *m* tree; mast; ~ **a camme** camshaft; ~ **a gomiti** crankshaft
albicocca (ahl-bee-*kok*-kah) *f* apricot
album (*ahl*-boom) *m* album; ~ **da disegno** sketch-book; ~ **per ritagli** scrap-book
alce (*ahl*-chay) *m* moose
alcool (*ahl*-koa-oal) *m* alcohol; ~ **metilico** methylated spirits
alcoolico (ahl-*kaw*-lee-koa) *adj* alcoholic
alcuno (ahl-*kōō*-noa) *adj* any; **alcuni** *adj* some; *pron* some
alfabeto (ahl-fah-*bai*-toa) *m* alphabet
algebra (*ahl*-jay-brah) *f* algebra
Algeria (ahl-jay-*ree*-ah) *f* Algeria
algerino (ahl-jay-*ree*-noa) *adj* Algerian; *m* Algerian
aliante (ah-*lyahn*-tay) *m* glider
alimentari (ah-lee-mayn-*taa*-ree) *mpl* groceries *pl*, foodstuffs *pl*
alimento (ah-lee-*mayn*-toa) *m* food; **alimenti** alimony
allacciare (ahl-laht-*chaa*-ray) *v* fasten
allargare (ahl-lahr-*gaa*-ray) *v* widen; extend; expand
allarmante (ahl-lahr-*mahn*-tay) *adj* scary
allarmare (ahl-lahr-*maa*-ray) *v* alarm
allarme (ahl-*lahr*-may) *m* alarm; ~ **d'incendio** fire-alarm
allattare (ahl-laht-*taa*-ray) *v* nurse
alleanza (ahl-lay-*ahn*-tsah) *f* alliance
alleato (ahl-lay-*aa*-toa) *m* associate; **Alleati** Allies *pl*
allegare (ahl-lay-*gaa*-ray) *v* enclose
allegato (ahl-lay-*gaa*-toa) *m* annex, enclosure
allegria (ahl-lay-*gree*-ah) *f* gaiety
allegro (ahl-*lāy*-groa) *adj* merry, joyful, gay, cheerful; jolly
allenatore (ahl-lay-nah-*tōā*-ray) *m* coach
allergia (ahl-layr-*jee*-ah) *f* allergy
allevare (ahl-lay-*vaa*-ray) *v* raise; rear; *breed
allibrare (ahl-lee-*braa*-ray) *v* book
allibratore (ahl-lee-brah-*tōā*-ray) *m* bookmaker
allievo (ahl-*lyai*-voa) *m* scholar
allodola (ahl-*law*-doa-lah) *f* lark
alloggiare (ahl-load-*jaa*-ray) *v* accommodate, lodge
alloggio (ahl-*lod*-joa) *m* accommodation, lodgings *pl*; apartment *nAm*; ~ **e colazione** bed and breakfast
allontanare (ahl-loan-tah-*naa*-ray) *v* remove; **allontanarsi** depart; deviate
allora (ahl *lōā*-rah) *adv* then; **da** ~ since
allungare (ahl-loong-*gaa*-ray) *v* lengthen; dilute
almanacco (ahl-mah-*nahk*-koa) *m* almanac
almeno (ahl-*māy*-noa) *adv* at least
alpinismo (ahl-pee-*nee*-zmoa) *m* mountaineering
alquanto (ahl-*kwahn*-toa) *adv* fairly, rather, pretty, quite; somewhat
alt! (ahlt) stop!

altalena (ahl-tah-*lāy*-nah) *f* swing; see-saw
altare (ahl-*taa*-ray) *m* altar
alternativa (ahl-tayr-nah-*tee*-vah) *f* alternative
alternato (ahl-tayr-*naa*-toa) *adj* alternate
altezza (ahl-*tayt*-tsah) *f* height
altezzoso (ahl-tayt-*tsōā*-soa) *adj* haughty
altitudine (ahl-tee-*tōō*-dee-nay) *f* altitude
alto (*ahl*-toa) *adj* high; tall; loud; **verso l'alto** up
altoparlante (ahl-toa-pahr-*lahn*-tay) *m* loud-speaker
altopiano (ahl-toa-*pyaa*-noa) *m* (pl altipiani) plateau, uplands *pl*
altrettanto (ahl-trayt-*tahn*-toa) *adv* as much
altrimenti (ahl-tree-*mayn*-tee) *adv* otherwise, else; *conj* otherwise
altro (*ahl*-troa) *adj* other; different; **l'un l'altro** each other; **l'uno o l'altro** either; **tra l'altro** among other things; **un ~** another
d'altronde (dahl-*troan*-day) besides
altrove (ahl-*trōā*-vay) *adv* elsewhere
altura (ahl-*tōō*-rah) *f* rise
alveare (ahl-vay-*aa*-ray) *m* beehive
alzare (ahl-*tsaa*-ray) *v* lift; **alzarsi** *get up, *rise
amabile (ah-*maa*-bee-lay) *adj* gentle
amaca (ah-*maa*-kah) *f* hammock
amante (ah-*mahn*-tay) *m* lover; *f* mistress
amare (ah-*maa*-ray) *v* love; *be fond of
amaro (ah-*maa*-roa) *adj* bitter
amato (ah-*maa*-toa) *adj* beloved
ambasciata (ahm-bahsh-*shaa*-tah) *f* embassy
ambasciatore (ahm-bahsh-shah-*tōā*-ray) *m* ambassador
ambiente (ahm-*byayn*-tay) *m* milieu, environment
ambiguo (ahm-*bee*-gwoa) *adj* ambiguous
ambizioso (ahm-bee-*tsyōā*-soa) *adj* ambitious
ambra (*ahm*-brah) *f* amber
ambulante (ahm-boo-*lahn*-tay) *adj* itinerant
ambulanza (ahm-boo-*lahn*-tsah) *f* ambulance
America (ah-*mai*-ree-kah) *f* America; ~ **Latina** Latin America
americano (ah-may-ree-*kaa*-noa) *adj* American; *m* American
ametista (ah-may-*tee*-stah) *f* amethyst
amianto (ah-*myahn*-toa) *m* asbestos
amica (ah-*mee*-kah) *f* friend
amichevole (ah-mee-*kāy*-voa-lay) *adj* friendly
amicizia (ah-mee-*chee*-tsyah) *f* friendship
amico (ah-*mee*-koa) *m* friend
amido (*aa*-mee-doa) *m* starch
ammaccare (ahm-mahk-*kaa*-ray) *v* bruise
ammaccatura (ahm-mahk-kah-*tōō*-rah) *f* dent
ammaestrare (ahm-mah[ay]-*straa*-ray) *v* train
ammainare (ahm-migh-*naa*-ray) *v* *strike
ammalato (ahm-mah-*laa*-toa) *adj* ill, sick
ammazzare (ahm-maht-*tsaa*-ray) *v* kill
***ammettere** (ahm-*mayt*-tay-ray) *v* admit; acknowledge
amministrare (ahm-mee-nee-*straa*-ray) *v* direct
amministrativo (ahm-mee-nee-strah-*tee*-voa) *adj* administrative
amministrazione (ahm-mee-nee-strah-*tsyōā*-nay) *f* administration; direction

ammiraglio (ahm-mee-*rah*-lʸoa) *m* admiral
ammirare (ahm-mee-*raa*-ray) *v* admire
ammirazione (ahm-mee-rah-*tsyōā*-nay) *f* admiration
ammissione (ahm-meess-*syōā*-nay) *f* admittance, admission
ammobiliare (ahm-moa-bee-*lʸaa*-ray) *v* furnish; **non ammobiliato** unfurnished
ammollare (ahm-moal-*laa*-ray) *v* soak
ammoniaca (ahm-moa-*nee*-ah-kah) *f* ammonia
ammonire (ahm-moa-*nee*-ray) *v* caution
ammontare (ahm-moan-*taa*-ray) *m* amount
ammontare a (ahm-moan-*taa*-ray) amount to
ammorbidire (ahm-moar-bee-*dee*-ray) *v* soften
ammortizzatore (ahm-moar-teed-dzah-*tōā*-ray) *m* shock absorber
ammucchiare (ahm-mook-*kyaa*-ray) *v* pile
ammuffito (ahm-moof-*fee*-toa) *adj* mouldy
ammutinamento (ahm-moo-tee-nah-*mayn*-toa) *m* mutiny
amnistia (ahm-nee-*stee*-ah) *f* amnesty
amo (*aa*-moa) *m* fishing hook; **pescare con l'amo** fish
amore (ah-*mōā*-ray) *m* love; darling, sweetheart
amoretto (ah-moa-*rayt*-toa) *m* affair
ampio (*ahm*-pyoa) *adj* extensive, broad
ampliamento (ahm-plyah-*mayn*-toa) *m* extension
ampliare (ahm-*plyaa*-ray) *v* enlarge
amuleto (ah-moo-*lāy*-toa) *m* charm
analfabeta (ah-nahl-fah-*bai*-tah) *m* illiterate
analisi (ah-*naa*-lee-zee) *f* analysis
analista (ah-nah-*lee*-stah) *m* analyst
analizzare (ah-nah-leed-*dzaa*-ray) *v* analyse; *break down
analogo (ah-*naa*-loa-goa) *adj* similar
ananas (*ah*-nah-nahss) *m* pineapple
anarchia (ah-nahr-*kee*-ah) *f* anarchy
anatomia (ah-nah-toa-*mee*-ah) *f* anatomy
anche (*ahng*-kay) *adv* too, also; even
ancora[1] (ahng-*kōā*-rah) *adv* yet, still; again; some more; ~ **una volta** once more
ancora[2] (*ahng*-koa-rah) *f* anchor
***andare** (ahn-*daa*-ray) *v* *go; ~ **a prendere** *get, fetch; ~ **carponi** crawl; ~ **in macchina** *ride; ***andarsene** *go away, depart
andata (ahn-*daa*-tah) *f* going
andatura (ahn-dah-*tōō*-rah) *f* walk; pace, gait
andirivieni (ahn-dee-ree-*vyai*-nee) *m* bustle
anello (ah-*nehl*-loa) *m* ring; ~ **di fidanzamento** engagement ring; ~ **per stantuffo** piston ring
anemia (ah-nay-*mee*-ah) *f* anaemia
anestesia (ah-nay-stay-*see*-ah) *f* anaesthesia
anestetico (ah-nay-*stai*-tee-koa) *m* anaesthetic
angelo (*ahn*-jay-loa) *m* angel
angolo (*ahng*-goa-loa) *m* corner; angle
angora (*ahng*-go-rah) *f* mohair
anguilla (ahng-*gweel*-lah) *f* eel
anguria (ahng-*gōō*-ryah) *f* watermelon
angusto (ahng-*goo*-stoa) *adj* narrow
anima (*aa*-nee-mah) *f* soul; essence
animale (ah-nee-*maa*-lay) *m* animal; beast; ~ **da preda** beast of prey; ~ **domestico** pet
animato (ah-nee-*maa*-toa) *adj* busy
animo (*aa*-nee-moa) *m* heart; intention; courage

anitra (*aa*-nee-trah) *f* duck
***annettere** (ahn-*neht*-tay-ray) *v* annex; attach
anniversario (ahn-nee-vayr-*saa*-ryoa) *m* anniversary; jubilee
anno (*ahn*-noa) *m* year; **all'anno** per annum; ~ **bisestile** leap-year; ~ **nuovo** New Year
annodare (ahn-noa-*daa*-ray) *v* knot, tie
annoiare (ahn-noa-*yaa*-ray) *v* annoy; bore
annotare (ahn-noa-*taa*-ray) *v* *write down, note
annuale (ahn-*nwaa*-lay) *adj* yearly, annual
annuario (ahn-*nwaa*-ryoa) *m* annual
annuire (ahn-*nwee*-ray) *v* nod
annullamento (ahn-nool-lah-*mayn*-toa) *m* cancellation
annullare (ahn-nool-*laa*-ray) *v* cancel
annunziare (ahn-noon-*tsyaa*-ray) *v* announce
annunzio (ahn-*noon*-tsyoa) *m* announcement; ~ **pubblicitario** commercial
anonimo (ah-*naw*-nee-moa) *adj* anonymous
anormale (ah-noar-*maa*-lay) *adj* abnormal
ansia (*ahn*-syah) *f* worry
ansietà (ahn-syay-*tah*) *f* anxiety, concern
ansimare (ahn-see-*maa*-ray) *v* pant
ansioso (ahn-*syōā*-soa) *adj* anxious, eager
d'anteguerra (dahn-tay-*gwehr*-rah) pre-war
antenato (ahn-tay-*naa*-toa) *m* ancestor
antenna (ahn-*tayn*-nah) *f* aerial
anteriore (ahn-tay-*ryōā*-ray) *adj* prior, previous
anteriormente (ahn-tay-ryoar-*mayn*-tay) *adv* formerly
antibiotico (ahn-tee-*byaw*-tee-koa) *m* antibiotic
anticaglia (ahn-tee-*kaa*-lyah) *f* antique
antichità (ahn-tee-kee-*tah*) *fpl* antiquities *pl*; **Antichità** *f* antiquity
anticipare (ahn-tee-chee-*paa*-ray) *v* anticipate
anticipatamente (ahn-tee-chee-pah-tah-*mayn*-tay) *adv* in advance
anticipo (ahn-*tee*-chee-poa) *m* advance; **in** ~ in advance
antico (ahn-*tee*-koa) *adj* ancient; antique; former
anticoncezionale (ahn-tee-koan-chay-tsyoa-*naa*-lay) *m* contraceptive
anticongelante (ahn-tee-koan-jay-*lahn*-tay) *m* antifreeze
antipasto (ahn-tee-*pah*-stoa) *m* hors-d'œuvre
antipatia (ahn-tee-pah-*tee*-ah) *f* antipathy, dislike
antipatico (ahn-tee-*paa*-tee-koa) *adj* unpleasant, nasty
antiquario (ahn-tee-*kwaa*-ryoa) *m* antique dealer
antiquato (ahn-tee-*kwaa*-toa) *adj* ancient, old-fashioned; quaint
antisettico (ahn-tee-*seht*-tee-koa) *m* antiseptic
antologia (ahn-toa-loa-*jee*-ah) *f* anthology
anzi (*ahn*-tsee) *adv* rather, on the contrary
anziano (ahn-*tsyaa*-noa) *adj* aged, elderly
ape (*aa*-pay) *f* bee
aperitivo (ah-pay-ree-*tee*-voa) *m* aperitif, drink
aperto (ah-*pehr*-toa) *adj* open; **all'aperto** outdoors
apertura (ah-payr-*tōō*-rah) *f* opening
apice (*aa*-pee-chay) *m* zenith
appagamento (ahp-pah-gah-*mayn*-toa) *m* satisfaction
apparato (ahp-pah-*raa*-toa) *m* ap-

pliance; pomp
apparecchio (ahp-pah-*rayk*-kyoa) *m* appliance, apparatus, machine
apparente (ahp-pah-*rehn*-tay) *adj* apparent
apparentemente (ahp-pah-rayn-tay-*mayn*-tay) *adv* apparently
apparenza (ahp-pah-*rehn*-tsah) *f* appearance; semblance
***apparire** (ahp-pah-*ree*-ray) *v* appear
apparizione (ahp-pah-ree-*tsyōā*-nay) *f* apparition
appartamento (ahp-pahr-tah-*mayn*-toa) *m* flat; suite; apartment *nAm*; **blocco di appartamenti** apartment house *Am*
***appartenere** (ahp-pahr-tay-*nāy*-ray) *v* belong
appassionato (ahp-pahss-syoa-*naa*-toa) *adj* passionate; keen
appello (ahp-*pehl*-loa) *m* appeal; call
appena (ahp-*pai*-nah) *adv* hardly, barely; just; **non** ~ as soon as
***appendere** (ahp-*pehn*-day-ray) *v* *hang
appendice (ahp-payn-*dee*-chay) *f* appendix
appendicite (ahp-payn-dee-*chee*-tay) *f* appendicitis
appetito (ahp-pay-*tee*-toa) *m* appetite
appetitoso (ahp-pay-tee-*tōā*-soa) *adj* appetizing
appezzamento (ahp-payt-tsah-*mayn*-toa) *m* plot
appiccicare (ahp-peet-chee-*kaa*-ray) *v* *stick
appiccicaticcio (ahp-peet-chee-kah-*teet*-choa) *adj* sticky
applaudire (ahp-plou-*dee*-ray) *v* clap
applauso (ahp-*plou*-zoa) *m* applause
applicare (ahp-plee-*kaa*-ray) *v* apply; **applicarsi** apply
applicazione (ahp-plee-kah-*tsyōā*-nay) *f* application
appoggiare (ahp-poad-*jaa*-ray) *v* support; **appoggiarsi** *lean
apposta (ahp-*po*-stah) *adv* on purpose
***apprendere** (ahp-*prehn*-day-ray) *v* learn; *hear
apprezzamento (ahp-prayt-tsah-*mayn*-toa) *m* appreciation
apprezzare (ahp-prayt-*tsaa*-ray) *v* appreciate
approfittare (ahp-proa-feet-*taa*-ray) *v* profit, benefit
appropriato (ahp-proa-*pryaa*-toa) *adj* appropriate, proper
approssimativo (ahp-proass-see-mah-*tee*-voa) *adj* approximate
approvare (ahp-proa-*vaa*-ray) *v* approve; approve of
approvazione (ahp-proa-vah-*tsyōā*-nay) *f* approval
appuntamento (ahp-poon-tah-*mayn*-toa) *m* appointment, date
appuntare (ahp-poon-*taa*-ray) *v* pin
appuntato (ahp-poon-*taa*-toa) *adj* pointed
appunto (ahp-*poon*-toa) *m* note; **blocco per appunti** pad, writing-pad
apribottiglie (ah-pree-boat-*tee*-lʸay) *m* bottle opener
aprile (ah-*pree*-lay) April
***aprire** (ah-*pree*-ray) *v* open; unlock; turn on
apriscatole (ah-pree-*skaa*-toa-lay) *m* tin-opener, can opener
aquila (*ah*-kwee-lah) *f* eagle
Arabia Saudita (ah-*raa*-byah sou-*dee*-tah) Saudi Arabia
arabo (*ah*-rah-boa) *adj* Arab; *m* Arab
arachide (ah-*raa*-kee-day) *f* peanut
aragosta (ah-rah-*goa*-stah) *f* lobster
aragostina (ah-rah-goa-*stee*-nah) *f* prawn
arancia (ah-*rahn*-chah) *f* orange
arancione (ah-rahn-*chōā*-nay) *adj* orange

arare (ah-*raa*-ray) *v* plough
aratro (ah-*raa*-troa) *m* plough
arazzo (ah-*raht*-tsoa) *m* tapestry
arbitrario (ahr-bee-*traa*-ryoa) *adj* arbitrary
arbitro (*ahr*-bee-troa) *m* umpire
arbusto (ahr-*boo*-stoa) *m* shrub
arcata (ahr-*kaa*-tah) *f* arch; arcade
arcato (ahr-*kaa*-toa) *adj* arched
archeologia (ahr-kay-oa-loa-*jee*-ah) *f* archaeology
archeologo (ahr-kay-*o*-loa-goa) *m* archaeologist
architetto (ahr-kee-*tayt*-toa) *m* architect
architettura (ahr-kee-tayt-*tōō*-rah) *f* architecture
archivio (ahr-*kee*-vyoa) *m* archives *pl*
arcivescovo (ahr-chee-*vay*-skoa-voa) *m* archbishop
arco (*ahr*-koa) *m* bow; arch
arcobaleno (ahr-koa-bah-*lāy*-noa) *m* rainbow
***ardere** (*ahr*-day-ray) *v* *burn; glow
ardesia (ahr-*dāy*-syah) *f* slate
ardore (ahr-*dōā*-ray) *m* glow
area (*aa*-ray-ah) *f* area
arena (ah-*rāy*-nah) *f* bullring
argenteria (ahr-jayn-tay-*ree*-ah) *f* silverware
argentiere (ahr-jayn-*tyai*-ray) *m* silversmith
Argentina (ahr-jayn-*tee*-nah) *f* Argentina
argentino (ahr-jayn-*tee*-noa) *adj* Argentinian; *m* Argentinian
argento (ahr-*jehn*-toa) *m* silver; **d'argento** silver
argilla (ahr-*jeel*-lah) *f* clay
argine (*ahr*-jee-nay) *m* dike, dam; river bank, embankment
argomentare (ahr-goa-mayn-*taa*-ray) *v* argue
argomento (ahr-goa-*mayn*-toa) *m* argument; theme
aria (*aa*-ryah) *f* air, sky; tune; **ad ~ condizionata** air-conditioned; **a tenuta d'aria** airtight; ***aver l'aria** look; **condizionamento dell'aria** air-conditioning
arido (*aa*-ree-doa) *adj* arid
arieggiare (ah-ryayd-*jaa*-ray) *v* air
aringa (ah-*reeng*-gah) *f* herring
arioso (ah-*ryōā*-soa) *adj* airy
aritmetica (ah-reet-*mai*-tee-kah) *f* arithmetic
arma (*ahr*-mah) *f* (pl armi) arm, weapon
armadio (ahr-*maa*-dyoa) *m* cupboard; closet *nAm*
armare (ahr-*maa*-ray) *v* arm
armatore (ahr-mah-*tōā*-ray) *m* shipowner
armonia (ahr-moa-*nee*-ah) *f* harmony
arnese (ahr-*nāy*-say) *m* tool, utensil; **cassetta degli arnesi** tool kit
aroma (ah-*raw*-mah) *m* aroma
arpa (*ahr*-pah) *f* harp
arrabbiato (ahr-rahb-*byaa*-toa) *adj* angry, cross
arrampicare (ahr-rahm-pee-*kaa*-ray) *v* climb
arrangiarsi con (ahr-rahn-*jahr*-see) *make do with
arredare (ahr-ray-*daa*-ray) *v* furnish
***arrendersi** (ahr-*rehn*-dayr-see) *v* surrender
arrestare (ahr-ray-*staa*-ray) *v* arrest
arresto (ahr-*reh*-stoa) *m* arrest
arretrato (ahr-ray-*traa*-toa) *adj* overdue
arricciacapelli (ahr-reet-chah-kah-*payl*-lee) *m* curling-tongs *pl*
arricciare (ahr-reet-*chaa*-ray) *v* curl
arrischiare (ahr-ree-*skyaa*-ray) *v* venture
arrivare (ahr-ree-*vaa*-ray) *v* arrive
arrivederci! (ahr-ree-vay-*dayr*-chee)

good-bye!
arrivo (ahr-*ree*-voa) *m* arrival; **in ~** due
arrogante (ahr-roa-*gahn*-tay) *adj* snooty
arrossire (ahr-roass-*see*-ray) *v* blush
arrostire (ahr-roa-*stee*-ray) *v* roast
arrotondato (ahr-roa-toan-*daa*-toa) *adj* rounded
arrugginito (ahr-rood-jee-*nee*-toa) *adj* rusty
arte (*ahr*-tay) *f* art; **arti e mestieri** arts and crafts; **belle arti** fine arts; **opera d'arte** work of art
arteria (ahr-*tai*-ryah) *f* artery; thoroughfare
articolazione (ahr-tee-koa-lah-*tsyōā*-nay) *f* joint
articolo (ahr-*tee*-koa-loa) *m* article; item; **articoli da toeletta** toiletry
artificiale (ahr-tee-fee-*chaa*-lay) *adj* artificial
artificio (ahr-tee-*fee*-choa) *m* artifice
artigianato (ahr-tee-jah-*naa*-toa) *m* handicraft
artiglio (ahr-*tee*-lʸoa) *m* claw
artista (ahr-*tee*-stah) *m* artist
artistico (ahr-*tee*-stee-koa) *adj* artistic
***ascendere** (ahsh-*shayn*-day-ray) *v* ascend
ascensione (ahsh-shayn-*syōā*-nay) *f* ascent
ascensore (ahsh-shayn-*sōā*-ray) *m* lift; elevator *nAm*
ascesa (ahsh-*shāy*-sah) *f* rise; climb; ascent
ascesso (ahsh-*shehss*-soa) *m* abscess
ascia (*ahsh*-shah) *f* axe
asciugacapelli (ahsh-shoo-gah-kah-*payl*-lee) *m* hair-dryer
asciugamano (ahsh-shoo-gah-*maa*-noa) *m* towel, bath towel
asciugare (ahsh-shoo-*gaa*-ray) *v* dry; wipe
asciutto (ahsh-*shoot*-toa) *adj* dry
ascoltare (ah-skoal-*taa*-ray) *v* listen
ascoltatore (ah-skoal-tah-*tōā*-ray) *m* listener
asfalto (ah-*sfahl*-toa) *m* asphalt
Asia (*aa*-zyah) *f* Asia
asiatico (ah-*zyaa*-tee-koa) *adj* Asian; *m* Asian
asilo (ah-*zee*-loa) *m* asylum; **~ infantile** kindergarten
asino (*aa*-see-noa) *m* ass, donkey
asma (*ah*-zmah) *f* asthma
asola (*aa*-zoa-lah) *f* buttonhole
asparago (ah-*spaa*-rah-goa) *m* asparagus
aspettare (ah-spayt-*taa*-ray) *v* wait, await; expect
aspettativa (ah-spayt-tah-*tee*-vah) *f* expectation
aspetto (ah-*speht*-toa) *m* look; appearance; aspect; **di bell'aspetto** good-looking
aspirapolvere (ah-spee-rah-*poal*-vay-ray) *m* vacuum cleaner; **pulire con l'aspirapolvere** hoover; vacuum *vAm*
aspirare (ah-spee-*raa*-ray) *v* inhale; aspire; **~ a** aim at
aspirazione (ahss-pee-rah-*tsyōā*-nay) *f* suction; aspiration
aspirina (ah-spee-*ree*-nah) *f* aspirin
aspro (*ah*-sproa) *adj* harsh
assaggiare (ahss-sahd-*jaa*-ray) *v* taste
assai (ahss-*sigh*) *adv* very, quite
***assalire** (ahss-sah-*lee*-ray) *v* attack
assassinare (ahss-sahss-see-*naa*-ray) *v* murder
assassinio (ahss-sahss-*see*-ñoa) *m* assassination, murder
assassino (ahss-sahss-*see*-noa) *m* murderer
asse (*ahss*-say) *m* axle; *f* plank, board
assedio (ahss-*sāy*-dyoa) *m* siege
assegnare (ahss-say-*ñaa*-ray) *v* allot;

~ **a** assign to
assegno (ahss-*sāy*-ñoa) *m* allowance; cheque; check *nAm*; ~ **turistico** traveller's cheque; **libretto di assegni** cheque-book; check-book *nAm*
assemblea (ahss-saym-*blai*-ah) *f* assembly, meeting
assennato (ahss-sayn-*naa*-toa) *adj* sober
assente (ahss-*sehn*-tay) *adj* absent
assenza (ahss-*sehn*-tsah) *f* absence
asserire (ahss-say-*ree*-ray) *v* claim
assetato (ahss-say-*taa*-toa) *adj* thirsty
assicurare (ahss-see-koo-*raa*-ray) *v* assure; insure; **assicurarsi** secure
assicurazione (ahss-see-koo-rah-*tsyōa*-nay) *f* insurance; ~ **sulla vita** life insurance; ~ **viaggi** travel insurance
assieme (ahss-*syai*-may) *m* set
assistente (ahss-see-*stehn*-tay) *m* assistant
assistenza (ahss-see-*stehn*-tsah) *f* assistance
***assistere** (ahss-*see*-stay-ray) *v* assist, aid; ~ **a** attend, assist at
associare (ahss-soa-*chaa*-ray) *v* associate; **associarsi** *v* join
associato (ahss-soa-*chaa*-toa) *adj* affiliated
associazione (ahss-soa-chah-*tsyōa*-nay) *f* association; society, club
assolutamente (ahss-soa-loo-tah-*mayn*-tay) *adv* absolutely
assoluto (ahss-soa-*lōō*-toa) *adj* sheer; total
assoluzione (ahss-soa-loo-*tsyōa*-nay) *f* acquittal
assomigliare a (ahss-soa-mee-*lʸaa*-ray) resemble
assonnato (ahss-soan-*naa*-toa) *adj* sleepy
assortimento (ahss-soar-tee-*mayn*-toa) *m* assortment
assortire (ahss-soar-*tee*-ray) *v* assort; sort
assortito (ahss-soar-*tee*-toa) *adj* varied
***assumere** (ahss-*sōō*-may-ray) *v* assume; engage
assurdo (ahss-*soor*-doa) *adj* absurd
asta (*ah*-stah) *f* auction
astemio (ah-*stai*-myoa) *m* teetotaller
***astenersi da** (ah-stay-*nayr*-see) abstain from
astore (ah-*stōa*-ray) *m* hawk
astratto (ah-*straht*-toa) *adj* abstract
astronomia (ah-stroa-noa-*mee*-ah) *f* astronomy
astuccio (ah-*stoot*-choa) *m* case; ~ **di toeletta** toilet case; ~ **per tabacco** tobacco pouch
astuto (ah-*stōō*-toa) *adj* sly
astuzia (ah-*stōō*-tsyah) *f* ruse
ateo (*aa*-tay-oa) *m* atheist
Atlantico (aht-*lahn*-tee-koa) *m* Atlantic
atleta (aht-*lai*-tah) *m* athlete
atletica (aht-*lai*-tee-kah) *f* athletics *pl*
atmosfera (aht-moa-*sfai*-rah) *f* atmosphere
atomico (ah-*taw*-mee-koa) *adj* atomic
atomizzatore (ah-toa-meed-dzah-*tōa*-ray) *m* atomizer
atomo (*aa*-toa-moa) *m* atom
atrio (*aa*-tryoa) *m* lobby
atroce (ah-*trōa*-chay) *adj* horrible
attaccapanni (aht-tahk-kah-*pahn*-nee) *m* hat rack; coat-hanger, hanger
attaccare (aht-tahk-*kaa*-ray) *v* attach; assault
attacco (aht-*tahk*-koa) *m* attack; fit; ~ **cardiaco** heart attack
atteggiamento (aht-tayd-jah-*mayn*-toa) *m* position
attempato (aht-taym-*paa*-toa) *adj* aged
***attendere** (aht-*tehn*-day-ray) *v* await, wait; ~ **a** attend to
attento (aht-*tehn*-toa) *adj* attentive;

careful; ***stare** ~ look out
attenzione (aht-tayn-*tsyōā*-nay) *f* attention; consideration, notice; ***fare** ~ mind, *pay attention, look out, beware; **prestare ~ a** attend to
atterrare (aht-tayr-*raa*-ray) *v* knock down; land
attesa (aht-*tāy*-sah) *f* waiting
attestato (aht-tay-*staa*-toa) *m* certificate
attillato (aht-teel-*laa*-toa) *adj* tight
attimo (*aht*-tee-moa) *m* moment
attinenza (aht-tee-*nehn*-tsah) *f* relation
attitudine (aht-tee-*tōō*-dee-nay) *f* faculty, talent; attitude
attività (aht-tee-vee-*tah*) *f* activity; work
attivo (aht-*tee*-voa) *adj* active
atto (*aht*-toa) *m* deed, act; certificate
attore (aht-*tōā*-ray) *m* actor
attorno (aht-*toar*-noa) *adv* about; **~ a** round
attraccare (aht-trahk-*kaa*-ray) *v* dock
attraente (aht-trah-*ehn*-tay) *adj* attractive
***attrarre** (aht-*trahr*-ray) *v* attract
attrattiva (aht-trah-*tee*-vah) *f* attraction
attraversare (aht-trah-vayr-*saa*-ray) *v* cross; pass through
attraverso (aht-trah-*vehr*-soa) *prep* across; through
attrazione (aht-trah-*tsyōā*-nay) *f* attraction
attrezzatura (aht-trayt-tsah-*tōō*-rah) *f* gear
attrezzo (aht-*trayt*-tsoa) *m* tool; **attrezzi da pesca** fishing tackle, fishing gear
attribuire a (aht-tree-*bwee*-ray) assign to
attrice (aht-*tree*-chay) *f* actress
attrito (aht-*tree*-toa) *m* friction
attuale (aht-*twaa*-lay) *adj* present; topical
attualmente (aht-twahl-*mayn*-tay) *adv* at present
attuare (aht-*twaa*-ray) *v* realize
audace (ou-*daa*-chay) *adj* brave
audacia (ou-*daa*-chah) *f* courage; nerve
auditorio (ou-dee-*tōā*-ryoa) *m* auditorium
augurare (ou-goo-*raa*-ray) *v* wish
aula (*ou*-lah) *f* classroom
aumentare (ou-mayn-*taa*-ray) *v* increase; raise
aumento (ou-*mayn*-toa) *m* rise, increase; raise *nAm*
aureo (*ou*-ray-oa) *adj* golden
aurora (ou-*raw*-rah) *f* daybreak, dawn; sunrise
Australia (ou-*straa*-lʸah) *f* Australia
australiano (ou-strah-*lʸaa*-noa) *adj* Australian; *m* Australian
Austria (*ou*-stryah) *f* Austria
austriaco (ou-*stree*-ah-koa) *adj* Austrian; *m* Austrian
autentico (ou-*tehn*-tee-koa) *adj* original, authentic; true
autista (ou-*tee*-stah) *m* driver, chauffeur
autobus (*ou*-toa-booss) *m* (pl ~) bus; coach
autocarro (ou-toa-*kahr*-roa) *m* lorry; truck *nAm*
autogoverno (ou-toa-goa-*vehr*-noa) *m* self-government
automatico (ou-toa-*maa*-tee-koa) *adj* automatic
automazione (ou-toa-mah-*tsyōā*-nay) *f* automation
automobile (ou-toa-*maw*-bee-lay) *f* automobile, motor-car; **~ club** automobile club
automobilismo (ou-toa-moa-bee-*lee*-zmoa) *m* motoring
automobilista (ou-toa-moa-bee-*lee*-

stah) *m* motorist
autonoleggio (ou-toa-noa-*layd*-joa) *m* car hire; car rental *Am*
autonomo (ou-*taw*-noa-moa) *adj* autonomous, independent
autore (ou-*tōā*-ray) *m* author
autorità (ou-toa-ree-*tah*) *f* authority
autoritario (ou-toa-ree-*taa*-ryoa) *adj* authoritarian
autorizzare (ou-toa-reed-*dzaa*-ray) *v* license
autorizzazione (ou-toa-reed-dzah-*tsyōā*-nay) *f* authorization, permission
autostello (ou-toa-*stehl*-loa) *m* motel
autostoppista (ou-toa-stoap-*pee*-stah) *m* hitchhiker; ***fare l'autostop** hitchhike
autostrada (ou-toa-*straa*-dah) *f* motorway; highway *nAm*
autunno (ou-*toon*-noa) *m* autumn; fall *nAm*
avanti (ah-*vahn*-tee) *adv* onwards, forward; ahead; ~ **dritto** straight on
avant'ieri (ah-vahn-*tyai*-ree) *adv* the day before yesterday
avanzamento (ah-vahn-tsah-*mayn*-toa) *m* advance
avanzare (ah-vahn-*tsaa*-ray) *v* advance; *get on
avanzo (ah-*vahn*-tsoa) *m* remainder
avaria (ah-vah-*ree*-ah) *f* breakdown
avaro (ah-*vaa*-roa) *adj* avaricious
avena (ah-*vāȳ*-nah) *f* oats *pl*
***avere** (ah-*vāȳ*-ray) *v* *have
avido (*aa*-vee-doa) *adj* greedy
aviogetto (ah-vyoa-*jeht*-toa) *m* jet
avorio (ah-*vaw*-ryoa) *m* ivory
avvelenare (ahv-vay-lay-*naa*-ray) *v* poison
avvenente (ahv-vay-*nehn*-tay) *adj* handsome
avvenimento (ahv-vay-nee-*mayn*-toa) *m* event
avvenire (ahv-vay-*nee*-ray) *m* future
***avvenire** (ahv-vay-*nee*-ray) *v* happen
avventato (ahv-vayn-*taa*-toa) *adj* rash
avventore (ahv-vayn-*tōā*-ray) *m* customer
avventura (ahv-vayn-*tōō*-rah) *f* adventure
avverbio (ahv-*vehr*-byoa) *m* adverb
avversario (ahv-vayr-*saa*-ryoa) *m* opponent
avversione (ahv-vayr-*syōā*-nay) *f* aversion, dislike
avversità (ahv-vayr-see-*tah*) *f* misfortune
avverso (ahv-*vehr*-soa) *adj* averse
avvertimento (ahv-vayr-tee-*mayn*-toa) *m* warning
avvertire (ahv-vayr-*tee*-ray) *v* warn; notice
avviatore (ahv-vyah-*taw*-ray) *m* starter motor
avvicinare (ahv-vee-chee-*naa*-ray) *v* approach
avvisare (ahv-vee-*zaa*-ray) *v* warn; notify
avviso (ahv-*vee*-zoa) *m* notice, announcement; advertisement
avvitare (ahv-vee-*taa*-ray) *v* screw
avvocato (ahv-voa-*kaa*-toa) *m* lawyer; barrister, solicitor, attorney
***avvolgere** (ahv-*vol*-jay-ray) *v* *wind; wrap
avvolgibile (ahv-voal-*jee*-bee-lay) *m* blind
avvoltoio (ahv-voal-*tōā*-yoa) *m* vulture
azienda (ah-*dzyehn*-dah) *f* concern, business
azione (ah-*tsyōā*-nay) *f* deed, action; share
azoto (ah-*dzaw*-toa) *m* nitrogen
azzardo (ahd-*dzahr*-doa) *m* chance
azzurro (ahd-*dzoor*-roa) *adj* sky-blue

B

babbo (*bahb*-boa) *m* dad
babordo (bah-*boar*-doa) *m* port
baby-pullman (*bay*-bee-pool-mahn) *m* carry-cot
bacca (*bahk*-kah) *f* berry
baccano (bahk-*kaa*-noa) *m* noise
bacheca (bah-*kai*-kah) *f* show-case
baciare (bah-*chaa*-ray) *v* kiss
bacino (bah-*chee*-noa) *m* basin; dock; pelvis
bacio (*baa* choa) *m* kiss
badare a (bah-*daa*-ray) tend, look after; mind
badia (bah-*dee*-ah) *f* abbey
baffi (*bahf*-fee) *mpl* moustache
bagagliaio (bah-gah-*lʸaa*-yoa) *m* luggage van; boot; trunk *nAm*
bagaglio (bah-*gaa*-lʸoa) *m* luggage, baggage; ~ **a mano** hand luggage; hand baggage *Am*
bagliore (bah-*lʸōā*-ray) *m* glare
bagnarsi (bah-*ñahr*-see) *v* bathe
bagnato (bah-*ñaa*-toa) *adj* wet; moist, damp
bagno (*baa*-ñoa) *m* bath; ~ **turco** Turkish bath; **costume da** ~ bathing-suit; **cuffia da** ~ bathing-cap; ***fare il** ~ bathe
baia (*baa*-yah) *f* bay
balbettare (bahl-bayt-*taa*-ray) *v* falter
balconata (bahl-koa-*naa*-tah) *f* circle
balcone (bahl-*kōā*-nay) *m* balcony
balena (bah-*lāȳ*-nah) *f* whale
baleno (bah-*lāȳ*-noa) *m* flash
ballare (bahl-*laa*-ray) *v* dance
balletto (bahl-*layt*-toa) *m* ballet
ballo (*bahl*-loa) *m* dance; ball
balzare (bahl-*dzaa*-ray) *v* *leap
bambina (bahm-*bee*-nah) *f* little girl
bambinaia (bahm-bee-*naa*-yah) *f* nurse; babysitter
bambino (bahm-*bee*-noa) *m* child; kid
bambola (*bahm*-boa-lah) *f* doll
bambù (bahm-*boo*) *m* bamboo
banana (bah-*naa*-nah) *f* banana
banca (*bahng*-kah) *f* bank
bancarella (bahng-kah-*rehl*-lah) *f* stall
banchetto (bahng-*kayt*-toa) *m* banquet
banchina (bahng-*kee*-nah) *f* platform
banco (*bahng*-koa) *m* bench; counter; stand; reef; ~ **di scuola** desk
banconota (bahng-koa-*naw*-tah) *f* banknote
banda (*bahn*-dah) *f* gang; band
bandiera (bahn-*dyai*-rah) *f* flag
bandito (bahn-*dee*-toa) *m* bandit
bar (bahr) *m* bar; saloon, café, pub
baracca (bah-*rahk*-kah) *f* shed; booth
baratro (*baa*-rah-troa) *m* chasm
barattare (bah-raht-*taa*-ray) *v* swap
barattolo (bah-*raht*-toa-loa) *m* tin, canister
barba (*bahr*-bah) *f* beard
barbabietola (bahr-bah-*byai*-toa-lah) *f* beetroot, beet
barbiere (bahr-*byai*-ray) *m* barber
barbone (bahr-*bōā*-nay) *m* tramp
barca (*bahr*-kah) *f* boat; ~ **a remi** rowing-boat; ~ **a vela** sailing-boat
barchetta (bahr-*kayt*-tah) *f* dinghy
barcollante (bahr-koal-*lahn*-tay) *adj* unsteady
bar-emporio (bahr-aym-*paw*-ryoa) *m* drugstore *nAm*
barile (bah-*ree*-lay) *m* cask, barrel
bariletto (bah-ree-*layt*-toa) *m* keg
barista (bah-*ree*-stah) *m* bartender, barman; *f* barmaid
baritono (bah-*ree*-toa-noa) *m* baritone
barocco (bah-*rok*-koa) *adj* baroque
barometro (bah-*raw*-may-troa) *m* barometer
barra (*bahr*-rah) *f* rod
barriera (bahr-*ryai*-rah) *f* barrier; ~ **di**

sicurezza crash barrier
basamento (bah-zah-*mayn*-toa) *m* crankcase
basare (bah-*zaa*-ray) *v* base
base (*baa*-zay) *f* base; basis
basette (bah-*zayt*-tay) *fpl* sideburns *pl*, whiskers *pl*
basilica (bah-*zee*-lee-kah) *f* basilica
basso (*bahss*-soa) *adj* low; short; *m* bass
bassopiano (bahss-soa-*pyaa*-noa) *m* lowlands *pl*
bastante (bah-*stahn*-tay) *adj* sufficient
bastardo (bah-*stahr*-doa) *m* bastard
bastare (bah-*staa*-ray) *v* suffice, *do
bastone (bah-*stōā*-nay) *m* stick; cane; ~ **da passeggio** walking-stick; **bastoni da sci** ski sticks; ski poles *Am*
battaglia (baht-*taa*-lyah) *f* battle
battello (baht-*tehl*-loa) *m* boat
battere (*baht*-tay-ray) *v* *beat; ~ **le mani** clap
batteria (baht-tay-*ree*-ah) *f* battery
batterio (baht-*tai*-ryoa) *m* bacterium
battesimo (baht-*tāy*-zee-moa) *m* christening, baptism
battezzare (baht-tayd-*dzaa*-ray) *v* christen, baptize
baule (bah-*ōō*-lay) *m* chest; trunk
becco (*bayk*-koa) *m* beak; nozzle; goat
beffare (bayf-*faa*-ray) *v* fool
beige (baizh) *adj* beige
belga (*behl*-gah) *adj* (pl belgi) Belgian; *m* Belgian
Belgio (*behl*-joa) *m* Belgium
bellezza (bayl-*layt*-tsah) *f* beauty
bellino (bayl-*lee*-noa) *adj* nice
bello (*behl*-loa) *adj* beautiful; fair, lovely, fine, pretty
benché (behng-*kay*) *conj* although, though
benda (*bayn*-dah) *f* band
bendare (bayn-*daa*-ray) *v* dress
bene (*bai*-nay) *adv* well; **va bene!** all right!
***benedire** (bay-nay-*dee*-ray) *v* bless
benedizione (bay-nay-dee-*tsyōā*-nay) *f* blessing
beneficiario (bay-nay-fee-*chaa*-ryoa) *m* payee
beneficio (bay-nay-*fee*-choa) *m* benefit
benessere (bay-*nehss*-say-ray) *m* welfare
benevolenza (bay-nay-voa-*lehn*-tsah) *f* goodwill
benevolo (bay-*nai*-voa-loa) *adj* kind
benvenuto (behn-vay-*nōō*-toa) *adj* welcome
benzina (bayn-*dzee*-nah) *f* fuel, petrol; gasoline *nAm*, gas *nAm*
***bere** (*bāy*-ray) *v* *drink
berretto (bayr-*rayt*-toa) *m* cap; beret
bersaglio (bayr-*saa*-lyoa) *m* mark; target
bestemmia (bay-*staym*-myah) *f* curse
bestemmiare (bay-staym-*myaa*-ray) *v* curse, *swear
bestia (*beh*-styah) *f* beast
bestiame (bay-*styaa*-may) *m* cattle *pl*
betulla (bay-*tool*-lah) *f* birch
bevanda (bay-*vahn*-dah) *f* beverage; **bevande alcooliche** spirits, liquor
biancheria (byahng-kay-*ree*-ah) *f* linen; lingerie; ~ **da letto** bedding; ~ **personale** underwear
bianco (*byahng*-koa) *adj* white
biasimare (byah-zee-*maa*-ray) *v* blame
biasimo (*byaa*-zee-moa) *m* blame
bibbia (*beeb*-byah) *f* bible
bibita (*bee*-bee-tah) *f* drink; ~ **analcoolica** soft drink
biblioteca (bee-blyoa-*tai*-kah) *f* library
bicchiere (beek-*kyai*-ray) *m* glass; tumbler
bicicletta (bee-chee-*klayt*-tah) *f* cycle, bicycle
biforcarsi (bee-foar-*kahr*-see) *v* fork

biglietteria (bee-lʸayt-tay-*ree*-ah) *f* box-office; ~ **automatica** ticket machine
biglietto (bee-*lʸayt*-toa) *m* note; ticket; ~ **da visita** visiting-card; ~ **gratuito** free ticket
bigodino (bee-goa-*dee*-noa) *m* curler
bilancia (bee-*lahn*-chah) *f* weighing-machine, scales *pl*
bilancio (bee-*lahn*-choa) *m* budget; balance
bile (*bee*-lay) *f* gall, bile
biliardo (bee-*lʸahr*-doa) *m* billiards *pl*
bilingue (bee-*leeng*-gway) *adj* bilingual
bimbetto (beem-*bayt*-toa) *m* tot
bimbo (*beem*-boa) *m* toddler
binario (bee-*naa*-ryoa) *m* track
binocolo (bee-*naw*-koa-loa) *m* binoculars *pl*; field glasses
biologia (byoa-loa-*jee*-ah) *f* biology
bionda (*byoan*-dah) *f* blonde
biondo (*byoan*-doa) *adj* fair
birbante (beer-*bahn*-tay) *m* rascal
birichinata (bee-ree-kee-*naa*-tah) *f* mischief
birra (*beer*-rah) *f* beer, ale
birreria (beer-ray-*ree*-ah) *f* brewery
bisaccia (bee-*zaht*-chah) *f* haversack
biscottino (bee-skoat-*tee*-noa) *m* biscuit; cracker *nAm*
biscotto (bee-*skot*-toa) *m* cookie *nAm*
bisognare (bee-zoa-*ñaa*-ray) *v* need
bisogno (bee-*zōā*-ñoa) *m* want; need; misery; ***aver** ~ **di** need
bistecca (bee-*stayk*-kah) *f* steak
bivio (*bee*-vyoa) *m* road fork, fork
bizzarro (beed-*dzahr*-roa) *adj* odd, strange, queer, quaint
bloccare (bloak-*kaa*-ray) *v* block
blu (bloo) *adj* blue
blusa (*blōō*-zah) *f* blouse
boa (*baw*-ah) *f* buoy
bocca (*boak*-kah) *f* mouth
boccale (boak-*kaa*-lay) *m* mug
boccaporto (boak-kah-*por*-toa) *m* porthole
bocchino (boak-*kee*-noa) *m* cigarette-holder
bocciare (boat-*chaa*-ray) *v* fail
bocciolo (boat-*chaw*-loa) *m* bud
boccone (boak-*kōā*-nay) *m* bite
boia (*boi*-ah) *m* (pl ~) executioner
Bolivia (boa-*lee*-vyah) *f* Bolivia
boliviano (boa-lee-*vyaa*-noa) *adj* Bolivian; *m* Bolivian
bolla (*boal*-lah) *f* bubble; blister
bollettino meteorologico (boal-layt-*tee*-noa may-tay-oa-roa-*law*-jee-koa) weather forecast
bollire (boal-*lee*-ray) *v* boil
bollitore (boal-lee-*tōā*-ray) *m* kettle
bomba (*boam*-bah) *f* bomb
bombardare (boam-bahr-*daa*-ray) *v* bomb
bordello (boar-*dehl*-loa) *m* brothel
bordo (*boar*-doa) *m* edge; border, verge; **a** ~ aboard
borghese (boar-*gāy*-say) *adj* middle-class, bourgeois; *m* civilian
borsa[1] (*boar*-sah) *f* bag; ~ **da ghiaccio** ice-bag; ~ **dell'acqua calda** hot-water bottle; ~ **per la spesa** shopping bag
borsa[2] (*boar*-sah) *f* grant; ~ **di studio** scholarship
borsa[3] (*boar*-sah) *f* exchange; stock market, stock exchange
borsellino (boar-sayl-*lee*-noa) *m* purse
borsetta (boar-*sayt*-tah) *f* handbag, bag
boschetto (boa-*skayt*-toa) *m* grove
bosco (*bo*-skoa) *m* wood
boscoso (boa-*skōā*-soa) *adj* wooded
botanica (boa-*taa*-nee-kah) *f* botany
botola (*bo*-toa-lah) *f* hatch
botte (*boat*-tay) *f* cask, barrel
bottega (boat-*tāy*-gah) *f* store

botteghino (boat-tay-*gee*-noa) *m* box-office
bottiglia (boat-*tee*-lʸah) *f* bottle
bottone (boat-*tōā*-nay) *m* button
boutique (boo-*teek*) *m* boutique
a braccetto (ah braht-*chayt*-toa) arm-in-arm
braccialetto (braht-chah-*layt*-toa) *m* bracelet, bangle
braccio[1] (*braht*-choa) *m* (pl le braccia) arm
braccio[2] (*braht*-choa) *m* (pl bracci) arm; tributary
brachetta (brah-*kayt*-tah) *f* fly
braciola (brah-*chaw*-lah) *f* chop
bramare (brah-*maa*-ray) *v* long for
bramosia (brah-moa-*zee*-ah) *f* longing
branchia (*brahng*-kyah) *f* gill
branda (*brahn*-dah) *f* camp-bed
brano (*braa*-noa) *m* excerpt, passage
branzino (brahn-*dzee*-noa) *m* bass
Brasile (brah-*zee*-lay) *m* Brazil
brasiliano (brah-zee-*lʸaa*-noa) *adj* Brazilian; *m* Brazilian
bravo (*braa*-voa) *adj* clever; honest
breccia (*brayt*-chah) *f* gap; breach
bretelle (bray-*tehl*-lay) *fpl* braces *pl*; suspenders *plAm*
breve (*brāȳ*-vay) *adj* brief; concise; **tra** ~ shortly
brevetto (bray-*vayt*-toa) *m* patent
brezza (*brayd*-dzah) *f* breeze
briciola (*bree*-choa-lah) *f* crumb
brillante (breel-*lahn*-tay) *adj* brilliant, bright
brillantina (breel-lahn-*tee*-nah) *f* hair cream
brillare (breel-*laa*-ray) *v* *shine
brindisi (*breen*-dee-zee) *m* toast
britannico (bree-*tahn*-nee-koa) *adj* British
britanno (bree-*tahn*-noa) *m* Briton
brivido (*bree*-vee-doa) *m* chill, shudder, shiver
brocca (*brok*-kah) *f* pitcher, jug
bronchite (broang-*kee*-tay) *f* bronchitis
brontolare (broan-toa-*laa*-ray) *v* growl; grumble
bronzeo (*broan*-dzay-oa) *adj* bronze
bronzo (*broan*-dzoa) *m* bronze
bruciare (broo-*chaa*-ray) *v* *burn
bruciatura (broo-chah-*tōō*-rah) *f* burn
brughiera (broo-*gyāȳ*-rah) *f* moor
bruna (*brōō*-nah) *f* brunette
bruno (*brōō*-noa) *adj* brown
brutale (broo-*taa*-lay) *adj* brutal
brutto (*broot*-toa) *adj* ugly; bad
buca (*bōō*-kah) *f* pit, hole; ~ **delle lettere** pillar-box
bucato (boo-*kaa*-toa) *adj* punctured; *m* washing, laundry
bucatura (boo-kah-*tōō*-rah) *f* flat tyre, puncture
buccia (*boot*-chah) *f* skin, peel
buco (*bōō*-koa) *m* hole; ~ **della serratura** keyhole
budella (boo-*dehl*-lah) *fpl* bowels *pl*
bue (*bōō*-ay) *m* ox
buffé (boof-*feh*) *m* buffet
buffo (*boof*-foa) *adj* funny
buffonata (boof-foa-*naa*-tah) *f* farce
buio (*bōō*-yoa) *adj* obscure, dark; *m* dark
bulbo (*bool*-boa) *m* bulb; light bulb
Bulgaria (bool-gah-*ree*-ah) *f* Bulgaria
bulgaro (*bool*-gah-roa) *adj* Bulgarian; *m* Bulgarian
bullone (bool-*lōā*-nay) *m* bolt
buongustaio (bwon-goo-*staa*-yoa) *m* gourmet
buono (*bwaw*-noa) *adj* good; kind; nice; *m* voucher
burocrazia (boo-roa-krah-*tsee*-ah) *f* bureaucracy
burrasca (boor-*rah*-skah) *f* gale
burro (*boor*-roa) *m* butter
bussare (booss-*saa*-ray) *v* knock, tap

bussola (*booss*-soa-lah) *f* compass
busta (*boo*-stah) *f* envelope; sleeve
busto (*boo*-stoa) *m* bust; corset, girdle
buttare (boot-*taa*-ray) *v* *throw; **da ~** disposable

C

cabaret (kah-bah-*ray*) *m* cabaret
cabina (kah-*bee*-nah) *f* booth, cabin; **~ di coperta** deck cabin; **~ telefonica** telephone booth
caccia (*kaht*-chah) *f* chase, hunt
cacciare (kaht-*chaa*-ray) *v* hunt; chase; **~ di frodo** poach
cacciatore (kaht-chah-*tōā*-ray) *m* hunter
cacciavite (kaht-chah-*vee*-tay) *m* screw-driver
cachemire (kahsh-*meer*) *m* cashmere
cadavere (kah-*daa*-vay-ray) *m* corpse
***cadere** (kah-*dāȳ*-ray) *v* *fall; ***far ~** drop
caduta (kah-*dōō*-tah) *f* fall
caffè (kahf-*feh*) *m* coffee; public house
caffeina (kahf-fay-*ee*-nah) *f* caffeine
cagna (*kah*-ñah) *f* bitch
calamità (kah-lah-mee-*tah*) *f* calamity
calare (kah-*laa*-ray) *v* lower
calce (*kahl*-chay) *f* lime
calcestruzzo (kahl-chay-*stroot*-tsoa) *m* concrete
calcio (*kahl*-choa) *m* kick; soccer; calcium; **~ d'inizio** kick-off; **~ di rigore** penalty kick; ***prendere a calci** kick
calcolare (kahl-koa-*laa*-ray) *v* calculate
calcolo (*kahl*-koa-loa) *m* calculation; **calcolo biliare** gallstone; ***fare i calcoli** reckon
caldo (*kahl*-doa) *adj* warm, hot; *m* heat
calendario (kah-layn-*daa*-ryoa) *m* calendar
callista (kahl-*lee*-stah) *m* chiropodist
callo (*kahl*-loa) *m* callus; corn
calma (*kahl*-mah) *f* calm
calmare (kahl-*maa*-ray) *v* calm down; **calmarsi** calm down
calmo (*kahl*-moa) *adj* calm; serene, quiet
calore (kah-*lōā*-ray) *m* warmth, heat
caloria (kah-loa-*ree*-ah) *f* calorie
calunnia (kah-*loon*-ñah) *f* slander
calvinismo (kahl-vee-*nee*-zmoa) *m* Calvinism
calvo (*kahl*-voa) *adj* bald
calza (*kahl*-tsah) *f* sock; stocking; **calze elastiche** support hose
calzamaglia (kahl-tsah-*maa*-l^{y}ah) *f* panty-hose, tights *pl*
calzatura (kahl-tsah-*tōō*-rah) *f* footwear
calzolaio (kahl-tsoa-*laa*-yoa) *m* shoemaker
calzoleria (kahl-tsoa-lay-*ree*-ah) *f* shoe-shop
calzoncini (kahl-tsoan-*chee*-nee) *mpl* shorts *pl*; trunks *pl*
calzoni (kahl-*tsōā*-nee) *mpl* slacks *pl*; pants *plAm*; **~ da sci** ski pants
cambiamento (kahm-byah-*mayn*-toa) *m* alteration, change
cambiare (kahm-*byaa*-ray) *v* change; alter, vary; exchange, switch; **~ marcia** change gear; **cambiarsi** change
cambio (*kahm*-byoa) *m* change; exchange; **~ di velocità** gear-box; **corso del ~** exchange rate; ***dare il ~** relieve
camera (*kaa*-may-rah) *f* room, chamber; **~ blindata** vault; **~ da letto** bedroom; **~ d'aria** inner tube; ~

degli ospiti guest-room; ~ **dei bambini** nursery
cameriera (kah-may-*ryai*-rah) *f* maid; chambermaid; waitress
cameriere (kah-may-*ryai*-ray) *m* valet; waiter
camerino (kah-may-*ree*-noa) *m* dressing-room
camicia (kah-*mee*-chah) *f* shirt; ~ **da notte** nightdress
camino (kah-*mee*-noa) *m* chimney
camionetta (kah-myoa-*nayt*-tah) *f* pick-up van
cammello (kahm-*mehl*-loa) *m* camel
cammeo (kahm-*mai*-oa) *m* cameo
camminare (kahm-mee-*naa*-ray) *v* *go, walk; step; hike
campagna (kahm-*paa*-ñah) *f* countryside, country; campaign
campana (kahm-*paa*-nah) *f* bell
campanello (kahm-pah-*nehl*-loa) *m* bell, doorbell
campanile (kahm-pah-*nee*-lay) *m* steeple
campeggiatore (kahm-payd-jah-*tōā*-ray) *m* camper
campeggio (kahm-*payd*-joa) *m* camping; camping site
campione (kahm-*pyōā*-nay) *m* champion; sample
campo (*kahm*-poa) *m* field; camp; ~ **di gioco** recreation ground; ~ **di golf** golf-course; ~ **di grano** cornfield; ~ **di tennis** tennis-court
camposanto (kahm-poa-*sahn*-toa) *m* churchyard
Canadà (kah-nah-*dah*) *m* Canada
canadese (kah-nah-*dāȳ*-zay) *adj* Canadian; *m* Canadian
canale (kah-*naa*-lay) *m* canal; channel
canapa (*kah*-nah-pah) *f* hemp
canarino (kah-nah-*ree*-noa) *m* canary
cancello (kahn-*chehl*-loa) *m* gate
cancro (*kahng*-kroa) *m* cancer
candela (kahn-*dāȳ*-lah) *f* candle; ~ **d'accensione** sparking-plug
candelabro (kahn-day-*laa*-broa) *m* candelabrum
candidato (kahn-dee-*daa*-toa) *m* candidate
cane (*kaa*-nay) *m* dog; ~ **guida** guide-dog
canguro (kahng-*gōō*-roa) *m* kangaroo
canile (kah-*nee*-lay) *m* kennel
canna (*kahn*-nah) *f* cane; ~ **da pesca** fishing rod
cannella (kahn-*nehl*-lah) *f* cinnamon
cannone (kahn-*nōā*-nay) *m* gun
canoa (kah-*nōā*-ah) *f* canoe
cantante (kahn-*tahn*-tay) *m* singer, vocalist
cantare (kahn-*taa*-ray) *v* *sing
canticchiare (kahn-teek-*kyaa*-ray) *v* hum
cantina (kahn-*tee*-nah) *f* cellar; wine-cellar
cantiniere (kahn-tee-*nyai*-ray) *m* wine-waiter
canto (*kahn*-toa) *m* song *c*
canzonare (kahn-tsoa-*naa*-ray) *v* mock
canzone (kahn-*tsōā*-nay) *f* song; ~ **popolare** folk song
caos (*kaa*-oass) *m* chaos
caotico (kah-*aw*-tee-koa) *adj* chaotic
capace (kah-*paa*-chay) *adj* able; capable
capacità (kah-pah-chee-*tah*) *f* capacity; faculty
capanna (kah-*pahn*-nah) *f* hut; cabin
caparbio (kah-*pahr*-byoa) *adj* obstinate
capello (kah-*payl*-loa) *m* hair; **fissatore per capelli** setting lotion
capigliatura (kah-pee-lʸah-*tōō*-rah) *f* hair-do
capire (kah-*pee*-ray) *v* *understand, *see, *take
capitale (kah-pee-*taa*-lay) *m* capital
capitalismo (kah-pee-tah-*lee*-zmoa) *m*

capitalism
capitano (kah-pee-*taa*-noa) *m* captain
capitare (kah-pee-*taa*-ray) *v* occur
capitolazione (kah-pee-toa-lah-*tsyōā*-nay) *f* capitulation
capitolo (kah-*pee*-toa-loa) *m* chapter
capo (*kaa*-poa) *m* head; manager, boss, chieftain, chief; cape; ~ **di stato** head of state
capocameriere (kah-poa-kah-may-*ryai*-ray) *m* head-waiter
capocuoco (kah-poa-*kwaw*-koa) *m* chef
capogiro (kah-poa-*jee*-roa) *m* dizziness
capolavoro (kah-poa-lah-*vōā*-roa) *m* masterpiece
capomastro (kah-poa-*mah*-stroa) *m* foreman
capostazione (kah-poa-stah-*tsyōā*-nay) *m* station-master
capoverso (kah-poa-*vehr*-soa) *m* paragraph
***capovolgere** (kah-poa-*vol*-jay-ray) *v* turn over
cappella (kahp-*pehl*-lah) *f* chapel
cappellano (kahp-payl-*laa*-noa) *m* chaplain
cappello (kahp-*pehl*-loa) *m* hat
cappotto (kahp-*pot*-toa) *m* coat; ~ **di pelliccia** fur coat
cappuccio (kahp-*poot*-choa) *m* hood
capra (*kaa*-prah) *f* goat
capretto (kah-*prayt*-toa) *m* kid
capriccio (kah-*preet*-choa) *m* fancy, fad, whim
capsula (*kah*-psoo-lah) *f* capsule
caraffa (kah-*rahf*-fah) *f* carafe
caramella (kah-rah-*mehl*-lah) *f* toffee; sweet; candy *nAm*
carato (kah-*raa*-toa) *m* carat
carattere (kah-*raht*-tay-ray) *m* character
caratteristica (kah-raht-tay-*ree*-stee-kah) *f* feature, characteristic, quality
caratteristico (kah-raht-tay-*ree*-stee-koa) *adj* typical, characteristic
caratterizzare (kah-raht-tay-reed-*dzaa*-ray) *v* mark, characterize
carbone (kahr-*bōā*-nay) *m* coal; ~ **di legno** charcoal
carburatore (kahr-boo-rah-*tōā*-ray) *m* carburettor
carcere (*kahr*-chay-ray) *m* gaol
carceriere (kahr-chay-*ryai*-ray) *m* jailer
carciofo (kahr-*chaw*-foa) *m* artichoke
cardinale (kahr-dee-*naa*-lay) *m* cardinal; *adj* cardinal
cardine (*kahr*-dee-nay) *m* hinge
cardo (*kahr*-doa) *m* thistle
carenza (kah-*rehn*-tsah) *f* shortage
caricare (kah-ree-*kaa*-ray) *v* load, charge; *wind
carico (*kaa*-ree-koa) *m* cargo, load, freight, charge
carillon (kah-ree-*yoyah*) *m* chimes *pl*
carino (kah-*ree*-noa) *adj* nice; pretty
carità (kah-ree-*tah*) *f* charity
carnagione (kahr-nah-*jōā*-nay) *f* complexion
carne (*kahr*-nay) *f* flesh; meat
carnevale (kahr-nay-*vaa*-lay) *m* carnival
caro (*kaa*-roa) *adj* dear; expensive; *m* darling
carota (kah-*raw*-tah) *f* carrot
carovana (kah-roa-*vah*-nah) *f* caravan
carpa (*kahr*-pah) *f* carp
carriera (kahr-*ryai*-rah) *f* career
carriola (kahr-*ryaw*-lah) *f* wheelbarrow
carro (*kahr*-roa) *m* cart
carrozza (kahr-*rot*-tsah) *f* coach, carriage
carrozzeria (kahr-roat-tsay-*ree*-ah) *f* coachwork; motor body *Am*
carrozzina (kahr-roat-*tsee*-nah) *f* pram; baby carriage *Am*
carrozzone (kahr-roat-*tsōā*-nay) *m* caravan
carrucola (kahr-*roo*-koa-lah) *f* pulley

carta (*kahr*-tah) *f* paper; map; menu; ~ **assorbente** blotting paper; ~ **carbone** carbon paper; ~ **da gioco** playing-card; ~ **da imballaggio** wrapping paper; ~ **da lettere** writing-paper; notepaper; ~ **da macchina** typing paper; ~ **da parati** wallpaper; ~ **di credito** credit card; charge plate *Am*; ~ **d'identità** identity card; ~ **igienica** toilet-paper; ~ **nautica** chart; ~ **stradale** road map; ~ **verde** green card; ~ **vetrata** sandpaper; **di** ~ paper
cartella (kahr-*tehl*-lah) *f* briefcase; satchel
cartello indicatore (kahr-*tehl*-loa een-dee-kah-*tōā*-ray) milepost, signpost
cartellone (kahr-tayl-*lōā*-nay) *m* poster
cartilagine (kahr-tee-*laa*-jee-nay) *f* cartilage
cartoleria (kahr-toa-lay-*ree*-ah) *f* stationer's; stationery
cartolina (kahr-toa-*lee*-nah) *f* card, postcard; ~ **illustrata** picture postcard
cartoncino (kahr-toan-*chee*-noa) *m* card
cartone (kahr-*tōā*-nay) *m* cardboard; ~ **animato** cartoon; **di** ~ cardboard
cartuccia (kahr-*toot*-chah) *f* cartridge
casa (*kaa*-sah) *f* house; home; **a** ~ home; ~ **di campagna** country house; ~ **di riposo** rest-home; ~ **galleggiante** houseboat; ~ **padronale** manor-house; **in** ~ at home
casalinga (kah-sah-*leeng*-gah) *f* housewife
casalingo (kah-sah-*leeng*-goa) *adj* home-made
cascata (kah-*skaa*-tah) *f* waterfall
cascina (kah-*shee*-nah) *f* farmhouse
casco (*kah*-skoa) *m* helmet
caseggiato (kah-sayd-*jaa*-toa) *m* block of flats
caserma (kah-*zehr*-mah) *f* barracks *pl*
casinò (kah-see-*noa*) *m* casino
caso *m* luck, chance; case, instance, event; ~ **di emergenza** emergency; **in** ~ **di** in case of; **in ogni** ~ anyway; **per** ~ by chance
cassa (*kahss*-sah) *f* pay-desk; ~ **di risparmio** savings bank; ~ **mobile** container
cassaforte (kahss-sah-*for*-tay) *f* safe
casseruola (kahss-say-*rwaw*-lah) *f* saucepan
cassetta postale (kahss-*sayt*-tah poa-*staa*-lay) letter-box; mailbox *nAm*
cassetto (kahss-*sayt*-toa) *m* drawer
cassettone (kahss-sayt-*tōā*-nay) *m* chest of drawers
cassiera (kahss-*syai*-rah) *f* cashier
cassiere (kahss-*syai*-ray) *m* cashier
castagna (kah-*staa*-ñah) *f* chestnut
castano (kah-*staa*-noa) *adj* auburn
castello (kah-*stehl*-loa) *m* castle
casto (*kah*-stoa) *adj* chaste, pure
castoro (kah-*staw*-roa) *m* beaver
catacomba (kah-tah-*koam*-bah) *f* catacomb
catalogo (kah-*taa*-loa-goa) *m* catalogue
catarro (kah-*tahr*-roa) *m* catarrh
catastrofe (kah-*tah*-stroa-fay) *f* catastrophe, disaster
categoria (kah-tay-goa-*ree*-ah) *f* category
categorico (kah-tay-*gaw*-ree-koa) *adj* explicit
catena (kah-*tāy*-nah) *f* chain; ~ **di montagne** mountain range
catino (kah-*tee*-noa) *m* basin
catrame (kah-*traa*-may) *m* tar
cattedra (*kaht*-tay-drah) *f* pulpit
cattedrale (kaht-tay-*draa*-lay) *f* cathedral
cattivo (kaht-*tee*-voa) *adj* bad; ill,

evil; naughty
cattolico (kaht-*taw*-lee-koa) *adj* Roman Catholic, catholic
cattura (kaht-*tōō*-rah) *f* capture
catturare (kaht-too-*raa*-ray) *v* capture
caucciù (kou-*choo*) *m* rubber
causa (*kou*-zah) *f* cause; reason; case; lawsuit; **a ~ di** owing to; because of, for, on account of
causare (kou-*zaa*-ray) *v* cause
cautela (kou-*tai*-lah) *f* caution
cauto (*kou*-toa) *adj* cautious
cauzione (kou-*tsyōā*-nay) *f* guarantee, security; bail
cava (*kaa*-vah) *f* quarry
cavalcare (kah-vahl-*kaa*-ray) *v* *ride
cavaliere (kah-vah-*lyai*-ray) *m* knight
cavalla (kah-*vahl*-lah) *f* mare
cavallerizzo (kah-vahl-lay-*reet*-tzoa) *m* rider, horseman
cavalletta (kah-vahl-*layt*-tah) *f* grasshopper
cavallino (kah-vahl-*lee*-noa) *m* pony
cavallo (kah-*vahl*-loa) *m* horse; **~ da corsa** race-horse; **~ vapore** horsepower
cavatappi (kah-vah-*tahp*-pee) *m* corkscrew
caverna (kah-*vehr*-nah) *f* cavern, cave
caviale (kah-*vyaa*-lay) *m* caviar
caviglia (kah-*vee*-lyah) *f* ankle
cavità (kah-vee-*tah*) *f* cavity
cavo (*kaa*-voa) *m* cable
cavolfiore (kah-voal-*fyōā*-ray) *m* cauliflower
cavolini (kah-voa-*lee*-nee) *mpl* sprouts *pl*
cavolo (*kaa*-voa-loa) *m* cabbage
ceco (*chai*-koa) *adj* Czech; *m* Czech
Cecoslovacchia (chay-koa-zloa-*vahk*-kyah) *f* Czechoslovakia
cedere (*chai*-day-ray) *v* *give in, indulge
cedola (*chai*-doa-lah) *f* coupon
cedro (*chāy*-droa) *m* lime
ceffone (chayf-*fōā*-nay) *m* smack
celare (chay-*laa*-ray) *v* *hide
celebrare (chay-lay-*braa*-ray) *v* celebrate
celebrazione (chay-lay-brah-*tsyōā*-nay) *f* celebration
celebre (*chai*-lay-bray) *adj* famous
celebrità (chay-lay-bree-*tah*) *f* celebrity
celibato (chay-lee-*baa*-toa) *m* celibacy
celibe (*chai*-lee-bay) *adj* single; *m* bachelor
cella (*chehl*-lah) *f* cell
cellofan (*chehl*-loa-fahn) *m* cellophane
cemento (chay-*mayn*-toa) *m* cement
cena (*chāy*-nah) *f* dinner, supper
cenere (*chāy*-nay-ray) *f* ash
cenno (*chayn*-noa) *m* sign
censura (chayn-*sōō*-rah) *f* censorship
centigrado (chayn-*tee*-grah-doa) *adj* centigrade
centimetro (chayn-*tee*-may-troa) *m* centimetre; tape-measure
cento (*chehn*-toa) *num* hundred
centrale (chayn-*traa*-lay) *adj* central; **~ elettrica** power-station
centralinista (chayn-trah-lee-*nee*-stah) *f* operator
centralino (chayn-trah-*lee*-noa) *m* telephone exchange
centralizzare (chayn-trah-leed-*dzaa*-ray) *v* centralize
centro (*chehn*-troa) *m* centre; **~ commerciale** shopping centre; **~ della città** town centre; **~ di ricreazione** recreation centre; **~ sanitario** health centre
ceppo (*chayp*-poa) *m* block; log
cera (*chāy*-rah) *f* wax
ceramica (chay-*raa*-mee-kah) *f* faience, ceramics *pl*, pottery
cerbiatto (chayr-*byaht*-toa) *m* fawn
cercare (chayr-*kaa*-ray) *v* look for; *seek, search, hunt for; look up

cerchio (*chayr*-kyoa) *m* circle, ring
cerchione (chayr-*kyōā*-nay) *m* rim
cerimonia (chay-ree-*maw*-ñah) *f* ceremony
cerotto (chay-*rot*-toa) *m* plaster, adhesive tape
certamente (chayr-tah-*mayn*-tay) *adv* surely
certezza (chayr-*tayt*-tsah) *f* certainty
certificato (chayr-tee-fee-*kaa*-toa) *m* certificate; ~ **di sanità** health certificate
certo (*chehr*-toa) *adj* certain
cervello (chayr-*vehl*-loa) *m* brain
cervo (*chehr*-voa) *m* deer
cespuglio (chay-*spōō*-l^{y}oa) *m* scrub, bush
cessare (chayss-*saa*-ray) *v* end; stop, discontinue, quit
cestino (chay-*stee*-noa) *m* wastepaper-basket
ceto (*chai*-toa) *m* rank; ~ **medio** middle class
cetriolo (chay-*tryaw*-loa) *m* cucumber
chalet (shah-*lay*) *m* chalet
champagne (shah~~ng~~-*pahñ*) *m* champagne
che (kay) *pron* that, who, which; how; *conj* that; as, than
chi (kee) *pron* who; **a** ~ whom
chiacchierare (kyahk-kyay-*raa*-ray) *v* chat
chiacchierata (kyahk-kyay-*raa*-tah) *f* chat
chiacchierone (kyahk-kyay-*rōā*-nay) *m* chatterbox
chiamare (kyah-*maa*-ray) *v* call; **chiamarsi** *be called
chiamata (kyah-*maa*-tah) *f* telephone call; ~ **locale** local call
chiarificare (kyah-ree-fee-*kaa*-ray) *v* clarify
chiarire (kyah-*ree*-ray) *v* clarify, explain
chiaro (*kyaa*-roa) *adj* clear; pale, light; plain, distinct; ~ **di luna** moonlight
chiasso (*kyahss*-soa) *m* noise, racket
chiave (*kyaa*-vay) *f* key; wrench; ~ **di casa** latchkey
chiavistello (kyah-vee-*stehl*-loa) *m* bolt
chiazza (*keeaht*-tsah) *f* spot
chiazzato (kyaht-*tsaa*-toa) *adj* spotted
***chiedere** (*kyai*-day-ray) *v* ask; beg; ***chiedersi** wonder
chierico (*kyai*-ree-koa) *m* clergyman
chiesa (*kyai*-zah) *f* church, chapel
chiglia (*kee*-l^{y}ah) *f* keel
chilo (*kee*-loa) *m* kilogram
chilometraggio (kee-loa-may-*trahd*-joa) *m* distance in kilometres
chilometro (kee-*law*-may-troa) *m* kilometre
chimica (*kee*-mee-kah) *f* chemistry
chimico (*kee*-mee-koa) *adj* chemical
chinarsi (kee-*nahr*-see) *v* *bend down
chinino (kee-*nee*-noa) *m* quinine
chiocciola di mare (*kyot*-choa-lah dee *maa*-ray) winkle
chiodo (*kyaw*-doa) *m* nail
chiosco (*kyo*-skoa) *m* kiosk
chirurgo (kee-*roor*-goa) *m* surgeon
chitarra (kee-*tahr*-rah) *f* guitar
***chiudere** (*kyōō*-day-ray) *v* close; fasten, *shut; turn off; ~ **a chiave** lock; lock up
chiunque (*kyoong*-kway) *pron* anybody, whoever; anyone
chiusa (*kyōō*-sah) *f* sluice, lock
chiuso (*kyōō*-soa) *adj* closed, shut
chiusura lampo (kyoo-*sōō*-rah *lahm*-poa) zip; zipper
ci (chee) *pron* ourselves, us
ciabatta (chah-*baht*-tah) *f* slipper
cialda (*chahl*-dah) *f* waffle
ciancia (*chahn*-chah) *f* chat
ciao! (*chaa*-oa) hello!
ciarlare (chahr-*laa*-ray) *v* chat

ciarlata (chahr-*laa*-tah) *f* chat
ciarlatano (chahr-lah-*taa*-noa) *m* quack
ciascuno (chah-*skōō*-noa) *adj* every, each
cibo (*chee*-boa) *m* fare, food; ~ **surgelato** frozen food
cicatrice (chee-kah-*tree*-chay) *f* scar
ciclista (chee-*klee*-stah) *m* cyclist
ciclo (*chee*-kloa) *m* cycle; bicycle
cicogna (chee-*kōā*-ñah) *f* stork
cieco (*chai*-koa) *adj* blind
cielo (*chai*-loa) *m* sky; heaven
cifra (*chee*-frah) *f* number, figure
ciglio (*chee*-lʸoa) *m* (pl le ciglia) eyelash
cigno (*chee*-ñoa) *m* swan
cigolare (chee-goa-*laa*-ray) *v* creak
Cile (*chee*-lay) *m* Chile
cileno (chee-*lāy*-noa) *adj* Chilean; *m* Chilean
ciliegia (chee-*lʸāy*-jah) *f* cherry
cilindro (chee-*leen*-droa) *m* cylinder
cima (*chee*-mah) *f* top; peak; **in ~ a** on top of
cimice (*chee*-mee-chay) *f* bug
cimitero (chee-mee-*tai*-roa) *m* graveyard, cemetery
Cina (*chee*-nah) *f* China
cinegiornale (chee-nay-joar-*naa*-lay) *m* newsreel
cinema (*chee*-nay-mah) *m* pictures; movie theater *Am*, movies *Am*
cinematografo (chee-nay-mah-*taw*-grah-foa) *m* cinema
cinepresa (chee-nay-*prāy*-sah) *f* camera
cinese (chee-*nāy*-say) *adj* Chinese; *m* Chinese
***cingere** (*cheen*-jay-ray) *v* encircle
cinghia (*cheeng*-gyah) *f* strap; belt; ~ **del ventilatore** fan belt
cinquanta (cheeng-*kwahn*-tah) *num* fifty
cinque (*cheeng*-kway) *num* five

ciò (cho) *pron* that, this
cioccolata (choak-koa-*laa*-tah) *f* chocolate
cioccolatino (choak-koa-lah-*tee*-noa) *m* chocolate
cioccolato (choak-koa-*laa*-toa) *m* chocolate
cioè (choa-*ai*) *adv* namely
ciottolo (*chot*-toa-loa) *m* pebble
cipolla (chee-*poal*-lah) *f* onion
cipollina (chee-poal-*lee*-nah) *f* chives *pl*
cipria (*chee*-pryah) *f* face-powder; **piumino da ~** powder-puff
circa (*cheer*-kah) *adv* approximately, about; *prep* about
circo (*cheer*-koa) *m* circus
circolazione (cheer-koa-lah-*tsyōā*-nay) *f* circulation; ~ **del sangue** circulation
circolo (*cheer*-koa-loa) *m* circle; club; ~ **nautico** yacht-club
circondare (cheer-koan-*daa*-ray) *v* circle, encircle, surround
circonvallazione (cheer-koan-vahl-lah-*tsyōā*-nay) *f* by-pass
circostante (cheer-koa-*stahn*-tay) *adj* surrounding
circostanza (cheer-koa-*stahn*-tsah) *f* circumstance, condition
cistifellea (chee-stee-*fehl*-lay-ah) *f* gall bladder
cistite (chee-*stee*-tay) *f* cystitis
citare (chee-*taa*-ray) *v* quote
citazione (chee-tah-*tsyōā*-nay) *f* mention, quotation; summons
città (cheet-*tah*) *f* city, town
cittadinanza (cheet-tah-dee-*nahn*-tsah) *f* townspeople *pl*; citizenship
cittadino (cheet-tah-*dee*-noa) *m* citizen
civico (*chee*-vee-koa) *adj* civic
civile (chee-*vee*-lay) *adj* civilian, civil
civilizzato (chee-vee-leed-*dzaa*-toa) *adj* civilized

civiltà (chee-veel-*tah*) *f* civilization
clacson (*klahk*-soan) *m* hooter; horn
classe (*klahss*-say) *f* class; grade; form; ~ **turistica** tourist class
classico (*klahss*-see-koa) *adj* classical
classificare (klahss-see-fee-*kaa*-ray) *v* classify, grade; sort
clausola (*klou*-zoa-lah) *f* clause
clava (*klaa*-vah) *f* club
clavicembalo (klah-vee-*chaym*-bah-loa) *m* harpsichord
clavicola (klah-*vee*-koa-lah) *f* collarbone
clemenza (klay-*mehn*-tsah) *f* mercy
cliente (*klyehn*-tay) *m* client, customer
clima (*klee*-mah) *m* climate
clinica (*klee*-nee-kah) *f* clinic
cloro (*klaw*-roa) *m* chlorine
coagulare (koa-ah-goo-*laa*-ray) *v* coagulate
cocaina (koa-kah-*ee*-nah) *f* cocaine
cocciuto (koat-*chōō*-toa) *adj* stubborn
cocco (*kok*-koa) *m* pet
coccodrillo (koak-koa-*dreel*-loa) *m* crocodile
coda (*kōā*-dah) *f* tail; queue; ***fare la** ~ queue; stand in line *Am*
codardo (koa-*dahr*-doa) *m* coward
codice (*kaw*-dee-chay) *m* code; ~ **postale** zip code *Am*
coerenza (koa-ay-*rehn*-tsah) *f* coherence
cofano (*kaw*-fah-noa) *m* bonnet; hood *nAm*
***cogliere** (*kaw*-lyay-ray) *v* pick; *catch
cognac (koa-*ñahk*) *m* cognac
cognata (koa-*ñaa*-tah) *f* sister-in-law
cognato (koa-*ñaa*-toa) *m* brother-in-law
cognome (koa-*ñōā*-may) *m* family name, surname; ~ **da nubile** maiden name
coincidenza (koa-een-chee-*dehn*-tsah) *f* connection
***coincidere** (koa-een-*chee*-day-ray) *v* coincide
***coinvolgere** (koa-een-*vol*-jay-ray) *v* involve
colapasta (koa-lah-*pah*-stah) *m* strainer
colazione (koa-lah-*tsyōā*-nay) *f* luncheon, lunch; **prima** ~ breakfast; **seconda** ~ lunch
colla (*koal*-lah) *f* gum, glue
collaborazione (koal-lah-boa-rah-*tsyōā*-nay) *f* collaboration
collana (koal-*laa*-nah) *f* beads *pl*, necklace
collare (koal-*laa*-ray) *m* collar
collega (koal-*lai*-gah) *m* colleague
collegare (koal-lay-*gaa*-ray) *v* connect, link
collera (*kol*-lay-rah) *f* anger, passion
collettivo (koal-layt-*tee*-voa) *adj* collective
colletto (koal-*layt*-toa) *m* collar; **bottoncino per** ~ collar stud
collettore (koal-layt-*tōā*-ray) *m* collector
collezione (koal-lay-*tsyōā*-nay) *f* collection; ~ **d'arte** art collection
collezionista (koal-lay-tsyoa-*nee*-stah) *m* collector
collina (koal-*lee*-nah) *f* hill
collinoso (koal-lee-*nōā*-soa) *adj* hilly
collisione (koal-lee-*zyōā*-nay) *f* collision
collo (*kol*-loa) *m* throat, neck
collocare (koal-loa-*kaa*-ray) *v* *lay, *put
colmo (*koal*-moa) *adj* full up; *m* height
Colombia (koa-*loam*-byah) *f* Colombia
colombiano (koa-loam-*byaa*-noa) *adj* Colombian; *m* Colombian
colonia (koa-*law*-ñah) *f* colony; ~ **di vacanze** holiday camp

colonna (koa-*lon*-nah) *f* pillar, column
colonnello (koa-loan-*nehl*-loa) *m* colonel
colore (koa-*lōā*-ray) *m* paint; colour; **di ~** coloured
colorito (koa-loa-*ree*-toa) *adj* colourful
colpa (*koal*-pah) *f* guilt, fault, blame
colpetto (koal-*payt*-toa) *m* tap
colpevole (koal-*pāy*-voa-lay) *adj* guilty; **dichiarare ~** convict
colpire (koal-*pee*-ray) *v* *hit; *strike; touch
colpo (*koal*-poa) *m* knock, blow; stroke; **~ di sole** sunstroke
coltello (koal-*tehl*-loa) *m* knife
coltivare (koal-tee-*vaa*-ray) *v* cultivate; *grow, raise
colto (*koal*-toa) *adj* cultured
coltura (koal-*tōō*-rah) *f* culture
coma (*kaw*-mah) *m* coma
comandante (koa-mahn-*dahn*-tay) *m* commander; captain
comandare (koa-mahn-*daa*-ray) *v* command, order
comando (koa-*mahn*-doa) *m* order; leadership
combattere (koam-*baht*-tay-ray) *v* combat, *fight, battle
combattimento (koam-baht-tee-*mayn*-toa) *m* combat, battle; fight, struggle
combinare (koam-bee-*naa*-ray) *v* combine
combinazione (koam-bee-nah-*tsyōā*-nay) *f* combination
combustibile (koam-boo-*stee*-bee-lay) *m* fuel
come (*kōā*-may) *adv* such as, like; how; *conj* as; **~ pure** as well; as well as; **~ se** as if
comico (*kaw*-mee-koa) *adj* comic, humorous; *m* comedian, entertainer
cominciare (koa-meen-*chaa*-ray) *v* *begin, start
comitato (koa-mee-*taa*-toa) *m* committee, commission
commedia (koam-*mai*-dyah) *f* comedy; **~ musicale** musical comedy, musical
commediante (koam-may-*dyahn*-tay) *m* comedian
commemorazione (koam-may-moa-rah-*tsyōā*-nay) *f* commemoration
commentare (koam-mayn-*taa*-ray) *v* comment
commento (koam-*mayn*-toa) *m* comment; note
commerciale (koam-mayr-*chaa*-lay) *adj* commercial
commerciante (koam-mayr-*chahn*-tay) *m* tradesman, merchant, dealer
commerciare (koam-mayr-*chaa*-ray) *v* trade
commercio (koam-*mehr*-choa) *m* trade, commerce, business; **~ al minuto** retail trade
commessa (koam-*mayss*-sah) *f* salesgirl
commesso (koam-*mayss*-soa) *m* salesman, shop assistant; **~ d'ufficio** clerk
commestibile (koam-may-*stee*-bee-lay) *adj* edible
***commettere** (koam-*mayt*-tay-ray) *v* commit
commissione (koam-meess-*syōā*-nay) *f* message, errand; committee
commovente (koam-moa-*vehn*-tay) *adj* touching
commozione (koam-moa-*tsyōā*-nay) *f* emotion; **~ cerebrale** concussion
***commuovere** (koam-*mwaw*-vay-ray) *v* move
comò (koa-*mo*) *m* (pl ~) bureau *nAm*
comodità (koa-moa-dee-*tah*) *f* comfort
comodo (*kaw*-moa-doa) *adj* convenient; comfortable, easy; *m* leisure
compagnia (koam-pah-*ñee*-ah) *f* com-

pany; society
compagno (koam-*paa*-ñoa) *m* companion; partner; comrade; ~ **di classe** class-mate
***comparire** (koam-pah-*ree*-ray) *v* appear
compassione (koam-pahss-*syōā*-nay) *f* sympathy; **provare ~ per** pity
compatire (koam-pah-*tee*-ray) *v* pity
compatriota (koam-pah-*tryaw*-tah) *m* countryman
compatto (koam-*paht*-toa) *adj* compact
compensare (koam-payn-*saa*-ray) *v* compensate, *make good
compensazione (koam-payn-sah-*tsyōā*-nay) *f* compensation
compera (*koam*-pay-rah) *f* purchase
competente (koam-pay-*tehn*-tay) *adj* expert; qualified
competere (koam-*pai*-tay-ray) *v* compete
competizione (koam-pay-tee-*tsyōā*-nay) *f* contest
compiacente (koam-pyah-*chehn*-tay) *adj* willing
compiere (*koam*-pyay-ray) *v* accomplish; commit; perform
compilare (koam-pee-*laa*-ray) *v* compile; *make up; fill out *Am*
compitare (koam-pee-*taa*-ray) *v* *spell
compito (*koam*-pee-toa) *m* duty, task
compleanno (koam-play-*ahn*-noa) *m* birthday
complesso (koam-*plehss*-soa) *adj* complex; *m* complex
completamente (koam-play-tah-*mayn*-tay) *adv* wholly, completely, quite
completare (koam-play-*taa*-ray) *v* complete, finish; fill in; fill out *Am*
completo (koam-*plai*-toa) *adj* total, complete, whole, utter
complicato (koam-plee-*kaa*-toa) *adj* complicated
complice (*kom*-plee-chay) *m* accessary
complimentare (koam-plee-mayn-*taa*-ray) *v* compliment
complimento (koam-plee-*mayn*-toa) *m* compliment
complotto (koam-*plot*-toa) *m* plot
componimento (koam-poa-nee-*mayn*-toa) *m* essay
***comporre** (koam-*poar*-ray) *v* compose
comportamento (koam-poar-tah-*mayn*-toa) *m* behaviour
comportare (koam-poar-*taa*-ray) *v* imply; **comportarsi** behave, act; **comportarsi male** misbehave
compositore (koam-poa-zee-*tōā*-ray) *m* composer
composizione (koam-poa-zee-*tsyōā*-nay) *f* composition
composto (koam-*poa*-stoa) *adj* sedate
comprare (koam-*praa*-ray) *v* *buy, purchase
compratore (koam-prah-*tōā*-ray) *m* buyer, purchaser
***comprendere** (koam-*prehn*-day-ray) *v* contain, include, comprise; conceive, *understand
comprensione (koam-prayn-*syōā*-nay) *f* understanding
comprensivo (koam-prayn-*see*-voa) *adj* comprehensive; sympathetic
compreso (koam-*prāȳ*-soa) *adj* inclusive
compromesso (koam-proa-*mayss*-soa) *m* compromise
computare (koam-poo-*taa*-ray) *v* calculate
comune (koa-*mōō*-nay) *adj* common
comunicare (koa-moo-nee-*kaa*-ray) *v* communicate, inform
comunicato (koa-moo-nee-*kaa*-toa) *m* communiqué
comunicazione (koa-moo-nee-kah-*tsyōā*-nay) *f* communication, infor-

mation
comunione (koa-moo-*nyōā*-nay) *f* congregation
comunismo (koa-moo-*nee*-zmoa) *m* communism
comunista (koa-moo-*nee*-stah) *m* communist
comunità (koa-moo-nee-*tah*) *f* community
comunque (koa-*moong*-kway) *adv* at any rate, any way; though, still
con (koan) *prep* with; by
***concedere** (koan-*chai*-day-ray) *v* grant
concentrare (koan-chayn-*traa*-ray) *v* concentrate
concentrazione (koan-chayn-trah-*tsyōā*-nay) *f* concentration
concepimento (koan-chay-pee-*mayn*-toa) *m* conception
concepire (koan-chay-*pee*-ray) *v* conceive
concernere (koan-*chehr*-nay-ray) *v* concern
concerto (koan-*chehr*-toa) *m* concert
concessione (koan-chayss-*syōā*-nay) *f* concession
concetto (koan-*cheht*-toa) *m* idea
concezione (koan-chay-*tsyōā*-nay) *f* conception
conchiglia (koang-*kee*-lʸah) *f* sea-shell, shell
concime (koan-*chee*-may) *m* manure
conciso (koan-*chee*-zoa) *adj* concise
***concludere** (koang-*klōō*-day-ray) *v* conclude
conclusione (koang-kloo-*zyōā*-nay) *f* conclusion, issue
concordanza (koang-koar-*dahn*-tsah) *f* agreement
concorrente (koang-koar-*rehn*-tay) *m* rival, competitor
concorrenza (koang-koar-*rehn*-tsah) *f* rivalry, competition
concorso (koang-*koar*-soa) *m* concurrence
concreto (koang-*krai*-toa) *adj* concrete
concupiscenza (koang-koo-peesh-*shehn*-tsah) *f* lust
condanna (koan-*dahn*-nah) *f* conviction
condannare (koan-dahn-*naa*-ray) *v* sentence
condannato (koan-dahn-*naa*-toa) *m* convict
condire (koan-*dee*-ray) *v* flavour
condito (koan-*dee*-toa) *adj* spiced
***condividere** (koan-dee-*vee*-day-ray) *v* share
condizionale (koan-dee-tsyoa-*naa*-lay) *adj* conditional
condizione (koan-dee-*tsyōā*-nay) *f* term, condition
condotta (koan-*doat*-tah) *f* conduct
***condurre** (koan-*door*-ray) *v* conduct, carry; *drive
conduttore (koan-doot-*tōā*-ray) *m* conductor
confederazione (koan-fay-day-rah-*tsyōā*-nay) *f* union, federation
conferenza (koan-fay-*rehn*-tsah) *f* lecture; conference; ~ **stampa** press conference
conferma (koan-*fayr*-mah) *f* confirmation
confermare (koan-fayr-*maa*-ray) *v* confirm, acknowledge
confessare (koan-fayss-*saa*-ray) *v* confess
confessione (koan-fayss-*syōā*-nay) *f* confession
confezionare (koan-fay-tsyoa-*naa*-ray) *v* manufacture
confezionato (koan-fay-tsyoa-*naa*-toa) *adj* ready-made
confidente (koan-fee-*dehn*-tay) *adj* confident
confidenziale (koan-fee-dayn-*tsyaa*-lay)

adj confidential; familiar
confine (koan-*fee*-nay) *m* border
confiscare (koan-fee-*skaa*-ray) *v* confiscate
conflitto (koan-*fleet*-toa) *m* conflict
***confondere** (koan-*foan*-day-ray) *v* *mistake, confuse
in conformità con (een koan-foar-mee-*tah* koan) in accordance with
confortevole (koan-foar-*tāy*-voa-lay) *adj* cosy, comfortable
conforto (koan-*for*-toa) *m* comfort
confronto (koan-*froan*-toa) *m* comparison; confrontation
confusione (koan-foo-*zyōā*-nay) *f* confusion, disorder
confuso (koan-*fōō*-zoa) *adj* confused
congedare (koan-jay-*daa*-ray) *v* dismiss
congedo (koan-*jai*-doa) *m* leave
congelarsi (koan-jay-*lahr*-see) *v* *freeze
congelato (koan-jay-*laa*-toa) *adj* frozen
congelatore (koan-jay-lah-*tōā*-ray) *m* deep-freeze
congettura (koan-jayt-*tōō*-rah) *f* guess
congetturare (koan-jayt-too-*raa*-ray) *v* guess
congiunto (koan-*joon*-toa) *adj* joint; related
congiura (koan-*jōō*-rah) *f* plot
congratularsi (koang-grah-too-*lahr*-see) *v* congratulate
congratulazione (koang-grah-too-lah-*tsyōā*-nay) *f* congratulation
congregazione (koang-gray-gah-*tsyōā*-nay) *f* congregation
congresso (koang-*grehss*-soa) *m* congress
coniglio (koa-*nee*-lʸoa) *m* rabbit
coniugi (*kaw*-ñoo-jee) *mpl* married couple
connessione (koan-nayss-*syōā*-nay) *f* connection
***connettere** (koan-*neht*-tay-ray) *v* connect; plug in
connotati (koan-noa-*taa*-tee) *mpl* description
conoscenza (koa-noash-*shehn*-tsah) *f* knowledge; acquaintance
***conoscere** (koa-*noash*-shay-ray) *v* *know
conquista (koang-*kwee*-stah) *f* conquest
conquistare (koang-kwee-*staa*-ray) *v* conquer
conquistatore (koang-kwee-stah-*tōā*-ray) *m* conqueror
consapevole (koan-sah-*pāy*-voa-lay) *adj* aware
conscio (*kon*-shoa) *adj* conscious
consegna (koan-*sāy*-ñah) *f* delivery
consegnare (koan-say-*ñaa*-ray) *v* deliver; commit
conseguentemente (koan-say-gwayn-tay-*mayn*-tay) *adv* consequently
conseguenza (koan-say-*gwehn*-tsah) *f* result, consequence; issue; **in ~ di** because of, for
conseguibile (koan-say-*gwee*-bee-lay) *adj* attainable
conseguire (koan-say-*gwee*-ray) *v* obtain
consenso (koan-*sehn*-soa) *m* consent
consentire (koan-sayn-*tee*-ray) *v* agree, consent
conservare (koan-sayr-*vaa*-ray) *v* preserve; *hold
conservatore (koan-sayr-vah-*tōā*-ray) *adj* conservative
conservatorio (koan-sayr-vah-*taw*-ryoa) *m* music academy
conserve (koan-*sehr*-vay) *fpl* tinned food; ***mettere in conserva** preserve
considerare (koan-see-day-*raa*-ray) *v* consider, regard; count, reckon
considerato (koan-see-day-*raa*-toa)

prep considering
considerazione (koan-see-day-rah-*tsyōā*-nay) *f* consideration
considerevole (koan-see-day-*rāy*-voa-lay) *adj* considerable
consigliare (koan-see-*lyaa*-ray) *v* recommend, advise
consigliere (koan-see-*lyai*-ray) *m* counsellor; councillor
consiglio (koan-*see*-lyoa) *m* board; advice; counsel, council
consistere in (koan-*see*-stay-ray) consist of
consolare (koan-soa-*laa*-ray) *v* comfort
consolato (koan-soa-*laa*-toa) *m* consulate
consolazione (koan-soa-lah-*tsyōā*-nay) *f* comfort
console (*kon*-soa-lay) *m* consul
consorte (koan-*sor*-tay) *f* wife
constante (koan-*stahn*-tay) *adj* constant
constatare (koan-stah-*taa*-ray) *v* ascertain
consueto (koan-*swai*-toa) *adj* habitual
consulta (koan-*sool*-tah) *f* consultation
consultare (koan-sool-*taa*-ray) *v* consult
consultazione (koan-sool-tah-*tsyōā*-nay) *f* consultation
consultorio (koan-sool-*taw*-ryoa) *m* surgery
consumare (koan-soo-*maa*-ray) *v* use up
consumato (koan-soo-*maa*-toa) *adj* worn
consumatore (koan-soo-mah-*tōā*-ray) *m* consumer
contadino (koan-tah-*dee*-noa) *m* peasant
contagioso (koan-tah-*jōā*-soa) *adj* contagious, infectious
contaminazione (koan-tah-mee-nah-*tsyōā*-nay) *f* pollution
contanti (koan-*tahn*-tee) *mpl* cash
contare (koan-*taa*-ray) *v* count; ~ **su** rely on
contattare (koan-taht-*taa*-ray) *v* contact
contatto (koan-*taht*-toa) *m* touch, contact
conte (*koan*-tay) *m* count, earl
contea (koan-*tai*-ah) *f* county
contemporaneo (koan-taym-poa-*raa*-nay-oa) *adj* contemporary; *m* contemporary
***contenere** (koan-tay-*nāy*-ray) *v* contain; comprise; restrain
contento (koan-*tehn*-toa) *adj* content; glad, happy
contenuto (koan-tay-*nōō*-toa) *m* contents *pl*
contessa (koan-*tayss*-sah) *f* countess
contiguo (koan-*tee*-gwoa) *adj* neighbouring
continentale (koan-tee-nayn-*taa*-lay) *adj* continental
continente (koan-tee-*nehn*-tay) *m* continent
continuamente (koan-tee-nwah-*mayn*-tay) *adv* all the time, continually
continuare (koan-tee-*nwaa*-ray) *v* continue, carry on; *go on, *go ahead, *keep on, *keep
continuazione (koan-tee-nwah-*tsyōā*-nay) *f* sequel
continuo (koan-*tee*-nwoa) *adj* continuous, continual
conto (*koan*-toa) *m* account; bill; check *nAm*; ~ **bancario** bank account; **per ~ di** on behalf of; ***rendere ~ di** account for
contorno (koan-*toar*-noa) *m* outline, contour
contrabbandare (koan-trahb-bahn-*daa*-ray) *v* smuggle
***contraddire** (koan-trahd-*dee*-ray) *v*

contradict
contraddittorio (koan-trahd-deet-*taw*-ryoa) *adj* contradictory
contraffatto (koan-trahf-*faht*-toa) *adj* false
contralto (koan-*trahl*-toa) *m* alto
contrario (koan-*traa*-ryoa) *adj* contrary, opposite; *m* reverse, contrary; **al** ~ on the contrary
***contrarre** (koan-*trahr*-ray) *v* contract
contrasto (koan-*trah*-stoa) *m* contrast
contratto (koan-*traht*-toa) *m* agreement, contract; ~ **di affitto** lease
contravvenzione (koan-trahv-vayn-*tsyōā*-nay) *f* ticket
contribuire (koan-tree-*bwee*-ray) *v* contribute
contributo (koan-tree-*bōō*-toa) *m* contribution
contribuzione (koan-tree-boo-*tsyōā*-nay) *f* contribution
contro (*koan*-troa) *prep* against; versus
controllare (koan-troal-*laa*-ray) *v* control
controllo (koan-*trol*-loa) *m* control, inspection; ~ **passaporti** passport control
controllore (koan-troal-*lōā*-ray) *m* ticket collector
controversia (koan-troa-*vehr*-syah) *f* dispute
controverso (koan-troa-*vehr*-soa) *adj* controversial
contusione (koan-too-*zyōā*-nay) *f* bruise
conveniente (koan-vay-*ñehn*-tay) *adj* convenient, proper
***convenire** (koan-vay-*nee*-ray) *v* suit, fit
convento (koan-*vehn*-toa) *m* convent; nunnery
conversazione (koan-vayr-sah-*tsyōā*-nay) *f* conversation, discussion, talk
convertire (koan-vayr-*tee*-ray) *v* convert; cash
***convincere** (koan-*veen*-chay-ray) *v* convince, persuade
convinzione (koan-veen-*tsyōā*-nay) *f* conviction, persuasion
convitto (koan-*veet*-toa) *m* boarding-school
convulsione (koan-vool-*syōā*-nay) *f* convulsion
cooperante (koa-oa-pay-*rahn*-tay) *adj* co-operative
cooperativa (koa-oa-pay-rah-*tee*-vah) *f* co-operative
cooperativo (koa-oa-pay-rah-*tee*-voa) *adj* co-operative
cooperatore (koa-oa-pay-rah-*tōā*-ray) *adj* co-operative
cooperazione (koa-oa-pay-rah-*tsyōā*-nay) *f* co-operation
coordinare (koa-oar-dee-*naa*-ray) *v* coordinate
coordinazione (koa-oar-dee-nah-*tsyōā*-nay) *f* co-ordination
coperchio (koa-*pehr*-kyoa) *m* top, cover, lid
coperta (koa-*pehr*-tah) *f* blanket; quilt; deck
copertina (koa-payr-*tee*-nah) *f* cover, jacket
coperto (koa-*pehr*-toa) *adj* overcast
copertone (koa-payr-*tōā*-nay) *m* tyre
copia (*kaw*-pyah) *f* copy; ~ **fotostatica** photostat
copiare (koa-*pyaa*-ray) *v* copy
coppa (*kop*-pah) *f* cup
coppia (*kop*-pyah) *f* couple
copriletto (koa-pree-*leht*-toa) *m* counterpane
***coprire** (koa-*pree*-ray) *v* cover
coraggio (koa-*rahd*-joa) *m* guts, courage
coraggioso (koa-rahd-*jōā*-soa) *adj* courageous; plucky, brave, bold

corallo (koa-*rahl*-loa) *m* coral
corazza (koa-*raht*-tsah) *f* armour
corda (*kor*-dah) *f* cord, rope; string
cordiale (koar-*dyaa*-lay) *adj* cordial; hearty, sympathetic
cordicella (koar-dee-*chehl*-lah) *f* line
cordoglio (koar-*daw*-lyoa) *m* grief
cordone elettrico (koar-*dōā*-nay ay-*leht*-tree-koa) electric cord
cornacchia (koar-*nahk*-kyah) *f* crow
cornice (koar-*nee*-chay) *f* frame
corno[1] (*kor*-noa) *m* (pl le corna) horn
corno[2] (*kor*-noa) *m* (pl i corni) horn
coro (*kaw*-roa) *m* choir
corona (koa-*rōā*-nah) *f* crown
coronare (koa-roa-*naa*-ray) *v* crown
corpo (*kor*-poa) *m* body
corpulento (koar-poo-*lehn*-toa) *adj* corpulent, stout
corredo (koar-*rai*-doa) *m* kit
***correggere** (koar-*rehd*-jay-ray) *v* correct
corrente (koar-*rehn*-tay) *adj* current; *f* current, stream; **con la** ~ downstream; **contro** ~ upstream; ~ **alternata** alternating current; ~ **continua** direct current; ~ **d'aria** draught; ***mettere al** ~ inform
***correre** (*koar*-ray-ray) *v* *run; *speed; * ~ **troppo** *speed
correttezza (koar-rayt-*tayt*-tsah) *f* correctness
corretto (koar-*reht*-toa) *adj* correct, right
correzione (koar-ray-*tsyōā*-nay) *f* correction
corrida (koar-*ree*-dah) *f* bullfight
corridoio (koar-ree-*dōā*-yoa) *m* corridor
corriera *f* coach
corrispondente (koar-ree-spoan-*dehn*-tay) *m* correspondent; reporter
corrispondenza (koar-ree-spoan-*dehn*-tsah) *f* correspondence
***corrispondere** (koar-ree-*spoan*-day-ray) *v* correspond, agree
***corrompere** (koar-*roam*-pay-ray) *v* corrupt, bribe
corrotto (koar-*roat*-toa) *adj* corrupt; vicious
corruzione (koar-roo-*tsyōā*-nay) *f* corruption, bribery
corsa (*koar*-sah) *f* ride; race; ~ **di cavalli** horserace
corsia (koar-*see*-ah) *f* lane
corso (*koar*-soa) *m* course; promenade; ~ **accelerato** intensive course; ~ **del cambio** exchange rate, rate of exchange
corte (*koar*-tay) *f* court
corteccia (koar-*tayt*-chah) *f* bark
corteo (koar-*tai*-oa) *m* procession
cortese (koar-*tāȳ*-zay) *adj* civil, courteous, polite
cortile (koar-*tee*-lay) *m* yard; ~ **di ricreazione** playground
corto (*koar*-toa) *adj* short; ~ **circuito** short circuit
corvo (*kor*-voa) *m* raven
cosa (*kaw*-sah) *f* thing; **che** ~ what; **qualunque** ~ anything
coscia (*kosh*-shah) *f* thigh
coscienza (koash-*shehn*-tsah) *f* consciousness; conscience
coscritto (koa-*skreet*-toa) *m* conscript
così (koa-*see*) *adv* so, thus, such; as; ~ **che** so that; **e** ~ **via** and so on
cosiddetto (koa-seed-*dayt*-toa) *adj* so-called
cosmetici (koa-*zmai*-tee-chee) *mpl* cosmetics *pl*
cospirare (koa-spee-*raa*-ray) *v* conspire
costa (*ko*-stah) *f* coast
costante (koa-*stahn*-tay) *adj* even
costare (koa-*staa*-ray) *v* *cost
costatare (koa-stah-*taa*-ray) *v* diagnose
costernato (koa-stayr-*naa*-toa) *adj* upset

costituire (koa-stee-*twee*-ray) *v* constitute
costituzione (koa-stee-too-*tsyōā*-nay) *f* constitution
costo (*ko*-stoa) *m* cost; charge
costola (*ko*-stoa-lah) *f* rib
costoletta (koa-stoa-*layt*-tah) *f* cutlet
costoso (koa-*stōā*-soa) *adj* expensive
***costringere** (koa-*streen*-jay-ray) *v* compel, force
costruire (koa-*strwee*-ray) *v* construct, *build
costruzione (koa-stroo-*tsyōā*-nay) *f* construction
costume (koa-*stōō*-may) *m* custom; ~ **da bagno** bathing-suit, swim-suit; ~ **nazionale** national dress; **costumi** *mpl* morals
cotoletta (koa-toa-*layt*-tah) *f* chop
cotone (koa-*tōā*-nay) *m* cotton; **di** ~ cotton
cozza (*koat*-tsah) *f* mussel
cozzare (koat-*tsaa*-ray) *v* collide, bump
crampo (*krahm*-poa) *m* cramp
cranio (*kraa*-ñoa) *m* skull
cratere (krah-*tai*-ray) *m* crater
cravatta (krah-*vaht*-tah) *f* tie, necktie; ~ **a farfalla** bow tie
cravattino (krah-vaht-*tee*-noa) *m* bow tie
creare (kray-*aa*-ray) *v* create
creatura (kray-ah-*tōō*-rah) *f* creature
credenza (kray-*dehn*-tsah) *f* closet
credere (*krāy*-day-ray) *v* believe; guess, reckon
credibile (kray-*dee*-bee-lay) *adj* credible
credito (*krāy*-dee-toa) *m* credit
creditore (kray-dee-*tōā*-ray) *m* creditor
credulo (*krai*-doo-loa) *adj* credulous
crema (*krai*-mah) *f* cream; ~ **da barba** shaving-cream; ~ **di bellezza** face-cream; ~ **idratante** moisturizing cream; ~ **per la notte** night-cream; ~ **per la pelle** skin cream; ~ **per le mani** hand cream
cremare (kray-*maa*-ray) *v* cremate
cremazione (kray-mah-*tsyōā*-nay) *f* cremation
cremisino (kray-mee-*zee*-noa) *adj* crimson
cremoso (kray-*mōā*-soa) *adj* creamy
crepa (*krai*-pah) *f* cleft
crepuscolo (kray-*poo*-skoa-loa) *m* twilight, dusk
***crescere** (*kraysh*-shay-ray) *v* *grow
crescione (kraysh-*shōā*-nay) *m* watercress
crescita (*kraysh*-shee-tah) *f* growth
cresta (*kray*-stah) *f* ridge
creta (*krāy*-tah) *f* chalk
cricco (*kreek*-koa) *m* jack
criminale (kree-mee-*naa*-lay) *adj* criminal; *m* criminal
criminalità (kree-mee-nah-lee-*tah*) *f* criminality
crimine (*kree*-mee-nay) *m* crime
crisi (*kree*-zee) *f* crisis
cristallino (kree-stahl-*lee*-noa) *adj* crystal
cristallo (kree-*stahl*-loa) *m* crystal
cristiano (kree-*styaa*-noa) *adj* Christian; *m* Christian
Cristo (*kree*-stoa) *m* Christ
critica (*kree*-tee-kah) *f* criticism
criticare (kree-tee-*kaa*-ray) *v* criticize
critico (*kree*-tee-koa) *adj* critical; *m* critic
croccante (kroak-*kahn*-tay) *adj* crisp
croce (*krōā*-chay) *f* cross
crocevia (kroa-chay-*vee*-ah) *m* junction, crossing
crociata (kroa-*chaa*-tah) *f* crusade
crocicchio (kroa-*cheek*-kyoa) *m* crossroads
crociera (kroa-*chai*-rah) *f* cruise
***crocifiggere** (kroa-chee-*feed*-jay-ray) *v* crucify

crocifissione (kroa-chee-feess-*syōā*-nay) *f* crucifixion
crocifisso (kroa-chee-*feess*-soa) *m* crucifix
crollare (kroal-*laa*-ray) *v* collapse
cromo (*kraw*-moa) *m* chromium
cronico (*kraw*-nee-koa) *adj* chronic
cronologico (kroa-noa-*law*-jee-koa) *adj* chronological
crosta (*kro*-stah) *f* crust
crostaceo (kroa-*staa*-chay-oa) *m* shellfish
crostino (kroa-*stee*-noa) *m* toast
crudele (kroo-*dai*-lay) *adj* cruel, harsh
crudo (*krōō*-doa) *adj* raw
cruscotto (kroo-*skot*-toa) *m* dashboard
Cuba (*kōō*-bah) *f* Cuba
cubano (koo-*baa*-noa) *adj* Cuban; *m* Cuban
cubo (*kōō*-boa) *m* cube
cuccetta (koot-*chayt*-tah) *f* berth, bunk
cucchiaiata (kook-kyah-*yaa*-tah) *f* spoonful
cucchiaino (kook-kyah-*ee*-noa) *m* teaspoon; teaspoonful
cucchiaio (kook-*kyaa*-yoa) *m* spoon, tablespoon; ~ **da minestra** soupspoon
cucina (koo-*chee*-nah) *f* kitchen; stove; ~ **a gas** gas cooker
cucinare (koo-chee-*naa*-ray) *v* cook; ~ **alla griglia** grill
cucire (koo-*chee*-ray) *v* sew
cucitura (koo-chee-*tōō*-rah) *f* seam; **senza** ~ seamless
cuculo (*kōō*-koo-loa) *m* cuckoo
cugina (koo-*jee*-nah) *f* cousin
cugino (koo-*jee*-noa) *m* cousin
cui (*koo*-ee) *pron* whose; of which; whom; to which
culla (*kool*-lah) *f* cradle
culmine (*kool*-mee-nay) *m* height
culto (*kool*-toa) *m* worship
cultura (kool-*tōō*-rah) *f* culture
cumulo (*koo*-moo-loa) *m* heap
cuneo (*kōō*-nay-oa) *m* wedge
cunetta (koo-*nayt*-tah) *f* gutter
cuoco (*kwaw*-koa) *m* cook
cuore (*kwaw*-ray) *m* heart
cupidigia (koo-pee-*dee*-jah) *f* greed
cupo (*kōō*-poa) *adj* gloomy
cupola (*kōō*-poa-lah) *f* dome
cura (*kōō*-rah) *f* care; cure; ***aver** ~ **di** *take care of; ~ **di bellezza** beauty treatment
curapipe (koo-rah-*pee*-pay) *m* pipe cleaner
curare (koo-*raa*-ray) *v* nurse; cure; ~ **le unghie** manicure
curato (koo-*raa*-toa) *adj* neat
curiosità (koo-ryoa-see-*tah*) *f* curiosity; sight, curio
curioso (koo-*ryōā*-soa) *adj* curious
curva (*koor*-vah) *f* bend; curve
curvare (koor-*vaa*-ray) *v* *bend
curvatura (koor-vah-*tōō*-rah) *f* bend
curvo (*koor*-voa) *adj* curved
cuscinetto (koosh-shee-*nayt*-toa) *m* pad
cuscino (koosh-*shee*-noa) *m* cushion; ~ **elettrico** heating pad
custode (koo-*staw*-day) *m* warden; custodian; caretaker
custodia (koo-*staw*-dyah) *f* custody
custodire (koo-stoa-*dee*-ray) *v* guard

D

da (dah) *prep* out of, from; at, to; as from; since; by
dabbasso (dahb-*bahss*-soa) *adv* downstairs; down
dacché (dahk-*kay*) *adv* since
dado (*daa*-doa) *m* nut
daltonico (dahl-*taw*-nee-koa) *adj* colour-blind

danese (dah-*nāy*-say) *adj* Danish; *m* Dane
Danimarca (dah-nee-*mahr*-kah) *f* Denmark
danneggiare (dahn-nayd-*jaa*-ray) *v* damage
danno (*dahn*-noa) *m* damage; mischief, harm
dannoso (dahn-*nōa*-soa) *adj* harmful
dappertutto (dahp-payr-*toot*-toa) *adv* throughout
***dare** (*daa*-ray) *v* *give
data (*daa*-tah) *f* date
dato (*daa*-toa) *m* data *pl*
dattero (*daht*-tay-roa) *m* date
dattilografa (daht-tee-*law*-grah-fah) *f* typist
dattilografare (daht-tee-loa-grah-*faa*-ray) *v* type
dattiloscritto (daht-tee-loa-*skreet*-toa) *adj* typewritten
davanti (dah-*vahn*-tee) *prep* before
davanzale (dah-vahn-*tsaa*-lay) *m* window-sill
davvero (dahv-*vāy*-roa) *adv* really
dazio (*daa*-tsyoa) *m* Customs duty, duty
dea (*dai*-ah) *f* goddess
debito (*dai*-bee-toa) *m* debt; debit
debole (*dāy*-boa-lay) *adj* weak; faint; dim
debolezza (day-boa-*layt*-tsah) *f* weakness
decaffeinizzato (day-kahf-fay-neet-*tsaa*-toa) *adj* decaffeinated
deceduto (day-chay-*dōo*-toa) *adj* dead
decente (day-*chehn*-tay) *adj* decent, proper
decenza (day-*chehn*-tsah) *f* decency
***decidere** (day-*chee*-day-ray) *v* decide
decimo (*dai*-chee-moa) *num* tenth
decisione (day-chee-*zyōa*-nay) *f* decision
deciso (day-*chee*-zoa) *adj* resolute
decollare (day-koal-*laa*-ray) *v* *take off
decollo (day-*kol*-loa) *m* take-off
decrepito (day-*krai*-pee-toa) *adj* dilapidated
***decrescere** (day-*kraysh*-shay-ray) *v* decrease
dedicare (day-dee-*kaa*-ray) *v* dedicate; devote
***dedurre** (day-*door*-ray) *v* infer, deduce
deferenza (day-fay-*rehn*-tsah) *f* respect
deficienza (day-fee-*chehn*-tsah) *f* deficiency, shortcoming
deficit (*dai*-fee-cheet) *m* deficit
definire (day-fee-*nee*-ray) *v* define
definitivo (day-fee-nee-*tee*-voa) *adj* definitive
definizione (day-fee-nee-*tsyōa*-nay) *f* definition
deformato (day-foar-*maa*-toa) *adj* deformed
deforme (day-*foar*-may) *adj* deformed
degno di (*day*-ñoa dee) worthy of
delegato (day-lay-*gaa*-toa) *m* delegate
delegazione (day-lay-gah-*tsyōa*-nay) *f* delegation
deliberare (day-lee-bay-*raa*-ray) *v* deliberate
deliberazione (day-lee-bay-rah-*tsyōa*-nay) *f* deliberation
delicato (day-lee-*kaa*-toa) *adj* delicate; tender; gentle
delinquente (day-leeng-*kwehn*-tay) *m* criminal
delizia (day-*lee*-tsyah) *f* delight, joy
deliziare (day-lee-*tsyaa*-ray) *v* delight
delizioso (day-lee-*tsyōa*-soa) *adj* delicious, lovely, wonderful
delucidare (day-loo-chee-*daa*-ray) *v* elucidate
***deludere** (day-*lōo*-day-ray) *v* disappoint, *let down; *be disappointing
delusione (day-loo-*zyōa*-nay) *f* disappointment

democratico (day-moa-*kraa*-tee-koa) *adj* democratic
democrazia (day-moa-krah-*tsee*-ah) *f* democracy
demolire (day-moa-*lee*-ray) *v* demolish
demolizione (day-moa-lee-*tsyōā*-nay) *f* demolition
denaro (day-*naa*-roa) *m* money
denominazione (day-noa-mee-nah-*tsyōā*-nay) *f* denomination
denso (*dehn*-soa) *adj* dense, thick
dente (*dehn*-tay) *m* tooth
dentiera (dayn-*tyai*-rah) *f* denture, false teeth
dentifricio (dayn-tee-*free*-choa) *m* toothpaste
dentista (dayn-*tee*-stah) *m* dentist
dentro (*dayn*-troa) *adv* in, inside; *prep* inside, within
denutrizione (day-noo-tree-*tsyōā*-nay) *f* malnutrition
deodorante (day-oa-doa-*rahn*-tay) *m* deodorant
deperibile (day-pay-*ree*-bee-lay) *adj* perishable
depositare (day-poa-zee-*taa*-ray) *v* deposit, bank
deposito (day-*paw*-zee-toa) *m* deposit; depot, warehouse; ~ **bagagli** left luggage office; baggage deposit office *Am*
depressione (day-prayss-*syōā*-nay) *f* depression
depresso (day-*prehss*-soa) *adj* depressed, blue
deprimente (day-pree-*mayn*-tay) *adj* depressing
***deprimere** (day-*pree*-may-ray) *v* depress
deputato (day-poo-*taa*-toa) *m* deputy; Member of Parliament
derisione (day-ree-*zyōā*-nay) *f* mockery
derivare (day-ree-*vaa*-ray) *v* divert; ~ **da** derive from
***descrivere** (day-*skree*-vay-ray) *v* describe
descrizione (day-skree-*tsyōā*-nay) *f* description
deserto (day-*zehr*-toa) *adj* desert; *m* desert
desiderabile (day-see-day-*raa*-bee-lay) *adj* desirable
desiderare (day-see-day-*raa*-ray) *v* want, desire, wish
desiderio (day-see-*dai*-ryoa) *m* desire, wish
desideroso (day-see-day-*rōā*-soa) *adj* eager
designare (day-see-*ñaa*-ray) *v* designate; appoint
desistere (day-*see*-stay-ray) *v* *give up
destarsi (day-*stahr*-see) *v* wake up
destinare (day-stee-*naa*-ray) *v* destine
destinatario (day-stee-nah-*taa*-ryoa) *m* addressee
destinazione (day-stee-nah-*tsyōā*-nay) *f* destination
destino (day-*stee*-noa) *m* fate, destiny, fortune
destro (*deh*-stroa) *adj* right; right-hand; skilful
detenuto (day-tay-*nōō*-toa) *m* prisoner
detenzione (day-tayn-*tsyōā*-nay) *f* custody
detergente (day-tayr-*jehn*-tay) *m* detergent
determinare (day-tayr-mee-*naa*-ray) *v* define, determine; **determinato** definite
determinazione (day-tayr-mee-nah-*tsyōā*-nay) *f* determination
detersivo (day-tayr-*see*-voa) *m* washing-powder
detestare (day-tay-*staa*-ray) *v* hate, dislike
dettagliante (dayt-tah-*lʸahn*-tay) *m* retailer

dettagliato (dayt-tah-*lʸaa*-toa) *adj* detailed
dettaglio (dayt-*taa*-lʸoa) *m* detail
dettare (dayt-*taa*-ray) *v* dictate
dettato (dayt-*taa*-toa) *m* dictation
deviare (day-*vyaa*-ray) *v* deviate
deviazione (day-vyah-*tsyōā*-nay) *f* detour, diversion
di (dee) *prep* of
diabete (dyah-*bai*-tay) *m* diabetes
diabetico (dyah-*bai*-tee-koa) *m* diabetic
diagnosi (*dyaa*-ñoa-zee) *f* diagnosis
diagnosticare (dyah-ñoa-stee-*kaa*-ray) *v* diagnose
diagonale (dyah-goa-*naa*-lay) *adj* diagonal; *f* diagonal
diagramma (dyah-*grahm*-mah) *m* chart; diagram
dialetto (dyah-*leht*-toa) *m* dialect
diamante (dyah-*mahn*-tay) *m* diamond
diapositiva (dyah-poa-zee-*tee*-vah) *f* slide
diario (*dyaa*-ryoa) *m* diary
diarrea (dyahr-*rai*-ah) *f* diarrhoea
diavolo (*dyaa*-voa-loa) *m* devil
dibattere (dee-*baht*-tay-ray) *v* discuss
dibattito (dee-*baht*-tee-toa) *m* debate, discussion
dicembre (dee-*chehm*-bray) December
diceria (dee-chay-*ree*-ah) *f* rumour
dichiarare (dee-kyah-*raa*-ray) *v* declare
dichiarazione (dee-kyah-rah-*tsyōā*-nay) *f* declaration, statement
diciannove (dee-chahn-*naw*-vay) *num* nineteen
diciannovesimo (dee-chahn-noa-*vai*-zee-moa) *num* nineteenth
diciassette (dee-chahss-*seht*-tay) *num* seventeen
diciassettesimo (dee-chahss-sayt-*tai*-zee-moa) *num* seventeenth
diciottesimo (dee-choat-*tai*-zee-moa) *num* eighteenth
diciotto (dee-*chot*-toa) *num* eighteen
didietro (dee-*dyai*-troa) *m* bottom
dieci (*dyai*-chee) *num* ten
dieta (*dyai*-tah) *f* diet
dietro (*dyai*-troa) *prep* behind
***difendere** (dee-*fehn*-day-ray) *v* defend
difensore (dee-fayn-*sōā*-ray) *m* champion
difesa (dee-*fāȳ*-sah) *f* defence; plea
difetto (dee-*feht*-toa) *m* fault
difettoso (dee-fayt-*tōā*-soa) *adj* defective, faulty
differente (deef-fay-*rehn*-tay) *adj* different
differenza (deef-fay-*rehn*-tsah) *f* difference; contrast, distinction
differire (deef-fay-*ree*-ray) *v* differ, vary; delay
difficile (deef-*fee*-chee-lay) *adj* difficult, hard
difficoltà (deef-fee-koal-*tah*) *f* difficulty
diffidare di (deef-fee-*daa*-ray) mistrust
***diffondere** (deef-*foan*-day-ray) *v* *shed
diffusione (deef-foo-*zyōā*-nay) *f* diffusion
difterite (deef-tay-*ree*-tay) *f* diphtheria
diga (*dee*-gah) *f* dike, dam
digeribile (dee-jay-*ree*-bee-lay) *adj* digestible
digerire (dee-jay-*ree*-ray) *v* digest
digestione (dee-jay-*styōā*-nay) *f* digestion
dignità (dee-ñee-*tah*) *f* dignity; rank
dignitoso (dee-ñee-*tōā*-soa) *adj* dignified
dilazione (dee-lah-*tsyōā*-nay) *f* respite
dilettevole (dee-layt-*tāȳ*-voa-lay) *adj* delightful
diletto (dee-*leht*-toa) *adj* dear; *m* delight, pleasure
diligente (dee-lee-*jehn*-tay) *adj* dili-

gent
diligenza (dee-lee-*jehn*-tsah) *f* diligence
diluire (dee-*lwee*-ray) *v* dilute
diluito (dee-*lwee*-toa) *adj* weak
dimagrire (dee-mah-*gree*-ray) *v* slim
dimensione (dee-mayn-*syōā*-nay) *f* extent, size
dimenticare (dee-mayn-tee-*kaa*-ray) *v* *forget
***dimettersi** (dee-*mayt*-tayr-see) *v* resign
dimezzare (dee-mayd-*dzaa*-ray) *v* halve
diminuire (dee-mee-*nwee*-ray) *v* reduce; decrease, lessen
diminuzione (dee-mee-noo-*tsyōā*-nay) *f* decrease
dimissioni (dee-meess-*syōā*-nee) *fpl* resignation
dimostrare (dee-moa-*straa*-ray) *v* demonstrate, prove, *show
dimostrazione (dee-moa-strah-*tsyōā*-nay) *f* demonstration; ***fare una** ~ demonstrate
dinamo (*dee*-nah-moa) *f* dynamo
dinanzi a (dee-*nahn*-tsee ah) before
dintorni (deen-*toar*-nee) *mpl* environment, surroundings *pl*
dio (*dee*-oa) *m* (pl dei) god
dipendente (dee-payn-*dehn*-tay) *adj* dependant
dipendenza (dee-payn-*dehn*-tsah) *f* annex
***dipendere da** (dee-*pehn*-day-ray) depend on
diploma (dee-*plaw*-mah) *m* certificate; diploma
diplomarsi (dee-ploa-*mahr*-see) *v* graduate
diplomatico (dee-ploa-*maa*-tee-koa) *m* diplomat
***dire** (*dee*-ray) *v* *say, *tell; ***voler** ~ *mean
direttamente (dee-rayt-tah-*mayn*-tay) *adv* straight away
direttiva (dee-rayt-*tee*-vah) *f* directive
diretto (dee-*reht*-toa) *adj* direct; ~ **a** bound for
direttore (dee-rayt-*tōā*-ray) *m* director, manager; executive; ~ **di scuola** head teacher, headmaster; ~ **d'orchestra** conductor
direzione (dee-ray-*tsyōā*-nay) *f* way, direction; management; **indicatore di** ~ trafficator; directional signal *Am*
dirigente (dee-ree-*jehn*-tay) *m* leader
***dirigere** (dee-*ree*-jay-ray) *v* direct, head, *lead; conduct; manage
diritto (dee-*reet*-toa) *adj* erect, upright; *m* right; ~ **amministrativo** administrative law; ~ **civile** civil law; ~ **commerciale** commercial law; ~ **elettorale** franchise; ~ **penale** criminal law; **sempre** ~ straight ahead
dirottare (dee-roat-*taa*-ray) *v* hijack
dirottatore (dee-roat-tah-*tōā*-ray) *m* hijacker
disabitato (dee-zah-bee-*taa*-toa) *adj* uninhabited
disadatto (dee-zah-*daht*-toa) *adj* unfit
disapprovare (dee-zahp-proa-*vaa*-ray) *v* disapprove
disastro (dee-*zah*-stroa) *m* disaster, calamity
disastroso (dee-zah-*strōā*-soa) *adj* disastrous
discendente (deesh-shayn-*dehn*-tay) *m* descendant
discendenza (deesh-shayn-*dehn*-tsah) *f* origin
discernimento (deesh-shayr-nee-*mayn*-toa) *m* sense
discesa (deesh-*shāȳ*-sah) *f* descent; **in** ~ downwards
disciplina (deesh-shee-*plee*-nah) *f* discipline

disco (*dee*-skoa) *m* disc; record
discorso (dee-*skoar*-soa) *m* speech; conversation
discussione (dee-skooss-*syōā*-nay) *f* argument, discussion
***discutere** (dee-*skōō*-tay-ray) *v* argue, discuss; dispute
disdegno (deez-*dāy*-ñoa) *m* contempt
***disdire** (deez-*dee*-ray) *v* cancel; check out
disegnare (dee-say-*ñaa*-ray) *v* sketch, *draw
disegno (dee-*sāy*-ñoa) *m* sketch, drawing; pattern; design; **puntina da disegno** drawing-pin; thumbtack *nAm*
disertare (dee-zayr-*taa*-ray) *v* desert
***disfare** (dee-*sfaa*-ray) *v* *undo; unpack, unwrap
disgelarsi (deez-jay-*lahr*-see) *v* thaw
disgelo (deez-*jai*-loa) *m* thaw
***disgiungere** (deez-*joon*-jay-ray) *v* disconnect
disgrazia (deez-*graa*-tsyah) *f* accident; disgrace
disgraziatamente (deez-grah-tsyah-tah-*mayn*-tay) *adv* unfortunately
disgustoso (deez-goo-*stōā*-soa) *adj* revolting, disgusting
disimparare (dee-zeem-pah-*raa*-ray) *v* unlearn
disinfettante (dee-zeen-fayt-*tahn*-tay) *m* disinfectant
disinfettare (dee-zeen-fayt-*taa*-ray) *v* disinfect
disinserire (dee-zeen-say-*ree*-ray) *v* disconnect
disinteressato (dee-zeen-tay-rayss-*saa*-toa) *adj* unselfish
disinvoltura (dee-zeen-voal-*tōō*-rah) *f* ease
disoccupato (dee-zoak-koo-*paa*-toa) *adj* unemployed
disoccupazione (dee-zoak-koo-pah-*tsyōā*-nay) *f* unemployment
disonesto (dee-zoa-*neh*-stoa) *adj* crooked, unfair, dishonest
disonore (dee-zoa-*nōā*-ray) *m* disgrace, shame
disordinato (dee-zoar-dee-*naa*-toa) *adj* sloppy, untidy
disordine (dee-*zoar*-dee-nay) *m* mess, disorder
disossare (dee-zoass-*saa*-ray) *v* bone
dispari (*dee*-spah-ree) *adj* odd
dispensa (dee-*spehn*-sah) *f* larder
dispensare (dee-spayn-*saa*-ray) *v* exempt
disperare (dee-spay-*raa*-ray) *v* despair
disperato (dee-spay-*raa*-toa) *adj* desperate; hopeless
disperazione (dee-spay-rah-*tsyōā*-nay) *f* despair
dispiacere (dee-spyah-*chāy*-ray) *m* sorrow
***dispiacere** (dee-spyah-*chāy*-ray) *v* displease
disponibile (dee-spoa-*nee*-bee-lay) *adj* available; spare
***disporre di** (dee-*spoar*-ray) dispose of
dispositivo (dee-spoa-zee-*tee*-voa) *m* apparatus
disposizione (dee-spoa-zee-*tsyōā*-nay) *f* disposal
disprezzare (dee-sprayt-*tsaa*-ray) *v* despise, scorn
disprezzo (dee-*spreht*-tsoa) *m* contempt, scorn
disputa (*dee*-spoo-tah) *f* argument, dispute
disputare (dee-spoo-*taa*-ray) *v* argue; dispute
dissenteria (deess-sayn-tay-*ree*-ah) *f* dysentery
dissentire (deess-sayn-*tee*-ray) *v* disagree
dissimile (deess-*see*-mee-lay) *adj* unlike

***dissuadere** (deess-swah-*dāy*-ray) *v* dissuade from
distante (dee-*stahn*-tay) *adj* far-away, remote
distanza (dee-*stahn*-tsah) *f* distance; space, way
***distinguere** (dee-*steeng*-gway-ray) *v* distinguish
distinto (dee-*steen*-toa) *adj* distinct; separate; distinguished
distinzione (dee-steen-*tsyōā*-nay) *f* difference, distinction
***distogliere** (dee-*staw*-l^y^ay-ray) *v* avert
distorsione (dee-stoar-*syōā*-nay) *f* sprain
distretto (dee-*strayt*-toa) *m* district
distribuire (dee-stree-*bwee*-ray) *v* *deal, distribute; issue
distributore (dee-stree-boo-*tōā*-ray) *m* distributor; ~ **automatico** slot-machine; ~ **di benzina** petrol station, filling station, service station
distribuzione (dee-stree-boo-*tsyōā*-nay) *f* distribution; disposition
***distruggere** (dee-*strood*-jay-ray) *v* destroy, wreck
distruzione (dee-stroo-*tsyōā*-nay) *f* destruction
disturbare (dee-stoor-*baa*-ray) *v* trouble, disturb; **disturbarsi** bother
disturbo (dee-*stoor*-boa) *m* disturbance
ditale (dee-*taa*-lay) *m* thimble
dito (*dee*-toa) *m* (pl le dita) finger; ~ **del piede** toe
ditta (*deet*-tah) *f* company, firm; business
dittafono (deet-*taa*-foa-noa) *m* dictaphone
dittatore (deet-tah-*tōā*-ray) *m* dictator
divano (dee-*vaa*-noa) *m* couch
***divenire** (dee-vay-*nee*-ray) *v* *become
diventare (dee-vayn-*taa*-ray) *v* *grow, *go, *get
diversione (dee-vayr-*syōā*-nay) *f* diversion
diverso (dee-*vehr*-soa) *adj* different; **diversi** several
divertente (dee-vayr-*tehn*-tay) *adj* funny, entertaining, enjoyable, amusing
divertimento (dee-vayr-tee-*mayn*-toa) *m* pleasure, fun, entertainment, amusement
divertire (dee-vayr-*tee*-ray) *v* entertain, amuse
***dividere** (dee-*vee*-day-ray) *v* divide
divieto (dee-*vyai*-toa) *m* prohibition; ~ **di sorpasso** no overtaking; no passing *Am*; ~ **di sosta** no parking
divino (dee-*vee*-noa) *adj* divine
divisa estera (dee-*vee*-zah *eh*-stay-rah) foreign currency
divisione (dee-vee-*zyōā*-nay) *f* division; agency
divisorio (dee-vee-*zaw*-ryoa) *m* partition
divorziare (dee-voar-*tsyaa*-ray) *v* divorce
divorzio (dee-*vor*-tsyoa) *m* divorce
dizionario (dee-tsyoa-*naa*-ryoa) *m* dictionary
doccia (*doat*-chah) *f* shower
docente (doa-*chehn*-tay) *m* teacher
documento (doa-koo-*mayn*-toa) *m* document
dodicesimo (doa-dee-*chai*-zee-moa) *num* twelfth
dodici (*dōā*-dee-chee) *num* twelve
dogana (doa-*gaa*-nah) *f* Customs *pl*
doganiere (doa-gah-*ñai*-ray) *m* Customs officer
doglie (*daw*-l^y^ay) *fpl* labour
dolce (*doal*-chay) *adj* sweet; gentle, tender; *m* cake; dessert, sweet
dolciumi (doal-*chōō*-mee) *mpl* sweets; candy *nAm*
***dolere** (doa-*lāy*-ray) *v* ache, *hurt

dolore (doa-*lōā*-ray) *m* pain, ache; grief, sorrow
doloroso (doa-loa-*rōā*-soa) *adj* sorrowful, painful
domanda (doa-*mahn*-dah) *f* inquiry, query; request; demand
domandare (doa-mahn-*daa*-ray) *v* ask; query
domani (doa-*maa*-nee) *adv* tomorrow
domenica (doa-*māy*-nee-kah) *f* Sunday
domestica (doa-*meh*-stee-kah) *f* housemaid
domestico (doa-*meh*-stee-koa) *adj* domestic; *m* domestic; **faccende domestiche** housekeeping
domicilio (doa-mee-*chee*-lyoa) *m* domicile
dominante (doa-mee-*nahn*-tay) *adj* leading
dominare (doa-mee-*naa*-ray) *v* master; rule
dominazione (doa-mee-nah-*tsyōā*-nay) *f* domination
dominio (doa-*mee*-ñoa) *m* rule, dominion
donare (doa-*naa*-ray) *v* donate
donatore (doa-nah-*tōā*-ray) *m* donor
donazione (doa-nah-*tsyōā*-nay) *f* donation
dondolare (doan-doa-*laa*-ray) *v* rock, *swing
donna (*don*-nah) *f* woman
dono (*dōā*-noa) *m* gift, present
dopo (*daw*-poa) *prep* after; ~ **che** after
doppio (*doap*-pyoa) *adj* double
dorato (doa-*raa*-toa) *adj* gilt
dormire (doar-*mee*-ray) *v* *sleep
dormitorio (doar-mee-*taw*-ryoa) *m* dormitory
dorso (*dawr*-soa) *m* back
dose (*daw*-zay) *f* dose
dotato (doa-*taa*-toa) *adj* talented
dottore (doat-*tōā*-ray) *m* doctor
dove (*dōā*-vay) *adv* where; *conj* where
dovere (doa-*vāy*-ray) *m* duty
***dovere** (doa-*vāy*-ray) *v* need to, *have to, *be obliged to, *be bound to, *must, *ought to, *should, *shall; owe
dovunque (doa-*voong*-kway) *adv* anywhere; *conj* wherever
dovuto (doa-*vōō*-toa) *adj* due
dozzina (doad-*dzee*-nah) *f* dozen
drago (*draa*-goa) *m* dragon
dramma (*drahm*-mah) *m* drama
drammatico (drahm-*maa*-tee-koa) *adj* dramatic
drammaturgo (drahm-mah-*toor*-goa) *m* playwright, dramatist
drapperia (drahp-pay-*ree*-ah) *f* drapery
drenare (dray-*naa*-ray) *v* drain
dritto (*dreet*-toa) *adj* straight; *adv* straight
drogheria (droa-gay-*ree*-ah) *f* grocer's
droghiere (droa-*gyai*-ray) *m* grocer
dubbio (*doob*-byoa) *m* doubt; ***mettere in** ~ query
dubbioso (doob-*byōā*-soa) *adj* doubtful
dubitare (doo-bee-*taa*-ray) *v* doubt
duca (*dōō*-kah) *m* (pl duchi) duke
duchessa (doo-*kayss*-sah) *f* duchess
due (*dōō*-ay) *num* two; **tutti e** ~ either
duna (*dōō*-nah) *f* dune
dunque (*doong*-kway) *conj* so; then
duomo (*dwaw*-moa) *m* cathedral
durante (doo-*rahn*-tay) *prep* for, during
durare (doo-*raa*-ray) *v* last
durata (doo-*raa*-tah) *f* duration
duraturo (doo-rah-*tōō*-roa) *adj* permanent, lasting
durevole (doo-*rāy*-voa-lay) *adj* lasting
duro (*dōō*-roa) *adj* tough, hard

E

e (ay) *conj* and
ebano (*ai*-bah-noa) *m* ebony
ebbene! (ayb-*bai*-nay) well!
ebraico (ay-*braa*-ee-koa) *adj* Jewish; *m* Hebrew
ebreo (ay-*brai*-oa) *m* Jew
eccedenza (ayt-chay-*dehn*-tsah) *f* surplus
eccedere (ayt-*chai*-day-ray) *v* exceed
eccellente (ayt-chayl-*lehn*-tay) *adj* excellent
***eccellere** (ayt-*chehl*-lay-ray) *v* excel
eccentrico (ayt-*chehn*-tree-koa) *adj* eccentric
eccessivo (ayt-chayss-*see*-voa) *adj* excessive
eccesso (ayt-*chehss*-soa) *m* excess; ~ **di velocità** speeding
eccetera (ayt-*chai*-tay-rah) etcetera
eccetto (ayt-*cheht*-toa) *prep* except
eccezionale (ayt-chayss-syoa-*naa*-lay) *adj* exceptional
eccezione (ayt-chayss-*syōā*-nay) *f* exception
eccitante (ayt-chee-*tahn*-tay) *adj* exciting
eccitare (ayt-chee-*taa*-ray) *v* excite
eccitazione (ayt-chee-tah-*tsyōā*-nay) *f* excitement
ecco (*ehk*-koa) here you are; *adv* here is
eclissi (ay-*kleess*-see) *f* eclipse
eco (*ai*-koa) *m/f* echo
economia (ay-koa-noa-*mee*-ah) *f* economy
economico (ay-koa-*naw*-mee-koa) *adj* economic; inexpensive, cheap, economical
economista (ay-koa-noa-*mee*-stah) *m* economist
economizzare (ay-koa-noa-meed-*dzaa*-ray) *v* economize
Ecuador (*ay*-kwah-doar) *m* Ecuador
ecuadoriano (ay-kwah-doa-*ryaa*-noa) *m* Ecuadorian
eczema (ayk-*jai*-mah) *m* eczema
edera (*ai*-day-rah) *f* ivy
edicola (ay-*dee*-koa-lah) *f* newsstand, bookstand
edificare (ay-dee-fee-*kaa*-ray) *v* construct
edificio (ay-dee-*fee*-choa) *m* construction, building
editore (ay-dee-*tōā*-ray) *m* publisher
edizione (ay-dee-*tsyōā*-nay) *f* issue, edition; ~ **del mattino** morning edition
educare (ay-doo-*kaa*-ray) *v* educate; *bring up
educazione (ay-doo-kah-*tsyōā*-nay) *f* education
effervescenza (ayf-fayr-vaysh-*shehn*-tsah) *f* fizz
effettivamente (ayf-fayt-tee-vah-*mayn*-tay) *adv* as a matter of fact; indeed
effetto (ayf-*feht*-toa) *m* effect; **effetti personali** belongings *pl*
effettuare (ayf-fayt-*twaa*-ray) *v* implement, effect; achieve
efficace (ayf-fee-*kaa*-chay) *adj* effective
efficiente (ayf-fee-*chehn*-tay) *adj* efficient
Egitto (ay-*jeet*-toa) *m* Egypt
egiziano (ay-jee-*tsyaa*-noa) *adj* Egyptian; *m* Egyptian
egli (*āȳ*-lyee) *pron* he; ~ **stesso** himself
egocentrico (ay-goa-*chehn*-tree-koa) *adj* self-centred
egoismo (ay-goa-*ee*-zmoa) *m* selfishness
egoista (ay-goa-*ee*-stah) *adj* selfish
egoistico (ay-goa-*ee*-stee-koa) *adj* ego-

istic
elaborare (ay-lah-boa-*raa*-ray) *v* elaborate
elasticità (ay-lah-stee-chee-*tah*) *f* elasticity
elastico (ay-*lah*-stee-koa) *adj* elastic; *m* rubber band, elastic
elefante (ay-lay-*fahn*-tay) *m* elephant
elegante (ay-lay-*gahn*-tay) *adj* smart, elegant
eleganza (ay-lay-*gahn*-tsah) *f* elegance
***eleggere** (ay-*lehd*-jay-ray) *v* elect
elementare (ay-lay-mayn-*taa*-ray) *adj* primary
elemento (ay-lay-*mayn*-toa) *m* element
elencare (ay-layng-*kaa*-ray) *v* list
elenco (ay-*lehng*-koa) *m* list; ~ **telefonico** telephone directory; telephone book *Am*
elettricista (ay-layt-tree-*chee*-stah) *m* electrician
elettricità (ay-layt-tree-chee-*tah*) *f* electricity
elettrico (ay-*leht*-tree-koa) *adj* electric
elettronico (ay-layt-*traw*-nee-koa) *adj* electronic
elevare (ay-lay-*vaa*-ray) *v* raise; elevate; **elevato** high; lofty
elevazione (ay-lay-vah-*tsyōā*-nay) *f* mound
elezione (ay-lay-*tsyōā*-nay) *f* election
elica (*ai*-lee-kah) *f* propeller
eliminare (ay-lee-mee-*naa*-ray) *v* eliminate
ella (*ayl*-lah) *pron* she
elogio (ay-*law*-joa) *m* praise
emancipazione (ay-mahn-chee-pah-*tsyōā*-nay) *f* emancipation
emblema (aym-*blai*-mah) *m* emblem
emergenza (ay-mayr-*jehn*-tsah) *f* emergency
***emergere** (ay-*mehr*-jay-ray) *v* appear, emerge; *stand out
***emettere** (ay-*mayt*-tay-ray) *v* utter
emicrania (ay-mee-*kraa*-ñah) *f* migraine
emigrante (ay-mee-*grahn*-tay) *m* emigrant
emigrare (ay-mee-*graa*-ray) *v* emigrate
emigrazione (ay-mee-grah-*tsyōā*-nay) *f* emigration
eminente (ay-mee-*nehn*-tay) *adj* outstanding
emissione (ay-meess-*syōā*-nay) *f* issue; broadcast
emorragia (ay-moar-rah-*jee*-ah) *f* haemorrhage
emorroidi (ay-moar-*raw*-ee-dee) *fpl* haemorrhoids *pl*, piles *pl*
emozione (ay-moa-*tsyōā*-nay) *f* emotion
enciclopedia (ayn-chee-kloa-pay-*dee*-ah) *f* encyclopaedia
energia (ay-nayr-*jee*-ah) *f* energy; power; ~ **nucleare** nuclear energy
energico (ay-*nehr*-jee-koa) *adj* energetic
enigma (ay-*neeg*-mah) *m* enigma, mystery; puzzle
enorme (ay-*nor*-may) *adj* tremendous, immense, enormous, huge
ente (*ehn*-tay) *m* being; society
entrambi (ayn-*trahm*-bee) *adj* both
entrare (ayn-*traa*-ray) *v* *go in, enter
entrata (ayn-*traa*-tah) *f* way in, entry, entrance; **entrate** revenue
entro (*ayn*-troa) *prep* in
entusiasmo (ayn-too-*zyah*-zmoa) *m* enthusiasm
entusiastico (ayn-too-*zyah*-stee-koa) *adj* enthusiastic
epico (*ai*-pee-koa) *adj* epic
epidemia (ay-pee-day-*mee*-ah) *f* epidemic
epilessia (ay-pee-layss-*seeah*) *f* epilepsy
epilogo (ay-*pee*-loa-goa) *m* epilogue
episodio (ay-pee-*zaw*-dyoa) *m* episode

epoca (*ai*-poa-kah) *f* period
eppure (ayp-*pōō*-ray) *conj* yet, however
equatore (ay-kwah-*tōā*-ray) *m* equator
equilibrio (ay-kwee-*lee*-bryoa) *m* balance
equipaggiamento (ay-kwee-pahd-jah-*mayn*-toa) *m* outfit, equipment
equipaggiare (ay-kwee-pahd-*jaa*-ray) *v* equip
equipaggio (ay-kwee-*pahd*-joa) *m* crew
equitazione (ay-kwee-tah-*tsyōā*-nay) *f* riding
equivalente (ay-kwee-vah-*lehn*-tay) *adj* equivalent
equivoco (ay-*kwee*-voa-koa) *adj* ambiguous
equo (*ai*-kwoa) *adj* right
erba (*ehr*-bah) *f* grass; herb
erbaccia (ayr-*baht*-chah) *f* weed
eredità (ay-ray-dee-*tah*) *f* inheritance
ereditare (ay-ray-dee-*taa*-ray) *v* inherit
ereditario (ay-ray-dee-*taa*-ryoa) *adj* hereditary
erica (*ai*-ree-kah) *f* heather
***erigere** (ay-*ree*-jay-ray) *v* erect
ernia (*ehr*-ñah) *f* hernia, slipped disc
eroe (ay-*raw*-ay) *m* hero
errare (ayr-*raa*-ray) *v* wander, err
erroneo (ayr-*raw*-nay-oa) *adj* mistaken, wrong
errore (ayr-*rōā*-ray) *m* mistake, error
erudito (ay-roo-*dee*-toa) *m* scholar
eruzione (ay-roo-*tsyōā*-nay) *f* rash
esagerare (ay-zah-jay-*raa*-ray) *v* exaggerate
esalare (ay-zah-*laa*-ray) *v* exhale
esame (ay-*zaa*-may) *m* examination; test
esaminare (ay-zah-mee-*naa*-ray) *v* examine
esantema (ay-zahn-*tai*-mah) *m* rash
esattamente (ay-*zaht*-tah-mayn-tay) *adv* just
esatto (ay-*zaht*-toa) *adj* exact, precise; correct, just
esaurire (ay-zou-*ree*-ray) *v* exhaust; **esaurito** sold out; **esausto** overtired, overstrung
esca (*ay*-skah) *f* bait
esclamare (ay-sklah-*maa*-ray) *v* exclaim
esclamazione (ay-sklah-mah-*tsyōā*-nay) *f* exclamation
***escludere** (ay-*sklōō*-day-ray) *v* exclude
esclusivamente (ay-skloo-zee-vah-*mayn*-tay) *adv* solely, exclusively
esclusivo (ay-skloo-*zee*-voa) *adj* exclusive
escogitare (ay-skoa-jee-*taa*-ray) *v* devise
escoriazione (ay-skoa-ryah-*tsyōā*-nay) *f* graze
escrescenza (ay-skraysh-*shehn*-tsah) *f* growth
escursione (ay-skoor-*syōā*-nay) *f* excursion
esecutivo (ay-zay-koo-*tee*-voa) *adj* executive
esecuzione (ay-zay-koo-*tsyōā*-nay) *f* execution
eseguire (ay-zay-*gwee*-ray) *v* execute, perform, carry out
esempio (ay-*zaym*-pyoa) *m* instance, example; **per** ~ for instance, for example
esemplare (ay-zaym-*plaa*-ray) *m* specimen
esentare (ay-zayn-*taa*-ray) *v* exempt
esente (ay-*zehn*-tay) *adj* exempt; ~ **da tassa** tax-free
esenzione (ay-zayn-*tsyōā*-nay) *f* exemption
esercitare (ay-zayr-chee-*taa*-ray) *v* exercise; **esercitarsi** practise
esercito (ay-*zehr*-chee-toa) *m* army
esercizio (ay-zayr-*chee*-tsyoa) *m* exer-

cise
esibire (ay-zee-*bee*-ray) *v* exhibit; *show
esigente (ay-zee-*jehn*-tay) *adj* particular
esigenza (ay-zee-*jehn*-tsah) *f* demand; requirement
***esigere** (ay-*zee*-jay-ray) *v* demand; require
esiguo (ay-*zee*-gwoa) *adj* minor
esilio (ay-*zee*-l^{y}oa) *m* exile
esistenza (ay-zee-*stehn*-tsah) *f* existence
***esistere** (ay-*zee*-stay-ray) *v* exist
esitare (ay-zee-*taa*-ray) *v* hesitate
esito (*ai*-zee-toa) *m* result; issue
esonerare da (ay-zoa-nay-*raa*-ray) discharge of
esotico (ay-*zaw*-tee-koa) *adj* exotic
***espandere** (ay-*spahn*-day-ray) *v* expand
***espellere** (ay-*spehl*-lay-ray) *v* expel
esperienza (ay-spay-*ryehn*-tsah) *f* experience
esperimento (ay-spay-ree-*mayn*-toa) *m* experiment
esperto (ay-*spehr*-toa) *adj* experienced; skilful, skilled; *m* expert
espirare (ay-spee-*raa*-ray) *v* expire
esplicazione (ay-splee-kah-*tsyōā*-nay) *f* explanation
esplicito (ay-*splee*-chee-toa) *adj* explicit; express, definite
***esplodere** (ay-*splaw*-day-ray) *v* explode
esplorare (ay-sploa-*raa*-ray) *v* explore
esplosione (ay-sploa-*zyōā*-nay) *f* explosion, blast
esplosivo (ay-sploa-*zee*-voa) *adj* explosive; *m* explosive
***esporre** (ay-*spoar*-ray) *v* exhibit, display
esportare (ay-spoar-*taa*-ray) *v* export
esportazione (ay-spoar-tah-*tsyōā*-nay) *f* exports *pl*, exportation, export
esposimetro (ay-spoa-*zee*-may-troa) *m* exposure meter
esposizione (ay-spoa-zee-*tsyōā*-nay) *f* exposition, exhibition, display, show; exposure
espressione (ay-sprayss-*syōā*-nay) *f* expression
espresso (ay-*sprehss*-soa) *adj* express; **per** ~ special delivery
***esprimere** (ay-*spree*-may-ray) *v* express
essa (*ayss*-sah) *pron* she; ~ **stessa** herself
essenza (ayss-*sehn*-tsah) *f* essence
essenziale (ayss-sayn-*tsyaa*-lay) *adj* essential
essenzialmente (ayss-sayn-tsyahl-*mayn*-tay) *adv* essentially
essere (*ehss*-say-ray) *m* creature; being; ~ **umano** human being
***essere** (*ehss*-say-ray) *v* *be
essi (*ayss*-see) *pron* they; ~ **stessi** themselves
essiccatoio (ayss-see-t^{y}ah-*tōā*-yoa) *m* dryer
est (ehst) *m* east
estasi (*eh*-stah-zee) *f* ecstasy
estate (ay-*staa*-tay) *f* summer; **piena** ~ midsummer
***estendere** (ay-*stehn*-day-ray) *v* extend; expand
esteriore (ay-stay-*ryōā*-ray) *adj* external; *m* outside
esterno (ay-*stehr*-noa) *adj* outward, exterior; *m* outside, exterior
all'estero (ahl-*leh*-stay-roa) abroad
esteso (ay-*stāȳ*-soa) *adj* broad
***estinguere** (ay-*steeng*-gway-ray) *v* extinguish
estintore (ay-steen-*tōā*-ray) *m* fire-extinguisher
***estorcere** (ay-*stor*-chay-ray) *v* extort
estorsione (ay-stoar-*syōā*-nay) *f* extor-

tion
estradare (ay-strah-*daa*-ray) *v* extradite
estraneo (ay-*straa*-nay-oa) *adj* foreign; *m* stranger
***estrarre** (ay-*strahr*-ray) *v* extract
estremità (ay-stray-mee-*tah*) *f* end
estremo (ay-*strāy*-moa) *adj* extreme; very, utmost; *m* extreme
estuario (ay-*stwaa*-ryoa) *m* estuary
esuberante (ay-zoo-bay-*rahn*-tay) *adj* exuberant
esule (*ai*-zoo-lay) *m* exile
età (ay-*tah*) *f* age
etere (*ai*-tay-ray) *m* ether
eternità (ay-tayr-nee-*tah*) *f* eternity
eterno (ay-*tehr*-noa) *adj* eternal
eterosessuale (ay-tay-roa-sayss-*swaa*-lay) *adj* heterosexual
etichetta (ay-tee-*kayt*-tah) *f* label, tag
etichettare (ay-tee-kayt-*taa*-ray) *v* label
Etiopia (ay-*tyaw*-pyah) *f* Ethiopia
etiopico (ay-*tyaw*-pee-koa) *adj* Ethiopian; *m* Ethiopian
Europa (ay^{oo}-*raw*-pah) *f* Europe
europeo (ay^{oo}-roa-*pai*-oa) *adj* European; *m* European
evacuare (ay-vah-*kwaa*-ray) *v* evacuate
evaporare (ay-vah-poa-*raa*-ray) *v* evaporate
evasione (ay-vah-*zyōā*-nay) *f* escape
evento (ay-*vehn*-toa) *m* occurrence, event, happening
eventuale (ay-vayn-*twaa*-lay) *adj* eventual, possible
evidente (ay-vee-*dehn*-tay) *adj* evident
evidentemente (ay-vee-dehn-tay-*mayn*-tay) *adv* apparently
evitare (ay-vee-*taa*-ray) *v* avoid
evoluzione (ay-voa-loo-*tsyōā*-nay) *f* evolution

F

fa (fah) *adv* ago
fabbrica (*fahb*-bree-kah) *f* factory, mill, works *pl*
fabbricante (fahb-bree-*kahn*-tay) *m* manufacturer
fabbricare (fahb-bree-*kaa*-ray) *v* construct; manufacture
fabbricazione (fahb-bree-kah-*tsyōā*-nay) *f* construction
fabbro (*fahb*-broa) *m* smith, blacksmith
faccenda (faht-*chehn*-dah) *f* matter, concern; **faccende di casa** housekeeping
facchino (fahk-*kee*-noa) *m* porter
faccia (*faht*-chah) *f* face; **in ~ a** *prep* facing
facciata (faht-*chaa*-tah) *f* façade; front
facile (*faa*-chee-lay) *adj* easy
facilità (fah-chee-lee-*tah*) *f* ease
facilone (fah-chee-*lōā*-nay) *adj* easygoing
facoltà (fah-koal-*tah*) *f* faculty
facoltativo (fah-koal-tah-*tee*-voa) *adj* optional
faggio (*fahd*-joa) *m* beech
fagiano (fah-*jaa*-noa) *m* pheasant
fagiolo (fah-*jaw*-loa) *m* bean
fagotto (fah-*got*-toa) *m* bundle
falcone (fahl-*kōā*-nay) *m* hawk
falegname (fah-lay-*ñaa*-may) *m* carpenter
fallace (fahl-*laa*-chay) *adj* false
fallimento (fahl-lee-*mayn*-toa) *m* failure
fallire (fahl-*lee*-ray) *v* fail
fallito (fahl-*lee*-toa) *adj* bankrupt
fallo (*fahl*-loa) *m* mistake
falsificare (fahl-see-fee-*kaa*-ray) *v* counterfeit, forge

falsificazione (fahl-see-fee-kah-*tsyōā*-nay) *f* fake
falso (*fahl*-soa) *adj* untrue; false
fama (*faa*-mah) *f* fame; reputation; **di ~ mondiale** world-famous
fame (*faa*-may) *f* hunger
famigerato (fah-mee-jay-*raa*-toa) *adj* notorious
famiglia (fah-*mee*-lʸah) *f* family
familiare (fah-mee-*lʸaa*-ray) *adj* familiar
famoso (fah-*mōā*-soa) *adj* famous
fanale (fah-*naa*-lay) *m* headlamp; **~ antinebbia** foglamp; **fanalino posteriore** rear-light
fanatico (fah-naa-tee-koa) *adj* fanatical
fanciulla (fahn-*chool*-lah) *f* young girl
fanciullo (fahn-*chool*-loa) *m* boy
fanfara (fahn-*faa*-rah) *f* brass band
fango (*fahng*-goa) *m* mud
fangoso (fahng-*gōā*-soa) *adj* muddy
fantasia (fahn-tah-*zee*-ah) *f* fantasy
fantasma (fahn-*tah*-zmah) *m* spirit, phantom
fantastico (fahn-*tah*-stee-koa) *adj* fantastic
fante (*fahn*-tay) *m* knave
fanteria (fahn-tay-*ree*-ah) *f* infantry
fantino (fahn-*tee*-noa) *m* jockey
***fare** (*faa*-ray) *v* *do; *make; *have
farfalla (fahr-*fahl*-lah) *f* butterfly
farina (fah-*ree*-nah) *f* flour
farmacia (fahr-mah-*chee*-ah) *f* pharmacy, chemist's; drugstore *nAm*
farmacista (fahr-mah-*chee*-stah) *m* chemist
farmaco (*fahr*-mah-koa) *m* drug
farmacologia (fahr-mah-koa-loa-*jee*-ah) *f* pharmacology
faro (*faa*-roa) *m* lighthouse; headlight
farsa (*fahr*-sah) *f* farce
fasciatura (fahsh-shah-*tōō*-rah) *f* bandage
fascino (*fahsh*-shee-noa) *m* glamour, charm
fascismo (fahsh-*shee*-zmoa) *m* fascism
fascista (fahsh-*shee*-stah) *m* fascist
fascistico (fahsh-*shee*-stee-koa) *adj* fascist
fase (*faa*-zay) *f* phase; stage
fastidioso (fah-stee-*dyōā*-soa) *adj* inconvenient, difficult
fata (*faa*-tah) *f* fairy
fatale (fah-*taa*-lay) *adj* fatal
fatica (fah-*tee*-kah) *f* strain
faticare (fah-tee-*kaa*-ray) *v* labour
faticoso (fah-tee-*kōā*-soa) *adj* tiring
fato (*faa*-toa) *m* fate
fatto (*faht*-toa) *m* fact
fattore (faht-*tōā*-ray) *m* factor; farmer
fattoressa (faht-toa-*rayss*-sah) *f* farmer's wife
fattoria (faht-toa-*ree*-ah) *f* farm
fattorino d'albergo (faht-toa-*ree*-noa dahl-*behr*-goa) bellboy
fattura (faht-*tōō*-rah) *f* bill, invoice
fatturare (faht-too-*raa*-ray) *v* bill
fauci (*fou*-chee) *fpl* mouth
favola (*fah*-voa-lah) *f* fable
favore (fah-*vōā*-ray) *m* favour; **a ~ di** on behalf of; **per ~** please
favorevole (fah-voa-*rāy*-voa-lay) *adj* favourable
favorire (fah-voa-*ree*-ray) *v* favour
favorito (fah-voa-*ree*-toa) *adj* pet; *m* favourite
fazzoletto (faht-tsoa-*layt*-toa) *m* handkerchief; **~ di carta** kleenex, tissue
febbraio (fayb-*braa*-yoa) February
febbre (*fehb*-bray) *f* fever; **~ del fieno** hay fever
febbricitante (fayb-bree-chee-*tahn*-tay) *adj* feverish
fecondo (fay-*koan*-doa) *adj* fertile
fede (*fāy*-day) *f* belief, faith; wedding-ring
fedele (fay-*dāy*-lay) *adj* true, faithful

federa (*fai*-day-rah) *f* pillow-case
federale (fay-day-*raa*-lay) *adj* federal
federazione (fay-day-rah-*tsyōā*-nay) *f* federation
fegato (*fāy*-gah-toa) *m* liver
felice (fay-*lee*-chay) *adj* happy
felicissimo (faylee-*cheess*-see-moa) *adj* delighted
felicità (fay-lee-chee-*tah*) *f* happiness
felicitarsi con (fay-lee-chee-*tahr*-see) compliment, congratulate
felicitazione (fay-lee-chee-tah-*tsyōā*-nay) *f* congratulation
feltro (*fayl*-troa) *m* felt
femmina (*faym*-mee-nah) *f* female; girl
femminile (faym-mee-*nee*-lay) *adj* female; feminine
***fendere** (*fayn*-day-ray) *v* *split
fenicottero (fay-nee-*kot*-tay-roa) *m* flamingo
fenomeno (fay-*naw*-may-noa) *m* phenomenon
ferie (*fai*-ryay) *fpl* holiday; **in ~** on holiday
ferire (fay-*ree*-ray) *v* injure, wound, *hurt
ferita (fay-*ree*-tah) *f* injury, wound
ferito (fay-*ree*-toa) *adj* injured
fermaglio (fayr-*maa*-lʸoa) *m* fastener; **~ per capelli** bobby pin *Am*
fermarsi (fayr-*mahr*-see) *v* halt, pull up
fermata (fayr-*maa*-tah) *f* stop
fermentare (fayr-mayn-*taa*-ray) *v* ferment
fermo (*fayr*-moa) *adj* steadfast; **~ posta** poste restante
feroce (fay-*rōā*-chay) *adj* wild, fierce
ferramenta (fayr-rah-*mayn*-tah) *fpl* hardware
ferriera (fayr-*ryai*-rah) *f* ironworks
ferro (*fehr*-roa) *m* iron; **di ~** iron; **~ da stiro** iron; **~ di cavallo** horseshoe; **rottame di ~** scrap-iron
ferrovia (fayr-roa-*vee*-ah) *f* railway; railroad *nAm*
fertile (*fehr*-tee-lay) *adj* fertile
fessura (fayss-*sōō*-rah) *f* crack, chink; slot
festa (*feh*-stah) *f* holiday; feast; party
festival (*fay*-stee-vahl) *m* festival
festivo (fay-*stee*-voa) *adj* festive
fetta (*fayt*-tah) *f* slice
feudale (fayᵒᵒ-*daa*-lay) *adj* feudal
fiaba (*fyaa*-bah) *f* fairytale
fiacco (*fyahk*-koa) *adj* feeble, faint
fiamma (*fyahm*-mah) *f* flame
fiammifero (fyahm-*mee*-fay-roa) *m* match
fianco (*fyahng*-koa) *m* hip
fiato (*fyaa*-toa) *m* breath
fibbia (*feeb*-byah) *f* buckle
fibra (*fee*-brah) *f* fibre
fico (*fee*-koa) *m* fig
fidanzamento (fee-dahn-tsah-*mayn*-toa) *m* engagement
fidanzata (fee-dahn-*tsaa*-tah) *f* fiancée
fidanzato (fee-dahn-*tsaa*-toa) *adj* engaged; *m* fiancé
fidarsi (fee-*dahr*-see) *v* trust
fidato (fee-*daa*-toa) *adj* trustworthy, reliable; **non ~** unreliable
fiducia (fee-*dōō*-chah) *f* faith, trust, confidence
fieno (*fyai*-noa) *m* hay
fiera (*fyai*-rah) *f* fair
fierezza (fyay-*rayt*-tsah) *f* pride
fiero (*fyai*-roa) *adj* proud
figlia (*fee*-lʸah) *f* daughter
figliastro (fee-*lʸah*-stroa) *m* stepchild
figliata (fee-*lʸaa*-tah) *f* litter
figlio (*fee*-lʸoa) *m* son
figliolo (fee-*lʸaw*-loa) *m* son; boy
figura (fee-*gōō*-rah) *f* figure; picture
figurarsi (fee-goo-*rahr*-see) *v* imagine; fancy
fila (*fee*-lah) *f* row, rank, file, line

filare (fee-*laa*-ray) *v* *spin
filippino (fee-leep-*pee*-noa) *adj* Philippine; *m* Filipino
film (feelm) *m* (pl ~) film, movie
filmare (feel-*maa*-ray) *v* film
filo (*fee*-loa) *m* thread, wire, yarn
filobus (fee-loa-*booss*) *m* trolley-bus
filosofia (fee-loa-zoa-*fee*-ah) *f* philosophy
filosofo (fee-*law*-zoa-foa) *m* philosopher
filtrare (feel-*traa*-ray) *v* strain
filtro (*feel*-troa) *m* filter; percolator; ~ **dell'aria** air-filter; ~ **dell'olio** oil filter
finale (fee-*naa*-lay) *adj* eventual, final
finalmente (fee-nahl-*mayn*-tay) *adv* at last
finanze (fee-*nahn*-tsay) *fpl* finances *pl*
finanziare (fee-nahn-*tsyaa*-ray) *v* finance
finanziario (fee-nahn-*tsyaa*-ryoa) *adj* financial
finanziatore (fee-nahn-tsyah-*tōā*-ray) *m* investor
finché (feeng-*kay*) *conj* until, till; ~ **non** till
fine (*fee*-nay) *f* ending, end; *m* purpose; **fine-settimana** weekend
finestra (fee-*nay*-strah) *f* window
***fingere** (*feen*-jay-ray) *v* pretend
finire (fee-*nee*-ray) *v* end, finish; expire; **finito** finished; over
finlandese (feen-lahn-*dāȳ*-say) *adj* Finnish; *m* Finn
Finlandia (feen-*lahn*-dyah) *f* Finland
fino (*fee*-noa) *adj* fine; sheer
fino a (*fee*-noa ah) *prep* until, to, till
finora (fee-*nōā*-rah) *adv* so far
finzione (feen-*tsyōā*-nay) *f* fiction
fioraio (fyoa-*raa*-yoa) *m* florist
fiore (*fyōā*-ray) *m* flower
fiorente (fyoa-*rehn*-tay) *adj* prosperous
firma (*feer*-mah) *f* signature
firmare (feer-*maa*-ray) *v* sign
fischiare (fee-*skyaa*-ray) *v* whistle
fischio (*fee*-skyoa) *m* whistle
fisica (*fee*-zee-kah) *f* physics
fisico (*fee*-zee-koa) *adj* physical; *m* physicist
fisiologia (fee-zyoa-loa-*jee*-ah) *f* physiology
fissare (feess-*saa*-ray) *v* gaze, stare; settle
fisso (*feess*-soa) *adj* permanent, fixed
fitta (*feet*-tah) *f* stitch
fiume (*fyōō*-may) *m* river
flacone (flah-*kōā*-nay) *m* flask
flagello (flah-*jehl*-loa) *m* plague
flanella (flah-*nehl*-lah) *f* flannel
flauto (*flou*-toa) *m* flute
flessibile (flayss-*see*-bee-lay) *adj* supple, flexible, elastic
floscio (*flosh*-shoa) *adj* limp
flotta (*flot*-tah) *f* fleet
fluente (*flwehn*-tay) *adj* fluent
fluido (*flōō*-ee-doa) *adj* fluid; *m* fluid
flusso (*slooss*-soa) *m* flood
foca (*faw*-kah) *f* seal
foce (*faw*-chay) *f* mouth
focolare (foa-koa-*laa*-ray) *m* fireplace, hearth
fodera (*faw*-day-rah) *f* lining
foglia (*faw*-lyah) *f* leaf
foglio (*faw*-lyoa) *m* sheet; ~ **di registrazione** registration form
fogna (*fōā*-ñah) *f* sewer
folklore (foal-*klaw*-ray) *m* folklore
folla (*fol*-lah) *f* crowd
folle (*fol*-lay) *adj* crazy, mad
folletto (foal-*layt*-toa) *m* elf
fondamentale (foan-dah-mayn-*taa*-lay) *adj* fundamental, essential, basic
fondamento (foan-dah-*mayn*-toa) *m* base; basis
fondare (foan-*daa*-ray) *v* found; **fondato** well-founded

fondazione (foan-dah-*tsyōā*-nay) *f* foundation
***fondere** (*foan*-day-ray) *v* melt
fondo (*foan*-doa) *m* ground, bottom; **fondi** fund; ~ **tinta** foundation cream
fonetico (foa-*nai*-tee-koa) *adj* phonetic
fontana (foan-*taa*-nah) *f* fountain
fonte (*foan*-tay) *f* spring; source
foratura (foa-rah-*tōō*-rah) *f* puncture, blow-out
forbici (*for*-bee-chee) *fpl* scissors *pl*; **forbicine per le unghie** nail-scissors *pl*
forca (*foar*-kah) *f* gallows *pl*
forchetta (foar-*kayt*-tah) *f* fork
forcina (foar-*chee*-nah) *f* hairpin, hair-grip
foresta (foa-*reh*-stah) *f* forest
forestiero (foa-ray-*styai*-roa) *m* foreigner
forfora (*foar*-foa-rah) *f* dandruff
forma (*foar*-mah) *f* form, shape; figure; condition
formaggio (foar-*mahd*-joa) *m* cheese
formale (foar-*maa*-lay) *adj* formal
formalità (foar-mah-lee-*tah*) *f* formality
formare (foar-*maa*-ray) *v* form, shape
formato (foar-*maa*-toa) *m* size
formazione (foar-mah-*tsyōā*-nay) *f* formation
formica (foar-*mee*-kah) *f* ant
formidabile (foar-mee-*daa*-bee-lay) *adj* terrific
formula (*for*-moo-lah) *f* formula
formulario (foar-moo-*laa*-ryoa) *m* form
fornace (foar-*naa*-chay) *f* furnace
fornello (foar-*nehl*-loa) *m* cooker; ~ **a gas** gas cooker; ~ **a spirito** spirit stove
fornire (foar-*nee*-ray) *v* furnish, provide, supply
fornitura (foar-nee-*tōō*-rah) *f* supply
forno (*foar*-noa) *m* oven
forse (*foar*-say) *adv* maybe, perhaps
forte (*for*-tay) *adj* strong, powerful; loud; *m* fort
fortezza (foar-*tayt*-tsah) *f* fortress
fortuito (foar-*tōō*-ee-toa) *adj* casual, accidental
fortuna (foar-*tōō*-nah) *f* lot; luck, fortune
fortunato (foar-too-*naa*-toa) *adj* lucky, fortunate
foruncolo (foa-*roong*-koa-loa) *m* boil
forza (*for*-tsah) *f* energy, strength, force; ~ **di volontà** will-power; ~ **motrice** driving force; **forze militari** military force
forzare (foar-*tsaa*-ray) *v* force; strain
foschia (foa-*skee*-ah) *f* mist, haze
fosco (*foa*-skoa) *adj* hazy
fossato (foass-*saa*-toa) *m* ditch; moat
fosso (*foass*-soa) *m* ditch
foto (*faw*-toa) *f* photo; ~ **per passaporto** passport photograph
fotografare (foa-toa-grah-*faa*-ray) *v* photograph
fotografia (foa-toa-grah-*fee*-ah) *f* photography; photograph
fotografo (foa-*taw*-grah-foa) *m* photographer
fra (frah) *prep* among; amid
fragile (*fraa*-jee-lay) *adj* fragile
fragola (*fraa*-goa-lah) *f* strawberry
***fraintendere** (frah-een-*tehn*-day-ray) *v* *misunderstand
frammento (frahm-*mayn*-toa) *m* fragment
francese (frahn-*chāy*-zay) *adj* French; *m* Frenchman
Francia (*frahn*-chah) *f* France
franco (*frahng*-koa) *adj* open; ~ **di dazio** duty-free; ~ **di porto** postage paid
francobollo (frahng-koa-*boal*-loa) *m* postage stamp

frangia (*frahn*-jah) *f* fringe
frappé (frahp-*pay*) *m* milk-shake
frase (*fraa*-zay) *f* sentence; phrase
fratello (frah-*tehl*-loa) *m* brother
fraternità (frah-tayr-nee-*tah*) *f* fraternity
frattanto (fraht-*tahn*-toa) *adv* meanwhile
nel frattempo (nayl fraht-*tehm*-poa) in the meantime
frattura (fraht-*tōō*-rah) *f* fracture; break
fratturare (fraht-too-*raa*-ray) *v* fracture
frazione (frah-*tsyōā*-nay) *f* fraction; hamlet
freccia (*frayt*-chah) *f* arrow; indicator
freddino (frayd-*dee*-noa) *adj* chilly
freddo (*frayd*-doa) *adj* cold; *m* cold
freno (*frāy*-noa) *m* brake; ~ **a mano** hand-brake; ~ **a pedale** foot-brake
frequentare (fray-kwayn-*taa*-ray) *v* mix with, associate with
frequente (fray-*kwehn*-tay) *adj* frequent
frequenza (fray-*kwehn*-tsah) *f* frequency; attendance
fresco (*fray*-skoa) *adj* fresh; cool
fretta (*frayt*-tah) *f* speed, haste, hurry; **in** ~ in a hurry
frettoloso (frayt-toa-*lōā*-soa) *adj* hasty
***friggere** (*freed*-jay-ray) *v* fry
frigorifero (free-goa-*ree*-fay-roa) *m* refrigerator, fridge
fringuello (freeng-*gwehl*-loa) *m* finch
frittata (freet-*taa*-tah) *f* omelette
frizione (free-*tsyōā*-nay) *f* clutch
frode (*fraw*-day) *f* fraud
fronte (*froan*-tay) *f* forehead; **di** ~ **a** in front of; opposite; ***far** ~ **a** face
frontiera (froan-*tyai*-rah) *f* frontier; boundary
frontone (froan-*tōā*-nay) *m* gable
frullatore (frool-lah-*tōā*-ray) *m* mixer
frumento (froo-*mayn*-toa) *m* corn, grain; wheat
frusta (*froo*-stah) *f* whip
frutta (*froot*-tah) *f* fruit
frutteto (froot-*tāy*-toa) *m* orchard
fruttivendolo (froot-tee-*vayn*-doa-loa) *m* greengrocer; vegetable merchant
frutto (*froot*-toa) *m* fruit
fruttuoso (froot-*twōā*-soa) *adj* profitable
fucile (foo-*chee*-lay) *m* gun, rifle
fuga (*fōō*-gah) *f* flight; leak
fuggire (food-*jee*-ray) *v* escape
fuggitivo (food-jee-*tee*-voa) *m* runaway
fulvo (*fool*-voa) *adj* fawn
fumare (foo-*maa*-ray) *v* smoke
fumatore (foo-mah-*tōā*-ray) *m* smoker; **compartimento per fumatori** smoking-compartment
fumo (*fōō*-moa) *m* smoke
funerale (foo-nay-*raa*-lay) *m* funeral
fungo (*foong*-goa) *m* toadstool, mushroom
funzionamento (foon-tsyoa-nah-*mayn*-toa) *m* working, operation
funzionare (foon-tsyoa-*naa*-ray) *v* work, operate
funzionario (foon-tsyoa-*naa*-ryoa) *m* civil servant
funzione (foon-*tsyōā*-nay) *f* function; office
fuoco (*fwaw*-koa) *m* fire; focus
fuori (*fwaw*-ree) *adv* out; outside; **al di** ~ outwards; ~ **di** outside, out of
furbo (*foor*-boa) *adj* cunning
furfante (foor-*fahn*-tay) *m* villain
furgone (foor-*gōā*-nay) *m* delivery van, van
furibondo (foo-ree-*boan*-doa) *adj* furious
furioso (foo-*ryōā*-soa) *adj* furious
furore (foo-*rōā*-ray) *m* rage
furto (*foor*-toa) *m* robbery, theft
fusibile (foo-*zee*-bee-lay) *m* fuse

fusione (foo-*zyōā*-nay) *f* merger
futile (*fōō*-tee-lay) *adj* insignificant, petty
futuro (foo-*tōō*-roa) *m* future; *adj* future

G

gabbia (*gahb*-byah) *f* cage; ~ **da imballaggio** crate
gabbiano (gahb-*byaa*-noa) *m* gull; seagull
gabinetto (gah-bee-*nayt*-toa) *m* toilet, bathroom, lavatory; cabinet; ~ **per signore** ladies' room, powder-room; ~ **per signori** men's room
gaiezza (gah-*yayt*-tsah) *f* gaiety
gaio (*gaa*-yoa) *adj* cheerful
galleggiante (gahl-layd-*jahn*-tay) *m* float
galleggiare (gahl-layd-*jaa*-ray) *v* float
galleria (gahl-lay-*ree*-ah) *f* tunnel; gallery; ~ **d'arte** art gallery
gallina (gahl-*lee*-nah) *f* hen
gallo (*gahl*-loa) *m* cock
galoppo (gah-*lop*-poa) *m* gallop
gamba (*gahm*-bah) *f* leg
gamberetto (gahm-bay-*rayt*-toa) *m* shrimp
gambero (*gahm*-bay-roa) *m* prawn
gambo (*gahm*-boa) *m* stem
gancio (*gahn*-choa) *m* peg
gara (*gaa*-rah) *f* competition; race
garante (gah-*rahn*-tay) *m* guarantor
garantire (gah-rahn-*tee*-ray) *v* guarantee
garanzia (gah-rahn-*tsee*-ah) *f* guarantee
gargarizzare (gahr-gah-reed-*dzaa*-ray) *v* gargle
garza (*gahr*-dzah) *f* gauze
gas (gahz) *m* gas; ~ **di scarico** exhaust gases
gastrico (*gah*-stree-koa) *adj* gastric
gatto (*gaht*-toa) *m* cat
gazza (*gahd*-dzah) *f* magpie
gelare (jay-*laa*-ray) *v* *freeze
gelatina (jay-lah-*tee*-nah) *f* jelly
gelato (jay-*laa*-toa) *m* ice-cream
gelo (*jai*-loa) *m* frost
gelone (jay-*lōā*-nay) *m* chilblain
gelosia (jay-loa-*see*-ah) *f* jealousy
geloso (jay-*lōā*-soa) *adj* envious, jealous
gemelli (jay-*mehl*-lee) *mpl* twins *pl*; cuff-links *pl*
gemere (*jai*-may-ray) *v* groan, moan
gemma (*jehm*-mah) *f* gem
generale (jay-nay-*raa*-lay) *adj* general; universal, broad, public; *m* general; **in** ~ in general
generalmente (jay-nay-rahl-*mayn*-tay) *adv* as a rule
generare (jay-nay-*raa*-ray) *v* generate
generatore (jay-nay-rah-*tōā*-ray) *m* generator
generazione (jay-nay-rah-*tsyōā*-nay) *f* generation
genere (*jai*-nay-ray) *m* sort, kind; gender
genero (*jai*-nay-roa) *m* son-in-law
generosità (jay-nay-roa-see-*tah*) *f* generosity
generoso (jay-nay-*rōā*-soa) *adj* generous, liberal
gengiva (jayn-*jee*-vah) *f* gum
genio (*jai*-ñoa) *m* genius
genitale (jay-nee-*taa*-lay) *adj* genital
genitori (jay-nee-*tōā*-ree) *mpl* parents *pl*
gennaio (jayn-*naa*-yoa) January
gente (*jehn*-tay) *f* pcoplc *pl*
gentile (jayn-*tee*-lay) *adj* good-natured; kind
genuino (jay-*nwee*-noa) *adj* genuine
geografia (jay-oa-grah-*fee*-ah) *f* ge-

ography
geologia (jay-oa-loa-*jee*-ah) *f* geology
geometria (jay-oa-may-*tree*-ah) *f* geometry
gerarchia (jay-rahr-*kee*-ah) *f* hierarchy
Germania (jayr-*maa*-nyah) *f* Germany
germe (*jehr*-may) *m* germ
gesso (*jehss*-soa) *m* plaster
gesticolare (jay-stee-koa-*laa*-ray) *v* gesticulate
gestione (jay-*styōā*-nay) *f* management
gesto (*jeh*-stoa) *m* sign
gettare (jayt-*taa*-ray) *v* toss, *throw, *cast
getto (*jeht*-toa) *m* spout, jet
gettone (jayt-*tōā*-nay) *m* token, chip
ghiacciaio (gyaht-*chaa*-yoa) *m* glacier
ghiaccio (*gyaht*-choa) *m* ice
ghiaia (*gyaa*-yah) *f* gravel
ghianda (*gyahn*-dah) *f* acorn
ghiandola (*gyahn*-doa-lah) *f* gland
ghignare (gee-*ñaa*-ray) *v* grin
ghiottoneria (gyoat-toa-nay-*ree*-ah) *f* delicacy
ghiribizzo (gee-ree-*beed*-dzoa) *m* whim
ghisa (*gee*-zah) *f* cast iron
già (jah) *adv* already; formerly
giacca (*jahk*-kah) *f* jacket; ~ **e calzoni** pant-suit; ~ **sportiva** blazer
giacché (jahk-*kay*) *conj* since
giacchetta (jahk-*kayt*-tah) *f* jacket; ~ **sportiva** sports-jacket
giaccone (jahk-*kōā*-nay) *m* cardigan
giacimento (jah-chee-*mayn*-toa) *m* deposit
giada (*jaa*-dah) *f* jade
giallo (*jahl*-loa) *adj* yellow
Giappone (jahp-*pōā*-nay) *m* Japan
giapponese (jahp-poa-*nāy*-say) *adj* Japanese; *m* Japanese
giara (*jaa*-rah) *f* jar
giardiniere (jahr-dee-*ñai*-ray) *m* gardener
giardino (jahr-*dee*-noa) *m* garden; ~ **d'infanzia** kindergarten; ~ **pubblico** public garden; ~ **zoologico** zoological gardens, zoo
gigante (jee-*gahn*-tay) *m* giant
gigantesco (jee-gahn-*tay*-skoa) *adj* gigantic
giglio (*jee*-lʸoa) *m* lily
ginecologo (jee-nay-*kaw*-loa-goa) *m* gynaecologist
ginnasta (jeen-*nah*-stah) *m* gymnast
ginnastica (jeen-*nah*-stee-kah) *f* gymnastics *pl*
ginocchio (jee-*nok*-kyoa) *m* (pl le ginocchia) knee
giocare (joa-*kaa*-ray) *v* play
giocatore (joa-kah-*tōā*-ray) *m* player
giocattolo (joa-*kaht*-toa-loa) *m* toy
gioco (*jaw*-koa) *m* play; **carta da ~** playing-card; ~ **della dama** draughts; checkers *plAm*; ~ **delle bocce** bowling
giogo (*jōā*-goa) *m* yoke
gioia (*jaw*-yah) *f* gladness, joy; **gioie** jewellery
gioielliere (joa-yayl-*lʸai*-ray) *m* jeweller
gioiello (joa-*yehl*-loa) *m* gem, jewel; **gioielli** jewellery
gioioso (joa-*yōā*-soa) *adj* joyful
Giordania (joar-*daa*-ñah) *f* Jordan
giordano (joar-*daa*-noa) *adj* Jordanian; *m* Jordanian
giornalaio (joar-nah-*laa*-yoa) *m* newsagent
giornale (joar-*naa*-lay) *m* paper, newspaper; journal; ~ **del mattino** morning paper
giornaliero (joar-nah-*lʸai*-roa) *adj* daily
giornalismo (joar-nah-*lee*-zmoa) *m* journalism
giornalista (joar-nah-*lee*-stah) *m* journalist
giornata (joar-*naa*-tah) *f* day
giorno (*joar*-noa) *m* day; **al ~** per

day; **di** ~ by day; ~ **feriale** weekday; ~ **lavorativo** working day; **quindicina di giorni** fortnight; **un** ~ some time; **un** ~ **o l'altro** some day
giostra (*jo*-strah) *f* merry-go-round
giovane (*jōā*-vah-nay) *adj* young; *m* lad; ~ **esploratore** boy scout; ~ **esploratrice** girl guide
giovanile (joa-vah-*nee*-lay) *adj* juvenile
giovanotto (joa-vah-*not*-toa) *m* youth
giovare (joa-*vaa*-ray) *v* *be of use
giovedì (joa-vay-*dee*) *m* Thursday
gioventù (joa-vayn-*too*) *f* youth
giovinezza (joa-vee-*nayt*-tsah) *f* youth
giradischi (jee-rah-*dee*-skee) *m* record-player
girare (jee-*raa*-ray) *v* turn; endorse; ***far** ~ *spin; ~ **intorno a** by-pass
giro (*jee*-roa) *m* turn; day trip; detour; ~ **d'affari** turnover
gita (*jee*-tah) *f* trip, excursion; ~ **turistica** tour
giù (joo) *adv* beneath, below, down; over; ~ **da** off; **in** ~ downwards, down
giudicare (joo-dee-*kaa*-ray) *v* judge
giudice (*jōō*-dee-chay) *m* judge
giudizio (joo-*dee*-tsyoa) *m* judgment
giugno (*jōō*-ñoa) June
giunco (*joong*-koa) *m* reed; rush
***giungere** (*joon*-jay-ray) *v* arrive
giungla (*joong*-glah) *f* jungle
giuoco (*jwaw*-koa) *m* game
giuramento (joo-rah-*mayn*-toa) *m* oath, vow
giurare (joo-*raa*-ray) *v* vow, *swear
giuria (joo-*ree*-ah) *f* jury
giuridico (joo-*ree*-dee-koa) *adj* legal
giurista (joo-*ree*-stah) *m* lawyer
giustamente (joo-stah-*mayn*-tay) *adv* rightly
giustificare (joo-stee-fee-*kaa*-ray) *v* justify
giustizia (joo-*stee*-tsyah) *f* justice
giusto (*joo*-stoa) *adj* righteous, right, fair, just; proper
glaciale (glah-*chaa*-lay) *adj* freezing
gli (lʸee) *pron* him
globale (gloa-*baa*-lay) *adj* overall
globo (*glaw*-boa) *m* globe
gloria (*glaw*-ryah) *f* glory
glossario (gloass-*saa*-ryoa) *m* vocabulary
goccia (*goat*-chah) *f* drop
godere (goa-*dāy*-ray) *v* enjoy
godimento (goa-dee-*mayn*-toa) *m* enjoyment
goffo (*gof*-foa) *adj* clumsy, awkward
gola (*gōā*-lah) *f* throat; gorge, glen
golf (goalf) *m* jumper; golf; **campo di** ~ golf-links
golfo (*goal*-foa) *m* gulf
goloso (goa-*lōā*-soa) *adj* greedy
gomito (*gaw*-mee-toa) *m* elbow
gomma (*goam*-mah) *f* gum; ~ **da masticare** chewing-gum; ~ **per cancellare** rubber, eraser
gommapiuma (goam-mah-*pyōō*-mah) *f* foam-rubber
gondola (*goan*-doa-lah) *f* gondola
gonfiabile (goan-*fyaa*-bee-lay) *adj* inflatable
gonfiare (goan-*fyaa*-ray) *v* inflate; *swell
gonfiore (goan-*fyōā*-ray) *m* swelling
gonna (*goan*-nah) *f* skirt
gotta (*goat*-tah) *f* gout
governante (goa-vayr-*nahn*-tay) *f* governess; housekeeper
governare (goa-vayr-*naa*-ray) *v* govern, rule; navigate
governatore (goa-vayr-nah-*tōā*-ray) *m* governor
governo (goa-*vehr*-noa) *m* government, rule
gradevole (grah-*dāy*-voa-lay) *adj*

pleasing, pleasant, enjoyable, agreeable
gradire (grah-*dee*-ray) *v* fancy, like
grado (*graa*-doa) *m* degree; ***essere in ~ di** *be able to
graduale (grah-*dwaa*-lay) *adj* gradual
graffetta (grahf-*fayt*-tah) *f* staple
graffiare (grahf-*fyaa*-ray) *v* scratch
graffio (*grahf*-fyoa) *m* scratch
grafico (*graa*-fee-koa) *adj* graphic; *m* graph, diagram
grammatica (grahm-*maa*-tee-kah) *f* grammar
grammaticale (grahm-mah-tee-*kaa*-lay) *adj* grammatical
grammo (*grahm*-moa) *m* gram
grammofono (grahm-*maw*-foa-noa) *m* gramophone
granaio (grah-*naa*-yoa) *m* barn
Gran Bretagna (grahn bray-*taa*-ñah) Great Britain, Britain
granchio (*grahng*-kyoa) *m* crab
grande (*grahn*-day) *adj* big; great, large, major
grandezza (grahn-*dayt*-tsah) *f* size
grandine (*grahn*-dee-nay) *f* hail
grandioso (grahn-*dyōā*-soa) *adj* magnificent, superb
granello (grah-*nehl*-loa) *m* corn, grain
graniglia (grah-*nee*-lʸah) *f* grit
granito (grah-*nee*-toa) *m* granite
grano (*graa*-noa) *m* corn, grain
granturco (grahn-*toor*-koa) *m* maize; **pannocchia di ~** corn on the cob
grasso (*grahss*-soa) *adj* fat; corpulent; greasy; *m* grease, fat
grassottello (grahss-soat-*tehl*-loa) *adj* plump
grata (*graa*-tah) *f* grate
gratis (*graa*-teess) *adj* gratis
gratitudine (grah-tee-*tōō*-dee-nay) *f* gratitude
grato (*graa*-toa) *adj* grateful
grattacielo (graht-tah-*chai*-loa) *m* skyscraper
grattugia (graht-*tōō*-jah) *f* grater
gratuito (grah-*tōō*-ee-toa) *adj* free of charge, free
grave (*graa*-vay) *adj* grave
gravità (grah-vee-*tah*) *f* gravity
grazia (*graa*-tsyah) *f* grace; pardon
grazie (*graa*-tsyay) thank you
grazioso (grah-*tsyōā*-soa) *adj* graceful
Grecia (*grai*-chah) *f* Greece
greco (*grai*-koa) *adj* (pl greci) Greek; *m* Greek
gregge (*grayd*-jay) *m* herd, flock
grembiule (graym-*byōō*-lay) *m* apron
gremito (gray-*mee*-toa) *adj* chock-full
gridare (gree-*daa*-ray) *v* cry; shout
grido (*gree*-doa) *m* cry, scream, shout
grigio (*gree*-joa) *adj* grey
griglia (*gree*-lʸah) *f* grill
grilletto (greel-*layt*-toa) *m* trigger
grillo (*greel*-loa) *m* cricket
grinza (*green*-tsah) *f* crease
grossa (*gross*-sah) *f* gross
grossista (groass-*see*-stah) *m* wholesale dealer
grosso (*gross*-soa) *adj* big, stout
grossolano (groass-soa-*laa*-noa) *adj* coarse; rude
grotta (*grot*-tah) *f* grotto
gru (groo) *f* crane
grullo (*grool*-loa) *adj* silly
grumo (*grōō*-moa) *m* lump
grumoso (groo-*mōā*-soa) *adj* lumpy
gruppo (*groop*-poa) *m* group, party, set; bunch
guadagnare (gwah-dah-*ñaa*-ray) *v* *make, earn; gain
guadagno (gwah-*daa*-ñoa) *m* profit
guadare (gwah-*daa*-ray) *v* wade
guado (*gwaa*-doa) *m* ford
guaio (*gwaa*-yoa) *m* trouble
guancia (*gwahn*-chah) *f* cheek
guanciale (gwahn-*chaa*-lay) *m* pillow
guanto (*gwahn*-toa) *m* glove

guardare (gwahr-*daa*-ray) *v* look; watch, look at, view; **guardarsi** beware
guardaroba (gwahr-dah-*raw*-bah) *m* wardrobe; checkroom *nAm*
guardia (*gwahr*-dyah) *f* attendant; ~ **del corpo** bodyguard; ~ **forestale** forester
guardiano (gwahr-*dyaa*-noa) *m* guard, warden
guarigione (gwah-ree-*jōā*-nay) *f* recovery, cure
guarire (gwah-*ree*-ray) *v* heal; recover
guastare (gwah-*staa*-ray) *v* *spoil; **guastarsi** *break down
guasto (*gwah*-stoa) *adj* broken; *m* breakdown
guerra (*gwehr*-rah) *f* war; ~ **mondiale** world war
gufo (*gōō*-foa) *m* owl
guglia (*gōō*-lʸah) *f* spire
guida (*gwee*-dah) *f* lead; guide; guidebook; **patente di** ~ driving licence
guidare (gwee-*daa*-ray) *v* guide, conduct; *drive
guinzaglio (gween-*tsaa*-lʸoa) *m* leash, lead
guscio (*goosh*-shoa) *m* shell; ~ **di noce** nutshell
gustare (goo-*staa*-ray) *v* enjoy
gusto (*goo*-stoa) *m* taste; flavour; zest
gustoso (goo-*stōā*-soa) *adj* enjoyable, tasty

I

icona (ee-*kōā*-nah) *f* icon
idea (ee-*dai*-ah) *f* idea; ~ **luminosa** brain-wave
ideale (ee-day-*aa*-lay) *adj* ideal; *m* ideal
identico (ee-*dehn*-tee-koa) *adj* identical
identificare (ee-dayn-tee-fee-*kaa*-ray) *v* identify
identificazione (ee-dayn-tee-fee-kah-*tsyōā*-nay) *f* identification
identità (ee-dayn-tee-*tah*) *f* identity
idillio (ee-*deel*-lʸoa) *m* romance
idioma (ee-*dyaw*-mah) *m* idiom
idiomatico (ee-dyoa-*maa*-tee-koa) *adj* idiomatic
idiota (ee-*dyaw*-tah) *adj* idiotic; *m* fool, idiot
idolo (*ee*-doa-loa) *m* idol
idoneo (ee-*daw*-nay-oa) *adj* adequate
idraulico (ee-*drou*-lee-koa) *m* plumber
idrogeno (ee-*draw*-jay-noa) *m* hydrogen
ieri (*yai*-ree) *adv* yesterday
igiene (ee-*jai*-nay) *f* hygiene
igienico (ee-*jai*-nee-koa) *adj* hygienic
ignorante (ee-ñoa-*rahn*-tay) *adj* ignorant
ignorare (ee-ñoa-*raa*-ray) *v* ignore
ignoto (ee-*ñaw*-toa) *adj* unknown
il (eel) *art* (f la;pl i, gli, le) the *art*
illecito (eel-*lāy*-chee-toa) *adj* unauthorized
illegale (eel-lay-*gaa*-lay) *adj* unlawful, illegal
illeggibile (eel-layd-*jee*-bee-lay) *adj* illegible
illimitato (eel-lee-mee-*taa*-toa) *adj* unlimited
illuminare (eel-loo-mee-*naa*-ray) *v* il-

luminate
illuminazione (eel-loo-mee-nah-*tsyōā*-nay) *f* lighting, illumination
illusione (eel-loo-*zyōā*-nay) *f* illusion
illustrare (eel-loo-*straa*-ray) *v* illustrate
illustrazione (eel-loo-strah-*tsyōā*-nay) *f* illustration; picture
illustre (eel-*loo*-stray) *adj* noted
imballaggio (eem-bahl-*lahd*-joa) *m* packing
imballare (eem-bahl-*laa*-ray) *v* pack up, pack
imbarazzante (eem-bah-raht-*tsahn*-tay) *adj* awkward, embarrassing; puzzling
imbarazzare (eem-bah-raht-*tsaa*-ray) *v* embarrass
imbarcare (eem-bahr-*kaa*-ray) *v* embark
imbarco (eem-*bahr*-koa) *m* embarkation
imbiancare (eem-byahng-*kaa*-ray) *v* bleach
imboscata (eem-boa-*skaa*-tah) *f* ambush
imbrogliare (eem-broa-*lʸaa*-ray) *v* cheat
imbroglio (eem-*braw*-lʸoa) *m* muddle
imbronciato (eem-broan-*chaa*-toa) *adj* cross
imbuto (eem-*bōō*-toa) *m* funnel
imitare (ee-mee-*taa*-ray) *v* copy, imitate
imitazione (ee-mee-tah-*tsyōā*-nay) *f* imitation
immacolato (eem-mah-koa-*laa*-toa) *adj* stainless, spotless
immagazzinare (eem-mah-gahd-dzee-*naa*-ray) *v* store
immaginare (eem-mah-jee-*naa*-ray) *v* fancy, imagine
immaginario (eem-mah-jee-*naa*-ryoa) *adj* imaginary
immaginazione (eem-mah-jee-nah-*tsyōā*-nay) *f* fancy, imagination
immagine (eem-*maa*-jee-nay) *f* image; ~ **riflessa** reflection
immangiabile (eem-mahn-*jaa*-bee-lay) *adj* inedible
immediatamente (eem-may-dyah-tah-*mayn*-tay) *adv* instantly, immediately
immediato (eem-may-*dyaa*-toa) *adj* immediate
immenso (eem-*mehn*-soa) *adj* vast, immense, huge
immigrante (eem-mee-*grahn*-tay) *m* immigrant
immigrare (eem-mee-*graa*-ray) *v* immigrate
immigrazione (eem-mee-grah-*tsyōā*-nay) *f* immigration
imminente (eem-mee-*nehn*-tay) *adj* oncoming
immobile (eem-*maw*-bee-lay) *m* house
immodesto (eem-moa-*deh*-stoa) *adj* immodest
immondizia (eem-moan-*dee*-tsyah) *f* rubbish, refuse, garbage
immunità (eem-moo-nee-*tah*) *f* immunity
immunizzare (eem-moo-need-*dzaa*-ray) *v* immunize
impalcatura (eem-pahl-kah-*tōō*-rah) *f* scaffolding
imparare (eem-pah-*raa*-ray) *v* *learn; ~ **a memoria** memorize
imparziale (eem-pahr-*tsyaa*-lay) *adj* impartial
impasticciare (eem-pah-steet-*chaa*-ray) *v* muddle
impasto (eem-*pah*-stoa) *m* batter
impaurito (eem-pou-*ree*-toa) *adj* afraid
impaziente (eem-pah-*tsyehn*-tay) *adj* eager, impatient
impeccabile (eem-payk-*kaa*-bee-lay) *adj* faultless
impedimento (eem-pay-dee-*mayn*-toa)

m impediment
impedire (eem-pay-*dee*-ray) *v* prevent; impede
impegnare (eem-pay-*ñaa*-ray) *v* pawn; **impegnarsi** engage
impegno (eem-*pāy*-ñoa) *m* engagement
imperatore (eem-pay-rah-*tōā*-ray) *m* emperor
imperatrice (eem-pay-rah-*tree*-chay) *f* empress
imperfetto (eem-payr-*feht*-toa) *adj* imperfect
imperfezione (eem-payr-fay-*tsyōā*-nay) *f* fault
imperiale (eem-pay-*ryaa*-lay) *adj* imperial
impermeabile (eem-payr-may-*aa*-bee-lay) *adj* waterproof, rainproof; *m* mackintosh, raincoat
impero (eem-*pai*-roa) *m* empire
impersonale (eem-payr-soa-*naa*-lay) *adj* impersonal
impertinente (eem-payr-tee-*nehn*-tay) *adj* insolent, impertinent
impertinenza (eem-payr-tee-*nehn*-tsah) *f* impertinence
impetuoso (eem-pay-*twōā*-soa) *adj* violent
impianto (eem-*pyahn*-toa) *m* plant
impiegare (eem-pyay-*gaa*-ray) *v* employ; *spend
impiegato (eem-pyay-*gaa*-toa) *m* clerk, employee
impiego (eem-*pyai*-goa) *m* job, post; employment; **domanda d'impiego** application
implicare (eem-plee-*kaa*-ray) *v* imply
imponente (eem-poa-*nehn*-tay) *adj* imposing, grand
impopolare (eem-poa-poa-*laa*-ray) *adj* unpopular
***imporre** (eem-*poar*-ray) *v* impose; order; ***imporsi** assert oneself
importante (eem-poar-*tahn*-tay) *adj* important, capital; big
importanza (eem-poar-*tahn*-tsah) *f* importance; ***avere** ~ matter
importare (eem-poar-*taa*-ray) *v* import
importatore (eem-poar-tah-*tōā*-ray) *m* importer
importazione (eem-poar-tah-*tsyōā*-nay) *f* import
importunare (eem-poar-too-*naa*-ray) *v* disturb, bother
impossibile (eem-poass-*see*-bee-lay) *adj* impossible
imposta[1] (eem-*po*-stah) *f* shutter
imposta[2] (eem-*poa*-stah) *f* taxation; ~ **sul reddito** income-tax
impostare (eem-poa-*staa*-ray) *v* mail, post
impostazione (eem-poa-stah-*tsyōā*-nay) *f* approach
impotente (eem-poa-*tehn*-tay) *adj* powerless; impotent
impotenza (eem-poa-*tehn*-tsah) *f* impotence
impraticabile (eem-prah-tee-*kaa*-bee-lay) *adj* impassable
imprenditore (eem-prayn-dee-*tōā*-ray) *m* contractor
impresa (eem-*prāy*-sah) *f* enterprise, concern, undertaking
impressionante (eem-prayss-syoa-*nahn*-tay) *adj* impressive; striking
impressionare (eem-prayss-syoa-*naa*-ray) *v* impress
impressione (eem-prayss-*syōā*-nay) *f* impression
imprigionamento (eem-pree-joa-nah-*mayn*-toa) *m* imprisonment
imprigionare (eem-pree-joa-*naa*-ray) *v* imprison
improbabile (eem-proa-*baa*-bee-lay) *adj* improbable, unlikely
improprio (eem-*praw*-pryoa) *adj* improper

improvvisamente (eem-proav-vee-zah-*mayn*-tay) *adv* suddenly
improvvisare (eem-proav-vee-*zaa*-ray) *v* improvise
improvviso (eem-proav-*vee*-zoa) *adj* sudden
impudente (eem-poo-*dehn*-tay) *adj* impudent
impugnare (eem-poo-*ñaa*-ray) *v* grip
impugnatura (eem-poo-ñah-*too*-rah) *f* handle
impulsivo (eem-pool-*see*-voa) *adj* impulsive
impulso (eem-*pool*-soa) *m* impulse; urge
in (een) *prep* in, into; at
inabilitato (ee-nah-bee-lee-*taa*-toa) *adj* disabled
inabitabile (ee-nah-bee-*taa*-bee-lay) *adj* uninhabitable
inaccessibile (ee-naht-chayss-*see*-bee-lay) *adj* inaccessible
inaccettabile (ee-naht-chayt-*taa*-bee-lay) *adj* unacceptable
inadatto (ee-nah-*daht*-toa) *adj* unsuitable
inadeguato (ee-nah-day-*gwaa*-toa) *adj* inadequate
inamidare (ee-nah-mee-*daa*-ray) *v* starch
inaspettato (ee-nah-spayt-*taa*-toa) *adj* unexpected
inatteso (ee-naht-*tay*-soa) *adj* unexpected
inaugurare (ee-nou-goo-*raa*-ray) *v* open, inaugurate
incantare (eeng-kahn-*taa*-ray) *v* bewitch
incantevole (eeng-kahn-*tay*-voa-lay) *adj* enchanting
incanto (eeng-*kahn*-toa) *m* spell, charm
incapace (eeng-kah-*paa*-chay) *adj* incapable, unable
incaricare (eeng-kah-ree-*kaa*-ray) *v* charge; **incaricarsi di** *take charge of; **incaricato di** in charge of
incarico (eeng-*kaa*-ree-koa) *m* assignment
incassare (eeng-kahss-*saa*-ray) *v* cash
incauto (eeng-*kou*-toa) *adj* unwise
incendio (een-*chehn*-dyoa) *m* fire
incenso (een-*chehn*-soa) *m* incense
incerto (een-*chehr*-toa) *adj* uncertain, doubtful
inchiesta (eeng-*kyeh*-stah) *f* enquiry, inquiry
inchinare (eeng-kee-*naa*-ray) *v* bow
inchiostro (eeng-*kyo*-stroa) *m* ink
inciampare (een-chahm-*paa*-ray) *v* stumble
incidentale (een-chee-dayn-*taa*-lay) *adj* incidental, casual
incidente (een-chee-*dehn*-tay) *m* accident; incident; ~ **aereo** plane crash
***incidere** (een-*chee*-day-ray) *v* engrave
incinta (een-*cheen*-tah) *adj* pregnant
incisione (een-chee-*zyoa*-nay) *f* cut; engraving
incisore (een-chee-*zoa*-ray) *m* engraver
incitare (een-chee-*taa*-ray) *v* incite
inclinare (eeng-klee-*naa*-ray) *v* slant; **inclinato** slanting, sloping
inclinazione (eeng-klee-nah-*tsyoa*-nay) *f* gradient; inclination, tendency
***includere** (eeng-*kloo*-day-ray) *v* count, include
incollare (eeng-koal-*laa*-ray) *v* paste, *stick
incolto (eeng-*koal*-toa) *adj* desert, waste, uncultivated; uneducated
incolume (eeng-*kaw*-loo-may) *adj* unhurt
incombustibile (eeng-koam-boo-*stee*-bee-lay) *adj* fireproof
incompetente (eeng-koam-pay-*tehn*-tay) *adj* incompetent; unqualified
incompleto (eeng-koam-*plai*-toa) *adj*

incomplete
inconcepibile (eeng-koan-chay-*pee*-bee-lay) *adj* inconceivable
incondizionato (eeng-koan-dee-tsyoa-*naa*-toa) *adj* unconditional
inconscio (eeng-*kon*-shoa) *adj* unconscious
inconsueto (eeng-koan-*swai*-toa) *adj* unusual
incontrare (eeng-koan-*traa*-ray) *v* *meet, run into, *come across, encounter
incontro (eeng-*koan*-troa) *m* meeting, encounter
inconveniente (eeng-koan-vay-*ñehn*-tay) *adj* inconvenient; *m* inconvenience
incoraggiare (eeng-koa-rahd-*jaa*-ray) *v* encourage
incoronare (eeng-koa-roa-*naa*-ray) *v* crown
incosciente (eeng-koash-*shehn*-tay) *adj* unaware
incredibile (eeng-kray-*dee*-bee-lay) *adj* incredible
incremento (eeng-kray-*mayn*-toa) *m* increase
increscioso (eeng-kraysh-*shōā*-soa) *adj* unpleasant
increspare (eeng-kray-*spaa*-ray) *v* crease
incrinarsi (eeng-kree-*nahr*-see) *v* crack
incrocio (eeng-*krōā*-choa) *m* junction
incurabile (eengkoo-*raa*-bee-lay) *adj* incurable
indaffarato (een-dahf-fah-*raa*-toa) *adj* busy
indagare (een-dah-*gaa*-ray) *v* enquire; inquire
indagine (een-*daa*-jee-nay) *f* inquiry; examination
indecente (een-day-*chehn*-tay) *adj* indecent
indefinito (een-day-fee-*nee*-toa) *adj* indefinite
indemoniato (een-day-moa-*ñaa*-toa) *adj* possessed
indennità (een-dayn-nee-*tah*) *f* indemnity, compensation
indesiderabile (een-day-see-day-*raa*-bee-lay) *adj* undesirable
India (*een*-dyah) *f* India
indiano (een-*dyaa*-noa) *adj* Indian; *m* Indian
indicare (een-dee-*kaa*-ray) *v* point out; indicate, declare
indicazione (een-dee-kah-*tsyōā*-nay) *f* indication; direction
indice (*een*-dee-chay) *m* index finger; index; table of contents
indietro (een-*dyai*-troa) *adv* behind; back; **all'indietro** backwards
indifeso (een-dee-*fāy*-soa) *adj* unprotected
indifferente (een-deef-fay-*rehn*-tay) *adj* indifferent
indigeno (een-*dee*-jay-noa) *m* native
indigestione (een-dee-jay-*styōā*-nay) *f* indigestion
indignazione (een-dee-ñah-*tsyōā*-nay) *f* indignation
indipendente (een-dee-payn-*dehn*-tay) *adj* independent, self-employed
indipendenza (een-dee-payn-*dehn*-tsah) *f* independence
indiretto (een-dee-*reht*-toa) *adj* indirect
indirizzare (een-dee-reet-*tsaa*-ray) *v* address
indirizzo (een-dee-*reet*-tsoa) *m* address
indispensabile (een-dee-spayn-*saa*-bee-lay) *adj* essential
indisposto (een-dee-*spoa*-stoa) *adj* unwell
individuale (een-dee-vee-*dwaa*-lay) *adj* individual
individuo (een-dee-*vee*-dwoa) *m* individual

indiziato (een-dee-*tsyaa*-toa) *m* suspect
indizio (een-*dee*-tsyoa) *m* indication
indole (*een*-doa-lay) *f* nature
indolenzito (een-doa-layn-*jee*-toa) *adj* sore
indolore (een-doa-*lōā*-ray) *adj* painless
Indonesia (een-doa-*nai*-zyah) *f* Indonesia
indonesiano (een-doa-nay-*zyaa*-noa) *adj* Indonesian; *m* Indonesian
indossare (een-doass-*saa*-ray) *v* *put on; *wear
indossatrice (een-doass-sah-*tree*-chay) *f* model, mannequin
indovinare (een-doa-vee-*naa*-ray) *v* guess
indovinello (een-doa-vee-*nehl*-loa) *m* riddle
indubbiamente (een-doob-byah-*mayn*-tay) *adv* undoubtedly
indugio (een-*dōō*-joa) *m* delay
***indurre a** (een-*door*-ray) cause to
industria (een-*doo*-stryah) *f* industry; ~ **mineraria** mining
industriale (een-doo-*stryaa*-lay) *adj* industrial
inefficace (een-ayf-fee-*kaa*-chay) *adj* inefficient
ineguale (ee-nay-*gwaa*-lay) *adj* uneven, unequal
inesatto (ee-nay-*zaht*-toa) *adj* incorrect, inaccurate
inesperto (ee-nay-*spehr*-toa) *adj* inexperienced
inesplicabile (ee-nay-splee-*kaa*-bee-lay) *adj* unaccountable
inestimabile (ee-nay-stee-*maa*-bee-lay) *adj* priceless
inevitabile (ee-nay-vee-*taa*-bee-lay) *adj* inevitable, unavoidable
infastidire (een-fah-stee-*dee*-ray) *v* annoy; bother
infatti (een-*faht*-tee) *conj* as a matter of fact, in fact
infedele (een-fay-*dai*-lay) *adj* unfaithful
infelice (een-fay-*lee*-chay) *adj* unhappy
inferiore (een-fay-*ryōā*-ray) *adj* inferior, bottom
infermeria (een-fayr-may-*ree*-ah) *f* infirmary
infermiera (een-fayr-*myai*-rah) *f* nurse
inferno (een-*fehr*-noa) *m* hell
inferriata (een-fayr-*ryaa*-tah) *f* railing
infettare (een-fayt-*taa*-ray) *v* infect
infezione (een-fay-*tsyōā*-nay) *f* infection
infiammabile (een-fyahm-*maa*-bee-lay) *adj* inflammable
infiammarsi (een-fyahm-*mahr*-see) *v* *become septic
infiammazione (een-fyahm-mah-*tsyōā*-nay) *f* inflammation
infierire (een-fyay-*ree*-ray) *v* rage
infilare (een-fee-*laa*-ray) *v* thread
infine (een-*fee*-nay) *adv* at last
infinito (een-fee-*nee*-toa) *adj* infinite, endless; *m* infinitive
inflazione (een-flah-*tsyōā*-nay) *f* inflation
influente (een-*flwehn*-tay) *adj* influential
influenza (een-*flwehn*-tsah) *f* influence; influenza, flu
influenzare (een-floo-ayn-*tsaa*-ray) *v* affect
influire (een-*flwee*-ray) *v* influence
informale (een-foar-*maa*-lay) *adj* informal, casual
informare (een-foar-*maa*-ray) *v* inform; **informarsi** enquire, inquire
informazione (een-foar-mah-*tsyōā*-nay) *f* information, enquiry
infornare (een-foar-*naa*-ray) *v* bake
infrangibile (een-frahn-*jee*-bee-lay) *adj* unbreakable
infrarosso (een-frah-*roass*-soa) *adj* in-

fra-red
infreddolito (een-frayd-doa-*lee*-toa) *adj* shivery
infrequente (een-fray-*kwehn*-tay) *adj* infrequent
infruttuoso (een-froot-*twōā*-soa) *adj* unsuccessful
ingannare (eeng-gahn-*naa*-ray) *v* deceive, cheat
inganno (eeng-*gahn*-noa) *m* deceit; illusion
ingegnere (een-jay-*ñai*-ray) *m* engineer
ingente (een-*jehn*-tay) *adj* enormous
ingenuo (een-*jai*-nwoa) *adj* simple, naïve
Inghilterra (eeng-geel-*tehr*-rah) *f* England
inghiottire (eeng-gyoat-*tee*-ray) *v* swallow
inginocchiarsi (een-jee-noak-*kyahr*-see) *v* *kneel
ingiuriare (een-joo-*ryaa*-ray) *v* call names
ingiustizia (een-joo-*stee*-tsyah) *f* injustice
ingiusto (een-*joo*-stoa) *adj* unjust, unfair
inglese (eeng-*glāy*-say) *adj* English; British; *m* Englishman; Briton
ingoiare (eeng-goa-*yaa*-ray) *v* swallow
ingorgo (eeng-*goar*-goa) *m* traffic jam; bottleneck
ingrandimento (eeng-grahn-dee-*mayn*-toa) *m* enlargement
ingrandire (eeng-grahn-*dee*-ray) *v* enlarge
ingrato (eeng-*graa*-toa) *adj* ungrateful
ingrediente (eeng-gray-*dyehn*-tay) *m* ingredient
ingresso (eeng-*grehss*-soa) *m* entry; entrance; appearance, admission; entrance-fee
ingrosso (eeng-*gross*-soa) *m* wholesale
inguine (*eeng*-gwee-nay) *m* groin
iniettare (ee-ñayt-*taa*-ray) *v* inject
iniezione (ee-ñay-*tsyōā*-nay) *f* injection, shot
ininterrotto (ee-neen-tayr-*roat*-toa) *adj* continuous
iniziale (ee-nee-*tsyaa*-lay) *adj* initial; *f* initial; ***apporre le iniziali** initial
iniziare (ee-nee-*tsyaa*-ray) *v* *begin, commence
iniziativa (ee-nee-tsyah-*tee*-vah) *f* initiative
inizio (ee-*nee*-tsyoa) *m* beginning, start
innalzare (een-nahl-*tsaa*-ray) *v* erect
innamorato (een-nah-moa-*raa*-toa) *adj* in love
innanzi (een-*nahn*-tsee) *adv* forwards; before; ~ **a** before
innato (een-*naa*-toa) *adj* natural
inno (*een*-noa) *m* hymn; ~ **nazionale** national anthem
innocente (een-noa-*chehn*-tay) *adj* innocent
innocenza (een-noa-*chehn*-tsah) *f* innocence
innocuo (een-*naw*-kwoa) *adj* harmless
inoculare (ee-noa-koo-*laa*-ray) *v* inoculate
inoculazione (ee-noa-koo-lah-*tsyōā*-nay) *f* inoculation
inoltrare (ee-noal-*traa*-ray) *v* forward
inoltre (ee-*noal*-tray) *adv* moreover, besides, furthermore; likewise
inondazione (ee-noan-dah-*tsyōā*-nay) *f* flood
inopportuno (ee-noap-poar-*tōō*-noa) *adj* misplaced
inquieto (eeng-kwee-*ai*-toa) *adj* restless, uneasy
inquietudine (eeng-kwee-ay-*tōō*-dee-nay) *f* unrest
inquilino (eeng-kwee-*lee*-noa) *m* tenant; lodger

inquinamento (eeng-kwee-nah-*mayn*-toa) *m* pollution
inquisitivo (eeng-kwee-zee-*tee*-voa) *adj* inquisitive
insalata (een-sah-*laa*-tah) *f* salad
insano (een-*saa*-noa) *adj* insane
insegnamento (een-say-ñah-*mayn*-toa) *m* tuition; teachings *pl*
insegnante (een-say-*ñahn*-tay) *m* teacher; master, schoolteacher, schoolmaster
insegnare (een-say-*ñaa*-ray) *v* *teach
inseguire (een-say-*gwee*-ray) *v* chase
insenatura (een-say-nah-*tōō*-rah) *f* creek, inlet
insensato (een-sayn-*saa*-toa) *adj* senseless; meaningless
insensibile (een-sayn-*see*-bee-lay) *adj* insensitive
inserire (een-say-*ree*-ray) *v* insert
insetticida (een-sayt-tee-*chee*-dah) *m* insecticide
insettifugo (een-sayt-tee-*fōō*-goa) *m* insect repellent
insetto (een-*seht*-toa) *m* insect; bug *nAm*
insieme (een-*syai*-may) *adv* together; jointly
insignificante (een-see-ñee-fee-*kahn*-tay) *adj* unimportant, insignificant; petty; inconspicuous
insipido (een-*see*-pee-doa) *adj* tasteless
insistere (een-*see*-stay-ray) *v* insist
insoddisfacente (een-soad-dee-sfah-*chehn*-tay) *adj* unsatisfactory
insolente (een-soa-*lehn*-tay) *adj* insolent, impertinent
insolenza (een-soa-*lehn*-tsah) *f* insolence
insolito (een-*saw*-lee-toa) *adj* uncommon, unusual
insomma (een-*soam*-mah) *adv* in short
insonne (een-*son*-nay) *adj* sleepless
insonnia (een-*son*-ñah) *f* insomnia
insonorizzato (een-soa-noa-reed-*jaa*-toa) *adj* soundproof
insopportabile (een-soap-poar-*taa*-bee-lay) *adj* unbearable
instabile (een-*staa*-bee-lay) *adj* unstable
installare (een-stahl-*laa*-ray) *v* install
installazione (een-stahl-lah-*tsyōā*-nay) *f* installation
insuccesso (een-soot-*chehss*-soa) *m* failure
insufficiente (een-soof-fee-*chehn*-tay) *adj* insufficient
insultante (een-sool-*tahn*-tay) *adj* offensive
insultare (een-sool-*taa*-ray) *v* insult
insulto (een-*sool*-toa) *m* insult
insuperato (een-soo-pay-*raa*-toa) *adj* unsurpassed
insurrezione (een-soor-ray-*tsyōā*-nay) *f* rising
intagliare (een-tah-*lyaa*-ray) *v* carve
intanto (een-*tahn*-toa) *adv* in the meantime
intatto (een-*taht*-toa) *adj* unbroken, whole, intact
intelletto (een-tayl-*leht*-toa) *m* intellect
intellettuale (een-tayl-layt-*twaa*-lay) *adj* intellectual
intelligente (een-tayl-lee-*jehn*-tay) *adj* intelligent; clever, smart, bright
intelligenza (een-tayl-lee-*jehn*-tsah) *f* intelligence; brain
***intendere** (een-*tehn*-day-ray) *v* *mean; intend
intenditore (een-tayn-dee-*tōā*-ray) *m* connoisseur
intensità (een-tayn-see-*tah*) *f* intensity
intenso (een-*tehn*-soa) *adj* intense, violent
intento (een-*tehn*-toa) *m* aim
intenzionale (een-tayn-tsyoa-*naa*-lay)

adj intentional
intenzione (een-tayn-*tsyōā*-nay) *f* intention, purpose
interamente (een-tay-rah-*mayn*-tay) *adv* completely, entirely, altogether, quite
interessamento (een-tay-rayss-sah-*mayn*-toa) *m* interest
interessante (een-tay-rayss-*sahn*-tay) *adj* interesting
interessare (een-tay-rayss-*saa*-ray) *v* interest; **interessato** concerned
interesse (een-tay-*rehss*-say) *m* interest
interferenza (een-tayr-fay-*rehn*-tsah) *f* interference
interferire (een-tayr-fay-*ree*-ray) *v* interfere
interim (*een*-tay-reem) *m* interim
interiora (een-tay-*ryōā*-rah) *fpl* insides
interiore (een-tay-*ryōā*-ray) *m* interior
intermediario (een-tayr-may-*dyaa*-ryoa) *m* intermediary; ***fare da** ~ mediate
intermezzo (een-tayr-*mehd*-dzoa) *m* interlude
internazionale (een-tayr-nah-tsyoa-*naa*-lay) *adj* international
interno (een-*tehr*-noa) *adj* inner, internal, inside; resident; domestic; *m* inside; **all'interno** within; **verso l'interno** inwards
intero (een-*tāȳ*-roa) *adj* entire, whole
interpretare (een-tayr-pray-*taa*-ray) *v* interpret
interprete (een-*tehr*-pray-tay) *m* interpreter
interrogare (een-tayr-roa-*gaa*-ray) *v* interrogate
interrogativo (een-tayr-roa-gah-*tee*-voa) *adj* interrogative
interrogatorio (een-tayr-roa-gah-*taw*-ryoa) *m* interrogation
interrogazione (een-tayr-roa-gah-*tsyōā*-nay) *f* examination
***interrompere** (een-tayr-*roam*-pay-ray) *v* interrupt; ***interrompersi** pause
interruttore (een-tayr-root-*tōā*-ray) *m* switch
interruzione (een-tayr-roo-*tsyōā*-nay) *f* interruption
intersezione (een-tayr-say-*tsyōā*-nay) *f* intersection
interurbana (een-tay-roor-*baa*-nah) *f* trunk-call
intervallo (een-tayr-*vahl*-loa) *m* interval; intermission, break; half-time
***intervenire** (een-tayr-vay-*nee*-ray) *v* intervene
intervista (een-tayr-*vee*-stah) *f* interview
intestino (een-tay-*stee*-noa) *m* gut, intestine; bowels *pl*
intimità (een-tee-mee-*tah*) *f* privacy
intimo (*een*-tee-moa) *adj* intimate; cosy
intirizzito (een-tee-reed-*dzee*-toa) *adj* numb
intollerabile (een-toal-lay-*raa*-bee-lay) *adj* intolerable
intonarsi con (een-toa-*nahr*-see) match
intorno (een-*toar*-noa) *adv* around; ~ **a** around, round, about
intorpidito (een-toar-pee-*dee*-toa) *adj* numb
intossicazione alimentare (een-toass-see-kah-*tsyōā*-nay ah-lee-mayn-*taa*-ray) food poisoning
***intraprendere** (een-trah-*prehn*-day-ray) *v* *undertake
***intrattenere** (een-traht-tay-*nāȳ*-ray) *v* entertain
***intravvedere** (een-trahv-vay-*dāȳ*-ray) *v* glimpse
intricato (een-tree-*kaa*-toa) *adj* complex
intrigo (een-*tree*-goa) *m* intrigue
***introdurre** (een-troa-*door*-ray) *v* in-

troduce
introduzione (een-troa-doo-*tsyōā*-nay) *f* introduction
intromettersi in (een-troa-*mayt*-tayr-see) interfere with
intuire (een-*twee*-ray) *v* *understand
inumidire (ee-noo-mee-*dee*-ray) *v* moisten, damp
inutile (ee-*nōō*-tee-lay) *adj* useless; vain
inutilmente (ee-noo-teel-*mayn*-tay) *adv* in vain
***invadere** (een-*vaa*-day-ray) *v* invade
invalido (een-*vaa*-lee-doa) *adj* disabled, invalid; *m* invalid
invano (een-*vaa*-noa) *adv* in vain
invasione (een-vah-*zyōā*-nay) *f* invasion
invece di (een-*vāy*-chay dee) instead of
inveire (een-vay-*ee*-ray) *v* scold
inventare (een-vayn-*taa*-ray) *v* invent
inventario (een-vayn-*taa*-ryoa) *m* inventory
inventivo (een-vayn-*tee*-voa) *adj* inventive
inventore (een-vayn-*tōā*-ray) *m* inventor
invenzione (een-vayn-*tsyōā*-nay) *f* invention
inverno (een-*vehr*-noa) *m* winter
inverso (een-*vehr*-soa) *adj* reverse
invertire (een-vayr-*tee*-ray) *v* invert
investigare (een-vay-stee-*gaa*-ray) *v* investigate
investigatore (een-vay-stee-gah-*tōā*-ray) *m* detective
investigazione (een-vay-stee-gah-*tsyōā*-nay) *f* enquiry, investigation
investimento (een-vay-stee-*mayn*-toa) *m* investment
investire (een-vay-*stee*-ray) *v* invest
inviare (een-*vyaa*-ray) *v* dispatch
inviato (een-*vyaa*-toa) *m* envoy
invidia (een-*vee*-dyah) *f* envy
invidiare (een-vee-*dyaa*-ray) *v* grudge, envy
invidioso (een-vee-*dyōā*-soa) *adj* envious
invio (een-*vee*-oa) *m* expedition
invisibile (een-vee-*zee*-bee-lay) *adj* invisible
invitare (een-vee-*taa*-ray) *v* ask, invite
invito (een-*vee*-toa) *m* invitation
invocare (een-voa-*kaa*-ray) *v* invoke
involontario (een-voa-loan-*taa*-ryoa) *adj* unintentional
inzuppare (een-tsoop-*paa*-ray) *v* soak
io (*ee*-oa) *pron* I; ~ **stesso** myself
iodio (*yaw*-dyoa) *m* iodine
ipocrisia (ee-poa-kree-*see*-ah) *f* hypocrisy
ipocrita (ee-*paw*-kree-tah) *m* hypocrite; *adj* hypocritical
ipoteca (ee-poa-*tai*-kah) *f* mortgage
ipotesi (ee-*paw*-tay-zee) *f* supposition
ippodromo (eep-*paw*-droa-moa) *m* race-course
ippoglosso (eep-poa-*gloss*-soa) *m* halibut
ira (*ee*-rah) *f* anger
iracheno (ee-rah-*kāy*-noa) *adj* Iraqi; *m* Iraqi
Iran (*ee*-rahn) *m* Iran
iraniano (ee-rah-*nyaa*-noa) *adj* Iranian; *m* Iranian
Iraq (*ee*-rahk) *m* Iraq
irascibile (ee-rahsh-*shee*-bee-lay) *adj* irascible, hot-tempered, quick-tempered
irato (ee-*raa*-toa) *adj* angry
Irlanda (eer-*lahn*-dah) *f* Ireland
irlandese (eer-lahn-*dāy*-say) *adj* Irish; *m* Irishman
ironia (ee-roa-*nee*-ah) *f* irony
ironico (ee-*raw*-nee-koa) *adj* ironical
irragionevole (eer-rah-joa-*nāy*-voa-lay) *adj* unreasonable
irreale (eer-ray-*aa*-lay) *adj* unreal

irregolare (eer-ray-goa-*laa*-ray) *adj* irregular; uneven
irreparabile (eer-ray-pah-*raa*-bee-lay) *adj* irreparable
irrequieto (eer-ray-kwee-*ai*-toa) *adj* restless
irrestringibile (eer-ray-streen-*jee*-bee-lay) *adj* shrinkproof
irrevocabile (eer-ray-voa-*kaa*-bee-lay) *adj* irrevocable
irrilevante (eer-ree-lay-*vahn*-tay) *adj* insignificant
irrisorio (eer-ree-*zaw*-ryoa) *adj* ludicrous
irritabile (eer-ree-*taa*-bee-lay) *adj* irritable
irritare (eer-ree-*taa*-ray) *v* irritate
irruzione (eer-roo-*tsyōā*-nay) *f* invasion, raid
***iscrivere** (ee-*skree*-vay-ray) *v* enter; **per iscritto** in writing, written
iscrizione (ee-skree-*tsyōā*-nay) *f* inscription
Islanda (ee-*zlahn*-dah) *f* Iceland
islandese (ee-zlahn-*dāȳ*-say) *adj* Icelandic; *m* Icelander
isola (*ee*-zoa-lah) *f* island
isolamento (ee-zoa-lah-*mayn*-toa) *m* isolation; insulation
isolare (ee-zoa-*laa*-ray) *v* isolate; insulate
isolato (ee-zoa-*laa*-toa) *adj* isolated; *m* house block *Am*
isolatore (ee-zoa-lah-*tōā*-ray) *m* insulator
Isole Filippine (*ee*-zoa-lay fee-leep-*pee*-nay) Philippines *pl*
ispessire (ee-spayss-*see*-ray) *v* thicken
ispettore (ee-spayt-*tōā*-ray) *m* inspector; supervisor
ispezionare (ee-spay-tsyoa-*naa*-ray) *v* inspect
ispezione (ee-spay-*tsyōā*-nay) *f* inspection
ispirare (ee-spee-*raa*-ray) *v* inspire
Israele (ee-zrah-*ai*-lay) *m* Israel
israeliano (ee-zrah-ay-*lʸaa*-noa) *adj* Israeli; *m* Israeli
issare (eess-*saa*-ray) *v* hoist
istantanea (ee-stahn-*taa*-nay-ah) *f* snapshot
istante (ee-*stahn*-tay) *m* instant, second; while; **all'istante** instantly
isterico (ee-*stai*-ree-koa) *adj* hysterical
istinto (ee-*steen*-toa) *m* instinct
istituire (ee-stee-*twee*-ray) *v* institute; found
istituto (ee-stee-*tōō*-toa) *m* institute; institution
istituzione (ee-stee-too-*tsyōā*-nay) *f* institution, institute
istmo (*eest*-moa) *m* isthmus
istruire (ee-*strwee*-ray) *v* instruct; educate
istruttivo (ee-stroot-*tee*-voa) *adj* instructive
istruttore (ee-stroot-*tōā*-ray) *m* instructor
istruzione (ee-stroo-*tsyōā*-nay) *f* instruction; background; **istruzioni per l'uso** directions for use
Italia (ee-*taa*-lʸah) *f* Italy
italiano (ee-tah-*lʸaa*-noa) *adj* Italian; *m* Italian
itinerario (ee-tee-nay-*raa*-ryoa) *m* itinerary
itterizia (eet-tay-*ree*-tsyah) *f* jaundice
Iugoslavia (yoo-goa-*zlaa*-vyah) *f* Yugoslavia, Jugoslavia
iugoslavo (yoo-goa-*zlaa*-voa) *adj* Jugoslav; *m* Yugoslav, Jugoslav

K

kaki (*kaa*-kee) *m* khaki
Kenia (*kai*-nyah) *m* Kenya

L

la (lah) *pron* her
là (lah) *adv* there; **al di** ~ beyond; **al di** ~ **di** past; **di** ~ there
labbro (*lahb*-broa) *m* (pl le labbra) lip; **pomata per le labbra** lipsalve
labirinto (lah-bee-*reen*-toa) *m* labyrinth, maze
laboratorio (lah-boa-rah-*taw*-ryoa) *m* laboratory; ~ **linguistico** language laboratory
laborioso (lah-boa-*ryōā*-soa) *adj* industrious
lacca (*lahk*-kah) *f* lacquer; varnish; ~ **per capelli** hair-spray
laccio (*laht*-choa) *m* lace
lacrima (*laa*-kree-mah) *f* tear
ladro (*laa*-droa) *m* robber, thief
laggiù (lahd-*joo*) *adv* over there
lagnanza (lah-*ñahn*-tsah) *f* complaint
lagnarsi (lah-*ñahr*-see) *v* complain
lago (*laa*-goa) *m* lake
laguna (lah-*gōō*-nah) *f* lagoon
lama (*laa*-mah) *f* blade; ~ **di rasoio** razor-blade
lamentevole (lah-mayn-*tāy*-voa-lay) *adj* lamentable
lamiera (lah-*myai*-rah) *f* plate
lamina (*laa*-mee-nah) *f* sheet
lampada (*lahm*-pah-dah) *f* lamp; ~ **da tavolo** reading-lamp; ~ **flash** flash-bulb; ~ **portatile** flash-light
lampadina (lahm-pah-*dee*-nah) *f* light bulb; ~ **tascabile** torch
lampante (lahm-*pahn*-tay) *adj* self-evident
lampione (lahm-*pyōā*-nay) *m* lamp-post
lampo (*lahm*-poa) *m* lightning
lampone (lahm-*pōā*-nay) *m* raspberry
lana (*laa*-nah) *f* wool; **di** ~ woollen; ~ **da rammendo** darning wool; ~ **pettinata** worsted
lancia (*lahn*-chah) *f* spear
lanciare (lahn-*chaa*-ray) *v* *throw, *cast; launch
lancio (*lahn*-choa) *m* cast
landa (*lahn*-dah) *f* moor, heath
lanterna (lahn-*tehr*-nah) *f* lantern; ~ **vento** hurricane lamp
lanugine (lah-*nōō*-jee-nay) *f* down
lapide (*laa*-pee-day) *f* gravestone
lardo (*lahr*-doa) *m* bacon
larghezza (lahr-*gayt*-tsah) *f* width, breadth
largo (*lahr*-goa) *adj* wide, broad; ***farsi** ~ push
laringite (lah-reen-*jee*-tay) *f* laryngitis
lasca (*lah*-skah) *f* roach
lasciare (lahsh-*shaa*-ray) *v* desert, *leave; *leave behind; allow to, *let
lassativo (lahss-sah-*tee*-voa) *m* laxative
lassù (lahss-*soo*) *adv* up there
lastricare (lah-stree-*kaa*-ray) *v* pave
lateralmente (lah-tay-rahl-*mayn*-tay) *adv* sideways
laterizio (lah-tay-*ree*-tsyoa) *m* brick
latino americano (lah-*tee*-noa ah-may-ree-*kaa*-noa) Latin-American
latitudine (lah-tee-*tōō*-dee-nāy) *f* latitude
lato (*laa*-toa) *m* way, side
latrare (lah-*traa*-ray) *v* bay
latta (*laht*-tah) *f* tin, can
lattaio (laht-*taa*-yoa) *m* milkman
latte (*laht*-tay) *m* milk
latteo (*laht*-tay-oa) *adj* milky
latteria (laht-tay-*ree*-ah) *f* dairy
lattuga (laht-*tōō*-gah) *f* lettuce
lavabile (lah-*vaa*-bee-lay) *adj* washable
lavaggio (lah-*vahd*-joa) *m* washing; **inalterabile al** ~ fast-dyed
lavagna (lah-*vaa*-ñah) *f* blackboard

lavanderia (lah-vahn-day-*ree*-ah) *f* laundry; ~ **automatica** launderette
lavandino (lah-vahn-*dee*-noa) *m* wash-stand; wash-basin
lavare (lah-*vaa*-ray) *v* wash; ~ **i piatti** wash up
lavatrice (lah-vah-*tree*-chay) *f* washing-machine
lavello (lah-*vehl*-loa) *m* sink
lavorare (lah-voa-*raa*-ray) *v* work; ~ **all'uncinetto** crochet; ~ **a maglia** *knit; ~ **sodo** labour; ~ **troppo** overwork
lavoratore (lah-voa-rah-*tōā*-ray) *m* worker
lavoro (lah-*vōā*-roa) *m* work; labour; job; **datore di** ~ employer; **lavori domestici** housework; ~ **fatto a mano** handwork; ~ **manuale** handicraft
Le (lay) *pron* you
le (lay) *pron* her
leale (lay-*aa*-lay) *adj* true, loyal
lebbra (*layb*-brah) *f* leprosy
leccare (layk-*kaa*-ray) *v* lick
leccornia (layk-*koar*-ñah) *f* delicatessen
lega (*lāȳ*-gah) *f* union, league
legale (lay-*gaa*-lay) *adj* lawful, legal; **procuratore** ~ solicitor
legalizzazione (lay-gah-leed-dzah-*tsyōā*-nay) *f* legalization
legame (lay-*gaa*-may) *m* link
legare (lay-*gaa*-ray) *v* *bind, tie; ~ **insieme** bundle
legato (lay-*gaa*-toa) *m* legacy
legatura (lay-gah-*tōō*-rah) *f* binding
legazione (lay-gah-*tsyōā*-nay) *f* legation
legge (*lehd*-jay) *f* law
leggenda (layd-*jehn*-dah) *f* legend; caption
***leggere** (*lehd*-jay-ray) *v* *read
leggero (layd-*jai*-roa) *adj* light; slight; gentle
leggibile (layd-*jee*-bee-lay) *adj* legible
leggio (layd-*jee*-oa) *m* desk
legittimo (lay-*jeet*-tee-moa) *adj* legitimate, legal
legname (lay-*ñaa*-may) *m* timber
legno (*lāȳ*-ñoa) *m* wood; **di** ~ wooden
Lei (*lai*-ee) *pron* you; ~ **stesso** yourself
lente (*lehn*-tay) *f* lens; ~ **d'ingrandimento** magnifying glass; **lenti a contatto** contact lenses
lento (*lehn*-toa) *adj* slack, slow
lenza (*lehn*-tsah) *f* fishing line
lenzuolo (layn-*tswaw*-loa) *m* sheet
leone (lay-*ōā*-nay) *m* lion
lepre (*lai*-pray) *f* hare
lesione (lay-*zyōā*-nay) *f* injury
letale (lay-*taa*-lay) *adj* mortal
letamaio (lay-tah-*maa*-yoa) *m* dunghill
letame (lay-*taa*-may) *m* dung
lettera (*leht*-tay-rah) *f* letter; **carta da lettere** notepaper; ~ **di credito** letter of credit; ~ **di raccomandazione** letter of recommendation
letterario (layt-tay-*raa*-ryoa) *adj* literary
letteratura (layt-tay-rah-*tōō*-rah) *f* literature
letto (*leht*-toa) *m* bed; **letti gemelli** twin beds; **lettino da campeggio** camp-bed; cot *nAm*
lettura (layt-*tōō*-rah) *f* reading
leva (*lāȳ*-vah) *f* lever; ~ **del cambio** gear lever
levare (lay-*vaa*-ray) *v* *take away
levata (lay-*vaa*-tah) *f* collection
levatrice (lay-vah-*tree*-chay) *f* midwife
levigato (lay-vee-*gaa*-toa) *adj* smooth
levriere (lay-*vryai*-ray) *m* greyhound
lezione (lay-*tsyōā*-nay) *f* lesson, lecture
li (lee) *pron* (f le) them
lì (lee) *adv* there

libanese (lee-bah-*nāy*-say) *adj* Lebanese; *m* Lebanese
Libano (*lee*-bah-noa) *m* Lebanon
libbra (*leeb*-brah) *f* pound
liberale (lee-bay-*raa*-lay) *adj* liberal
liberare (lee-bay-*raa*-ray) *v* deliver
liberazione (lee-bay-rah-*tsyōā*-nay) *f* liberation; delivery
Liberia (lee-*bai*-ryah) *f* Liberia
liberiano (lee-bay-*ryaa*-noa) *adj* Liberian; *m* Liberian
libero (*lee*-bay-roa) *adj* free
libertà (lee-bayr-*tah*) *f* freedom, liberty
libraio (lee-*braa*-yoa) *m* bookseller
libreria (lee-bray-*ree*-ah) *f* bookstore
libro (*lee*-broa) *m* book; ~ **dei reclami** complaints book; ~ **di cucina** cookery-book; cookbook *nAm*; ~ **in brossura** paperback
licenza (lee-*chehn*-tsah) *f* permission, licence
licenziare (lee-chayn-*tsyaa*-ray) *v* fire
lieto (*lyai*-toa) *adj* pleased, glad
lieve (*lyai*-vay) *adj* light
lievito (*lyai*-vee-toa) *m* yeast
lilla (*leel*-lah) *adj* mauve
lima (*lee*-mah) *f* file; **limetta per le unghie** nail-file
limitare (lee-mee-*taa*-ray) *v* limit
limite (*lee*-mee-tay) *m* boundary, bound; limit; ~ **di velocità** speed limit
limonata (lee-moa-*naa*-tah) *f* lemonade
limone (lee-*mōā*-nay) *m* lemon
limpido (*leem*-pee-doa) *adj* limpid
lindo (*leen*-doa) *adj* neat
linea (*lee*-nayah) *f* line; ~ **aerea** airline; ~ **di navigazione** shipping line; ~ **principale** main line
lineetta (lee-nay-*ayt*-tah) *f* dash; hyphen
lingua (*leeng*-gwah) *f* tongue; language; ~ **materna** mother tongue, native language
linguaggio (leeng-*gwahd*-joa) *m* speech
lino (*lee*-noa) *m* linen
liquido (*lee*-kwee-doa) *adj* liquid
liquirizia (lee-kwee-*ree*-tsyah) *f* liquorice
liquore (lee-*kwaw*-ray) *m* liqueur; **spaccio di liquori** off-licence
lisca (*lee*-skah) *f* fishbone
liscio (*leesh*-shoa) *adj* smooth
liso (*lee*-zoa) *adj* threadbare
lista (*lee*-stah) *f* strip; list; ~ **dei vini** wine-list; ~ **di attesa** waiting-list; **listino prezzi** price list
lite (*lee*-tay) *f* row, dispute, quarrel
litigare (lee-tee-*gaa*-ray) *v* quarrel
litigio (lee-*tee*-joa) *m* quarrel
litorale (lee-toa-*raa*-lay) *m* sea-coast
litro (*lee*-troa) *m* litre
livella (lee-*vehl*-lah) *f* level
livellare (lee-vayl-*laa*-ray) *v* level
livello (lee-*vehl*-loa) *m* level; ~ **di vita** standard of living
livido (*lee*-vee-doa) *m* bruise
lo (loa) *pron* him
locale (loa-*kaa*-lay) *adj* local
località (loa-kah-lee-*tah*) *f* spot, locality
localizzare (loa-kah-leed-*dzaa*-ray) *v* locate
locanda (loa-*kahn*-dah) *f* inn, roadhouse; roadside restaurant
locazione (loa-kah-*tsyōā*-nay) *f* lease; ***dare in** ~ lease
locomotiva (loa-koa-moa-*tee*-vah) *f* locomotive
locomotrice (loa-koa-moa-*tree*-chay) *f* engine
lodare (loa-*daa*-ray) *v* praise
lode (*law*-day) *f* glory
loggione (load-*jōā*-nay) *m* gallery
logica (*law*-jee-kah) *f* logic

logico (*law*-jee-koa) *adj* logical
logorare (loa-goa-*raa*-ray) *v* wear out
lombaggine (loam-*bahd*-jee-nay) *f* lumbago
longitudine (loan-jee-*tōō*-dee-nay) *f* longitude
lontano (loan-*taa*-noa) *adj* far-off, far, distant
loquace (loa-*kwaa*-chay) *adj* talkative
lordo (*loar*-doa) *adj* gross
loro (*lōā*-roa) *adj* their; *pron* them
lotta (*lot*-tah) *f* combat, fight, battle; contest, struggle, strife
lottare (loat-*taa*-ray) *v* *fight, struggle
lotteria (loat-tay-*ree*-ah) *f* lottery
lozione (loa-*tsyōā*-nay) *f* lotion; ~ **dopo barba** aftershave lotion
lubrificante (loo-bree-fee-*kahn*-tay) *m* lubrication oil
lubrificare (loo-bree-fee-*kaa*-ray) *v* grease, lubricate
lubrificazione (loo-bree-fee-kah-*tsyōā*-nay) *f* lubrication
lucchetto (look-*kayt*-toa) *m* padlock
luccio (*loot*-choa) *m* pike
luce (*lōō*-chay) *f* light; ~ **del giorno** daylight; ~ **del sole** sunshine, sunlight; ~ **di posizione** parking light; ~ **laterale** sidelight; ~ **posteriore** tail-light; **luci di arresto** brake lights
lucentezza (loo-chayn-*tayt*-tsah) *f* gloss
lucidare (loo-chee-*daa*-ray) *v* polish
lucido (*lōō*-chee-doa) *adj* bright; glossy
luglio (*lōō*-lʸoa) July
lui (looæʰ) *pron* him; he
lumaca (loo-*maa*-kah) *f* snail
lume (*lōō*-may) *m* light; lamp
luminoso (loo-mee-*nōā*-soa) *adj* luminous
luna (*lōō*-nah) *f* moon; ~ **di miele** honeymoon
lunedì (loo-nay-*dee*) *m* Monday
lunghezza (loong-*gayt*-tsah) *f* length; ~ **d'onda** wave-length
lungo (*loong*-goa) *adj* long; tall; *prep* along, past; **di gran lunga** by far; **per il** ~ lengthways
lungofiume (loong-goa-*fyōō*-may) *m* riverside
luogo (*lwaw*-goa) *m* spot; ***aver** ~ *take place; **in nessun** ~ nowhere; ~ **di nascita** place of birth; ~ **di riunione** meeting-place; ~ **di villeggiatura** holiday resort
lupo (*lōō*-poa) *m* wolf
luppolo (*loop*-poa-loa) *m* hop
lusso (*looss*-soa) *m* luxury
lussuoso (looss-*swōā*-soa) *adj* luxurious
lutto (*loot*-toa) *m* mourning

M

ma (mah) *conj* but; yet
macchia (*mahk*-kyah) *f* stain, spot, blot
macchiare (mahk-*kyaa*-ray) *v* stain
macchina (*mahk*-kee-nah) *f* engine, machine; car; ~ **da cucire** sewing-machine; ~ **da scrivere** typewriter; ~ **fotografica** camera; ~ **sportiva** sports-car
macchinario (mahk-kee-*naa*-ryoa) *m* machinery
macchiolina (mahk-kyoa-*lee*-nah) *f* speck
macellaio (mah-chayl-*laa*-yoa) *m* butcher
macinare (mah-chee-*naa*-ray) *v* *grind
macinino (mah-chee-*nee*-noa) *m* mill
madre (*maa*-dray) *f* mother
madreperla (mah-dray-*pehr*-lah) *f* mother-of-pearl
maestro (mah-*eh*-stroa) *m* master;

schoolmaster, teacher
magari (mah-*gaa*-ree) *adv* even; *conj* even if
magazzinaggio (mah-gahd-dzee-*nahd*-joa) *m* storage
magazzino (mah-gahd-*dzee*-noa) *m* depository, warehouse, store-house; **grande** ~ department store; ***tenere in** ~ stock
maggio (*mahd*-joa) May
maggioranza (mahd-joa-*rahn*-tsah) *f* majority
maggiore (mahd-*jōā*-ray) *adj* major, main, superior; elder; eldest; *m* major
maggiorenne (mahd-joa-*rehn*-nay) *adj* of age
magia (mah-*jee*-ah) *f* magic
magico (*maa*-jee-koa) *adj* magic
magistrato (mah-jee-*straa*-toa) *m* magistrate
maglia (*maa*-lʸah) *f* link; mesh; vest
maglieria (mah-lʸay-*ree*-ah) *f* hosiery
maglietta (mah-*lʸayt*-tah) *f* undershirt
maglio (*maa*-lʸoa) *m* mallet
maglione (mah-*lʸōā*-nay) *m* jersey, pullover, sweater
magnete (mah-*ñai*-tay) *m* magneto
magnetico (mah-*ñai*-tee-koa) *adj* magnetic
magnetofono (mah-ñay-*taw*-foa-noa) *m* recorder, tape-recorder
magnifico (mah-*ñee*-fee-koa) *adj* gorgeous, splendid, magnificent, swell
magro (*maa*-groa) *adj* thin, lean
mai (migh) *adv* ever; **non...** ~ never
maiale (mah-*yaa*-lay) *m* pig
maiuscola (mah-*yoo*-skoa-lah) *f* capital letter
malacca (mah-*lahk*-kah) *f* rattan
malagevole (mah-lah-*jāȳ*-voa-lay) *adj* rough
malaria (mah-*laa*-ryah) *f* malaria
malato (mah-*laa*-toa) *adj* ill
malattia (mah-laht-*tee*-ah) *f* disease, ailment, illness; ~ **venerea** venereal disease
male (*maa*-lay) *m* mischief, evil, harm; sickness; **mal d'aria** air-sickness; **mal di denti** toothache; **mal di gola** sore throat; **mal di mare** seasickness; **mal di pancia** stomach-ache; **mal di schiena** backache; **mal di stomaco** stomach-ache; **mal di testa** headache; **mal d'orecchi** earache
***maledire** (mah-lay-*dee*-ray) *v* curse
malese (mah-*lāȳ*-say) *adj* Malaysian; *m* Malay
Malesia (mah-*lai*-zyah) *f* Malaysia
malessere (mah-*lehss*-say-ray) *m* hangover
malevolo (mah-*lāȳ*-voa-loa) *adj* spiteful, malicious
malfermo (mahl-*fayr*-moa) *adj* unsteady
malfido (mahl-*fee*-doa) *adj* untrustworthy
malgrado (mahl-*graa*-doa) *prep* in spite of, despite
maligno (mah-*lee*-ñoa) *adj* malignant
malinconia (mah-leeng-koa-*nee*-ah) *f* melancholy
malinconico (mah-leeng-*kaw*-nee-koa) *adj* sad
malinteso (mah-leen-*tāȳ*-soa) *m* misunderstanding
malizia (mah-*lee*-tsyah) *f* mischief
malizioso (mah-lee-*tsyōā*-soa) *adj* mischievous
malsano (mahl-*saa*-noa) *adj* unsound, unhealthy
malsicuro (mahl-see-*kōō*-roa) *adj* unsafe
malvagio (mahl-*vaa*-joa) *adj* evil, ill
mamma (*mahm*-mah) *f* mum
mammifero (mahm-*mee*-fay-roa) *m* mammal

mammut (mahm-*moot*) *m* mammoth
mancante (mahng-*kahn*-tay) *adj* missing
mancanza (mahng-*kahn*-tsah) *f* want, lack, shortage; fault
mancare (mahng-*kaa*-ray) *v* lack; fail
mancia (*mahn*-chah) *f* gratuity, tip
manciata (mahn-*chaa*-tah) *f* handful
mancino (mahn-*chee*-noa) *adj* left-handed
mandare (mahn-*daa*-ray) *v* *send
mandarino (mahn-dah-*ree*-noa) *m* mandarin, tangerine
mandato (mahn-*daa*-toa) *m* mandate
mandorla (*mahn*-doar-lah) *f* almond
maneggevole (mah-nayd-*jāy*-voa-lay) *adj* handy
maneggiabile (mah-nayd-*jaa*-bee-lay) *adj* manageable
maneggiare (mah-nayd-*jaa*-ray) *v* handle
manette (mah-*nayt*-tay) *fpl* handcuffs *pl*
mangiare (mahn-*jaa*-ray) *v* *eat; *m* food
mangiatoia (mahn-jah-*tōā*-yah) *f* manger
mania (mah-*nee*-ah) *f* craze
manica (*maa*-nee-kah) *f* sleeve; **La Manica** English Channel
manico (*maa*-nee-koa) *m* handle
manicure (mah-nee-*kōō*-ray) *f* manicure
maniera (mah-*ñāy*-rah) *f* way, manner; **maniere** manners *pl*
manifestare (mah-nee-fay-*staa*-ray) *v* express
manifestazione (mah-nee-fay-stah-*tsyōā*-nay) *f* expression
mano (*maa*-noa) *f* hand; **fatto a ~** hand-made
manopola (mah-*naw*-poa-lah) *f* knob
manoscritto (mah-noa-*skreet*-toa) *m* manuscript

mansueto (mahn-*swai*-toa) *adj* tame
mantella (mahn-*tehl*-lah) *f* cape
mantello (mahn-*tehl*-loa) *m* cloak
***mantenere** (mahn-tay-*nāy*-ray) *v* maintain; *keep
mantenimento (mahn-tay-nee-*mayn*-toa) *m* upkeep
manuale (mah-*nwaa*-lay) *adj* manual; *m* handbook, textbook; **~ di conversazione** phrase-book
manutenzione (mah-noo-tayn-*tsyōā*-nay) *f* maintenance
manzo (*mahn*-dzoa) *m* beef
mappa (*mahp*-pah) *f* map
marca (*mahr*-kah) *f* brand
marcare (mahr-*kaa*-ray) *v* mark; score
marchio (*mahr*-kyoa) *m* brand; **~ di fabbrica** trademark
marcia (*mahr*-chah) *f* march; ***far ~ indietro** reverse; **~ indietro** reverse
marciapiede (mahr-chah-*pyai*-day) *m* pavement; sidewalk *nAm*
marciare (mahr-*chaa*-ray) *v* march
marcio (*mahr*-choa) *adj* rotten
mare (*maa*-ray) *m* sea; **riva del ~** seaside
marea (mah-*rai*-ah) *f* tide; **alta ~** high tide; **bassa ~** low tide
margarina (mahr-gah-*ree*-nah) *f* margarine
margine (*mahr*-jee-nay) *m* edge; margin; **~ della strada** wayside, roadside
marina (mah-*ree*-nah) *f* navy; seascape
marinaio (mah-ree-*naa*-yoa) *m* sailor, seaman
marito (mah-*ree*-toa) *m* husband
marittimo (mah-*reet*-tee-moa) *adj* maritime
marmellata (mahr-mayl-*laa*-tah) *f* marmalade, jam
marmo (*mahr*-moa) *m* marble
marocchino (mah-roak-*kee*-noa) *adj*

Moroccan; *m* Moroccan
Marocco (mah-*rok*-koa) *m* Morocco
martedì (mahr-tay-*dee*) *m* Tuesday
martello (mahr-*tehl*-loa) *m* hammer
martire (*mahr*-tee-ray) *m* martyr
marzo (*mahr*-tsoa) March
mascalzone (mah-skahl-*tsōā*-nay) *m* bastard
mascella (mahsh-*shehl*-lah) *f* jaw
maschera (*mah*-skay-rah) *f* mask; usherette; ~ **di bellezza** face-pack
maschile (mah-*skee*-lay) *adj* masculine
maschio (*mah*-skyoa) male
massa (*mahss*-sah) *f* lot, bulk; mass, crowd
massaggiare (mahss-sahd-*jaa*-ray) *v* massage
massaggiatore (mahss-sahd-jah-*tōā*-ray) *m* masseur
massaggio (mahss-*sahd*-joa) *m* massage; ~ **facciale** face massage
massiccio (mahss-*seet*-choa) *adj* solid, massive
massimo (*mahss*-see-moa) *adj* greatest; **al** ~ at most
masso (*mahss*-soa) *m* boulder
masticare (mah-stee-*kaa*-ray) *v* chew
matematica (mah-tay-*maa*-tee-kah) *f* mathematics
matematico (mah-tay-*maa*-tee-koa) *adj* mathematical
materasso (mah-tay-*rahss*-soa) *m* mattress
materia (mah-*tai*-ryah) *f* matter; ~ **prima** raw material
materiale (mah-tay-*ryaa*-lay) *adj* material, substantial; *m* material
matita (mah-*tee*-tah) *f* pencil; ~ **per gli occhi** eye-pencil
matrice (mah-*tree*-chay) *f* stub
matrigna (mah-*tree*-ñah) *f* stepmother
matrimoniale (mah-tree-moa-*ñaa*-lay) *adj* matrimonial
matrimonio (mah-tree-*maw*-ñoa) *m* marriage; matrimony; wedding
mattina (maht-*tee*-nah) *f* morning
mattino (maht-*tee*-noa) *m* morning
matto (*maht*-toa) *adj* mad
mattone (maht-*tōā*-nay) *m* brick
mattonella (maht-toa-*nehl*-lah) *f* tile
mattutino (maht-too-*tee*-noa) *adj* early
maturità (mah-too-ree-*tah*) *f* maturity
maturo (mah-*tōō*-roa) *adj* ripe, mature
mausoleo (mou-zoa-*lai*-oa) *m* mausoleum
mazza (*maht*-tsah) *f* club; ~ **da golf** golf-club
mazzo (*maht*-tsoa) *m* bunch, bouquet
me (may) *pron* me
meccanico (mayk-*kaa*-nee-koa) *adj* mechanical; *m* mechanic
meccanismo (mayk-kah-*nee*-zmoa) *m* mechanism, machinery
medaglia (may-*daa*-lyah) *f* medal
medesimo (may-*dāȳ*-zee-moa) *adj* same
media (*mai*-dyah) *f* average, mean; **in** ~ on the average
mediante (may-*dyahn*-tay) *prep* by means of
mediatore (may-dyah-*tōā*-ray) *m* mediator; broker
medicamento (may-dee-kah-*mayn*-toa) *m* medicine
medicina (may-dee-*chee*-nah) *f* medicine
medico (*mai*-dee-koa) *adj* medical; *m* physician, doctor; ~ **generico** general practitioner
medicone (may-dee-*kōā*-nay) *m* quack
medievale (may-dyay-*vaa*-lay) *adj* mediaeval
medio (*mai*-dyoa) *adj* medium; average
mediocre (may-*dyaw*-kray) *adj* moderate, medium
medioevo (may-dyoa-*ai*-voa) *m* Mid-

dle Ages
meditare (may-dee-*taa*-ray) *v* meditate
Mediterraneo (may-dee-tayr-*raa*-nay-oa) *m* Mediterranean
medusa (may-*doo*-zah) *f* jelly-fish
meglio (*mai*-lʸoa) *adv* better; best
mela (*may*-lah) *f* apple
melanzana (may-lahn-*tsaa*-nah) *f* egg-plant
melma (*mayl*-mah) *f* muck
melodia (may-loa-*dee*-ah) *f* tune, melody
melodioso (may-loa-*dyoa*-soa) *adj* tuneful
melodramma (may-loa-*drahm*-mah) *m* melodrama
melone (may-*loa*-nay) *m* melon
membrana (maym-*braa*-nah) *f* diaphragm
membro[1] (*mehm*-broa) *m* (pl le membra) limb
membro[2] (*mehm*-broa) *m* (pl i membri) member; **qualità di ~** membership
memorabile (may-moa-*raa*-bee-lay) *adj* memorable
memoria (may-*maw*-ryah) *f* memory; **a ~** by heart
ménage (may-*naazh*) *m* household
mendicante (mayn-dee-*kahn*-tay) *m* beggar
mendicare (mayn-dee-*kaa*-ray) *v* beg
meno (*may*-noa) *adv* less; minus; **a ~ che** unless; ***fare a ~ di** spare
mensa (*mayn*-sah) *f* canteen
mensile (mayn-*see*-lay) *adj* monthly
menta (*mayn*-tah) *f* mint; **~ peperina** peppermint
mentale (mayn-*taa*-lay) *adj* mental
mente (*mayn*-tay) *f* mind
mentire (mayn-*tee*-ray) *v* lie
mento (*mayn*-toa) *m* chin
mentre (*mayn*-tray) *conj* whilst, while
menu (may-*noo*) *m* menu
menzionare (mayn-tsyoa-*naa*-ray) *v* mention
menzione (mayn-*tsyoa*-nay) *f* mention
menzogna (mayn-*tsoa*-ñah) *f* lie
meraviglia (may-rah-*vee*-lʸah) *f* surprise; marvel
meravigliarsi (may-rah-vee-*lʸahr*-see) *v* marvel
meraviglioso (may-rah-vee-*lʸoa*-soa) *adj* marvellous, fine, wonderful
mercante (mayr-*kahn*-tay) *m* trader, merchant; **~ di vini** wine-merchant
mercanteggiare (mayr-kahn-tayd-*jaa*-ray) *v* bargain
mercanzia (mayr-kahn-*tsee*-ah) *f* merchandise
mercato (mayr-*kaa*-toa) *m* market; **a buon ~** cheap; **~ nero** black market
merce (*mehr*-chay) *f* merchandise; **merci** goods *pl*, wares *pl*
merceria (mayr-chay-*ree*-ah) *f* haberdashery
mercoledì (mayr-koa-lay-*dee*) *m* Wednesday
mercurio (mayr-*koo*-ryoa) *m* mercury
merenda (may-*rehn*-dah) *f* tea
meridionale (may-ree-dyoa-*naa*-lay) *adj* southern, southerly
meritare (may-ree-*taa*-ray) *v* deserve, merit
merito (*mai*-ree-toa) *m* merit
merlano (mayr-*laa*-noa) *m* whiting
merletto (mayr-*layt*-toa) *m* lace
merlo (*mehr*-loa) *m* blackbird
merluzzo (mayr-*loot*-tsoa) *m* cod; haddock
meschino (may-*skee*-noa) *adj* mean; narrow-minded
mescolare (may-skoa-*laa*-ray) *v* mix; stir; shuffle
mese (*may*-say) *m* month
messa (*mayss*-sah) *f* Mass
messaggero (mayss-sahd-*jai*-roa) *m*

messenger
messaggio (mayss-*sahd*-joa) *m* message
messicano (mayss-see-*kaa*-noa) *adj* Mexican; *m* Mexican
Messico (*mehss*-see-koa) *m* Mexico
mestiere (may-*styai*-ray) *m* trade; business
mesto (*meh*-stoa) *adj* sad
mestruazione (may-strwah-*tsyōā*-nay) *f* menstruation
metà (may-*tah*) *f* half; **a** ~ half
metallico (may-*tahl*-lee-koa) *adj* metal
metallo (may-*tahl*-loa) *m* metal
meticoloso (may-tee-koa-*lōā*-soa) *adj* precise
metodico (may-*taw*-dee-koa) *adj* methodical
metodo (*mai*-toa-doa) *m* method
metrico (*mai*-tree-koa) *adj* metric
metro (*mai*-troa) *m* metre; meter; ~ **a nastro** tape-measure
metropolitana (may-troa-poa-lee-*taa*-nah) *f* underground; subway *nAm*
***mettere** (*mayt*-tay-ray) *v* *set, *put; *lay; ~ **in imbarazzo** embarrass
mezzanino (mayd-dzah-*nee*-noa) *m* mezzanine
mezzanotte (mayd-dzah-*not*-tay) *f* midnight
mezzo (*mehd*-dzoa) *adj* half; middle; *m* midst, middle; means; **in** ~ **a** amid; among
mezzogiorno (mayd-dzoa-*joar*-noa) *m* midday, noon
mi (mee) *pron* me; myself
miccia (*meet*-chah) *f* fuse
micia (*mee*-chah) *f* pussy-cat
microfono (mee-*kraw*-foa-noa) *m* microphone
micromotore (mee-kroa-moa-*tōā*-ray) *m* moped
microsolco (mee-kroa-*soal*-koa) *m* long-playing record
midollo (mee-*doal*-loa) *m* marrow
miele (*myai*-lay) *m* honey
miglio (*mee*-lʸoa) *m* (pl le miglia) mile; **distanza in miglia** mileage
miglioramento (mee-lʸoa-rah-*mayn*-toa) *m* improvement
migliorare (mee-lʸoa-*raa*-ray) *v* improve
migliore (mee-*lʸōā*-ray) *adj* better; superior
mignolo (*mee*-ñoa-loa) *m* little finger
milionario (mee-lʸoa-*naa*-ryoa) *m* millionaire
milione (mee-*lʸōā*-nay) *m* million
militare (mee-lee-*taa*-ray) *adj* military; *m* soldier
mille (*meel*-lay) *num* thousand
minaccia (mee-*naht*-chah) *f* threat
minacciare (mee-naht-*chaa*-ray) *v* threaten
minaccioso (mee-naht-*chōā*-soa) *adj* threatening
minatore (mee-nah-*tōā*-ray) *m* miner
minerale (mee-nay-*raa*-lay) *m* mineral; ore
minestra (mee-*neh*-strah) *f* soup
miniatura (mee-ñah-*tōō*-rah) *f* miniature
miniera (mee-*ñai*-rah) *f* mine, pit; ~ **d'oro** goldmine
minimo (*mee*-nee-moa) *adj* least; *m* minimum
ministero (mee-nee-*stai*-roa) *m* ministry
ministro (mee-*nee*-stroa) *m* minister; **primo** ~ Prime Minister, premier
minoranza (mee-noa-*rahn*-tsah) *f* minority
minore (mee-*nōā*-ray) *adj* minor; junior
minorenne (mee-noa-*rehn*-nay) *adj* under age; *m* minor
minuscolo (mee-*noo*-skoa-loa) *adj* tiny
minuto (mee-*nōō*-toa) *adj* minute; *m*

minute
minuzioso (mee-noo-*tsyōā*-soa) *adj* thorough
mio (*mee*-oa) *adj* (f mia; pl miei, mie) my
miope (*mee*-oa-pay) *adj* short-sighted
miracolo (mee-*raa*-koa-loa) *m* miracle, wonder
miracoloso (mee-rah-koa-*lōā*-soa) *adj* miraculous
mirare a (mee-*raa*-ray) aim at
mirino (mee-*ree*-noa) *m* view-finder
miscuglio (mee-*skōō*-lʸoa) *m* mixture
miserabile (mee-zay-*raa*-bee-lay) *adj* miserable
miseria (mee-*zai*-ryah) *f* misery
misericordia (mee-zay-ree-*kor*-dyah) *f* mercy
misericordioso (mee-zay-ree-koar-*dyōā*-soa) *adj* merciful
misero (*mee*-zay-roa) *adj* miserable; poor
missione (meess-*syōā*-nay) *f* mission
misterioso (mee-stay-*ryōā*-soa) *adj* mysterious
mistero (mee-*stai*-roa) *m* mystery
misto (*mee*-stoa) *adj* mixed, miscellaneous
misura (mee-*zōō*-rah) *f* measure; size; **fatto su ~** made to order, tailor-made
misurare (mee-zoo-*raa*-ray) *v* measure
misuratore (mee-zoo-rah-*tōā*-ray) *m* gauge
mite (*mee*-tay) *adj* mild
mitigare (mee-tee-*gaa*-ray) *v* relieve
mito (*mee*-toa) *m* myth
mobile (*maw*-bee-lay) *adj* mobile; movable
mobilia (moa-*bee*-lʸah) *f* furniture
moda (*maw*-dah) *f* fashion; **alla ~** fashionable; **fuori ~** out of date
modellare (moa-dayl-*laa*-ray) *v* model
modello (moa-*dehl*-loa) *m* model
moderato (moa-day-*raa*-toa) *adj* moderate
moderno (moa-*dehr*-noa) *adj* modern
modestia (moa-*deh*-styah) *f* modesty
modesto (moa-*deh*-stoa) *adj* modest
modifica (moa-*dee*-fee-kah) *f* alteration
modificare (moa-dee-fee-*kaa*-ray) *v* modify, change, alter
modista (moa-*dee*-stah) *f* milliner
modo (*maw*-doa) *m* way, fashion, manner; **ad ogni ~** at any rate; **in nessun ~** by no means; **in ogni ~** anyhow; **nello stesso ~** likewise
moglie (*mōā*-lʸay) *f* wife
molare (moa-*laa*-ray) *m* molar
molesto (moa-*leh*-stoa) *adj* troublesome
molla (*mol*-lah) *f* spring
molleggio (moal-*layd*-joa) *m* suspension
molo (*maw*-loa) *m* pier, jetty; wharf, quay
moltiplicare (moal-tee-plee-*kaa*-ray) *v* multiply
moltiplicazione (moal-tee-plee-kah-*tsyōā*-nay) *f* multiplication
molto (*moal*-toa) *adj* much; *adv* very, quite; far, much; **molti** *adj* many
momentaneo (moa-mayn-*taa*-nay-oa) *adj* momentary
momento (moa-*mayn*-toa) *m* moment; **a momenti** presently
monaca (*maw*-nah-kah) *f* nun
monaco (*maw*-nah-koa) *m* monk
monarca (moa-*nahr*-kah) *m* monarch, ruler
monarchia (moa-nahr-*kee*-ah) *f* monarchy
monastero (moa-nah-*stai*-roa) *m* cloister, monastery
mondiale (moan-*dyaa*-lay) *adj* worldwide
mondo (*moan*-doa) *m* world

monello (moa-*nehl*-loa) *m* rascal
moneta (moa-*nāy*-tah) *f* coin; ~ **spicciola** petty cash
monetario (moa-nay-*taa*-ryoa) *adj* monetary
monologo (moa-*naw*-loa-goa) *m* monologue
monopattino (moa-noa-*paht*-tee-noa) *m* scooter
monopolio (moa-noa-*paw*-lyoa) *m* monopoly
monotono (moa-*naw*-toa-noa) *adj* monotonous, dull
montagna (moan-*taa*-ñah) *f* mountain
montagnoso (moan-tah-*ñōā*-soa) *adj* mountainous
montare (moan-*taa*-ray) *v* mount; *get on; assemble
montatura (moan-tah-*tōō*-rah) *f* frame
monte (*moan*-tay) *m* mount
montone (moan-*tōā*-nay) *m* mutton
monumento (moa-noo-*mayn*-toa) *m* monument; ~ **commemorativo** memorial
mora (*maw*-rah) *f* mulberry; blackberry
morale (moa-*raa*-lay) *adj* moral; *f* moral; *m* spirits
moralità (moa-rah-lee-*tah*) *f* morality
morbido (*mor*-bee-doa) *adj* soft, smooth
morbillo (moar-*beel*-loa) *m* measles
***mordere** (*mor*-day-ray) *v* *bite
morfina (moar-*fee*-nah) *f* morphine, morphia
***morire** (moa-*ree*-ray) *v* die
mormorare (moar-moa-*raa*-ray) *v* whisper
morsa (*mor*-sah) *f* clamp
morsetto (moar-*sayt*-toa) *m* clamp
morso (*mor*-soa) *m* bite
mortale (moar-*taa*-lay) *adj* fatal; mortal
morte (*mor*-tay) *f* death
morto (*mor*-toa) *adj* dead
mosaico (moa-*zaa*-ee-koa) *m* mosaic
mosca (*moa*-skah) *f* fly
moschea (moa-*skai*-ah) *f* mosque
mossa (*moss*-sah) *f* move
mostra (*moa*-strah) *f* display; exhibition; ***mettere in** ~ display; ~ **d'arte** art exhibition
mostrare (moa-*straa*-ray) *v* display, *show; **mostrarsi** prove
motivo (moa-*tee*-voa) *m* cause, occasion; **a** ~ **di** owing to
moto (*maw*-toa) *m* motion
motocicletta (moa-toa-chee-*klayt*-tah) *f* motor-cycle
motonave (moa-toa-*naa*-vay) *f* launch
motore (moa-*tōā*-ray) *m* motor, engine
motorino (moa-toa-*ree*-noa) *m* motorbike *nAm*
motoscafo (moa-toa-*skaa*-foa) *m* motor-boat
motto (*mot*-toa) *m* motto, slogan
movente (moa-*vehn*-tay) *m* motive
movimento (moa-vee-*mayn*-toa) *m* movement
mozione (moa-*tsyōā*-nay) *f* motion
mucchio (*mook*-kyoa) *m* pile, heap
muffa (*moof*-fah) *f* mildew
muffole (*moof*-foa-lay) *fpl* mittens *pl*
mugghiare (moog-*gyaa*-ray) *v* roar
mugnaio (moo-*ñaa*-yoa) *m* miller
mulino a vento (moo-*lee*-noa ah *vayn*-toa) windmill
mulo (*mōō*-loa) *m* mule
multa (*mool*-tah) *f* fine
municipale (moo-nee-chee-*paa*-lay) *adj* municipal
municipalità (moo-nee-chee-pah-lee-*tah*) *f* municipality
municipio (moo-nee-*chee*-pyoa) *m* town hall
munifico (moo-*nee*-fee-koa) *adj* generous
***muovere** (*mwaw*-vay-ray) *v* move,

stir
murare (moo-*raa*-ray) *v* *lay bricks
muratore (moo-rah-*tōā*-ray) *m* bricklayer
muro (*mōō*-roa) *m* wall
muschio (*moo*-skyoa) *m* moss
muscolo (*moo*-skoa-loa) *m* muscle
muscoloso (moo-skoa-*lōā*-soa) *adj* muscular
museo (moo-*zai*-oa) *m* museum; ~ **delle cere** waxworks *pl*
musica (*mōō*-zee-kah) *f* music
musicale (moo-zee-*kaa*-lay) *adj* musical
musicista (moo-zee-*chee*-stah) *m* musician
muso (*mōō*-zoa) *m* snout
mussolina (mooss-soa-*lee*-nah) *f* muslin
mutamento (moo-tah-*mayn*-toa) *m* variation
mutande (moo-*tahn*-day) *fpl* drawers; panties *pl*, pants *pl*; shorts *plAm*
mutandine (moo-tahn-*dee*-nay) *fpl* panties *pl*, briefs *pl*; knickers *pl*; underpants *plAm*; ~ **da bagno** bathing-trunks, swimming-trunks
mutare (moo-*taa*-ray) *v* change
muto (*mōō*-toa) *adj* mute, dumb; speechless
mutuo (*mōō*-twoa) *adj* mutual

N

nafta (*nahf*-tah) *f* fuel oil
nailon (*nigh*-loan) *m* nylon
nano (*naa*-noa) *m* dwarf
narciso (nahr-*chee*-zoa) *m* daffodil
narcosi (nahr-*kaw*-zee) *f* narcosis
narcotico (nahr-*kaw*-tee-koa) *m* narcotic, drug
narice (nah-*ree*-chay) *f* nostril
* **nascere** (*nahsh*-shay-ray) *v* *be born
nascita (*nahsh*-shee-tah) *f* birth
* **nascondere** (nah-*skoan*-day-ray) *v* *hide; conceal
naso (*naa*-soa) *m* nose
nastro (*nah*-stroa) *m* ribbon; tape; ~ **adesivo** adhesive tape
Natale (nah-*taa*-lay) Xmas, Christmas
natica (*naa*-tee-kah) *f* buttock
nativo (nah-*tee*-voa) *adj* native
nato (*naa*-toa) *adj* born
natura (nah-*tōō*-rah) *f* nature
naturale (nah-too-*raa*-lay) *adj* natural
naturalmente (nah-too-rahl-*mayn*-tay) *adv* of course, naturally
nausea (*nou*-zay-ah) *f* nausea, sickness
nauseante (nou-zay-*ahn*-tay) *adj* disgusting
nauseato (nou-zay-*aa*-toa) *adj* sick
navale (nah-*vaa*-lay) *adj* naval; **cantiere** ~ shipyard
nave (*naa*-vay) *f* ship; vessel; ~ **da guerra** man-of-war; ~ **di linea** liner
navigabile (nah-vee-*gaa*-bee-lay) *adj* navigable
navigare (nah-vee-*gaa*-ray) *v* sail, navigate
navigazione (nah-vee-gah-*tsyōā*-nay) *f* navigation
nazionale (nah-tsyoa-*naa*-lay) *adj* national
nazionalità (nah-tsyōā-nah-lee-*tah*) *f* nationality
nazionalizzare (nah-tsyoa-nah-leed-*dzaa*-ray) *v* nationalize
nazione (nah-*tsyōā*-nay) *f* nation
ne (nay) *pron* of it; about him
né... né (nay) neither ... nor
neanche (nay-*ahng*-kay) *adv* not even; *conj* nor
nebbia (*nayb*-byah) *f* mist, fog
nebbioso (nayb-*byōā*-soa) *adj* misty, hazy, foggy

necessario (nay-chayss-*saa*-ryoa) *adj* necessary
necessità (nay-chayss-see-*tah*) *f* necessity; need
necroscopia (nay-kroa-skoa-*pee*-ah) *f* autopsy
negare (nay-*gaa*-ray) *v* deny
negativa (nay-gah-*tee*-vah) *f* negative
negativo (nay-gah-*tee*-voa) *adj* negative
negligente (nay-glee-*jehn*-tay) *adj* neglectful
negligenza (nay-glee-*jehn*-tsah) *f* neglect
negoziante (nay-goa-*tsyahn*-tay) *m* dealer; shopkeeper; ~ **di stoffe** draper
negoziare (nay-goa-*tsyaa*-ray) *v* negotiate
negozio (nay-*gaw*-tsyoa) *m* shop; ~ **di ferramenta** hardware store; ~ **di fiori** flower-shop; ~ **di giocattoli** toyshop
negro (*nāy*-groa) *m* Negro
nemico (nay-*mee*-koa) *m* enemy
nemmeno (naym-*māy*-noa) *adv* not even; *conj* nor
neon (*nai*-oan) *m* neon
neonato (nay-oa-*naa*-toa) *m* infant
neppure (nayp-*pōō*-ray) *adv* not even; *conj* nor
nero (*nāy*-roa) *adj* black
nervo (*nehr*-voa) *m* nerve
nervoso (nayr-*vōā*-soa) *adj* nervous
nessuno (nayss-*sōō*-noa) *adj* no; *pron* none, nobody, no one
nettare (nayt-*taa*-ray) *v* clean
netto (*nayt*-toa) *adj* net
neutrale (nay^oo^-*traa*-lay) *adj* neutral
neutro (*neh^oo^*-troa) *adj* neuter
neve (*nāy*-vay) *f* snow; ~ **fangosa** slush
nevicare (nay-vee-*kaa*-ray) *v* snow
nevoso (nay-*vōā*-soa) *adj* snowy
nevralgia (nay-vrahl-*jee*-ah) *f* neuralgia
nevrosi (nay-*vraw*-zee) *f* neurosis
nichelio (nee-*kai*-l^y^oa) *m* nickel
nicotina (nee-koa-*tee*-nah) *f* nicotine
nido (*nee*-doa) *m* nest; nursery
niente (*ñehn*-tay) *pron* nothing; nil
Nigeria (nee-*jai*-ryah) *f* Nigeria
nigeriano (nee-jay-*ryaa*-noa) *adj* Nigerian; *m* Nigerian
nipote (nee-*pōā*-tay) *m* grandson; nephew; *f* granddaughter; niece
nipotina (nee-poa-*tee*-nah) *f* granddaughter
nipotino (nee-poa-*tee*-noa) *m* grandson
no (no) no
nobile (*naw*-bee-lay) *adj* noble
nobiltà (noa-beel-*tah*) *f* nobility
nocca (*nok*-kah) *f* knuckle
nocciola (noat-*chaw*-lah) *f* hazelnut
nocciolo (*not*-choa-loa) *m* stone; essence, heart
noce (*nōā*-chay) *f* nut; walnut; ~ **di cocco** coconut; ~ **moscata** nutmeg
nocivo (noa-*chee*-voa) *adj* harmful, hurtful
nodo (*naw*-doa) *m* knot; lump; ~ **scorsoio** loop
noi (noi) *pron* we; ~ **stessi** ourselves
noia (*naw*-yah) *f* annoyance; bother
noioso (noa-*yōā*-soa) *adj* annoying, dull, boring
noleggiare (noa-layd-*jaa*-ray) *v* hire
a nolo (ah *naw*-loa) for hire
nome (*nōā*-may) *m* name; first name; denomination; noun; **a** ~ **di** in the name of, on behalf of; ~ **di battesimo** Christian name
nomignolo (noa-*mee*-ñoa-loa) *m* nickname
nomina (*naw*-mee-nah) *f* appointment, nomination
nominale (noa-mee-*naa*-lay) *adj* nom-

inal
nominare (noa-mee-*naa*-ray) *v* mention, name; appoint, nominate
non (noan) not; ~... **mai** never; ~... **più** no longer
nonché (noang-*kay*) *conj* as well as
noncurante (noang-koo-*rahn*-tay) *adj* careless
nonna (*non*-nah) *f* grandmother
nonno (*non*-noa) *m* grandfather, granddad; **nonni** grandparents *pl*
nono (*naw*-noa) *num* ninth
nonostante (noa-noa-*stahn*-tay) *prep* in spite of
nord (nord) *m* north; **polo Nord** North Pole
nord-est (nor-*dehst*) *m* north-east
nordico (*nor*-dee-koa) *adj* northern
nord-ovest (nor-*daw*-vayst) *m* north-west
norma (*nor*-mah) *f* standard; **di** ~ as a rule
normale (noar-*maa*-lay) *adj* normal; standard, regular
norvegese (noar-vay-*jāy*-say) *adj* Norwegian; *m* Norwegian
Norvegia (noar-*vāy*-jah) *f* Norway
nostalgia (noa-stahl-*jee*-ah) *f* homesickness
nostro (*no*-stroa) *adj* our
nota (*naw*-tah) *f* memo
notaio (noa-*taa*-yoa) *m* notary
notare (noa-*taa*-ray) *v* note; notice
notevole (noa-*tāy*-voa-lay) *adj* considerable, remarkable, noticeable, striking
notificare (noa-tee-fee-*kaa*-ray) *v* notify
notizia (noa-*tee*-tsyah) *f* notice; **notizie** tidings *pl*, news
notiziario (noa-tee-*tsyaa*-ryoa) *m* news
noto (*naw*-toa) *adj* well-known
notte (*not*-tay) *f* night; **di** ~ by night; overnight
notturno (noat-*toor*-noa) *adj* nightly; **locale** ~ nightclub
novanta (noa-*vahn*-tah) *num* ninety
nove (*naw*-vay) *num* nine
novembre (noa-*vehm*-bray) November
novità (noa-vee-*tah*) *f* news
nozione (noa-*tsyōa*-nay) *f* notion; idea
nubifragio (noo-bee-*fraa*-joa) *m* cloudburst
nuca (*nōo*-kah) *f* nape of the neck
nucleare (noo-klay-*aa*-ray) *adj* nuclear
nucleo (*nōo*-klay-oa) *m* core, nucleus
nudo (*nōo*-doa) *adj* nude, bare, naked; *m* nude
nulla (*nool*-lah) *m* nothing
nullo (*nool*-loa) *adj* invalid, void
numerale (noo-may-*raa*-lay) *m* numeral
numero (*nōo*-may-roa) *m* number; digit; quantity; act; ~ **di targa** registration number; licence number *Am*
numeroso (noo-may-*rōa*-soa) *adj* numerous
***nuocere** (*nwaw*-chay-ray) *v* harm
nuotare (nwoa-*taa*-ray) *v* *swim
nuotatore (nwoa-tah-*tōa*-ray) *m* swimmer
nuoto (*nwaw*-toa) *m* swimming; ~ **a farfalla** butterfly stroke; ~ **a rana** breaststroke
nuovamente (nwaw-vah-*mayn*-tay) *adv* again
Nuova Zelanda (*nwaw*-vah tsay-*lahn*-dah) New Zealand
nuovo (*nwaw*-voa) *adj* new; **di** ~ again; ~ **fiammante** brand-new
nutriente (noo-*tryehn*-tay) *adj* nutritious, nourishing
nutrire (noo-*tree*-ray) *v* *feed
nuvola (*nōo*-voa-lah) *f* cloud
nuvoloso (noo-voa-*lōa*-soa) *adj* cloudy

O

o (oa) *conj* or; ~... **o** either ... or
oasi (*aw*-ah-zee) *f* oasis
obbligare (oab-blee-*gaa*-ray) *v* oblige
obbligatorio (oab-blee-gah-*taw*-ryoa) *adj* compulsory, obligatory
obbligazione (oab-blee-gah-*tsyōā*-nay) *f* bond
obbligo (*ob*-blee-goa) *m* obligation
obeso (oa-*bai*-zoa) *adj* corpulent, stout
obiettare (oa-byayt-*taa*-ray) *v* object
obiettivo (oa-byayt-*tee*-voa) *m* objective, object
obiezione (oa-byay-*tsyōā*-nay) *f* objection; ***fare** ~ **a** mind
obliquo (oa-*blee*-kwoa) *adj* slanting
oblungo (oa-*bloong*-goa) *adj* oblong
oca (*aw*-kah) *f* goose
occasionalmente (oak-kah-zyoa-nahl-*mayn*-tay) *adv* occasionally
occasione (oak-kah-*zyōā*-nay) *f* chance, occasion, opportunity; **d'occasione** second-hand
occhiali (oak-*kyaa*-lee) *mpl* spectacles, glasses; ~ **da sole** sun-glasses *pl*; ~ **di protezione** goggles *pl*
occhiata (oak-*kyaa*-tah) *f* glimpse, glance, look; ***dare un'occhiata** glance
occhio (*ok*-kyoa) *m* eye; ~ **di pernice** corn; ***tenere d'occhio** watch
occidentale (oat-chee-dayn-*taa*-lay) *adj* western; westerly
occidente (oat-chee-*dehn*-tay) *m* west
***occorrere** (oak-*koar*-ray-ray) *v* need
occupante (oak-koo-*pahn*-tay) *m* occupant
occupare (oak-koo-*paa*-ray) *v* occupy, *take up; **occuparsi di** attend to, look after, see to, *take care of; **occupato** *adj* busy, engaged; occupied
occupazione (oak-koo-pah-*tsyōā*-nay) *f* occupation; employment
oceano (oa-*chai*-ah-noa) *m* ocean; **Oceano Pacifico** Pacific Ocean
oculista (oa-koo-*lee*-stah) *m* oculist
odiare (oa-*dyaa*-ray) *v* hate
odio (*aw*-dyoa) *m* hatred, hate
odorare (oa-doa-*raa*-ray) *v* *smell
odore (oa-*dōā*-ray) *m* odour, smell
***offendere** (oaf-*fehn*-day-ray) *v* injure, offend, wound, *hurt
offensiva (oaf-fayn-*see*-vah) *f* offensive
offensivo (oaf-fayn-*see*-voa) *adj* offensive
offerta (oaf-*fehr*-tah) *f* offer; supply
offesa (oaf-*fāȳ*-sah) *f* offence
officina (oaf-feet-*chee*-nah) *f* workshop; ~ **del gas** gasworks
***offrire** (oaf-*free*-ray) *v* offer
offuscato (oaf-foo-*skaa*-toa) *adj* dim
oggettivo (oad-jayt-*tee*-voa) *adj* objective
oggetto (oad-*jeht*-toa) *m* object; **oggetti smarriti** lost and found
oggi (*od*-jee) *adv* today
oggigiorno (oad-jee-*joar*-noa) *adv* nowadays
ogni (*ōā*-ñee) *adj* every, each
ogniqualvolta (oa-ñee-kwahl-*vol*-tah) *conj* whenever
ognuno (oa-*ñōō*-noa) *pron* everyone, everybody
Olanda (oa-*lahn*-dah) *f* Holland
olandese (oa-lahn-*dāȳ*-say) *adj* Dutch; *m* Dutchman
oleoso (oa-lay-*ōā*-soa) *adj* oily
olio (*aw*-lʸoa) *m* oil; ~ **abbronzante** suntan oil; ~ **da tavola** salad-oil; ~ **d'oliva** olive oil; ~ **per capelli** hair-oil
oliva (oa-*lee*-vah) *f* olive
olmo (*oal*-moa) *m* elm

oltraggio (oal-*trahd*-joa) *m* outrage
oltre (*oal*-tray) *prep* beyond; over; ~ **a** besides
oltremarino (oal-tray-mah-*ree*-noa) *adj* overseas
oltrepassare (oal-tray-pahss-*saa*-ray) *v* *overtake; pass *vAm*
omaggio (oa-*mahd*-joa) *m* tribute, homage
ombelico (oam-bay-*lee*-koa) *m* navel
ombra (*oam*-brah) *f* shadow, shade
ombreggiato (oam-brayd-*jaa*-toa) *adj* shady
ombrellino (oam-brayl-*lee*-noa) *m* sunshade
ombrello (oam-*brehl*-loa) *m* umbrella
ombretto (oam-*brayt*-toa) *m* eye-shadow
***omettere** (oa-*mayt*-tay-ray) *v* omit, *leave out; skip
omosessuale (oa-moa-sayss-*swaa*-lay) *adj* homosexual
onda (*oan*-dah) *f* wave
ondulare (oan-doo-*laa*-ray) *v* curl
ondulato (oan-doo-*laa*-toa) *adj* wavy, undulating
onestà (oa-nay-*stah*) *f* honesty
onesto (oa-*neh*-stoa) *adj* honest; fair, straight; honourable
onice (*aw*-nee-chay) *f* onyx
onnipotente (oan-nee-poa-*tehn*-tay) *adj* omnipotent
onorare (oa-noa-*raa*-ray) *v* honour
onorario (oa-noa-*raa*-ryoa) *m* fee
onore (oa-*nōā*-ray) *m* glory, honour
onorevole (oa-noa-*rāȳ*-voa-lay) *adj* honourable
opaco (oa-*paa*-koa) *adj* dim, mat
opale (oa-*paa*-lay) *m* opal
opera (*aw*-pay-rah) *f* opera
operaio (oa-pay-*raa*-yoa) *m* labourer, workman
operare (oa-pay-*rah*-ray) *v* operate
operazione (oa-pay-rah-*tsyōā*-nay) *f* surgery, operation
operetta (oa-pay-*rayt*-tah) *f* operetta
opinione (oa-pee-*ñōā*-nay) *f* view, opinion
***opporsi** (oap-*poar*-see) *v* oppose; ~ **a** object to
opportunità (oap-poar-too-nee-*tah*) *f* chance, opportunity
opportuno (oap-poar-*tōō*-noa) *adj* opportune
opposizione (oap-poa-zee-*tsyōā*-nay) *f* opposition
opposto (oap-*poa*-stoa) *adj* opposite
***opprimere** (oap-*pree*-may-ray) *v* oppress
oppure (oap-*pōō*-ray) *conj* or
opuscolo (oa-*poo*-skoa-loa) *m* brochure
ora (*ōā*-rah) *f* hour; *adv* now; **d'ora innanzi** henceforth; ~ **di arrivo** time of arrival; ~ **di partenza** time of departure; ~ **di punta** rush-hour, peak hour; **ore di visita** visiting hours; **ore d'ufficio** office hours, business hours; **quarto d'ora** quarter of an hour
orale (oa-*raa*-lay) *adj* oral
oramai (oa-rah-*mahæë*) *adv* by now; by then
orario (oa-*raa*-ryoa) *m* timetable, schedule; ~ **di apertura** business hours; ~ **di ricevimento** consultation hours; ~ **estivo** summer time
orchestra (oar-*keh*-strah) *f* orchestra
ordinare (oar-dee-*naa*-ray) *v* arrange; order
ordinario (oar-dee-*naa*-ryoa) *adj* ordinary; plain, common, simple
ordinato (oar-dee-*naa*-toa) *adj* tidy
ordinazione (oar-dee-nah-*tsyōā*-nay) *f* order; **modulo di** ~ order-form
ordine (*oar*-dee-nay) *m* order; method; command; **in** ~ in order; ***mettere in** ~ arrange

orecchino (oa-rayk-*kee*-noa) *m* earring
orecchio (oa-*rayk*-kyoa) *f* ear
orecchioni (oa-rayk-*kyōā*-nee) *mpl* mumps
orefice (oa-*rāȳ*-fee-chay) *m* goldsmith
orfano (*or*-fah-noa) *m* orphan
organico (oar-*gaa*-nee-koa) *adj* organic
organismo (oar-gah-*nee*-zmoa) *m* organism
organizzare (oar-gah-need-*dzaa*-ray) *v* organize; arrange
organizzazione (oar-gah-need-dzah-*tsyōā*-nay) *f* organization
organo (*or*-gah-noa) *m* organ; **organetto di Barberia** street-organ
orgoglio (oar-*gaw*-lʸoa) *m* pride
orgoglioso (oar-goa-*lʸōā*-soa) *adj* proud
orientale (oa-ryayn-*taa*-lay) *adj* eastern; easterly; oriental
orientarsi (oa-ryayn-*tahr*-see) *v* orientate
oriente (oa-*ryehn*-tay) *m* east; Orient
originale (oa-ree-jee-*naa*-lay) *adj* original
originariamente (oa-ree-jee-nah-ryah-*mayn*-tay) *adv* originally
origine (oa-*ree*-jee-nay) *f* origin
origliare (oa-ree-*lʸaa*-ray) *v* eavesdrop
orizzontale (oa-reed-dzoan-*taa*-lay) *adj* horizontal
orizzonte (oa-reed-*dzoan*-tay) *m* horizon
orlo (*oar*-loa) *m* rim, brim; hem; ~ **del marciapiede** curb
orlon (*or*-loan) *m* orlon
ornamentale (oar-nah-mayn-*taa*-lay) *adj* ornamental
ornamento (oar-nah-*mayn*-toa) *m* decoration, ornament
oro (*aw*-roa) *m* gold; ~ **laminato** gold leaf
orologiaio (oa-roa-loa-*jaa*-yoa) *m* watch-maker
orologio (oa-roa-*law*-joa) *m* watch; clock; **cinturino da** ~ watch-strap; ~ **da polso** wrist-watch; ~ **da tasca** pocket-watch
orrendo (oar-*rehn*-doa) *adj* hideous
orribile (oar-*ree*-bee-lay) *adj* horrible
orrore (oar-*rōā*-ray) *m* horror
orso (*oar*-soa) *m* bear
orticoltura (oar-tee-koal-*tōō*-rah) *f* horticulture
orto (*or*-toa) *m* kitchen garden
ortodosso (oar-toa-*doss*-soa) *adj* orthodox
ortografia (oar-toa-grah-*fee*-ah) *f* spelling
orzo (*or*-dzoa) *m* barley
osare (oa-*zaa*-ray) *v* dare
osceno (oash-*shai*-noa) *adj* obscene
oscurità (oa-skoo-ree-*tah*) *f* gloom, dark
oscuro (oa-*skōō*-roa) *adj* dim, dark; obscure
ospedale (oa-spay-*daa*-lay) *m* hospital
ospitale (oa-spee-*taa*-lay) *adj* hospitable
ospitalità (oa-spee-tah-lee-*tah*) *f* hospitality
ospitare (oa-spee-*taa*-ray) *v* entertain
ospite (*o*-spee-tay) *f* hostess, host; *m* guest; **camera degli ospiti** spare room
ospizio (oa-*spee*-tsyoa) *m* asylum, home
osservare (oass-sayr-*vaa*-ray) *v* observe; watch, regard; remark, note
osservatorio (oass-sayr-vah-*tōā*-ryoa) *m* observatory
osservazione (oass-sayr-vah-*tsyōā*-nay) *f* observation; remark
ossessione (oass-sayss-*syōā*-nay) *f* obsession
ossia (oass-*see*-ah) *conj* that is; or rather
ossigeno (oass-*see*-jay-noa) *m* oxygen

osso (*oss*-soa) *m* (pl le ossa) bone
ostacolare (oa-stah-koa-*laa*-ray) *v* hinder, embarrass
ostacolo (oa-*staa*-koa-loa) *m* obstacle
ostaggio (oa-*stahd*-joa) *m* hostage
ostello (oa-*stehl*-loa) *m* hostel; ~ **della gioventù** youth hostel
ostia (*o*-styah) *f* wafer
ostile (oa-*stee*-lay) *adj* hostile
ostinato (oa-stee-*naa*-toa) *adj* obstinate, dogged
ostrica (*o*-stree-kah) *f* oyster
ostruire (oa-*strwee*-ray) *v* block
ottanta (oat-*tahn*-tah) *num* eighty
ottavo (oat-*taa*-voa) *num* eighth
***ottenere** (oat-tay-*nāy*-ray) *v* *get, obtain; acquire
ottenibile (oat-tay-*nee*-bee-lay) *adj* available, obtainable
ottico (*ot*-tee-koa) *m* optician
ottimismo (oat-tee-*mee*-zmoa) *m* optimism
ottimista (oat-tee-*mee*-stah) *m* optimist
ottimistico (oat-tee-*mee*-stee-koa) *adj* optimistic
ottimo (*ot*-tee-moa) *adj* excellent, first-rate, fine; best
otto (*ot*-toa) *num* eight
ottobre (oat-*tōā*-bray) October
ottoname (oat-toa-*naa*-may) *m* brassware
ottone (oat-*tōā*-nay) *m* brass
otturazione (oat-too-rah-*tsyōā*-nay) *f* filling
ottuso (oat-*tōō*-zoa) *adj* blunt; slow, dumb
ovale (oa-*vaa*-lay) *adj* oval
ovatta (oa-*vaht*-tah) *f* cotton-wool
ovest (*aw*-vayst) *m* west
ovunque (oa-*voong*-kway) *adv* anywhere, everywhere
ovvio (*ov*-vyoa) *adj* obvious, apparent
ozioso (oa-*tsyōā*-soa) *adj* idle

P

pacchetto (pahk-*kayt*-toa) *m* parcel, packet
pacco (*pahk*-koa) *m* parcel, package
pace (*paa*-chay) *f* peace
pachistano (pah-kee-*staa*-noa) *adj* Pakistani; *m* Pakistani
pacifico (pah-*chee*-fee-koa) *adj* peaceful
pacifismo (pah-chee-*fee*-zmoa) *m* pacifism
pacifista (pah-chee-*fee*-stah) *m* pacifist; *adj* pacifist
padella (pah-*dehl*-lah) *f* frying-pan
padiglione (pah-dee-*lʸōā*-nay) *m* pavilion
padre (*paa*-dray) *m* father; dad
padrino (pah-*dree*-noa) *m* godfather
padrona (pah-*drōā*-nah) *f* mistress
padrone (pah-*drōā*nay) *m* master, boss; ~ **di casa** landlord
paesaggio (pah^ay^-*zahd*-joa) *m* landscape, scenery
paese (pah-*āy*-zay) *m* country, land; ~ **natio** native country
Paesi Bassi (pah-*āy*-zee *bahss*-see) the Netherlands
paga (*paa*-gah) *f* pay
pagamento (pah-gah-*mayn*-toa) *m* payment
pagano (pah-*gaa*-noa) *adj* pagan, heathen; *m* pagan, heathen
pagare (pah-*gaa*-ray) *v* *pay; ***far** ~ charge; ~ **a rate** *pay on account; **pagato in anticipo** prepaid
paggio (*pahd*-joa) *m* page-boy
pagina (*paa*-jee-nah) *f* page
paglia (*paa*-lʸah) *f* straw
pagliaccio (pah-*lʸaht*-choa) *m* clown
pagnotta (pah-*ñot*-tah) *f* loaf

paio (*paa*-yoa) *m* (pl le paia) pair
Pakistan (pah-kee-*stahn*) *m* Pakistan
pala (*paa*-lah) *f* shovel
palazzo (pah-*laht*-tsoa) *m* palace; mansion
palco (*pahl*-koa) *m* antlers *pl*
palestra (pah-*leh*-strah) *f* gymnasium
palla (*pahl*-lah) *f* ball
pallido (*pahl*-lee-doa) *adj* pale; dim, mat, dull
pallina (pahl-*lee*-nah) *f* marble
pallino (pahl-*lee*-noa) *m* hobby-horse
palloncino (pahl-loan-*chee*-noa) *m* balloon
pallone (pahl-*lōā*-nay) *m* football
pallottola (pahl-*lot*-toa-lah) *f* bullet
palma (*pahl*-mah) *f* palm
palo (*paa*-loa) *m* pole, post
palpabile (pahl-*paa*-bee-lay) *adj* palpable
palpare (pahl-*paa*-ray) *v* *feel
palpebra (*pahl*-pay-brah) *f* eyelid
palpitazione (pahl-pee-tah-*tsyōā*-nay) *f* palpitation
palude (pah-*lōō*-day) *f* marsh, swamp, bog
paludoso (pah-loo-*dōā*-soa) *adj* marshy
pancia (*pahn*-chah) *f* belly
panciotto (pahn-*chot*-toa) *m* waistcoat; vest *nAm*
pane (*paa*-nay) *m* bread; ~ **integrale** wholemeal bread
panetteria (pah-nayt-tay-*ree*-ah) *f* bakery
panettiere (pah-nayt-*tyai*-ray) *m* baker
panfilo (*pahn*-fee-loa) *m* yacht
panico (*paa*-nee-koa) *m* panic
paniere (pah-*ñai*-ray) *m* hamper, basket
panino (pah-*nee*-noa) *m* roll, bun
panna (*pahn*-nah) *f* cream
pannello (pahn-*nehl*-loa) *m* panel; **rivestimento a pannelli** panelling
panno (*pahn*-noa) *m* cloth
pannolino (pahn-noa-*lee*-noa) *m* nappy; diaper *nAm*; ~ **igienico** sanitary towel
pantaloni (pahn-tah-*lōā*-nee) *mpl* trousers *pl*
pantofola (pahn-*taw*-foa-lah) *f* slipper
Papa (*paa*-pah) *m* pope
papà (pah-*pah*) *m* daddy
papavero (pah-*paa*-vay-roa) *m* poppy
pappagallo (pahp-pah-*gahl*-loa) *m* parrot
parabrezza (pah-rah-*brayd*-dzah) *m* windscreen; windshield *nAm*
parafango (pah-rah-*fahng*-goa) *m* mud-guard
paragonare (pah-rah-goa-*naa*-ray) *v* compare
paragone (pah-rah-*gōā*-nay) *m* comparison
paragrafo (pah-*raa*-grah-foa) *m* paragraph
paralitico (pah-rah-*lee*-tee-koa) *adj* lame
paralizzare (pah-rah-leed-*dzaa*-ray) *v* paralise
parallela (pah-rahl-*lai*-lah) *f* parallel
parallelo (pah-rahl-*lai*-loa) *adj* parallel
paralume (pah-rah-*lōō*-may) *m* lampshade
parata (pah-*raa*-tah) *f* parade
paraurti (pah-rah-*oor*-tee) *m* fender, bumper
parcheggio (pahr-*kehd*-joa) *m* parking; car park; parking lot *Am*
parchimetro (pahr-*kee*-may-troa) *m* parking meter
parco (*pahr*-koa) *m* park; ~ **nazionale** national park
parecchi (pah-*rayk*-kee) *adj* several, various
pareggiare (pah-rayd-*jaa*-ray) *v* level; equalize
parente (pah-*rehn*-tay) *m* relative,

relation
parere (pah-*rāy*-ray) *m* view, opinion
***parere** (pah-*rāy*-ray) *v* seem
parete (pah-*rāy*-tay) *f* wall
pari (*paa*-ree) *adj* even
parlamentare (pahr-lah-mayn-*taa*-ray) *adj* parliamentary
parlamento (pahr-lah-*mayn*-toa) *m* parliament
parlare (pahr-*laa*-ray) *v* *speak, talk
parola (pah-*raw*-lah) *f* word; speech; ~ **d'ordine** password
parrocchetto (pahr-roak-*kayt*-toa) *m* parakeet
parrocchia (pahr-*rok*-kyah) *f* parish
parrucca (pahr-*rook*-kah) *f* wig
parrucchiere (pahr-rook-*kyai*-ray) *m* hairdresser
parsimonioso (pahr-see-moa-*nyōa*-soa) *adj* thrifty, economical
parte (*pahr*-tay) *f* part; share; side; **a** ~ apart, separately; **dall'altra** ~ across; **dall'altra** ~ **di** across; **da** ~ aside; **in** ~ partly; **una** ~ some
partecipante (pahr-tay-chee-*pahn*-tay) *m* participant
partecipare (pahr-tay-chee-*paa*-ray) *v* participate
partenza (pahr-*tehn*-tsah) *f* departure
particolare (pahr-tee-koa-*laa*-ray) *adj* particular, special, peculiar; *m* detail; **in** ~ in particular
particolareggiato (pahr-tee-koa-lah-rayd-*jaa*-toa) *adj* detailed
particolarmente (pahr-tee-koa-lahr-*mayn*-tay) *adv* specially
partire (pahr-*tee*-ray) *v* depart, *leave; *set out; pull out; **a** ~ **da** as from
partita (pahr-*tee*-tah) *f* batch; match; ~ **di calcio** football match; ~ **di pugilato** boxing match
partito (pahr-*tee*-toa) *m* party
parto (*pahr*-toa) *m* delivery, childbirth
parziale (pahr-*tsyaa*-lay) *adj* partial
pascolare (pah-skoa-*laa*-ray) *v* graze
pascolo (*pah*-skoa-loa) *m* pasture
Pasqua (*pah*-skwah) Easter
passaggio (pahss-*sahd*-joa) *m* passage; aisle; ~ **a livello** level crossing; ~ **pedonale** crossing, pedestrian crossing; crosswalk *nAm*
passante (pahss-*sahn*-tay) *m* passer-by
passaporto (pahss-sah-*por*-toa) *m* passport
passare (pahss-*saa*-ray) *v* pass; ~ **accanto** pass by
passarella (pahss-sah-*rehl*-lah) *f* gangway
passatempo (pahss-sah-*tehm*-poa) *m* entertainment, amusement; hobby
passato (pahss-*saa*-toa) *adj* past; *m* past
passeggero (pahss-sayd-*jāy*-roa) *m* passenger
passeggiare (pahss-sayd-*jaa*-ray) *v* walk, stroll
passeggiata (pahss-sayd-*jaa*-tah) *f* walk, stroll
passera di mare (*pahss*-say-rah dee *maa*-ray) plaice
passero (*pahss*-say-roa) *m* sparrow
passione (pahss-*syōa*-nay) *f* passion
passivo (pahss-*see*-voa) *adj* passive
passo (*pahss*-soa) *m* pace, step; gait; mountain pass; extract; ***stare al** ~ **con** *keep up with
pasta (*pah*-stah) *f* dough; paste
pasticca (pah-*steek*-kah) *f* tablet
pasticceria (pah-steet-chay-*ree*-ah) *f* pastry, cake; pastry shop, sweetshop; candy store *Am*
pasticciare (pah-steet-*chaa*-ray) *v* mess up
pasticciere (pah-steet-*chai*-ray) *m* confectioner
pasticcio (pah-*steet*-choa) *m* muddle
pasto (*pah*-stoa) *m* meal
pastore (pah-*stōa*-ray) *m* shepherd;

clergyman, parson, minister, rector
patata (pah-*taa*-tah) *f* potato; **patatine fritte** chips
patria (*paa*-tryah) *f* fatherland, native country
patrigno (pah-*tree*-ñoa) *m* stepfather
patriota (pah-*tryaw*-tah) *m* patriot
patrocinatore (pah-troa-chee-nah-*tōā*-ray) *m* advocate
pattinaggio (paht-tee-*nahd*-joa) *m* skating; ~ **a rotelle** roller-skating
pattinare (paht-tee-*naa*-ray) *v* skate
pattino (*paht*-tee-noa) *m* skate
patto (*paht*-toa) *m* agreement; term
pattuglia (paht-*tōō*-lʸah) *f* patrol
pattugliare (paht-too-*lʸaa*-ray) *v* patrol
pattumiera (paht-too-*myai*-rah) *f* rubbish-bin, dustbin; trash can *Am*
paura (pah-*ōō*-rah) *f* fear, fright; ***aver** ~ *be afraid
pausa (*pou*-zah) *f* pause
pavimentare (pah-vee-mayn-*taa*-ray) *v* pave
pavimento (pah-vee-*mayn*-toa) *m* floor; pavement
pavoncella (pah-voan-*chehl*-lah) *f* pewit
pavone (pah-*vōā*-nay) *m* peacock
paziente (pah-*tsyehn*-tay) *adj* patient; *m* patient
pazienza (pah-*tsyehn*-tsah) *f* patience
pazzia (paht-*tsee*-ah) *f* madness, lunacy
pazzo (*paht*-tsoa) *adj* crazy, mad, lunatic; *m* lunatic
peccato (payk-*kaa*-toa) *m* sin; **peccato**! what a pity!
pecora (*pai*-koa-rah) *f* sheep
pedaggio (pay-*dahd*-joa) *m* toll
pedale (pay-*daa*-lay) *m* pedal
pedata (pay-*daa*-tah) *f* kick
pedicure (pay-dee-*kōō*-ray) *m* pedicure
pedina (pay-*dee*-nah) *f* pawn
pedone (pay-*dōā*-nay) *m* pedestrian
peggio (*pehd*-joa) *adv* worse; worst
peggiore (payd-*jōā*-ray) *adj* worse
pelle (*pehl*-lay) *f* skin; hide; leather; **di** ~ leather; ~ **di cinghiale** pigskin; ~ **di vacca** cow-hide; ~ **di vitello** calf skin; ~ **d'oca** goose-flesh; ~ **scamosciata** suede
pellegrinaggio (payl-lay-gree-*nahd*-joa) *m* pilgrimage
pellegrino (payl-lay-*gree*-noa) *m* pilgrim
pellicano (payl-lee-*kaa*-noa) *m* pelican
pelliccia (payl-*leet*-chah) *f* fur
pellicciaio (payl-lee-*chaa*-yoa) *m* furrier
pellicola (payl-*lee*-koa-lah) *f* film; ~ **a colori** colour film
peloso (pay-*lōā*-soa) *adj* hairy
peltro (*payl*-troa) *m* pewter
pena (*pāȳ*-nah) *f* trouble, pains, difficulty; penalty; ~ **di morte** death penalty; ***valer la** ~ *be worthwhile
penalità (pay-nah-lee-*tah*) *f* penalty
pendente (payn-*dehn*-tay) *adj* slanting; *m* pendant
pendere (*pehn*-day-ray) *v* *hang; slope
pendio (payn-*dee*-oa) *m* incline, hillside, slope
pendolare (payn-doa-*laa*-ray) *m* commuter
penetrare (pay-nay-*traa*-ray) *v* penetrate
penetrazione (pay-nay-trah-*tsyōā*-nay) *f* insight
penicillina (pay-nee-cheel-*lee*-nah) *f* penicillin
penisola (pay-*nee*-zoa-lah) *f* peninsula
penna (*payn*-nah) *f* feather; pen; ~ **a sfera** Biro, ballpoint-pen; ~ **stilografica** fountain-pen
pennello (payn-*nehl*-loa) *m* brush; paint-brush; ~ **da barba** shaving-

brush
penoso (pay-*nōā*-soa) *adj* painful
pensare (payn-*saa*-ray) *v* *think; ~ **a** *think of
pensatore (payn-sah-*tōā*-ray) *m* thinker
pensiero (payn-*syai*-roa) *m* thought, idea
pensieroso (payn-syay-*rōā*-soa) *adj* thoughtful
pensionante (payn-syoa-*nahn*-tay) *m* boarder
pensionato (payn-syoa-*naa*-toa) *adj* retired
pensione (payn-*syōā*-nay) *f* board; guest-house, pension, boarding-house; ~ **completa** bed and board, full board, board and lodging
Pentecoste (payn-tay-*ko*-stay) *f* Whitsun
pentimento (payn-tee-*mayn*-toa) *m* repentance
pentola (*pehn*-toa-lah) *f* pot; ~ **a pressione** pressure-cooker
penuria (pay-*nōō*-ryah) *f* scarcity
pepe (*pāȳ*-pay) *m* pepper
per (payr) *prep* for; to; with; times
pera (*pāȳ*-rah) *f* pear
percento (payr-*chehn*-toa) *m* percent
percentuale (payr-chayn-*twaa*-lay) *f* percentage
percepire (payr-chay-*pee*-ray) *v* perceive, sense
percettibile (payr-chayt-*tee*-bee-lay) *adj* perceptible, noticeable
percezione (payr-chay-*tsyōā*-nay) *f* perception
perché (payr-*kay*) *adv* what for, why; *conj* because
perciò (payr-*cho*) *conj* therefore
***percorrere** (payr-*koar*-ray-ray) *v* cover; *go through
***percuotere** (payr-*kwaw*-tay-ray) *v* thump
perdente (payr-*dehn*-tay) *adj* leaky
***perdere** (*pehr*-day-ray) *v* *lose
perdita (*pehr*-dee-tah) *f* loss
perdonare (payr-doa-*naa*-ray) *v* *forgive
perdono (payr-*dōā*-noa) *m* pardon; grace
perfetto (payr-*feht*-toa) *adj* perfect; faultless
perfezione (payr-fay-*tsyōā*-nay) *f* perfection
perfido (*pehr*-fee-doa) *adj* foul
perforare (payr-foa-*raa*-ray) *v* pierce
pericolo (pay-*ree*-koa-loa) *m* danger; risk, peril; distress
pericoloso (pay-ree-koa-*lōā*-soa) *adj* perilous, dangerous
periodico (pay-*ryaw*-dee-koa) *adj* periodical; *m* periodical
periodo (pay-*ree*-oa-doa) *m* period, term
perire (pay-*ree*-ray) *v* perish
perito (pay-*ree*-toa) *m* expert
perla (*pehr*-lah) *f* pearl
perlina (payr-*lee*-nah) *f* bead
perlustrare (payr-loo-*straa*-ray) *v* search
permanente (payr-mah-*nehn*-tay) *adj* permanent; *f* permanent wave
permesso (payr-*mayss*-soa) *m* authorization, permission; permit; ***avere il** ~ **di** *be allowed to; ~ **di lavoro** work permit; labor permit *Am*; ~ **di pesca** fishing licence; ~ **di soggiorno** residence permit
***permettere** (payr-*mayt*-tay-ray) *v* allow, permit; ***permettersi** afford
pernice (payr-*nee*-chay) *f* partridge
però (pay-*roa*) *conj* but; only, yet
perorare (pay-roa-*raa*-ray) *v* plead
perpendicolare (payr-payn-dee-koa-*laa*-ray) *adj* perpendicular
perquisire (payr-kwee-*zee*-ray) *v* search
perseguire (payr-say-*gwee*-ray) *v* pur-

sue
perseverare (payr-say-vay-*raa*-ray) *v* *keep up
Persia (*pehr*-syah) *f* Persia
persiana (payr-*syaa*-nah) *f* shutter, blind
persiano (payr-*syaa*-noa) *adj* Persian; *m* Persian
persistere (payr-*see*-stay-ray) *v* insist
persona (payr-*sōā*-nah) *f* person; **per ~** per person
personaggio (payr-soa-*nahd*-joa) *m* personality; character
personale (payr-soa-*naa*-lay) *adj* personal, private; *m* staff, personnel
personalità (payr-soa-nah-lee-*tah*) *f* personality
perspicace (payr-spee-*kaa*-chay) *adj* clever
***persuadere** (payr-swah-*dāy*-ray) *v* persuade
pesante (pay-*sahn*-tay) *adj* heavy
pesare (pay-*saa*-ray) *v* weigh
pesca[1] (*peh*-skah) *f* peach
pesca[2] (*pay*-skah) *f* fishing industry
pescare (pay-*skaa*-ray) *v* fish; **~ con l'amo** angle
pescatore (pay-skah-*tōā*-ray) *m* fisherman
pesce (*paysh*-shay) *m* fish; **~ persico** perch
pescecane (paysh-shay-*kaa*-nay) *m* shark
pescheria (pay-skay-*ree*-ah) *f* fish shop
pesciolino (paysh-shoa-*lee*-noa) *m* whitebait
peso (*pāy*-soa) *m* weight; load, burden
pessimismo (payss-see-*mee*-zmoa) *m* pessimism
pessimista (payss-see-*mee*-stah) *m* pessimist
pessimistico (payss-see-*mee*-stee-koa) *adj* pessimistic
pessimo (*pehss*-see-moa) *adj* worst
pestare (pay-*staa*-ray) *v* stamp
petalo (*pai*-tah-loa) *m* petal
petizione (pay-tee-*tsyōā*-nay) *f* petition
petroliera (pay-troa-*lʸai*-rah) *f* tanker
petrolio (pay-*traw*-lʸoa) *m* petroleum; oil; paraffin, kerosene
pettegolare (payt-tay-goa-*laa*-ray) *v* gossip
pettegolezzo (payt-tay-goa-*layt*-tsoa) *m* gossip
pettinare (payt-tee-*naa*-ray) *v* comb
pettine (*peht*-tee-nay) *m* comb; **~ tascabile** pocket-comb
pettirosso (payt-tee-*roass*-soa) *m* robin
petto (*peht*-toa) *m* chest, bosom
pezzetto (payt-*tsayt*-toa) *m* bit; morsel, scrap
pezzo (*peht*-tsoa) *m* piece; part, lump; fragment; **in due pezzi** two-piece; **~ di ricambio** spare part
piacere (pyah-*chāy*-ray) *m* pleasure; **con ~** gladly
***piacere** (pyah-*chāy*-ray) *v* please
piacevole (pyah-*chāy*-voa-lay) *adj* pleasant, enjoyable, nice
piacevolissimo (pyah-chay-voa-*leess*-see-moa) *adj* delightful
piaga (*pyaa*-gah) *f* sore
pianeta (pyah-*nāy*-tah) *m* planet
***piangere** (*pyahn*-jay-ray) *v* *weep, cry
pianista (pyah-*nee*-stah) *m* pianist
piano (*pyaa*-noa) *adj* plane, smooth, even, flat, level; *m* floor, storey; project; **primo ~** foreground
pianoforte (pyah-noa-*for*-tay) *m* piano; **~ a coda** grand piano
pianta (*pyahn*-tah) *f* plant; map, plan
piantagione (pyahn-tah-*jōā*-nay) *f* plantation
piantare (pyahn-*taa*-ray) *v* plant
pianterreno (pyahn-tayr-*rāy*-noa) *m* ground floor

pianura (pyah-*nōō*-rah) *f* plain
piattino (pyaht-*tee*-noa) *m* saucer
piatto (*pyaht*-toa) *adj* even, flat, level; *m* plate, dish
piazza (*pyaht*-tsah) *f* square; ~ **del mercato** market-place
piccante (peek-*kahn*-tay) *adj* savoury; spicy
picchiare (peek-*kyaa*-ray) *v* *strike, *beat; smack
piccino (peet-*chee*-noa) *m* baby
piccione (peet-*chōā*-nay) *m* pigeon
piccolo (*peek*-koa-loa) *adj* small, little; minor, petty
piccone (peek-*kōā*-nay) *m* pick-axe
***fare un picnic** picnic
pidocchio (pee-*dok*-kyoa) *m* louse
piede (*pyai*-day) *m* foot; leg; **a piedi** walking, on foot; **in piedi** upright; ~ **di porco** crowbar
piega (*pyai*-gah) *f* fold; crease
piegare (pyay-*gaa*-ray) *v* fold
pieghevole (pyay-*gāȳ*-voa-lay) *adj* flexible, supple
pieno (*pyai*-noa) *adj* full; ***fare il** ~ fill up; ~ **zeppo** chock-full
pietà (pyay-*tah*) *f* pity
pietanza (pyay-*tahn*-tsah) *f* dish
pietra (*pyai*-trah) *f* stone; **di** ~ stone; ~ **miliare** milestone; landmark; ~ **pomice** pumice stone; ~ **preziosa** stone; ~ **sepolcrale** tombstone
pietrina (pyay-*tree*-nah) *f* flint
pigiama (pee-*jaa*-mah) *m* pyjamas *pl*
pigliare (pee-*lʸaa*-ray) *v* *take
pigro (*pee*-groa) *adj* lazy; idle
pila (*pee*-lah) *f* stack
pilastro (pee-*lah*-stroa) *m* column, pillar
pillola (*peel*-loa-lah) *f* pill
pilota (pee-*law*-tah) *m* pilot
pinguedine (peeng-*gwai*-dee-nay) *f* fatness
pinguino (peeng-*gwee*-noa) *m* penguin
pinze (*peen*-tsay) *fpl* pliers *pl*, tongs *pl*
pinzette (peen-*tsayt*-tay) *fpl* tweezers *pl*
pio (*pee*-oa) *adj* pious
pioggerella (pyoad-jay-*rehl*-lah) *f* drizzle
pioggia (*pyod*-jah) *f* rain
piombo (*pyoam*-boa) *m* lead
pioniere (pyoa-*ñai*-ray) *m* pioneer
***piovere** (*pyaw*-vay-ray) *v* rain
piovoso (pyoa-*vōā*-soa) *adj* rainy
pipa (*pee*-pah) *f* pipe
pirata (pee-*raa*-tah) *m* pirate
piroscafo (pee-*raw*-skah-foa) *m* steamer
piscina (peesh-*shee*-nah) *f* swimming pool
pisello (pee-*sehl*-loa) *m* pea
pisolino (pee-zoa-*lee*-noa) *m* nap
pista (*pee*-stah) *f* track; ring; ~ **da corsa** race-course, race-track; ~ **di bocce** bowling alley; ~ **di decollo** runway; ~ **di pattinaggio** skating-rink
pistola (pee-*staw*-lah) *f* pistol
pittore (peet-*tōā*-ray) *m* painter
pittoresco (peet-toa-*ray*-skoa) *adj* picturesque, scenic
pittura (peet-*tōō*-rah) *f* painting, picture; ~ **ad olio** oil-painting
pitturare (peet-too-*raa*-ray) *v* paint
più (pyoo) *adv* more; *prep* plus; **il** ~ most; **per lo** ~ mostly; ~ **... più** the ... the; ~ **in là di** beyond; ~ **lontano** further; **sempre** ~ more and more; **tutt'al** ~ at most
piuttosto (pee^{oo}t-*to*-stoa) *adv* sooner, rather; fairly, pretty, quite
pizzicare (peet-tsee-*kaa*-ray) *v* pinch
planetario (plah-nay-*taa*-ryoa) *m* planetarium
plasmare (plah-*zmaa*-ray) *v* model
plastica (*plah*-stee-kah) *f* plastic

plastico (*plah*-stee-koa) *adj* plastic
platino (*plaa*-tee-noa) *m* platinum
plurale (ploo-*raa*-lay) *m* plural
pneumatico (pnay°°-*maa*-tee-koa) *adj* pneumatic; *m* tire; ~ **di ricambio** spare tyre
poco (*paw*-koa) *adj* little; *m* bit; **pochi** *adj* few; **press'a** ~ about; **tra** ~ soon
poderoso (poa-day-*rōā*-soa) *adj* mighty, powerful
poema (poa-*ai*-mah) *m* poem; ~ **epico** epic
poesia (poa-ay-*zee*-ah) *f* poetry
poeta (poa-*ai*-tah) *m* poet
poi (poi) *adv* then; afterwards
poiché (poay-*kay*) *conj* as, since, because; for
polacco (poa-*lahk*-koa) *adj* Polish; *m* Pole
polio (*paw*-lʸoa) *f* polio
polipo (*paw*-lee-poa) *m* octopus
politica (poa-*lee*-tee-kah) *f* politics; policy
politico (poa-*lee*-tee-koa) *adj* political
polizia (poa-lee-*tsee*-ah) *f* police *pl*
poliziotto (poa-lee-*tsyot*-toa) *m* policeman
polizza (poa-*leet*-tsah) *f* policy; ~ **di assicurazione** insurance policy
pollame (poal-*laa*-may) *m* fowl; poultry
pollice (*pol*-lee-chay) *m* thumb
pollivendolo (poal-lee-*vayn*-doa-loa) *m* poulterer
pollo (*poal*-loa) *m* chicken
polmone (poal-*mōā*-nay) *m* lung
polmonite (poal-moa-*nee*-tay) *f* pneumonia
Polonia (poa-*law*-ñah) *f* Poland
polpaccio (poal-*paht*-choa) *m* calf
polposo (poal-*pōā*-soa) *adj* mellow
polsino (poal-*see*-noa) *m* cuff
polso (*poal*-soa) *m* pulse; wrist
poltrona (poal-*trōā*-nah) *f* armchair, easy chair; ~ **d'orchestra** orchestra seat *Am*; stall
polvere (*poal*-vay-ray) *f* dust; powder; ~ **da sparo** gunpowder; ~ **dentifricia** toothpowder
polveroso (poal-vay-*rōā*-soa) *adj* dusty
pomeriggio (poa-may-*reed*-joa) *m* afternoon; **oggi nel** ~ this afternoon
pomodoro (poa-moa-*daw*-roa) *m* tomato
pompa (*poam*-pah) *f* pump; ~ **ad acqua** water pump; ~ **di benzina** petrol pump; gas pump *Am*
pompare (poam-*paa*-ray) *v* pump
pompelmo (poam-*pehl*-moa) *m* grapefruit
pompieri (poam-*pyai*-ree) *mpl* fire-brigade
ponderare (poan-day-*raa*-ray) *v* deliberate
ponte (*poan*-tay) *m* bridge; ~ **di coperta** main deck; ~ **levatoio** drawbridge; ~ **sospeso** suspension bridge
pontefice (poan-*tāy*-fee-chay) *m* pontiff
popelina (poa-pay-*lee*-nah) *f* poplin
popolano (poa-poa-*laa*-noa) *adj* vulgar
popolare (poa-poa-*laa*-ray) *adj* popular; **danza** ~ folk-dance
popolazione (poa-poa-lah-*tsyōā*-nay) *f* population
popolo (*paw*-poa-loa) *m* people; nation, folk
popoloso (poa-poa-*lōā*-soa) *adj* populous
porcellana (poar-chayl-*laa*-nah) *f* porcelain, china
porcellino (poar-chayl-*lee*-noa) *m* piglet; ~ **d'India** guinea-pig
porco (*por*-koa) *m* (pl porci) pig
porcospino (poar-koa-*spee*-noa) *m* porcupine

***porgere** (*por*-jay-ray) *v* hand, *give
porporino (poar-poa-*ree*-noa) *adj* purple
***porre** (*poar*-ray) *v* place; *put
porta (*por*-tah) *f* door; ~ **girevole** revolving door; ~ **scorrevole** sliding door
portabagagli (poar-tah-bah-*gaa*-lyee) *m* luggage rack
portacarte (poar-tah-*kahr*-tay) *m* attaché case
portacenere (poar-tah-*chāy*-nay-ray) *m* ashtray
portacipria (poar-tah-*chee*-pryah) *m* powder compact
portafoglio (poar-tah-*fōā*-lyoa) *m* pocket-book, wallet
portafortuna (poar-tah-foar-*tōō*-nah) *m* lucky charm
portalampada (poar-tah-*lahm*-pah-dah) *m* socket
portare (poar-*taa*-ray) *v* *bring; fetch; carry, *bear; **portar via** *take away
portasigarette (poar-tah-see-gah-*rayt*-tay) *m* cigarette-case
portata (poar-*taa*-tah) *f* course; reach, range
portatile (poar-*taa*-tee-lay) *adj* portable
portatore (poar-tah-*tōā*-ray) *m* bearer
portauovo (poar-tah-*waw*-voa) *m* egg-cup
portico (*por*-tee-koa) *m* arcade
portiere (poar-*tyai*-ray) *m* porter; goalkeeper
portinaio (poar-tee-*naa*-yoa) *m* concierge, janitor; doorman, door-keeper
porto (*por*-toa) *m* harbour, port; ~ **di mare** seaport
Portogallo (poar-toa-*gahl*-loa) *m* Portugal
portoghese (poar-toa-*gāy*-say) *adj* Portuguese; *m* Portuguese
portuale (poar-*twaa*-lay) *m* docker
porzione (poar-*tsyōā*-nay) *f* portion, helping
posare (poa-*saa*-ray) *v* *lay, *put; place
posate (poa-*saa*-tay) *fpl* cutlery
positiva (poa-zee-*tee*-vah) *f* positive, print
positivo (poa-zee-*tee*-voa) *adj* positive
posizione (poa-zee-*tsyōā*-nay) *f* position; site, location
***possedere** (poass-say-*dāy*-ray) *v* possess, own
possedimenti (poass-say-dee-*mayn*-tee) *mpl* possessions
possesso (poass-*sehss*-soa) *m* possession
possibile (poass-*see*-bee-lay) *adj* possible
possibilità (poass-see-bee-lee-*tah*) *f* possibility
posta (*po*-stah) *f* post, mail; bet; ~ **aerea** airmail
posteggiare (poa-stayd-*jaa*-ray) *v* park
posteggio di autopubbliche (poa-*stayd*-joa dee ou-toa-*poob*-blee-kay) taxi rank; taxi stand *Am*
posteriore (poa-stay-*ryōā*-ray) *adj* rear; later
postino (poa-*stee*-noa) *m* postman
posto (*poa*-stoa) *m* place; seat; station; **in qualche** ~ somewhere; ***mettere a** ~ *put away; ~ **di polizia** police-station; ~ **di pronto soccorso** first-aid post; ~ **libero** vacancy
potabile (poa-*taa*-bee-lay) *adj* for drinking
potente (poa-*tehn*-tay) *adj* powerful
potenza (poa-*tehn*-tsah) *f* might; power; capacity
potere (poa-*tāy*-ray) *m* authority, power; faculty
***potere** (poa-*tāy*-ray) *v* *can, *be able to; *might, *may

povero (*paw*-vay-roa) *adj* poor
povertà (poa-vayr-*tah*) *f* poverty
pozzanghera (poat-*tsahng*-gay-rah) *f* puddle
pozzo (*poat*-tsoa) *m* well; ~ **di petrolio** oil-well
pranzare (prahn-*dzaa*-ray) *v* *eat; dine
pranzo (*prahn*-dzoa) *m* dinner; lunch; ~ **a prezzo fisso** set menu
pratica (*praa*-tee-kah) *f* practice
praticamente (prah-tee-kah-*mayn*-tay) *adv* practically
praticare (prah-tee-*kaa*-ray) *v* practise
pratico (*praa*-tee-koa) *adj* practical
prato (*praa*-toa) *m* meadow; lawn
precario (pray-*kaa*-ryoa) *adj* critical, precarious
precauzione (pray-kou-*tsyōā*-nay) *f* precaution
precedente (pray-chay-*dehn*-tay) *adj* previous, former, preceding
precedentemente (pray-chay-dayn-tay-*mayn*-tay) *adv* before
precedenza (pray-chay-*dehn*-tsah) *f* right of way; priority
precedere (pray-*chai*-day-ray) *v* precede
precettore (pray-chayt-*tōā*-ray) *m* tutor
precipitare (pray-chee-pee-*taa*-ray) *v* crash; **precipitarsi** dash
precipitazione (pray-chee-pee-tah-*tsyōā*-nay) *f* shower; precipitation
precipizio (pray-chee-*pee*-tsyoa) *m* precipice
precisamente (pray-chee-zah-*mayn*-tay) *adv* exactly
precisare (pray-chee-*zaa*-ray) *v* specify
precisione (pray-chee-*zyōā*-nay) *f* precision
preciso (pray-*chee*-zoa) *adj* very, precise
predecessore (pray-day-chayss-*sōā*-ray) *m* predecessor
predicare (pray-dee-*kaa*-ray) *v* preach
***predire** (pray-*dee*-ray) *v* predict
preferenza (pray-fay-*rehn*-tsah) *f* preference
preferibile (pray-fay-*ree*-bee-lay) *adj* preferable
preferire (pray-fay-*ree*-ray) *v* prefer; **preferito** favourite
prefisso (pray-*feess*-soa) *m* prefix; area code
pregare (pray-*gaa*-ray) *v* ask; pray
preghiera (pray-*gyai*-rah) *f* prayer
pregiudizio (pray-joo-*dee*-tsyoa) *m* prejudice
preliminare (pray-lee-mee-*naa*-ray) *adj* preliminary
prematuro (pray-mah-*tōō*-roa) *adj* premature
premeditato (pray-may-dee-*taa*-toa) *adj* deliberate
premere (*prai*-may-ray) *v* press
premio (*prai*-myoa) *m* award, prize; premium; ~ **di consolazione** consolation prize
premura (pray-*mōō*-rah) *f* haste
premuroso (pray-moo-*rōā*-soa) *adj* thoughtful
***prendere** (*prehn*-day-ray) *v* *take; *catch; capture
prenotare (pray-noa-*taa*-ray) *v* reserve, book
prenotazione (pray-noa-tah-*tsyōā*-nay) *f* reservation, booking
preoccuparsi (pray-oak-koo-*pahr*-see) *v* worry; ~ **di** care about
preoccupato (pray-oak-koo-*paa*-toa) *adj* concerned, anxious, worried
preoccupazione (pray-oak-koo-pah-*tsyōā*-nay) *f* worry; trouble, care
preparare (pray-pah-*raa*-ray) *v* prepare; cook
preparazione (pray-pah-rah-*tsyōā*-nay) *f* preparation
preposizione (pray-poa-zee-*tsyōā*-nay) *f* preposition

presa (*prāy*-sah) *f* grip; capture
presbiterio (pray-zbee-*tai*-ryoa) *m* parsonage, rectory, vicarage
a prescindere da (ah pray-*sheen*-day-ray dah) apart from
***prescrivere** (pray-*skree*-vay-ray) *v* prescribe
presentare (pray-zayn-*taa*-ray) *v* offer, present; introduce; **presentarsi** report; appear
presentazione (pray-zayn-tah-*tsyōā*-nay) *f* introduction
presente (pray-*zehn*-tay) *adj* present; *m* present
presenza (pray-*zehn*-tsah) *f* presence
preservazione (pray-zayr-vah-*tsyōā*-nay) *f* preservation
preside (*prai*-see-day) *m* headmaster, principal
presidente (pray-see-*dehn*-tay) *m* chairman, president
pressante (prayss-*sahn*-tay) *adj* pressing
pressione (prayss-*syōā*-nay) *f* pressure; ~ **atmosferica** atmospheric pressure; ~ **dell'olio** oil pressure; ~ **gomme** tyre pressure; ~ **sanguigna** blood pressure
presso (*prehss*-soa) *prep* with
prestare (pray-*staa*-ray) *v* *lend
prestazione (pray-stah-*tsyōā*-nay) *f* feat
prestigiatore (pray-stee-jah-*tōā*-ray) *m* magician
prestigio (pray-*stee*-joa) *m* prestige
prestito (*preh*-stee-toa) *m* loan; ***prendere in** ~ borrow
presto (*preh*-stoa) *adv* soon, shortly
***presumere** (pray-*zōō*-may-ray) *v* assume
presumibile (pray-zoo-*mee*-bee-lay) *adj* presumable
presuntuoso (pray-zoon-*twōā*-soa) *adj* conceited, presumptuous
prete (*prai*-tay) *m* priest
***pretendere** (pray-*tehn*-day-ray) *v* pretend
pretesa (pray-*tāy*-sah) *f* pretence; claim
pretesto (pray-*teh*-stoa) *m* pretext
***prevedere** (pray-vay-*dāy*-ray) *v* forecast; anticipate
***prevenire** (pray-vay-*nee*-ray) *v* anticipate, prevent
preventivo (pray-vayn-*tee*-voa) *adj* preventive; *m* budget
previo (*prai*-vyoa) *adj* previous
previsione (pray-vee-*zyōā*-nay) *f* forecast
prezioso (pray-*tsyōā*-soa) *adj* valuable, precious
prezzare (prayt-*tsaa*-ray) *v* price
prezzemolo (prayt-*tsāy*-moa-loa) *m* parsley
prezzo (*preht*-tsoa) *m* price-list; cost, rate; **calo di** ~ slump; ~ **d'acquisto** purchase price; ~ **del biglietto** fare; ~ **del coperto** cover charge
prigione (pree-*jōā*-nay) *m* jail, prison
prigioniero (pree-joa-*ñai*-roa) *m* prisoner; ***far** ~ capture
prima (*pree*-mah) *adv* at first; before; ~ **che** before; ~ **di** before
primario (pree-*maa*-ryoa) *adj* primary
primato (pree-*maa*-toa) *m* record
primavera (pree-mah-*vāy*-rah) *f* springtime, spring
primitivo (pree-mee-*tee*-voa) *adj* primitive
primo (*pree*-moa) *num* first, foremost, primary, chief
principale (preent-shee-*paa*-lay) *adj* leading, main, cardinal, principal, primary, chief
principalmente (preen-chee-pahl-*mayn*-tay) *adv* mainly
principe (*preen*-chee-pay) *m* prince
principessa (preen-chee-*payss*-sah) *f*

princess
principiante (preen-chee-*pyahn*-tay) *m* beginner, learner
principio (preen-*chee*-pyoa) *m* beginning; principle; **al** ~ at first
priorità (pryoa-ree-*tah*) *f* priority
privare di (pree-*vaa*-ray) deprive of
privato (pree-*vaa*-toa) *adj* private
privazioni (pree-vah-*tsyōā*-nee) *fpl* exposure
privilegiare (pree-vee-lay-*jaa*-ray) *v* favour
privilegio (pree-vee-*lai*-joa) *m* privilege
probabile (proa-*baa*-bee-lay) *adj* probable, likely
probabilmente (proa-bah-beel-*mayn*-tay) *adv* probably
problema (proa-*blai*-mah) *m* problem, question
procedere (proa-*chai*-day-ray) *v* proceed
procedimento (proa-chay-dee-*mayn*-toa) *m* procedure; process
processione (proa-chayss-*syōā*-nay) *f* procession
processo (proa-*chehss*-soa) *m* trial, lawsuit; process
proclamare (proa-klah-*maa*-ray) *v* proclaim
procurare (proa-koo-*raa*-ray) *v* furnish
prodigo (*praw*-dee-goa) *adj* lavish; liberal
prodotto (proa-*doat*-toa) *m* product; produce
***produrre** (proa-*door*-ray) *v* produce
produttore (proa-doot-*tōā*-ray) *m* producer
produzione (proa-doo-*tsyōā*-nay) *f* production, output; ~ **in serie** mass production
profano (proa-*faa*-noa) *m* layman
professare (proa-fayss-*saa*-ray) *v* confess
professionale (proa-fayss-syoa-*naa*-lay) *adj* professional
professione (proa-fayss-*syōā*-nay) *f* profession
professore (proa-fayss-*sōā*-ray) *m* master; professor
professoressa (proa-fayss-soa-*rayss*-sah) *f* teacher
profeta (proa-*fai*-tah) *m* prophet
profitto (proa-*feet*-toa) *m* benefit, gain; profit
profondità (proa-foan-dee-*tah*) *f* depth
profondo (proa-*foan*-doa) *adj* deep; profound
profumo (proa-*fōō*-moa) *m* scent; perfume
progettare (proa-jayt-*taa*-ray) *v* plan; design
progetto (proa-*jeht*-toa) *m* plan, scheme; project
programma (proa-*grahm*-mah) *m* programme
progredire (proa-gray-*dee*-ray) *v* *get on
progressista (proa-grayss-*see*-stah) *adj* progressive
progressivo (proa-grayss-*see*-voa) *adj* progressive
progresso (proa-*grehss*-soa) *m* progress
proibire (proa-ee-*bee*-ray) *v* *forbid, prohibit; **proibito passare** no entry
proibitivo (proa-ee-bee-*tee*-voa) *adj* prohibitive
proiettore (proa-yayt-*tōā*-ray) *m* spotlight
prolunga (proa-*loong*-gah) *f* extension cord
prolungamento (proa-loong-gah-*mayn*-toa) *m* extension
promessa (proa-*mayss*-sah) *f* promise; vow
***promettere** (proa-*mayt*-tay-ray) *v* promise
promontorio (proa-moan-*taw*-ryoa) *m*

headland
promozione (proa-moa-*tsyōā*-nay) *f* promotion
***promuovere** (proa-*mwaw*-vay-ray) *v* promote
pronome (proa-*nōā*-may) *m* pronoun
pronto (*proan*-toa) *adj* ready; prompt
pronuncia (proa-*noon*-chah) *f* pronunciation
pronunciare (proa-noon-*chaa*-ray) *v* pronounce
propaganda (proa-pah-*gahn*-dah) *f* propaganda
propenso (proa-*pehn*-soa) *adj* inclined
***proporre** (proa-*poar*-ray) *v* propose
proporzionale (proa-poar-tsyoa-*naa*-lay) *adj* proportional
proporzione (proa-poar-*tsyōā*-nay) *f* proportion
proposito (proa-*paw*-zee-toa) *m* purpose; **a** ~ by the way
proposta (proa-*poa*-stah) *f* proposition, proposal
proprietà (proa-pryay-*tah*) *f* property; estate
proprietario (proa-pryay-*taa*-ryoa) *m* proprietor, owner; landlord
proprio (*pro*-pryoa) *adj* own
propulsare (proa-pool-*saa*-ray) *v* propel
prosaico (proa-*zigh*-koa) *adj* matter-of-fact
prosciugare (proash-shoo-*gaa*-ray) *v* drain
prosciutto (proash-*shoot*-toa) *m* ham
proseguire (proa-say-*gwee*-ray) *v* continue, carry on
prosperità (proa-spay-ree-*tah*) *f* prosperity
prospettiva (proa-spayt-*tee*-vah) *f* perspective; prospect, outlook
prospetto (proa-*speht*-toa) *m* prospectus
prossimamente (proass-see-mah-*mayn*-tay) *adv* shortly
prossimità (proass-see-mee-*tah*) *f* vicinity
prossimo (*pross*-see-moa) *adj* next
prostituta (proa-stee-*tōō*-tah) *f* prostitute
protagonista (proa-tah-goa-*nee*-stah) *m* protagonist
***proteggere** (proa-*tehd*-jay-ray) *v* protect
proteina (proa-tay-*ee*-nah) *f* protein
protesta (proa-*teh*-stah) *f* protest
protestante (proa-tay-*stahn*-tay) *adj* Protestant
protestare (proa-tay-*staa*-ray) *v* protest
protezione (proa-tay-*tsyōā*-nay) *f* protection
protuberanza (proa-too-bay-*rahn*-tsah) *f* lump
prova (*praw*-vah) *f* trial, experiment, test; evidence, token, proof; rehearsal; ***fare le prove** rehearse; **in** ~ on approval
provare (proa-*vaa*-ray) *v* attempt, test; prove; experience; try on
provenienza (proa-vay-*ñehn*-tsah) *f* origin
***provenire da** (proa-vay-*nee*-ray) *come from; originate from
proverbio (proa-*vehr*-byoa) *m* proverb
provincia (proa-*veen*-chah) *f* province
provinciale (proa-veen-*chaa*-lay) *adj* provincial
provocare (proa-voa-*kaa*-ray) *v* cause
***provvedere** (proav-vay-*dāy*-ray) *v* provide; ~ **di** furnish with
provvedimento (proav-vay-dee-*mayn*-toa) *m* measure
provvisioni (proav-vee-*zyōā*-nee) *fpl* provisions *pl*
provvisorio (proav-vee-*zaw*-ryoa) *adj* provisional, temporary
provvista (proav-*vee*-stah) *f* supply
prudente (proo-*dehn*-tay) *adj* wary

prudere (*proō*-day-ray) *v* itch
prurito (proo-*ree*-toa) *m* itch
psichiatra (psee-*kyaa*-trah) *m* psychiatrist
psichico (*psee*-kee-koa) *adj* psychic
psicoanalista (psee-koa-ah-nah-*lee*-stah) *m* psychoanalyst
psicologia (psee-koa-loa-*jee*-ah) *f* psychology
psicologico (psee-koa-*law*-jee-koa) *adj* psychological
psicologo (psee-*kaw*-loa-goa) *m* psychologist
pubblicare (poob-blee-*kaa*-ray) *v* publish
pubblicazione (poob-blee-kah-*tsyoā*-nay) *f* publication
pubblicità (poob-blee-chee-*tah*) *f* advertising, publicity
pubblico (*poob*-blee-koa) *adj* public; *m* public
pudore (poo-*doā*-ray) *m* shame
pugno (*poō*-ñoa) *m* fist; punch; **sferrare pugni** punch
pulcino (pool-*chee*-noa) *m* chicken
pulire (poo-*lee*-ray) *v* clean; ~ **a secco** dry-clean
pulito (poo-*lee*-toa) *adj* clean
pulitura (poo-lee-*toō*-rah) *f* cleaning
pulizia (poo-lee-*tsee*-ah) *f* cleaning
pulpito (*pool*-pee-toa) *m* pulpit
pulsante (pool-*sahn*-tay) *m* push-button
***pungere** (*poon*-jay-ray) *v* *sting, prick
punire (poo-*nee*-ray) *v* punish
punizione (poo-nee-*tsyoā*-nay) *f* punishment
punta (*poon*-tah) *f* point, tip
puntare su (poon-*taa*-ray) aim at
punteggio (poon-*tehd*-joa) *m* score
punto (*poon*-toa) *m* point; period, full stop; item, issue; stitch; ~ **decisivo** turning-point; ~ **di congelamento** freezing-point; ~ **di partenza** starting-point; ~ **di riferimento** landmark; ~ **di vista** point of view, outlook; ~ **e virgola** semi-colon; ~ **interrogativo** question mark
puntuale (poon-*twaa*-lay) *adj* punctual
puntura (poon-*toō*-rah) *f* bite, sting
purché (poor-*kay*) *conj* provided that
pure (*poō*-ray) *adv* as well, also
puro (*poō*-roa) *adj* clean, pure; neat, sheer
purosangue (poo-roa-*sahng*-gway) *adj* thoroughbred
pus (pooss) *m* pus
pustoletta (poo-stoa-*layt*-tah) *f* pimple
puttana (poot-*taa*-nah) *f* whore
puzzare (poot-*tsaa*-ray) *v* *smell, *stink
puzzle (pahzl) jigsaw puzzle
puzzolente (poot-tsoa-*lehn*-tay) *adj* smelly

Q

qua (kwah) *adv* here
quadrato (kwah-*draa*-toa) *adj* square; *m* square
quadrettato (kwah-drayt-*taa*-toa) *adj* chequered
quadretto (kwah-*drayt*-toa) *m* check
quadro (*kwaa*-droa) *m* picture; cadre; ~ **di distribuzione** switchboard
quaglia (*kwaa*-lʸah) *f* quail
qualche (*kwahl*-kay) *adj* some
qualcosa (kwahl-*kaw*-sah) *pron* something
qualcuno (kwahl-*koō*-noa) *pron* someone, somebody
quale (*kwaa*-lay) *pron* which
qualifica (kwah-*lee*-fee-kah) *f* qualification
qualificato (kwah-lee-fee-*kaa*-toa) *adj*

qualified; **non** ~ unskilled
qualità (kwah-lee-*tah*) *f* quality; **di prima** ~ first-rate, first-class
qualora (kwah-*lōā*-rah) *conj* when, in case
qualsiasi (kwahl-*see*-ah-see) *adj* whatever; whichever
quando (*kwahn*-doa) *adv* when; *conj* when
quantità (kwahn-tee-*tah*) *f* amount, quantity; number; lot
quanto (*kwahn*-toa) *adj* how much, how many
quantunque (kwahn-*toong*-kway) *conj* though
quaranta (kwah-*rahn*-tah) *num* forty
quarantena (kwah-rahn-*tai*-nah) *f* quarantine
quartiere (kwahr-*tyai*-ray) *m* district, quarter; ~ **generale** headquarters *pl*; ~ **povero** slum
quarto (*kwahr*-toa) *num* fourth; *m* quarter
quasi (*kwaa*-zee) *adv* almost, nearly
quattordicesimo (kwaht-toar-dee-*chai*-zee-moa) *num* fourteenth
quattordici (kwaht-*tor*-dee-chee) *num* fourteen
quattro (*kwaht*-troa) *num* four
quello[1] (*kwayl*-loa) *pron* that; **quelli** those; ~ **che** what
quello[2] (*kwayl*-loa) *adj* that; **quei** *adj* those
quercia (*kwehr*-chah) *f* oak
questione (kway-*styōā*-nay) *f* matter, issue, question
questo (*kway*-stoa) *adj* this; **questi** these
qui (kwee) *adv* here
quiete (kwee-*ai*-tay) *f* stillness, quiet
quieto (kwee-*ai*-toa) *adj* quiet
quindi (*kween*-dee) *conj* therefore
quindicesimo (kween-dee-*chai*-zee-moa) *num* fifteenth
quindici (*kween*-dee-chee) *num* fifteen
quinto (*kween*-toa) *num* fifth
quota (*kwaw*-tah) *f* quota
quotidiano (kwoa-tee-*dyaa*-noa) *adj* daily; everyday; *m* daily

R

rabarbaro (rah-*bahr*-bah-roa) *m* rhubarb
rabbia (*rahb*-byah) *f* anger, rage; rabies
rabbioso (rahb-*byōā*-soa) *adj* mad
rabbrividire (rahb-bree-vee-*dee*-ray) *v* shiver
raccapricciante (rahk-kahp-preet-*chahn*-tay) *adj* creepy
raccapriccio (rahk-kahp-*preet*-choa) *m* horror
racchetta (rahk-*kayt*-tah) *f* racquet
***raccogliere** (rahk-*kaw*-lyay-ray) *v* pick up; gather; collect; ***raccogliersi** gather
raccolta (rahk-*kol*-tah) *f* crop; ~ **di documenti** file
raccolto (rahk-*kol*-toa) *m* harvest
raccomandare (rahk-koa-mahn-*daa*-ray) *v* recommend; register
raccomandata (rahk-koa-mahn-*daa*-tah) *f* registered letter
raccomandazione (rahk-koa-mahn-dah-*tsyōā*-nay) *f* recommendation
raccontare (rahk-koan-*taa*-ray) *v* relate, *tell
racconto (rahk-*koan*-toa) *m* story, tale; ~ **a fumetti** comics *pl*
raccorciare (rahk-koar-*chaa*-ray) *v* shorten; trim
***radere** (*raa*-day-ray) *v* shave
radiatore (rah-dyah-*tōā*-ray) *m* radiator
radicale (rah-dee-*kaa*-lay) *adj* radical

radice (rah-*dee*-chay) *f* root
radio (*raa*-dyoa) *f* wireless, radio
radiografare (rah-dyoa-grah-*faa*-ray) *v* X-ray
radiografia (rah-dyoa-grah-*fee*-ah) *f* X-ray
raduno (rah-*dōō*-noa) *m* rally
radura (rah-*dōō*-rah) *f* clearing
rafano (*raa*-fah-noa) *m* horseradish
raffermo (rahf-*fayr*-moa) *adj* stale
raffica (*rahf*-fee-kah) *f* gust, blow
raffigurare (rahf-fee-goo-*raa*-ray) *v* represent
raffineria (rahf-fee-nay-*ree*-ah) *f* refinery; ~ **di petrolio** oil-refinery
raffreddore (rahf-frayd-*dōā*-ray) *m* cold; ***prendere un** ~ catch a cold
ragazza (rah-*gaht*-tsah) *f* girl
ragazzino (rah-gaht-*tsee*-noa) *m* boy
ragazzo (rah-*gaht*-tsoa) *m* lad, boy
raggio (*rahd*-joa) *m* beam, ray; radius; spoke
***raggiungere** (rahd-*joon*-jay-ray) *v* attain, achieve, reach
raggiungibile (rahd-joon-*jee*-bee-lay) *adj* attainable
ragguaglio (rahg-*gwaa*-lʸoa) *m* information
ragionamento (rah-joa-nah-*mayn*-toa) *m* reasoning
ragionare (rah-joa-*naa*-ray) *v* reason
ragione (rah-*jōā*-nay) *f* reason, wits *pl*, sense; cause; ***avere** ~ * be right
ragionevole (rah-joa-*nāy*-voa-lay) *adj* reasonable; sensible
ragnatela (rah-ñah-*tāy*-lah) *f* cobweb, spider's web
ragno (*raa*-ñoa) *m* spider
raion (*raa*-yoan) *m* rayon
rallegrare (rahl-lay-*graa*-ray) *v* cheer up
rallentare (rahl-layn-*taa*-ray) *v* slow down
rame (*raa*-may) *m* copper
rammendare (rahm-mayn-*daa*-ray) *v* mend, darn
rammentare (rahm-mayn-*taa*-ray) *v* remind of; **rammentarsi** remember
ramo (*raa*-moa) *m* branch, bough
ramoscello (rah-moash-*shehl*-loa) *m* twig
rampa (*rahm*-pah) *f* ramp
rana (*raa*-nah) *f* frog
rancido (*rahn*-chee-doa) *adj* rancid
randello (rahn-*dehl*-loa) *m* cudgel
rapida (*raa*-pee-dah) *f* rapids *pl*
rapidità (rah-pee-dee-*tah*) *f* speed
rapido (*raa*-pee-doa) *adj* fast; swift, rapid
rapina (rah-*pee*-nah) *f* robbery, hold-up
rappezzare (rahp-payt-*tsaa*-ray) *v* patch
rapporto (rahp-*por*-toa) *m* report; affair, intercourse
rappresentante (rahp-pray-zayn-*tahn*-tay) *m* agent
rappresentanza (rahp-pray-zayn-*tahn*-tsah) *f* representation
rappresentare (rahp-pray-zayn-*taa*-ray) *v* represent
rappresentativo (rahp-pray-zayn-tah-*tee*-voa) *adj* representative
rappresentazione (rahp-pray-zayn-tah-*tsyōā*-nay) *f* performance, show; ~ **di marionette** puppet-show; ~ **teatrale** play
raramente (rah-rah-*mayn*-tay) *adv* seldom, rarely
raro (*raa*-roa) *adj* uncommon, rare
raschiare (rah-*skyaa*-ray) *v* scrape
raso (*raa*-soa) *m* satin
rasoio (rah-*sōā*-yoa) *m* safety-razor, razor; ~ **elettrico** electric razor; shaver
raspare (rah-*spaa*-ray) *v* grate
rassegna (rahss-*sāy*-ñah) *f* survey
rassomiglianza (rahss-soa-mee-*lʸahn*-

tsah) *f* similarity
rastrello (rah-*strehl*-loa) *m* (pl ~n) rake
rata (*raa*-tah) *f* instalment
ratto (*raht*-toa) *m* rat
rauco (*rou*-koa) *adj* hoarse
ravanello (rah-vah-*nehl*-loa) *m* radish
razione (rah-*tsyōā*-nay) *f* ration
razza (*raht*-tsah) *f* breed, race
razziale (raht-*tsyaa*-lay) *adj* racial
razzo (*raht*-tsoa) *m* rocket
re (ray) *m* (pl ~) king
reale (ray-*aa*-lay) *adj* true, factual, actual, substantial, real; royal
realizzabile (ray-ah-leed-*dzaa*-bee-lay) *adj* feasible, realizable
realizzare (ray-ah-leed-*dzaa*-ray) *v* realize
realtà (ray-ahl-*tah*) *f* reality; **in** ~ actually, in effect; really
reato (ray-*aa*-toa) *m* offence
reazione (ray-ah-*tsyōā*-nay) *f* reaction
recapitare (ray-kah-pee-*taa*-ray) *v* deliver
recare (ray-*kaa*-ray) *v* *bring; cause; **recarsi** *go
recensione (ray-chayn-*syōā*-nay) *f* review
recente (ray-*chehn*-tay) *adj* recent; **di** ~ recently
recentemente (ray-chayn-tay-*mayn*-tay) *adv* lately, recently
recessione (ray-chayss-*syōā*-nay) *f* recession
recinto (ray-*cheen*-toa) *m* fence
recipiente (ray-chee-*pyehn*-tay) *m* container, vessel
reciproco (ray-*chee*-proa-koa) *adj* mutual
recital (ray-see-*tahl*) *m* recital
recitare (ray-chee-*taa*-ray) *v* act
reclamare (ray-klah-*maa*-ray) *v* claim
recluta (*ray*-kloo-tah) *f* recruit
redattore (ray-daht-*tōā*-ray) *m* editor
reddito (*rehd*-dee-toa) *m* revenue, income; **redditi** earnings *pl*
***redigere** (ray-*dee*-jay-ray) *v* *draw up
***redimere** (ray-*dee*-may-ray) *v* redeem
refe (*rāy*-fay) *m* thread
referenza (ray-fay-*rehn*-tsah) *f* reference
regalo (ray-*gaa*-loa) *m* gift, present
regata (ray-*gaa*-tah) *f* regatta
***reggersi** (*rehd*-jayr-see) *v* *hold on
reggicalze (rayd-jee-*kahl*-tsay) *m* suspender belt; garter belt *Am*
reggipetto (rayd-jee-*peht*-toa) *m* brassiere, bra
reggiseno (rayd-jee-*sāy*-noa) *m* brassiere, bra
regia (ray-*jee*-ah) *f* direction
regime (ray-*jee*-may) *m* rule, régime
regina (ray-*jee*-nah) *f* queen
regionale (ray-joa-*naa*-lay) *adj* regional
regione (ray-*jōā*-nay) *f* region; country, district
regista (ray-*jee*-stah) *m* director
registrare (ray-jee-*straa*-ray) *v* record, book; **registrarsi** register, check in
registrazione (ray-jee-strah-*tsyōā*-nay) *f* registration; record, entry; recording
regnare (ray-*ñaa*-ray) *v* reign
regno (*rāy*-ñoa) *m* kingdom; reign
regola (*rai*-goa-lah) *f* rule
regolamentazione (ray-goa-lah-mayn-tah-*tsyōā*-nay) *f* regulation
regolamento (ray-goa-lah-*mayn*-toa) *m* regulation
regolare (ray-goa-*laa*-ray) *adj* regular; *v* regulate; adjust; **regolato** regular
relativo (ray-lah-*tee*-voa) *adj* relative; comparative
relazione (ray-lah-*tsyōā*-nay) *f* relation; reference, connection; report; **in** ~ **a** regarding
religione (ray-lee-*jōā*-nay) *f* religion

religioso (ray-lee-*jōā*-soa) *adj* religious
reliquia (ray-*lee*-kwee-ah) *f* relic
relitto (ray-*leet*-toa) *m* wreck
remare (ray-*maa*-ray) *v* row
remo (*rai*-moa) *m* oar; paddle
remoto (ray-*maw*-toa) *adj* remote, out of the way
***rendere** (*rehn*-day-ray) *v* reimburse; *pay; ~ **conto di** account for; ~ **omaggio** honour
rene (*rai*-nay) *m* kidney
renna (*rehn*-nah) *f* reindeer
reparto (ray-*pahr*-toa) *m* section, division
repellente (ray-payl-*lehn*-tay) *adj* repellent
repertorio (ray-payr-*taw*-ryoa) *m* repertory
***reprimere** (ray-*pree*-may-ray) *v* suppress
repubblica (ray-*poob*-blee-kah) *f* republic
repubblicano (ray-poob-blee-*kaa*-noa) *adj* republican
reputare (ray-poo-*taa*-ray) *v* consider
reputazione (ray-poo-tah-*tsyōā*-nay) *f* fame, reputation
resa (*rāȳ*-sah) *f* surrender
residente (ray-see-*dehn*-tay) *adj* resident; *m* resident
residenza (ray-see-*dehn*-tsah) *f* residence
residuo (ray-*see*-dwoa) *m* remnant, remainder
resina (*rai*-zee-nah) *f* resin
resistenza (ray-see-*stehn*-tsah) *f* resistance; strength
resistere (ray-*see*-stay-ray) *v* resist
resoconto (ray-soa-*koan*-toa) *m* account
***respingere** (ray-*speen*-jay-ray) *v* turn down, reject
respirare (ray-spee-*raa*-ray) *v* breathe
respiratore (ray-spee-rah-*tōā*-ray) *m* snorkel
respirazione (ray-spee-rah-*tsyōā*-nay) *f* respiration, breathing
respiro (ray-*spee*-roa) *m* breath
responsabile (ray-spoan-*saa*-bee-lay) *adj* responsible; liable
responsabilità (ray-spoan-sah-bee-lee-*tah*) *f* responsibility; liability
restare (ray-*staa*-ray) *v* remain
restauro (ray-*stou*-roa) *m* repair
restio (ray-*stee*-oa) *adj* unwilling
resto (*reh*-stoa) *m* rest; remnant, remainder
***restringersi** (ray-*streen*-jayr-see) *v* *shrink; tighten
restrizione (ray-stree-*tsyōā*-nay) *f* restriction, qualification
rete (*rāȳ*-tay) *f* net; network; goal; ~ **da pesca** fishing net; ~ **stradale** road system
reticella (ray-tee-*chehl*-lah) *f* hair-net
retina (*rai*-tee-nah) *f* retina
rettangolare (rayt-tahng-goa-*laa*-ray) *adj* rectangular
rettangolo (rayt-*tahng*-goa-loa) *m* rectangle, oblong
rettifica (rayt-*tee*-fee-kah) *f* correction
rettile (*reht*-tee-lay) *m* reptile
retto (*reht*-toa) *adj* right; *m* rectum
reumatismo (ray°°-mah-*tee*-zmoa) *m* rheumatism
revisionare (ray-vee-zyoa-*naa*-ray) *v* revise, overhaul
revisione (ray-vee-*zyōā*-nay) *f* revision
revocare (ray-voa-*kaa*-ray) *v* recall
rialzo (*ryahl*-tsoa) *m* rise
riassunto (ryahss-*soon*-toa) *m* résumé
ribassare (ree-bahss-*saa*-ray) *v* lower
ribasso (ree-*bahss*-soa) *m* reduction
ribellione (ree-bayl-*lʸōā*-nay) *f* revolt, rebellion
ribes (*ree*-bayss) *m* currant; ~ **nero** black-currant
ributtante (ree-boot-*tahn*-tay) *adj*

creepy, repulsive
ricamare (ree-kah-*maa*-ray) *v* embroider
ricambio (ree-*kahm*-byoa) *m* refill
ricamo (ree-*kaa*-moa) *m* embroidery
ricattare (ree-kaht-*taa*-ray) *v* blackmail
ricatto (ree-*kaht*-toa) *m* blackmail
ricchezza (reek-*kayt*-tsah) *f* riches *pl*, wealth, fortune
riccio (*reet*-choa) *m* hedgehog; ~ **di mare** sea-urchin
ricciolo (*reet*-choa-loa) *m* curl; wave
ricciuto (reet-*chōō*-toa) *adj* curly
ricco (*reek*-koa) *adj* rich, wealthy
ricerca (ree-*chehr*-kah) *f* research; search
ricetta (ree-*cheht*-tah) *f* prescription; recipe
ricevere (ree-*chāy*-vay-ray) *v* receive
ricevimento (ree-chay-vee-*mayn*-toa) *m* reception, receipt; **capo ufficio** ~ receptionist
ricevitore (ree-chay-vee-*tōā*-ray) *m* receiver
ricevuta (ree-chay-*vōō*-tah) *f* receipt; voucher
richiamare (ree-kyah-*maa*-ray) *v* recall
richiamo (ree-*kyah*-moa) *m* recall *m*; allurement; cross-reference
***richiedere** (ree-*kyai*-day-ray) *v* request; demand
richiesta (ree-*kyeh*-stah) *f* request; application
richiesto (ree-*keeeh*-stoa) *adj* requisite
ricominciare (ree-koa-meen-*chaa*-ray) *v* recommence
ricompensa (ree-koam-*pehn*-sah) *f* reward, prize
ricompensare (ree-koam-payn-*saa*-ray) *v* reward
riconciliazione (ree-koan-chee-lyah-*tsyōā*-nay) *f* reconciliation
riconoscente (ree-koa-noash-*shehn*-tay) *adj* grateful, thankful
***riconoscere** (ree-koa-*noash*-shay-ray) *v* recognize; acknowledge; admit, confess
riconoscimento (ree-koa-noash-shee-*mayn*-toa) *m* recognition
ricordare (ree-koar-*daa*-ray) *v* remember; *think of; ***far** ~ remind; **ricordarsi** recollect, remember, recall
ricordo (ree-*kor*-doa) *m* memory, remembrance; souvenir
***ricorrere** (ree-*koar*-ray-ray) *v* recur; appeal; ~ **a** apply to
ricostruire (ree-koa-*strwee*-ray) *v* *rebuild; reconstruct
ricreazione (ree-kray-ah-*tsyōā*-nay) *f* recreation
ricuperare (ree-koo-pay-*raa*-ray) *v* recover
ricusare (ree-koo-*zaa*-ray) *v* deny
ridacchiare (ree-dahk-*kyaa*-ray) *v* giggle, chuckle
***ridere** (*ree*-day-ray) *v* laugh
ridicolizzare (ree-dee-koa-leed-*dzaa*-ray) *v* ridicule
ridicolo (ree-*dee*-koa-loa) *adj* ridiculous, ludicrous
ridondante (ree-doan-*dahn*-tay) *adj* redundant
ridotto (ree-*doat*-toa) *m* lobby, foyer
***ridurre** (ree-*door*-ray) *v* reduce, *cut
riduzione (ree-doo-*tsyōā*-nay) *f* discount, reduction, rebate
rieducazione (ryay-doo-kah-*tsyōā*-nay) *f* rehabilitation
riempire (ryaym-*pee*-ray) *v* fill
rientrare (ryayn-*traa*-ray) *v* return; ~ **in** *be part of
riferimento (ree-fay-ree-*mayn*-toa) *m* reference
riferire (ree-fay-*ree*-ray) *v* report
rifiutare (ree-fyoo-*taa*-ray) *v* deny, refuse; reject
rifiuto (ree-*fyōō*-toa) *m* refusal; **rifiuti** litter

riflessione (ree-flayss-*syōā*-nay) *f* deliberation
riflesso (ree-*flehss*-soa) *m* reflection
***riflettere**[1] (ree-*fleht*-tay-ray) *v* (pp riflesso) reflect
***riflettere**[2] (ree-*fleht*-tay-ray) *v* (pp riflettuto) *think
riflettore (ree-flayt-*tōā*-ray) *m* searchlight; reflector
riforma (ree-*foar*-mah) *f* reformation
rifornimento (ree-foar-nee-*mayn*-toa) *m* supply
rifugiarsi (ree-foo-*jahr*-see) *v* *seek refuge
rifugio (ree-*fōō*-joa) *m* cover, shelter
riga (*ree*-gah) *f* line; ruler
rigettare (ree-jayt-*taa*-ray) *v* reject; vomit
rigido (*ree*-jee-doa) *adj* stiff; bleak; strict
rigirarsi (ree-jee-*rahr*-see) *v* turn round
rigoroso (ree-goa-*rōā*-soa) *adj* severe
riguardare (ree-gwahr-*daa*-ray) *v* concern, affect; **per quanto riguarda** as regards; **riguardante** concerning
riguardo (ree-*gwahr*-doa) *m* regard, consideration; ~ **a** regarding; concerning, with reference to
riguardoso (ree-gwahr-*dōā*-soa) *adj* considerate
rilassamento (ree-lahss-sah-*mayn*-toa) *m* relaxation
rilassarsi (ree-lahss-*sahr*-see) *v* relax
rilevante (ree-lay-*vahn*-tay) *adj* important
rilevare (ree-lay-*vaa*-ray) *v* notice; collect, pick up; *take over
rilievo (ree-*l^{y}ai*-voa) *m* relief; importance
rima (*ree*-mah) *f* rhyme
rimandare (ree-mahn-*daa*-ray) *v* postpone; ~ **a** refer to
rimanente (ree-mah-*nehn*-tay) *adj* remaining
rimanenza (ree-mah-*nehn*-tsah) *f* remnant
***rimanere** (ree-mah-*nāȳ*-ray) *v* stay, remain
rimborsare (reem-boar-*saa*-ray) *v* reimburse, refund, *repay
rimborso (reem-*boar*-soa) *m* refund, repayment
rimedio (ree-*māȳ*-dyoa) *m* remedy
rimessa (ree-*mayss*-sah) *f* remittance; garage; ***mettere in** ~ garage
***rimettere** (ree-*mayt*-tay-ray) *v* remit
rimorchiare (ree-moar-*kyaa*-ray) *v* tug
rimorchiatore (ree-moar-kyah-*tōā*-ray) *m* tug
rimorchio (ree-*mor*-kyoa) *m* trailer
***rimpiangere** (reem-*pyahn*-jay-ray) *v* regret; miss
rimpianto (reem-*pyahn*-toa) *m* regret
rimproverare (reem-proa-vay-*raa*-ray) *v* reproach, reprimand; blame
rimprovero (reem-*praw*-vay-roa) *m* reproach
rimunerare (ree-moo-nay-*raa*-ray) *v* remunerate
rimunerativo (ree-moo-nay-rah-*tee*-voa) *adj* paying
rimunerazione (ree-moo-nay-rah-*tsyōā*-nay) *f* remuneration
rincasare (reeng-kah-*saa*-ray) *v* *go home
***rinchiudere** (reeng-*kyōō*-day-ray) *v* *shut in
rinfrescare (reen-fray-*skaa*-ray) *v* refresh
rinfresco (reen-*fray*-skoa) *m* refreshment
ringhiera (reeng-*gyai*-rah) *f* banisters *pl*, rail
ringraziare (reeng-grah-*tsyaa*-ray) *v* thank
rinnovare (reen-noa-*vaa*-ray) *v* renew
rinoceronte (ree-noa-chay-*roan*-tay) *m* rhinoceros

rinomanza (ree-noa-*mahn*-tsah) *f* fame
rinorragia (ree-noar-rah-*jee*-ah) *f* nosebleed
rintracciare (reen-traht-*chaa*-ray) *v* trace
rinviare (reen-*vyaa*-ray) *v* *send back; adjourn, *put off
rinvio (reen-*vee*-oa) *m* delay
riordinare (ryoar-dee-*naa*-ray) *v* tidy up
riparare (ree-pah-*raa*-ray) *v* shelter; mend, repair, fix
riparazione (ree-pah-rah-*tsyōā*-nay) *f* reparation
riparo (ree-*paa*-roa) *m* shelter; screen
ripartire (ree-pahr-*tee*-ray) *v* divide
riparto (ree-*pahr*-toa) *m* department
ripensare (ree-payn-*saa*-ray) *v* *think over
ripetere (ree-*pai*-tay-ray) *v* repeat
ripetizione (ree-pay-tee-*tsyōā*-nay) *f* repetition
ripetutamente (ree-pay-too-tah-*mayn*-tay) *adv* again and again
ripido (*ree*-pee-doa) *adj* steep
ripieno (ree-*pyai*-noa) *adj* stuffed; *m* filling; stuffing
riportare (ree-poar-*taa*-ray) *v* *bring back
riposante (ree-poa-*sahn*-tay) *adj* restful
riposarsi (ree-poa-*sahr*-see) *v* rest
riposo (ree-*paw*-soa) *m* rest
***riprendere** (ree-*prehn*-day-ray) *v* resume
ripresa (ree-*prāy*-sah) *f* round
ripristino (ree-pree-*stee*-noa) *m* revival
***riprodurre** (ree-proa-*door*-ray) *v* reproduce
riproduzione (ree-proa-doo-*tsyōā*-nay) *f* reproduction
riprovare (ree-proa-*vaa*-ray) *v* scold
ripugnante (ree-poo-*ñahn*-tay) *adj* repellent
ripugnanza (ree-poo-*ñahn*-tsah) *f* dislike
risarcimento (ree-sahr-chee-*mayn*-toa) *m* indemnity
risata (ree-*saa*-tah) *f* laughter
riscaldamento (ree-skahl-dah-*mayn*-toa) *m* heating
riscaldatore (ree-skahl-dah-*tōā*-ray) *m* heater
riscatto (ree-*skaht*-toa) *m* ransom
rischiare (ree-*skyaa*-ray) *v* risk
rischio (*ree*-skyoa) *m* risk; chance, hazard
rischioso (ree-*skyōā*-soa) *adj* risky
***riscuotere** (ree-*skwaw*-tay-ray) *v* cash, raise
risentirsi per (ree-sayn-*teer*-see) resent
riserva (ree-*sehr*-vah) *f* reserve; store; qualification; **di** ~ spare; ~ **di selvaggina** game reserve
riservare (ree-sayr-*vaa*-ray) *v* reserve, engage
riservato (ree-sayr-*vaa*-toa) *adj* reserved; modest
riso[1] (*ree*-soa) *m* laugh
riso[2] (*ree*-soa) *m* rice
risoluto (ree-soa-*lōō*-toa) *adj* determined, resolute
***risolvere** (ree-*sol*-vay-ray) *v* solve
risparmi (ree-*spahr*-mee) *mpl* savings *pl*
risparmiare (ree-spahr-*myaa*-ray) *v* save
rispedire (ree-spay-*dee*-ray) *v* *send back
rispettabile (ree-spayt-*taa*-bee-lay) *adj* respectable
rispettare (ree-spayt-*taa*-ray) *v* respect
rispettivo (ree-spayt-*tee*-voa) *adj* respective
rispetto (ree-*speht*-toa) *m* esteem, respect
rispettoso (ree-spayt-*tōā*-soa) *adj* respectful

risplendere (ree-*splehn*-day-ray) *v* *shine
***rispondere** (ree-*spoan*-day-ray) *v* answer; reply
risposta (ree-*spoa*-stah) *f* answer, reply; **in** ~ in reply; **senza** ~ unanswered
ristorante (ree-stoa-*rahn*-tay) *m* restaurant
risultare (ree-sool-*taa*-ray) *v* result; appear
risultato (ree-sool-*taa*-toa) *m* result; issue, effect, outcome
risvolta (ree-*svol*-tah) *f* lapel
ritardare (ree-tahr-*daa*-ray) *v* delay
ritardo (ree-*tahr*-doa) *m* delay; **in** ~ late, overdue
***ritenere** (ree-tay-*nay*-ray) *v* consider
ritirare (ree-tee-*raa*-ray) *v* *withdraw; *draw
ritmo (*reet*-moa) *m* rhythm
ritornare (ree-toar-*naa*-ray) *v* turn back, return
ritorno (ree-*toar*-noa) *m* return; way back; **andata e** ~ round trip *Am*
ritratto (ree-*traht*-toa) *m* portrait
ritrovare (ree-troa-*vaa*-ray) *v* recover, *find back
ritto (*reet*-toa) *adj* erect
riunione (ryoo-*nyōā*-nay) *f* assembly, meeting
riunire (ryoo-*nee*-ray) *v* reunite; assemble; join
***riuscire** (ryoosh-*shee*-ray) *v* manage, succeed; *make; **riuscito** successful
riva (*ree*-vah) *f* bank, shore; ~ **del mare** seashore
rivale (ree-*vaa*-lay) *m* rival
rivaleggiare (ree-vah-layd-*jaa*-ray) *v* rival
rivalità (ree-vah-lee-*tah*) *f* rivalry
***rivedere** (ree-vay-*day*-ray) *v* check
rivelare (ree-vay-*laa*-ray) *v* reveal
rivelazione (ree-vay-lah-*tsyōā*-nay) *f* revelation
rivendicare (ree-vayn-dee-*kaa*-ray) *v* claim
rivendicazione (ree-vayn-dee-kah-*tsyōā*-nay) *f* claim
rivenditore (ree-vayn-dee-*tōā*-ray) *m* retailer
rivista (ree-*vee*-stah) *f* magazine, review; revue; ~ **mensile** monthly magazine
***rivolgersi a** (ree-*vol*-jayr-see) address
rivolgimento (ree-voal-jee-*mayn*-toa) *m* reverse
rivolta (ree-*vol*-tah) *f* revolt, rebellion
rivoltante (ree-voal-*tahn*-tay) *adj* revolting
rivoltarsi (ree-voal-*tahr*-see) *v* revolt
rivoltella (ree-voal-*tehl*-lah) *f* gun, revolver
rivoluzionario (ree-voa-loo-tsyoa-*naa*-ryoa) *adj* revolutionary
rivoluzione (ree-voa-loo-*tsyōā*-nay) *f* revolution
roba (*raw*-bah) *f* stuff
robaccia (roa-*baht*-chah) *f* trash
robusto (roa-*boo*-stoa) *adj* robust, solid, strong
roccaforte (roak-kah-*for*-tay) *f* stronghold
rocchetto (roak-*kayt*-toa) *m* spool
roccia (*rot*-chah) *f* rock
roccioso (roat-*chōā*-soa) *adj* rocky
roco (*raw*-koa) *adj* hoarse
Romania (roa-mah-*nee*-ah) *f* Rumania
romantico (roa-*mahn*-tee-koa) *adj* romantic
romanziere (roa-mahn-*dzyai*-ray) *m* novelist
romanzo (roa-*mahn*-dzoa) *m* novel; ~ **a puntate** serial; ~ **poliziesco** detective story
rombo[1] (*roam*-boa) *m* roar
rombo[2] (*roam*-boa) *m* brill
romeno (roa-*mai*-noa) *adj* Rumanian;

m Rumanian
***rompere** (*roam*-pay-ray) *v* *break
rompicapo (roam-pee-*kaa*-poa) *m* puzzle
rondine (*roan*-dee-nay) *f* swallow
rosa (*raw*-zah) *f* rose; *adj* rose, pink
rosario (roa-*zaa*-ryoa) *m* rosary, beads *pl*
rosolaccio (roa-zoa-*laht*-choa) *m* poppy
rospo (*ro*-spoa) *m* toad
rossetto (roass-*sayt*-toa) *m* lipstick; rouge
rosso (*roass*-soa) *adj* red
rosticceria (roa-steet-chay-*ree*-ah) *f* grill-room
rotabile (roa-*taa*-bee-lay) *f* carriage-way; roadway *nAm*
rotolare (roa-toa-*laa*-ray) *v* roll
rotolo (*raw*-toa-loa) *m* roll
rotonda (roa-*toan*-dah) *f* roundabout
rotondo (roa-*toan*-doa) *adj* round
rotta (*roat*-tah) *f* route; course
rotto (*roat*-toa) *adj* broken
rottura (roat-*tōō*-rah) *f* break
rotula (*raw*-too-lah) *f* kneecap
roulette (roo-*leht*) *f* roulette
roulotte (roo-*lot*-tay) *f* trailer *nAm*
rovesciare (roa-vaysh-*shaa*-ray) *v* *spill, knock over; *overthrow; turn inside out; **rovesciarsi** overturn
rovescio (roa-*vehsh*-shoa) *m* reverse; **alla rovescia** the other way round; inside out
rovina (roa-*vee*-nah) *f* destruction, ruination, ruin; **rovine** ruins
rovinare (roa-vee-*naa*-ray) *v* ruin
rozzo (*road*-dzoa) *adj* gross
rubare (roo-*baa*-ray) *v* *steal; rob
rubinetto (roo-bee-*nayt*-toa) *m* tap; faucet *nAm*
rubino (roo-*bee*-noa) *m* ruby
rubrica (roo-*bree*-kah) *f* column
ruga (*rōō*-gah) *f* wrinkle
ruggine (*rood*-jee-nay) *f* rust
ruggire (rood-*jee*-ray) *v* roar
ruggito (rood-*jee*-toa) *m* roar
rugiada (roo-*jaa*-dah) *f* dew
rumore (roo-*mōā*-ray) *m* noise
rumoroso (roo-moa-*rōā*-soa) *adj* noisy
ruota (*rwaw*-tah) *f* wheel; ~ **di ricambio** spare wheel
rurale (roo-*raa*-lay) *adj* rural
ruscello (roosh-*shehl*-loa) *m* brook, stream
russare (rooss-*saa*-ray) *v* snore
Russia (*rooss*-syah) *f* Russia
russo (*rooss*-soa) *adj* Russian; *m* Russian
rustico (*roo*-stee-koa) *adj* rustic
ruvido (*rōō*-vee-doa) *adj* uneven

S

sabato (*saa*-bah-toa) *m* Saturday
sabbia (*sahb*-byah) *f* sand
sabbioso (sahb-*byōā*-soa) *adj* sandy
saccarina (sahk-kah-*ree*-nah) *f* saccharin
sacchetto (sahk-*kayt*-toa) *m* paper bag; pouch
sacco (*sahk*-koa) *m* bag, sack; ~ **a pelo** sleeping-bag
sacerdote (sah-chayr-*daw*-tay) *m* priest
sacrificare (sah-kree-fee-*kaa*-ray) *v* sacrifice
sacrificio (sah-kree-*fee*-choa) *m* sacrifice
sacrilegio (sah-kree-*lai*-joa) *m* sacrilege
sacro (*saa*-kroa) *adj* sacred
saggezza (sahd-*jayt*-tsah) *f* wisdom
saggiare (sahd-*jaa*-ray) *v* test
saggio (*sahd*-joa) *adj* wise; *m* essay
sagrestano (sah-gray-*staa*-noa) *m* sex-

ton
sala (*saa*-lah) *f* hall; ~ **da ballo** ballroom; ~ **da banchetto** banqueting-hall; ~ **da concerti** concert hall; ~ **da pranzo** dining-room; ~ **d'aspetto** waiting-room; ~ **da tè** tea-shop; ~ **di esposizione** showroom; ~ **di lettura** reading-room; ~ **per fumatori** smoking-room
salariato (sah-lah-*ryaa*-toa) *m* employee
salario (sah-*laa*-ryoa) *m* salary, pay
salassare (sah-lahss-*saa*-ray) *v* *bleed
salato (sah-*laa*-toa) *adj* salty
saldare (sahl-*daa*-ray) *v* weld, solder; *pay off
saldatore (sahl-dah-*tōā*-ray) *m* soldering-iron
saldatura (sahl-dah-*tōō*-rah) *f* joint
saldo (*sahl*-doa) *adj* firm; *m* balance; **saldi** sales
sale (*saa*-lay) *m* salt; **sali da bagno** bath salts
saliera (sah-*lyai*-rah) *f* salt-cellar
***salire** (sah-*lee*-ray) *v* ascend; *rise, increase
saliva (sah-*lee*-vah) *f* spit
salmone (sahl-*mōā*-nay) *m* salmon
salone (sah-*lōā*-nay) *m* salon; lounge; ~ **di bellezza** beauty salon, beauty parlour
salotto (sah-*lot*-toa) *m* drawing-room, living-room; **salottino di prova** fitting room
salsa (*sahl*-sah) *f* sauce
salsiccia (sahl-*seet*-chah) *f* sausage
saltare (sahl-*taa*-ray) *v* jump
saltellare (sahl-tayl-*laa*-ray) *v* skip, hop
saltello (sahl-*tehl*-loa) *m* hop
salto (*sahl*-toa) *m* leap, jump
salubre (sah-*lōō*-bray) *adj* wholesome
salutare (sah-loo-*taa*-ray) *v* greet; salute
salute (sah-*lōō*-tay) *f* health
saluto (sah-*lōō*-toa) *m* greeting
salvare (sahl-*vaa*-ray) *v* save, rescue
salvataggio (sahl-vah-*tahd*-joa) *m* rescue; **cintura di** ~ lifebelt
salvatore (sahl-vah-*tōā*-ray) *m* saviour
salvo (*sahl*-voa) *prep* except
sanatorio (sah-nah-*taw*-ryoa) *m* sanatorium
sandalo (*sahn*-dah-loa) *m* sandal
sangue (*sahng*-gway) *m* blood
sanguinare (sahng-gwee-*naa*-ray) *v* *bleed
sanitario (sah-nee-*taa*-ryoa) *adj* sanitary
sano (*saa*-noa) *adj* healthy; well
santo (*sahn*-toa) *adj* holy; *m* saint
santuario (sahn-*twaa*-ryoa) *m* shrine
***sapere** (sah-*pāȳ*-ray) *v* taste; *know; *be able to
sapone (sah-*pōā*-nay) *m* soap; ~ **da barba** shaving-soap; ~ **in polvere** soap powder
sapore (sah-*pōā*-ray) *m* taste
saporito (sah-poa-*ree*-toa) *adj* savoury, tasty
sardina (sahr-*dee*-nah) *f* sardine
sarta (*sahr*-tah) *f* dressmaker
sarto (*sahr*-toa) *m* tailor
sasso (*sahss*-soa) *m* stone
satellite (sah-*tehl*-lee-tay) *m* satellite
saudita (sou-*dee*-tah) *adj* Saudi Arabian
sauna (*sou*-nah) *f* sauna
sbadigliare (zbah-dee-*lyaa*-ray) *v* yawn
sbagliarsi (zbah-*lyahr*-see) *v* *be mistaken
sbagliato (zbah-*lyaa*-toa) *adj* false, wrong; misplaced
sbaglio (*zbaa*-lyoa) *m* mistake, error
sbalordire (zbah-loar-*dee*-ray) *v* astonish
sbarcare (zbahr-*kaa*-ray) *v* land, disembark
sbarra (*zbahr*-rah) *f* bar; rail

sbattere (*zbaht*-tay-ray) *v* slam; whip
sbiadire (zbyah-*dee*-ray) *v* fade
sbottonare (zboat-toa-*naa*-ray) *v* unbutton
sbucciare (zboot-*chaa*-ray) *v* peel
scaccato (skahk-*kaa*-toa) *adj* chequered
scacchi (*skahk*-kee) *mpl* chess
scacchiera (skahk-*kyai*-rah) *f* draughtboard; checkerboard *nAm*
scacciare (skaht-*chaa*-ray) *v* chase
scacco! (*skahk*-koa) check!
scadente (skah-*dehn*-tay) *adj* poor
scadenza (skah-*dehn*-tsah) *f* expiry
***scadere** (skah-*dāy*-ray) *v* expire
scaffale (skahf-*faa*-lay) *m* shelf
scala (*skaa*-lah) *f* stairs *pl*, staircase; ladder; scale; ~ **di sicurezza** fire-escape; ~ **mobile** escalator; ~ **musicale** scale
scaldare (skahl-*daa*-ray) *v* warm, heat; **scaldacqua ad immersione** immersion heater
scalfire (skahl-*fee*-ray) *v* scratch
scalfittura (skahl-feet-*tōō*-rah) *f* scratch
scalino (skah-*lee*-noa) *m* step
scalo (*skaa*-loa) *m* dock
scalpello (skahl-*pehl*-loa) *m* chisel
scalpore (skahl-*pōā*-ray) *m* fuss
scambiare (skahm-*byaa*-ray) *v* exchange
scambio (*skahm*-byoa) *m* exchange; points *pl*
scandalo (*skahn*-dah-loa) *m* scandal; offence
Scandinavia (skahn-dee-*naa*-vyah) *f* Scandinavia
scandinavo (skahn-dee-*naa*-voa) *adj* Scandinavian; *m* Scandinavian
scappamento (skahp-pah-*mayn*-toa) *m* exhaust
scappare (skahp-*paa*-ray) *v* escape; slip
scarabeo (skah-rah-*bai*-oa) *m* beetle
scaricare (skah-ree-*kaa*-ray) *v* discharge, unload
scarlatto (skahr-*laht*-toa) *adj* scarlet
scarpa (*skahr*-pah) *f* shoe; **lucido per scarpe** shoe polish; **scarpe da ginnastica** gym shoes, plimsolls *pl*; sneakers *plAm*; **scarpe da tennis** tennis shoes; **stringa per scarpe** shoe-lace
scarrozzata (skahr-roat-*tsaa*-tah) *f* drive
scarsamente (skahr-sah-*mayn*-tay) *adv* scarcely
scarsezza (skahr-*sayt*-tsah) *f* want
scarso (*skahr*-soa) *adj* scarce; slight, small
scartare (skahr-*taa*-ray) *v* discard
scassinare (skahss-see-*naa*-ray) *v* burgle
scassinatore (skahss-see-nah-*tōā*-ray) *m* burglar
scatola (*skaa*-toa-lah) *f* box; ~ **di colori** paint-box; ~ **di fiammiferi** match-box
scatolone (skah-toa-*lōā*-nay) *m* carton
scavare (skah-*vaa*-ray) *v* *dig
scavo (*skaa*-voa) *m* excavation
***scegliere** (*shai*-lʸay-ray) *v* *choose; pick, select; elect
scellerato (shayl-lay-*raa*-toa) *adj* wicked
scelta (*shayl*-tah) *f* choice; pick, selection
scelto (*shayl*-toa) *adj* select
scena (*shai*-nah) *f* scene; stage
scenario (shay-*naa*-ryoa) *m* setting
***scendere** (*shayn*-day-ray) *v* descend; *get off
scheggia (*skayd*-jah) *f* splinter, chip
scheggiare (skayd-*jaa*-ray) *v* chip
scheletro (*skai*-lay-troa) *m* skeleton
schema (*skai*-mah) *m* scheme; diagram

schermo (*skayr*-moa) *m* screen
scherno (*skayr*-noa) *m* scorn
scherzare (skayr-*tsaa*-ray) *v* joke
scherzo (*skayr*-tsoa) *m* joke; fun
schiaccianoci (skyaht-chah-*nōā*-chee) *m* nutcrackers *pl*
schiacciare (skyaht-*chaa*-ray) *v* mash; press; overwhelm
schiaffeggiare (skyahf-fayd-*jaa*-ray) *v* slap
schiaffo (*skyahf*-foa) *m* slap
schiarimento (skyah-ree-*mayn*-toa) *m* explanation
schiavo (*skyaa*-voa) *m* slave
schioccare (skyoak-*kaa*-ray) *v* crack
schiocco (*skyok*-koa) *m* crack
schiuma (*skyōō*-mah) *f* lather, foam, froth
schivo (*skee*-voa) *adj* shy
schizzare (skeet-*tsaa*-ray) *v* splash
schizzo (*skeet*-tsoa) *m* sketch
sci (shee) *m* ski; skiing; **scarponi da** ~ ski boots; ~ **d'acqua** water ski
sciacquare (shahk-*kwaa*-ray) *v* rinse
sciacquata (shahk-*kwaa*-tah) *f* rinse
sciagura (shah-*gōō*-rah) *f* disaster
scialle (*shahl*-lay) *m* scarf, shawl
sciare (*shyaa*-ray) *v* ski
sciarpa (*shahr*-pah) *f* scarf
sciatore (shyah-*tōā*-ray) *m* skier
sciatto (*shaht*-toa) *adj* slovenly
scientifico (shayn-*tee*-fee-koa) *adj* scientific
scienza (*shehn*-tsah) *f* science
scienziato (shayn-*tsyaa*-toa) *m* scientist
scimmia (*sheem*-myah) *f* monkey
scintilla (sheen-*teel*-lah) *f* spark
scintillante (sheen-teel-*lahn*-tay) *adj* sparkling
scintillare (sheen-teel-*laa*-ray) *v* *shine
sciocchezza (shoak-*kayt*-tsah) *f* rubbish, nonsense
sciocco (*shok*-koa) *adj* crazy, foolish, silly; *m* fool
***sciogliere** (*shaw*-lʸay-ray) *v* dissolve
scioperare (shoa-pay-*raa*-ray) *v* *strike
sciopero (*shaw*-pay-roa) *m* strike
sciroppo (shee-*rop*-poa) *m* syrup
scivolare (shee-voa-*laa*-ray) *v* glide, slip; skid
scivolata (shee-voa-*laa*-tah) *f* slide
scivolo (*shee*-voa-loa) *m* slide
scodella (skoa-*dehl*-lah) *f* soup-plate
scogliera (skoa-*lʸāȳ*-rah) *f* cliff
scoglio (*skaw*-lʸoa) *m* cliff
scoiattolo (skoa-*yaht*-toa-loa) *m* squirrel
scolara (skoa-*laa*-rah) *f* schoolgirl
scolaro (skoa-*laa*-roa) *m* schoolboy; pupil
scolo (*skōā*-loa) *m* drain
scolorirsi (skoa-loa-*reer*-see) *v* fade, discolour
scommessa (skoam-*mayss*-sah) *f* bet
***scommettere** (skoam-*mayt*-tay-ray) *v* *bet
scomodità (skoa-moa-dee-*tah*) *f* inconvenience
scomodo (*skaw*-moa-doa) *adj* uncomfortable
***scomparire** (skoam-pah-*ree*-ray) *v* disappear
scompartimento (skoam-pahr-tee-*mayn*-toa) *m* compartment; ~ **per fumatori** smoker
scomparto (skoam-*pahr*-toa) *m* section
***sconfiggere** (skoan-*feed*-jay-ray) *v* defeat
sconfinato (skoan-fee-*naa*-toa) *adj* unlimited
sconfitta (skoan-*feet*-tah) *f* defeat
sconosciuto (skoa-noash-*shōō*-toa) *adj* unfamiliar
sconsiderato (skoan-see-day-*raa*-toa) *adj* rash
scontentare (skoan-tayn-*taa*-ray) *v* displease

scontento (skoan-*tehn*-toa) *adj* dissatisfied, discontented
sconto (*skoan*-toa) *m* discount, rebate; **tasso di ~** bank-rate
scontrarsi (skoan-*trahr*-see) *v* crash
scontro (*skoan*-troa) *m* collision, crash
scopa (*skōā*-pah) *f* broom
scopare (skoa-*paa*-ray) *v* *sweep
scoperta (skoa-*pehr*-tah) *f* discovery
scopo (*skaw*-poa) *m* design; **allo ~ di** to, in order to
scoppiare (skoap-*pyaa*-ray) *v* *burst
scoppio (*skop*-pyoa) *m* outbreak
***scoprire** (skoa-*pree*-ray) *v* uncover; detect, discover
***scorgere** (*skor*-jay-ray) *v* perceive
***scorrere** (*skoar*-ray-ray) *v* flow, stream
scorretto (skoar-*reht*-toa) *adj* incorrect
scorso (*skoar*-soa) *adj* past, last
scorta (*skor*-tah) *f* escort; stock
scortare (skoar-*taa*-ray) *v* escort
scortese (skoar-*tāȳ*-zay) *adj* unkind, impolite
scossa (*skoss*-sah) *f* shock
Scozia (*skaw*-tsyah) *f* Scotland
scozzese (skoat-*tsāȳ*-say) *adj* Scottish, Scotch; *m* Scot
scriminatura (skree-mee-nah-*tōō*-rah) *f* parting
scritto (*skreet*-toa) *m* writing
scrittoio (skreet-*tōā*-yoa) *m* bureau
scrittore (skreet-*tōā*-ray) *m* writer
scrittura (skreet-*tōō*-rah) *f* handwriting
scrivania (skree-vah-*nee*-ah) *f* desk
scrivano (skree-*vaa*-noa) *m* clerk
***scrivere** (*skree*-vay-ray) *v* *write
scrupoloso (skroo-poa-*lōā*-soa) *adj* careful
sculacciata (skoo-laht-*chaa*-tah) *f* spanking
scultore (skool-*tōā*-ray) *m* sculptor
scultura (skool-*tōō*-rah) *f* sculpture; ~ **in legno** wood-carving, carving
scuola (*skwaw*-lah) *f* school; **marinare la ~** play truant; **~ di equitazione** riding-school; **~ media** secondary school
***scuotere** (*skwaw*-tay-ray) *v* shock
scuro (*skōō*-roa) *adj* obscure
scusa (*skōō*-zah) *f* apology, excuse
scusare (skoo-*zaa*-ray) *v* excuse; **scusa**! sorry!; **scusarsi** apologize
sdolcinatura (zdoal-chee-nah-*tōō*-rah) *f* tear-jerker
sdraiarsi (zdrah-*yahr*-see) *v* *lie down
sdrucciolevole (zdroot-choa-*lāȳ*-voa-lay) *adj* slippery
se (say) *conj* if; whether; **se … o** whether … or
sé (say) *pron* oneself
sebbene (sayb-*bai*-nay) *conj* though, although
seccatore (sayk-kah-*tōā*-ray) *m* bore
seccatura (sayk-kah-*tōō*-rah) *f* nuisance
secchio (*sayk*-kyoa) *m* pail, bucket
secolo (*sai*-koa-loa) *m* century
secondario (say-koan-*daa*-ryoa) *adj* secondary, subordinate
secondo[1] (say-*koan*-doa) *num* second
secondo[2] (say-*koan*-doa) *prep* according to
secondo[3] (say-*koan*-doa) *m* second
sedano (*sai*-dah-noa) *m* celery
sedativo (say-dah-*tee*-voa) *m* sedative
sede (*sai*-day) *f* seat
sedere (say-*dāȳ*-ray) *m* bottom
***sedere** (say-*dāȳ*-ray) *v* *sit; ***sedersi** *sit down
sedia (*sai*-dyah) *f* chair, seat; **~ a rotelle** wheelchair; **~ a sdraio** deck chair
sedicesimo (say-dee-*chai*-zee-moa) *num* sixteenth
sedici (*sāȳ*-dee-chee) *num* sixteen
sedimento (say-dee-*mayn*-toa) *m* de-

posit
***sedurre** (say-*door*-ray) *v* seduce
seduta (say-*dōō*-tah) *f* session
sega (*sāy*-gah) *f* saw
segatura (say-gah-*tōō*-rah) *f* sawdust
seggio (*sehd*-joa) *m* chair
segheria (say-gay-*ree*-ah) *f* saw-mill
segmento (sayg-*mayn*-toa) *m* stretch
segnalare (say-ñah-*laa*-ray) *v* signal; indicate
segnale (say-*ñaa*-lay) *m* signal; ~ **di soccorso** distress signal
segnare (say-*ñaa*-ray) *v* tick off, mark
segno (*sāy*-ñoa) *m* sign; mark; token, signal
segretaria (say-gray-*taa*-ryah) *f* secretary
segretario (say-gray-*taa*-ryoa) *m* clerk, secretary
segreto (say-*grāy*-toa) *adj* secret; *m* secret
seguente (say-*gwehn*-tay) *adj* following
seguire (say-*gwee*-ray) *v* follow; **in seguito** then, afterwards
seguitare (say-gooæh-*taa*-ray) *v* continue
sei (say) *num* six
selezionare (say-lay-tsyoa-*naa*-ray) *v* select; **selezionato** select
selezione (say-lay-*tsyōā*-nay) *f* selection; choice
sella (*sehl*-lah) *f* saddle
selvaggina (sayl-vahd-*jee*-nah) *f* game
selvaggio (sayl-*vahd*-joa) *adj* fierce, savage
selvatico (sayl-*vaa*-tee-koa) *adj* wild
semaforo (say-*maa*-foa-roa) *m* traffic light
sembrare (saym-*braa*-ray) *v* appear, seem, look
seme (*sāy*-may) *m* pip
semenza (say-*mehn*-tsah) *f* seed
semi- (say-mee) semi-
semicerchio (say-mee-*chehr*-kyoa) *m* semicircle
seminare (say-mee-*naa*-ray) *v* *sow
seminterrato (say-meen-tayr-*raa*-toa) *m* basement
semplice (*saym*-plee-chay) *adj* simple; plain
sempre (*sehm*-pray) *adv* always, ever; ~ **diritto** straight ahead
senape (*sai*-nah-pay) *f* mustard
senato (say-*naa*-toa) *m* senate
senatore (say-nah-*tōā*-ray) *m* senator
senile (say-*nee*-lay) *adj* senile
seno (*sāy*-noa) *m* breast, bosom
sensato (sayn-*saa*-toa) *adj* down-to-earth
sensazionale (sayn-sah-tsyoa-*naa*-lay) *adj* sensational
sensazione (sayn-sah-*tsyōā*-nay) *f* feeling; sensation
sensibile (sayn-*see*-bee-lay) *adj* sensitive
sensibilità (sayn-see-bee-lee-*tah*) *f* sensibility
senso (*sehn*-soa) *m* sense; reason; ~ **unico** one-way traffic
sentenza (sayn-*tehn*-tsah) *f* sentence, verdict
sentiero (sayn-*tyai*-roa) *m* trail, path, lane, footpath
sentimentale (sayn-tee-mayn-*taa*-lay) *adj* sentimental
sentimento (sayn-tee-*mayn*-toa) *m* feeling
sentire (sayn-*tee*-ray) *v* *feel; listen
senza (*sehn*-tsah) *prep* without; **senz'altro** without fail
separare (say-pah-*raa*-ray) *v* part, separate, divide; **separato** separate
separatamente (say-pah-rah-tah-*mayn*-tay) *adv* apart
sepoltura (say-poal-*tōō*-rah) *f* burial
seppellimento (sayp-payl-lee-*mayn*-toa) *m* burial

seppellire (sayp-payl-*lee*-ray) *v* bury
sequenza (say-*kwehn*-tsah) *f* shot
sequestrare (say-kway-*straa*-ray) *v* confiscate, impound
sera (*sāy*-rah) *f* evening, night
serbatoio (sayr-bah-*tōā*-yoa) *m* reservoir, tank; ~ **di benzina** petrol tank
sereno (say-*rāy*-noa) *adj* serene
serie (*sai*-ryay) *f* (pl~) series, sequence
serietà (say-ryay-*tah*) *f* seriousness; gravity
serio (*sai*-ryoa) *adj* serious
sermone (sayr-*mōā*-nay) *m* sermon
serpeggiante (sayr-payd-*jahn*-tay) *adj* winding
serpente (sayr-*pehn*-tay) *m* snake
serra (*sehr*-rah) *f* greenhouse
serrare (sayr-*raa*-ray) *v* tighten
serratura (sayr-rah-*tōō*-rah) *f* lock
servire (sayr-*vee*-ray) *v* attend on, serve, wait on
servitore (sayr-vee-*tōā*-ray) *m* servant
servizievole (sayr-vee-*tsyāy*-voa-lay) *adj* obliging, helpful
servizio (sayr-*vee*-tsyoa) *m* service; service charge; ~ **da tavola** dinner-service; ~ **da tè** tea-set; ~ **in camera** room service; ~ **postale** postal service
servo (*sehr*-voa) *m* boy
sessanta (sayss-*sahn*-tah) *num* sixty
sessione (sayss-*syōā*-nay) *f* session
sesso (*sehss*-soa) *m* sex
sessuale (sayss-*swaa*-lay) *adj* sexual
sessualità (sayss-swah-lee-*tah*) *f* sexuality
sesto (*seh*-stoa) *num* sixth
seta (*sāy*-tah) *f* silk; **di** ~ silken
setacciare (sayt-taht-*chaa*-ray) *v* sieve
setaccio (say-*taht*-choa) *m* sieve
sete (*sāy*-tay) *f* thirst
settanta (sayt-*tahn*-tah) *num* seventy
sette (*seht*-tay) *num* seven
settembre (sayt-*tehm*-bray) September
settentrionale (sayt-tayn-tryoa-*naa*-lay) *adj* northerly, north
settentrione (sayt-tayn-*tryōā*-nay) *m* north
setticemia (sayt-tee-chay-*mee*-ah) *f* blood-poisoning
settico (*seht*-tee-koa) *adj* septic
settimana (sayt-tee-*maa*-nah) *f* week
settimanale (sayt-tee-mah-*naa*-lay) *adj* weekly
settimo (*seht*-tee-moa) *num* seventh
settore (sayt-*tōā*-ray) *m* field
severo (say-*vai*-roa) *adj* harsh, strict, severe
sezione (say-*tsyōā*-nay) *f* department; section
sfacciato (sfaht-*chaa*-toa) *adj* bold
sfavorevole (sfah-voa-*rāy*-voa-lay) *adj* unfavourable
sfera (*sfai*-rah) *f* sphere
sfida (*sfee*-dah) *f* challenge
sfidare (sfee-*daa*-ray) *v* challenge, dare
sfilacciarsi (sfee-laht-*chahr*-see) *v* fray
sfiorare (sfyoa-*raa*-ray) *v* skim over; touch on
sfondo (*sfoan*-doa) *m* background
sfortuna (sfoar-*tōō*-nah) *f* bad luck, misfortune
sfortunato (sfoar-too-*naa*-toa) *adj* unfortunate, unlucky
sforzarsi (sfoar-*tsahr*-see) *v* try
sforzo (*sfor*-tsoa) *m* effort; strain
sfrontato (sfroan-*taa*-toa) *adj* bold
sfruttare (sfroot-*taa*-ray) *v* exploit
sfuggire (sfood-*jee*-ray) *v* escape
sfumatura (sfoo-mah-*tōō*-rah) *f* nuance
sgangerato (zgahng-gay-*raa*-toa) *adj* ramshackle
sgarbato (zgahr-*baa*-toa) *adj* unkind
sgocciolamento (zgoat-choa-lah-*mayn*-toa) *m* leak
sgombrare (zgoam-*braa*-ray) *v* vacate

sgombro (*zgoam*-broa) *m* mackerel
sgomentare (zgoa-mayn-*taa*-ray) *v* terrify
sgradevole (zgrah-*dāy*-voa-lay) *adj* disagreeable, unpleasant, nasty
sguardo (*zgwahr*-doa) *m* look
si (see) *pron* himself; herself; themselves
sì (see) yes
sia ... sia (*see*-ah) both ... and
Siam (syahm) *m* Siam
siamese (syah-*māy*-zay) *adj* Siamese; *m* Siamese
siccità (seet-chee-*tah*) *f* drought
siccome (seek-*kōā*-may) *conj* as
sicurezza (see-koo-*rayt*-tsah) *f* safety, security; **cintura di ~** safety-belt, seat-belt
sicuro (see-*kōō*-roa) *adj* safe, secure; sure
siepe (*syai*-pay) *f* hedge
siero (*syai*-roa) *m* serum
sifone (see-*fōā*-nay) *m* siphon, syphon
sigaretta (see-gah-*rayt*-tah) *f* cigarette
sigaro (*see*-gah-roa) *m* cigar
sigillo (see-*jeel*-loa) *m* seal
significare (see-ñee-fee-*kaa*-ray) *v* *mean
significativo (see-ñee-fee-kah-*tee*-voa) *adj* significant
significato (see-ñee-fee-*kaa*-toa) *m* meaning, sense
signora (see-*ñōā*-rah) *f* lady; mistress; madam
signore (see-*ñōā*-ray) *m* gentleman; mister; sir
signorina (see-ñoa-*ree*-nah) *f* miss
silenziatore (see-layn-tsyah-*tōā*-ray) *m* silencer; muffler *nAm*
silenzio (see-*lehn*-tsyoa) *m* silence
silenzioso (see-layn-*tsyōā*-soa) *adj* silent
sillaba (*seel*-lah-bah) *f* syllable
simbolo (*seem*-boa-loa) *m* symbol
simile (*see*-mee-lay) *adj* alike, like; such; similar
simpatia (seem-pah-*tee*-ah) *f* sympathy
simpatico (seem-*paa*-tee-koa) *adj* pleasant, nice
simulare (see-moo-*laa*-ray) *v* simulate
simultaneo (see-mool-*taa*-nay-oa) *adj* simultaneous
sinagoga (see-nah-*gaw*-gah) *f* synagogue
sincero (seen-*chai*-roa) *adj* honest, sincere
sindacato (seen-dah-*kaa*-toa) *m* trade-union
sindaco (*seen*-dah-koa) *m* mayor
sinfonia (seen-foa-*nee*-ah) *f* symphony
singhiozzo (seeng-*geeot*-tsoa) *m* hiccup
singolare (seeng-goa-*laa*-ray) *adj* queer; *m* singular
singolarità (seeng-goa-lah-ree-*tah*) *f* peculiarity
singolo (*seeng*-goa-loa) *adj* individual, single; *m* individual
sinistro (see-*nee*-stroa) *adj* left-hand, left; ominous, sinister; **a sinistra** left-hand
sino a (*see*-noa ah) as far as, till
sinonimo (see-*naw*-nee-moa) *m* synonym
sintetico (seen-*tai*-tee-koa) *adj* synthetic
sintomo (*seen*-toa-moa) *m* symptom
sintonizzare (seen-toa-need-*dzaa*-ray) *v* tune in
sipario (see-*paa*-ryoa) *m* curtain
sirena (see-*rai*-nah) *f* siren; mermaid
Siria (*see*-ryah) *f* Syria
siriano (see-*ryaa*-noa) *adj* Syrian; *m* Syrian
siringa (see-*reeng*-gah) *f* syringe
sistema (see-*stai*-mah) *m* system; **~ decimale** decimal system; **~ di raf-**

freddamento cooling system; ~ **lubrificante** lubrication system
sistemare (see-stay-*maa*-ray) *v* settle; **sistemarsi** settle down
sistematico (see-stay-*maa*-tee-koa) *adj* systematic
sistemazione (see-stay-mah-*tsyōā*-nay) *f* accommodation
sito (*see*-toa) *m* site
situato (see-*twaa*-toa) *adj* situated
situazione (see-twah-*tsyōā*-nay) *f* situation; position
slacciare (zlaht-*chaa*-ray) *v* unfasten, untie
slegare (zlay-*gaa*-ray) *v* loosen; **slegato** loose
slip (zleep) *mpl* briefs *pl*
slitta (*zleet*-tah) *f* sleigh, sledge
slittare (zleet-*taa*-ray) *v* *slide
slogato (zloa-*gaa*-toa) *adj* dislocated
smacchiatore (zmahk-kyah-*tōā*-ray) *m* stain remover, cleaning fluid
smaltare (zmahl-*taa*-ray) *v* glaze; **smaltato** enamelled
smalto (*zmahl*-toa) *m* enamel; ~ **per unghie** nail-polish
smarrire (zmahr-*ree*-ray) *v* *lose; *mislay; **smarrito** lost
smemorato (zmay-moa-*raa*-toa) *adj* forgetful
smeraldo (zmay-*rahl*-doa) *m* emerald
***smettere** (*zmayt*-tay-ray) *v* cease, stop, quit
smisurato (zmee-zoo-*raa*-toa) *adj* immense
smoking (*zmo*-keeng) *m* dinner-jacket; tuxedo *nAm*
smorfia (*zmoar*-fyah) *f* grin
smorto (*zmor*-toa) *adj* dull
smussato (zmooss-*saa*-toa) *adj* dull
snello (*znehl*-loa) *adj* slim, slender
sobborgo (soab-*boar*-goa) *m* suburb; outskirts *pl*
sobrio (*saw*-bryoa) *adj* sober
soccombere (soak-*koam*-bay-ray) *v* succumb
soccorso (soak-*koar*-soa) *m* assistance, aid; **equipaggiamento di pronto** ~ first-aid kit; **pronto** ~ first-aid
sociale (soa-*chaa*-lay) *adj* social
socialismo (soa-chah-*lee*-zmoa) *m* socialism
socialista (soa-chah-*lee*-stah) *adj* socialist; *m* socialist
società (soa-chyay-*tah*) *f* community; society; company
socio (*saw*-choa) *m* associate; partner
***soddisfare** (soad-dee-*sfaa*-ray) *v* satisfy
soddisfazione (soad-dee-sfah-*tsyōā*-nay) *f* satisfaction
sofà (soa-*fah*) *m* sofa
sofferenza (soaf-fay-*rehn*-tsah) *f* suffering
soffiare (soaf-*fyaa*-ray) *v* *blow
soffione (soaf-*fyōā*-nay) *m* dandelion
soffitta (soaf-*feet*-tah) *f* attic
soffitto (soaf-*feet*-toa) *m* ceiling
soffocare (soaf-foa-*kaa*-ray) *v* choke
***soffrire** (soaf-*free*-ray) *v* suffer
soggetto (soad-*jeht*-toa) *m* topic, subject; **soggetto a** subject to, liable to
soggiornare (soad-joar-*naa*-ray) *v* stay
soggiorno (soad-*joar*-noa) *m* stay; sitting-room, living-room
soglia (*saw*-lʸah) *f* threshold
sogliola (*saw*-lʸoa-lah) *f* sole
sognare (soa-*ñaa*-ray) *v* *dream
sogno (*sōā*-ñoa) *m* dream
solamente (soa-lah-*mayn*-tay) *adv* only
solco (*soal*-koa) *m* groove
soldato (soal-*daa*-toa) *m* soldier
sole (*sōā*-lay) *m* sun
soleggiato (soa-layd-*jaa*-toa) *adj* sunny
solenne (soa-*lehn*-nay) *adj* solemn
solido (*saw*-lee-doa) *adj* sound, solid, firm; *m* solid

solitario (soa-lee-*taa*-ryoa) *adj* lonely
solito (*saw*-lee-toa) *adj* customary, usual, ordinary
solitudine (soa-lee-*tōō*-dee-nay) *f* loneliness
sollecito (soal-*lāy*-chee-toa) *adj* prompt
solleticare (soal-lay-tee-*kaa*-ray) *v* tickle
sollevare (soal-lay-*vaa*-ray) *v* lift, raise; *bring up
sollievo (soal-*lʸai*-voa) *m* relief
solo (*sōā*-loa) *adj* only; *adv* only, alone
soltanto (soal-*tahn*-toa) *adv* only, merely
solubile (soa-*lōō*-bee-lay) *adj* soluble
soluzione (soa-loo-*tsyōā*-nay) *f* solution
somiglianza (soa-mee-*lʸahn*-tsah) *f* resemblance
somma (*soam*-mah) *f* amount, sum; ~ **globale** lump sum
sommario (soam-*maa*-ryoa) *m* summary
somministrare (soam-mee-nee-*straa*-ray) *v* administer
sommo (*soam*-moa) *adj* top
sommossa (soam-*moss*-sah) *f* riot
sonare (soa-*naa*-ray) *v* play
sonnifero (soan-*nee*-fay-roa) *m* sleeping-pill
sonno (*soan*-noa) *m* sleep
sonoro (soa-*naw*-roa) *adj* noisy
sopportare (soap-poar-*taa*-ray) *v* *bear, sustain, endure; *go through
sopra (*sōā*-prah) *prep* over; *adv* above; **al di** ~ over; **di** ~ upstairs
soprabito (soa-*praa*-bee-toa) *m* coat; topcoat, overcoat
sopracciglio (soa-praht-*chee*-lʸoa) *m* eyebrow
***sopraffare** (soa-prahf-*faa*-ray) *v* overwhelm
soprappeso (soa-prahp-*pāy*-soa) *m* overweight
soprattutto (soa-praht-*toot*-toa) *adv* most of all, especially
sopravvivenza (soa-prahv-vee-*vehn*-tsah) *f* survival
***sopravvivere** (soa-prahv-*vee*-vay-ray) *v* survive
soprintendenza (soa-preen-tayn-*dehn*-tsah) *f* supervision
***soprintendere** (soa-preen-*tehn*-day-ray) *v* supervise
sordido (*sor*-dee-doa) *adj* filthy
sordo (*soar*-doa) *adj* deaf
sorella (soa-*rehl*-lah) *f* sister
sorgente (soar-*jehn*-tay) *f* source, spring, fountain
***sorgere** (*sor*-jay-ray) *v* *rise; *arise
sorpassare (soar-pahss-*saa*-ray) *v* pass
sorprendente (soar-prayn-*dehn*-tay) *adj* astonishing
***sorprendere** (soar-*prehn*-day-ray) *v* surprise
sorpresa (soar-*prāy*-sah) *f* astonishment, surprise
***sorridere** (soar-*ree*-day-ray) *v* smile
sorriso (soar-*ree*-soa) *m* smile
sorsetto (soar-*sayt*-toa) *m* sip
sorte (*sor*-tay) *f* destiny, lot
sorteggio (soar-*tayd*-joa) *m* draw
sorveglianza (soar-vay-*lʸahn*-tsah) *f* supervision
sorvegliare (soar-vay-*lʸaa*-ray) *v* patrol
***sospendere** (soa-*spehn*-day-ray) *v* discontinue, suspend
sospensione (soa-spayn-*syōā*-nay) *f* suspension
sospettare (soa-spayt-*taa*-ray) *v* suspect
sospetto (soa-*speht*-toa) *adj* suspicious; *m* suspicion
sospettoso (soa-spayt-*tōā*-soa) *adj* suspicious
sostanza (soa-*stahn*-tsah) *f* substance

sostanziale (soa-stahn-*tsyaa*-lay) *adj* substantial
sostare (soa-*staa*-ray) *v* stop
sostegno (soa-*stay*-ñoa) *m* support
***sostenere** (soa-stay-*nay*-ray) *v* *hold up, support
sostituire (soa-stee-*twee*-ray) *v* replace, substitute
sostituto (soa-stee-*too*-toa) *m* deputy, substitute
sottaceti (soat-tah-*chay*-tee) *mpl* pickles *pl*
sotterraneo (soa-tayr-*raa*-nay-oa) *adj* underground
sottile (soat-*tee*-lay) *adj* thin, sheer; subtle
sotto (*soat*-toa) *prep* beneath, below, under; *adv* underneath
sottolineare (soat-toa-lee-nay-*aa*-ray) *v* underline; stress, emphasize
***sottomettere** (soat-toa-*mayt*-tay-ray) *v* subject; ***sottomettersi** submit
***sottoporre** (soat-toa-*poar*-ray) *v* subject; submit
sottoscritto (soat-toa-*skreet*-toa) *m* undersigned
***sottoscrivere** (soat-toa-*skree*-vay-ray) *v* sign
sottosopra (soat-toa-*soa*-prah) upside-down
sottotitolo (soat-toa-*tee*-toa-loa) *m* subtitle
sottovalutare (soat-toa-vah-loo-*taa*-ray) *v* underestimate
sottoveste (soat-toa-*veh*-stay) *f* slip
***sottrarre** (soat-*trahr*-ray) *v* subtract; deduct
sovietico (soa-*vyai*-tee-koa) *adj* Soviet
sovrano (soa-*vraa*-noa) *m* sovereign; ruler
sovvenzione (soav-vayn-*tsyoa*-nay) *f* subsidy
sozzo (*soad*-dzoa) *adj* dirty
spaccare (spahk-*kaa*-ray) *v* crack; chop; **spaccarsi** *burst
spada (*spaa*-dah) *f* sword
Spagna (*spaa*-ñah) *f* Spain
spagnolo (spah-*ñoa*-loa) *adj* Spanish; *m* Spaniard
spago (*spaa*-goa) *m* twine, cord, string
spalancare (spah-lahng-*kaa*-ray) *v* open wide
spalla (*spahl*-lah) *f* shoulder
***spandere** (*spahn*-day-ray) *v* *spill
sparare (spah-*raa*-ray) *v* fire, *shoot
***spargere** *v* *strew; *shed, spill; *spread
sparire (spah-*ree*-ray) *v* disappear, vanish
sparo (*spaa*-roa) *m* shot
sparpagliare (spahr-pah-*lyaa*-ray) *v* scatter
spaventare (spah-vayn-*taa*-ray) *v* scare, frighten; **spaventarsi** *be frightened
spaventevole (spah-vayn-*tay*-voa-lay) *adj* horrible, terrifying
spavento (spah-*vehn*-toa) *m* scare, fright
spaventoso (spah-vayn-*toa*-soa) *adj* dreadful, terrible
spaziare (spah-*tsyaa*-ray) *v* space
spazio (*spaa*-tsyoa) *m* room, space
spazioso (spah-*tsyoa*-soa) *adj* roomy, spacious, large
spazzare (spaht-*tsaa*-ray) *v* wipe
spazzatura (spaht-tsah-*too*-rah) *f* junk, garbage
spazzola (*spaht*-tsoa-lah) *f* brush; ~ **per capelli** hairbrush; ~ **per vestiti** clothes-brush; **spazzolino da denti** toothbrush; **spazzolino per le unghie** nailbrush
spazzolare (spaht-tsoa-*laa*-ray) *v* brush
specchio (*spehk*-kyoa) *m* mirror, looking-glass
speciale (spay-*chaa*-lay) *adj* particular, special, peculiar

specialista (spay-chah-*lee*-stah) *m* specialist
specialità (spay-chah-lee-*tah*) *f* speciality
specializzarsi (spay-chah-leed-*dzahr*-see) *v* specialize
specialmente (spay-chahl-*mayn*-tay) *adv* especially
specie (*spai*-chay) *f* (pl ~) species, breed; sort
specifico (spay-*chee*-fee-koa) *adj* specific
speculare (spay-koo-*laa*-ray) *v* speculate
spedire (spay-*dee*-ray) *v* despatch, dispatch, *send off, *send; ship
spedizione (spay-dee-*tsyōā*-nay) *f* consignment; expedition
***spegnere** (*spai*-ñay-ray) *v* extinguish; *put out, switch off
spelonca (spay-*loang*-kah) *f* cave
***spendere** (*spehn*-day-ray) *v* *spend
spendereccio (spayn-day-*rayt*-choa) *adj* wasteful
spensierato (spayn-syay-*raa*-toa) *adj* carefree
speranza (spay-*rahn*-tsah) *f* hope
speranzoso (spay-rahn-*tsōā*-soa) *adj* hopeful
sperare (spay-*raa*-ray) *v* hope
spergiuro (spayr-*jōō*-roa) *m* perjury
sperimentare (spay-ree-mayn-*taa*-ray) *v* experiment; experience
spesa (*spāȳ*-sah) *f* expense, expenditure; ***fare la** ~ shop; **spese** expenses *pl*, expenditure; **spese di viaggio** fare; travelling expenses
spesso (*spayss*-soa) *adj* thick; *adv* often
spessore (spayss-*sōā*-ray) *m* thickness
spettacolo (spayt-*taa*-koa-loa) *m* spectacle, show; sight; ~ **di varietà** floor show, variety show
spettatore (spayt-tah-*tōā*-ray) *m* spectator
spettro (*speht*-troa) *m* spook, ghost
spezie (*spai*-tsyay) *fpl* spices
spezzare (spayt-*tsaa*-ray) *v* *break; interrupt
spia (*spee*-ah) *f* spy
spiacente (spyah-*chehn*-tay) *adj* sorry
spiacevole (spyah-*chāȳ*-voa-lay) *adj* unpleasant
spiaggia (*spyahd*-jah) *f* beach; ~ **per nudisti** nudist beach
spianata (spyah-*naa*-tah) *f* esplanade
spianato (spyah-*naa*-toa) *adj* level
spiare (*spyaa*-ray) *v* peep
spicciarsi (speet-*chahr*-see) *v* hurry
spiccioli (*speet*-choa-lee) *mpl* change
spiedo (*spyai*-doa) *m* spit
spiegabile (spyay-*gaa*-bee-lay) *adj* accountable
spiegare (spyay-*gaa*-ray) *v* unfold; explain
spiegazione (spyay-gah-*tsyōā*-nay) *f* explanation
spietato (spyay-*taa*-toa) *adj* heartless
spilla (*speel*-lah) *f* brooch
spillo (*speel*-loa) *m* pin; ~ **di sicurezza** safety-pin
spina (*spee*-nah) *f* thorn; plug; ~ **di pesce** fishbone; ~ **dorsale** spine, backbone
spinaci (spee-*naa*-chee) *mpl* spinach
***spingere** (*speen*-jay-ray) *v* push
spinta (*speen*-tah) *f* push
spirare (spee-*raa*-ray) *v* expire
spirito (*spee*-ree-toa) *m* spirit; soul; humour; ghost
spiritoso (spee-ree-*tōā*-soa) *adj* witty, humorous
spirituale (spee-ree-*twaa*-lay) *adj* spiritual
splendido (*splehn*-dee-doa) *adj* splendid; glorious, magnificent, lovely
splendore (splayn-*dōā*-ray) *m* glare; splendour

spogliarsi (spoa-*lʸahr*-see) *v* undress
spogliatoio (spoa-lʸah-*tōā*-yoa) *m* cloakroom
spoglio (*spaw*-lʸoa) *adj* bare, naked
sponda (*spoan*-dah) *f* shore
sporco (*spor*-koa) *adj* dirty, foul
***sporgere** (*spor*-jay-ray) *v* *put out; protrude
sport (sport) *m* sport; ~ **invernali** winter sports; ~ **velico** yachting
sportivo (spoar-*tee*-voa) *m* sportsman
sposa (*spaw*-zah) *f* bride
sposalizio (spoa-zah-*lee*-tsyoa) *m* wedding
sposare (spoa-*zaa*-ray) *v* marry
sposo (*spaw*-zoa) *m* bridegroom
spostamento (spoa-stah-*mayn*-toa) *m* removal
spostare (spoa-*staa*-ray) *v* move, remove
sprecare (spray-*kaa*-ray) *v* waste
spreco (*sprai*-koa) *m* waste
spruzzatore (sproot-tsah-*tōā*-ray) *m* atomizer
spugna (*spōō*-ñah) *f* sponge; towelling
spumante (spoo-*mahn*-tay) *adj* sparkling
spumare (spoo-*maa*-ray) *v* foam
spuntato (spoon-*taa*-toa) *adj* blunt
spuntino (spoon-*tee*-noa) *m* snack
sputare (spoo-*taa*-ray) *v* *spit
sputo (*spōō*-toa) *m* spit
squadra (*skwaa*-drah) *f* team; shift, gang; soccer team
squadriglia (skwah-*dree*-lʸah) *f* squadron
squama (*skwaa*-mah) *f* scale
squattrinato (skwaht-tree-*naa*-toa) *adj* broke
squisito (skwee-*zee*-toa) *adj* exquisite, delicious
stabile (*staa*-bee-lay) *adj* steady, stable, permanent; *m* premises *pl*
stabilire (stah-bee-*lee*-ray) *v* establish; determine
staccare (stahk-*kaa*-ray) *v* detach
stadio (*staa*-dyoa) *m* stadium; stage
staffa (*stahf*-fah) *f* stirrup
stagione (stah-*jōā*-nay) *f* season; **alta** ~ peak season, high season; **bassa** ~ low season; **fuori** ~ off season
stagno (*staa*-ñoa) *m* tin; pond
stagnola (stah-*ñaw*-lah) *f* tinfoil
stalla (*stahl*-lah) *f* stable
stamani (stah-*maa*-nee) *adv* this morning
stampa (*stahm*-pah) *f* press; picture, print, engraving; **stampe** printed matter
stampare (stahm-*paa*-ray) *v* print
stampella (stahm-*pehl*-lah) *f* crutch
stancare (stahng-*kaa*-ray) *v* tire
stanco (*stahng*-koa) *adj* weary, tired
stanotte (stah-*not*-tay) *adv* tonight
stantio (stahn-*tee*-oa) *adj* stuffy
stantuffo (stahn-*toof*-foa) *m* piston; **asta dello** ~ piston-rod
stanza (*stahn*-tsah) *f* room; ~ **da bagno** bathroom
stappare (stahp-*paa*-ray) *v* uncork
***stare** (*staa*-ray) *v* stay; **lasciar** ~ *keep off; ***star disteso** *lie; ~ **attento a** *pay attention to; ~ **in guardia** watch out; ~ **in piedi** *stand
starnutire (stahr-noo-*tee*-ray) *v* sneeze
stasera (stah-*sai*-rah) *adv* tonight
statale (stah-*taa*-lay) *adj* national
statistica (stah-*tee*-stee-kah) *f* statistics *pl*
Stati Uniti (*staa*-tee oo-*nee*-tee) United States, the States
stato (*staa*-toa) *m* state; condition; ~ **di emergenza** emergency
statua (*staa*-twah) *f* statue
stazionario (stah-tsyoa-*naa*-ryoa) *adj* stationary

stazione (stah-*tsyōā*-nay) *f* station; depot *nAm*; ~ **balneare** seaside resort; ~ **centrale** central station; ~ **di servizio** gas station *Am*; ~ **termale** spa
stecca (*stayk*-kah) *f* rod; splint; carton
steccato (stayk-*kaa*-toa) *m* fence
stella (*stayl*-lah) *f* star
stendardo (stayn-*dahr*-doa) *m* banner
***stendere** (*stehn*-day-ray) *v* *spread
stenografia (stay-noa-grah-*fee*-ah) *f* shorthand
stenografo (stay-*naw*-grah-foa) *m* stenographer
sterile (*stai*-ree-lay) *adj* sterile
sterilizzare (stay-ree-leed-*dzaa*-ray) *v* sterilize
stesso (*stayss*-soa) *adj* same
stile (*stee*-lay) *m* style
stima (*stee*-mah) *f* esteem, respect; ***fare la** ~ estimate
stimare (stee-*maa*-ray) *v* esteem
stimolante (stee-moa-*lahn*-tay) *m* stimulant
stimolare (stee-moa-*laa*-ray) *v* stimulate, urge
stimolo (*stee*-moa-loa) *m* impulse
stipendio (stee-*pehn*-dyoa) *m* salary, wages *pl*
stipulare (stee-poo-*laa*-ray) *v* stipulate
stipulazione (stee-poo-lah-*tsyōā*-nay) *f* stipulation
stirare (stee-*raa*-ray) *v* iron, press; **non si stira** wash and wear, drip-dry; **senza stiratura** drip-dry; **stiratura permanente** permanent press
stitichezza (stee-tee-*kayt*-tsah) *f* constipation
stitico (*stee*-tee-koa) *adj* constipated
stiva (*stee*-vah) *f* hold
stivale (stee-*vaa*-lay) *m* boot
stizza (*steet*-tsah) *f* temper
stoffa (*stof*-fah) *f* cloth, fabric, material
stola (*staw*-lah) *f* stole
stolto (*stoal*-toa) *adj* foolish
stomachevole (stoa-mah-*kāȳ*-voa-lay) *adj* revolting
stomaco (*staw*-mah-koa) *m* stomach; **bruciore di** ~ heartburn
***storcere** (*stor*-chay-ray) *v* wrench; sprain
stordito (stoar-*dee*-toa) *adj* giddy, dizzy
storia (*staw*-ryah) *f* history; tale; ~ **d'amore** love-story; ~ **dell'arte** art history
storico (*staw*-ree-koa) *adj* historical, historic; *m* historian
stornello (stoar-*nehl*-loa) *m* starling
storta (*stor*-tah) *f* wrench
storto (*stor*-toa) *adj* crooked
stoviglie (stoa-*vee*-lʸay) *fpl* pottery; **canovaccio per** ~ tea-cloth
strabico (*straa*-bee-koa) *adj* cross-eyed
straccio (*straht*-choa) *m* rag
strada (*straa*-dah) *f* road, street; drive; **a mezza** ~ halfway; ~ **a pedaggio** turnpike *nAm*; ~ **ferrata** railroad *nAm*; ~ **in riparazione** road up; ~ **maestra** thoroughfare
strangolare (strahng-goa-*laa*-ray) *v* strangle
straniero (strah-*ñai*-roa) *adj* alien, foreign; *m* alien, stranger, foreigner
strano (*straa*-noa) *adj* strange; odd, curious, peculiar, queer, singular, funny
straordinario (strah-oar-dee-*naa*-ryoa) *adj* extraordinary, exceptional
strappare (strahp-*paa*-ray) *v* rip, *tear
strappo (*strahp*-poa) *m* tear
strato (*straa*-toa) *m* layer
strattone (straht-*tōā*-nay) *m* tug
stravagante (strah-vah-*gahn*-tay) *adj* extravagant

strega (*strāy*-gah) *f* witch
stregare (stray-*gaa*-ray) *v* bewitch
stretta (*strayt*-tah) *f* clutch, grip, grasp; ~ **di mano** handshake
strettamente (strayt-tah-*mayn*-tay) *adv* tight
stretto (*strayt*-toa) *adj* narrow; tight
stria (*stree*-ah) *f* stripe
striato (*stryaa*-toa) *adj* striped
strillare (streel-*laa*-ray) *v* scream, yell, shriek
strillo (*streel*-loa) *m* scream, yell, shriek
***stringere** (*streen*-jay-ray) *v* tighten
striscia (*streesh*-shah) *f* strip
strisciare (streesh-*shaa*-ray) *v* *creep
strofa (*straw*-fah) *f* stanza
strofinare (stroa-fee-*naa*-ray) *v* rub, scrub; wipe
strozzare (stroat-*tsaa*-ray) *v* choke
strumento (stroo-*mayn*-toa) *m* implement; instrument; ~ **musicale** musical instrument
struttura (stroot-*tōō*-rah) *f* fabric, structure, texture
struzzo (*stroot*-tsoa) *m* ostrich
stucco (*stook*-koa) *m* plaster
studente (stoo-*dehn*-tay) *m* student
studentessa (stoo-dayn-*tayss*-sah) *f* student
studiare (stoo-*dyaa*-ray) *v* study
studio (*stōō*-dyoa) *m* study
stufa (*stoo*-fah) *f* stove; ~ **a gas** gas stove
stufo di (*stōō*-foa dee) fed up with, tired of
stuoia (*stwaw*-yah) *f* mat
***stupefare** (stoo-pay-*faa*-ray) *v* amaze
stupendo (stoo-*pehn*-doa) *adj* wonderful
stupidaggini (stoo-pee-*dahd*-jee-nee) *fpl* rubbish; ***dire** ~ talk rubbish
stupido (*stōō*-pee-doa) *adj* stupid; foolish, dumb
stupire (stoo-*pee*-ray) *v* amaze, surprise
stupore (stoo-*pōā*-ray) *m* amazement, wonder
stuzzicadenti (stoot-tsee-kah-*dehn*-tee) *m* toothpick
stuzzicare (stoot-tsee-*kaa*-ray) *v* kid, tease
stuzzichino (stoot-tsee-*kee*-noa) *m* appetizer
su (soo) *prep* on, upon, in; above; about; *adv* up; upstairs; **in** ~ upwards, up; overhead
subacqueo (soo-*bahk*-kway-oa) *adj* underwater
subalterno (soo-bahl-*tehr*-noa) *adj* subordinate
subire (soo-*bee*-ray) *v* suffer
subito (*sōō*-bee-toa) *adv* at once, instantly, straight away, presently, immediately
subordinato (soo-boar-dee-*naa*-toa) *adj* minor
suburbano (soo-boor-*baa*-noa) *adj* suburban
***succedere** (soot-*chai*-day-ray) *v* succeed; happen, occur
successione (soot-chayss-*syōā*-nay) *f* sequence
successivo (soot-chayss-*see*-voa) *adj* following, subsequent
successo (soot-*chehss*-soa) *m* success; hit
succhiare (sook-*kyaa*-ray) *v* suck
succo (*sook*-koa) *m* juice; ~ **di frutta** squash
succoso (sook-*kōā*-soa) *adj* juicy
succursale (sook-koor-*saa*-lay) *f* branch
sud (sood) *m* south; **polo Sud** South Pole
sudare (soo-*daa*-ray) *v* perspire, sweat
suddito (*sood*-dee-toa) *m* subject
sud-est (soo-*dehst*) *m* south-east

sudicio (*sōō*-dee-choa) *adj* dirty; filthy, unclean, soiled
sudiciume (soo-dee-*chōō*-may) *m* dirt
sudore (soo-*dōā*-ray) *m* perspiration, sweat
sud-ovest (sood-*aw*-vayst) *m* south-west
sufficiente *adj* enough, sufficient
suffragio (soof-*fraa*-joa) *m* suffrage
suggerimento (sood-jay-ree-*mayn*-toa) *m* suggestion
suggerire (sood-jay-*ree*-ray) *v* suggest
sughero (*sōō*-gay-roa) *m* cork
sugo (*sōō*-goa) *m* gravy
suicidio (swee-*chee*-dyoa) *m* suicide
sunto (*soon*-toa) *m* summary
suo (*sōō*-oa) *adj* (f sua;pl suoi,sue) his; her; **Suo** *adj* your
suocera (*swaw*-chay-rah) *f* mother-in-law
suocero (*swaw*-chay-roa) *m* father-in-law; **suoceri** parents-in-law *pl*
suola (*swaw*-lah) *f* sole
suolo (*swaw*-loa) *m* soil, earth
suonare (swoa-*naa*-ray) *v* sound; *ring; ~ **il clacson** hoot; toot *vAm*, honk *vAm*
suono (*swaw*-noa) *m* sound
superare (soo-pay-*raa*-ray) *v* exceed, *outdo
superbo (soo-*pehr*-boa) *adj* superb
superficiale (soo-payr-fee-*chaa*-lay) *adj* superficial
superficie (soo-payr-*fee*-chay) *f* surface
superfluo (soo-*pehr*-flwoa) *adj* unnecessary, superfluous
superiore (soo-pay-*ryōā*-ray) *adj* upper, superior
superlativo (soo-payr-lah-*tee*-voa) *adj* superlative; *m* superlative
supermercato (soo-payr-mayr-*kaa*-toa) *m* supermarket
superstizione (soo-payr-stee-*tsyōā*-nay) *f* superstition
supplementare (soop-play-mayn-*taa*-ray) *adj* extra, additional
supplemento (soop-play-*mayn*-toa) *m* supplement; surcharge
supplicare (soop-plee-*kaa*-ray) *v* beg
***supporre** (soop-*poar*-ray) *v* suppose; suspect; **supposto che** supposing that
supposta (soop-*poa*-stah) *f* suppository
suscitare (soosh-shee-*taa*-ray) *v* stir up
susina (soo-*see*-nah) *f* plum
sussidio (sooss-*see*-dyoa) *m* grant
sussistenza (sooss-see-*stehn*-tsah) *f* livelihood
sussurro (sooss-*soor*-roa) *m* whisper
suturare (soo-too-*raa*-ray) *v* sew up
svago (*zvaa*-goa) *m* recreation
svalutare (zvah-loo-*taa*-ray) *v* devalue
svalutazione (zvah-loo-tah-*tsyōā*-nay) *f* devaluation
svantaggio (zvahn-*tahd*-joa) *m* disadvantage
svedese (zvay-*dāy*-zay) *adj* Swedish; *m* Swede
sveglia (*zvāy*-l^{y}ah) *f* alarm-clock
svegliare (zvay-*l^{y}aa*-ray) *v* *awake, *wake; **svegliarsi** wake up
sveglio (*zvāy*-l^{y}oa) *adj* awake; clever, smart, bright
svelare (zvay-*laa*-ray) *v* reveal
svelto (*zvehl*-toa) *adj* quick
svendita (*zvayn*-dee-tah) *f* clearance sale
***svenire** (zvay-*nee*-ray) *v* faint
sventolare (zvayn-toa-*laa*-ray) *v* wave
Svezia (*zvai*-tsyah) *f* Sweden
sviluppare (zvee-loop-*paa*-ray) *v* develop
sviluppo (zvee-*loop*-poa) *m* development
svista (*zvee*-stah) *f* slip, oversight
svitare (zvee-*taa*-ray) *v* unscrew
Svizzera (*zveet*-tsay-rah) *f* Switzerland

svizzero (*zveet*-tsay-roa) *adj* Swiss; *m* Swiss
***svolgere** (*zvol*-jay-ray) *v* *unwind; treat; carry out
svolta (*zvol*-tah) *f* turning, curve
swahili (zvah-*ee*-lee) *m* Swahili

T

tabaccaio (tah-bahk-*kaa*-yoa) *m* tobacconist
tabaccheria (tah-bahk-kay-*ree*-ah) *f* tobacconist's, cigar shop
tabacco (tah-*bahk*-koa) *m* tobacco; ~ **da pipa** pipe tobacco
tabella (tah-*behl*-lah) *f* chart, table; ~ **di conversione** conversion chart
tabù (tah-*boo*) *m* taboo
taccagno (tahk-*kaa*-ñoa) *adj* stingy
tacchino (tahk-*kee*-noa) *m* turkey
tacco (*tahk*-koa) *m* heel
taccuino (tahk-*kwee*-noa) *m* notebook
***tacere** (tah-*chāy*-ray) *v* *keep quiet, *be silent; ***far** ~ silence
tachimetro (tah-*kee*-may-troa) *m* speedometer
tagliacarte (tah-lʸah-*kahr*-tay) *m* paper-knife
tagliando (tah-*lʸahn*-doa) *m* coupon
tagliare (tah-*lʸaa*-ray) *v* *cut; *cut off, carve, chip
taglio (*taa*-lʸoa) *m* cut; ~ **di capelli** haircut
tailandese (tigh-lahn-*dāy*-say) *adj* Thai; *m* Thai
Tailandia (tigh-*lahn*-dyah) *f* Thailand
talco (*tahl*-koa) *m* talc powder; ~ **per piedi** foot powder
tale (*taa*-lay) *adj* such
talento (tah-*lehn*-toa) *m* gift, talent; **di** ~ gifted
talloncino (tahl-loan-*cheenoa*) *m* counterfoil
tallone (tahl-*lōa*-nay) *m* heel
talmente (tahl-*mayn*-tay) *adv* so
taluni (tah-*lōō*-nee) *pron* some
talvolta (tahl-*vol*-tah) *adv* sometimes
tamburo (tahm-*bōō*-roa) *m* drum; ~ **del freno** brake drum
tampone (tahm-*pōa*-nay) *m* tampon
tana (*taa*-nah) *f* den
tangibile (tahn-*jee*-bee-lay) *adj* tangible
tanto (*tahn*-toa) *adv* as much; **di** ~ **in tanto** now and then; **ogni** ~ occasionally
tappa (*tahp*-pah) *f* stage
tappeto (tahp-*pāy*-toa) *m* carpet; rug
tappezzare (tahp-payt-*tsaa*-ray) *v* upholster
tappezzeria (tahp-payt-tsay-*ree*-ah) *f* tapestry
tappo (*tahp*-poa) *m* cork, stopper
tardi (*tahr*-dee) *adv* late
tardivo (tahr-*dee*-voa) *adj* late
tardo (*tahr*-doa) *adj* late; slow
targa automobilistica (*tahr*-gah ou-toa-moa-bee-*lee*-stee-kah) registration plate; licence plate *Am*
tariffa (tah-*reef*-fah) *f* tariff, rate; ~ **del parcheggio** parking fee; ~ **doganale** Customs duty; ~ **notturna** night rate
tarma (*tahr*-mah) *f* moth
tartaruga (tahr-tah-*rōō*-gah) *f* turtle
tasca (*tah*-skah) *f* pocket
tassa (*tahss*-sah) *f* tax; ~ **sugli affari** turnover tax, sales tax; ~ **di scambio** sales tax
tassabile (tahs-*saa*-bee-lay) *adj* dutiable
tassametro (tahss-*saa*-may-troa) *m* taxi-meter
tassare (tahss-*saa*-ray) *v* tax
tassì (tahss-*see*) *m* cab, taxi
tassista (tahss-*see*-stah) *m* cab-driver,

taxi-driver
tattica (*taht*-tee-kah) *f* tactics *pl*
tatto (*taht*-toa) *m* touch
taverna (tah-*vehr*-nah) *f* public house, pub; tavern
tavola (*taa*-voa-lah) *f* table; ~ **calda** snack-bar, cafeteria
tavoletta (tah-voa-*layt*-tah) *f* board
tazza (*taht*-tsah) *f* cup; mug; **tazzina da tè** teacup
te (tay) *pron* you
tè (teh) *m* tea
teatro (tay-*aa*-troa) *m* theatre; drama; ~ **dell'opera** opera house; ~ **di varietà** music-hall, variety theatre
tecnica (*tehk*-nee-kah) *f* technique
tecnico (*tehk*-nee-koa) *adj* technical; *m* technician
tecnologia (tayk-noa-loa-*jee*-ah) *f* technology
tedesco (tay-*day*-skoa) *adj* German; *m* German
tegame (tay-*gaa*-may) *m* pan
tegola (*tāȳ*-goa-lah) *f* tile
teiera (tay-*yai*-rah) *f* teapot
telaio (tay-*laa*-yoa) *m* chassis
telefonare (tay-lay-foa-*naa*-ray) *v* ring up, phone, call; call up *Am*
telefonata (tay-lay-foa-*naa*-tah) *f* call
telefonista (tay-lay-foa-*nee*-stah) *f* telephonist, telephone operator
telefono (tay-*lai*-foa-noa) *m* phone, telephone; ~ **interno** extension
telegrafare (tay-lay-grah-*faa*-ray) *v* cable, telegraph
telegramma (tay-lay-*grahm*-mah) *m* cable, telegram
telemetro (tay-*lai*-may-troa) *m* range-finder
teleobbiettivo (tay-lay-oab-byayt-*tee*-voa) *m* telephoto lens
telepatia (tay-lay-pah-*tee*-ah) *f* telepathy
televisione (tay-lay-vee-*zyōā*-nay) *f* television
televisore (tay-lay-vee-*zōā*-ray) *m* television set
telex (tay-*lehks*) *m* telex
tema (*tai*-mah) *m* theme
temerario (tay-may-*raa*-ryoa) *adj* daring
temere (tay-*māȳ*-ray) *v* fear, dread
temperamatite (taym-pay-rah-mah-*tee*-tay) *m* pencil-sharpener
temperatura (taym-pay-rah-*tōō*-rah) *f* temperature; ~ **ambientale** room temperature
temperino (taym-pay-*ree*-noa) *m* pocket-knife, penknife
tempesta (taym-*peh*-stah) *f* storm, tempest
tempestoso (taym-pay-*stōā*-soa) *adj* stormy
tempia (*tehm*-pyah) *f* temple
tempio (*tehm*-pyoa) *m* temple
tempo (*tehm*-poa) *m* time; weather; **in** ~ in time; ~ **libero** spare time
temporale (taym-poa-*raa*-lay) *m* thunderstorm
temporalesco (taym-poa-rah-*lay*-skoa) *adj* thundery
temporaneo (taym-poa-*raa*-nay-oa) *adj* temporary
tenace (tay-*naa*-chay) *adj* tough
tenaglie (tay-*naa*-lyay) *fpl* pincers *pl*
tenda (*tehn*-dah) *f* curtain; tent; ~ **di riparo** awning
tendenza (tayn-*dehn*-tsah) *f* tendency
***tendere** (*tehn*-day-ray) *v* stretch; *be inclined to; * ~ **a** tend to
tendine (tayn-*dee*-nay) *m* sinew, tendon
***tenere** (tay-*nāȳ*-ray) *v* *keep; *hold
tenero (*tai*-nay-roa) *adj* tender
tennis (*tehn*-neess) *m* tennis; **campo di** ~ tennis-court; ~ **da tavolo** ping-pong
tensione (tayn-*syōā*-nay) *f* tension;

stress, pressure
tentare (tayn-*taa*-ray) *v* try, attempt; tempt
tentativo (tayn-tah-*tee*-voa) *m* try, attempt, effort
tentazione (tayn-tah-*tsyōā*-nay) *f* temptation
teologia (tay-oa-loa-*jee*-ah) *f* theology
teoria (tay-oa-*reeah*) *f* theory
teorico (tay-*aw*-ree-koa) *adj* theoretical
terapia (tay-rah-*pee*-ah) *f* therapy
tergicristallo (tayr-jee-kree-*stahl*-loa) *m* windscreen wiper; windshield wiper *Am*
terital (tay-ree-*tahl*) *m* terylene
terminare (tayr-mee-*naa*-ray) *v* finish; stop
termine (*tehr*-mee-nay) *m* term; finish, end; terminal
termometro (tayr-*maw*-may-troa) *m* thermometer
termos (*tehr*-moass) *m* vacuum flask, thermos flask
termostato (tayr-*mo*-stah-toa) *m* thermostat
terra (*tehr*-rah) *f* earth; land; ground, soil; **a ~** ashore; down
terracotta (tayr-rah-*kot*-tah) *f* faience
terraferma (tayr-rah-*fayr*-mah) *f* mainland
terraglie (tayr-*raa*-lʸay) *fpl* crockery, ceramics *pl*, earthenware
terrazza (tayr-*raht*-tsah) *f* terrace
terremoto (tayr-ray-*maw*-toa) *m* earthquake
terreno (tayr-*rāy*-noa) *m* soil; grounds, terrain
terribile (tayr-*ree*-bee-lay) *adj* terrible; awful, dreadful, frightful
territorio (tayr-ree-*taw*-ryoa) *m* territory
terrore (tayr-*rōā*-ray) *m* terror
terrorismo (tayr-roa-*ree*-zmoa) *m* terrorism
terrorista (tayr-roa-*ree*-stah) *m* terrorist
terzo (*tehr*-tsoa) *num* third
tesi (*tai*-zee) *f* thesis
teso (*tāy*-soa) *adj* tense
tesoriere (tay-zoa-*ryai*-ray) *m* treasurer
tesoro (tay-*zaw*-roa) *m* treasure; **Tesoro** *m* treasury
tessere (*tehss*-say-ray) *v* *weave
tessitore (tayss-see-*tōā*-ray) *m* weaver
tessuto (tayss-*sōō*-toa) *m* tissue; textile
testa (*teh*-stah) *f* head; **in ~ a** ahead of; **~ cilindro** cylinder head
testamento (tay-stah-*mayn*-toa) *m* will
testardo (tay-*stahr*-doa) *adj* pig-headed, head-strong
testimone (tay-stee-*maw*-nay) *m* witness; **~ oculare** eye-witness
testimoniare (tay-stee-moa-*ñaa*-ray) *v* testify
testo (*teh*-stoa) *m* text
tetro (*tai*-troa) *adj* sombre
tetto (*tayt*-toa) *m* roof; **~ di paglia** thatched roof
ti (tee) *pron* you; yourself
tiepido (*tyai*-pee-doa) *adj* lukewarm, tepid
tifoidea (tee-foa-ee-*dai*-ah) *f* typhoid
tifoso (tee-*fōā*-soa) *m* fan; supporter
tiglio (*tee*-lʸoa) *m* limetree, lime
tigre (*tee*-gray) *f* tiger
timbro (*teem*-broa) *m* stamp; tone
timidezza (tee-mee-*dayt*-tsah) *f* timidity, shyness
timido (*tee*-mee-doa) *adj* timid, shy
timo (*tee*-moa) *m* thyme
timone (tee-*mōā*-nay) *m* rudder, helm
timoniere (tee-moa-*ñai*-ray) *m* steersman, helmsman
timore (tee-*mōā*-ray) *m* fear, dread
timpano (*teem*-pah-noa) *m* ear-drum
***tingere** (*teen*-jay-ray) *v* dye

tinta (*teen*-tah) *f* shade; **a ~ solida** fast-dyed
tintoria (teen-toa-*ree*-ah) *f* dry-cleaner's
tintura (teen-*tōō*-rah) *f* colourant, dye
tipico (*tee*-pee-koa) *adj* typical, characteristic
tipo (*tee*-poa) *m* type; guy, fellow
tiranno (tee-*rahn*-noa) *m* tyrant
tirare (tee-*raa*-ray) *v* *draw, pull; *blow; **~ di scherma** fence
tiratura (tee-rah-*tōō*-rah) *f* issue
tiro (*tee*-roa) *m* throw; trick
titolo (*tee*-toa-loa) *m* title; headline, heading; degree; **titoli** stocks and shares
tizio (*tee*-tsyoa) *m* chap
toccare (toak-*kaa*-ray) *v* touch; *hit
tocco (*toak*-koa) *m* touch
***togliere** (*taw*-lʸay-ray) *v* *take out, *take away
toletta (toa-*leht*-tah) *f* dressing-table; washroom *nAm*
tollerabile (toal-lay-*raa*-bee-lay) *adj* tolerable
tollerare (toal-lay-*raa*-ray) *v* *bear
tomba (*toam*-bah) *f* grave, tomb
tonico (*taw*-nee-koa) *m* tonic; **~ per capelli** hair tonic
tonnellata (toan-nayl-*laa*-tah) *f* ton
tonno (*toan*-noa) *m* tuna
tono (*taw*-noa) *m* tone; note
tonsille (toan-*seel*-lay) *fpl* tonsils *pl*
tonsillite (toan-seel-*lee*-tay) *f* tonsilitis
topo (*taw*-poa) *m* mouse
torace (toa-*raa*-chay) *m* chest
***torcere** (*tor*-chay-ray) *v* twist
torcia (*tor*-chah) *f* torch
tordo (*toar*-doa) *m* thrush
tormenta (toar-*mayn*-tah) *f* blizzard, snowstorm
tormentare (toar-mayn-*taa*-ray) *v* torment
tormento (toar-*mayn*-toa) *m* torment
tornante (toar-*nahn*-tay) *m* turn
tornare (toar-*naa*-ray) *v* *go back, *get back
torneo (toar-*nai*-oa) *m* tournament
toro (*taw*-roa) *m* bull
torre (*toar*-ray) *f* tower
torrone (toar-*rōā*-nay) *m* nougat
torsione (toar-*syōā*-nay) *f* twist
torsolo (*toar*-soa-loa) *m* core
torta (*toar*-tah) *f* cake
torto (*tor*-toa) *m* wrong; ***avere ~** *be wrong; ***fare un ~** wrong
tortuoso (toar-*twōā*-soa) *adj* crooked
tortura (toar-*tōō*-rah) *f* torture
torturare (toar-too-*raa*-ray) *v* torture
tosse (*toass*-say) *f* cough
tossico (*toss*-see-koa) *adj* toxic
tossire (toass-*see*-ray) *v* cough
totale (toa-*taa*-lay) *adj* total; utter; *m* whole; total
totalitario (toa-tah-lee-*taa*-ryoa) *adj* totalitarian
totalizzatore (toa-tah-leed-dzah-*tōā*-ray) *m* totalizator
totalmente (toa-tahl-*mayn*-tay) *adv* completely
toupet (too-*pay*) *m* hair piece
tovaglia (toa-*vaa*-lʸah) *f* table-cloth
tovagliolo (toa-vah-*lʸaw*-loa) *m* napkin, serviette; **~ di carta** paper napkin
tra (trah) *prep* between; among, amid
traccia (*traht*-chah) *f* trail, trace
tradimento (trah-dee-*mayn*-toa) *m* treason
tradire (trah-*dee*-ray) *v* betray; *give away
traditore (trah-dee-*tōā*-ray) *m* traitor
tradizionale (trah-dee-tsyoa-*naa*-lay) *adj* traditional
tradizione (trah-dee-*tsyōā*-nay) *f* tradition
***tradurre** (trah-*door*-ray) *v* translate
traduttore (trah-doot-*tōā*-ray) *m* trans-

lator
traduzione (trah-doo-*tsyōā*-nay) *f* translation, version
traffico (*trahf*-fee-koa) *m* traffic
tragedia (trah-*jai*-dyah) *f* tragedy; drama
traghetto (trah-*gayt*-toa) *m* ferry-boat
tragico (*traa*-jee-koa) *adj* tragic
traguardo (trah-*gwahr*-doa) *m* finish; goal
trainare (trigh-*naa*-ray) *v* tow, haul
tralasciare (trah-lahsh-*shaa*-ray) *v* fail
tram (trahm) *m* tram; streetcar *nAm*
trama (*traa*-mah) *f* plot
trambusto (trahm-*boo*-stoa) *m* fuss
tramezzino (trah-mayd-*dzee*-noa) *m* sandwich
tramonto (trah-*moan*-toa) *m* sunset
tranne (*trahn*-nay) *prep* but
tranquillante (trahng-kweel-*lahn*-tay) *m* tranquillizer
tranquillità (trahng-kweel-lee-*tah*) *f* quiet
tranquillizzare (trahng-kweel-leed-*dzaa*-ray) *v* reassure
tranquillo (trahng-*kweel*-loa) *adj* calm; still, tranquil, quiet
transatlantico (trahn-saht-*lahn*-tee-koa) *adj* transatlantic
transazione (trahn-sah-*tsyōā*-nay) *f* transaction
transizione (trahn-see-*tsyōā*-nay) *f* transition
trapanare (trah-pah-*naa*-ray) *v* drill, bore
trapano (*traa*-pah-noa) *m* drill
trapassare (trah-pahss-*saa*-ray) *v* depart
trappola (*trahp*-poa-lah) *f* trap
***trarre** (*trahr*-ray) *v* *draw
trascinare (trahsh-shee-*naa*-ray) *v* drag
***trascorrere** (trah-*skoar*-ray-ray) *v* pass
trascurare (trah-skoo-*raa*-ray) *v* neglect; overlook; **trascurato** careless
trasferire (trah-sfay-*ree*-ray) *v* transfer
trasformare (trah-sfoar-*maa*-ray) *v* transform
trasformatore (trah-sfoar-mah-*tōā*-ray) *m* transformer
trasgredire (trahz-gray-*dee*-ray) *v* trespass, offend
trasgressore (trah-zgrayss-*sōā*-ray) *m* trespasser
traslocare (trah-zloa-*kaa*-ray) *v* move
trasloco (trah-*zlaw*-koa) *m* move
***trasmettere** (trah-*zmayt*-tay-ray) *v* transmit, *broadcast
trasmettitore (trah-zmayt-tee-*tōā*-ray) *m* transmitter
trasmissione (trah-zmeess-*syōā*-nay) *f* transmission
trasparente (trah-spah-*rehn*-tay) *adj* transparent, sheer
traspirare (trah-spee-*raa*-ray) *v* perspire
traspirazione (trah-spee-rah-*tsyōā*-nay) *f* perspiration
trasportare (trah-spoar-*taa*-ray) *v* transport
trasporto (trah-*spor*-toa) *m* transportation, transport
tratta (*traht*-tah) *f* draft
trattamento (traht-tah-*mayn*-toa) *m* treatment
trattare (traht-*taa*-ray) *v* handle, treat; ~ **con** *deal with
trattativa (traht-tah-*tee*-vah) *f* negotiation
trattato (traht-*taa*-toa) *m* essay; treaty
***trattenere** (traht-tay-*nāy*-ray) *v* restrain; ***trattenersi** stay
tratto (*traht*-toa) *m* line; feature, trait; ~ **del carattere** characteristic
trattore (traht-*tōā*-ray) *m* tractor
trave (*traa*-vay) *f* beam
traversa (trah-*vehr*-sah) *f* side-street
traversata (trah-vayr-*saa*-tah) *f* pass-

age, crossing

travestimento (trah-vay-stee-*mayn*-toa) *m* disguise

travestirsi (trah-vay-*steer*-see) *v* disguise

tre (tray) *num* three; ~ **quarti** three-quarter

tredicesimo (tray-dee-*chai*-zee-moa) *num* thirteenth

tredici (*trāy*-dee-chee) *num* thirteen

tremare (tray-*maa*-ray) *v* tremble, shiver

tremendo (tray-*mehn*-doa) *adj* terrible

trementina (tray-mayn-*tee*-nah) *f* turpentine

treno (*trai*-noa) *m* train; ~ **direttissimo** express train; ~ **diretto** through train; ~ **locale** local train; ~ **merci** goods train; freight-train *nAm*; ~ **notturno** night train; ~ **passeggeri** passenger train

trenta (*trayn*-tah) *num* thirty

trentesimo (trayn-*tai*-zee-moa) *num* thirtieth

triangolare (tryahng-goa-*laa*-ray) *adj* triangular

triangolo (*tryahng*-goa-loa) *m* triangle

tribordo (tree-*boar*-doa) *m* starboard

tribù (tree-*boo*) *f* tribe

tribuna (tree-*bōō*-nah) *f* stand

tribunale (tree-boo-*naa*-lay) *m* law court

trifoglio (tree-*faw*-lʸoa) *m* clover; shamrock

triglia (*tree*-lʸah) *f* mullet

trimestrale (tree-may-*straa*-lay) *adj* quarterly

trimestre (tree-*meh*-stray) *m* quarter

trinciato (treen-*chaa*-toa) *m* cigarette tobacco

trionfante (tryoan-*fahn*-tay) *adj* triumphant

trionfare (tryoan-*faa*-ray) *v* triumph

trionfo (*tryoan*-foa) *m* triumph

triste (*tree*-stay) *adj* sad

tristezza (tree-*stayt*-tsah) *f* sadness, sorrow

tritare (tree-*taa*-ray) *v* *grind, mince

triviale (tree-*vyaa*-lay) *adj* vulgar

tromba (*troam*-bah) *f* trumpet

troncare (troang-*kaa*-ray) *v* *cut off

tronco (*troang*-koa) *m* trunk

trono (*traw*-noa) *m* throne

tropicale (troa-pee-*kaa*-lay) *adj* tropical

tropici (*traw*-pee-chee) *mpl* tropics *pl*

troppo (*trop*-poa) *adv* too

trota (*traw*-tah) *f* trout

trovare (troa-*vaa*-ray) *v* *find, *come across

trovata (troa-*vaa*-tah) *f* idea

trucco (*trook*-koa) *m* make-up; trick

truffa (*troof*-fah) *f* swindle

truffare (troof-*faa*-ray) *v* swindle

truffatore (troof-fah-*tōā*-ray) *m* swindler

truppe (*troop*-pay) *fpl* troops *pl*

tu (too) *pron* you; ~ **stesso** yourself

tubatura (too-bah-*tōō*-rah) *f* pipe

tubercolosi (too-bayr-koa-*law*-zee) *f* tuberculosis

tubetto (too-*bayt*-toa) *m* tube

tubo (*tōō*-boa) *m* tube

tuffare (toof-*faa*-ray) *v* dive

tulipano (too-lee-*paa*-noa) *m* tulip

tumore (too-*mōā*-ray) *m* tumour

tumulto (too-*mool*-toa) *m* disturbance

tunica (*tōō*-nee-kah) *f* tunic

Tunisia (too-nee-*zee*-ah) *f* Tunisia

tunisino (too-nee-*zee*-noa) *adj* Tunisian; *m* Tunisian

tuo (*tōō*-oa) *adj* (f tua;pl tuoi,tue) your

tuonare (twoa-*naa*-ray) *v* thunder

tuono (*twaw*-noa) *m* thunder

tuorlo (*twor*-loa) *m* egg-yolk

turbare (toor-*baa*-ray) *v* upset

turbina (toor-*bee*-nah) *f* turbine

turbolento (toor-boa-*lehn*-toa) *adj* rowdy
Turchia (toor-*kee*-ah) *f* Turkey
turco (*toor*-koa) *adj* Turkish; *m* Turk
turismo (too-*ree*-zmoa) *m* tourism
turista (too-*ree*-stah) *m* tourist
turno (*toor*-noa) *m* turn
tuta (*tōō*-tah) *f* overalls *pl*
tutela (too-*tai*-lah) *f* custody
tutore (too-*tōā*-ray) *m* guardian, tutor
tuttavia (toot-tah-*vee*-ah) *adv* however, nevertheless
tutto (*toot*-toa) *adj* all; entire; *pron* everything; **in** ~ altogether; ~ **compreso** all in
tuttora (toot-*tōā*-rah) *adv* still
tweed (tweed) *m* tweed

U

ubbidiente (oob-bee-*dyehn*-tay) *adj* obedient
ubbidienza (oob-bee-*dyehn*-tsah) *f* obedience
ubbidire (oob-bee-*dee*-ray) *v* obey
ubicazione (oo-bee-kah-*tsyōā*-nay) *f* situation
ubriaco (oo-*bryaa*-koa) *adj* intoxicated, drunk
uccello (oot-*chehl*-loa) *m* bird; ~ **marino** sea-bird
***uccidere** (oot-*chee*-day-ray) *v* kill
udibile (oo-*dee*-bee-lay) *adj* audible
udienza (oo-*dyehn*-tsah) *f* audience
***udire** (oo-*dee*-ray) *v* *hear
udito (oo-*dee*-toa) *m* hearing
uditore (oo-dee-*tōā*-ray) *m* auditor
ufficiale (oof-fee-*chaa*-lay) *adj* official; *m* officer
ufficio (oof-*fee*-choa) *m* office; ~ **cambio** money exchange, exchange office; ~ **di collocamento** employment exchange; ~ **informazioni** inquiry office, information bureau; ~ **oggetti smarriti** lost property office; ~ **postale** post-office; ~ **ricevimento** reception office; ~ **turistico** tourist office
ufficioso (oof-fee-*chōā*-soa) *adj* unofficial
uguaglianza (oo-gwah-*lʸahn*-tsah) *f* equality
uguagliare (oo-gwah-*lʸaa*-ray) *v* equal
uguale (oo-*gwaa*-lay) *adj* even, equal; alike
ulcera (*ool*-chay-rah) *f* ulcer, sore; ~ **gastrica** gastric ulcer
ulteriore (ool-tay-*ryōā*-ray) *adj* further
ultimamente (ool-tee-mah-*mayn*-tay) *adv* lately
ultimo (*ool*-tee-moa) *adj* last, ultimate
ultravioletto (ool-trah-vyoa-*layt*-toa) *adj* ultraviolet
umanità (oo-mah-nee-*tah*) *f* humanity, mankind
umano (oo-*maa*-noa) *adj* human
umidità (oo-mee-dee-*tah*) *f* moisture, humidity, damp
umido (*ōō*-mee-doa) *adj* wet, moist, humid, damp
umile (*ōō*-mee-lay) *adj* humble
umore (oo-*mōā*-ray) *m* spirit, mood; **di buon** ~ good-tempered, good-humoured
un (oon) *art* (uno;f una) a *art*
unanime (oo-*naa*-nee-may) *adj* unanimous; like-minded
uncino (oon-*chee*-noa) *m* hook
undicesimo (oon-dee-*chai*-zee-moa) *num* eleventh
undici (*oon*-dee-chee) *num* eleven
ungherese (oong-gay-*rāȳ*-zay) *adj* Hungarian; *m* Hungarian
Ungheria (oong-gay-*ree*-ah) *f* Hungary
unghia (*oong*-gyah) *f* nail
unguento (oong-*gwehn*-toa) *m* salve,

ointment
unicamente (oo-nee-kah-*mayn*-tay) *adv* exclusively
unico (*ōō*-nee-koa) *adj* sole; unique
uniforme (oo-nee-*foar*-may) *adj* uniform; *f* uniform
unilaterale (oo-nee-lah-tay-*raa*-lay) *adj* one-sided
unione (oo-*ñōā*-nay) *f* union
Unione Sovietica (oo-*ñōā*-nay soa-*vyai*-tee-kah) Soviet Union
unire (oo-*nee*-ray) *v* join; unite; combine; **unirsi a** join
unità (oo-nee-*tah*) *f* unity; unit; ~ **monetaria** monetary unit
unito (oo-*nee*-toa) *adj* joint
universale (oo-nee-vayr-*saa*-lay) *adj* universal, global; all-round
università (oo-nee-vayr-see-*tah*) *f* university
universo (oo-nee-*vehr*-soa) *m* universe
uno (*ōō*-noa) *num* one; *pron* one
unto (*oon*-toa) *adj* greasy
untuoso (oon-*twōā*-soa) *adj* fatty
uomo (*waw*-moa) *m* (pl uomini) man; ~ **d'affari** businessman; ~ **di stato** statesman; ~ **politico** politician
uovo (*waw*-voa) *m* (pl le uova) egg; **uova di pesce** roe
uragano (oo-rah-*gaa*-noa) *m* hurricane
urbano (oor-*baa*-noa) *adj* urban
urgente (oor-*jehn*-tay) *adj* urgent, pressing
urgenza (oor-*jehn*-tsah) *f* urgency
urina (oo-*ree*-nah) *f* urine
urlare (oor-*laa*-ray) *v* scream, shout
urlo (*oor*-loa) *m* cry
urtante (oor-*tahn*-tay) *adj* shocking
urtare (oor-*taa*-ray) *v* bump
urto (*oor*-toa) *m* bump; push
uruguaiano (oo-roo-gwah-*yaa*-noa) *adj* Uruguayan; *m* Uruguayan
Uruguay (oo-roo-*gwaa*-ee) *m* Uruguay
usabile (oo-*zaa*-bee-lay) *adj* usable
usanza (oo-*zahn*-tsah) *f* usage
usare (oo-*zaa*-ray) *v* use; **usato** worn-out
usciere (oosh-*shai*-ray) *m* usher; bailiff
uscio (*oosh*-shoa) *m* door
* **uscire** (oosh-*shee*-ray) *v* *go out
uscita (oosh-*shee*-tah) *f* way out, exit; issue; ~ **di sicurezza** emergency exit
usignolo (oo-zee-*ñōā*-loa) *m* nightingale
uso (*ōō*-zoa) *m* use; **fuori** ~ out of order
usuale (oo-*zwaa*-lay) *adj* customary
utensile (oo-tayn-*see*-lay) *m* utensil, implement
utente (oo-*tehn*-tay) *m* user
utero (*ōō*-tay-roa) *m* womb
utile (*ōō*-tee-lay) *adj* useful
utilità (oo-tee-lee-*tah*) *f* utility, use
utilizzare (oo-tee-leed-*dzaa*-ray) *v* utilize, employ; exploit
uva (*ōō*-vah) *f* grapes *pl*; ~ **di Corinto** currant; ~ **spina** gooseberry
uvetta (oo-*vayt*-tah) *f* raisin

V

vacante (vah-*kahn*-tay) *adj* unoccupied, vacant
vacanza (vah-*kahn*-tsah) *f* vacation
vacca (*vahk*-kah) *f* cow
vaccinare (vaht-chee-*naa*-ray) *v* vaccinate
vaccinazione (vaht-chee-nah-*tsyōā*-nay) *f* vaccination
vacillante (vah-cheel-*lahn*-tay) *adj* shaky; unsteady
vacillare (vah-cheel-*laa*-ray) *v* falter
vagabondaggio (vah-gah-boan-*dahd*-joa) *m* vagrancy

vagabondare (vah-gah-boan-*daa*-ray) *v* roam, tramp
vagabondo (vah-gah-*boan*-doa) *m* tramp
vagare (vah-*gaa*-ray) *v* wander
vaglia (*vaa*-lʸah) *m* money order; ~ **postale** postal order; mail order *Am*
vagliare (vah-*lʸaa*-ray) *v* sift
vago (*vaa*-goa) *adj* faint, vague
vagone (vah-*gōā*-nay) *m* coach, carriage; waggon; passenger car *Am*; ~ **letto** sleeping-car; ~ **ristorante** dining-car
vaiolo (vah-*yaw*-loa) *m* smallpox
valanga (vah-*lahng*-gah) *f* avalanche
***valere** (vah-*lāy*-ray) *v* *be worth
valido (*vaa*-lee-doa) *adj* valid
valigia (vah-*lee*-jah) *f* bag, case, suitcase
valle (*vahl*-lay) *f* valley
valletto (vahl-*layt*-toa) *m* valet
valore (vah-*lōā*-ray) *m* value, worth; **senza**~ worthless; **valori** valuables *pl*
valoroso (vah-loa-*rōā*-soa) *adj* courageous
valuta (vah-*lōō*-tah) *f* currency
valutare (vah-loo-*taa*-ray) *v* evaluate, estimate, appreciate, value
valutazione (vah-loo-tah-*tsyōā*-nay) *f* estimate
valvola (*vahl*-voa-lah) *f* valve; ~ **dell'aria** choke
valzer (*vahl*-tsayr) *m* waltz
vanga (*vahng*-gah) *f* spade
vangelo (vahn-*jai*-loa) *m* gospel
vaniglia (vah-*nee*-lʸah) *f* vanilla
vanità (vah-nee-*tah*) *f* vanity
vano (*vaa*-noa) *adj* vain, idle; *m* room
vantaggio (vahn-*tahd*-joa) *m* benefit, advantage; profit; lead
vantaggioso (vahn-tahd-*jōā*-soa) *adj* advantageous
vantarsi (vahn-*tahr*-see) *v* boast
vapore (vah-*pōā*-ray) *m* steam, vapour
vaporizzatore (vah-poa-reed-dzah-*tōā*-ray) *m* atomizer
vari (*vaa*-ree) *adj* various
variabile (vah-*ryaa*-bee-lay) *adj* variable
variare (vah-*ryaa*-ray) *v* vary
variazione (vah-ryah-*tsyōā*-nay) *f* variation
varicella (vah-ree-*chehl*-lah) *f* chickenpox
varietà (vah-ryay-*tah*) *f* variety
varo (*vaa*-roa) *m* launching
vascello (vahsh-*shehl*-loa) *m* vessel
vasellame (vah-zayl-*laa*-may) *m* crockery
vasellina (vah-zayl-*lee*-nah) *f* vaseline
vaso (*vaa*-zoa) *m* vase; bowl; ~ **sanguigno** blood-vessel
vassoio (vahss-*sōā*-yoa) *m* tray
vasto (*vah*-stoa) *adj* vast; extensive, wide
vecchiaia (vayk-*kyaa*-yah) *f* old age
vecchio (*vehk*-keeoa) *adj* old; ancient
***vedere** (vay-*dāy*-ray) *v* *see; notice; ***far** ~ *show
vedova (*vāy*-doa-vah) *f* widow
vedovo (*vāy*-doa-voa) *m* widower
veduta (vay-*dōō*-tah) *f* sight
veemente (vay-ay-*mayn*-tay) *adj* fierce, intense
vegetariano (vay-jay-tah-*ryaa*-noa) *m* vegetarian
vegetazione (vay-jay-tah-*tsyōā*-nay) *f* vegetation
veicolo (vay-*ee*-koa-loa) *m* vehicle
vela (*vāy*-lah) *f* sail; ~ **di trinchetto** foresail
veleno (vay-*lāy*-noa) *m* poison
velenoso (vay-lay-*nōā*-soa) *adj* poisonous
velivolo (vay-*lee*-voa-loa) *m* aircraft
velluto (vayl-*lōō*-toa) *m* velvet; ~ **a**

coste corduroy; ~ **di cotone** velveteen
velo (*vāy*-loa) *m* veil
veloce (vay-*lōā*-chay) *adj* fast, rapid
velocità (vay-loa-chee-*tah*) *f* speed; pace, rate; gear; **limite di** ~ speed limit; ~ **di crociera** cruising speed
vena (*vāy*-nah) *f* vein; ~ **varicosa** varicose vein
vendemmia (vayn-*daym*-myah) *f* vintage
vendere (*vayn*-day-ray) *v* *sell; ~ **al minuto** retail
vendetta (vayn-*dayt*-tah) *f* revenge
vendibile (vayn-*dee*-bee-lay) *adj* saleable
vendita (*vayn*-dee-tah) *f* sale; **in** ~ for sale; ~ **al minuto** retail trade
venerabile (vay-nay-*raa*-bee-lay) *adj* venerable
venerare (vay-nay-*raa*-ray) *v* worship
venerdì (vay-nayr-*dee*) *m* Friday
venezolano (vay-nay-tsoa-*laa*-noa) *adj* Venezuelan; *m* Venezuelan
Venezuela (vay-nay-*tswai*-lah) *m* Venezuela
***venire** (vay-*nee*-ray) *v* *come; ***far** ~ *send for
ventaglio (vayn-*taa*-lʸoa) *m* fan
ventesimo (vayn-*tai*-zee-moa) *num* twentieth
venti (*vayn*-tee) *num* twenty
ventilare (vayn-tee-*laa*-ray) *v* ventilate
ventilatore (vayn-tee-lah-*tōā*-ray) *m* fan, ventilator
ventilazione (vayn-tee-lah-*tsyōā*-nay) *f* ventilation
vento (*vehn*-toa) *m* wind
ventoso (vayn-*tōā*-soa) *adj* gusty, windy
veramente (vay-rah-*mayn*-tay) *adv* really
veranda (vay-*rahn*-dah) *f* veranda
verbale (vayr-*baa*-lay) *adj* verbal; *m* minutes
verbo (*vehr*-boa) *m* verb
verde (*vayr*-day) *adj* green
verdetto (vayr-*dayt*-toa) *m* verdict
verdura (vayr-*dōō*-rah) *f* greens *pl*, vegetable
vergine (*vehr*-jee-nay) *f* virgin
vergogna (vayr-*gōā*-ñah) *f* shame; ***aver** ~ *be ashamed; **vergogna!** shame!
vergognoso (vayr-goa-*ñōā*-soa) *adj* ashamed
verificare (vay-ree-fee-*kaa*-ray) *v* check, verify
verità (vay-ree-*tah*) *f* truth
veritiero (vay-ree-*tyai*-roa) *adj* truthful
verme (*vehr*-may) *m* worm
vernice (vayr-*nee*-chay) *f* varnish
verniciare (vayr-nee-*chaa*-ray) *v* varnish, paint
vero (*vāy*-roa) *adj* true; very
versamento (vayr-sah-*mayn*-toa) *m* deposit
versare (vayr-*saa*-ray) *v* pour; *shed
versione (vayr-*syōā*-nay) *f* version
verso[1] (*vehr*-soa) *prep* to; at, towards
verso[2] (*vehr*-soa) *m* verse
verticale (vayr-tee-*kaa*-lay) *adj* vertical
vertigine (vayr-*tee*-jee-nay) *f* vertigo; giddiness
vescica (vaysh-*shee*-kah) *f* bladder
vescovo (*vāy*-skoa-voa) *m* bishop
vespa (*vay*-spah) *f* wasp
vestaglia (vay-*staa*-lʸah) *f* negligee; dressing-gown
veste (*veh*-stay) *f* frock; robe
vestibolo (vayss-*tee*-boa-loa) *m* hall
vestire (vay-*stee*-ray) *v* dress; *wear
vestiti (vayss-*tee*-tee) *mpl* clothes *pl*; **vestito da donna** gown, dress; **vestito da uomo** *m* suit
veterinario (vay-tay-ree-*naa*-ryoa) *m* veterinary surgeon
vetrina (vay-*tree*-nah) *f* shop-window

vetro (*vāy*-troa) *m* glass; pane; **di ~** glass; **~ colorato** stained glass
vetta (*vayt*-tah) *f* peak, summit
vezzeggiare (vayt-tsayd-*jaa*-ray) *v* cuddle
vi (vee) *pron* you; yourselves
via[1] (*vee*-ah) *f* way; **~ d'acqua** waterway; **~ principale** main street; **~ selciata** causeway
via[2] (*vee*-ah) *adv* away, gone, off; *prep* via
viadotto (vyah-*doat*-toa) *m* viaduct
viaggiare (veeahd-*jaa*-ray) *v* travel
viaggiatore (vyahd-jah-*tōā*-ray) *m* traveller
viaggio (*vyahd*-joa) *m* journey; trip, voyage; **~ d'affari** business trip; **~ di ritorno** return journey
viale (*vyaa*-lay) *m* avenue
vibrare (vee-*braa*-ray) *v* tremble, vibrate
vibrazione (vee-brah-*tsyōā*-nay) *f* vibration
vicario (vee-*kaa*-ryoa) *m* vicar
vicenda (vee-*chehn*-dah) *f* vicissitude; event
vicepresidente (vee-chay-pray-see-*dehn*-tay) *m* vice-president
vicinanza (vee-chee-*nahn*-tsah) *f* vicinity
vicinato (vee-chee-*naa*-toa) *m* neighbourhood
vicino (vee-*chee*-noa) *adj* close, nearby, near; *m* neighbour; **~ a** near; beside, next to, by
vicolo (*vee*-koa-loa) *m* lane, alley; **~ cieco** cul-de-sac
video (*vee*-day-oa) *m* screen
vietato (vyay-*taa*-toa) *adj* prohibited; **~ ai pedoni** no pedestrians; **~ fumare** no smoking; **~ l'ingresso** no admittance
vigilante (vee-jee-*lahn*-tay) *adj* vigilant
vigna (*vee*-ñah) *f* vineyard
vigore (vee-*gōā*-ray) *m* stamina
vile (*vee*-lay) *adj* cowardly
villa (*veel*-lah) *f* villa
villaggio (veel-*lahd*-joa) *m* village
villino (veel-*lee*-noa) *m* cottage
***vincere** (*veen*-chay-ray) *v* conquer, *overcome; *win
vincita (*veen*-chee-tah) *f* winnings *pl*
vincitore (veen-chee-*tōā*-ray) *m* winner
vino (*vee*-noa) *m* wine
violazione (vyoa-lah-*tsyōā*-nay) *f* violation
violentare (vyoa-layn-*taa*-ray) *v* rape
violento (vyoa-*lehn*-toa) *adj* violent, severe
violenza (vyoa-*lehn*-tsah) *f* violence
violetta (vyoa-*layt*-tah) *f* violet
violetto (vyoa-*layt*-toa) *adj* violet
violino (vyoa-*lee*-noa) *m* violin
virgola (*veer*-goa-lah) *f* comma
virgolette (veer-goa-*layt*-tay) *fpl* quotation marks
virtù (veer-*too*) *f* virtue
virtuoso (veer-*twōā*-soa) *adj* good
viscido (*veesh*-shee-doa) *adj* slippery
visibile (vee-*zee*-bee-lay) *adj* visible
visibilità (vee-zee-bee-lee-*tah*) *f* visibility
visione (vee-*zyōā*-nay) *f* vision
visita (*vee*-zee-tah) *f* visit, call; **~ medica** check-up
visitare (vee-zee-*taa*-ray) *v* call on; visit
visitatore (vee-zee-tah-*tōā*-ray) *m* visitor
viso (*vee*-zoa) *m* face
visone (vee-*zōā*-nay) *m* mink
vista (*vee*-stah) *f* sight; view
vistare (vee-*staa*-ray) *v* endorse
visto (*vee*-stoa) *m* visa
vistoso (vee-*stōā*-soa) *adj* striking
vita (*vee*-tah) *f* life; waist
vitale (vee-*taa*-lay) *adj* vital
vitamina (vee-tah-*mee*-nah) *f* vitamin

vite (*vee*-tay) *f* screw; vine
vitello (vee-*tehl*-loa) *m* calf; veal
vittima (*veet*-tee-mah) *f* victim; casualty
vitto (*veet*-toa) *m* fare, food; ~ **e alloggio** room and board, bed and board, board and lodging
vittoria (veet-*taw*-ryah) *f* victory
vivace (vee-*vaa*-chay) *adj* active, brisk, lively; gay
vivaio (vee-*vaa*-yoa) *m* nursery
vivente (vee-*vehn*-tay) *adj* alive
***vivere** (*vee*-vay-ray) *v* live
vivido (*vee*-vee-doa) *adj* vivid
vivo (*vee*-voa) *adj* alive, live
viziare (vee-*tsyaa*-ray) *v* *spoil
vizio (*vee*-tsıæħ) *m* vice
vocabolario (voa-kah-boa-*laa*-ryoa) *m* vocabulary
vocale (voa-*kaa*-lay) *adj* vocal; *f* vowel
voce (*vōā*-chay) *f* voice; **ad alta ~** aloud
voglia (*vaw*-lʸah) *f* fancy; ***aver ~ di** fancy, *feel like
voi (*vōā*-ee) *pron* you; ~ **stessi** yourselves
volante (voa-*lahn*-tay) *m* steering-wheel
volare (voa-*laa*-ray) *v* *fly
volentieri (voa-layn-*tyai*-ree) *adv* gladly, willingly
***volere** (voa-*lāy*-ray) *v* *will, want; ***voler bene** care for, like
volgare (voal-*gaa*-ray) *adj* coarse, vulgar
***volgere** (*vol*-jay-ray) *v* turn
volo (*vōā*-loa) *m* flight; ~ **charter** charter flight; ~ **di ritorno** return flight; ~ **notturno** night flight
volontà (voa-loan-*tah*) *f* will
volontario (voa-loan-*taa*-ryoa) *adj* voluntary; *m* volunteer
volpe (*voal*-pay) *f* fox
volt (voalt) *m* volt
volta (*vol*-tah) *f* time; vault; **ancora una ~** once more; **due volte** twice; **qualche ~** sometimes; **una ~** once
voltaggio (voal-*tahd*-joa) *m* voltage
voltare (voal-*taa*-ray) *v* turn; turn round
volume (voa-*lōō*-may) *m* volume
voluminoso (voa-loo-mee-*nōā*-soa) *adj* big, bulky
vomitare (voa-mee-*taa*-ray) *v* vomit
vostro (*vo*-stroa) *adj* your
votare (voa-*taa*-ray) *v* vote
votazione (voa-tah-*tsyōā*-nay) *f* vote
voto (*vōā*-toa) *m* vote; mark
vulcano (vool-*kaa*-noa) *m* volcano
vulnerabile (vool-nay-*raa*-bee-lay) *adj* vulnerable
vuotare (vwo-*taa*-ray) *v* empty
vuoto (*vwaw*-toa) *adj* empty; hollow; *m* vacuum

Z

zaffiro (dzahf-*fee*-roa) *m* sapphire
zaino (*dzigh*-noa) *m* rucksack, knapsack
zampa (*tsahm*-pah) *f* paw
zampillo (tsahm-*peel*-loa) *m* squirt
zanzara (dzahn-*dzaa*-rah) *f* mosquito
zanzariera (dzahn-dzah-*ryai*-rah) *f* mosquito-net
zappa (*tsahp*-pah) *f* spade
zattera (*tsaht*-tay-rah) *f* raft
zebra (*dzai*-brah) *f* zebra
zelante (dzay-*lahn*-tay) *adj* diligent, zealous
zelo (*dzai*-loa) *m* diligence, zeal
zenit (*dzai*-neet) *m* zenith
zenzero (*dzehn*-dzay-roa) *m* ginger
zero (*dzai*-roa) *m* nought, zero
zia (*tsee*-ah) *f* aunt

zigomo (*dzee*-goa-moa) *m* cheek-bone
zigzagare (dzeeg-dzah-*gaa*-ray) *v* *wind
zinco (*dzeeng*-koa) *m* zinc
zingaro (*tseeng*-gah-roa) *m* gipsy
zio (*tsee*-oa) *m* uncle
zitella (tsee-*tehl*-lah) *f* spinster
zitto (*tseet*-toa) *adj* silent
zoccolo (*tsok*-koa-loa) *m* wooden shoe; hoof
zodiaco (dzoa-*dee*-ah-koa) *m* zodiac
zona (*dzōā*-nah) *f* zone; area; ~ **di parcheggio** parking zone; ~ **industriale** industrial area
zoologia (dzoa-oa-loa-*jee*-ah) *f* zoology
zoom (zōōm) *m* zoom lens
zoppicante (tsoap-pee-*kahn*-tay) *adj* lame
zoppicare (tsoap-pee-*kaa*-ray) *v* limp
zoppo (*tsop*-poa) *adj* crippled, lame
zuccherare (tsook-kay-*raa*-ray) *v* sweeten
zucchero (*tsook*-kay-roa) *m* sugar; **zolletta di** ~ lump of sugar

Menu Reader

Food

abbacchio grilled lam
  ~ **alla cacciatora** pieces of lamb, often braised with garlic, rosemary, white wine, anchovy paste and hot peppers
(all') abruzzese Abruzzi style; with red peppers and sometimes ham
acciughe anchovies
  ~ **al limone** fresh anchovies served with a sauce of lemon, oil, breadcrumbs and oregano
(all')aceto (in) vinegar
acetosella sorrel
acquacotta soup of bread and vegetables, sometimes with eggs and cheese
affettati sliced cold meat, ham and salami (US cold cuts)
affumicato smoked
agliata garlic sauce; garlic mashed with breadcrumbs
aglio garlic
agnello lamb
agnolotti kind of ravioli with savoury filling of vegetables, chopped meats, sometimes with garlic and herbs
(all')agro dressing of lemon juice and oil
agrodolce sweet-sour dressing of caramelized sugar, vinegar and flour to which capers, raisins or lemon may be added
al, all', alla in the style of: with
ala wing
albicocca apricot
alice anchovy
allodola lark
alloro bay leaf
ananas pineapple
anguilla eel
  ~ **alla veneziana** braised with tunny (tuna) and lemon sauce
anguria watermelon
anice aniseed
animelle (di vitello) (veal) sweetbreads
anitra duck
  ~ **selvatica** wild duck
annegati slices of meat in white wine or Marsala wine
antipasto hors-d'oeuvre
  ~ **di mare** seafood
  ~ **a scelta** to one's own choosing
arachide peanuts
aragosta spiny lobster
arancia orange
aringa herring

arista loin of pork
arrosto roast(ed)
arsella kind of mussel
asiago cheese made of skimmed milk, semi hard to hard, sweet when young
asparago asparagus
assortito assorted
astice lobster
attorta flaky pastry filled with fruit and almonds
avellana hazelnut
babbaluci snails in olive-oil sauce with tomatoes and onions
baccalà stockfish, dried cod
~ **alla fiorentina** floured and fried in oil
~ **alla vicentina** poached in milk with onion, garlic, parsley, anchovies and cinnamon
(con) bagna cauda simmering sauce of butter, olive oil, garlic and chopped anchovies, into which raw vegetables and bread are dipped
barbabietola beetroot
basilico basil
beccaccia woodcock
Bel Paese smooth cheese with delicate taste
ben cotto well-done
(alla) besciamella (with) white sauce
bigoli in salsa noodles with an anchovy or sardine sauce
biscotto rusk, biscuit (US zwieback, cookie)
bistecca steak, usually beef, but may be another kind of meat
~ **di manzo** beef steak
~ **(alla) pizzaiola** with tomatoes, basil and sometimes garlic
~ **di vitello** veal scallop
bocconcini diced meat with herbs
bollito 1) boiled 2) meat or fish stew
(alla) bolognese in a sauce of tomatoes and meat or ham and cheese
(alla) brace on charcoal
braciola di maiale pork chop
bracioletta small slice of meat
~ **a scottadito** charcoal-grilled lamb chops
braciolone alla napoletana breaded rumpsteak with garlic, parsley, ham and currants; rolled, sautéed and stewed
branzino bass
brasato braised
broccoletti strascinati brocoli sautéed with pork fat and garlic
brodetto fish soup with onions and tomato pulp
brodo bouillon, broth, soup
~ **vegetale** vegetable broth
bruschetta a thick slice of countrystyle bread, grilled, rubbed with garlic and sprinkled with olive oil
budino blancmange, custard
bue beef
burrida fish casserole strongly flavoured with spices and herbs
burro butter
~ **maggiordomo** with lemon juice and parsley
busecca thick tripe and vegetable soup
cacciagione game
(alla) cacciatora often with mushrooms, herbs, shallots, wine, tomatoes, strips of ham and tongue
cacciucco spicy fish soup, usually with onions, green pepper, garlic and red wine topped with garlic flavoured croutons

caciocavallo firm, slightly sweet cheese from cow's or sheep's milk
calamaretto young squid
calamaro squid
caldo hot
calzone pizza dough envelope with ham, cheese, herbs and baked
(alla) campagnola with vegetables, especially onions and tomatoes
canederli dumplings made from ham, sausage and breadcrumbs
cannella cinnamon
cannelloni tubular dough stuffed with meat, cheese or vegetables, covered with a white sauce and baked
~ **alla Barbaroux** with chopped ham, veal, cheese and covered with white sauce
~ **alla laziale** with meat and onion filling and baked in tomato sauce
~ **alla napoletana** with cheese and ham filling in tomato and herb sauce
cannolo rolled pastry filled with sweet, white cheese, sometimes nougat and crystallized fruit
capitone large eel
capocollo smoked salt pork
caponata aubergine, green pepper, tomato, vegetable marrow, garlic, oil and herbs; usually served cold
cappelletti small ravioli filled with meat, herbs, cheese and eggs
cappero caper
cappon magro pyramid of cooked vegetables and fish salad
cappone capon
capretto kid
~ **ripieno al forno** stuffed with herbs and roasted
caprino a soft goat's cheese
~ **romano** hard goat's milk cheese
capriolo roebuck
caramellato caramelized
(alla) carbonara *pasta* with smoked ham, cheese, eggs and olive oil
carbonata 1) grilled pork chop 2) beef stew in red wine
carciofo artichoke
~ **alla romana** stuffed, sautéed in oil, garlic and white wine
carciofino small artichoke
cardo cardoon
carne meat
~ **a carrargiu** spit-roasted
carota carrot
carpa, carpione carp
(della) casa chef's speciality
(alla) casalinga home-made
cassata ice-cream with a crystallized fruit filling
~ **(alla) siciliana** sponge cake garnished with sweet cream cheese, chocolate and crystallized fruit
(in) casseruola (in a) casserole
castagnaccio chestnut cake with pine kernels, raisins, nuts, cooked in oil
castagne chestnuts
caviale caviar
cavolfiore cauliflower
cavolino di Bruxelles brussels sprout
cavolo cabbage
cazzoeula a casserole of pork, celery, onions, cabbage and spices
cece chick-pea
cena dinner, supper
cerfoglio chervil
cervella brains

cervo stag
cetriolino gherkin (US pickle)
cetriolo cucumber
chiodo di garofano cloves
ciambella ringshaped bun
cicoria endive (US chicory)
ciliegia cherry
cima cold, stuffed veal
~ **alla genovese** stuffed with eggs, sausage and mushrooms
cinghiale (wild) boar
cioccolata chocolate
cipolla onion
cipollina pearl onion
ciuppin thick fish soup
cocomero watermelon
coda di bue oxtail
colazione lunch
composta stewed fruit
coniglio rabbit
~ **all'agro** stewed in red wine, with the addition of lemon juice
contorno garnish
copata small wafer of honey and nuts
coppa kind of raw ham, usually smoked
corda lamb tripes roasted or braised in tomato sauce with peas
cornetti 1) string beans 2) crescent rolls
cosce di rana frogs' legs
coscia leg, thigh
cosciotto leg
costata beef steak or chop, entrecôte
~ **alla fiorentina** grilled over an olive-wood fire, served with lemon juice and parsley
~ **alla pizzaiola** braised in sauce with tomatoes, marjoram, parsley and *mozzarella* cheese
~ **al prosciutto** with ham, cheese and truffles; breaded and fried
costoletta cutlet, chop (veal or pork)
~ **alla bolognese** breaded veal cutlet topped with a slice of ham, cheese and tomato sauce
~ **alla milanese** veal cutlet, breaded, then fried
~ **alla parmigiana** breaded and baked with parmesan cheese
~ **alla valdostana** with ham and *fontina* cheese
~ **alla viennese** breaded veal scallop, wiener schnitzel
cotechino spiced pork sausage, served hot in slices
cotto cooked
~ **a puntino** medium (done)
cozza mussel
cozze alla marinara mussels cooked in white wine with parsley and garlic
crauti sauerkraut
crema cream, custard
cremino 1) soft cheese 2) type of ice-cream bar
crescione watercress
crespolino spinach-filled pancake baked in cheese sauce
crocchetta potato or rice croquette
crostaceo shellfish
crostata pie, flan
crostini small pieces of toast, croutons
~ **in brodo** broth with croutons
~ **alla provatura** diced bread and *provatura* cheese toasted on a spit
crostino alla napoletana small toast with anchovies and melted cheese
crudo raw
culatello type of raw ham, cured

in white wine
cuore heart
~ **di sedano** celery heart
cuscusu di Trapani fish soup with semolina flakes
dattero date
datteri di mare mussels, small clams
dentice dentex (Mediterranean fish, similar to sea bream)
(alla) diavola usually grilled with a lavish amount of pepper, chili pepper or pimento
diverso varied
dolce sweet, dessert
dolci pastries, cakes
(alla) Doria with cucumbers
dragoncello tarragon
fagiano pheasant
fagiolino French bean (US green bean)
fagiolo haricot bean
faraona guinea hen
farcito stuffed
farsumagru rolled beef or veal stuffed with bacon, ham, eggs, cheese, parsley and onions; braised with tomatoes
fatto in casa home-made
fava broad bean
favata casserole of beans, bacon, sausage and seasoning
fegatelli di maiale alla Fiorentina pork liver grilled on a skewer with bay leaves and diced, fried croutons
fegato liver
~ **alla veneziana** slices of calf's liver fried with onions
(ai) ferri on the grill, grilled
fesa round cut taken from leg of veal
~ **in gelatina** roast veal in aspic jelly
fettina small slice
fettuccine flat narrow noodles
~ **verdi** green noodles
fico fig
filetto fillet
finocchio fennel
~ **in salsa bianca** in white sauce
(alla) fiorentina with herbs, oil and often spinach
focaccia 1) flat bread, sprinkled with olive oil, sometimes with fried chopped onions or cheese 2) sweet ring-shaped cake
~ **di vitello** veal patty
fondo di carciofo artichoke heart (US bottom)
fonduta melted cheese with egg-yolk, milk and truffles
fontina a soft, creamy cheese from Piedmont, chiefly used in cooking
formaggio cheese
(al) forno baked
forte hot, spicy
fra diavolo with a spicy tomato sauce
fragola strawberry
~ **di bosco** wild
frattaglie giblets
fregula soup with semolina and saffron dumplings
fresco cool, fresh, uncooked
frittata omelet
~ **semplice** plain
frittatina di patate potato omelet
frittella fritter, pancake, often filled with ham and cheese or with an apple
fritto deep-fried
~ **alla milanese** breaded
~ **misto** deep-fried bits of sea-food, vegetables or meat
~ **alla napoletana** fried fish, vegetables and cheese

~ **alla romana** sweetbread, artichokes and cauliflower
~ **di verdura** fried vegetables
frutta fruit
~ **candita** crystallized (US candied)
~ **cotta** stewed
frutti di mare shellfish
fungo mushroom
galantina tartufata truffles in aspic jelly
gallina hen
gallinaccio 1) chanterelle mushroom 2) woodcock
gallinella water-hen
gallo cedrone grouse
gamberetto shrimp
gambero crayfish, crawfish
garofolato beef stew with cloves
(in) gelatina (in) aspic jelly
gelato ice-cream; iced dessert
(alla) genovese with basil and other herbs, pine kernels, garlic and oil
ghiacciato iced, chilled
ginepro juniper (berry)
girello round steak from the leg
gnocchi dumplings
gorgonzola most famous of the Italian blue-veined cheese, rich with a tangy flavour
grana hard cheese; also known as *parmigiano(-reggiano)*
granchio crab
grasso rich with fat or oil
(alla) graticola grilled
gratinata sprinkled with breadcrumbs and grated cheese and oven-browned
grattugiato grated
(alla) griglia from the grill
grissino breadstick
gruviera mild cheese with holes, Italian version of Swiss *gruyère*
guazzetto meat stew with garlic, rosemary, tomatoes and pimentos
incasciata layers of dough, meat sauce, hard-boiled eggs and grated cheese
indivia chicory (US endive)
insalata salad
~ **all'americana** mayonnaise and shrimps
~ **russa** diced boiled vegetables in mayonnaise
~ **verde** green
~ **di verdura cotta** boiled vegetables
involtino stuffed meat or ham roll
lampone raspberry
lampreda lamprey
lardo bacon
lasagne thin layers of generally green noodle dough alternating with tomato, sausage meat, ham, white sauce and grated cheese; baked in the oven
latte alla portoghese baked custard with liquid caramel
lattuga lettuce
lauro bay leaf
(alla) laziale with onions
legume vegetable
lenticchia lentil
lepre hare
~ **al lardo con funghi** with bacon and mushrooms
~ **in salmì** jugged
leprotto leveret
lesso 1) boiled 2) meat or fish stew
limone lemon
lingua tongue
linguine flat noodles
lista dei vini wine list
lodigiano kind of parmesan cheese
lombata loin
luganega pork sausage

lumaca snail
lupo di mare sea perch
maccheroni macaroni
macedonia di frutta fruit salad
maggiorana marjoram
magro 1) lean 2) dish without meat
maiale pork
~ **al latte** cooked in milk
~ **ubriaco** cooked in red wine
maionese mayonnaise
mandarino mandarin
mandorla almond
manzo beef
~ **arrosto ripieno** stuffed roast
~ **lesso** boiled
~ **salato** corned beef
(alla) marinara sauce of tomatoes, olives, garlic, clams and mussels
marinato marinated
maritozzo soft roll
marmellata jam
~ **d'arance** marmalade
marrone chestnut
mascarpone soft, butter-coloured cheese, often served as a sweet dish
medaglione round fillet of beef or veal
mela apple
~ **cotogna** quince
melanzana aubergine (US eggplant)
melanzane alla parmigiana aubergines baked with tomatoes, parmesan cheese and spices
melanzane ripiene stuffed with various ingredients and gratinéed
melone melon
~ **con prosciutto** with cured ham
menta mint
meringa meringue
merlano whiting
merluzzo cod
messicani veal scallops rolled around a meat, cheese or herb stuffing
midollo marrow (bone)
miele honey
(alla) milanese 1) Milanese style of cooking 2) breaded (of meat)
millefoglie custard slice (US napoleon)
minestra soup
~ **in brodo** bouillon with noodles or rice and chicken liver
~ **di funghi** cream of mushroom
minestrone thick vegetable soup
~ **alla genovese** with spinach, basil, macaroni
~ **verde** with French beans and herbs
mirtillo bilberry (US blueberry)
misto mixed
mitilo mussel
(alla) montanara with different root vegetables
montone mutton
mora blackberry, mulberry
mortadella bologna (sausage)
mostarda mustard
~ **di frutta** spiced crystallized fruits (US candied fruits) in a sweet-sour syrup
mozzarella soft, unripened cheese with a bland, slightly sweet flavour, made from buffalo's milk in southern Italy, elsewhere with cow's milk
(alla) napoletana with cheese, tomatoes, herbs and sometimes anchovies
nasello whiting
naturale plain, without sauce or

filling
navone yellow turnip
nocciola hazelnut
noce nut
  ~ **di cocco** coconut
  ~ **moscata** nutmeg
nostrano local, home-grown
oca goose
olio oil
  ~ **d'arachide** peanut oil
  ~ **di semi** seed oil
olive agrodolci olives in vinegar and sugar
olive ripiene stuffed olives (e.g. with meat, cheese, pimento)
ombrina umbrine (fish)
orata John Dory (fish)
origano oregano
osso bone
  ~ **buco** veal shanks cooked in various ways depending on the region
ostrica oyster
ovalina small *mozzarella* cheese from buffalo's milk
ovolo egg mushroom
(alla) paesana with bacon, potatoes, carrots, vegetable marrow and other root vegetables
pagliarino medium-soft cheese from Piedmont
palomba wood-pigeon, ring-dove
pan di Genova almond cake
pan di Spagna sponge cake
pan tostato toasted Italian bread
pancetta bacon
pandolce heavy cake with dried fruit and pine kernels
pane bread
  ~ **casareccio** home-made
  ~ **scuro** dark
  ~ **di segale** rye
panettone tall light cake with a few raisins and crystallized fruit
panforte di Siena flat round slab made mostly of spiced crystallized fruit
pangrattato breadcrumbs
panicielli d'uva passula grapes wrapped in citron leaves and baked
panino roll
  ~ **imbottito** sandwich
panna cream
  ~ **montata** whipped
panzarotti fried or baked large dough envelopes often with a filling of pork, eggs, cheese, anchovies and tomatoes
pappardelle long, broad noodles
  ~ **con la lepre** garnished with spiced hare
parmigiano(-reggiano) parmesan, a hard cheese generally grated for use in hot dishes
passatelli pasta made from a mixture of egg, parmesan cheese, breadcrumbs, often with a pinch of nutmeg
passato purée, creamed
  ~ **di verdura** mashed vegetable soup, generally with croutons
pasta the traditional Italian first course; essentially a dough consisting of flour, water, oil (or butter) and eggs; produced in a variety of shapes and sizes (e.g. spaghetti, macaroni, broad noodles, ravioli, shell- and star-shaped *pasta*); may be eaten on its own, in a bouillon, seasoned with butter or olive oil, stuffed or accompanied by a savoury sauce, sprinkled with grated cheese
  ~ **asciutta** any pasta not eaten in a bouillon; served with any of various dressings

pasticcino tart, cake, small pastry
pasticcio 1) pie 2) type of *pasta* like *lasagne*
pastina small *pasta* in various shapes used principally as a bouillon or soup ingredient
pasto meal
patate potatoes
~ **fritte** deep fried
~ **lesse** boiled
~ **novelle** new
~ **in padella** fried in a pan
~ **rosolate** roasted
~ **saltate** sliced and sautéed
patatine small, new potatoes
pecorino a hard cheese made from sheep's milk
pepato peppered
pepe pepper
peperonata stew of peppers, tomatoes and sometimes onions
peperone green or red sweet pepper
~ **arrostito** roasted sweet pepper
~ **ripieno** stuffed, usually with rice and chopped meat
pera pear
pernice partridge
pesca peach
~ **melba** peach-halves poached in syrup over vanilla ice-cream, topped with raspberry sauce and whipped cream
pescatrice angler fish, frog fish
pesce fish
~ **spada** swordfish
pesto sauce of basil leaves, garlic, cheese and sometimes with pine kernels and majoram; used in *minestrone* or with *pasta*
petto breast
(a) piacere to your own choosing
piatto dish
~ **del giorno** the day's speciality
~ **principale** main course
primo ~ first course
piccante highly seasoned
piccata thin veal scallop
~ **al marsala** braised in Marsala sauce
piccione pigeon (US squab)
piede trotter (US foot)
(alla) piemontese Piedmontese style; with truffles and rice
pignoli pine kernels
pinoccate pine kernel and almond cake
pisello pea
pistacchi pistachio nuts
piviere plover (bird)
pizza flat, open(-faced) pie, tart, flan; bread dough bottom with any of a wide variety of toppings
pizzetta small *pizza*
polenta pudding of maizemeal (US cornmeal)
~ **pasticciata** *polenta*, sliced and served with meat sauce, mushrooms, white sauce, butter and cheese
~ **e uccelli** small birds spit-roasted and served with *polenta*
pollame fowl
pollo chicken
~ **alla diavola** highly spiced and grilled
~ **novello** spring chicken
polpetta di carne meatball
polpettone meat loaf of seasoned beef or veal
polpo octopus
~ **in purgatorio** sautéed in oil with tomatoes, parsley, garlic and peppers
(salsa di) pommarola tomato sauce

for *pasta*
pomodoro tomato
pompelmo grapefruit
popone melon
porchetta roast suck(l)ing pig
porcini boletus mushrooms
porro leek
pranzo lunch or dinner
prezzemolo parsley
prezzo price
~ **fisso** fixed price
prima colazione breakfast
primizie spring fruit or vegetables
profiterole filled cream puff
~ **alla cioccolata** with chocolate frosting
prosciutto ham
~ **affumicato** cured, smoked
~ **di cinghiale** smoked wild boar
~ **di Parma** cured ham from Parma
provatura soft, mild and slightly sweet cheese made from buffalo's milk
provolone white, medium-hard cheese
prugna plum
~ **secca** prune
punte di asparagi asparagus tips
purè di patate mashed potatoes
quaglia quail
rabarbaro rhubarb
rafano horse-radish
ragù meat sauce for *pasta*
ragusano hard and slightly sweet cheese
rapa turnip
ravanello radish
raviggiolo cheese made from sheep's or goat's milk
razza ray
ribes currants
~ **neri** blackcurrants
~ **rossi** redcurrants
riccio di mare sea urchin
ricotta soft cow's or sheep's milk cheese
rigaglie giblets
rigatoni 1) type of *pasta* similar to *cannelloni* 2) type of macaroni
ripieno stuffing, stuffed
risi e bisi rice and peas cooked in chicken bouillon
riso rice
~ **in bianco** white rice with butter
risotto dish made of boiled rice served as a first course, with various ingredients according to the region
(brodo) ristretto consommé
robiola soft, rich and sweet sheep's milk cheese
robiolina goat's or sheep's milk cheese
rognoni kidneys
(alla) romana with vegetables, particularly onions, mint and sometimes anchovies
rombo turbot, brill
rosbif roast beef
rosmarino rosemary
rotolo rolled, stuffed meat
salame salami
salato salted
sale salt
salmone salmon
salsa sauce
salsiccia any spiced pork sausage to be served cooked
saltimbocca veal slices with ham, sage, herbs and wine
~ **alla romana** veal cutlet flavoured with ham and sage, sautéed in butter and white wine
(al) sangue underdone (US rare)
sarda pilchard, sardine

sardina small sardine
sardo sheep's milk cheese, hard, pungent and aromatic
sartù oven-baked rice with tomatoes, meat balls, chicken giblets, mushrooms and peas
scalogno shallot
scaloppa, scaloppina veal scallop
~ **alla fiorentina** with spinach and white sauce
scamorza aged *mozzarella*, firmer and saltier
scampi Dublin Bay prawns
scapece fried fish preserved in white vinegar with saffron
(allo) sciroppo in syrup
scorfano rascasse, a Mediterranean fish, used for fish soup
scorzonera salsify
sedano celery
selvaggina game
senape mustard
seppia cuttlefish, squid
servizio (non) compreso service (not) included
sfogliatelle puff pastry with custard or fruit-preserve filling
sgombro mackerel
silvano chocolate meringue or tart
soffritto sautéed
sogliola sole
~ **arrosto** baked in olive oil, herbs and white wine
~ **dorata** breaded and fried
~ **ai ferri** grilled
~ **alla mugnaia** sautéed in butter with lemon juice and parsley
soppressata 1) sausage 2) preserved pig's head with pistachio nuts
sottaceti pickled vegetables
sottaceto pickled
spaghetti spaghetti
~ **aglio e olio** with olive oil and fried garlic
~ **all'amatriciana** with tomato sauce, garlic and parmesan cheese
~ **alla carbonara** with oil, cheese, bacon and eggs
~ **pomodoro e basilico** fresh tomatoes and basil leaves
~ **alle vongole** with clam or mussel sauce, tomatoes, garlic and pimento
spalla shoulder
specialità speciality
spezzatino meat or fowl stew
spiedino pieces of meat grilled or roasted on a skewer
~ **di mare** pieces of fish and seafood skewered and roasted
(allo) spiedo (on a) spit
spigola sea bass
spinaci spinach
spugnola morel mushroom
spumone foamy ice-cream dessert with crystallized fruit, whipped cream and nuts
(di) stagione (in) season
stellette star-shaped *pasta*
stinco knuckle (of veal), shin (of beef)
stoccafisso stockfish, dried cod
storione sturgeon
stracchino creamy, soft to medium-soft cheese
stracciatella consommé with semolina or breadcrumbs, eggs and grated cheese
stracotto meat stew, slowly cooked for several hours
strascinati shell-shaped fresh *pasta* with different sauces
stufato 1) stew(ed) 2) beef stew
succu tunnu soup with semolina and saffron dumplings

sufflé soufflé
sugo sauce, gravy
(carne di) suino pork
suppli rice croquettes with *mozzarella* cheese and meat sauce
suprema di pollo in gelatina chicken breast in aspic jelly
susina plum
tacchino turkey
tagliatelle flat noodles
tagliolini thin flat noodles
taleggio medium-hard cheese with a mild flavour
tartaruga turtle
tartina open(-faced) sandwich
tartufo truffle
tartufi di mare cockles or small clams
(al) tegame sautéed
(alla) teglia fried in a pan
testa di vitello calf's head
timo thyme
tinca tench (fish)
tonnato in tunny (tuna) sauce
tonno tunny (US tuna)
topinambur Jerusalem artichoke
tordo thrush
torrone nougat
torta pie, tart, flan
tortelli small fritters
tortellini ringlets of dough filled with seasoned minced meat
tortiglione almond cake
tortino savoury tart filled with cheese and vegetables
~ **di carciofi** fried artichokes mixed with beaten eggs
(alla) toscana with tomatoes, celery and herbs
tostato toasted
totano young squid
tramezzino small sandwich
trenette noodles
triglia red mullet
trippe alla fiorentina slowly braised tripe and minced beef with tomato sauce, marjoram, parmesan cheese
trippe alla milanese tripe stewed with onions, leek, carrots, tomatoes, beans, sage and nutmeg
trippe alla romana cooked in sweet-and-sour sauce with cheese
tritato minced
trota trout
~ **alle mandorle** stuffed, seasoned, baked in cream and topped with almonds
~ **di ruscello** river trout
tutto compreso everything included
uccelletti, uccelli small birds, usually spit-roasted
~ **in umido** stewed
uovo egg
~ **affogato nel vino** poached in wine
~ **al burro** fried in butter
~ **in camicia** poached
~ **alla coque** boiled
~ **alla fiorentina** fried, served on a bed of spinach
~ **(al) forno** baked
~ **fritto** fried
~ **molle** soft-boiled
~ **ripieno** stuffed
~ **sodo** hard-boiled
~ **strapazzato** scrambled
uva grape
vaniglia vanilla
vario assorted
(alla) veneziana with onions or shallots, white wine and mint
verdura green vegetables
vermicelli thin noodles
verza green cabbage
vitello veal

~ **all'uccelletto** diced veal, sage, simmered in wine
vongola small clam
zaba(gl)ione dessert of egg-yolks, sugar and Marsala wine; served warm
zampone pig's trotter filled with seasoned pork, boiled and served in slices
zèppola fritter, doughnut
zimino fish stew
zucca pumpkin, gourd
zucchero sugar
zucchino small vegetable marrow (US zucchini)
zuppa soup
~ **fredda** cold
~ **di frutti di mare** seafood
~ **inglese** sponge cake steeped in rum with candied fruit and custard or whipped cream
~ **alla pavese** consommé with poached egg, croutons and grated cheese
~ **di vongole** clam soup with white wine

Drinks

abboccato medium dry (wine)
acqua water
~ **fredda** ice-cold
~ **gasata** soda water
acquavite brandy, spirits
Aleatico a dessert wine made from muscat grapes
amabile slightly sweet (wine)
Americano a popular aperitif made with *Campari*, vermouth, angostura and lemon peel
aperitivo aperitif
aranciata orangeade
asciutto dry (wine)
Asti Spumante the renowned sparkling white wine from Piedmont
Aurum an orange liqueur
Barbaresco a red wine from Piedmont resembling *Barolo*, but lighter and slightly drier
Barbera a dark red, full-bodied wine from Piedmont and Lombardy with a rich bouquet
Bardolino a very pale red wine, from the Lago di Garda near Verona
Barolo a high quality red wine from Piedmont, can be compared to wines from the Rhone Valley
bibita beverage, drink
birra beer
~ **di barile** draught (US draft)
~ **chiara** lager, light
~ **scura** dark
~ **alla spina** draught (US draft)
caffè coffee
~ **corretto** espresso laced with a shot of liquor or brandy
~ **freddo** iced
~ **macchiato** with a few drops of warm milk
~ **nero** black

~ **ristretto** small and concentrated
caffellatte coffee with milk
Campania the region around Naples is noted for its fine red and white wines like *Capri*, *Falerno* and *Lacrima Christi*
Campari a reddish bitter aperitif with a quinine taste
cappuccino black coffee and whipped milk, sometimes with grated chocolate
caraffa carafe
Castelli Romani a common dry white wine from south-east of Rome
Centerbe a strong, green herb liqueur
Cerasella a cherry liqueur
Certosino a yellow or green herb liqueur
Chianti the renowned red and white table wines of Tuscany, traditionally bottled in a *fiasco;* there are many different qualities depending on the vineyards
Chiaretto one of Italy's most famous rosé wines; best when drunk very young; produced south of Lago di Garda
Cortese a dry white wine from Piedmont with limited production
dolce sweet (wine)
Emilia-Romagna the region around Bologna produces chiefly red wine like *Lambrusco*, which is sparkling and has a certain tang, and *Sangiovese*, a still type
Est! Est! Est! a semi-sweet white wine from the region north of Rome
Etna wines from the west slopes of Mount Etna (Sicily)
Falerno red and white dry wines produced in Campagnia
Fernet-Branca a bitter digestive
fiasco a straw-covered flask
frappè milk shake
Frascati a *Castelli Romani* white wine which can be dry or slightly sweet
Freisa red wines from Piedmont; one type is dry and fruity, the other is lighter and can be slightly sweet or semi-sparkling; one of Italy's best red wines produced south-west of Lago Maggiore
frizzante semi-sparkling (wine)
Gattinara a red, high-quality full-bodied wine from Piedmont, south-east of Lago Maggiore
granatina, granita fruit syrup or coffee served over crushed ice
grappa spirit distilled from grape mash
Grignolino good quality red wine with a special character and scent; often with a high alcoholic content
Lacrima Christi the most well-known wine from the Vesuvian slopes (Campania); the white wine is the best, but there are also red and rosé versions
Lago di Caldaro light red wine produced in the Italian Tyrol
Lagrein Rosato a good rosé from the region around Bolzano in the Italian Tyrol
Lambrusco a sparkling and tingling red wine from Emilia-Romagna
latte milk
~ **al cacao** chocolate drink
Lazio Latium; the region princi-

pally to the south of Rome produces chiefly white wine like *Castelli Romani, Est! Est! Est!* and *Frascati*

limonata lemonade

Lombardia Lombardy; the region around Milan produces various red wines like the *Bonarda, Inferno, Spanna* and *Valtellina*, the rosé *Chiaretto* and the white *Lugana*

Lugana a good dry white wine from the region of Lago di Garda

Marsala the renowned red dessert wine from Sicily

Martini a brand-name of white and red vermouth

Millefiori a liqueur distilled from herbs and alpine flowers

Moscatello, Moscato muscatel; name for different dessert and table wines produced from the muscat grapes; there are some red, but most are white

Orvieto light, white wine from Umbria; three versions exist: dry, slightly sweet and sweet

Piemonte Piedmont; the north-western region of Italy reputedly produces the highest quality wine in the country and is best known for its sparkling wine *Asti Spumante;* among its red wines are *Barbaresco, Barbera, Barolo, Dolcetto, Freisa, Gattinara, Grignolino, Nebbiolo; Cortese* is a light white wine

porto port (wine)

Puglia Apulia; at the south-eastern tip of Italy, this region produces the greatest quantity of the nation's wine, mainly table wine and some dessert wine

Punt e Mès a brand-name vermouth

Sangiovese a red table wine from Emilia-Romagna

Santa Giustina a good red table wine from the Italian Tyrol

Santa Maddalena a good quality red wine from the Italian Tyrol, light in colour and rather fruity

sciroppo fruit syrup diluted with water

secco dry (wine)

Sicilia Sicily; this island is noted for its dessert wine, particularly the celebrated *Marsala;* among many table wines the red, white and rosé *Etna* wines are the best known

sidro cider

Silvestro a herb and mint liqueur

Soave very good dry white wine, which is best when drunk young (from the east ov Verona)

spremuta fresh fruit drink

spumante sparkling

Stock a wine-distilled brandy

Strega a strong herb liqueur

succo juice

tè tea

~ **al latte** with milk

~ **al limone** with lemon

Terlano Tyrolean white wine, renowned, well balanced, greenish yellow in colour and with a delicate taste

Toscana Tuscany; the region around Florence is particularly noted for its red and white *Chianti*, a good table wine, and the dessert wines *Aleatico* and *Vin Santo*

Traminer a Tyrolean white wine from the region which gave the grape and the name to the renowned Alsatian *Traminer* and *Gewürztraminer* white wines

Trentino-Alto Adige the alpine region produces red wines like *Lago di Caldaro, Santa Giustina, Santa Maddalena; Terlano* and *Traminer* are notable white wines; *Lagrein Rosato* is a rosé to remember while *Vin Santo* is a good dessert wine

Valpolicella a light red wine with a rich cherry colour and a trace of bitterness; it is best when drunk young

Valtellina region near the Swiss border which produces good, dark red wine

Vecchia Romagna a wine-distilled brandy

Veneto the north-eastern region of Italy produces high quality wines; among its red wines are *Amarone, Bardolino, Merlot, Pinot Nero, Valpolicella;* among the whites, *Pinot Grigio, Soave. Recioto* is a sparkling red wine

Vin Santo (Vinsanto) a fine dessert wine produced chiefly in Tuscany but also in Trentino, the Italian Tyrol

vino wine
- ~ **aperto** open
- ~ **bianco** white
- ~ **del paese** local
- ~ **rosatello, rosato** rosé
- ~ **rosso** red

Italian Verbs

Below is a list of Italian verbs in three regular conjugations, grouped by families according to their infinitive endings, *-are, -ere* and *-ire*. Within the *-ire* group is one category that lengthens its stem by the addition of *-isc-* in the singular and the third person plural of the present tense (e.g. *fiorire – fiorisco*). Verbs which do not follow the conjugations below are considered irregular (see irregular verb list). Note that there are some verbs which follow the regular conjugation of the category they belong to, but present some minor changes in spelling. Examples: *mangiare, mangerò; cominciare, comincerò; navigare, navigherò.* The personal pronoun is not generally expressed since the verb endings clearly indicate the person.

	1st conj.	2nd conj.	3rd conj.
Infinitive	**am are**	**tem ere**	**vest ire**
	(love)	*(fear)*	*(dress)*
Present	(io) am **o**	tem **o**	vest **o**
	(tu) am **i**	tem **i**	vest **i**
	(egli) am **a**	tem **e**	vest **e**
	(noi) am **iamo**	tem **iamo**	vest **iamo**
	(voi) am **ate**	tem **ete**	vest **ite**
	(essi) am **ano**	tem **ono**	vest **ono**
Imperfect	(io) am **avo**	tem **evo**	vest **ivo**
	(tu) am **avi**	tem **evi**	vest **ivi**
	(egli) am **ava**	tem **eva**	vest **iva**
	(noi) am **avamo**	tem **evamo**	vest **ivamo**
	(voi) am **avate**	tem **evate**	vest **ivate**
	(essi) am **avano**	tem **evano**	vest **ivano**
Past Definit	(io) am **ai**	tem **ei**	vest **ii**
	(tu) am **asti**	tem **esti**	vest **isti**
	(egli) am **ò**	tem **è**	vest **ì**
	(noi) am **ammo**	tem **emmo**	vest **immo**
	(voi) am **aste**	tem **este**	vest **iste**
	(essi) am **arono**	tem **erono**	vest **irono**
Future	(io) am **erò**	tem **erò**	vest **irò**
	(tu) am **erai**	tem **erai**	vest **irai**
	(egli) am **erà**	tem **erà**	vest **irà**
	(noi) am **eremo**	tem **eremo**	vest **iremo**
	(voi) am **erete**	tem **erete**	vest **irete**
	(essi) am **eranno**	tem **eranno**	vest **iranno**
Conditional	(io) am **erei**	tem **erei**	vest **irei**
	(tu) am **eresti**	tem **eresti**	vest **iresti**
	(egli) am **erebbe**	tem **erebbe**	vest **irebbe**
	(noi) am **eremmo**	tem **eremmo**	vest **iremmo**
	(voi) am **ereste**	tem **ereste**	vest **ireste**
	(essi) am **erebbero**	tem **erebbero**	vest **irebbero**

Pres. subj.	(io) am **i**	tem **a**	vest **a**
	(tu) am **i**	tem **a**	vest **a**
	(egli) am **i**	tem **a**	vest **a**
	(noi) am **iamo**	tem **iamo**	vest **iamo**
	(voi) am **iate**	tem **iate**	vest **iate**
	(essi) am **ino**	tem **ano**	vest **ano**
Pres. part./gerund	am **ando**	tem **endo**	vest **endo**
Past. part.	am **ato**	tem **uto**	vest **ito**

Auxiliary Verbs

	avere *(to have)*		**essere** *(to be)*	
	Present	*Imperfect*	*Present*	*Imperfect*
(io)	ho	avevo	sono	ero
(tu)	hai	avevi	sei	eri
(egli)	ha	aveva	è	era
(noi)	abbiamo	avevamo	siamo	eravamo
(voi)	avete	avevate	siete	eravate
(essi)	hanno	avevano	sono	erano
	Future	*Conditional*	*Future*	*Conditional*
(io)	avrò	avrei	sarò	sarei
(tu)	avrai	avresti	sarai	saresti
(egli)	avrà	avrebbe	sarà	sarebbe
(noi)	avremo	avremmo	saremo	saremmo
(voi)	avrete	avreste	sarete	sareste
(essi)	avranno	avrebbero	saranno	sarebbero
	Pres. subj.	*Pres. perf.*	*Pres. subj.*	*Pres. perf.*
(io)	abbia	ho avuto	sia	sono stato
(tu)	abbia	hai avuto	sia	sei stato
(egli)	abbia	ha avuto	sia	è stato
(noi)	abbiamo	abbiamo avuto	siamo	siamo stati
(voi)	abbiate	avete avuto	siate	siete stati
(essi)	abbiano	hanno avuto	siano	sono stati
	Past definit		*Past definit*	
(io)	ebbi		fui	
(tu)	avesti		fosti	
(egli)	ebbe		fu	
(noi)	avemmo		fummo	
(voi)	aveste		foste	
(essi)	ebbero		furono	

Irregular Verbs

Below is a list of the verbs and tenses commonly used in spoken Italian. In the listing, a) stands for the present tense, b) for the past definit, c) for the future, d) for the conditional and e) for the past participle. Certain verbs are considered irregular although often only their past participles have an irregular form while, for the rest, they are conjugated like regular verbs. A few verbs are conjugated irregularly in the present tense. Such cases are shown below in all persons, the first person singular only is given for all other tenses. Unless otherwise indicated, the verbs with prefixes like *ac-, am-, ap-, as-, at-, av-, co-, com-, con-, cor-, de-, di-, dis-, e-, es-, im-, in-, inter-, intra-, ot-, per-, pro-, re-, ri-, sopra-, sup-, tra(t)-*, etc. are conjugated like the stem verb.

accendere *light* — a) accendo; b) accesi; c) accenderò; d) accenderei; e) acceso

accludere *enclose* — a) accludo; b) acclusi; c) accluderò; d) accluderei; e) accluso

accorgersi *perceive* — a) mi accorgo, ti accorgi, si accorge, ci accorgiamo, vi accorgete, si accorgono; b) mi accorsi; c) mi accorgerò; d) mi accorgerei; e) accorto

addurre *bring, result in* — a) adduco; b) addussi; c) addurrò; d) addurrei; e) addotto

affliggere *afflict, upset* — a) affliggo; b) afflissi; c) affliggerò; d) affliggerei; e) afflitto

alludere *allude* — a) alludo; b) allusi; c) alluderò; d) alluderei; e) alluso

andare *go* — a) vado, vai, va, andiamo, andate, vanno; b) andai; c) andrò; d) andrei; e) andato

annettere *annex* — a) annetto; b) annettei; c) annetterò; d) annetterei; e) annesso

apparire *appear* — a) appaio, apparisci, appare, appariamo, apparite, appaiono; b) apparsi; c) apparirò; d) apparirei; e) apparso

appendere *hang* — a) appendo; b) appesi; c) appenderò; d) appenderei; e) appeso

aprire *open* — a) apro; b) aprii; c) aprirò; d) aprirei; e) aperto

ardere *burn* — a) ardo; b) arsi; c) arderò; d) arderei; e) arso

assistere *assist* — a) assisto; b) assistei; c) assisterò; d) assisterei; e) assistito

assolvere *absolve* — a) assolvo; b) assolsi; c) assolverò; d) assolverei; e) assolto

assumere *employ; assume* — a) assumo; b) assunsi; c) assumerò; d) assumerei; e) assunto

avere *have* — a) ho, hai, ha, abbiamo, avete, hanno; b) ebbi; c) avrò; d) avrei; e) avuto

bere *drink* — a) bevo, bevi, beve, beviamo, bevete, bevono; b) bevvi; c) berrò; d) berrei; e) bevuto

cadere *fall* — a) cado; b) caddi; c) cadrò; d) cadrei; e) caduto

capire *understand* — a) capisco, capisci, capisce, capiamo, capite, capiscono; b) capii; c) capirò; d) capirei; e) capito

chiedere *ask* — a) chiedo; b) chiesi; c) chiederò; d) chiederei; e) chiesto

chiudere *close* — a) chiudo; b) chiusi; c) chiuderò; d) chiuderei; e) chiuso

cingere *gird* — a) cingo; b) cinsi; c) cingerò; d) cingerei; e) cinto

cogliere *pick* — a) colgo, cogli, coglie, cogliamo, cogliete, colgono; b) colsi; c) coglierò; d) coglierei; e) colto

compiere *complete, do* — a) compio, compi, compie, compiamo, compiete, compiono; b) compiei; c) compierò; d) compierei; e) compiuto

comprimere *squeeze; press* — a) comprimo; b) compressi; c) comprimerò; d) comprimerei; e) compresso

concludere *conclude* — → chiudere

condurre *escort, drive* — a) conduco; b) condussi; c) condurrò; d) condurrei; e) condotto

connetere *connect, join* — a) connetto; b) connessi; c) connetterò; d) connetterei; e) connesso

conoscere *know, be aware of* — a) conosco; b) conobbi; c) conoscerò; d) conoscerei; e) conosciuto

coprire *cover* — a) copro; b) coprii; c) coprirò; d) coprirei; e) coperto

correre *run* — a) corro; b) corsi; c) correrò; d) correrei; e) corso

costruire *construct* — → capire

crescere *grow* — a) cresco; b) crebbi; c) crescerò; d) crescerei; e) cresciuto

cucire *sew* — a) cucio, cuci, cuce, cuciamo, cucite, cuciono; b) cucii; c) cucirò; d) cucirei; e) cucito

cuocere *cook* — a) cuocio, cuoci, cuoce, cuociamo, cuocete, cuociono; b) cossi; c) cuocerò; d) cuocerei; e) cotto

dare *give* — a) do, dai, dà, diamo, date, danno; b) diedi; c) darò; d) darei; e) dato

decidere a) decido; b) decisi; c) deciderò; d) deciderei; e) deciso
decide

dedurre → condurre
deduct

deludere → alludere
disappoint

deprimere → comprimere
depress

difendere a) difendo; b) difesi; c) difenderò; d) difenderei; e) difeso
defend

dipendere → appendere
depend

dipingere a) dipingo; b) dipinsi; c) dipingerò; d) dipingerei; e) dipinto
paint

dire a) dico, dici, dice, diciamo, dite, dicono; b) dissi; c) dirò; d) direi; e) detto
say, tell

dirigere a) dirigo; b) diressi; c) dirigerò; d) dirigerei; e) diretto
manage; conduct

discutere a) discuto; b) discussi; c) discuterò; d) discuterei; e) discusso
discuss

dissuadere a) dissuado; b) dissuasi; c) dissuaderò; d) dissuaderei; e) dissuaso
dissuade

distinguere a) distinguo; b) distinsi; c) distinguerò; d) distinguerei; e) distinto
distinguish

dividere a) divido; b) divisi; c) dividerò; d) divederei; e) diviso
divide

dolere a) dolgo, duoli, duole, dogliamo, dolete, dolgono; b) dolsi; c) dorrò; d) dorrei; e) doluto
hurt; ache

dovere a) devo, devi, deve, dobbiamo, dovete, debbono (devono); b) dovetti; c) dovrò; d) dovrei; e) dovuto
have to, ought to

eccellere a) eccello; b) eccelsi; c) eccellerò; d) eccellerei; e) eccelso
excel, outshine

emergere a) emergo; b) emersi; c) emergerò; d) emergerei; e) emerso
rise; distinguish oneself

erigere a) erigo; b) eressi; c) erigerò; d) erigerei; e) eretto
erect, build

escludere → alludere
exclude

esigere a) esigo; b) esigei; c) esigerò; d) esigerei; e) esatto
demand, require

esistere a) esisto; b) esistei; c) esisterò; d) esisterei; e) esistito
exist, live

espellere a) espello; b) espulsi; c) espellerò; d) espellerei; d) espulso
expel

esplodere a) esplodo; b) esplosi; c) esploderò; d) esploderei; e) esploso
explode

esprimere →comprimere
express

essere a) sono, sei, è, siamo, siete, sono; b) fui; c) sarò; d) sarei; e) stato
be

estinguere →distinguere
extinguish

fare a) faccio, fai, fa, facciamo, fate, fanno; b) feci; c) farò; d) farei; e) fatto
do, make

fendere a) fendo; b) fendei; c) fenderò; d) fenderei; e) fesso
split

ferire →capire
wound, hurt

figgere a) figgo; b) fissi; c) figgerò; d) figgerei; e) fitto
fasten

fingere a) fingo; b) finsi; c) fingerò; d) fingerei; e) finto
pretend

flettere a) fletto; b) flettei; c) fletterò; d) fletterei; e) flesso
bend

fondere a) fondo; b) fusi; c) fonderò; d) fonderei; e) fuso
melt

frangere a) frango; b) fransi; c) frangerò; d) frangerei; e) franto
break

friggere → affliggere
fry

giacere a) giaccio, giaci, giace, giaciamo, giacete, giacciono; b) giacqui; c) giacerò; d) giacerei; e) giaciuto
lie, rest

giungere a) giungo; b) giunsi; c) giungerò; d) giungerei; e) giunto
arrive

immergere a) immergo; b) immersi; c) immergerò; d) immergerei; e) immerso
dip, immerse

incidere a) incido; b) incisi; c) inciderò; d) inciderei; e) inciso
engrave; record; have influence

includere → alludere
include

indurre → condurre
induce

introdurre →condurre
insert, introduce

invadere a) invado; b) invasi; c) invaderò; d) invaderei; e) invaso
invade

leggere a) leggo; b) lessi; c) leggerò; d) leggerei; e) letto
read

mettere a) metto; b) misi; c) metterò; d) metterei; e) messo
put

mordere a) mordo; b) morsi; c) morderò; d) morderei; e) morso
bite

morire a) muoio, muori, muore, moriamo, morite, muoiono; b) morii; c) morirò; d) morirei; e) morto
die

muovere →mordere; e) mosso
move

nascere →conoscere; e) nato
be born

nascondere →mordere; e) nascosto
hide

nuocere a) nuoccio, nuoci, nuoce, nociamo, nocete, nuociono; b) nocqui; c) nocerò; d) nocerei; e) nuociuto
harm, damage

nutrire →capire
nourrish

offendere a) offendo; b) offesi; c) offenderò; d) offenderei; e) offeso
offend

offrire a) offro; b) offrii; c) offrirò; d) offrirei; e) offerto
offer

opprimere →comprimere
oppress

parere a) paio, pari, pare, paiamo, parete, paiono; b) parvi; c) parrò; d) parrei; e) parso
seem

percuotere a) percuoto; b) percossi; c) percuoterò; d) percuoterei; e) percosso
hit, strike

perdere a) perdo; b) persi; c) perderò; d) perderei; e) perso
lose

persuadere →dissuadere
persuade

piacere a) piaccio, piaci, piace, piacciamo, piacete, piacciono; b) piacqui; c) piacerò; d) piacerei; e) piaciuto
like; please

piangere a) piango; b) piansi; c) piangerò; d) piangerei; e) pianto
cry

piovere a) piove; b) piovve; c) pioverà; d) pioverebbe; e) piovuto
rain

porgere →leggere; e) porto
hand over, offer

porre a) pongo, poni, pone, poniamo, ponete, pongono; b) posi; c) porrò; d) porrei; e) posto
place, put

potere a) posso, puoi, può, possiamo, potete, possono; b) potei; c) potrò; d) potrei; e) potuto
be able to

prendere *take*	a) prendo; b) presi; c) prenderò; d) prenderei; e) preso
presumere *presume*	→assumere
produrre *produce*	→condurre
proteggere *protect*	a) proteggo; b) protessi; c) proteggerò; d) proteggerei; e) protetto
pungere *sting*	a) pungo; b) punsi; c) pungerò; d) pungerei; e) punto
radere *shave, raze*	a) rado; b) rasi; c) raderò; d) raderei; e) raso
redigere *edit, write*	a) redigo; b) redassi; c) redigerò; d) redigerei; e) redatto
redimere *redeem*	a) redimo; b) redensi; c) redimerò; d) redimerei; e) redento
reggere *uphold, support*	→leggere
rendere *render, give up*	→prendere
reprimere *repress*	→comprimere
retrocedere *retreat*	a) retrocedo; b) retrocedei; c) retrocederò; d) retrocederei; e) retroceduto
ridere *laugh*	→prendere
ridurre *reduce*	→condurre
rimanere *remain*	a) rimango, rimani, rimane, rimaniamo, rimanete, rimangono; b) rimasi; c) rimarrò; d) rimarrei; e) rimasto
riprodurre *reproduce*	→condurre
risolvere *resolve*	→assolvere
rispondere *answer*	a) rispondo; b) risposi; c) risponderò; d) risponderei; e) risposto
rompere *break*	a) rompo; b) ruppi; c) romperò; d) romperei; e) rotto
salire *go up, climb*	a) salgo, sali, sale, saliamo, salite, salgono; b) salii; c) salirò; d) salirei; e) salito
sapere *know*	a) so, sai, sa, sappiamo, sapete, sanno; b) seppi; c) saprò; d) saprei; e) saputo
scegliere *choose*	a) scelgo, scegli, sceglie, scegliamo, scegliete, scelgono; b) scelsi; c) sceglierò; d) sceglierei; e) scelto

scendere a) scendo; b) scesi; c) scenderò; d) scenderei; e) sceso
get down

sciogliere →cogliere
solve

scomparire →apparire
disappear

scoprire →coprire
dis-, uncover

scorgere a) scorgo; b) scorsi; c) scorgerò; d) scorgerei; e) scorto
notice, see

scrivere →leggere
write

scuotere →percuotere
shake

sedere a) siedo, siedi, siede, sediamo, sedete, siedono; b) sedei; c) sederò; d) sederei; e) seduto
sit

sedurre →condurre
seduce

smettere →mettere
put a stop to

soffrire →offrire
suffer

solere a) soglio, suoli, suole, sogliamo, solete, sogliono; b) solei; c) –; d) –; e) solito
be used to

sommergere →immergere
flood, sink

sopprimere →comprimere
suppress, abolish

sorgere →leggere; e) sorto
rise, ascend; be due to

sospendere →appendere
suspend

spandere a) spando; b) spansi; c) spanderò; d) spanderei; e) spanto
spread

spargere a) spargo; b) sparsi; c) spargerò; d) spargerei; e) sparso
scatter, strew

spegnere a) spengo, spegni, spegne, spegniamo, spegnete, spengono; b) spensi; c) spegnerò; d) spegnerei; e) spento
extinguish

spendere a) spendo; b) spesi; c) spenderò; d) spenderei; e) speso
spend; make use of

spingere a) spingo; b) spinsi; c) spingerò; d) spingerei; c) spinto
push

stare a) sto, stai, sta, stiamo, state, stanno; b) stetti; c) starò; d) starei; e) stato
stand, remain

stendere *stretch*	→tendere
stringere *press, tighten*	a) stringo; b) strinsi; c) stringerò; d) stringerei; e) stretto
struggere *melt; torment*	a) struggo; b) strussi; c) struggerò; d) struggerei; e) strutto
succedere *happen, succeed*	a) succedo; b) successi; c) succederò; d) succederei; e) successo
tacere *be silent*	a) taccio, taci, tace, tacciamo, tacete, tacciono; b) tacqui; c) tacerò; d) tacerei; e) taciuto
tendere *stretch*	a) tendo; b) tesi; c) tenderò; d) tenderei; e) teso
tenere *keep*	a) tengo, tieni, tiene, teniamo, tenete, tengono; b) tenni; c) terrò; d) terrei; e) tenuto
tingere *dye*	a) tingo; b) tinsi; c) tingerò; d) tingerei; e) tinto
togliere *take away*	→cogliere
torcere *wring*	a) torco; b) torsi; c) torcerò; d) torcerei; e) torto
tradurre *translate*	→condurre
trarre *draw, haul in*	a) traggo, trai, trae, traiamo, traete, traggono; b) trassi; c) trarrò; d) trarrei; e) tratto
uccidere *kill*	a) uccido; b) uccisi; c) ucciderò; d) ucciderei; e) ucciso
udire *hear, listen to*	a) odo, odi, ode, udiamo, udite, odono; b) udii; c) udirò; d) udirei; e) udito
uscire *go, come out*	a) esco, esci, esce, usciamo, uscite, escono; b) uscii; c) uscirò; d) uscirei; e) uscito
valere *be worth*	a) valgo, vali, vale, valiamo, valete, valgono; b) valsi; c) varrò; d) varrei; e) valuto (valso)
vedere *see*	a) vedo; b) vidi; c) vedrò; d) vedrei; e) visto
venire *come, arrive*	a) vengo, vieni, viene, veniamo, venite, vengono; b) venni; c) verrò; d) verrei; e) venuto
vincere *win, conquer*	a) vinco; b) vinsi; c) vincerò; d) vincerei; e) vinto
vivere *live*	a) vivo; b) vissi; c) vivrò; d) vivrei; e) vissuto (vivuto)
volere *want*	a) voglio, vuoi, vuole, vogliamo, volete, vogliono; b) volli (volsi); c) vorrò; d) vorrei; e) voluto (volsuto)
volgere *turn*	a) volgo; b) volsi; c) volgerò; d) volgerei; e) volto

Italian Abbreviations

ab.	*abitanti*	inhabitants, population
abb.	*abbonamento*	subscription
a.C.	*avanti Cristo*	B.C.
A.C.I.	*Automobile Club d'Italia*	Italian Automobile Association
A.D.	*anno Domini*	Anno Domini
A.G.I.P.	*Azienda Generale Italiana Petroli*	Italian National Oil Company
all.	*allegato*	enclosure, enclosed
A.N.A.S.	*Azienda Nazionale Autonoma della Strada*	National Road Board
A.N.S.A.	*Azienda Nazionale Stampa Associata*	Italian News Agency
Avv.	*Avvocato*	lawyer, solicitor, barrister
C.A.I.	*Club Alpino Italiano*	Italian Alpine Club
cat.	*categoria*	category
Cav.	*Cavaliere*	title of nobility corresponding to knight
C.C.I.	*Camera di Commercio Internazionale*	International Chamber of Commerce
cfr.	*confronta*	compare
C.I.T.	*Compagnia Italiana Turismo*	Italian Tourist Information Office
c.m.	*corrente mese*	instant, of this month
Com. in Prov.	*Comune in provincia di...*	township in the province of...
C.O.N.I.	*Comitato Olimpico Nazionale Italiano*	Italian Olympic Games Committee
C.P.	*casella postale*	post office box
C.so	*Corso*	main street
c.c.	*conto corrente*	current account
d.C.	*dopo Cristo*	A.D.
dott., dr.	*dottore*	doctor
dott.ssa	*dottoressa*	lady doctor
dozz.	*dozzina*	dozen
ecc.	*eccetera*	and so on
Ed.	*editore*	publisher
EE	*Escursionisti Esteri*	licence plate for foreigners temporarily living in Italy
Fed.	*federale*	federal
F.S.	*Ferrovie dello Stato*	Italian State Railways

I.C.E.	*Istituto Italiano per il Commercio Estero*	Italian Institute for Foreign Trade
I.V.A.	*Imposta sul Valore Aggiunto*	VAT, value added tax
L., Lit.	*Lira italiana*	lira
M.E.C.	*Mercato Comune Europeo*	Common Market
mod.	*modulo*	form
n/, ns.	*nostro*	our(s)
p.	*pagina*	page
P.T.	*Poste & Telecomunicazioni*	Post and Telecommunications
P.za	*piazza*	square
racc.	*raccomandata*	registered (letter)
R.A.I.	*Radio Audizioni Italiane*	Italian Broadcasting Corporation
Rep.	*Repubblica*	republic
Rev.	*Reverendo*	reverend
S.	*Santo*	saint
S.E.	*Sua Eccellenza*	His/Her Excellency
sec.	*secolo*	century
Sig.	*Signor*	Mr.
Sig.na	*Signorina*	Miss
Sig.a	*Signora*	Mrs.
S.p.A.	*Società per Azioni*	Ltd., Inc.
S.r.l.	*Società a responsabilità limitata*	limited liability company
S.S.	*Sua Santità*	His Holiness
T.C.I.	*Touring Club Italiano*	Italian Touring Club
v/, vs.	*vostro*	your(s)
V.le	*Viale*	boulevard, avenue
v.p.	*vedi pagina*	see page
v.r.	*vedi retro*	P.T.O., please turn over

Numerals

Cardinal numbers

0	zero
1	uno
2	due
3	tre
4	quattro
5	cinque
6	sei
7	sette
8	otto
9	nove
10	dieci
11	undici
12	dodici
13	tredici
14	quattordici
15	quindici
16	sedici
17	diciassette
18	diciotto
19	diciannove
20	venti
21	ventuno
22	ventidue
28	ventotto
30	trenta
31	trentuno
32	trentadue
40	quaranta
50	cinquanta
60	sessanta
70	settanta
80	ottanta
90	novanta
100	cento
101	centuno
230	duecentotrenta
1.000	mille
1.001	milleuno
2.000	duemila
1.000.000	un milione

Ordinal numbers

1º	primo
2º	secondo
3º	terzo
4º	quarto
5º	quinto
6º	sesto
7º	settimo
8º	ottavo
9º	nono
10º	decimo
11º	undicesimo
12º	dodicesimo
13º	tredicesimo
14º	quattordicesimo
15º	quindicesimo
16º	sedicesimo
17º	diciassettesimo
18º	diciottesimo
19º	diciannovesimo
20º	ventesimo
21º	ventunesimo
22º	ventiduesimo
23º	ventitreesimo
24º	ventiquattresimo
30º	trentesimo
31º	trentunesimo
32º	trentaduesimo
33º	trentatreesimo
40º	quarantesimo
50º	cinquantesimo
60º	sessantesimo
70º	settantesimo
80º	ottantesimo
90º	novantesimo
100º	centesimo
101º	centunesimo
102º	centoduesimo
230º	duecentotrentesimo
1.000º	millesimo
1.001º	milleunesimo

Time

In everyday conversation the 12-hour clock is generally used, but you will notice that the 24-hour system is employed elsewhere (e.g., 14.00 = 2 p.m.).

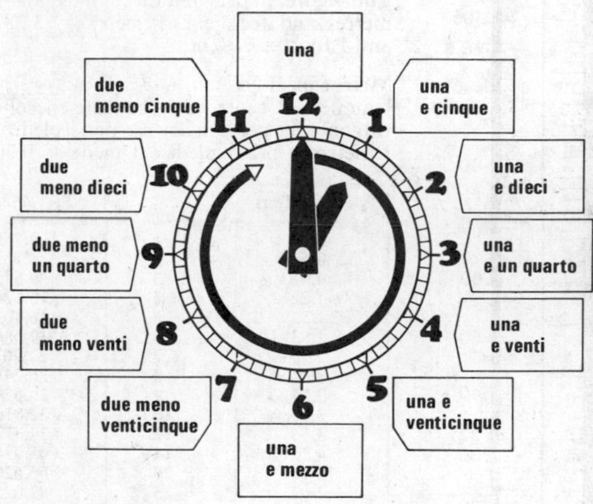

If you have to indicate that it is a.m. or p.m., add *del mattino, del pomeriggio* or *di sera.*

otto del mattino	8 a.m.
due del pomeriggio	2 p.m.
otto di sera	8 p.m.

Days of the Week

domenica	Sunday
lunedì	Monday
martedì	Tuesday
mercoledì	Wednesday
giovedì	Thursday
venerdì	Friday
sabato	Saturday

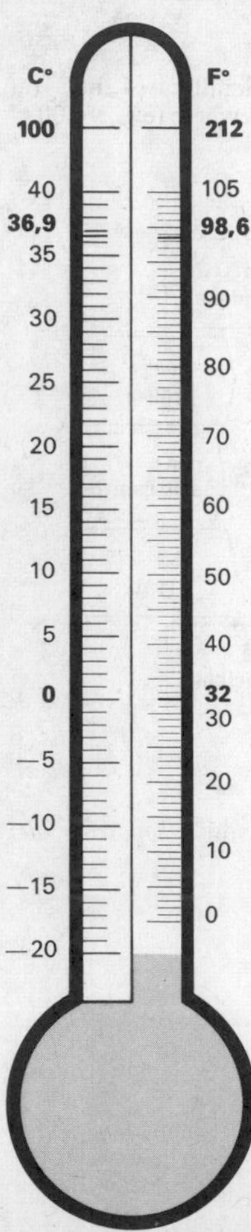

Conversion tables/ Tavole di trasformazione

Metres and feet
The figure in the middle stands for both metres and feet, e.g. 1 metre = 3.281 ft. and 1 foot = 0.30 m.

Metri e piedi
I numeri al centro del seguente specchietto valgono sia per i metri sia per i piedi. Es.: 1 metro = 3,281 piedi e 1 piede = 0,30 m.

Metres/Metri		Feet/Piedi
0.30	**1**	3.281
0.61	**2**	6.563
0.91	**3**	9.843
1.22	**4**	13.124
1.52	**5**	16.403
1.83	**6**	19.686
2.13	**7**	22.967
2.44	**8**	26.248
2.74	**9**	29.529
3.05	**10**	32.810
3.66	**12**	39.372
4.27	**14**	45.934
6.10	**20**	65.620
7.62	**25**	82.023
15.24	**50**	164.046
22.86	**75**	246.069
30.48	**100**	328.092

Temperature
To convert Centigrade to Fahrenheit, multiply by 1.8 and add 32.
To convert Fahrenheit to Centigrade, subtract 32 from Fahrenheit and divide by 1.8.

Temperatura
Per trasformare i gradi centigradi in Fahrenheit moltiplicare i centigradi per 1,8 e aggiungere 32.
Per convertire i Fahrenheit in centigradi sottrarre 32 dai Fahrenheit e dividere per 1,8.

Some Basic Phrases	Alcune espressioni utili
Please.	Per favore.
Thank you very much.	Mille grazie.
Don't mention it.	Prego.
Good morning.	Buongiorno *(di mattina)*.
Good afternoon.	Buongiorno *(di pomeriggio)*.
Good evening.	Buona sera.
Good night.	Buona notte.
Good-bye.	Arrivederci.
See you later.	A più tardi.
Where is/Where are…?	Dov'è/Dove sono...?
What do you call this?	Come si chiama questo?
What does that mean?	Cosa significa?
Do you speak English?	Parla inglese?
Do you speak German?	Parla tedesco?
Do you speak French?	Parla francese?
Do you speak Spanish?	Parla spagnolo?
Do you speak Italian?	Parla italiano?
Could you speak more slowly, please?	Può parlare più adagio, per piacere?
I don't understand.	Non capisco.
Can I have…?	Posso avere...?
Can you show me…?	Può indicarmi...?
Can you tell me…?	Può dirmi...?
Can you help me, please?	Può aiutarmi, per piacere?
I'd like…	Vorrei...
We'd like…	Vorremmo...
Please give me…	Per favore, mi dia...
Please bring me…	Per favore, mi porti...
I'm hungry.	Ho fame.
I'm thirsty.	Ho sete.
I'm lost.	Mi sono perso.
Hurry up!	Si affretti!
There is/There are…	C'è/Ci sono...
There isn't/There aren't…	Non c'è/Non ci sono...

Arrival	**L'arrivo**
Your passport, please.	Il passaporto, per favore.
Have you anything to declare?	Ha qualcosa da dichiarare?
No, nothing at all.	No, non ho nulla.
Can you help me with my luggage, please?	Può prendere le mie valige, per favore?
Where's the bus to the centre of town, please?	Dov'è l'autobus per il centro della città, per favore?
This way, please.	Da questa parte, per piacere.
Where can I get a taxi?	Dove posso trovare un taxi?
What's the fare to...?	Quanto costa la corsa per...?
Take me to this address, please.	Mi porti a questo indirizzo, per favore.
I'm in a hurry.	Ho fretta.

Hotel	**L'albergo**
My name is...	Mi chiamo...
Have you a reservation?	Ha fatto la prenotazione?
I'd like a room with a bath.	Vorrei una camera con bagno.
What's the price per night?	Qual è il prezzo per una notte?
May I see the room?	Posso vedere la camera?
What's my room number, please?	Qual è il numero della mia camera?
There's no hot water.	Non c'è acqua calda.
May I see the manager, please?	Posso vedere il direttore, per piacere?
Did anyone telephone me?	Mi ha telefonato qualcuno?
Is there any mail for me?	C'è posta per me?
May I have my bill (check), please?	Posso avere il conto, per favore?

Eating out	**Al ristorante**
Do you have a fixed-price menu?	Avete un menù a prezzo fisso?
May I see the menu?	Posso vedere il menù a scelta?

May we have an ashtray, please?	Possiamo avere un portacenere, per favore?
Where's the toilet, please?	Dove sono i gabinetti, per favore?
I'd like an hors d'œuvre (starter).	Vorrei degli antipasti.
Have you any soup?	Ha un brodo?
I'd like some fish.	Vorrei del pesce.
What kind of fish do you have?	Che pesce ha?
I'd like a steak.	Vorrei una bistecca.
What vegetables have you got?	Quali verdure ha?
Nothing more, thanks.	Nient'altro. Grazie.
What would you like to drink?	Cosa desidera bere?
I'll have a beer, please.	Mi dia una birra, per piacere.
I'd like a bottle of wine.	Vorrei una bottiglia di vino.
May I have the bill (check), please?	Posso avere il conto, per piacere?
Is service included?	È compreso il servizio?
Thank you, that was a very good meal.	Grazie. Abbiamo mangiato molto bene.

Travelling	**In viaggio**
Where's the railway station, please?	Dove si trova la stazione, per favore?
Where's the ticket office, please?	Dove si trova lo sportello dei biglietti, per favore?
I'd like a ticket to…	Vorrei un biglietto per...
First or second class?	Di prima o di seconda classe?
First class, please.	Di prima classe, per piacere.
Single or return (one way or roundtrip)?	Andata o andata e ritorno?
Do I have to change trains?	Devo cambiare treno?
What platform does the train for… leave from?	Da che binario parte il treno per...?
Where's the nearest underground (subway) station?	Dov'è la più vicina stazione della metropolitana?
Where's the bus station, please?	Dov'è la stazione degli autobus, per piacere?

When's the first bus to…?	Quando passa il primo autobus per...?
Please let me off at the next stop.	Mi faccia scendere alla prossima fermata, per piacere.

Relaxing	**Gli svaghi**
What's on at the cinema (movies)?	Cosa danno al cinema?
What time does the film begin?	A che ora incomincia il film?
Are there any tickets for tonight?	Ci sono ancora posti liberi per questa sera?
Where can we go dancing?	Dove possiamo andare a ballare?

Meeting people	**Incontri**
How do you do.	Buongiorno.
How are you?	Come sta?
Very well, thank you. And you?	Molto bene. Grazie. E lei?
May I introduce…?	Posso presentarle...?
My name is…	Mi chiamo...
I'm very pleased to meet you.	Sono molto lieto di fare la sua conoscenza.
How long have you been here?	Da quanto tempo è qui?
It was nice meeting you.	Sono lieto di aver fatto la sua conoscenza.
Do you mind if I smoke?	Le disturba se fumo?
Do you have a light, please?	Mi fa accendere, per piacere?
May I get you a drink?	Posso offrirle da bere?
May I invite you for dinner tonight?	Posso invitarla a cena questa sera?
Where shall we meet?	Dove possiamo incontrarci?

Shops, stores and services	**Negozi, grandi magazzini e altro**
Where's the nearest bank, please?	Dov'è la banca più vicina, per favore?
Where can I cash some travellers' cheques?	Dove posso incassare dei travellers' cheque?

Can you give me some small change, please?	Potrebbe darmi della moneta spicciola, per favore?
Where's the nearest chemist's (pharmacy)?	Dov'è la più vicina farmacia?
How do I get there?	Come ci si può arrivare?
Is it within walking distance?	Ci si può andare anche a piedi?
Can you help me, please?	Può aiutarmi, per piacere?
How much is this? And that?	Quanto costa questo? E quello?
It's not quite what I want.	Non è quello che volevo.
I like it.	Questo mi piace.
Can you recommend something for sunburn?	Può consigliarmi qualcosa per una scottatura di sole?
I'd like a haircut, please.	Vorrei farmi tagliare i capelli, per favore.
I'd like a manicure, please.	Vorrei una manicure, per favore.

Street directions	**Indicazioni stradali**
Can you show me on the map where I am?	Può indicarmi sulla cartina dove mi trovo?
You are on the wrong road.	È sulla strada sbagliata.
Go/Walk straight ahead.	Continui diritto.
It's on the left/on the right.	È a sinistra/a destra.

Emergencies	**Urgenze**
Call a doctor quickly.	Chiami subito un medico.
Call an ambulance.	Chiami un'ambulanza.
Please call the police.	Per piacere, chiami la polizia.

inglese-italiano

english-italian

Introduzione

Questo dizionario è stato compilato in modo da rispondere quanto meglio possibile a necessità di ordine pratico. Sono state volontariamente omesse informazioni linguistiche ritenute non indispensabili. Le voci sono collocate in ordine alfabetico, siano esse costituite da una parola sola, o da più parole separate o no tra loro da una lineetta. Come unica eccezione a questa regola, alcune espressioni idiomatiche sono state classificate come voci principali nella posizione alfabetica della parola più significativa nell'espressione stessa. Quando ad una voce susseguono accezioni varie come espressioni e locuzioni particolari, esse sono egualmente collocate in ordine alfabetico.

Ad ogni vocabolo fa seguito la trascrizione fonetica (vedasi la Guida di pronuncia) la quale a sua volta precede, salvo eccezioni, la definizione della categoria grammaticale del vocabolo (nome, verbo, aggettivo, ecc.). Quando un vocabolo rappresenta più di una categoria, le varie traduzioni sono raggruppate dopo le rispettive categorie.

Quando irregolare, la forma plurale di un nome è sempre indicata, com'è pure indicata nei casi in cui il lettore possa emettere un dubbio.

La tilde (~) è usata per rappresentare una voce ogni qualvolta essa si ripeta, in forme plurali irregolari o in accezioni varie.

Nei plurali irregolari dei nomi composti, è scritta per intero solo la parte che cambia, mentre quella che rimane immutata è rappresentata da una lineetta.

Un verbo irregolare è segnalato da un asterisco (*) posto dinnanzi. Per dettagli, ci si può riferire all'elenco dei verbi irregolari.

Il dizionario segue le norme dell'ortografia britannica. Ogni vocabolo o significato di esso che sia prevalentemente americano è stato contrassegnato come tale (vedasi l'elenco delle abbreviazioni usate nel testo).

Abbreviazioni

adj	aggettivo	*num*	numerale
adv	avverbio	*p*	passato
Am	Americano	*pl*	plurale
art	articolo	*plAm*	plurale (Americano)
conj	congiunzione	*pp*	participio passato
f	femminile	*pr*	presente
fpl	femminile plurale	*pref*	prefisso
m	maschile	*prep*	preposizione
mpl	maschile plurale	*pron*	pronome
n	nome	*v*	verbo
nAm	nome (Americano)	*vAm*	verbo (Americano)

Guida della pronuncia

Ogni lemma di questa parte del dizionario è accompagnato da una trascrizione fonetica che ne indica la pronuncia e che si deve leggere come l'italiano. Diamo spiegazioni (sotto) solo per le lettere e i simboli ambigui o particolarmente difficili da comprendere.

Le lineette indicano le divisioni fra le sillabe, che sono stampate in *corsivo* quando si devono pronunciare accentuate.

Certo, i suoni delle due lingue non coincidono mai perfettamente, ma seguendo alla lettera le nostre indicazioni, potrete pronunciare le parole straniere in modo da farvi comprendere. Per facilitarvi il compito, talvolta le nostre trascrizioni semplificano leggermente il sistema fonetico della lingua pur riflettendo le differenze di suono essenziali.

Consonanti

ð	una **s** blesa come in ro**s**a; mettete la punta della lingua contro i denti incisivi centrali superiori e soffiate leggermente facendo vibrare le corde vocali come per pronunciare **d**
gh	come in **gh**iro
h	come **c** nella pronuncia toscana di **c**asa (**h**asa); espirate udibilmente, come se aveste appena fatto una corsa
ng	come **ng** in lu**ng**o, ma senza pronunciare la **g** finale
r	mettete la lingua nella posizione come per pronunciare **ʒ** (vedi sotto), poi aprite leggermente la bocca e abbassate la lingua
s	sempre sonora, come in ro**s**a, mai come in **s**i
ʃ	come **sc** in **sc**i
θ	come **ð**, ma senza far vibrare le corde vocali
ʒ	il suono dolce della **g** toscana; come **g** in **g**iro, ma senza far sentire la **d** che compone all'inizio tale suono

Vocali e dittonghi

æ	fra **a** in c**a**so ed **e** in b**e**lla
ê	come **e** in b**e**lla (aperta)
o	come in p**o**rta (aperta)
ô	come **o** in s**o**le (chiusa)
ö	un suono neutro, come la vocale di f**uo**co nei dialetti settentrionali («f**oe**ch»)

1) Le vocali lunghe sono stampate doppie.

2) Le lettere rialzate (es. $^{\mathbf{u}}$**i**, **u**$^{\breve{o}}$) si devono pronunciare rapidamente.

3) Alcune parole inglesi derivanti dal francese hanno vocali nasali, che abbiamo trascritto col simbolo della vocale più **ng** (es. **ang**). Questo **ng** *non* si deve pronunciare: serve unicamente a indicare il suono nasale della vocale da pronunciare simultaneamente attraverso la bocca e il naso.

Pronuncia americana

La nostra trascrizione fonetica segue le norme usuali della pronunzia britannica. Benchè vi siano numerose variazioni secondo le regioni, l'inglese parlato in America presenta un certo numero di differenze generali. Eccone alcune:

1) La **r**, sia essa posta dinnanzi a consonante o in fine di parola, si pronunzia sempre (contrariamente all'usanza britannica).

2) In numerose parole (quali ad es. *ask*, *castle*, *laugh*, ecc.) **aa** diventa **ææ**.

3) Il suono britannico **o** si pronunzia **a**, spesso anche **oo**.

4) In vocaboli come *duty*, *tune*, *new*, ecc., $^{\mathbf{i}}$**uu** diventa sovente una sola **uu**.

5) Infine, talune parole sono accentuate diversamente.

A

a (ei,ö) *art* (an) un *art*
abbey (*æ*-bi) *n* badia *f*
abbreviation (ö-brii-vi-*ei*-ʃön) *n* abbreviazione *f*
aberration (æ-bö-*rei*-ʃön) *n* aberrazione *f*
ability (ö-*bi*-lö-ti) *n* abilità *f*
able (*ei*-böl) *adj* capace; abile; ***be ~ to** *essere in grado di; *sapere, *potere
abnormal (æb-*noo*-möl) *adj* anormale
aboard (ö-*bood*) *adv* a bordo
abolish (ö-*bo*-liʃ) *v* abolire
abortion (ö-*boo*-ʃön) *n* aborto *m*
about (ö-*baut*) *prep* su; circa; intorno a; *adv* press'a poco, circa; attorno
above (ö-*bav*) *prep* su; *adv* sopra
abroad (ö-*brood*) *adv* all'estero
abscess (*æb*-ssêss) *n* ascesso *m*
absence (*æb*-ssönss) *n* assenza *f*
absent (*æb*-ssönt) *adj* assente
absolutely (*æb*-ssö-luut-li) *adv* assolutamente
abstain from (öb-*sstein*) *astenersi da
abstract (*æb*-sstrækt) *adj* astratto
absurd (öb-*ssööd*) *adj* assurdo
abundance (ö-*ban*-dönss) *n* abbondanza *f*
abundant (ö-*ban*-dönt) *adj* abbondante
abuse (ö-*b*ʲ*uuss*) *n* abuso *m*
abyss (ö-*biss*) *n* abisso *m*
academy (ö-*kæ*-dö-mi) *n* accademia *f*
accelerate (ök-*ssê*-lö-reit) *v* accelerare
accelerator (ök-*ssê*-lö-rei-tö) *n* acceleratore *m*
accent (*æk*-ssönt) *n* accento *m*
accept (ök-*ssêpt*) *v* accettare; *accogliere
access (*æk*-ssêss) *n* accesso *m*
accessary (ök-*ssê*-ssö-ri) *n* complice *m*
accessible (ök-*ssê*-ssö-böl) *adj* accessibile
accessories (ök-*ssê*-ssö-ris) *pl* accessori *mpl*
accident (*æk*-ssi-dönt) *n* incidente *m*
accidental (æk-ssi-*dên*-töl) *adj* fortuito
accommodate (ö-*ko*-mö-deit) *v* alloggiare
accommodation (ö-ko-mö-*dei*-ʃön) *n* sistemazione *f*, alloggio *m*
accompany (ö-*kam*-pö-ni) *v* accompagnare
accomplish (ö-*kam*-pliʃ) *v* compiere; adempiere
in accordance with (in ö-*koo*-dönss ᵘið) in conformità con
according to (ö-*koo*-ding tuu) secondo
account (ö-*kaunt*) *n* conto *m*; resoconto *m*; **~ for** *rendere conto di;

on ~ of a causa di
accountable (ö-*kaun*-tö-böl) *adj* spiegabile
accurate (*æ*-k'u-röt) *adj* accurato
accuse (ö-*k'uus*) *v* accusare
accused (ö-*k'uusd*) *n* accusato *m*
accustom (ö-*ka*-sstöm) *v* abituare
ache (eik) *v* *dolere; *n* dolore *m*
achieve (ö-*tʃiiv*) *v* *raggiungere; effettuare
achievement (ö-*tʃiiv*-mönt) *n* adempimento *m*
acid (*æ*-ssid) *n* acido *m*
acknowledge (ök-*no*-lidʒ) *v* *riconoscere; *ammettere; confermare
acne (*æk*-ni) *n* acne *f*
acorn (*ei*-koon) *n* ghianda *f*
acquaintance (ö-*k^uein*-tönss) *n* conoscenza *f*
acquire (ö-*k^uai^ö*) *v* *ottenere
acquisition (æ-k^ui-*si*-ʃön) *n* acquisizione *f*
acquittal (ö-*k^ui*-töl) *n* assoluzione *f*
across (ö-*kross*) *prep* attraverso; dall'altra parte di; *adv* dall'altra parte
act (ækt) *n* atto *m*; numero *m*; *v* agire; comportarsi; recitare
action (*æk*-ʃön) *n* azione *f*
active (*æk*-tiv) *adj* attivo; vivace
activity (æk-*ti*-vö-ti) *n* attività *f*
actor (*æk*-tö) *n* attore *m*
actress (*æk*-triss) *n* attrice *f*
actual (*æk*-tʃu-öl) *adj* reale
actually (*æk*-tʃu-ö-li) *adv* in realtà
acute (ö-*k'uut*) *adj* acuto
adapt (ö-*dæpt*) *v* adattare
add (æd) *v* addizionare; *aggiungere
adding-machine (*æ*-ding-mö-ʃiin) *n* addizionatrice *f*
addition (ö-*di*-ʃön) *n* addizione *f*; aggiunta *f*
additional (ö-*di*-ʃö-nöl) *adj* supplementare; accessorio
address (ö-*drêss*) *n* indirizzo *m*; *v* indirizzare; *rivolgersi a
addressee (æ-drê-*ssii*) *n* destinatario *m*
adequate (*æ*-di-k^uöt) *adj* adeguato; idoneo
adjective (*æ*-dʒik-tiv) *n* aggettivo *m*
adjourn (ö-*dʒöön*) *v* rinviare
adjust (ö-*dʒasst*) *v* regolare; adattare
administer (öd-*mi*-ni-sstö) *v* somministrare
administration (öd-mi-ni-*sstrei*-ʃön) *n* amministrazione *f*
administrative (öd-*mi*-ni-sströ-tiv) *adj* amministrativo; **~ law** diritto amministrativo
admiral (*æd*-mö-röl) *n* ammiraglio *m*
admiration (æd-mö-*rei*-ʃön) *n* ammirazione *f*
admire (öd-*mai^ö*) *v* ammirare
admission (öd-*mi*-ʃön) *n* ingresso *m*; ammissione *f*
admit (öd-*mit*) *v* *ammettere; *riconoscere
admittance (öd-*mi*-tönss) *n* ammissione *f*; **no ~** vietato l'ingresso
adopt (ö-*dopt*) *v* adottare
adorable (ö-*doo*-rö-böl) *adj* adorabile
adult (*æ*-dalt) *n* adulto *m*; *adj* adulto
advance (öd-*vaanss*) *n* avanzamento *m*; anticipo *m*; *v* avanzare; **in ~** anticipatamente, in anticipo
advanced (öd-*vaansst*) *adj* avanzato
advantage (öd-*vaan*-tidʒ) *n* vantaggio *m*
advantageous (æd-vön-*tei*-dʒöss) *adj* vantaggioso
adventure (öd-*vên*-tʃö) *n* avventura *f*
adverb (*æd*-vööb) *n* avverbio *m*
advertisement (öd-*vöö*-tiss-mönt) *n* avviso *m*
advertising (*æd*-vö-tai-sing) *n* pubblicità *f*
advice (öd-*vaiss*) *n* consiglio *m*
advise (öd-*vais*) *v* consigliare

advocate (*æd*-vö-köt) *n* patrocinatore *m*
aerial (*êö*-ri-öl) *n* antenna *f*
aeroplane (*êö*-rö-plein) *n* aeroplano *m*
affair (ö-*fêö*) *n* affare *m*; rapporto *m*, amoretto *m*
affect (ö-*fêkt*) *v* influenzare; riguardare
affected (ö-*fêk*-tid) *adj* affettato
affection (ö-*fêk*-ʃön) *n* affezione *f*; affetto *m*
affectionate (ö-*fêk*-ʃö-nit) *adj* affettuoso
affiliated (ö-*fi*-li-ei-tid) *adj* associato
affirmative (ö-*föö*-mö-tiv) *adj* affermativo
affliction (ö-*flik*-ʃön) *n* afflizione *f*
afford (ö-*food*) *v* *permettersi
afraid (ö-*freid*) *adj* impaurito; ***be** ~ *aver paura
Africa (*æ*-fri-kö) Africa *f*
African (*æ*-fri-kön) *adj* africano
after (*aaf*-tö) *prep* dopo; *conj* dopo che
afternoon (aaf-tö-*nuun*) *n* pomeriggio *m*; **this** ~ oggi nel pomeriggio
afterwards (*aaf*-tö-ᵘöds) *adv* poi; in seguito
again (ö-*ghên*) *adv* ancora; di nuovo; ~ **and again** ripetutamente
against (ö-*ghênsst*) *prep* contro
age (eidʒ) *n* età *f*; vecchiaia *f*; **of** ~ maggiorenne; **under** ~ minorenne
aged (*ei*-dʒid) *adj* attempato; anziano
agency (*ei*-dʒön-ssi) *n* agenzia *f*; divisione *f*
agenda (ö-*dʒên*-dö) *n* agenda *f*
agent (*ei*-dʒönt) *n* agente *m*, rappresentante *m*
aggressive (ö-*ghrê* ssiv) *adj* aggressivo
ago (ö-*ghou*) *adv* fa
agrarian (ö-*ghrêö*-ri-ön) *adj* agricolo
agree (ö-*ghrii*) *v* accordarsi; consentire; *corrispondere
agreeable (ö-*ghrii*-ö-böl) *adj* gradevole
agreement (ö-*ghrii*-mönt) *n* contratto *m*; accordo *m*; concordanza *f*
agriculture (*æ*-ghri-kal-tʃö) *n* agricoltura *f*
ahead (ö-*hêd*) *adv* avanti; ~ **of** in testa a; ***go** ~ continuare; **straight** ~ sempre diritto
aid (eid) *n* soccorso *m*; *v* *assistere, aiutare
ailment (*eil*-mönt) *n* affezione *f*; malattia *f*
aim (eim) *n* intento *m*; ~ **at** puntare su, mirare a; aspirare a
air (êö) *n* aria *f*; *v* arieggiare
air-conditioning (*êö*-kön-di-ʃö-ning) *n* condizionamento dell'aria; **air-conditioned** *adj* ad aria condizionata
aircraft (*êö*-kraaft) *n* (pl ~) velivolo *m*; aereo *m*
airfield (*êö*-fiild) *n* aerodromo *m*
air-filter (*êö*-fil-tö) *n* filtro dell'aria
airline (*êö*-lain) *n* linea aerea
airmail (*êö*-meil) *n* posta aerea
airplane (*êö*-plein) *nAm* aeroplano *m*
airport (*êö*-poot) *n* aeroporto *m*
air-sickness (*êö*-ssik-nöss) *n* mal d'aria
airtight (*êö*-tait) *adj* a tenuta d'aria
airy (*êö*-ri) *adj* arioso
aisle (ail) *n* navata laterale; passaggio *m*
alarm (ö-*laam*) *n* allarme *m*; *v* allarmare
alarm-clock (ö-*laam*-klok) *n* sveglia *f*
album (*æl*-böm) *n* album *m*
alcohol (*æl*-kö-hol) *n* alcool *m*
alcoholic (æl-kö-*ho*-lik) *adj* alcoolico
ale (eil) *n* birra *f*
algebra (*æl*-dʒi-brö) *n* algebra *f*
Algeria (æl-*dʒiö*-ri-ö) Algeria *f*

Algerian (æl-*dʒiᵒ*-ri-ön) *adj* algerino
alien (*ei*-li-ön) *n* straniero *m*; *adj* straniero
alike (ö-*laik*) *adj* uguale, simile; *adv* ugualmente
alimony (*æ*-li-mö-ni) *n* alimenti
alive (ö-*laiv*) *adj* vivo, vivente
all (ool) *adj* tutto; ~ **in** tutto compreso; ~ **right**! va bene!; **at** ~ affatto
allergy (*æ*-lö-dʒi) *n* allergia *f*
alley (*æ*-li) *n* vicolo *m*
alliance (ö-*lai*-önss) *n* alleanza *f*
Allies (*æ*-lais) *pl* Alleati
allot (ö-*lot*) *v* assegnare
allow (ö-*lau*) *v* *permettere; ~ **to** lasciare; ***be allowed** *essere permesso; ***be allowed to** *avere il permesso di
allowance (ö-*lau*-önss) *n* assegno *m*
all-round (ool-*raund*) *adj* universale
almanac (*ool*-mö-næk) *n* almanacco *m*
almond (*aa*-mönd) *n* mandorla *f*
almost (*ool*-mousst) *adv* quasi
alone (ö-*loun*) *adv* solo
along (ö-*long*) *prep* lungo
aloud (ö-*laud*) *adv* ad alta voce
alphabet (*æl*-fö-bêt) *n* alfabeto *m*
already (ool-*rê*-di) *adv* già
also (*ool*-ssou) *adv* anche; pure
altar (*ool*-tö) *n* altare *m*
alter (*ool*-tö) *v* cambiare, modificare
alteration (ool-tö-*rei*-ʃön) *n* cambiamento *m*, modifica *f*
alternate (ool-*töö*-nöt) *adj* alternato
alternative (ool-*töö*-nö-tiv) *n* alternativa *f*
although (ool-*ðou*) *conj* benché, sebbene
altitude (*æl*-ti-tʲuud) *n* altitudine *f*
alto (*æl*-tou) *n* (pl ~s) contralto *m*
altogether (ool-tö-*ghê*-ðö) *adv* interamente; in tutto
always (*ool*-ᵘeis) *adv* sempre
am (æm) *v* (pr be)
amaze (ö-*meis*) *v* stupire, *stupefare
amazement (ö-*meis*-mönt) *n* stupore *m*
ambassador (æm-*bæ*-ssö-dö) *n* ambasciatore *m*
amber (*æm*-bö) *n* ambra *f*
ambiguous (æm-*bi*-ghʲu-öss) *adj* ambiguo; equivoco
ambitious (æm-*bi*-ʃöss) *adj* ambizioso
ambulance (*æm*-bʲu-lönss) *n* ambulanza *f*
ambush (*æm*-buʃ) *n* imboscata *f*
America (ö-*mê*-ri-kö) America *f*
American (ö-*mê*-ri-kön) *adj* americano
amethyst (*æ*-mi-θisst) *n* ametista *f*
amid (ö-*mid*) *prep* fra; tra, in mezzo a
ammonia (ö-*mou*-ni-ö) *n* ammoniaca *f*
amnesty (*æm*-ni-ssti) *n* amnistia *f*
among (ö-*mang*) *prep* tra; fra, in mezzo a; ~ **other things** tra l'altro
amount (ö-*maunt*) *n* quantità *f*; ammontare *m*, somma *f*; ~ **to** ammontare a
amuse (ö-*mʲuus*) *v* divertire
amusement (ö-*mʲuus*-mönt) *n* passatempo *m*, divertimento *m*
amusing (ö-*mʲuu*-sing) *adj* divertente
anaemia (ö-*nii*-mi-ö) *n* anemia *f*
anaesthesia (æ-niss-*θii*-si-ö) *n* anestesia *f*
anaesthetic (æ-niss-*θê*-tik) *n* anestetico *m*
analyse (*æ*-nö-lais) *v* analizzare
analysis (ö-*næ*-lö-ssiss) *n* (pl -ses) analisi *f*
analyst (*æ*-nö-lisst) *n* analista *m*; psicoanalista *m*
anarchy (*æ*-nö-ki) *n* anarchia *f*
anatomy (ö-*næ*-tö-mi) *n* anatomia *f*
ancestor (*æn*-ssê-sstö) *n* antenato *m*
anchor (*æng*-kö) *n* ancora *f*

anchovy (*æn*-tʃö-vi) *n* acciuga *f*
ancient (*ein*-ʃönt) *adj* vecchio, antico; antiquato
and (ænd, önd) *conj* e
angel (*ein*-dʒöl) *n* angelo *m*
anger (*æng*-ghö) *n* collera *f*, rabbia *f*; ira *f*
angle (*æng*-ghöl) *v* pescare con l'amo; *n* angolo *m*
angry (*æng*-ghri) *adj* irato, arrabbiato
animal (*æ*-ni-möl) *n* animale *m*
ankle (*æng*-köl) *n* caviglia *f*
annex[1] (*æ*-nêkss) *n* dipendenza *f*; allegato *m*
annex[2] (ö-*nêkss*) *v* *annettere
anniversary (æ-ni-*vöö*-ssö-ri) *n* anniversario *m*
announce (ö-*naunss*) *v* annunziare
announcement (ö-*naunss*-mönt) *n* annunzio *m*, avviso *m*
annoy (ö-*noi*) *v* infastidire, annoiare
annoyance (ö-*noi*-önss) *n* noia *f*
annoying (ö-*noi*-ing) *adj* noioso
annual (*æ*-nⁱu-öl) *adj* annuale; *n* annuario *m*
per annum (pör *æ*-nöm) all'anno
anonymous (ö-*no*-ni-möss) *adj* anonimo
another (ö-*na*-ðö) *adj* un altro
answer (*aan*-ssö) *v* *rispondere a; *n* risposta *f*
ant (ænt) *n* formica *f*
anthology (æn-*θo*-lö-dʒi) *n* antologia *f*
antibiotic (æn-ti-bai-*o*-tik) *n* antibiotico *m*
anticipate (æn-*ti*-ssi-peit) *v* *prevedere, anticipare; *prevenire
antifreeze (*æn*-ti-friis) *n* anticongelante *m*
antipathy (æn-*ti*-pö-θi) *n* antipatia *f*
antique (æn-*tiik*) *adj* antico; *n* anticaglia *f*; ~ **dealer** antiquario *m*
antiquity (æn-*ti*-kᵘö-ti) *n* Antichità *f*;
antiquities *pl* antichità *fpl*
antiseptic (æn-ti-*ssêp*-tik) *n* antisettico *m*
antlers (*ænt*-lös) *pl* palco *m*
anxiety (æng-*sai*-ö-ti) *n* ansietà *f*
anxious (*ængk*-ʃöss) *adj* ansioso; preoccupato
any (*ê*-ni) *adj* alcuno
anybody (*ê*-ni-bo-di) *pron* chiunque
anyhow (*ê*-ni-hau) *adv* in ogni modo
anyone (*ê*-ni-ᵘan) *pron* chiunque
anything (*ê*-ni-θing) *pron* qualunque cosa
anyway (*ê*-ni-ᵘei) *adv* in ogni caso
anywhere (*ê*-ni-ᵘêᵒ) *adv* dovunque; ovunque
apart (ö-*paat*) *adv* a parte, separatamente; ~ **from** a prescindere da
apartment (ö-*paat*-mönt) *nAm* appartamento *m*, alloggio *m*; ~ **house** *Am* blocco di appartamenti
aperitif (ö-*pê*-rö-tiv) *n* aperitivo *m*
apologize (ö-*po*-lö-dʒais) *v* scusarsi
apology (ö-*po*-lö-dʒi) *n* scusa *f*
apparatus (æ-pö-*rei*-töss) *n* dispositivo *m*, apparecchio *m*
apparent (ö-*pæ*-rönt) *adj* apparente; ovvio
apparently (ö-*pæ*-rönt-li) *adv* apparentemente; evidentemente
apparition (æ-pö-*ri*-ʃön) *n* apparizione *f*
appeal (ö-*piil*) *n* appello *m*
appear (ö-*piᵒ*) *v* sembrare; risultare; *apparire; presentarsi
appearance (ö-*piᵒ*-rönss) *n* apparenza *f*; aspetto *m*; ingresso *m*
appendicitis (ö-pên-di-*ssai*-tiss) *n* appendicite *f*
appendix (ö-*pên*-dikss) *n* (pl -dices, -dixes) appendice *f*
appetite (*æ*-pö-tait) *n* appetito *m*
appetizer (*æ*-pö-tai-sö) *n* stuzzichino *m*

appetizing (*æ*-pö-tai-sing) *adj* appetitoso
applause (ö-*ploos*) *n* applauso *m*
apple (*æ*-pöl) *n* mela *f*
appliance (ö-*plai*-önss) *n* apparecchio *m*
application (æ-pli-*kei*-ʃön) *n* applicazione *f*; richiesta *f*; domanda d'impiego
apply (ö-*plai*) *v* applicare; inoltrare una domanda d'impiego; applicarsi
appoint (ö-*point*) *v* designare, nominare
appointment (ö-*point*-mönt) *n* appuntamento *m*; nomina *f*
appreciate (ö-*prii*-ʃi-eit) *v* valutare; apprezzare
appreciation (ö-prii-ʃi-*ei*-ʃön) *n* apprezzamento *m*
approach (ö-*prouʧ*) *v* avvicinare; *n* impostazione *f*; accesso *m*
appropriate (ö-*prou*-pri-öt) *adj* adatto, appropriato
approval (ö-*pruu*-völ) *n* approvazione *f*; accordo *m*; **on** ~ in prova
approve (ö-*pruuv*) *v* approvare
approximate (ö-*prok*-ssi-möt) *adj* approssimativo
approximately (ö-*prok*-ssi-möt-li) *adv* circa, approssimativamente
apricot (*ei*-pri-kot) *n* albicocca *f*
April (*ei*-pröl) aprile
apron (*ei*-prön) *n* grembiule *m*
Arab (*æ*-röb) *adj* arabo
arbitrary (*aa*-bi-trö-ri) *adj* arbitrario
arcade (aa-*keid*) *n* portico *m*, arcata *f*
arch (aatʃ) *n* arco *m*; arcata *f*
archaeologist (aa-ki-*o*-lö-dʒisst) *n* archeologo *m*
archaeology (aa-ki-*o*-lö-dʒi) *n* archeologia *f*
archbishop (aatʃ-*bi*-ʃöp) *n* arcivescovo *m*
arched (aatʃt) *adj* arcato
architect (*aa*-ki-têkt) *n* architetto *m*
architecture (*aa*-ki-têk-tʃö) *n* architettura *f*
archives (*aa*-kaivs) *pl* archivio *m*
are (aa) *v* (pr be)
area (*êö*-ri-ö) *n* area *f*; zona *f*; ~ **code** prefisso *m*
Argentina (aa-dʒön-*tii*-nö) Argentina *f*
Argentinian (aa-dʒön-*ti*-ni-ön) *adj* argentino
argue (*aa*-ghʲuu) *v* argomentare, *discutere; disputare
argument (*aa*-ghʲu-mönt) *n* argomento *m*; discussione *f*; disputa *f*
arid (*æ*-rid) *adj* arido
***arise** (ö-*rais*) *v* *sorgere
arithmetic (ö-*riθ*-mö-tik) *n* aritmetica *f*
arm (aam) *n* braccio *m*; arma *f*; *v* armare
armchair (*aam*-tʃêö) *n* poltrona *f*
armed (aamd) *adj* armato; ~ **forces** forze armate
armour (*aa*-mö) *n* corazza *f*
army (*aa*-mi) *n* esercito *m*
aroma (ö-*rou*-mö) *n* aroma *m*
around (ö-*raund*) *prep* intorno a; *adv* intorno
arrange (ö-*reindʒ*) *v* ordinare, *mettere in ordine; organizzare
arrangement (ö-*reindʒ*-mönt) *n* accomodamento *m*
arrest (ö-*rêsst*) *v* arrestare; *n* arresto *m*
arrival (ö-*rai*-völ) *n* arrivo *m*
arrive (ö-*raiv*) *v* arrivare
arrow (*æ*-rou) *n* freccia *f*
art (aat) *n* arte *f*; abilità *f*; ~ **collection** collezione d'arte; ~ **exhibition** mostra d'arte; ~ **gallery** galleria d'arte; ~ **history** storia dell'arte; **arts and crafts** arti e mestieri; ~ **school** accademia di belle arti
artery (*aa*-tö-ri) *n* arteria *f*

artichoke (*aa*-ti-tʃouk) *n* carciofo *m*
article (*aa*-ti-köl) *n* articolo *m*
artifice (*aa*-ti-fiss) *n* artificio *m*
artificial (aa-ti-*fi*-ʃöl) *adj* artificiale
artist (*aa*-tisst) *n* artista *m*
artistic (aa-*ti*-sstik) *adj* artistico
as (æs) *conj* come; così; che; poiché, siccome; ~ **from** a partire da; da; ~ **if** come se
asbestos (æs-*bê*-sstoss) *n* amianto *m*
ascend (ö-*ssênd*) *v* *salire; *ascendere
ascent (ö-*ssênt*) *n* ascensione *f*; ascesa *f*
ascertain (æ-ssö-*tein*) *v* constatare; accertarsi di, accertare
ash (æʃ) *n* cenere *f*
ashamed (ö-*ʃeimd*) *adj* vergognoso; ***be** ~ *aver vergogna
ashore (ö-*ʃoo*) *adv* a terra
ashtray (*æʃ*-trei) *n* portacenere *m*
Asia (*ei*-ʃö) Asia *f*
Asian (*ei*-ʃön) *adj* asiatico
aside (ö-*ssaid*) *adv* da parte
ask (aassk) *v* domandare; pregare, *chiedere; invitare
asleep (ö-*ssliip*) *adj* addormentato
asparagus (ö-*sspæ*-rö-ghöss) *n* asparago *m*
aspect (*æ*-sspêkt) *n* aspetto *m*
asphalt (*æss*-fælt) *n* asfalto *m*
aspire (ö-*sspaiö*) *v* aspirare
aspirin (*æ*-sspö-rin) *n* aspirina *f*
ass (æss) *n* asino *m*
assassination (ö-ssæ-ssi-*nei*-ʃön) *n* assassinio *m*
assault (ö-*ssoolt*) *v* attaccare; aggredire
assemble (ö-*ssêm*-böl) *v* riunire; montare
assembly (ö-*ssêm*-bli) *n* riunione *f*, assemblea *f*
assignment (ö-*ssain*-mönt) *n* incarico *m*
assign to (ö-*ssain*) assegnare a; attribuire a
assist (ö-*ssisst*) *v* *assistere
assistance (ö-*ssi*-sstönss) *n* aiuto *m*; soccorso *m*, assistenza *f*
assistant (ö-*ssi*-sstönt) *n* assistente *m*
associate (ö-*ssou*-ʃi-öt) *n* socio *m*; alleato *m*; *v* associare; ~ **with** frequentare
association (ö-ssou-ssi-*ei*-ʃön) *n* associazione *f*
assort (ö-*ssoot*) *v* assortire
assortment (ö-*ssoot*-mönt) *n* assortimento *m*
assume (ö-*ssiuum*) *v* *assumere, *presumere
assure (ö-*ʃuö*) *v* assicurare
asthma (*æss*-mö) *n* asma *f*
astonish (ö-*ssto*-niʃ) *v* sbalordire
astonishing (ö-*ssto*-ni-ʃing) *adj* sorprendente
astonishment (ö-*ssto*-niʃ-mönt) *n* sorpresa *f*
astronomy (ö-*sstro*-nö-mi) *n* astronomia *f*
asylum (ö-*ssai*-löm) *n* asilo *m*; ospizio *m*
at (æt) *prep* in, da, a; verso
ate (êt) *v* (p eat)
atheist (*ei*-θi-isst) *n* ateo *m*
athlete (*æθ*-liit) *n* atleta *m*
athletics (æθ-*lê*-tikss) *pl* atletica *f*
Atlantic (öt-*læn*-tik) Atlantico *m*
atmosphere (*æt*-möss-fiö) *n* atmosfera *f*
atom (*æ*-töm) *n* atomo *m*
atomic (ö-*to*-mik) *adj* atomico
atomizer (*æ*-tö-mai-sö) *n* atomizzatore *m*; spruzzatore *m*, vaporizzatore *m*
attach (ö-*tætʃ*) *v* attaccare; *annettere; **attached to** affezionato a
attack (ö-*tæk*) *v* *assalire; *n* attacco *m*

attain (ö-*tein*) *v* *raggiungere
attainable (ö-*tei*-nö-böl) *adj* raggiungibile; conseguibile
attempt (ö-*têmpt*) *v* tentare; provare; *n* tentativo *m*
attend (ö-*tênd*) *v* *assistere a; ~ **on** servire; ~ **to** accudire a, occuparsi di; prestare attenzione a
attendance (ö-*tên*-dönss) *n* frequenza *f*
attendant (ö-*tên*-dönt) *n* guardia *f*
attention (ö-*tên*-ʃön) *n* attenzione *f*; ***pay** ~ *fare attenzione
attentive (ö-*tên*-tiv) *adj* attento
attic (*æ*-tik) *n* soffitta *f*
attitude (*æ*-ti-tʲuud) *n* attitudine *f*
attorney (ö-*töö*-ni) *n* avvocato *m*
attract (ö-*trækt*) *v* *attrarre
attraction (ö-*træk*-ʃön) *n* attrattiva *f*; attrazione *f*
attractive (ö-*træk*-tiv) *adj* attraente
auburn (*oo*-bön) *adj* castano
auction (*ook*-ʃön) *n* asta *f*
audible (*oo*-di-böl) *adj* udibile
audience (*oo*-di-önss) *n* udienza *f*
auditor (*oo*-di-tö) *n* uditore *m*
auditorium (oo-di-*too*-ri-öm) *n* auditorio *m*
August (*oo*-ghösst) agosto
aunt (aant) *n* zia *f*
Australia (o-*sstrei*-li-ö) Australia *f*
Australian (o-*sstrei*-li-ön) *adj* australiano
Austria (*o*-sstri-ö) Austria *f*
Austrian (*o*-sstri-ön) *adj* austriaco
authentic (oo-*θên*-tik) *adj* autentico
author (*oo*-θö) *n* autore *m*
authoritarian (oo-θo-ri-*têö*-ri-ön) *adj* autoritario
authority (oo-*θo*-rö-ti) *n* autorità *f*; potere *m*
authorization (oo-θö-rai-*sei*-ʃön) *n* autorizzazione *f*; permesso *m*
automatic (oo-tö-*mæ*-tik) *adj* automatico
automation (oo-tö-*mei*-ʃön) *n* automazione *f*
automobile (*oo*-tö-mö-biil) *n* automobile *f*; ~ **club** automobile club
autonomous (oo-*to*-nö-möss) *adj* autonomo
autopsy (*oo*-to-pssi) *n* necroscopia *f*
autumn (*oo*-töm) *n* autunno *m*
available (ö-*vei*-lö-böl) *adj* ottenibile, disponibile
avalanche (*æ*-vö-laanʃ) *n* valanga *f*
avaricious (æ-vö-*ri*-ʃöss) *adj* avaro
avenue (*æ*-vö-nʲuu) *n* viale *m*
average (*æ*-vö-ridʒ) *adj* medio; *n* media *f*; **on the** ~ in media
averse (ö-*vööss*) *adj* avverso
aversion (ö-*vöö*-ʃön) *n* avversione *f*
avert (ö-*vööt*) *v* *distogliere
avoid (ö-*void*) *v* evitare
await (ö-*ᵘeit*) *v* aspettare
awake (ö-*ᵘeik*) *adj* sveglio
***awake** (ö-*ᵘeik*) *v* svegliare
award (ö-*ᵘood*) *n* premio *m*; *v* aggiudicare
aware (ö-*ᵘêö*) *adj* consapevole
away (ö-*ᵘei*) *adv* via; ***go** ~ *andarsene
awful (*oo*-föl) *adj* terribile
awkward (*oo*-kᵘöd) *adj* imbarazzante; goffo
awning (*oo*-ning) *n* tenda di riparo
axe (ækss) *n* ascia *f*
axle (*æk*-ssöl) *n* asse *m*

B

baby (*bei*-bi) *n* piccino *m*; ~ **carriage** *Am* carrozzina *f*
babysitter (*bei*-bi-ssi-tö) *n* bambinaia *f*
bachelor (*bæ*-tʃö-lö) *n* celibe *m*

back (bæk) *n* dorso *m*; *adv* indietro; ***go** ~ tornare
backache (*bæ*-keik) *n* mal di schiena
backbone (*bæk*-boun) *n* spina dorsale
background (*bæk*-ghraund) *n* sfondo *m*; istruzione *f*
backwards (*bæk*-^{u}öds) *adv* all'indietro
bacon (*bei*-kön) *n* lardo *m*
bacterium (bæk-*tii*-ri-öm) *n* (pl -ria) batterio *m*
bad (bæd) *adj* cattivo; brutto
bag (bægh) *n* sacco *m*; borsetta *f*, borsa *f*; valigia *f*
baggage (*bæ*-ghidʒ) *n* bagaglio *m*; ~ **deposit office** *Am* deposito bagagli; **hand** ~ *Am* bagaglio a mano
bail (beil) *n* cauzione *f*
bailiff (*bei*-lif) *n* usciere *m*
bait (beit) *n* esca *f*
bake (beik) *v* infornare
baker (*bei*-kö) *n* panettiere *m*
bakery (*bei*-kö-ri) *n* panetteria *f*
balance (*bæ*-lönss) *n* equilibrio *m*; bilancio *m*; saldo *m*
balcony (*bæl*-kö-ni) *n* balcone *m*
bald (boold) *adj* calvo
ball (bool) *n* palla *f*; ballo *m*
ballet (*bæ*-lei) *n* balletto *m*
balloon (bö-*luun*) *n* palloncino *m*
ballpoint-pen (*bool*-point-pên) *n* penna a sfera
ballroom (*bool*-ruum) *n* sala da ballo
bamboo (bæm-*buu*) *n* (pl ~s) bambù *m*
banana (bö-*naa*-nö) *n* banana *f*
band (bænd) *n* banda *f*; benda *f*
bandage (*bæn*-didʒ) *n* fasciatura *f*
bandit (*bæn*-dit) *n* bandito *m*
bangle (*bæng*-ghöl) *n* braccialetto *m*
banisters (*bæ*-ni-sstös) *pl* ringhiera *f*
bank (bængk) *n* riva *f*; banca *f*; *v* depositare; ~ **account** conto bancario
banknote (*bængk*-nout) *n* banconota *f*
bank-rate (*bængk*-reit) *n* tasso di sconto
bankrupt (*bængk*-rapt) *adj* fallito
banner (*bæ*-nö) *n* stendardo *m*
banquet (*bæng*-k^{u}it) *n* banchetto *m*
banqueting-hall (*bæng*-k^{u}i-ting-hool) *n* sala da banchetto
baptism (*bæp*-ti-söm) *n* battesimo *m*
baptize (bæp-*tais*) *v* battezzare
bar (baa) *n* bar *m*; sbarra *f*
barber (*baa*-bö) *n* barbiere *m*
bare (bê^{ö}) *adj* nudo; spoglio
barely (*bê^{ö}*-li) *adv* appena
bargain (*baa*-ghin) *n* affare *m*; *v* mercanteggiare
baritone (*bæ*-ri-toun) *n* baritono *m*
bark (baak) *n* corteccia *f*; *v* abbaiare
barley (*baa*-li) *n* orzo *m*
barmaid (*baa*-meid) *n* barista *f*
barman (*baa*-mön) *n* (pl -men) barista *m*
barn (baan) *n* granaio *m*
barometer (bö-*ro*-mi-tö) *n* barometro *m*
baroque (bö-*rok*) *adj* barocco
barracks (*bæ*-rökss) *pl* caserma *f*
barrel (*bæ*-röl) *n* botte *f*, barile *m*
barrier (*bæ*-ri-ö) *n* barriera *f*
barrister (*bæ*-ri-sstö) *n* avvocato *m*
bartender (*baa*-tên-dö) *n* barista *m*
base (beiss) *n* base *f*; fondamento *m*; *v* basare
baseball (*beiss*-bool) *n* baseball *m*
basement (*beiss*-mönt) *n* seminterrato *m*
basic (*bei*-ssik) *adj* fondamentale
basilica (bö-*si*-li-kö) *n* basilica *f*
basin (*bei*-ssön) *n* bacino *m*, catino *m*
basis (*bei*-ssiss) *n* (pl bases) fondamento *m*, base *f*
basket (*baa*-sskit) *n* paniere *m*
bass[1] (beiss) *n* basso *m*
bass[2] (bæss) *n* (pl ~) branzino *m*

bastard (*baa*-sstöd) *n* bastardo *m*; mascalzone *m*

batch (bætʃ) *n* partita *f*

bath (baaθ) *n* bagno *m*; ~ **salts** sali da bagno; ~ **towel** asciugamano *m*

bathe (beið) *v* bagnarsi, *fare il bagno

bathing-cap (*bei*-ðing-kæp) *n* cuffia da bagno

bathing-suit (*bei*-ðing-ssuut) *n* costume da bagno

bathing-trunks (*bei*-ðing-trangkss) *n* mutandine da bagno

bathrobe (*baaθ*-roub) *n* accappatoio *m*

bathroom (*baaθ*-ruum) *n* stanza da bagno; gabinetto *m*

batter (*bæ*-tö) *n* impasto *m*

battery (*bæ*-tö-ri) *n* batteria *f*; accumulatore *m*

battle (*bæ*-töl) *n* battaglia *f*; lotta *f*, combattimento *m*; *v* combattere

bay (bei) *n* baia *f*; *v* latrare

***be** (bii) *v* *essere

beach (biitʃ) *n* spiaggia *f*; **nudist** ~ spiaggia per nudisti

bead (biid) *n* perlina *f*; **beads** *pl* collana *f*; rosario *m*

beak (biik) *n* becco *m*

beam (biim) *n* raggio *m*; trave *f*

bean (biin) *n* fagiolo *m*

bear (bê^{ö}) *n* orso *m*

***bear** (bê^{ö}) *v* portare; tollerare; sopportare

beard (bi^{ö}d) *n* barba *f*

bearer (*bê^{ö}*-rö) *n* portatore *m*

beast (biisst) *n* animale *m*; ~ **of prey** animale da preda

***beat** (biit) *v* picchiare; battere

beautiful (*b^{i}uu*-ti-föl) *adj* bello

beauty (*b^{i}uu*-ti) *n* bellezza *f*; ~ **parlour** salone di bellezza; ~ **salon** salone di bellezza; ~ **treatment** cura di bellezza

beaver (*bii*-vö) *n* castoro *m*

because (bi-*kos*) *conj* perché; poiché; ~ **of** in conseguenza di, a causa di

***become** (bi-*kam*) *v* *divenire; *addirsi

bed (bêd) *n* letto *m*; ~ **and board** vitto e alloggio, pensione completa; ~ **and breakfast** alloggio e colazione

bedding (*bê*-ding) *n* biancheria da letto

bedroom (*bêd*-ruum) *n* camera da letto

bee (bii) *n* ape *f*

beech (bii-tʃ) *n* faggio *m*

beef (biif) *n* manzo *m*

beehive (*bii*-haiv) *n* alveare *m*

been (biin) *v* (pp be)

beer (bi^{ö}) *n* birra *f*

beet (biit) *n* barbabietola *f*

beetle (*bii*-töl) *n* scarabeo *m*

beetroot (*biit*-ruut) *n* barbabietola *f*

before (bi-*foo*) *prep* prima di; davanti; *conj* prima che; *adv* prima; precedentemente

beg (bêgh) *v* mendicare; supplicare; *chiedere

beggar (*bê*-ghö) *n* mendicante *m*

***begin** (bi-*ghin*) *v* cominciare; iniziare

beginner (bi-*ghi*-nö) *n* principiante *m*

beginning (bi-*ghi*-ning) *n* inizio *m*; principio *m*

on behalf of (on bi-*haaf* ov) a nome di, per conto di; a favore di

behave (bi-*heiv*) *v* comportarsi

behaviour (bi-*hei*-v^{i}ö) *n* comportamento *m*

behind (bi-*haind*) *prep* dietro; *adv* indietro

beige (beiʒ) *adj* beige

being (*bii*-ing) *n* essere *m*

Belgian (*bêl*-dʒön) *adj* belga

Belgium (*bêl*-dʒöm) Belgio *m*

belief (bi-*liif*) *n* fede *f*
believe (bi-*liiv*) *v* credere
bell (bêl) *n* campana *f*; campanello *m*
bellboy (*bêl*-boi) *n* fattorino d'albergo
belly (*bê*-li) *n* pancia *f*
belong (bi-*long*) *v* *appartenere
belongings (bi-*long*-ings) *pl* effetti personali
beloved (bi-*lavd*) *adj* amato
below (bi-*lou*) *prep* sotto; *adv* giù
belt (bêlt) *n* cinghia *f*; **garter** ~ *Am* reggicalze *m*
bench (bêntʃ) *n* banco *m*
bend (bênd) *n* curva *f*; curvatura *f*
***bend** (bênd) *v* curvare; ~ **down** chinarsi
beneath (bi-*niiθ*) *prep* sotto; *adv* giù
benefit (*bê*-ni-fit) *n* profitto *m*, beneficio *m*; vantaggio *m*; *v* approfittare
bent (bênt) *adj* (pp bend) curvato
beret (*bê*-rei) *n* berretto *m*
berry (*bê*-ri) *n* bacca *f*
berth (bööθ) *n* cuccetta *f*
beside (bi-*ssaid*) *prep* vicino a
besides (bi-*ssaids*) *adv* inoltre; d'altronde; *prep* oltre a
best (bêsst) *adj* ottimo
bet (bêt) *n* scommessa *f*; posta *f*
***bet** (bêt) *v* *scommettere
betray (bi-*trei*) *v* tradire
better (*bê*-tö) *adj* migliore
between (bi-*tᵘiin*) *prep* tra
beverage (*bê*-vö-ridʒ) *n* bevanda *f*
beware (bi-*ᵘêö*) *v* guardarsi, *fare attenzione
bewitch (bi-*ᵘitʃ*) *v* stregare, incantare
beyond (bi-*ⁱond*) *prep* più in là di; oltre; in aggiunta a; *adv* al di là
bible (*bai*-böl) *n* bibbia *f*
bicycle (*bai*-ssi-köl) *n* bicicletta *f*; ciclo *m*
big (bigh) *adj* grande; voluminoso; grosso; importante
bile (bail) *n* bile *f*
bilingual (bai-*ling*-ghᵘöl) *adj* bilingue
bill (bil) *n* fattura *f*; conto *m*; *v* fatturare
billiards (*bil*-ⁱöds) *pl* biliardo *m*
***bind** (baind) *v* legare
binding (*bain*-ding) *n* legatura *f*
binoculars (bi-*no*-kⁱö-lös) *pl* binocolo *m*
biology (bai-*o*-lö-dʒi) *n* biologia *f*
birch (böötʃ) *n* betulla *f*
bird (bööd) *n* uccello *m*
Biro (*bai*-rou) *n* penna a sfera
birth (bööθ) *n* nascita *f*
birthday (*bööθ*-dei) *n* compleanno *m*
biscuit (*biss*-kit) *n* biscottino *m*
bishop (*bi*-ʃöp) *n* vescovo *m*
bit (bit) *n* pezzetto *m*; poco *m*
bitch (bitʃ) *n* cagna *f*
bite (bait) *n* boccone *m*; morso *m*; puntura *f*
***bite** (bait) *v* *mordere
bitter (*bi*-tö) *adj* amaro
black (blæk) *adj* nero; ~ **market** mercato nero
blackberry (*blæk*-bö-ri) *n* mora *f*
blackbird (*blæk*-bööd) *n* merlo *m*
blackboard (*blæk*-bood) *n* lavagna *f*
black-currant (blæk-*ka*-rönt) *n* ribes nero
blackmail (*blæk*-meil) *n* ricatto *m*; *v* ricattare
blacksmith (*blæk*-ssmiθ) *n* fabbro *m*
bladder (*blæ*-dö) *n* vescica *f*
blade (bleid) *n* lama *f*; ~ **of grass** filo d'erba
blame (bleim) *n* colpa *f*; biasimo *m*; *v* biasimare, rimproverare
blank (blængk) *adj* in bianco
blanket (*blæng*-kit) *n* coperta *f*
blast (blaasst) *n* esplosione *f*
blazer (*blei*-sö) *n* giacca sportiva
bleach (bliitʃ) *v* imbiancare

bleak (bliik) *adj* rigido
***bleed** (bliid) *v* sanguinare; salassare
bless (blêss) *v* *benedire
blessing (*blê*-ssing) *n* benedizione *f*
blind (blaind) *n* avvolgibile *m*, persiana *f*; *adj* cieco; *v* abbagliare
blister (*bli*-sstö) *n* bolla *f*
blizzard (*bli*-söd) *n* tormenta *f*
block (blok) *v* ostruire, bloccare; *n* ceppo *m*; ~ **of flats** caseggiato *m*
blonde (blond) *n* bionda *f*
blood (blad) *n* sangue *m*; ~ **pressure** pressione sanguigna
blood-poisoning (*blad*-poi-sö-ning) *n* setticemia *f*
blood-vessel (*blad*-vê-ssöl) *n* vaso sanguigno
blot (blot) *n* macchia *f*; **blotting paper** carta assorbente
blouse (blaus) *n* blusa *f*
blow (blou) *n* colpo *m*; raffica *f*
***blow** (blou) *v* soffiare; tirare
blow-out (*blou*-aut) *n* foratura *f*
blue (bluu) *adj* blu; depresso
blunt (blant) *adj* ottuso; spuntato
blush (blaʃ) *v* arrossire
board (bood) *n* asse *f*; tavoletta *f*; pensione *f*; consiglio *m*; ~ **and lodging** pensione completa, vitto e alloggio
boarder (*boo*-dö) *n* pensionante *m*
boarding-house (*boo*-ding-hauss) *n* pensione *f*
boarding-school (*boo*-ding-sskuul) *n* convitto *m*
boast (bousst) *v* vantarsi
boat (bout) *n* battello *m*, barca *f*
body (*bo*-di) *n* corpo *m*
bodyguard (*bo*-di-ghaad) *n* guardia del corpo
bog (bogh) *n* palude *f*
boil (boil) *v* bollire; *n* foruncolo *m*
bold (bould) *adj* coraggioso; sfrontato, sfacciato
Bolivia (bö-*li*-vi-ö) Bolivia *f*
Bolivian (bö-*li*-vi-ön) *adj* boliviano
bolt (boult) *n* chiavistello *m*; bullone *m*
bomb (bom) *n* bomba *f*; *v* bombardare
bond (bond) *n* obbligazione *f*
bone (boun) *n* osso *m*; lisca *f*; *v* disossare
bonnet (*bo*-nit) *n* cofano *m*
book (buk) *n* libro *m*; *v* prenotare; registrare, allibrare
booking (*bu*-king) *n* prenotazione *f*
bookmaker (*buk*-mei-kö) *n* allibratore *m*
bookseller (*buk*-ssê-lö) *n* libraio *m*
bookstand (*buk*-sstænd) *n* edicola *f*
bookstore (*buk*-sstoo) *n* libreria *f*
boot (buut) *n* stivale *m*; bagagliaio *m*
booth (buuð) *n* baracca *f*; cabina *f*
border (*boo*-dö) *n* confine *m*; bordo *m*
bore[1] (boo) *v* annoiare; trapanare; *n* seccatore *m*
bore[2] (boo) *v* (p bear)
boring (*boo*-ring) *adj* noioso
born (boon) *adj* nato
borrow (*bo*-rou) *v* *prendere in prestito; adottare
bosom (*bu*-söm) *n* petto *m*; seno *m*
boss (boss) *n* capo *m*, padrone *m*
botany (*bo*-tö-ni) *n* botanica *f*
both (bouθ) *adj* entrambi; **both … and** sia … sia
bother (*bo*-ðö) *v* infastidire, importunare; disturbarsi; *n* noia *f*
bottle (*bo*-töl) *n* bottiglia *f*; ~ **opener** apribottiglie *m*; **hot-water** ~ borsa dell'acqua calda
bottleneck (*bo*-töl-nêk) *n* ingorgo *m*
bottom (*bo*-töm) *n* fondo *m*; didietro *m*, sedere *m*; *adj* inferiore
bough (bau) *n* ramo *m*
bought (boot) *v* (p, pp buy)

boulder (*boul*-dö) *n* masso *m*
bound (baund) *n* limite *m*; ***be ~ to** *dovere; **~ for** diretto a
boundary (*baun*-dö-ri) *n* limite *m*; frontiera *f*
bouquet (bu-*kei*) *n* mazzo *m*
bourgeois (*bu*ö-ʒuaa) *adj* borghese
boutique (bu-*tiik*) *n* boutique *m*
bow[1] (bau) *v* inchinare
bow[2] (bou) *n* arco *m*; **~ tie** cravattino *m*, cravatta a farfalla
bowels (bauöls) *pl* intestino *m*, budella *fpl*
bowl (boul) *n* vaso *m*
bowling (*bou*-ling) *n* bowling *m*, gioco delle bocce; **~ alley** pista di bocce
box[1] (bokss) *v* *fare del pugilato; **boxing match** partita di pugilato
box[2] (bokss) *n* scatola *f*
box-office (*bokss*-o-fiss) *n* botteghino *m*, biglietteria *f*
boy (boi) *n* ragazzo *m*; ragazzino *m*, fanciullo *m*; servo *m*; **~ scout** giovane esploratore
bra (braa) *n* reggipetto *m*, reggiseno *m*
bracelet (*breiss*-lit) *n* braccialetto *m*
braces (*brei*-ssis) *pl* bretelle *fpl*
brain (brein) *n* cervello *m*; intelligenza *f*
brain-wave (*brein*-ueiv) *n* idea luminosa
brake (breik) *n* freno *m*; **~ drum** tamburo del freno; **~ lights** luci di arresto
branch (braantʃ) *n* ramo *m*; succursale *f*
brand (brænd) *n* marca *f*; marchio *m*
brand-new (brænd-*n*i*uu*) *adj* nuovo fiammante
brass (braass) *n* ottone *m*; **~ band** *n* fanfara *f*
brassiere (*bræ*-siö) *n* reggipetto *m*, reggiseno *m*
brassware (*braass*-uêö) *n* ottoname *m*
brave (breiv) *adj* audace, coraggioso
Brazil (brö-*sil*) Brasile *m*
Brazilian (brö-*sil*-iön) *adj* brasiliano
breach (briitʃ) *n* breccia *f*
bread (brêd) *n* pane *m*; **wholemeal** ~ pane integrale
breadth (brêdθ) *n* larghezza *f*
break (breik) *n* frattura *f*; intervallo *m*
***break** (breik) *v* *rompere; **~ down** guastarsi; analizzare
breakdown (*breik*-daun) *n* guasto *m*, avaria *f*
breakfast (*brêk*-fösst) *n* prima colazione
bream (briim) *n* (pl ~) abramide *m*
breast (brêsst) *n* seno *m*
breaststroke (*brêsst*-sstrouk) *n* nuoto a rana
breath (brêθ) *n* respiro *m*; fiato *m*
breathe (briið) *v* respirare
breathing (*brii*-ðing) *n* respirazione *f*
breed (briid) *n* razza *f*; specie *f*
***breed** (briid) *v* allevare
breeze (briis) *n* brezza *f*
brew (bruu) *v* *fare la birra
brewery (*bruu*-ö-ri) *n* birreria *f*
bribe (braib) *v* *corrompere
bribery (*brai*-bö-ri) *n* corruzione *f*
brick (brik) *n* laterizio *m*, mattone *m*
bricklayer (*brik*-leiö) *n* muratore *m*
bride (braid) *n* sposa *f*
bridegroom (*braid*-ghruum) *n* sposo *m*
bridge (bridʒ) *n* ponte *m*; bridge *m*
brief (briif) *adj* breve
briefcase (*briif*-keiss) *n* cartella *f*
briefs (briifss) *pl* slip *mpl*, mutandine *fpl*
bright (brait) *adj* brillante; lucido; sveglio, intelligente
brill (bril) *n* rombo *m*
brilliant (*bril*-iönt) *adj* brillante

brim (brim) *n* orlo *m*
***bring** (bring) *v* portare; ~ **back** riportare; ~ **up** educare; sollevare
brisk (brissk) *adj* vivace
Britain (*bri*-tön) Gran Bretagna
British (*bri*-tiʃ) *adj* britannico; inglese
Briton (*bri*-tön) *n* britanno *m*; inglese *m*
broad (brood) *adj* largo; ampio, esteso; generale
broadcast (*brood*-kaasst) *n* emissione *f*
***broadcast** (*brood*-kaasst) *v* *trasmettere
brochure (*brou*-ʃuᵒ) *n* opuscolo *m*
broke[1] (brouk) *v* (p break)
broke[2] (brouk) *adj* squattrinato
broken (*brou*-kön) *adj* (pp break) guasto, rotto
broker (*brou*-kö) *n* mediatore *m*
bronchitis (brong-*kai*-tiss) *n* bronchite *f*
bronze (brons) *n* bronzo *m*; *adj* bronzeo
brooch (broutʃ) *n* spilla *f*
brook (bruk) *n* ruscello *m*
broom (bruum) *n* scopa *f*
brothel (*bro*-θöl) *n* bordello *m*
brother (*bra*-ðö) *n* fratello *m*
brother-in-law (*bra*-ðö-rin-loo) *n* (pl brothers-) cognato *m*
brought (broot) *v* (p, pp bring)
brown (braun) *adj* bruno
bruise (bruus) *n* livido *m*, contusione *f*; *v* ammaccare
brunette (bruu-*nêt*) *n* bruna *f*
brush (braʃ) *n* spazzola *f*; pennello *m*; *v* spazzolare
brutal (*bruu*-töl) *adj* brutale
bubble (*ba*-böl) *n* bolla *f*
bucket (*ba*-kit) *n* secchio *m*
buckle (*ba*-köl) *n* fibbia *f*
bud (bad) *n* bocciolo *m*
budget (*ba*-dʒit) *n* preventivo *m*, bilancio *m*
buffet (*bu*-fei) *n* buffé *m*
bug (bagh) *n* cimice *f*; *nAm* insetto *m*
***build** (bild) *v* costruire
building (*bil*-ding) *n* edificio *m*
bulb (balb) *n* bulbo *m*; **light** ~ lampadina *f*
Bulgaria (bal-*ghêᵒ*-ri-ö) Bulgaria *f*
Bulgarian (bal-*ghêᵒ*-ri-ön) *adj* bulgaro
bulk (balk) *n* massa *f*; maggior parte
bulky (*bal*-ki) *adj* voluminoso
bull (bul) *n* toro *m*
bullet (*bu*-lit) *n* pallottola *f*
bullfight (*bul*-fait) *n* corrida *f*
bullring (*bul*-ring) *n* arena *f*
bump (bamp) *v* urtare; cozzare; *n* urto *m*
bumper (*bam*-pö) *n* paraurti *m*
bumpy (*bam*-pi) *adj* accidentato
bun (ban) *n* panino *m*
bunch (bantʃ) *n* mazzo *m*; gruppo *m*
bundle (*ban*-döl) *n* fagotto *m*; *v* legare insieme, affastellare
bunk (bangk) *n* cuccetta *f*
buoy (boi) *n* boa *f*
burden (*böö*-dön) *n* peso *m*
bureau (*bⁱuᵒ*-rou) *n* (pl ~x, ~s) scrittoio *m*; *nAm* comò *m*
bureaucracy (bⁱuᵒ-*ro*-krö-ssi) *n* burocrazia *f*
burglar (*böö*-ghlö) *n* scassinatore *m*
burgle (*böö*-ghöl) *v* scassinare
burial (*bê*-ri-öl) *n* seppellimento *m*, sepoltura *f*
burn (böön) *n* bruciatura *f*
***burn** (böön) *v* *ardere; bruciare
***burst** (böösst) *v* scoppiare; spaccarsi
bury (*bê*-ri) *v* seppellire
bus (bass) *n* autobus *m*
bush (buʃ) *n* cespuglio *m*
business (*bis*-nöss) *n* affari, commercio *m*; azienda *f*, ditta *f*; mestiere *m*; affare *m*; ~ **hours** orario di

apertura, ore d'ufficio; ~ **trip** viaggio d'affari; **on** ~ per affari
businessman (*bis*-nöss-mön) *n* (pl -men) uomo d'affari
bust (basst) *n* busto *m*
bustle (*ba*-ssöl) *n* andirivieni *m*
busy (*bi*-si) *adj* occupato; animato, indaffarato
but (bat) *conj* ma; però; *prep* tranne
butcher (*bu*-tʃö) *n* macellaio *m*
butter (*ba*-tö) *n* burro *m*
butterfly (*ba*-tö-flai) *n* farfalla *f*; ~ **stroke** nuoto a farfalla
buttock (*ba*-tök) *n* natica *f*
button (*ba*-tön) *n* bottone *m*; *v* abbottonare
buttonhole (*ba*-tön-houl) *n* asola *f*
***buy** (bai) *v* comprare; acquistare
buyer (*bai*-ö) *n* compratore *m*
by (bai) *prep* da; con; vicino a
by-pass (*bai*-paass) *n* circonvallazione *f*; *v* girare intorno a

C

cab (kæb) *n* tassì *m*
cabaret (*kæ*-bö-rei) *n* cabaret *m*
cabbage (*kæ*-bidʒ) *n* cavolo *m*
cab-driver (*kæb*-drai-vö) *n* tassista *m*
cabin (*kæ*-bin) *n* cabina *f*; capanna *f*
cabinet (*kæ*-bi-nöt) *n* gabinetto *m*
cable (*kei*-böl) *n* cavo *m*; telegramma *m*; *v* telegrafare
cadre (*kaa*-dö) *n* quadro *m*
café (*kæ*-fei) *n* bar *m*
cafeteria (kæ-fö-*tiö*-ri-ö) *n* tavola calda
caffeine (*kæ*-fiin) *n* caffeina *f*
cage (keidʒ) *n* gabbia *f*
cake (keik) *n* dolce *m*; pasticceria *f*, torta *f*
calamity (kö-*læ*-mö-ti) *n* calamità *f*, disastro *m*
calcium (*kæl*-ssi-öm) *n* calcio *m*
calculate (*kæl*-kiu-leit) *v* computare, calcolare
calculation (kæl-kiu-*lei*-ʃön) *n* calcolo *m*
calendar (*kæ*-lön-dö) *n* calendario *m*
calf (kaaf) *n* (pl calves) vitello *m*; polpaccio *m*; ~ **skin** pelle di vitello
call (kool) *v* chiamare; telefonare; *n* appello *m*; visita *f*; telefonata *f*; ***be called** chiamarsi; ~ **names** ingiuriare; ~ **on** visitare; ~ **up** *Am* telefonare
callus (*kæ*-löss) *n* callo *m*
calm (kaam) *adj* tranquillo, calmo; ~ **down** calmare
calorie (*kæ*-lö-ri) *n* caloria *f*
Calvinism (*kæl*-vi-ni-söm) *n* calvinismo *m*
came (keim) *v* (p come)
camel (*kæ*-möl) *n* cammello *m*
cameo (*kæ*-mi-ou) *n* (pl ~s) cammeo *m*
camera (*kæ*-mö-rö) *n* macchina fotografica; cinepresa *f*; ~ **shop** negozio di articoli fotografici
camp (kæmp) *n* campo *m*; *v* accamparsi
campaign (kæm-*pein*) *n* campagna *f*
camp-bed (kæmp-*bêd*) *n* lettino da campeggio, branda *f*
camper (*kæm*-pö) *n* campeggiatore *m*
camping (*kæm*-ping) *n* campeggio *m*; ~ **site** campeggio *m*
camshaft (*kæm*-ʃaaft) *n* albero a camme
can (kæn) *n* latta *f*; ~ **opener** apriscatole *m*
***can** (kæn) *v* *potere
Canada (*kæ*-nö-dö) Canadà *m*
Canadian (kö-*nei*-di-ön) *adj* canadese
canal (kö-*næl*) *n* canale *m*
canary (kö-*nêö*-ri) *n* canarino *m*

cancel (*kæn*-ssöl) *v* annullare; *disdire
cancellation (kæn-ssö-*lei*-ʃön) *n* annullamento *m*
cancer (*kæn*-ssö) *n* cancro *m*
candelabrum (kæn-dö-*laa*-bröm) *n* (pl -bra) candelabro *m*
candidate (*kæn*-di-döt) *n* candidato *m*
candle (*kæn*-döl) *n* candela *f*
candy (*kæn*-di) *nAm* caramella *f*; dolciumi *mpl*; ~ **store** *Am* pasticceria *f*
cane (kein) *n* canna *f*; bastone *m*
canister (*kæ*-ni-sstö) *n* barattolo *m*
canoe (kö-*nuu*) *n* canoa *f*
canteen (kæn-*tiin*) *n* mensa *f*
canvas (*kæn*-vöss) *n* tela di canapa
cap (kæp) *n* berretto *m*
capable (*kei*-pö-böl) *adj* capace
capacity (kö-*pæ*-ssö-ti) *n* capacità *f*; potenza *f*; abilità *f*
cape (keip) *n* mantella *f*; capo *m*
capital (*kæ*-pi-töl) *n* capitale *f*; capitale *m*; *adj* importante, capitale; ~ **letter** maiuscola *f*
capitalism (*kæ*-pi-tö-li-söm) *n* capitalismo *m*
capitulation (kö-pi-tʲu-*lei*-ʃön) *n* capitolazione *f*
capsule (*kæp*-ssʲuul) *n* capsula *f*
captain (*kæp*-tin) *n* capitano *m*; comandante *m*
capture (*kæp*-tʃö) *v* *far prigioniero, catturare; *prendere; *n* cattura *f*; presa *f*
car (kaa) *n* macchina *f*; ~ **hire** autonoleggio *m*; ~ **park** parcheggio *m*; ~ **rental** *Am* autonoleggio *m*
carafe (kö-*ræf*) *n* caraffa *f*
caramel (*kæ*-rö-möl) *n* caramella di zucchero
carat (*kæ*-röt) *n* carato *m*
caravan (*kæ*-rö-væn) *n* carovana *f*; carrozzone *m*
carburettor (kaa-bʲu-*rê*-tö) *n* carburatore *m*
card (kaad) *n* cartoncino *m*; cartolina *f*
cardboard (*kaad*-bood) *n* cartone *m*; *adj* di cartone
cardigan (*kaa*-di-ghön) *n* giaccone *m*
cardinal (*kaa*-di-nöl) *n* cardinale *m*; *adj* cardinale, principale
care (kêᵒ) *n* cura *f*; preoccupazione *f*; ~ **about** preoccuparsi di; ~ **for** *voler bene; ***take** ~ **of** *aver cura di, occuparsi di
career (kö-*riᵒ*) *n* carriera *f*
carefree (*kêᵒ*-frii) *adj* spensierato
careful (*kêᵒ*-föl) *adj* attento; scrupoloso, accurato
careless (*kêᵒ*-löss) *adj* noncurante, trascurato
caretaker (*kêᵒ*-tei-kö) *n* custode *m*
cargo (*kaa*-ghou) *n* (pl ~es) carico *m*
carnival (*kaa*-ni-völ) *n* carnevale *m*
carp (kaap) *n* (pl ~) carpa *f*
carpenter (*kaa*-pin-tö) *n* falegname *m*
carpet (*kaa*-pit) *n* tappeto *m*
carriage (*kæ*-ridʒ) *n* vagone *m*; carrozza *f*
carriageway (*kæ*-ridʒ-ᵘei) *n* rotabile *f*
carrot (*kæ*-röt) *n* carota *f*
carry (*kæ*-ri) *v* portare; *condurre; ~ **on** continuare; proseguire; ~ **out** eseguire
carry-cot (*kæ*-ri-kot) *n* baby-pullman *m*
cart (kaat) *n* carro *m*
cartilage (*kaa*-ti-lidʒ) *n* cartilagine *f*
carton (*kaa*-tön) *n* scatolone *m*; stecca *f*
cartoon (kaa-*tuun*) *n* cartone animato
cartridge (*kaa*-tridʒ) *n* cartuccia *f*
carve (kaav) *v* tagliare; intagliare
carving (*kaa*-ving) *n* scultura in legno
case (keiss) *n* caso *m*; causa *f*; vali-

gia *f*; astuccio *m*; **attaché** ~ portacarte *m*; **in** ~ qualora; **in** ~ **of** in caso di
cash (kæʃ) *n* contanti *mpl*; *v* convertire, *riscuotere, incassare
cashier (kæ-*ʃiö*) *n* cassiere *m*; cassiera *f*
cashmere (*kæʃ*-miö) *n* cachemire *m*
casino (kö-*ssii*-nou) *n* (pl ~s) casinò *m*
cask (kaassk) *n* barile *m*, botte *f*
cast (kaasst) *n* lancio *m*
***cast** (kaasst) *v* lanciare, gettare; **cast iron** ghisa *f*
castle (*kaa*-ssöl) *n* castello *m*
casual (*kæ*-ʒu-öl) *adj* informale; incidentale, fortuito
casualty (*kæ*-ʒu-öl-ti) *n* vittima *f*
cat (kæt) *n* gatto *m*
catacomb (*kæ*-tö-koum) *n* catacomba *f*
catalogue (*kæ*-tö-logh) *n* catalogo *m*
catarrh (kö-*taa*) *n* catarro *m*
catastrophe (kö-*tæ*-sströ-fi) *n* catastrofe *f*
***catch** (kætʃ) *v* acchiappare; afferrare; *cogliere
category (*kæ*-ti-ghö-ri) *n* categoria *f*
cathedral (kö-*θii*-dröl) *n* duomo *m*, cattedrale *f*
catholic (*kæ*-θö-lik) *adj* cattolico
cattle (*kæ*-töl) *pl* bestiame *m*
caught (koot) *v* (p, pp catch)
cauliflower (*ko*-li-flauö) *n* cavolfiore *m*
cause (koos) *v* causare; provocare; *n* causa *f*; ragione *f*, motivo *m*; ~ **to** *indurre a
causeway (*koos*-ᵘei) *n* via selciata
caution (*koo*-ʃön) *n* cautela *f*; *v* ammonire
cautious (*koo*-ʃöss) *adj* cauto
cave (keiv) *n* caverna *f*; spelonca *f*
cavern (*kæ*-vön) *n* caverna *f*
caviar (*kæ*-vi-aa) *n* caviale *m*
cavity (*kæ*-vö-ti) *n* cavità *f*
cease (ssiiss) *v* *smettere
ceiling (*ssii*-ling) *n* soffitto *m*
celebrate (*ssê*-li-breit) *v* celebrare
celebration (ssê-li-*brei*-ʃön) *n* celebrazione *f*
celebrity (ssi-*lê*-brö-ti) *n* celebrità *f*
celery (*ssê*-lö-ri) *n* sedano *m*
celibacy (*ssê*-li-bö-ssi) *n* celibato *m*
cell (ssêl) *n* cella *f*
cellar (*ssê*-lö) *n* cantina *f*
cellophane (*ssê*-lö-fein) *n* cellofan *m*
cement (ssi-*mênt*) *n* cemento *m*
cemetery (*ssê*-mi-tri) *n* cimitero *m*
censorship (*ssên*-ssö-ʃip) *n* censura *f*
centigrade (*ssên*-ti-ghreid) *adj* centigrado
centimetre (*ssên*-ti-mii-tö) *n* centimetro *m*
central (*ssên*-tröl) *adj* centrale; ~ **heating** riscaldamento centrale; ~ **station** stazione centrale
centralize (*ssên*-trö-lais) *v* centralizzare
centre (*ssên*-tö) *n* centro *m*
century (*ssên*-tʃö-ri) *n* secolo *m*
ceramics (ssi-*ræ*-mikss) *pl* terraglie *fpl*, ceramica *f*
ceremony (*ssê*-rö-mö-ni) *n* cerimonia *f*
certain (*ssöö*-tön) *adj* certo
certificate (ssö-*ti*-fi-köt) *n* attestato *m*; certificato *m*, atto *m*, diploma *m*
chain (tʃein) *n* catena *f*
chair (tʃêö) *n* sedia *f*; seggio *m*
chairman (*tʃêö*-mön) *n* (pl -men) presidente *m*
chalet (*ʃæ*-lei) *n* chalet *m*
chalk (tʃook) *n* creta *f*
challenge (*tʃæ*-löndʒ) *v* sfidare; *n* sfida *f*
chamber (*tʃeim*-bö) *n* camera *f*

chambermaid (*tʃeim*-bö-meid) *n* cameriera *f*
champagne (ʃæm-*pein*) *n* champagne *m*
champion (*tʃæm*-pⁱön) *n* campione *m*; difensore *m*
chance (tʃaanss) *n* caso *m*; opportunità *f*, occasione *f*; rischio *m*; azzardo *m*; **by** ~ per caso
change (tʃeindʒ) *v* modificare, cambiare; cambiarsi; *n* cambiamento *m*, cambio *m*; spiccioli *mpl*
channel (*tʃæ*-nöl) *n* canale *m*; **English Channel** La Manica
chaos (*kei*-oss) *n* caos *m*
chaotic (kei-*o*-tik) *adj* caotico
chap (tʃæp) *n* tizio *m*
chapel (*tʃæ*-pöl) *n* chiesa *f*, cappella *f*
chaplain (*tʃæ*-plin) *n* cappellano *m*
character (*kæ*-rök-tö) *n* carattere *m*
characteristic (kæ-rök-tö-*ri*-sstik) *adj* tipico, caratteristico; *n* caratteristica *f*; tratto del carattere
characterize (*kæ*-rök-tö-rais) *v* caratterizzare
charcoal (*tʃaa*-koul) *n* carbone di legno
charge (tʃaadʒ) *v* *far pagare; incaricare; accusare; caricare; *n* costo *m*; carico *m*; accusa *f*; ~ **plate** *Am* carta di credito; **free of** ~ gratuito; **in** ~ **of** incaricato di; ***take** ~ **of** incaricarsi di
charity (*tʃæ*-rö-ti) *n* carità *f*
charm (tʃaam) *n* incanto *m*, fascino *m*; amuleto *m*
charming (*tʃaa*-ming) *adj* affascinante
chart (tʃaat) *n* tabella *f*; diagramma *m*; carta nautica; **conversion** ~ tabella di conversione
chase (tʃeiss) *v* inseguire; scacciare, cacciare; *n* caccia *f*
chasm (*kæ*-söm) *n* baratro *m*
chassis (*ʃæ*-ssi) *n* (pl ~) telaio *m*
chaste (tʃeisst) *adj* casto
chat (tʃæt) *v* chiacchierare, ciarlare; *n* ciancia *f*, ciarlata *f*, chiacchierata *f*
chatterbox (*tʃæ*-tö-bokss) *n* chiacchierone *m*
chauffeur (*ʃou*-fö) *n* autista *m*
cheap (tʃiip) *adj* a buon mercato; economico
cheat (tʃiit) *v* ingannare; imbrogliare
check (tʃêk) *v* verificare, *rivedere; *n* quadretto *m*; *nAm* conto *m*; assegno *m*; **check!** scacco!; ~ **in** registrarsi; ~ **out** *disdire
check-book (*tʃêk*-buk) *nAm* libretto di assegni
checkerboard (*tʃê*-kö-bood) *nAm* scacchiera *f*
checkers (*tʃê*-kös) *plAm* gioco della dama
checkroom (*tʃêk*-ruum) *nAm* guardaroba *m*
check-up (*tʃê*-kap) *n* visita medica
cheek (tʃiik) *n* guancia *f*
cheek-bone (*tʃiik*-boun) *n* zigomo *m*
cheer (tʃiᵒ) *v* acclamare; ~ **up** rallegrare
cheerful (*tʃiᵒ*-föl) *adj* gaio, allegro
cheese (tʃiis) *n* formaggio *m*
chef (ʃêf) *n* capocuoco *m*
chemical (*kê*-mi-köl) *adj* chimico
chemist (*kê*-misst) *n* farmacista *m*; **chemist's** farmacia *f*
chemistry (*kê*-mi-sstri) *n* chimica *f*
cheque (tʃêk) *n* assegno *m*
cheque-book (*tʃêk*-buk) *n* libretto di assegni
chequered (*tʃê*-köd) *adj* quadrettato, scaccato
cherry (*tʃê*-ri) *n* ciliegia *f*
chess (tʃêss) *n* scacchi *mpl*
chest (tʃêsst) *n* petto *m*; torace *m*; baule *m*; ~ **of drawers** cassettone *m*

chestnut (*tʃêss*-nat) *n* castagna *f*
chew (tʃuu) *v* masticare
chewing-gum (*tʃuu*-ing-gham) *n* gomma da masticare
chicken (*tʃi*-kin) *n* pollo *m*; pulcino *m*
chickenpox (*tʃi*-kin-pokss) *n* varicella *f*
chief (tʃiif) *n* capo *m*; *adj* primo, principale
chieftain (*tʃiif*-tön) *n* capo *m*
chilblain (*tʃil*-blein) *n* gelone *m*
child (tʃaild) *n* (pl children) bambino *m*
childbirth (*tʃaild*-bööθ) *n* parto *m*
childhood (*tʃaild*-hud) *n* infanzia *f*
Chile (*tʃi*-li) Cile *m*
Chilean (*tʃi*-li-ön) *adj* cileno
chill (tʃil) *n* brivido *m*
chilly (*tʃi*-li) *adj* freddino
chimes (tʃaims) *pl* carillon *m*
chimney (*tʃim*-ni) *n* camino *m*
chin (tʃin) *n* mento *m*
China (*tʃai*-nö) Cina *f*
china (*tʃai*-nö) *n* porcellana *f*
Chinese (tʃai-*niis*) *adj* cinese
chink (tʃingk) *n* fessura *f*
chip (tʃip) *n* scheggia *f*; gettone *m*; *v* tagliare, scheggiare; **chips** patatine fritte
chiropodist (ki-*ro*-pö-disst) *n* callista *m*
chisel (*tʃi*-söl) *n* scalpello *m*
chives (tʃaivs) *pl* cipollina *f*
chlorine (*kloo*-riin) *n* cloro *m*
chock-full (tʃok-*ful*) *adj* gremito, pieno zeppo
chocolate (*tʃo*-klöt) *n* cioccolata *f*; cioccolatino *m*
choice (tʃoiss) *n* scelta *f*; selezione *f*
choir (kᵘaiᵒ) *n* coro *m*
choke (tʃouk) *v* soffocare; strozzare; *n* valvola dell'aria
***choose** (tʃuus) *v* *scegliere
chop (tʃop) *n* cotoletta *f*, braciola *f*; *v* spaccare
Christ (kraisst) Cristo *m*
christen (*kri*-ssön) *v* battezzare
christening (*kri*-ssö-ning) *n* battesimo *m*
Christian (*kriss*-tʃön) *adj* cristiano; ~ **name** nome di battesimo
Christmas (*kriss*-möss) Natale
chromium (*krou*-mi-öm) *n* cromo *m*
chronic (*kro*-nik) *adj* cronico
chronological (kro-nö-*lo*-dʒi-köl) *adj* cronologico
chuckle (*tʃa*-köl) *v* ridacchiare
chunk (tʃangk) *n* grosso pezzo
church (tʃöötʃ) *n* chiesa *f*
churchyard (*tʃöötʃ*-ⁱaad) *n* camposanto *m*
cigar (ssi-*ghaa*) *n* sigaro *m*; ~ **shop** tabaccheria *f*
cigarette (ssi-ghö-*rêt*) *n* sigaretta *f*; ~ **tobacco** trinciato *m*
cigarette-case (ssi-ghö-*rêt*-keiss) *n* portasigarette *m*
cigarette-holder (ssi-ghö-*rêt*-houl-dö) *n* bocchino *m*
cigarette-lighter (ssi-ghö-*rêt*-lai-tö) *n* accendino *m*
cinema (*ssi*-nö-mö) *n* cinematografo *m*
cinnamon (*ssi*-nö-mön) *n* cannella *f*
circle (*ssöö*-köl) *n* cerchio *m*; circolo *m*; balconata *f*; *v* accerchiare, circondare
circulation (ssöö-kⁱu-*lei*-ʃön) *n* circolazione *f*; circolazione del sangue
circumstance (*ssöö*-köm-sstænss) *n* circostanza *f*
circus (*ssöö*-köss) *n* circo *m*
citizen (*ssi*-ti-sön) *n* cittadino *m*
citizenship (*ssi*-ti-sön-ʃip) *n* cittadinanza *f*
city (*ssi*-ti) *n* città *f*
civic (*ssi*-vik) *adj* civico

civil (*ssi*-völ) *adj* civile; cortese; ~ **law** diritto civile; ~ **servant** funzionario *m*
civilian (ssi-*vil*-ⁱön) *adj* civile; *n* borghese *m*
civilization (ssi-vö-lai-*sei*-ʃön) *n* civiltà *f*
civilized (*ssi*-vö-laisd) *adj* civilizzato
claim (kleim) *v* rivendicare, reclamare; asserire; *n* rivendicazione *f*, pretesa *f*
clamp (klæmp) *n* morsa *f*; morsetto *m*
clap (klæp) *v* battere le mani, applaudire
clarify (*klæ*-ri-fai) *v* chiarire, chiarificare
class (klaass) *n* classe *f*
classical (*klæ*-ssi-köl) *adj* classico
classify (*klæ*-ssi-fai) *v* classificare
class-mate (*klaass*-meit) *n* compagno di classe
classroom (*klaass*-ruum) *n* aula *f*
clause (kloos) *n* clausola *f*
claw (kloo) *n* artiglio *m*
clay (klei) *n* argilla *f*
clean (kliin) *adj* puro, pulito; *v* nettare, pulire
cleaning (*klii*-ning) *n* pulizia *f*, pulitura *f*; ~ **fluid** smacchiatore *m*
clear (kliᵒ) *adj* chiaro; *v* sgombrare
clearing (*kliᵒ*-ring) *n* radura *f*
cleft (klêft) *n* crepa *f*
clergyman (*klöö*-dʒi-mön) *n* (pl -men) pastore *m*; chierico *m*
clerk (klaak) *n* commesso d'ufficio, impiegato *m*; scrivano *m*; segretario *m*
clever (*klê*-vö) *adj* intelligente; perspicace, sveglio
client (*klai*-önt) *n* cliente *m*
cliff (klif) *n* scoglio *m*, scogliera *f*
climate (*klai*-mit) *n* clima *m*
climb (klaim) *v* arrampicarsi; arrampicare
clinic (*kli*-nik) *n* clinica *f*
cloak (klouk) *n* mantello *m*
cloakroom (*klouk*-ruum) *n* spogliatoio *m*
clock (klok) *n* orologio *m*; **at … o'-clock** alle …
cloister (*kloi*-sstö) *n* monastero *m*
close[1] (klous) *v* *chiudere
close[2] (klouss) *adj* vicino
closet (*klo*-sit) *n* credenza *f*
cloth (kloθ) *n* stoffa *f*; panno *m*
clothes (klouðs) *pl* abiti, vestiti *mpl*
clothes-brush (*klouðs*-braʃ) *n* spazzola per vestiti
clothing (*klou*-ðing) *n* vestiti *mpl*
cloud (klaud) *n* nuvola *f*
cloud-burst (*klaud*-böösst) *n* nubifragio *m*
cloudy (*klau*-di) *adj* nuvoloso
clover (*klou*-vö) *n* trifoglio *m*
clown (klaun) *n* pagliaccio *m*
club (klab) *n* circolo *m*; associazione *f*; clava *f*, mazza *f*
clumsy (*klam*-si) *adj* goffo
clutch (klatʃ) *n* frizione *f*; stretta *f*
coach (koutʃ) *n* autobus *m*; vagone *m*; carrozza *f*; allenatore *m*
coachwork (*koutʃ*-ᵘöök) *n* carrozzeria *f*
coagulate (kou-*æ*-ghⁱu-leit) *v* coagulare
coal (koul) *n* carbone *m*
coarse (kooss) *adj* grossolano; volgare
coast (kousst) *n* costa *f*
coat (kout) *n* cappotto *m*, soprabito *m*
coat-hanger (*kout*-hæng-ö) *n* attaccapanni *m*
cobweb (*kob*-ᵘêb) *n* ragnatela *f*
cocaine (kou-*kein*) *n* cocaina *f*
cock (kok) *n* gallo *m*
cocktail (*kok*-teil) *n* cocktail *m*

coconut (*kou*-kö-nat) *n* noce di cocco
cod (kod) *n* (pl ~) merluzzo *m*
code (koud) *n* codice *m*
coffee (*ko*-fi) *n* caffè *m*
cognac (*ko*-nʲæk) *n* cognac *m*
coherence (kou-*hiö*-rönss) *n* coerenza *f*
coin (koin) *n* moneta *f*
coincide (kou-in-*ssaid*) *v* *coincidere
cold (kould) *adj* freddo; *n* freddo *m*; raffreddore *m*; **catch a ~** *prendere un raffreddore
collapse (kö-*læpss*) *v* crollare
collar (*ko*-lö) *n* collare *m*; colletto *m*; **~ stud** bottoncino per colletto
collarbone (*ko*-lö-boun) *n* clavicola *f*
colleague (*ko*-liigh) *n* collega *m*
collect (kö-*lêkt*) *v* *raccogliere; rilevare, *andare a prendere; *fare una colletta
collection (kö-*lêk*-ʃön) *n* collezione *f*; levata *f*
collective (kö-*lêk*-tiv) *adj* collettivo
collector (kö-*lêk*-tö) *n* collezionista *m*; collettore *m*
college (*ko*-lidʒ) *n* collegio *m*
collide (kö-*laid*) *v* cozzare
collision (kö-*li*-ʒön) *n* scontro *m*, collisione *f*
Colombia (kö-*lom*-bi-ö) Colombia *f*
Colombian (kö-*lom*-bi-ön) *adj* colombiano
colonel (*köö*-nöl) *n* colonnello *m*
colony (*ko*-lö-ni) *n* colonia *f*
colour (*ka*-lö) *n* colore *m*; *v* colorare; **~ film** pellicola a colori
colourant (*ka*-lö-rönt) *n* tintura *f*
colour-blind (*ka*-lö-blaind) *adj* daltonico
coloured (*ka*-löd) *adj* di colore
colourful (*ka*-lö-föl) *adj* pieno di colore, colorito
column (*ko*-löm) *n* pilastro *m*, colonna *f*; rubrica *f*
coma (*kou*-mö) *n* coma *m*
comb (koum) *v* pettinare; *n* pettine *m*
combat (*kom*-bæt) *n* lotta *f*, combattimento *m*; *v* combattere
combination (kom-bi-*nei*-ʃön) *n* combinazione *f*
combine (köm-*bain*) *v* combinare; unire
***come** (kam) *v* *venire; **~ across** incontrare; trovare
comedian (kö-*mii*-di-ön) *n* commediante *m*; comico *m*
comedy (*ko*-mö-di) *n* commedia *f*; **musical ~** commedia musicale
comfort (*kam*-föt) *n* agio *m*, comodità *f*, conforto *m*; consolazione *f*; *v* consolare
comfortable (*kam*-fö-tö-böl) *adj* confortevole, comodo
comic (*ko*-mik) *adj* comico
comics (*ko*-mikss) *pl* racconto a fumetti
coming (*ka*-ming) *n* venuta *f*
comma (*ko*-mö) *n* virgola *f*
command (kö-*maand*) *v* comandare; *n* ordine *m*
commander (kö-*maan*-dö) *n* comandante *m*
commemoration (kö-mê-mö-*rei*-ʃön) *n* commemorazione *f*
commence (kö-*mênss*) *v* iniziare
comment (*ko*-mênt) *n* commento *m*; *v* commentare
commerce (*ko*-mööss) *n* commercio *m*
commercial (kö-*möö*-ʃöl) *adj* commerciale; *n* annunzio pubblicitario; **~ law** diritto commerciale
commission (kö-*mi*-ʃön) *n* comitato *m*
commit (kö-*mit*) *v* affidare, consegnare; *commettere, compiere
committee (kö-*mi*-ti) *n* commissione

f, comitato *m*
common (*ko*-mön) *adj* comune; abituale; ordinario
commune (*ko*-m[i]uun) *n* comune *f*
communicate (kö-*m[i]uu*-ni-keit) *v* comunicare
communication (kö-m[i]uu-ni-*kei*-ʃön) *n* comunicazione *f*
communiqué (kö-*m[i]uu*-ni-kei) *n* comunicato *m*
communism (*ko*-m[i]u-ni-söm) *n* comunismo *m*
communist (*ko*-m[i]u-nisst) *n* comunista *m*
community (kö-*m[i]uu*-nö-ti) *n* società *f*, comunità *f*
commuter (kö-*m[i]uu*-tö) *n* pendolare *m*
compact (*kom*-pækt) *adj* compatto
companion (köm-*pæ*-n[i]ön) *n* compagno *m*
company (*kam*-pö-ni) *n* compagnia *f*; ditta *f*, società *f*
comparative (köm-*pæ*-rö-tiv) *adj* relativo
compare (köm-*pê*[ö]) *v* paragonare
comparison (köm-*pæ*-ri-ssön) *n* paragone *m*
compartment (köm-*paat*-mönt) *n* scompartimento *m*
compass (*kam*-pöss) *n* bussola *f*
compel (köm-*pêl*) *v* *costringere
compensate (*kom*-pön-sseit) *v* compensare
compensation (kom-pön-*ssei*-ʃön) *n* compensazione *f*; indennità *f*
compete (köm-*piit*) *v* competere
competition (kom-pö-*ti*-ʃön) *n* gara *f*; concorrenza *f*
competitor (köm-*pê*-ti-tör) *n* concorrente *m*
compile (köm-*pail*) *v* compilare
complain (köm-*plein*) *v* lagnarsi
complaint (köm-*pleint*) *n* lagnanza *f*; reclamo *m*

complaints book libro dei reclami
complete (köm-*pliit*) *adj* completo; *v* completare
completely (köm-*pliit*-li) *adv* interamente, totalmente, completamente
complex (*kom*-plêkss) *n* complesso *m*; *adj* intricato, complesso
complexion (köm-*plêk*-ʃön) *n* carnagione *f*
complicated (*kom*-pli-kei-tid) *adj* complicato
compliment (*kom*-pli-mönt) *n* complimento *m*; *v* complimentare, felicitarsi con
compose (köm-*pous*) *v* *comporre
composer (köm-*pou*-sö) *n* compositore *m*
composition (kom-pö-*si*-ʃön) *n* composizione *f*
comprehensive (kom-pri-*hên*-ssiv) *adj* comprensivo
comprise (köm-*prais*) *v* *comprendere, *contenere
compromise (*kom*-prö-mais) *n* compromesso *m*
compulsory (köm-*pal*-ssö-ri) *adj* obbligatorio
comrade (*kom*-reid) *n* compagno *m*
conceal (kön-*ssiil*) *v* *nascondere
conceited (kön-*ssii*-tid) *adj* presuntuoso
conceive (kön-*ssiiv*) *v* concepire, *comprendere
concentrate (*kon*-ssön-treit) *v* concentrare
concentration (kon-ssön-*trei*-ʃön) *n* concentrazione *f*
conception (kön-*ssêp*-ʃön) *n* concezione *f*; concepimento *m*
concern (kön-*ssöön*) *v* riguardare, concernere; *n* ansietà *f*; faccenda *f*; azienda *f*, impresa *f*
concerned (kön-*ssöönd*) *adj* preoccupato; interessato

concerning (kön-*ssöö*-ning) *prep* riguardo a, riguardante
concert (*kon*-ssöt) *n* concerto *m*; ~ **hall** sala da concerti
concession (kön-*ssê*-ʃön) *n* concessione *f*
concierge (kong-ssi-*ê*ö ʒ) *n* portinaio *m*
concise (kön-*ssaiss*) *adj* conciso, breve
conclusion (köng-*kluu*-ʒön) *n* conclusione *f*
concrete (*kong*-kriit) *adj* concreto; *n* calcestruzzo *m*
concurrence (köng-*ka*-rönss) *n* concorso *m*
concussion (köng-*ka*-ʃön) *n* commozione cerebrale
condition (kön-*di*-ʃön) *n* condizione *f*; stato *m*, forma *f*; circostanza *f*
conditional (kön-*di*-ʃö-nöl) *adj* condizionale
conduct[1] (*kon*-dakt) *n* condotta *f*
conduct[2] (kön-*dakt*) *v* *condurre; guidare; *dirigere
conductor (kön-*dak*-tö) *n* conduttore *m*; direttore d'orchestra
confectioner (kön-*fêk*-ʃö-nö) *n* pasticciere *m*
conference (*kon*-fö-rönss) *n* conferenza *f*
confess (kön-*fêss*) *v* *riconoscere; confessare; professare
confession (kön-*fê*-ʃön) *n* confessione *f*
confidence (*kon*-fi-dönss) *n* fiducia *f*
confident (*kon*-fi-dönt) *adj* confidente
confidential (kon-fi-*dên*-ʃöl) *adj* confidenziale
confirm (kön-*fööm*) *v* confermare
confirmation (kon-fö-*mei*-ʃön) *n* conferma *f*
confiscate (*kon*-fi-sskeit) *v* sequestrare, confiscare
conflict (*kon*-flikt) *n* conflitto *m*
confuse (kön-*fiuus*) *v* *confondere; **confused** *adj* confuso
confusion (kön-*fiuu*-ʒön) *n* confusione *f*
congratulate (köng-*ghræ*-tʃu-leit) *v* congratularsi, felicitarsi con
congratulation (köng-ghræ-tʃu-*lei*-ʃön) *n* congratulazione *f*, felicitazione *f*
congregation (kong-ghri-*ghei*-ʃön) *n* comunione *f*, congregazione *f*
congress (*kong*-ghrêss) *n* congresso *m*
connect (kö-*nêkt*) *v* *connettere; collegare
connection (kö-*nêk*-ʃön) *n* relazione *f*; connessione *f*; coincidenza *f*
connoisseur (ko-nö-*ssöö*) *n* intenditore *m*
connotation (ko-nö-*tei*-ʃön) *n* significato secondario
conquer (*kong*-kö) *v* conquistare; *vincere
conqueror (*kong*-kö-rö) *n* conquistatore *m*
conquest (*kong*-kuêsst) *n* conquista *f*
conscience (*kon*-ʃönss) *n* coscienza *f*
conscious (*kon*-ʃöss) *adj* conscio
consciousness (*kon*-ʃöss-nöss) *n* coscienza *f*
conscript (*kon*-sskript) *n* coscritto *m*
consent (kön-*ssênt*) *v* consentire; acconsentire; *n* consenso *m*
consequence (*kon*-ssi-kuönss) *n* conseguenza *f*
consequently (*kon*-ssi-kuönt-li) *adv* conseguentemente
conservative (kön-*ssöö*-vö-tiv) *adj* conservatore
consider (kön-*ssi*-dö) *v* considerare; reputare, *ritenere
considerable (kön-*ssi*-dö-rö-böl) *adj* considerevole; notevole
considerate (kön-*ssi*-dö-röt) *adj* riguardoso
consideration (kön-ssi-dö-*rei*-ʃön) *n*

considerazione *f*; riguardo *m*, attenzione *f*
considering (kön-*ssi*-dö-ring) *prep* considerato
consignment (kön-*ssain*-mönt) *n* spedizione *f*
consist of (kön-*ssisst*) consistere in
conspire (kön-*sspai*^{ö}) *v* cospirare
constant (*kon*-sstönt) *adj* constante
constipated (*kon*-ssti-pei-tid) *adj* stitico
constipation (kon-ssti-*pei*-ʃön) *n* stitichezza *f*
constituency (kön-*ssti*-tʃu-ön-ssi) *n* circoscrizione elettorale
constitution (kon-ssti-*t*^{i}*uu*-ʃön) *n* costituzione *f*
construct (kön-*sstrakt*) *v* costruire; edificare, fabbricare
construction (kön-*sstrak*-ʃön) *n* costruzione *f*; fabbricazione *f*; edificio *m*
consul (*kon*-ssöl) *n* console *m*
consulate (*kon*-ss^{i}u-löt) *n* consolato *m*
consult (kön-*ssalt*) *v* consultare
consultation (kon-ssöl-*tei*-ʃön) *n* consultazione *f*; consulta *f*; ~ **hours** *n* orario di ricevimento
consumer (kön-*ss*^{i}*uu*-mö) *n* consumatore *m*
contact (*kon*-tækt) *n* contatto *m*; accensione *f*; *v* contattare; ~ **lenses** lenti a contatto
contagious (kön-*tei*-dʒöss) *adj* contagioso
contain (kön-*tein*) *v* *contenere; *comprendere
container (kön-*tei*-nö) *n* recipiente *m*; cassa mobile
contemporary (kön-*têm*-pö-rö-ri) *adj* contemporaneo; di allora; *n* contemporaneo *m*
contempt (kön-*têmpt*) *n* disprezzo *m*, disdegno *m*
content (kön-*tênt*) *adj* contento
contents (*kon*-têntss) *pl* contenuto *m*
contest (*kon*-têsst) *n* lotta *f*; competizione *f*
continent (*kon*-ti-nönt) *n* continente *m*
continental (kon-ti-*nên*-töl) *adj* continentale
continual (kön-*ti*-n^{i}u-öl) *adj* continuo
continue (kön-*ti*-n^{i}uu) *v* continuare; proseguire
continuous (kön-*ti*-n^{i}u-öss) *adj* continuo, ininterrotto
contour (*kon*-tu^{ö}) *n* contorno *m*
contraceptive (kon-trö-*ssêp*-tiv) *n* anticoncezionale *m*
contract[1] (*kon*-trækt) *n* contratto *m*
contract[2] (kön-*trækt*) *v* *contrarre
contractor (kön-*træk*-tö) *n* imprenditore *m*
contradict (kon-trö-*dikt*) *v* *contraddire
contradictory (kon-trö-*dik*-tö-ri) *adj* contraddittorio
contrary (*kon*-trö-ri) *n* contrario *m*; *adj* contrario; **on the** ~ al contrario
contrast (*kon*-traasst) *n* contrasto *m*; differenza *f*
contribution (kon-tri-*b*^{i}*uu*-ʃön) *n* contribuzione *f*
control (kön-*troul*) *n* controllo *m*; *v* controllare
controversial (kon-trö-*vöö*-ʃöl) *adj* controverso
convenience (kön-*vii*-n^{i}önss) *n* comodità *f*
convenient (kön-*vii*-n^{i}önt) *adj* comodo; conveniente
convent (*kon*-vönt) *n* convento *m*
conversation (kon-vö-*ssei*-ʃön) *n* discorso *m*, conversazione *f*
convert (kön-*vööt*) *v* convertire
convict[1] (kön-*vikt*) *v* dichiarare colpe-

vole
convict[2] (*kon*-vikt) *n* condannato *m*
conviction (kön-*vik*-ʃön) *n* convinzione *f*; condanna *f*
convince (kön-*vinss*) *v* *convincere
convulsion (kön-*val*-ʃön) *n* convulsione *f*
cook (kuk) *n* cuoco *m*; *v* cucinare; preparare
cookbook (*kuk*-buk) *nAm* libro di cucina
cooker (*ku*-kö) *n* fornello *m*; **gas ~** cucina a gas
cookery-book (*ku*-kö-ri-buk) *n* libro di cucina
cookie (*ku*-ki) *nAm* biscotto *m*
cool (kuul) *adj* fresco; **cooling system** sistema di raffreddamento
co-operation (kou-o-pö-*rei*-ʃön) *n* cooperazione *f*
co-operative (kou-*o*-pö-rö-tiv) *adj* cooperativo; cooperante, cooperatore; *n* cooperativa *f*
co-ordinate (kou-*oo*-di-neit) *v* coordinare
co-ordination (kou-oo-di-*nei*-ʃön) *n* coordinazione *f*
copper (*ko*-pö) *n* rame *m*
copy (*ko*-pi) *n* copia *f*; *v* copiare; imitare; **carbon ~** copia *f*
coral (*ko*-röl) *n* corallo *m*
cord (kood) *n* corda *f*; spago *m*
cordial (*koo*-di-öl) *adj* cordiale
corduroy (*koo*-dö-roi) *n* velluto a coste
core (koo) *n* nucleo *m*; torsolo *m*
cork (kook) *n* sughero *m*; tappo *m*
corkscrew (*kook*-sskruu) *n* cavatappi *m*
corn (koon) *n* granello *m*; frumento *m*, grano *m*; occhio di pernice, callo *m*; **~ on the cob** pannocchia di granturco
corner (*koo*-nö) *n* angolo *m*
cornfield (*koon*-fiild) *n* campo di grano
corpse (koopss) *n* cadavere *m*
corpulent (*koo*-pʲu-lönt) *adj* corpulento; grasso, obeso
correct (kö-*rêkt*) *adj* esatto, corretto; *v* *correggere
correction (kö-*rêk*-ʃön) *n* correzione *f*; rettifica *f*
correctness (kö-*rêkt*-nöss) *n* correttezza *f*
correspond (ko-ri-*sspond*) *v* *corrispondere
correspondence (ko-ri-*sspon*-dönss) *n* corrispondenza *f*
correspondent (ko-ri-*sspon*-dönt) *n* corrispondente *m*
corridor (*ko*-ri-doo) *n* corridoio *m*
corrupt (kö-*rapt*) *adj* corrotto; *v* *corrompere
corruption (kö-*rap*-ʃön) *n* corruzione *f*
corset (*koo*-ssit) *n* busto *m*
cosmetics (kos-*mê*-tikss) *pl* cosmetici *mpl*
cost (kosst) *n* costo *m*; prezzo *m*
***cost** (kosst) *v* costare
cosy (*kou*-si) *adj* intimo, confortevole
cot (kot) *nAm* lettino da campeggio
cottage (*ko*-tidʒ) *n* villino *m*
cotton (*ko*-tön) *n* cotone *m*; di cotone
cotton-wool (*ko*-tön-ᵘul) *n* ovatta *f*
couch (kautʃ) *n* divano *m*
cough (kof) *n* tosse *f*; *v* tossire
could (kud) *v* (p can)
council (*kaun*-ssöl) *n* consiglio *m*
councillor (*kaun*-ssö-lö) *n* consigliere *m*
counsel (*kaun*-ssöl) *n* consiglio *m*
counsellor (*kaun*-ssö-lö) *n* consigliere *m*
count (kaunt) *v* contare; addizionare; *includere; considerare; *n* conte *m*
counter (*kaun*-tö) *n* banco *m*
counterfeit (*kaun*-tö-fiit) *v* falsificare

counterfoil (*kaun*-tö-foil) *n* talloncino *m*
counterpane (*kaun*-tö-pein) *n* copriletto *m*
countess (*kaun*-tiss) *n* contessa *f*
country (*kan*-tri) *n* paese *m*; campagna *f*; regione *f*; ~ **house** casa di campagna
countryman (*kan*-tri-mön) *n* (pl -men) compatriota *m*
countryside (*kan*-tri-ssaid) *n* campagna *f*
county (*kaun*-ti) *n* contea *f*
couple (*ka*-pöl) *n* coppia *f*
coupon (*kuu*-pon) *n* cedola *f*, tagliando *m*
courage (*ka*-ridʒ) *n* audacia *f*, coraggio *m*
courageous (kö-*rei*-dʒöss) *adj* valoroso, coraggioso
course (kooss) *n* rotta *f*; portata *f*; corso *m*; **intensive** ~ corso accelerato; **of** ~ naturalmente
court (koot) *n* tribunale *m*; corte *f*
courteous (*köö*-ti-öss) *adj* cortese
cousin (*ka*-sön) *n* cugina *f*, cugino *m*
cover (*ka*-vö) *v* *coprire; *n* rifugio *m*; coperchio *m*; copertina *f*; ~ **charge** prezzo del coperto
cow (kau) *n* vacca *f*
coward (*kau*-öd) *n* codardo *m*
cowardly (*kau*-öd-li) *adj* vile
cow-hide (*kau*-haid) *n* pelle di vacca
crab (kræb) *n* granchio *m*
crack (kræk) *n* schiocco *m*; fessura *f*; *v* schioccare; spaccare, incrinarsi
cracker (*kræ*-kö) *nAm* biscottino *m*
cradle (*krei*-döl) *n* culla *f*
cramp (kræmp) *n* crampo *m*
crane (krein) *n* gru *f*
crankcase (*krængk*-keiss) *n* basamento *m*
crankshaft (*krængk*-ʃaaft) *n* albero a gomiti
crash (kræʃ) *n* scontro *m*; *v* scontrarsi; precipitare; ~ **barrier** barriera di sicurezza
crate (kreit) *n* gabbia da imballaggio
crater (*krei*-tö) *n* cratere *m*
crawl (krool) *v* *andare carponi; *n* crawl *m*
craze (kreis) *n* mania *f*
crazy (*krei*-si) *adj* pazzo; sciocco, folle
creak (kriik) *v* cigolare
cream (kriim) *n* crema *f*; panna *f*; *adj* color crema
creamy (*krii*-mi) *adj* cremoso
crease (kriiss) *v* increspare; *n* piega *f*; grinza *f*
create (kri-*eit*) *v* creare
creature (*krii*-tʃö) *n* creatura *f*; essere *m*
credible (*krê*-di-böl) *adj* credibile
credit (*krê*-dit) *n* credito *m*; *v* accreditare; ~ **card** carta di credito
creditor (*krê*-di-tö) *n* creditore *m*
credulous (*krê*-dʲu-löss) *adj* credulo
creek (kriik) *n* insenatura *f*
***creep** (kriip) *v* strisciare
creepy (*krii*-pi) *adj* ributtante, raccapricciante
cremate (kri-*meit*) *v* cremare
cremation (kri-*mei*-ʃön) *n* cremazione *f*
crew (kruu) *n* equipaggio *m*
cricket (*kri*-kit) *n* cricket *m*; grillo *m*
crime (kraim) *n* crimine *m*
criminal (*kri*-mi-nöl) *n* delinquente *m*, criminale *m*; *adj* criminale; ~ **law** diritto penale
criminality (kri-mi-*næ*-lö-ti) *n* criminalità *f*
crimson (*krim*-sön) *adj* cremisino
crippled (*kri*-pöld) *adj* zoppo
crisis (*krai*-ssiss) *n* (pl crises) crisi *f*
crisp (krissp) *adj* croccante
critic (*kri*-tik) *n* critico *m*
critical (*kri*-ti-köl) *adj* critico; precario

criticism (*kri*-ti-ssi-söm) *n* critica *f*
criticize (*kri*-ti-ssais) *v* criticare
crochet (*krou*-ʃei) *v* lavorare all'uncinetto
crockery (*kro*-kö-ri) *n* terraglie *fpl*, vasellame *m*
crocodile (*kro*-kö-dail) *n* coccodrillo *m*
crooked (*kru*-kid) *adj* tortuoso, storto; disonesto
crop (krop) *n* raccolta *f*
cross (kross) *v* attraversare; *adj* arrabbiato, imbronciato; *n* croce *f*
cross-eyed (*kross*-aid) *adj* strabico
crossing (*kro*-ssing) *n* traversata *f*; crocevia *m*; passaggio pedonale; passaggio a livello
crossroads (*kross*-rouds) *n* crocicchio *m*
crosswalk (*kross*-ᵘook) *nAm* passaggio pedonale
crow (krou) *n* cornacchia *f*
crowbar (*krou*-baa) *n* piede di porco
crowd (kraud) *n* massa *f*, folla *f*
crowded (*krau*-did) *adj* affollato
crown (kraun) *n* corona *f*; *v* incoronare; coronare
crucifix (*kruu*-ssi-fikss) *n* crocifisso *m*
crucifixion (kruu-ssi-*fik*-ʃön) *n* crocifissione *f*
crucify (*kruu*-ssi-fai) *v* *crocifiggere
cruel (kruᵒl) *adj* crudele
cruise (kruus) *n* crociera *f*
crumb (kram) *n* briciola *f*
crusade (kruu-*sseid*) *n* crociata *f*
crust (krasst) *n* crosta *f*
crutch (kratʃ) *n* stampella *f*
cry (krai) *v* *piangere; gridare; *n* urlo *m*, grido *m*
crystal (*kri*-sstöl) *n* cristallo *m*; *adj* cristallino
Cuba (*kⁱuu*-bö) Cuba *f*
Cuban (*kⁱuu*-bön) *adj* cubano
cube (kⁱuub) *n* cubo *m*
cuckoo (*ku*-kuu) *n* cuculo *m*
cucumber (*kⁱuu*-köm-bö) *n* cetriolo *m*
cuddle (*ka*-döl) *v* vezzeggiare
cudgel (*ka*-dʒöl) *n* randello *m*
cuff (kaf) *n* polsino *m*
cuff-links (*kaf*-lingkss) *pl* gemelli *mpl*
cul-de-sac (*kal*-dö-ssæk) *n* vicolo cieco
cultivate (*kal*-ti-veit) *v* coltivare
culture (*kal*-tʃö) *n* cultura *f*; coltura *f*
cultured (*kal*-tʃöd) *adj* colto
cunning (*ka*-ning) *adj* furbo
cup (kap) *n* tazza *f*; coppa *f*
cupboard (*ka*-böd) *n* armadio *m*
curb (kööb) *n* orlo del marciapiede; *v* frenare
cure (kⁱuᵒ) *v* curare; *n* cura *f*; guarigione *f*
curio (*kⁱuᵒ*-ri-ou) *n* (pl ~s) curiosità *f*
curiosity (kⁱuᵒ-ri-*o*-ssö-ti) *n* curiosità *f*
curious (*kⁱuᵒ*-ri-öss) *adj* curioso; strano
curl (kööl) *v* ondulare; arricciare; *n* ricciolo *m*
curler (*köö*-lö) *n* bigodino *m*
curling-tongs (*köö*-ling-tongs) *pl* arricciacapelli *m*
curly (*köö*-li) *adj* ricciuto
currant (*ka*-rönt) *n* uva di Corinto; ribes *m*
currency (*ka*-rön-ssi) *n* valuta *f*; **foreign** ~ divisa estera
current (*ka*-rönt) *n* corrente *f*; *adj* corrente; **alternating** ~ corrente alternata; **direct** ~ corrente continua
curry (*ka*-ri) *n* curry *m*
curse (kööss) *v* bestemmiare; *maledire; *n* bestemmia *f*
curtain (*köö*-tön) *n* tenda *f*; sipario *m*
curve (kööv) *n* curva *f*; svolta *f*
curved (köövd) *adj* curvo
cushion (*ku*-ʃön) *n* cuscino *m*
custodian (ka-*sstou*-di-ön) *n* custode *m*

custody (*ka*-sstö-di) *n* detenzione *f*; custodia *f*; tutela *f*
custom (*ka*-sstöm) *n* costume *m*; abitudine *f*
customary (*ka*-sstö-mö-ri) *adj* usuale, solito, abituale
customer (*ka*-sstö-mö) *n* cliente *m*; avventore *m*
Customs (*ka*-sstöms) *pl* dogana *f*; ~ **duty** dazio *m*; ~ **officer** doganiere *m*
cut (kat) *n* incisione *f*; taglio *m*
***cut** (kat) *v* tagliare; *ridurre; ~ **off** tagliare; troncare
cutlery (*kat*-lö-ri) *n* posate *fpl*
cutlet (*kat*-löt) *n* costoletta *f*
cycle (*ssai*-köl) *n* ciclo *m*; bicicletta *f*
cyclist (*ssai*-klisst) *n* ciclista *m*
cylinder (*ssi*-lin-dö) *n* cilindro *m*; ~ **head** testa cilindro
cystitis (ssi-*sstai*-tiss) *n* cistite *f*
Czech (tʃêk) *adj* ceco
Czechoslovakia (tʃê-kö-sslö-*vaa*-ki-ö) Cecoslovacchia *f*

D

dad (dæd) *n* padre *m*
daddy (*dæ*-di) *n* papà *m*
daffodil (*dæ*-fö-dil) *n* narciso *m*
daily (*dei*-li) *adj* giornaliero, quotidiano; *n* quotidiano *m*
dairy (*dê*ö-ri) *n* latteria *f*
dam (dæm) *n* argine *m*; diga *f*
damage (*dæ*-midʒ) *n* danno *m*; *v* danneggiare
damp (dæmp) *adj* umido; bagnato; *n* umidità *f*; *v* inumidire
dance (daanss) *v* ballare; *n* ballo *m*
dandelion (*dæn*-di-lai-ön) *n* soffione *m*
dandruff (*dæn*-dröf) *n* forfora *f*
Dane (dein) *n* danese *m*
danger (*dein*-dʒö) *n* pericolo *m*
dangerous (*dein*-dʒö-röss) *adj* pericoloso
Danish (*dei*-niʃ) *adj* danese
dare (dêö) *v* osare; sfidare
daring (*dê*ö-ring) *adj* temerario
dark (daak) *adj* buio, oscuro; *n* oscurità *f*, buio *m*
darling (*daa*-ling) *n* amore *m*, caro *m*
darn (daan) *v* rammendare
dash (dæʃ) *v* precipitarsi; *n* lineetta *f*
dashboard (*dæʃ*-bood) *n* cruscotto *m*
data (*dei*-tö) *pl* dato *m*
date[1] (deit) *n* data *f*; appuntamento *m*; *v* datare; **out of** ~ fuori moda
date[2] (deit) *n* dattero *m*
daughter (*doo*-tö) *n* figlia *f*
dawn (doon) *n* alba *f*; aurora *f*
day (dei) *n* giorno *m*; **by** ~ di giorno; ~ **trip** giro *m*; **per** ~ al giorno; **the** ~ **before yesterday** avant'ieri
daybreak (*dei*-breik) *n* aurora *f*
daylight (*dei*-lait) *n* luce del giorno
dead (dêd) *adj* morto; deceduto
deaf (dêf) *adj* sordo
deal (diil) *n* accordo *m*, affare *m*
***deal** (diil) *v* distribuire; ~ **with** *v* trattare con; *fare affari con
dealer (*dii*-lö) *n* negoziante *m*, commerciante *m*
dear (diö) *adj* caro; diletto
death (dêθ) *n* morte *f*; ~ **penalty** pena di morte
debate (di-*beit*) *n* dibattito *m*
debit (*dê*-bit) *n* debito *m*
debt (dêt) *n* debito *m*
decaffeinated (dii-*kæ*-fi-nei-tid) *adj* decaffeinizzato
deceit (di-*ssiit*) *n* inganno *m*
deceive (di-*ssiiv*) *v* ingannare
December (di-*ssêm*-bö) dicembre
decency (*dii*-ssön-ssi) *n* decenza *f*
decent (*dii*-ssönt) *adj* decente

decide (di-*ssaid*) *v* *decidere
decision (di-*ssi*-ʒön) *n* decisione *f*
deck (dêk) *n* coperta *f*; ~ **cabin** cabina di coperta; ~ **chair** sedia a sdraio
declaration (dê-klö-*rei*-ʃön) *n* dichiarazione *f*
declare (di-*klêö*) *v* dichiarare; indicare
decoration (dê-kö-*rei*-ʃön) *n* ornamento *m*
decrease (dii-*kriiss*) *v* diminuire; *decrescere; *n* diminuzione *f*
dedicate (*dê*-di-keit) *v* dedicare
deduce (di *d'uuss*) *v* *dedurre
deduct (di-*dakt*) *v* *sottrarre
deed (diid) *n* azione *f*, atto *m*
deep (diip) *adj* profondo
deep-freeze (diip-*friis*) *n* congelatore *m*
deer (diö) *n* (pl ~) cervo *m*
defeat (di-*fiit*) *v* *sconfiggere; *n* sconfitta *f*
defective (di-*fêk*-tiv) *adj* difettoso
defence (di-*fênss*) *n* difesa *f*
defend (di-*fênd*) *v* *difendere
deficiency (di-*fi*-ʃön-ssi) *n* deficienza *f*
deficit (*dê*-fi-ssit) *n* deficit *m*
define (di-*fain*) *v* definire, determinare
definite (*dê*-fi-nit) *adj* determinato; esplicito
definition (dê-fi-*ni*-ʃön) *n* definizione *f*
deformed (di-*foomd*) *adj* deformato, deforme
degree (di-*ghrii*) *n* grado *m*; titolo *m*
delay (di-*lei*) *v* ritardare; differire; *n* indugio *m*, ritardo *m*; rinvio *m*
delegate (*dê*-li-ghöt) *n* delegato *m*
delegation (dê-li-*ghei*-ʃön) *n* delegazione *f*
deliberate[1] (di-*li*-bö-reit) *v* deliberare, ponderare
deliberate[2] (di-*li*-bö-röt) *adj* premeditato
deliberation (di-li-bö-*rei*-ʃön) *n* riflessione *f*, deliberazione *f*
delicacy (*dê*-li-kö-ssi) *n* ghiottoneria *f*
delicate (*dê*-li-köt) *adj* delicato
delicatessen (dê-li-kö-*tê*-ssön) *n* leccornia *f*; negozio di specialità gastronomiche
delicious (di-*li*-ʃöss) *adj* squisito, delizioso
delight (di-*lait*) *n* diletto *m*, delizia *f*; *v* deliziare; **delighted** felicissimo
delightful (di-*lait*-föl) *adj* dilettevole, piacevolissimo
deliver (di-*li*-vö) *v* recapitare, consegnare; liberare
delivery (di-*li*-vö-ri) *n* consegna *f*; parto *m*; liberazione *f*; ~ **van** furgone *m*
demand (di-*maand*) *v* *richiedere, *esigere; *n* esigenza *f*; domanda *f*
democracy (di-*mo*-krö-ssi) *n* democrazia *f*
democratic (dê-mö-*kræ*-tik) *adj* democratico
demolish (di-*mo*-liʃ) *v* demolire
demolition (dê-mö-*li*-ʃön) *n* demolizione *f*
demonstrate (*dê*-mön-sstreit) *v* dimostrare; *fare una dimostrazione
demonstration (dê-mön-*sstrei*-ʃön) *n* dimostrazione *f*
den (dên) *n* tana *f*
Denmark (*dên*-maak) Danimarca *f*
denomination (di-no-mi-*nei*-ʃön) *n* denominazionc *f*
dense (dênss) *adj* denso
dent (dênt) *n* ammaccatura *f*
dentist (*dên*-tisst) *n* dentista *m*
denture (*dên*-tʃö) *n* dentiera *f*
deny (di-*nai*) *v* negare; rifiutare, ricusare
deodorant (dii-*ou*-dö-rönt) *n* deodo-

rante *m*
depart (di-*paat*) *v* *andarsene, partire; trapassare
department (di-*paat*-mönt) *n* sezione *f*, riparto *m*; ~ **store** grande magazino
departure (di-*paa*-tʃö) *n* partenza *f*
dependant (di-*pên*-dönt) *adj* dipendente
depend on (di-*pênd*) *dipendere da
deposit (di-*po*-sit) *n* versamento *m*; deposito *m*; sedimento *m*, giacimento *m*; *v* depositare
depository (di-*po*-si-tö-ri) *n* magazzino *m*
depot (*dê*-pou) *n* deposito *m*; *nAm* stazione *f*
depress (di-*prêss*) *v* *deprimere
depression (di-*prê*-ʃön) *n* depressione *f*
deprive of (di-*praiv*) privare di
depth (dêpθ) *n* profondità *f*
deputy (*dê*-p$^\text{i}$u-ti) *n* deputato *m*; sostituto *m*
descend (di-*ssênd*) *v* *scendere
descendant (di-*ssên*-dönt) *n* discendente *m*
descent (di-*ssênt*) *n* discesa *f*
describe (di-*sskraib*) *v* *descrivere
description (di-*sskrip*-ʃön) *n* descrizione *f*; connotati *mpl*
desert^{1} (*dê*-söt) *n* deserto *m*; *adj* incolto, deserto
desert^{2} (di-*sööt*) *v* disertare; lasciare
deserve (di-*söölv*) *v* meritare
design (di-*sain*) *v* progettare; *n* disegno *m*; scopo *m*
designate (*dê*-sigh-neit) *v* designare
desirable (di-*sai*$^\text{ö}$-rö-böl) *adj* desiderabile
desire (di-*sai*$^\text{ö}$) *n* desiderio *m*; *v* desiderare
desk (dêssk) *n* scrivania *f*; leggio *m*; banco di scuola
despair (di-*sspê*$^\text{ö}$) *n* disperazione *f*; *v* disperare
despatch (di-*sspætʃ*) *v* spedire
desperate (*dê*-sspö-röt) *adj* disperato
despise (di-*sspais*) *v* disprezzare
despite (di-*sspait*) *prep* malgrado
dessert (di-*sööt*) *n* dolce *m*
destination (dê-ssti-*nei*-ʃön) *n* destinazione *f*
destine (*dê*-sstin) *v* destinare
destiny (*dê*-ssti-ni) *n* destino *m*, sorte *f*
destroy (di-*sstroi*) *v* *distruggere
destruction (di-*sstrak*-ʃön) *n* distruzione *f*; rovina *f*
detach (di-*tætʃ*) *v* staccare
detail (*dii*-teil) *n* particolare *m*, dettaglio *m*
detailed (*dii*-teild) *adj* particolareggiato, dettagliato
detect (di-*têkt*) *v* *scoprire
detective (di-*têk*-tiv) *n* investigatore *m*; ~ **story** romanzo poliziesco
detergent (di-*töö*-dʒönt) *n* detergente *m*
determine (di-*töö*-min) *v* stabilire, determinare
determined (di-*töö*-mind) *adj* risoluto
detour (*dii*-tu$^\text{ö}$) *n* giro *m*; deviazione *f*
devaluation (dii-væl-$^\text{i}$u-*ei*-ʃön) *n* svalutazione *f*
devalue (dii-*væl*-$^\text{i}$uu) *v* svalutare
develop (di-*vê*-löp) *v* sviluppare
development (di-*vê*-löp-mönt) *n* sviluppo *m*
deviate (*dii*-vi-eit) *v* deviare
devil (*dê*-völ) *n* diavolo *m*
devise (di-*vais*) *v* escogitare
devote (di-*vout*) *v* dedicare
dew (d$^\text{i}$uu) *n* rugiada *f*
diabetes (dai-ö-*bii*-tiis) *n* diabete *m*
diabetic (dai-ö-*bê*-tik) *n* diabetico *m*
diagnose (dai-ögh-*nous*) *v* diagnosti-

care; costatare
diagnosis (dai-ögh-*nou*-ssiss) *n* (pl -ses) diagnosi *f*
diagonal (dai-*æ*-ghö-nöl) *n* diagonale *f*; *adj* diagonale
diagram (*dai*-ö-ghræm) *n* diagramma *m*; schema *m*, grafico *m*
dialect (*dai*-ö-lêkt) *n* dialetto *m*
diamond (*dai*-ö-mönd) *n* diamante *m*
diaper (*dai*-ö-pö) *nAm* pannolino *m*
diaphragm (*dai*-ö-fræm) *n* membrana *f*
diarrhoea (dai-ö-*ri*-ö) *n* diarrea *f*
diary (*dai*-ö-ri) *n* agenda *f*; diario *m*
dictaphone (*dik*-tö-foun) *n* dittafono *m*
dictate (dik-*teit*) *v* dettare
dictation (dik-*tei*-ʃön) *n* dettato *m*
dictator (dik-*tei*-tö) *n* dittatore *m*
dictionary (*dik*-ʃö-nö-ri) *n* dizionario *m*
did (did) *v* (p do)
die (dai) *v* *morire
diesel (*dii*-söl) *n* diesel *m*
diet (*dai*-öt) *n* dieta *f*
differ (*di*-fö) *v* differire
difference (*di*-fö-rönss) *n* differenza *f*; distinzione *f*
different (*di*-fö-rönt) *adj* differente; altro
difficult (*di*-fi-költ) *adj* difficile; fastidioso
difficulty (*di*-fi-köl-ti) *n* difficoltà *f*; pena *f*
***dig** (digh) *v* scavare
digest (di-*dʒêsst*) *v* digerire
digestible (di-*dʒê*-sstö-böl) *adj* digeribile
digestion (di-*dʒêss*-tʃön) *n* digestione *f*
digit (*di*-dʒit) *n* numero *m*
dignified (*digh*-ni-faid) *adj* dignitoso
dike (daik) *n* diga *f*; argine *m*
dilapidated (di-*læ*-pi-dei-tid) *adj* decrepito
diligence (*di*-li-dʒönss) *n* zelo *m*, diligenza *f*
diligent (*di*-li-dʒönt) *adj* zelante, diligente
dilute (dai-*l^i uut*) *v* allungare, diluire
dim (dim) *adj* pallido, opaco; oscuro, debole, offuscato
dine (dain) *v* pranzare
dinghy (*ding*-ghi) *n* barchetta *f*
dining-car (*dai*-ning-kaa) *n* vagone ristorante
dining-room (*dai*-ning-ruum) *n* sala da pranzo
dinner (*di*-nö) *n* pranzo *m*; cena *f*
dinner-jacket (*di*-nö-dʒæ-kit) *n* smoking *m*
dinner-service (*di*-nö-ssöö-viss) *n* servizio da tavola
diphtheria (dif-*θi^ö*-ri-ö) *n* difterite *f*
diploma (di-*plou*-mö) *n* diploma *m*
diplomat (*di*-plö-mæt) *n* diplomatico *m*
direct (di-*rêkt*) *adj* diretto; *v* *dirigere; amministrare
direction (di-*rêk*-ʃön) *n* direzione *f*; indicazione *f*; regia *f*; amministrazione *f*; **directional signal** *Am* indicatore di direzione; **directions for use** istruzioni per l'uso
directive (di-*rêk*-tiv) *n* direttiva *f*
director (di-*rêk*-tö) *n* direttore *m*; regista *m*
dirt (dööt) *n* sudiciume *m*
dirty (*döö*-ti) *adj* sozzo, sudicio, sporco
disabled (di-*ssei*-böld) *adj* inabilitato, invalido
disadvantage (di-ssöd-*vaan*-tidʒ) *n* svantaggio *m*
disagree (di-ssö-*ghrii*) *v* non *essere d'accordo, dissentire
disagreeable (di-ssö-*ghrii*-ö-böl) *adj* sgradevole

disappear (di-ssö-*piö*) *v* sparire
disappoint (di-ssö-*point*) *v* *deludere
disappointment (di-ssö-*point*-mönt) *n* delusione *f*
disapprove (di-ssö-*pruuv*) *v* disapprovare
disaster (di-*saa*-sstö) *n* disastro *m*; catastrofe *f*, sciagura *f*
disastrous (di-*saa*-sströss) *adj* disastroso
disc (dissk) *n* disco *m*; **slipped ~** ernia *f*
discard (di-*sskaad*) *v* scartare
discharge (diss-*tʃaadʒ*) *v* scaricare; **~ of** esonerare da
discipline (*di*-ssi-plin) *n* disciplina *f*
discolour (di-*sska*-lö) *v* scolorirsi
disconnect (di-sskö-*nêkt*) *v* *disgiungere; disinserire
discontented (di-sskön-*tên*-tid) *adj* scontento
discontinue (di-sskön-*ti*-n[i]uu) *v* *sospendere, cessare
discount (*di*-sskaunt) *n* sconto *m*, riduzione *f*
discover (di-*sska*-vö) *v* *scoprire
discovery (di-*sska*-vö-ri) *n* scoperta *f*
discuss (di-*sskass*) *v* *discutere; dibattere
discussion (di-*sska*-ʃön) *n* discussione *f*; conversazione *f*, dibattito *m*
disease (di-*siis*) *n* malattia *f*
disembark (di-ssim-*baak*) *v* sbarcare
disgrace (diss-*ghreiss*) *n* disonore *m*
disguise (diss-*ghais*) *v* travestirsi; *n* travestimento *m*
disgusting (diss-*gha*-ssting) *adj* nauseante, disgustoso
dish (diʃ) *n* piatto *m*; pietanza *f*
dishonest (di-*sso*-nisst) *adj* disonesto
disinfect (di-ssin-*fêkt*) *v* disinfettare
disinfectant (di-ssin-*fêk*-tönt) *n* disinfettante *m*
dislike (di-*sslaik*) *v* detestare, non amare; *n* ripugnanza *f*, avversione *f*, antipatia *f*
dislocated (*di*-sslö-kei-tid) *adj* slogato
dismiss (diss-*miss*) *v* congedare
disorder (di-*ssoo*-dö) *n* disordine *m*; confusione *f*
dispatch (di-*sspætʃ*) *v* inviare, spedire
display (di-*ssplei*) *v* *mettere in mostra, *esporre; mostrare; *n* esposizione *f*, mostra *f*
displease (di-*sspliis*) *v* scontentare, *dispiacere
disposable (di-*sspou*-sö-böl) *adj* da buttare
disposal (di-*sspou*-söl) *n* disposizione *f*
dispose of (di-*sspous*) *disporre di
dispute (di-*ssp[i]uut*) *n* disputa *f*; lite *f*, controversia *f*; *v* *discutere, disputare
dissatisfied (di-*ssæ*-tiss-faid) *adj* scontento
dissolve (di-*solv*) *v* *sciogliere
dissuade from (di-*ss[u]eid*) *dissuadere
distance (*di*-sstönss) *n* distanza *f*; **~ in kilometres** chilometraggio *m*
distant (*di*-sstönt) *adj* lontano
distinct (di-*sstingkt*) *adj* chiaro; distinto
distinction (di-*sstingk*-ʃön) *n* distinzione *f*, differenza *f*
distinguish (di-*ssting*-gh[u]iʃ) *v* *distinguere
distinguished (di-*ssting*-gh[u]iʃt) *adj* distinto
distress (di-*sstrêss*) *n* pericolo *m*; **~ signal** segnale di soccorso
distribute (di-*sstri*-b[i]uut) *v* distribuire
distributor (di-*sstri*-b[i]u-tö) *n* distributore *m*
district (*di*-sstrikt) *n* distretto *m*; regione *f*; quartiere *m*
disturb (di-*sstööb*) *v* importunare, disturbare

disturbance (di-*sstöö*-bönss) *n* disturbo *m*; tumulto *m*
ditch (ditʃ) *n* fosso *m*, fossato *m*
dive (daiv) *v* tuffare
diversion (dai-*vöö*-ʃön) *n* deviazione *f*; diversione *f*
divide (di-*vaid*) *v* *dividere; ripartire; separare
divine (di-*vain*) *adj* divino
division (di-*vi*-ʒön) *n* divisione *f*; reparto *m*
divorce (di-*vooss*) *n* divorzio *m*; *v* divorziare
dizziness (*di*-si-nöss) *n* capogiro *m*
dizzy (*di*-si) *adj* stordito
***do** (duu) *v* *fare; bastare
dock (dok) *n* bacino *m*; scalo *m*; *v* attraccare
docker (*do*-kö) *n* portuale *m*
doctor (*dok*-tö) *n* medico *m*, dottore *m*
document (*do*-k[i]u-mönt) *n* documento *m*
dog (dogh) *n* cane *m*
dogged (*do*-ghid) *adj* ostinato
doll (dol) *n* bambola *f*
dome (doum) *n* cupola *f*
domestic (dö-*mê*-sstik) *adj* domestico; interno; *n* domestico *m*
domicile (*do*-mi-ssail) *n* domicilio *m*
domination (do-mi-*nei*-ʃön) *n* dominazione *f*
dominion (dö-*mi*-n[i]ön) *n* dominio *m*
donate (dou-*neit*) *v* donare
donation (dou-*nei*-ʃön) *n* donazione *f*
done (dan) *v* (pp do)
donkey (*dong*-ki) *n* asino *m*
donor (*dou*-nö) *n* donatore *m*
door (doo) *n* porta *f*; **revolving** ~ porta girevole; **sliding** ~ porta scorrevole
doorbell (*doo*-bêl) *n* campanello *m*
door-keeper (*doo*-kii-pö) *n* portinaio *m*
doorman (*doo*-mön) *n* (pl -men) portinaio *m*
dormitory (*doo*-mi-tri) *n* dormitorio *m*
dose (douss) *n* dose *f*
dot (dot) *n* punto *m*
double (*da*-böl) *adj* doppio
doubt (daut) *v* dubitare di, dubitare; *n* dubbio *m*; **without** ~ senza dubbio
doubtful (*daut*-föl) *adj* dubbioso; incerto
dough (dou) *n* pasta *f*
down[1] (daun) *adv* giù; in giù, dabbasso, a terra; *adj* abbattuto; *prep* lungo, giù da; ~ **payment** acconto *m*
down[2] (daun) *n* lanugine *f*
downpour (*daun*-poo) *n* acquazzone *m*
downstairs (daun-*sstê*[ö]*s*) *adv* dabbasso
downstream (daun-*sstriim*) *adv* con la corrente
down-to-earth (daun-tu-*ööθ*) *adj* sensato
downwards (*daun*-[u]öds) *adv* in giù, in discesa
dozen (*da*-sön) *n* (pl ~, ~s) dozzina *f*
draft (draaft) *n* tratta *f*
drag (drægh) *v* trascinare
dragon (*dræ*-ghön) *n* drago *m*
drain (drein) *v* prosciugare; drenare; *n* scolo *m*
drama (*draa*-mö) *n* dramma *m*; tragedia *f*; teatro *m*
dramatic (drö-*mæ*-tik) *adj* drammatico
dramatist (*dræ*-mö-tisst) *n* drammaturgo *m*
drank (drængk) *v* (p drink)
draper (*drei*-pö) *n* negoziante di stoffe
drapery (*drei*-pö-ri) *n* drapperia *f*
draught (draaft) *n* corrente d'aria;

draughts gioco della dama
draught-board (*draaft*-bood) *n* scacchiera *f*
draw (droo) *n* sorteggio *m*
***draw** (droo) *v* disegnare; tirare; ritirare; ~ **up** *redigere
drawbridge (*droo*-bridʒ) *n* ponte levatoio
drawer (*droo*-ö) *n* cassetto *m*; **drawers** mutande *fpl*
drawing (*droo*-ing) *n* disegno *m*
drawing-pin (*droo*-ing-pin) *n* puntina da disegno
drawing-room (*droo*-ing-ruum) *n* salotto *m*
dread (drêd) *v* temere; *n* timore *m*
dreadful (*drêd*-föl) *adj* terribile, spaventoso
dream (driim) *n* sogno *m*
***dream** (driim) *v* sognare
dress (drêss) *v* vestire; abbigliarsi, vestirsi, abbigliare; bendare; *n* abito femminile, vestito da donna
dressing-gown (*drê*-ssing-ghaun) *n* vestaglia *f*
dressing-room (*drê*-ssing-ruum) *n* camerino *m*
dressing-table (*drê*-ssing-tei-böl) *n* toletta *f*
dressmaker (*drêss*-mei-kö) *n* sarta *f*
drill (dril) *v* trapanare; addestrare; *n* trapano *m*
drink (dringk) *n* aperitivo *m*, bibita *f*
***drink** (dringk) *v* *bere
drinking-water (*dring*-king-^{u}oo-tö) *n* acqua potabile
drip-dry (drip-*drai*) *adj* non si stira, senza stiratura
drive (draiv) *n* strada *f*; scarrozzata *f*
***drive** (draiv) *v* guidare; *condurre
driver (*drai*-vö) *n* autista *m*
drizzle (*dri*-söl) *n* pioggerella *f*
drop (drop) *v* *far cadere; *n* goccia *f*
drought (draut) *n* siccità *f*
drown (draun) *v* affogare; ***be drowned** affogarsi
drug (dragh) *n* narcotico *m*; farmaco *m*
drugstore (*dragh*-sstoo) *nAm* bar-emporio *m*, farmacia *f*; emporio *m*
drum (dram) *n* tamburo *m*
drunk (drangk) *adj* (pp drink) ubriaco
dry (drai) *adj* asciutto; *v* asciugare
dry-clean (drai-*kliin*) *v* pulire a secco
dry-cleaner's (drai-*klii*-nös) *n* tintoria *f*
dryer (*drai*-ö) *n* essiccatoio *m*
duchess (da-tʃiss) *n* duchessa *f*
duck (dak) *n* anitra *f*
due (d^{i}uu) *adj* in arrivo; dovuto
dues (d^{i}uus) *pl* diritti *mpl*
dug (dagh) *v* (p, pp dig)
duke (d^{i}uuk) *n* duca *m*
dull (dal) *adj* monotono, noioso; smorto, pallido; smussato
dumb (dam) *adj* muto; ottuso, stupido
dune (d^{i}uun) *n* duna *f*
dung (dang) *n* letame *m*
dunghill (*dang*-hil) *n* letamaio *m*
duration (d^{i}u-*rei*-ʃön) *n* durata *f*
during (*d^{i}u^{ö}*-ring) *prep* durante
dusk (dassk) *n* crepuscolo *m*
dust (dasst) *n* polvere *f*
dustbin (*dasst*-bin) *n* pattumiera *f*
dusty (*da*-ssti) *adj* polveroso
Dutch (datʃ) *adj* olandese
Dutchman (*datʃ*-mön) *n* (pl -men) olandese *m*
dutiable (*d^{i}uu*-ti-ö-böl) *adj* tassabile
duty (*d^{i}uu*-ti) *n* dovere *m*; compito *m*; dazio *m*; **Customs** ~ tariffa doganale
duty-free (d^{i}uu-ti-*frii*) *adj* franco di dazio
dwarf (d^{u}oof) *n* nano *m*
dye (dai) *v* *tingere; *n* tintura *f*
dynamo (*dai*-nö-mou) *n* (pl ~s) dina-

mo *f*
dysentery (*di*-ssön-tri) *n* dissenteria *f*

E

each (iitʃ) *adj* ogni, ciascuno; ~ **other** l'un l'altro
eager (*ii*-ghö) *adj* desideroso, ansioso, impaziente
eagle (*ii*-ghöl) *n* aquila *f*
ear (iö) *n* orecchio *f*
earache (*iö*-reik) *n* mal d'orecchi
ear-drum (*iö*-dram) *n* timpano *m*
earl (ööl) *n* conte *m*
early (*öö*-li) *adj* mattutino
earn (öön) *v* guadagnare
earnest (*öö*-nisst) *n* serietà *f*
earnings (*öö*-nings) *pl* redditi, guadagni *mpl*
earring (*iö*-ring) *n* orecchino *m*
earth (ööθ) *n* terra *f*; suolo *m*
earthenware (*öö*-θön-ᵘêö) *n* terraglie *fpl*
earthquake (*ööθ*-kᵘeik) *n* terremoto *m*
ease (iis) *n* disinvoltura *f*, facilità *f*; agio *m*
east (iisst) *n* oriente *m*, est *m*
Easter (*ii*-sstö) Pasqua
easterly (*ii*-sstö-li) *adj* orientale
eastern (*ii*-sstön) *adj* orientale
easy (*ii*-si) *adj* facile; comodo; ~ **chair** poltrona *f*
easy-going (*ii*-si-ghou-ing) *adj* facilone
***eat** (iit) *v* mangiare; pranzare
eavesdrop (*iivs*-drop) *v* origliare
ebony (*ê*-bö-ni) *n* ebano *m*
eccentric (ik-*ssên*-trik) *adj* eccentrico
echo (*ê*-kou) *n* (pl ~es) eco *m/f*
eclipse (i-*klipss*) *n* eclissi *f*
economic (ii-kö-*no*-mik) *adj* economico
economical (ii-kö-*no*-mi-köl) *adj* parsimonioso, economico
economist (i-*ko*-nö-misst) *n* economista *m*
economize (i-*ko*-nö-mais) *v* economizzare
economy (i-*ko*-nö-mi) *n* economia *f*
ecstasy (*êk*-sstö-si) *n* estasi *f*
Ecuador (*ê*-kᵘö-doo) Ecuador *m*
Ecuadorian (ê-kᵘö-*doo*-ri-ön) *n* ecuadoriano *m*
eczema (*êk*-ssi-mö) *n* eczema *m*
edge (êdʒ) *n* bordo *m*, margine *m*
edible (*ê*-di-böl) *adj* commestibile
edition (i-*di*-ʃön) *n* edizione *f*; **morning** ~ edizione del mattino
editor (*ê*-di-tö) *n* redattore *m*
educate (*ê*-dʒu-keit) *v* istruire, educare
education (ê-dʒu-*kei*-ʃön) *n* educazione *f*
eel (iil) *n* anguilla *f*
effect (i-*fêkt*) *n* risultato *m*, effetto *m*; *v* effettuare; **in** ~ in realtà
effective (i-*fêk*-tiv) *adj* efficace
efficient (i-*fi*-ʃönt) *adj* efficiente
effort (*ê*-föt) *n* sforzo *m*; tentativo *m*
egg (êgh) *n* uovo *m*
egg-cup (*êgh*-kap) *n* portauovo *m*
eggplant (*êgh*-plaant) *n* melanzana *f*
egg-yolk (*êgh*-ⁱouk) *n* tuorlo *m*
egoistic (ë-ghou-*i*-sstik) *adj* egoistico
Egypt (*ii*-dʒipt) Egitto *m*
Egyptian (i-*dʒip*-ʃön) *adj* egiziano
eiderdown (*ai*-dö-daun) *n* trapunta di piume *m*
eight (eit) *num* otto
eighteen (ei-*tiin*) *num* diciotto
eighteenth (ei-*tiinθ*) *num* diciottesimo
eighth (eitθ) *num* ottavo
eighty (*ei*-ti) *num* ottanta
either (*ai*-ðö) *pron* l'uno o l'altro;

either ... or o... o
elaborate (i-*læ*-bö-reit) *v* elaborare
elastic (i-*læ*-sstik) *adj* elastico; flessibile; elastico *m*
elasticity (ê-læ-*ssti*-ssö-ti) *n* elasticità *f*
elbow (*êl*-bou) *n* gomito *m*
elder (*êl*-dö) *adj* maggiore
elderly (*êl*-dö-li) *adj* anziano
eldest (*êl*-disst) *adj* maggiore
elect (i-*lêkt*) *v* *scegliere, *eleggere
election (i-*lêk*-ʃön) *n* elezione *f*
electric (i-*lêk*-trik) *adj* elettrico; ~ **razor** rasoio elettrico; ~ **cord** cordone elettrico
electrician (i-lêk-*tri*-ʃön) *n* elettricista *m*
electricity (i-lêk-*tri*-ssö-ti) *n* elettricità *f*
electronic (i-lêk-*tro*-nik) *adj* elettronico
elegance (*ê*-li-ghönss) *n* eleganza *f*
elegant (*ê*-li-ghönt) *adj* elegante
element (*ê*-li-mönt) *n* elemento *m*
elephant (*ê*-li-fönt) *n* elefante *m*
elevator (*ê*-li-vei-tö) *nAm* ascensore *m*
eleven (i-*lê*-vön) *num* undici
eleventh (i-*lê*-vönθ) *num* undicesimo
elf (êlf) *n* (pl elves) folletto *m*
eliminate (i-*li*-mi-neit) *v* eliminare
elm (êlm) *n* olmo *m*
else (êlss) *adv* altrimenti
elsewhere (êl-*ssuêö*) *adv* altrove
elucidate (i-*luu*-ssi-deit) *v* delucidare
emancipation (i-mæn-ssi-*pei*-ʃön) *n* emancipazione *f*
embankment (im-*bængk*-mönt) *n* argine *m*
embargo (êm-*baa*-ghou) *n* (pl ~es) embargo *m*
embark (im-*baak*) *v* imbarcarsi; imbarcare
embarkation (êm-baa-*kei*-ʃön) *n* imbarco *m*
embarrass (im-*bæ*-röss) *v* imbarazzare; *mettere in imbarazzo; ostacolare
embassy (*êm*-bö-ssi) *n* ambasciata *f*
emblem (*êm*-blöm) *n* emblema *m*
embrace (im-*breiss*) *v* abbracciare; *n* abbraccio *m*
embroider (im-*broi*-dö) *v* ricamare
embroidery (im-*broi*-dö-ri) *n* ricamo *m*
emerald (*ê*-mö-röld) *n* smeraldo *m*
emergency (i-*möö*-dʒön-ssi) *n* caso di emergenza, emergenza *f*; stato di emergenza; ~ **exit** uscita di sicurezza
emigrant (*ê*-mi-ghrönt) *n* emigrante *m*
emigrate (*ê*-mi-ghreit) *v* emigrare
emigration (ê-mi-*ghrei*-ʃön) *n* emigrazione *f*
emotion (i-*mou*-ʃön) *n* commozione *f*, emozione *f*
emperor (*êm*-pö-rö) *n* imperatore *m*
emphasize (*êm*-fö-ssais) *v* sottolineare
empire (*êm*-paiö) *n* impero *m*
employ (im-*ploi*) *v* impiegare; utilizzare
employee (êm-ploi-*ii*) *n* salariato *m*, impiegato *m*
employer (im-*ploi*-ö) *n* datore di lavoro
employment (im-*ploi*-mönt) *n* impiego *m*, occupazione *f*; ~ **exchange** ufficio di collocamento
empress (*êm*-priss) *n* imperatrice *f*
empty (*êmp*-ti) *adj* vuoto; *v* vuotare
enable (i-*nei*-böl) *v* abilitare
enamel (i-*næ*-möl) *n* smalto *m*
enamelled (i-*næ*-möld) *adj* smaltato
enchanting (in-*tʃaan*-ting) *adj* affascinante, incantevole
encircle (in-*ssöö*-köl) *v* *cingere, circondare; accerchiare

enclose (ing-*klous*) *v* *accludere, allegare
enclosure (ing-*klou*-ʒö) *n* allegato *m*
encounter (ing-*kaun*-tö) *v* incontrare; *n* incontro *m*
encourage (ing-*ka*-ridʒ) *v* incoraggiare
encyclopaedia (ên-ssai-klö-*pii*-di-ö) *n* enciclopedia *f*
end (ênd) *n* fine *f*, estremità *f*; termine *m*; *v* finire; cessare
ending (*ên*-ding) *n* fine *f*
endless (*ênd*-löss) *adj* infinito
endorse (in-*dooss*) *v* vistare, girare
endure (in-*d*ʲ*u*ö) *v* sopportare
enemy (*ê*-nö-mi) *n* nemico *m*
energetic (ê-nö-*dʒê*-tik) *adj* energico
energy (*ê*-nö-dʒi) *n* energia *f*; forza *f*
engage (ing-*gheidʒ*) *v* *assumere; riservare; impegnarsi; **engaged** fidanzato; occupato
engagement (ing-*gheidʒ*-mönt) *n* fidanzamento *m*; impegno *m*; ~ **ring** anello di fidanzamento
engine (*ên*-dʒin) *n* macchina *f*, motore *m*; locomotrice *f*
engineer (ên-dʒi-*ni*ö) *n* ingegnere *m*
England (*ing*-ghlönd) Inghilterra *f*
English (*ing*-ghliʃ) *adj* inglese
Englishman (*ing*-ghliʃ-mön) *n* (pl -men) inglese *m*
engrave (ing-*ghreiv*) *v* *incidere
engraver (ing-*ghrei*-vö) *n* incisore *m*
engraving (ing-*ghrei*-ving) *n* stampa *f*; incisione *f*
enigma (i-*nigh*-mö) *n* enigma *m*
enjoy (in-*dʒoi*) *v* godere, gustare
enjoyable (in-*dʒoi*-ö-böl) *adj* piacevole, gradevole, divertente; gustoso
enjoyment (in-*dʒoi*-mönt) *n* godimento *m*
enlarge (in-*laadʒ*) *v* ingrandire; ampliare
enlargement (in-*laadʒ*-mönt) *n* ingrandimento *m*
enormous (i-*noo*-möss) *adj* ingente, enorme
enough (i-*naf*) *adv* abbastanza; *adj* sufficiente
enquire (ing-*k*ᵘ*ai*ö) *v* informarsi; indagare
enquiry (ing-*k*ᵘ*ai*ö-ri) *n* informazione *f*; investigazione *f*; inchiesta *f*
enter (*ên*-tö) *v* entrare; *iscrivere
enterprise (*ên*-tö-prais) *n* impresa *f*
entertain (ên-tö-*tein*) *v* divertire, *intrattenere; ospitare
entertainer (ên-tö-*tei*-nö) *n* comico *m*
entertaining (ên-tö-*tei*-ning) *adj* divertente
entertainment (ên-tö-*tein*-mönt) *n* divertimento *m*, passatempo *m*
enthusiasm (in-*θ*ʲ*uu*-si-æ-söm) *n* entusiasmo *m*
enthusiastic (in-θʲuu-si-*æ*-sstik) *adj* entusiastico
entire (in-*tai*ö) *adj* tutto, intero
entirely (in-*tai*ö-li) *adv* interamente
entrance (*ên*-trönss) *n* entrata *f*; accesso *m*; ingresso *m*
entrance-fee (*ên*-trönss-fii) *n* ingresso *m*
entry (*ên*-tri) *n* entrata *f*; ingresso *m*; registrazione *f*; **no** ~ proibito passare
envelope (*ên*-vö-loup) *n* busta *f*
envious (*ên*-vi-öss) *adj* invidioso, geloso
environment (in-*vai*ö-rön-mönt) *n* ambiente *m*; dintorni *mpl*
envoy (*ên*-voi) *n* inviato *m*
envy (*ên*-vi) *n* invidia *f*; *v* invidiare
epic (*ê*-pik) *n* poema epico; *adj* epico
epidemic (ê-pi-*dê*-mik) *n* epidemia *f*
epilepsy (*ê*-pi-lêp-ssi) *n* epilessia *f*
epilogue (*ê*-pi-logh) *n* epilogo *m*
episode (*ê*-pi-ssoud) *n* episodio *m*
equal (*ii*-kᵘöl) *adj* uguale; *v* uguagliare

equality (i-*k^u^o*-lö-ti) *n* uguaglianza *f*
equalize (*ii*-k^u^ö-lais) *v* pareggiare
equally (*ii*-k^u^ö-li) *adv* ugualmente
equator (i-*k^u^ei*-tö) *n* equatore *m*
equip (i-*k^u^ip*) *v* equipaggiare
equipment (i-*k^u^ip*-mönt) *n* equipaggiamento *m*
equivalent (i-*k^u^i*-vö-lönt) *adj* equivalente
eraser (i-*rei*-sö) *n* gomma per cancellare
erect (i-*rêkt*) *v* innalzare, *erigere; *adj* ritto, diritto
err (öö) *v* errare
errand (*ê*-rönd) *n* commissione *f*
error (*ê*-rö) *n* sbaglio *m*, errore *m*
escalator (*ê*-sskö-lei-tö) *n* scala mobile
escape (i-*sskeip*) *v* scappare; fuggire, sfuggire; *n* evasione *f*
escort[1] (*ê*-sskoot) *n* scorta *f*
escort[2] (i-*sskoot*) *v* scortare
especially (i-*sspê*-ʃö-li) *adv* soprattutto, specialmente
esplanade (ê-ssplö-*neid*) *n* spianata *f*
essay (*ê*-ssei) *n* saggio *m*; trattato *m*, componimento *m*
essence (*ê*-ssönss) *n* essenza *f*; nocciolo *m*, anima *f*
essential (i-*ssên*-ʃöl) *adj* indispensabile; fondamentale, essenziale
essentially (i-*ssên*-ʃö-li) *adv* essenzialmente
establish (i-*sstæ*-bliʃ) *v* stabilire
estate (i-*ssteit*) *n* proprietà *f*
esteem (i-*sstiim*) *n* rispetto *m*, stima *f*; *v* stimare
estimate[1] (*ê*-ssti-meit) *v* *fare la stima, valutare
estimate[2] (*ê*-ssti-möt) *n* valutazione *f*
estuary (*êss*-tʃu-ö-ri) *n* estuario *m*
etcetera (êt-*ssê*-tö-rö) eccetera
etching (*ê*-tʃing) *n* acquaforte *f*
eternal (i-*töö*-nöl) *adj* eterno
eternity (i-*töö*-nö-ti) *n* eternità *f*
ether (*ii*-θö) *n* etere *m*
Ethiopia (i-θi-*ou*-pi-ö) Etiopia *f*
Ethiopian (i-θi-*ou*-pi-ön) *adj* etiopico
Europe (*^i^u^ö^*-röp) Europa *f*
European (^i^u^ö^-rö-*pii*-ön) *adj* europeo
evacuate (i-*væ*-k^i^u-eit) *v* evacuare
evaluate (i-*væl*-^i^u-eit) *v* valutare
evaporate (i-*væ*-pö-reit) *v* evaporare
even (*ii*-vön) *adj* piano, piatto, uguale; costante; pari; *adv* anche
evening (*iiv*-ning) *n* sera *f*; ~ **dress** abito da sera
event (i-*vênt*) *n* evento *m*; caso *m*
eventual (i-*vên*-tʃu-öl) *adj* eventuale; finale
ever (*ê*-vö) *adv* mai; sempre
every (*êv*-ri) *adj* ciascuno, ogni
everybody (*êv*-ri-bo-di) *pron* ognuno
everyday (*êv*-ri-dei) *adj* quotidiano
everyone (*êv*-ri-^u^an) *pron* ognuno
everything (*êv*-ri-θing) *pron* tutto
everywhere (*êv*-ri-^u^ê^ö^) *adv* ovunque
evidence (*ê*-vi-dönss) *n* prova *f*
evident (*ê*-vi-dönt) *adj* evidente
evil (*ii*-völ) *n* male *m*; *adj* cattivo, malvagio
evolution (ii-vö-*luu*-ʃön) *n* evoluzione *f*
exact (igh-*sækt*) *adj* esatto
exactly (igh-*sækt*-li) *adv* precisamente
exaggerate (igh-*sæ*-dʒö-reit) *v* esagerare
examination (igh-sæ-mi-*nei*-ʃön) *n* esame *m*; indagine *f*; interrogazione *f*
examine (igh-*sæ*-min) *v* esaminare
example (igh-*saam*-pöl) *n* esempio *m*; **for** ~ per esempio
excavation (êkss-kö-*vei*-ʃön) *n* scavo *m*
exceed (ik-*ssiid*) *v* eccedere; superare
excel (ik-*ssêl*) *v* *eccellere
excellent (*êk*-ssö-lönt) *adj* ottimo, ec-

cellente
except (ik-*ssêpt*) *prep* eccetto, salvo
exception (ik-*ssêp*-ʃön) *n* eccezione *f*
exceptional (ik-*ssêp*-ʃö-nöl) *adj* straordinario, eccezionale
excerpt (*êk*-ssööpt) *n* brano *m*
excess (ik-*ssêss*) *n* eccesso *m*
excessive (ik-*ssê*-ssiv) *adj* eccessivo
exchange (ikss-*tʃeindʒ*) *v* scambiare, cambiare; *n* cambio *m*; borsa *f*; ~ **office** ufficio cambio; ~ **rate** corso del cambio
excite (ik-*ssait*) *v* eccitare
excitement (ik-*ssait*-mönt) *n* agitazione *f*, eccitazione *f*
exciting (ik-*ssai*-ting) *adj* eccitante
exclaim (ik-*sskleim*) *v* esclamare
exclamation (êk-ssklö-*mei*-ʃön) *n* esclamazione *f*
exclude (ik-*sskluud*) *v* *escludere
exclusive (ik-*sskluu*-ssiv) *adj* esclusivo
exclusively (ik-*sskluu*-ssiv-li) *adv* esclusivamente, unicamente
excursion (ik-*ssköö*-ʃön) *n* gita *f*, escursione *f*
excuse[1] (ik-*sskⁱuuss*) *n* scusa *f*
excuse[2] (ik-*sskⁱuus*) *v* scusare
execute (*êk*-ssi-kⁱuut) *v* eseguire
execution (êk-ssi-*kⁱuu*-ʃön) *n* esecuzione *f*
executioner (êk-ssi-*kⁱuu*-ʃö-nö) *n* boia *m*
executive (igh-*sê*-kⁱu-tiv) *adj* esecutivo; *n* potere esecutivo; direttore *m*
exempt (igh-*ʒêmpt*) *v* dispensare, esentare; *adj* esente
exemption (igh-*sêmp*-ʃön) *n* esenzione *f*
exercise (*êk*-ssö-ssais) *n* esercizio *m*; *v* esercitare
exhale (êkss-*heil*) *v* esalare
exhaust (igh-*soosst*) *n* scappamento *m*; *v* esaurire; ~ **gases** gas di scarico
exhibit (igh-*si*-bit) *v* *esporre; esibire
exhibition (êk-ssi-*bi*-ʃön) *n* mostra *f*, esposizione *f*
exile (*êk*-ssail) *n* esilio *m*; esule *m*
exist (igh-*sisst*) *v* *esistere
existence (igh-*si*-sstönss) *n* esistenza *f*
exit (*êk*-ssit) *n* uscita *f*
exotic (igh-*so*-tik) *adj* esotico
expand (ik-*sspænd*) *v* *espandere; *estendere; allargare
expect (ik-*sspêkt*) *v* aspettare
expectation (êk-sspêk-*tei*-ʃön) *n* aspettativa *f*
expedition (êk-sspö-*di*-ʃön) *n* invio *m*; spedizione *f*
expel (ik-*sspêl*) *v* *espellere
expenditure (ik-*sspên*-di-tʃö) *n* spesa *f*
expense (ik-*sspênss*) *n* spesa *f*
expensive (ik-*sspên*-ssiv) *adj* caro; costoso
experience (ik-*sspiᵒ̈*-ri-önss) *n* esperienza *f*; *v* provare, sperimentare; **experienced** esperto
experiment (ik-*sspê*-ri-mönt) *n* prova *f*, esperimento *m*; *v* sperimentare
expert (*êk*-sspööt) *n* perito *m*, esperto *m*; *adj* competente
expire (ik-*sspaiᵒ̈*) *v* spirare, finire, *scadere; espirare; **expired** scaduto
expiry (ik-*sspaiᵒ̈*-ri) *n* scadenza *f*
explain (ik-*ssplein*) *v* chiarire, spiegare
explanation (êk-ssplö-*nei*-ʃön) *n* schiarimento *m*, esplicazione *f*, spiegazione *f*
explicit (ik-*sspli*-ssit) *adj* categorico, esplicito
explode (ik-*ssploud*) *v* *esplodere
exploit (ik-*ssploit*) *v* sfruttare, utilizzare
explore (ik-*ssploo*) *v* esplorare
explosion (ik-*ssplou*-ʒön) *n* esplosione *f*
explosive (ik-*ssplou*-ssiv) *adj* esplosivo; *n* esplosivo *m*

export[1] (ik-*sspoot*) *v* esportare
export[2] (*êk*-sspoot) *n* esportazione *f*
exportation (êk-sspoo-*tei*-ʃön) *n* esportazione *f*
exports (*êk*-sspootss) *pl* esportazione *f*
exposition (êk-sspö-*si*-ʃön) *n* esposizione *f*
exposure (ik-*sspou*-ʒö) *n* privazioni *fpl*; esposizione *f*; ~ **meter** esposimetro *m*
express (ik-*ssprêss*) *v* *esprimere; manifestare; *adj* espresso; esplicito; ~ **train** treno direttissimo
expression (ik-*ssprê*-ʃön) *n* espressione *f*; manifestazione *f*
exquisite (ik-*sskᵘi*-sit) *adj* squisito
extend (ik-*sstênd*) *v* *estendere; allargare; accordare
extension (ik-*sstên*-ʃön) *n* prolungamento *m*; ampliamento *m*; telefono interno; ~ **cord** prolunga *f*
extensive (ik-*sstên*-ssiv) *adj* ampio; vasto
extent (ik-*sstênt*) *n* dimensione *f*
exterior (êk-*sstiᵒ*-ri-ö) *adj* esterno; *n* esterno *m*
external (êk-*sstöö*-nöl) *adj* esteriore
extinguish (ik-*ssting*-ghᵘiʃ) *v* *spegnere, *estinguere
extort (ik-*sstoot*) *v* *estorcere
extortion (ik-*sstoo*-ʃön) *n* estorsione *f*
extra (*êk*-sströ) *adj* supplementare
extract[1] (ik-*sstrækt*) *v* *estrarre
extract[2] (*êk*-sstrækt) *n* passo *m*
extradite (*êk*-sströ-dait) *v* estradare
extraordinary (ik-*sstroo*-dön-ri) *adj* straordinario
extravagant (ik-*sstræ*-vö-ghönt) *adj* esagerato, stravagante
extreme (ik-*sstriim*) *adj* estremo; *n* estremo *m*
exuberant (igh-*sʲuu*-bö-rönt) *adj* esuberante
eye (ai) *n* occhio *m*
eyebrow (*ai*-brau) *n* sopracciglio *m*
eyelash (*ai*-læʃ) *n* ciglio *m*
eyelid (*ai*-lid) *n* palpebra *f*
eye-pencil (*ai*-pên-ssöl) *n* matita per gli occhi
eye-shadow (*ai*-ʃæ-dou) *n* ombretto *m*
eye-witness (*ai*-ᵘit-nöss) *n* testimone oculare

F

fable (*fei*-böl) *n* favola *f*
fabric (*fæ*-brik) *n* stoffa *f*; struttura *f*
façade (fö-*ssaad*) *n* facciata *f*
face (feiss) *n* faccia *f*; *v* *far fronte a; ~ **massage** massaggio facciale; **facing** in faccia a
face-cream (*feiss*-kriim) *n* crema di bellezza
face-pack (*feiss*-pæk) *n* maschera di bellezza
face-powder (*feiss*-pau-dö) *n* cipria *f*
facility (fö-*ssi*-lö-ti) *n* agevolazione *f*
fact (fækt) *n* fatto *m*; **in** ~ infatti
factor (*fæk*-tö) *n* fattore *m*
factory (*fæk*-tö-ri) *n* fabbrica *f*
factual (*fæk*-tʃu-öl) *adj* reale
faculty (*fæ*-köl-ti) *n* potere *m*; capacità *f*, attitudine *f*, facoltà *f*
fad (fæd) *n* capriccio *m*
fade (feid) *v* scolorirsi, sbiadire
faience (fai-*angss*) *n* ceramica *f*, terracotta *f*
fail (feil) *v* fallire; mancare; tralasciare; bocciare; **without** ~ senz'altro
failure (*feil*-ʲö) *n* insuccesso *m*; fallimento *m*
faint (feint) *v* *svenire; *adj* fiacco, vago, debole
fair (fêᵒ) *n* fiera *f*; *adj* giusto, onesto;

biondo; bello
fairly (*fêö*-li) *adv* alquanto, piuttosto, abbastanza
fairy (*fêö*-ri) *n* fata *f*
fairytale (*fêö*-ri-teil) *n* fiaba *f*
faith (feiθ) *n* fede *f*; fiducia *f*
faithful (*feiθ*-ful) *adj* fedele
fake (feik) *n* falsificazione *f*
fall (fool) *n* caduta *f*; *nAm* autunno *m*
***fall** (fool) *v* *cadere
false (foolss) *adj* falso; sbagliato, fallace, contraffatto; ~ **teeth** dentiera *f*
falter (*fool*-tö) *v* vacillare; balbettare
fame (feim) *n* rinomanza *f*, fama *f*; reputazione *f*
familiar (fö-*mil*-ⁱö) *adj* familiare; confidenziale
family (*fæ*-mö-li) *n* famiglia *f*; ~ **name** cognome *m*
famous (*fei*-möss) *adj* famoso
fan (fæn) *n* ventilatore *m*; ventaglio *m*; tifoso *m*; ~ **belt** cinghia del ventilatore
fanatical (fö-*næ*-ti-köl) *adj* fanatico
fancy (*fæn*-ssi) *v* gradire, *aver voglia di; figurarsi, immaginare; *n* capriccio *m*; immaginazione *f*
fantastic (fæn-*tæ*-sstik) *adj* fantastico
fantasy (*fæn*-tö-si) *n* fantasia *f*
far (faa) *adj* lontano; *adv* molto; **by** ~ di gran lunga; **so** ~ finora
far-away (*faa*-rö-ᵘei) *adj* distante
farce (faass) *n* farsa *f*, buffonata *f*
fare (fêö) *n* spese di viaggio, prezzo del biglietto; vitto *m*, cibo *m*
farm (faam) *n* fattoria *f*
farmer (*faa*-mö) *n* fattore *m*; **farmer's wife** fattoressa *f*
farmhouse (*faam*-hauss) *n* cascina *f*
far-off (*faa*-rof) *adj* lontano
fascinate (*fæ*-ssi-neit) *v* affascinare
fascism (*fæ*-ʃi-söm) *n* fascismo *m*
fascist (*fæ*-ʃisst) *adj* fascistico; *n* fascista *m*
fashion (*fæ*-ʃön) *n* moda *f*; modo *m*
fashionable (*fæ*-ʃö-nö-böl) *adj* alla moda
fast (faasst) *adj* rapido, veloce; fisso
fast-dyed (faasst-*daid*) *adj* inalterabile al lavaggio, a tinta solida
fasten (*faa*-ssön) *v* allacciare; *chiudere
fastener (*faa*-ssö-nö) *n* fermaglio *m*
fat (fæt) *adj* grasso; *n* grasso *m*
fatal (*fei*-töl) *adj* fatale, mortale
fate (feit) *n* fato *m*, destino *m*
father (*faa*-ðö) *n* padre *m*
father-in-law (*faa*-ðö-rin-loo) *n* (pl fathers-) suocero *m*
fatherland (*faa*-ðö-lönd) *n* patria *f*
fatness (*fæt*-nöss) *n* pinguedine *f*
fatty (*fæ*-ti) *adj* untuoso
faucet (*foo*-ssit) *nAm* rubinetto *m*
fault (foolt) *n* colpa *f*; imperfezione *f*, difetto *m*, mancanza *f*
faultless (*foolt*-löss) *adj* impeccabile; perfetto
faulty (*fool*-ti) *adj* difettoso
favour (*fei*-vö) *n* favore *m*; *v* privilegiare, favorire
favourable (*fei*-vö-rö-böl) *adj* favorevole
favourite (*fei*-vö-rit) *n* favorito *m*; *adj* preferito
fawn (foon) *adj* fulvo; *n* cerbiatto *m*
fear (fiö) *n* timore *m*, paura *f*; *v* temere
feasible (*fii*-sö-böl) *adj* realizzabile
feast (fiisst) *n* festa *f*
feat (fiit) *n* prestazione *f*
feather (*fê*-ðö) *n* penna *f*
feature (*fii*-tʃö) *n* caratteristica *f*; tratto *m*
February (*fê*-bru-ö-ri) febbraio
federal (*fê*-dö-röl) *adj* federale
federation (fê-dö-*rei*-ʃön) *n* federazio-

ne *f*; confederazione *f*
fee (fii) *n* onorario *m*
feeble (*fii*-böl) *adj* fiacco
***feed** (fiid) *v* nutrire; **fed up with** stufo di
***feel** (fiil) *v* sentire; palpare; ~ **like** *aver voglia di
feeling (*fii*-ling) *n* sensazione *f*
fell (fêl) *v* (p fall)
fellow (*fê*-lou) *n* tipo *m*
felt[1] (fêlt) *n* feltro *m*
felt[2] (fêlt) *v* (p, pp feel)
female (*fii*-meil) *adj* femminile
feminine (*fê*-mi-nin) *adj* femminile
fence (fênss) *n* recinto *m*; steccato *m*; *v* tirare di scherma
fender (*fên*-dö) *n* paraurti *m*
ferment (föö-*mênt*) *v* fermentare
ferry-boat (*fê*-ri-bout) *n* traghetto *m*
fertile (*föö*-tail) *adj* fertile
festival (*fê*-ssti-völ) *n* festival *m*
festive (*fê*-sstiv) *adj* festivo
fetch (fêtʃ) *v* portare; *andare a prendere
feudal (*f*ʲ*uu*-döl) *adj* feudale
fever (*fii*-vö) *n* febbre *f*
feverish (*fii*-vö-riʃ) *adj* febbricitante
few (fʲuu) *adj* pochi
fiancé (fi-~~*ang*~~-ssei) *n* fidanzato *m*
fiancée (fi-~~*ang*~~-ssei) *n* fidanzata *f*
fibre (*fai*-bö) *n* fibra *f*
fiction (*fik*-ʃön) *n* finzione *f*
field (fiild) *n* campo *m*; settore *m*; ~ **glasses** binocolo *m*
fierce (fiᵒss) *adj* feroce; selvaggio, veemente
fifteen (fif-*tiin*) *num* quindici
fifteenth (fif-*tiinθ*) *num* quindicesimo
fifth (fifθ) *num* quinto
fifty (*fif*-ti) *num* cinquanta
fig (figh) *n* fico *m*
fight (fait) *n* combattimento *m*, lotta *f*
***fight** (fait) *v* combattere, lottare
figure (*fi*-ghö) *n* forma *f*, figura *f*; cifra *f*
file (fail) *n* lima *f*; raccolta di documenti; fila *f*
Filipino (fi-li-*pii*-nou) *n* filippino *m*
fill (fil) *v* riempire; ~ **in** completare; **filling station** distributore di benzina; ~ **out** *Am* completare, compilare; ~ **up** *fare il pieno
filling (*fi*-ling) *n* otturazione *f*; ripieno *m*
film (film) *n* film *m*; pellicola *f*; *v* filmare
filter (*fil*-tö) *n* filtro *m*
filthy (*fil*-θi) *adj* sordido, sudicio
final (*fai*-nöl) *adj* finale
finance (fai-*nænss*) *v* finanziare
finances (fai-*næn*-ssis) *pl* finanze *fpl*
financial (fai-*næn*-ʃöl) *adj* finanziario
finch (fintʃ) *n* fringuello *m*
***find** (faind) *v* trovare
fine (fain) *n* multa *f*; *adj* fino; bello; ottimo, meraviglioso; ~ **arts** belle arti
finger (*fing*-ghö) *n* dito *m*; **little** ~ mignolo *m*
fingerprint (*fing*-ghö-print) *n* impronta digitale
finish (*fi*-niʃ) *v* completare, finire; terminare; *n* termine *m*; traguardo *m*
Finland (*fin*-lönd) Finlandia *f*
Finn (fin) *n* finlandese *m*
Finnish (*fi*-niʃ) *adj* finlandese
fire (faiᵒ) *n* fuoco *m*; incendio *m*; *v* sparare; licenziare
fire-alarm (*fai*ᵒ-rö-laam) *n* allarme d'incendio
fire-brigade (*fai*ᵒ-bri-gheid) *n* pompieri *mpl*
fire-escape (*fai*ᵒ-ri-sskeip) *n* scala di sicurezza
fire-extinguisher (*fai*ᵒ-rik-ssting-ghᵘi-ʃö) *n* estintore *m*
fireplace (*fai*ᵒ-pleiss) *n* focolare *m*

fireproof (*fai*ö-pruuf) *adj* incombustibile
firm (fööm) *adj* saldo; solido; *n* ditta *f*
first (föösst) *num* primo; **at** ~ prima; al principio; ~ **name** nome *m*
first-aid (föösst-*eid*) *n* pronto soccorso; ~ **kit** equipaggiamento di pronto soccorso; ~ **post** posto di pronto soccorso
first-class (föösst-*klaass*) *adj* di prima qualità
first-rate (föösst-*reit*) *adj* ottimo, di prima qualità
fir-tree (*föö*-trii) *n* abete *m*
fish[1] (fiʃ) *n* (pl ~, ~es) pesce *m*; ~ **shop** pescheria *f*
fish[2] (fiʃ) *v* pescare; pescare con l'amo; **fishing gear** attrezzi da pesca; **fishing hook** amo *m*; **fishing industry** pesca *f*; **fishing licence** permesso di pesca; **fishing line** lenza *f*; **fishing net** rete da pesca; **fishing rod** canna da pesca; **fishing tackle** attrezzi da pesca
fishbone (*fiʃ*-boun) *n* lisca *f*, spina di pesce
fisherman (*fi*-ʃö-mön) *n* (pl -men) pescatore *m*
fist (fisst) *n* pugno *m*
fit (fit) *adj* adatto; *n* attacco *m*; *v* *convenire; **fitting room** salottino di prova
five (faiv) *num* cinque
fix (fikss) *v* riparare
fixed (fiksst) *adj* fisso
fizz (fis) *n* effervescenza *f*
fjord (fⁱood) *n* fiordo *m*
flag (flægh) *n* bandiera *f*
flame (fleim) *n* fiamma *f*
flamingo (flö-*ming*-ghou) *n* (pl ~s, ~es) fenicottero *m*
flannel (*flæ*-nöl) *n* flanella *f*
flash (flæʃ) *n* baleno *m*
flash-bulb (*flæʃ*-balb) *n* lampada flash
flash-light (*flæʃ*-lait) *n* lampada portatile
flask (flaassk) *n* flacone *m*; **thermos** ~ termos *m*
flat (flæt) *adj* piano, piatto; *n* appartamento *m*; ~ **tyre** bucatura *f*
flavour (*flei*-vö) *n* gusto *m*; *v* condire
fleet (fliit) *n* flotta *f*
flesh (flêʃ) *n* carne *f*
flew (fluu) *v* (p fly)
flex (flêkss) *n* cordone elettrico
flexible (*flêk*-ssi-böl) *adj* flessibile; pieghevole
flight (flait) *n* volo *m*; **charter** ~ volo charter
flint (flint) *n* pietrina *f*
float (flout) *v* galleggiare; *n* galleggiante *m*
flock (flok) *n* gregge *m*
flood (flad) *n* inondazione *f*; flusso *m*
floor (floo) *n* pavimento *m*; piano *m*; ~ **show** spettacollo di varietà
florist (*flo*-risst) *n* fioraio *m*
flour (flauö) *n* farina *f*
flow (flou) *v* *scorrere
flower (flauö) *n* fiore *m*
flowerbed (*flau*ö-bêd) *n* aiola *f*
flower-shop (*flau*ö-ʃop) *n* negozio di fiori
flown (floun) *v* (pp fly)
flu (fluu) *n* influenza *f*
fluent (*fluu*-önt) *adj* fluente
fluid (*fluu*-id) *adj* fluido; *n* fluido *m*
flute (fluut) *n* flauto *m*
fly (flai) *n* mosca *f*; brachetta *f*
***fly** (flai) *v* volare
foam (foum) *n* schiuma *f*; *v* spumare
foam-rubber (*foum*-ra-bö) *n* gommapiuma *f*
focus (*fou*-köss) *n* fuoco *m*
fog (fogh) *n* nebbia *f*
foggy (*fo*-ghi) *adj* nebbioso
foglamp (*fogh*-læmp) *n* fanale anti-

nebbia
fold (fould) *v* piegare; *n* piega *f*
folk (fouk) *n* popolo *m*; ~ **song** canzone popolare
folk-dance (*fouk*-daanss) *n* danza popolare
folklore (*fouk*-loo) *n* folklore *m*
follow (*fo*-lou) *v* seguire; **following** *adj* successivo, seguente
***be fond of** (bii fond ov) amare
food (fuud) *n* cibo *m*; mangiare *m*, vitto *m*; ~ **poisoning** intossicazione alimentare
foodstuffs (*fuud*-sstafss) *pl* alimentari *mpl*
fool (fuul) *n* idiota *m*, sciocco *m*; *v* beffare
foolish (*fuu*-liʃ) *adj* stolto, stupido; sciocco
foot (fut) *n* (pl feet) piede *m*; ~ **powder** talco per piedi; **on** ~ a piedi
football (*fut*-bool) *n* pallone *m*; ~ **match** partita di calcio
foot-brake (*fut*-breik) *n* freno a pedale
footpath (*fut*-paaθ) *n* sentiero *m*
footwear (*fut*-ᵘêᵒ) *n* calzatura *f*
for (foo, fö) *prep* per; durante; a causa di, in conseguenza di; *conj* poiché
***forbid** (fö-*bid*) *v* proibire
force (fooss) *v* *costringere, forzare; *n* forza *f*; **by** ~ per forza; **driving** ~ forza motrice
ford (food) *n* guado *m*
forecast (*foo*-kaasst) *n* previsione *f*; *v* *prevedere
foreground (*foo*-ghraund) *n* primo piano
forehead (*fo*-rêd) *n* fronte *f*
foreign (*fo*-rin) *adj* straniero; estraneo
foreigner (*fo*-ri-nö) *n* straniero *m*; forestiero *m*
foreman (*foo*-mön) *n* (pl -men) capomastro *m*
foremost (*foo*-mousst) *adj* primo
foresail (*foo*-sseil) *n* vela di trinchetto
forest (*fo*-risst) *n* foresta *f*
forester (*fo*-ri-sstö) *n* guardia forestale
forge (foodʒ) *v* falsificare
***forget** (fö-*ghêt*) *v* dimenticare
forgetful (fö-*ghêt*-föl) *adj* smemorato
***forgive** (fö-*ghiv*) *v* perdonare
fork (fook) *n* forchetta *f*; bivio *m*; *v* biforcarsi
form (foom) *n* forma *f*; formulario *m*; classe *f*; *v* formare
formal (*foo*-möl) *adj* formale
formality (foo-*mæ*-lö-ti) *n* formalità *f*
former (*foo*-mö) *adj* antico; precedente; **formerly** anteriormente, già
formula (*foo*-mⁱu-lö) *n* (pl ~e, ~s) formula *f*
fort (foot) *n* forte *m*
fortnight (*foot*-nait) *n* quindicina di giorni
fortress (*foo*-triss) *n* fortezza *f*
fortunate (*foo*-tʃö-nöt) *adj* fortunato
fortune (*foo*-tʃuun) *n* ricchezza *f*; destino *m*, fortuna *f*
forty (*foo*-ti) *num* quaranta
forward (*foo*-ᵘöd) *adv* in avanti, avanti; *v* inoltrare
fought (foot) *v* (p, pp fight)
foul (faul) *adj* sporco; perfido
found[1] (faund) *v* (p, pp find)
found[2] (faund) *v* fondare, istituire
foundation (faun-*dei*-ʃön) *n* fondazione *f*; ~ **cream** fondo tinta
fountain (*faun*-tin) *n* fontana *f*; sorgente *f*
fountain-pen (*faun*-tin-pên) *n* penna stilografica
four (foo) *num* quattro
fourteen (foo-*tiin*) *num* quattordici
fourteenth (foo-*tiinθ*) *num* quattordicesimo
fourth (fooθ) *num* quarto

fowl (faul) *n* (pl ~s, ~) pollame *m*
fox (fokss) *n* volpe *f*
foyer (*foi*-ei) *n* ridotto *m*
fraction (*fræk*-ʃön) *n* frazione *f*
fracture (*fræk*-tʃö) *v* fratturare; *n* frattura *f*
fragile (*fræ*-dʒail) *adj* fragile
fragment (*frægh*-mönt) *n* frammento *m*; pezzo *m*
frame (freim) *n* cornice *f*; montatura *f*
France (fraanss) Francia *f*
franchise (*fræn*-tʃais) *n* diritto elettorale
fraternity (frö-*töö*-nö-ti) *n* fraternità *f*
fraud (frood) *n* frode *f*
fray (frei) *v* sfilacciarsi
free (frii) *adj* libero; gratuito; ~ **of charge** gratuito; ~ **ticket** biglietto gratuito
freedom (*frii*-döm) *n* libertà *f*
***freeze** (friis) *v* gelare; congelarsi
freezing (*frii*-sing) *adj* glaciale
freezing-point (*frii*-sing-point) *n* punto di congelamento
freight (freit) *n* carico *m*
freight-train (*freit*-trein) *nAm* treno merci
French (frêntʃ) *adj* francese
Frenchman (*frêntʃ*-mön) *n* (pl -men) francese *m*
frequency (*frii*-kᵘön-ssi) *n* frequenza *f*
frequent (*frii*-kᵘönt) *adj* frequente
fresh (frêʃ) *adj* fresco; ~ **water** acqua dolce
friction (*frik*-ʃön) *n* attrito *m*
Friday (*frai*-di) venerdì *m*
fridge (fridʒ) *n* frigorifero *m*
friend (frênd) *n* amico *m*; amica *f*
friendly (*frênd*-li) *adj* affabile; amichevole
friendship (*frênd*-ʃip) *n* amicizia *f*
fright (frait) *n* paura *f*, spavento *m*
frighten (*frai*-tön) *v* spaventare
frightened (*frai*-tönd) *adj* spaventato; ***be** ~ spaventarsi
frightful (*frait*-föl) *adj* terribile
fringe (frindʒ) *n* frangia *f*
frock (frok) *n* veste *f*
frog (frogh) *n* rana *f*
from (from) *prep* da
front (frant) *n* facciata *f*; **in ~ of** di fronte a
frontier (*fran*-tiᵒ) *n* frontiera *f*
frost (frosst) *n* gelo *m*
froth (froθ) *n* schiuma *f*
frozen (*frou*-sön) *adj* congelato; ~ **food** cibo surgelato
fruit (fruut) *n* frutta *f*; frutto *m*
fry (frai) *v* *friggere
frying-pan (*frai*-ing-pæn) *n* padella *f*
fuel (*fⁱuu*-öl) *n* combustibile *m*; benzina *f*; ~ **pump** *Am* pompa di alimentazione
full (ful) *adj* pieno; ~ **board** pensione completa; ~ **stop** punto *m*; ~ **up** colmo
fun (fan) *n* divertimento *m*; scherzo *m*
function (*fangk*-ʃön) *n* funzione *f*
fund (fand) *n* fondi
fundamental (fan-dö-*mên*-töl) *adj* fondamentale
funeral (*fⁱuu*-nö-röl) *n* funerale *m*
funnel (*fa*-nöl) *n* imbuto *m*
funny (*fa*-ni) *adj* buffo, divertente; strano
fur (föö) *n* pelliccia *f*; ~ **coat** cappotto di pelliccia; **furs** pelliccia *f*
furious (*fⁱuᵒ*-ri-öss) *adj* furibondo, furioso
furnace (*föö*-niss) *n* fornace *f*
furnish (*föö*-niʃ) *v* fornire, procurare; arredare, ammobiliare; ~ **with** *provedere di
furniture (*föö*-ni-tʃö) *n* mobilia *f*
furrier (*fa*-ri-ö) *n* pellicciaio *m*
further (*föö*-ðö) *adj* più lontano; ulte-

riore
furthermore (*föö*-ðö-moo) *adv* inoltre
furthest (*föö*-ðisst) *adj* il più lontano
fuse (f'uus) *n* fusibile *m*; miccia *f*
fuss (fass) *n* trambusto *m*; scalpore *m*
future (*f'uu*-tʃö) *n* futuro *m*; *adj* futuro

G

gable (*ghei*-böl) *n* frontone *m*
gadget (*ghæ*-dʒit) *n* aggeggio *m*
gaiety (*ghei*-ö-ti) *n* gaiezza *f*, allegria *f*
gain (ghein) *v* guadagnare; *n* profitto *m*
gait (gheit) *n* andatura *f*, passo *m*
gale (gheil) *n* burrasca *f*
gall (ghool) *n* bile *f*; ~ **bladder** cistifellea *f*
gallery (*ghæ*-lö-ri) *n* loggione *m*; galleria *f*
gallop (*ghæ*-löp) *n* galoppo *m*
gallows (*ghæ*-lous) *pl* forca *f*
gallstone (*ghool*-sstoun) *n* calcolo biliare
game (gheim) *n* giuoco *m*; selvaggina *f*; ~ **reserve** riserva di selvaggina
gang (ghæng) *n* banda *f*; squadra *f*
gangway (*ghæng*-ᵘei) *n* passarella *f*
gaol (dʒeil) *n* carcere *m*
gap (ghæp) *n* breccia *f*
garage (*ghæ*-raaʒ) *n* rimessa *f*; *v* *mettere in rimessa
garbage (*ghaa*-bidʒ) *n* spazzatura *f*, immondizia *f*
garden (*ghaa*-dön) *n* giardino *m*; **public** ~ giardino pubblico; **zoological gardens** giardino zoologico
gardener (*ghaa*-dö-nö) *n* giardiniere *m*
gargle (*ghaa*-ghöl) *v* gargarizzare
garlic (*ghaa*-lik) *n* aglio *m*
gas (ghæss) *n* gas *m*; *nAm* benzina *f*; ~ **cooker** fornello a gas; ~ **pump** *Am* pompa di benzina; ~ **station** *Am* stazione di servizio; ~ **stove** stufa a gas
gasoline (*ghæ*-ssö-liin) *nAm* benzina *f*
gastric (*ghæ*-sstrik) *adj* gastrico; ~ **ulcer** ulcera gastrica
gasworks (*ghæss*-ᵘöökss) *n* officina del gas
gate (gheit) *n* cancello *m*
gather (*ghæ*-ðö) *v* *raccogliere; *raccogliersi
gauge (gheidʒ) *n* misuratore *m*
gauze (ghoos) *n* garza *f*
gave (gheiv) *v* (p give)
gay (ghei) *adj* allegro; vivace
gaze (gheis) *v* fissare
gazetteer (ghæ-sö-*tiᵒ*) *n* dizionario geografico
gear (ghiᵒ) *n* velocità *f*; attrezzatura *f*; **change** ~ cambiare marcia; ~ **lever** leva del cambio
gear-box (*ghiᵒ*-bokss) *n* cambio di velocità
gem (dʒêm) *n* gioiello *m*, gemma *f*
gender (*dʒên*-dö) *n* genere *m*
general (*dʒê*-nö-röl) *adj* generale; *n* generale *m*; ~ **practitioner** medico generico; **in** ~ in generale
generate (*dʒê*-nö-reit) *v* generare
generation (dʒê-nö-*rei*-ʃön) *n* generazione *f*
generator (*dʒê*-nö-rei-tör) *n* generatore *m*
generosity (dʒê-nö-*ro*-ssö-ti) *n* generosità *f*
generous (*dʒê*-nö-röss) *adj* munifico, generoso
genital (*dʒê*-ni-töl) *adj* genitale
genius (*dʒii*-ni-öss) *n* genio *m*

gentle (*dʒên*-töl) *adj* amabile; dolce, leggero; delicato
gentleman (*dʒên*-töl-mön) *n* (pl -men) signore *m*
genuine (*dʒê*-nʲu-in) *adj* genuino
geography (dʒi-*o*-ghrö-fi) *n* geografia *f*
geology (dʒi-*o*-lö-dʒi) *n* geologia *f*
geometry (dʒi-*o*-mö-tri) *n* geometria *f*
germ (dʒööm) *n* germe *m*
German (*dʒöö*-mön) *adj* tedesco
Germany (*dʒöö*-mö-ni) Germania *f*
gesticulate (dʒi-*ssti*-kʲu-leit) *v* gesticolare
***get** (ghêt) *v* *ottenere; *andare a prendere; diventare; ~ **back** tornare; ~ **off** *scendere; ~ **on** montare; avanzare, progredire; ~ **up** alzarsi
ghost (ghousst) *n* spettro *m*; spirito *m*
giant (*dʒai*-önt) *n* gigante *m*
giddiness (*ghi*-di-nöss) *n* vertigine *f*
giddy (*ghi*-di) *adj* stordito
gift (ghift) *n* regalo *m*, dono *m*; talento *m*
gifted (*ghif*-tid) *adj* di talento
gigantic (dʒai-*ghæn*-tik) *adj* gigantesco
giggle (*ghi*-ghöl) *v* ridacchiare
gill (ghil) *n* branchia *f*
gilt (ghilt) *adj* dorato
ginger (*dʒin*-dʒö) *n* zenzero *m*
gipsy (*dʒip*-ssi) *n* zingaro *m*
girdle (*ghöö*-döl) *n* busto *m*
girl (ghööl) *n* ragazza *f*; ~ **guide** giovane esploratrice
***give** (ghiv) *v* *dare; *porgere; ~ **away** tradire; ~ **in** cedere; ~ **up** desistere
glacier (*ghlæ*-ssi-ö) *n* ghiacciaio *m*
glad (ghlæd) *adj* lieto, contento; **gladly** con piacere, volentieri
gladness (*ghlæd*-nöss) *n* gioia *f*
glamorous (*ghlæ*-mö-röss) *adj* affascinante
glamour (*ghlæ*-mö) *n* fascino *m*
glance (ghlaanss) *n* occhiata *f*; *v* *dare un'occhiata
gland (ghlænd) *n* ghiandola *f*
glare (ghlêᵒ) *n* bagliore *m*; splendore *m*
glaring (*ghlêᵒ*-ring) *adj* abbagliante
glass (ghlaass) *n* bicchiere *m*; vetro *m*; di vetro; **glasses** occhiali *mpl*; **magnifying** ~ lente d'ingrandimento
glaze (ghleis) *v* smaltare
glen (ghlên) *n* gola *f*
glide (ghlaid) *v* scivolare
glider (*ghlai*-dö) *n* aliante *m*
glimpse (ghlimpss) *n* occhiata *f*; visione fugace; *v* *intravvedere
global (*ghlou*-böl) *adj* universale
globe (ghloub) *n* globo *m*
gloom (ghluum) *n* oscurità *f*
gloomy (*ghluu*-mi) *adj* cupo
glorious (*ghloo*-ri-öss) *adj* splendido
glory (*ghloo*-ri) *n* gloria *f*; onore *m*, lode *f*
gloss (ghloss) *n* lucentezza *f*
glossy (*ghlo*-ssi) *adj* lucido
glove (ghlav) *n* guanto *m*
glow (ghlou) *v* *ardere; *n* ardore *m*
glue (ghluu) *n* colla *f*
***go** (ghou) *v* *andare; camminare; diventare; ~ **ahead** continuare; ~ **away** *andarsene; ~ **back** tornare; ~ **home** rincasare; ~ **in** entrare; ~ **on** continuare; ~ **out** *uscire; ~ **through** sopportare
goal (ghoul) *n* traguardo *m*, rete *f*
goalkeeper (*ghoul*-kii-pö) *n* portiere *m*
goat (ghout) *n* becco *m*, capra *f*
god (ghod) *n* dio *m*
goddess (*gho*-diss) *n* dea *f*
godfather (*ghod*-faa-ðö) *n* padrino *m*
goggles (*gho*-ghöls) *pl* occhiali di pro-

tezione
gold (ghould) *n* oro *m*; ~ **leaf** oro laminato
golden (*ghoul*-dön) *adj* aureo
goldmine (*ghould*-main) *n* miniera d'oro
goldsmith (*ghould*-ssmiθ) *n* orefice *m*
golf (gholf) *n* golf *m*
golf-club (*gholf*-klab) *n* mazza da golf
golf-course (*gholf*-kooss) *n* campo di golf
golf-links (*gholf*-lingkss) *n* campo di golf
gondola (*ghon*-dö-lö) *n* gondola *f*
gone (ghon) *adv* (pp go) via
good (ghud) *adj* buono; virtuoso
good-bye! (ghud-*bai*) arrivederci!
good-humoured (ghud-*h'uu*-möd) *adj* di buon umore
good-looking (ghud-*lu*-king) *adj* di bell'aspetto
good-natured (ghud-*nei*-tʃöd) *adj* gentile
goods (ghuds) *pl* merci; ~ **train** treno merci
good-tempered (ghud-*têm*-pöd) *adj* di buon umore
goodwill (ghud-*ᵘil*) *n* benevolenza *f*
goose (ghuuss) *n* (pl geese) oca *f*
gooseberry (*ghus*-bö-ri) *n* uva spina
goose-flesh (*ghuuss*-flêʃ) *n* pelle d'oca
gorge (ghoodʒ) *n* gola *f*
gorgeous (*ghoo*-dʒöss) *adj* magnifico
gospel (*gho*-sspöl) *n* vangelo *m*
gossip (*gho*-ssip) *n* pettegolezzo *m*; *v* pettegolare
got (ghot) *v* (p, pp get)
gourmet (*ghuᵒ*-mei) *n* buongustaio *m*
gout (ghaut) *n* gotta *f*
govern (*gha*-vön) *v* governare
governess (*gha*-vö-niss) *n* governante *f*
government (*gha*-vön-mönt) *n* governo *m*
governor (*gha*-vö-nö) *n* governatore *m*
gown (ghaun) *n* vestito da donna
grace (ghreiss) *n* grazia *f*; perdono *m*
graceful (*ghreiss*-föl) *adj* grazioso
grade (ghreid) *n* classe *f*; *v* classificare
gradient (*ghrei*-di-önt) *n* inclinazione *f*
gradual (*ghræ*-dʒu-öl) *adj* graduale
graduate (*ghræ*-dʒu-eit) *v* diplomarsi
grain (ghrein) *n* granello *m*, frumento *m*, grano *m*
gram (ghræm) *n* grammo *m*
grammar (*ghræ*-mö) *n* grammatica *f*
grammatical (ghrö-*mæ*-ti-köl) *adj* grammaticale
gramophone (*ghræ*-mö-foun) *n* grammofono *m*
grand (ghrænd) *adj* imponente
granddad (*ghræn*-dæd) *n* nonno *m*
granddaughter (*ghræn*-doo-tö) *n* nipotina *f*, nipote *f*
grandfather (*ghræn*-faa-ðö) *n* nonno *m*
grandmother (*ghræn*-ma-ðö) *n* nonna *f*
grandparents (*ghræn*-pêᵒ-röntss) *pl* nonni
grandson (*ghræn*-ssan) *n* nipotino *m*, nipote *m*
granite (*ghræ*-nit) *n* granito *m*
grant (ghraant) *v* accordare; *concedere; *n* sussidio *m*, borsa *f*
grapefruit (*ghreip*-fruut) *n* pompelmo *m*
grapes (ghreipss) *pl* uva *f*
graph (ghræf) *n* grafico *m*
graphic (*ghræ*-fik) *adj* grafico
grasp (ghraassp) *v* afferrare; *n* stretta *f*
grass (ghraass) *n* erba *f*
grasshopper (*ghraass*-ho-pö) *n* cavalletta *f*

grate (ghreit) *n* grata *f*; *v* raspare
grateful (*ghreit*-föl) *adj* grato, riconoscente
grater (*ghrei*-tö) *n* grattugia *f*
gratis (*ghræ*-tiss) *adj* gratis
gratitude (*ghræ*-ti-t'uud) *n* gratitudine *f*
gratuity (ghrö-*t'uu*-ö-ti) *n* mancia *f*
grave (ghreiv) *n* tomba *f*; *adj* grave
gravel (*ghræ*-völ) *n* ghiaia *f*
gravestone (*ghreiv*-sstoun) *n* lapide *f*
graveyard (*ghreiv*-'aad) *n* cimitero *m*
gravity (*ghræ*-vö-ti) *n* gravità *f*; serietà *f*
gravy (*ghrei*-vi) *n* sugo *m*
graze (ghreis) *v* pascolare; *n* escoriazione *f*
grease (ghriiss) *n* grasso *m*; *v* lubrificare
greasy (*ghrii*-ssi) *adj* grasso, unto
great (ghreit) *adj* grande; **Great Britain** Gran Bretagna
Greece (ghriiss) Grecia *f*
greed (ghriid) *n* cupidigia *f*
greedy (*ghrii*-di) *adj* avido; goloso
Greek (ghriik) *adj* greco
green (ghriin) *adj* verde; ~ **card** carta verde
greengrocer (*ghriin*-ghrou-ssö) *n* fruttivendolo *m*
greenhouse (*ghriin*-hauss) *n* serra *f*
greens (ghriins) *pl* verdura *f*
greet (ghriit) *v* salutare
greeting (*ghrii*-ting) *n* saluto *m*
grey (ghrei) *adj* grigio
greyhound (*ghrei*-haund) *n* levriere *m*
grief (ghriif) *n* cordoglio *m*; afflizione *f*, dolore *m*
grieve (ghriiv) *v* *affliggersi
grill (ghril) *n* griglia *f*; *v* cucinare alla griglia
grill-room (*ghril*-ruum) *n* rosticceria *f*
grin (ghrin) *v* ghignare; *n* smorfia *f*
***grind** (ghraind) *v* macinare; tritare
grip (ghrip) *v* impugnare; *n* presa *f*, stretta *f*; *nAm* valigetta a mano *f*
grit (ghrit) *n* graniglia *f*
groan (ghroun) *v* gemere
grocer (*ghrou*-ssö) *n* droghiere *m*; **grocer's** drogheria *f*
groceries (*ghrou*-ssö-ris) *pl* alimentari *mpl*
groin (ghroin) *n* inguine *m*
groove (ghruuv) *n* solco *m*
gross[1] (ghrouss) *n* (pl ~) grossa *f*
gross[2] (ghrouss) *adj* rozzo; lordo
grotto (*ghro*-tou) *n* (pl ~es, ~s) grotta *f*
ground[1] (ghraund) *n* fondo *m*, terra *f*; ~ **floor** pianterreno *m*; **grounds** terreno *m*
ground[2] (ghraund) *v* (p, pp grind)
group (ghruup) *n* gruppo *m*
grove (ghrouv) *n* boschetto *m*
***grow** (ghrou) *v* *crescere; coltivare; diventare
growl (ghraul) *v* brontolare
grown-up (*ghroun*-ap) *adj* adulto; *n* adulto *m*
growth (ghrouθ) *n* crescita *f*; escrescenza *f*
grudge (ghradʒ) *v* invidiare
grumble (*ghram*-böl) *v* brontolare
guarantee (ghæ-rön-*tii*) *n* garanzia *f*; cauzione *f*; *v* garantire
guarantor (ghæ-rön-*too*) *n* garante *m*
guard (ghaad) *n* guardiano *m*; *v* custodire
guardian (*ghaa*-di-ön) *n* tutore *m*
guess (ghêss) *v* indovinare; credere, congetturare; *n* congettura *f*
guest (ghêsst) *n* ospite *m*
guest-house (*ghêsst*-hauss) *n* pensione *f*
guest-room (*ghêsst*-ruum) *n* camera degli ospiti
guide (ghaid) *n* guida *f*; *v* guidare
guidebook (*ghaid*-buk) *n* guida *f*

guide-dog (*ghaid*-dogh) *n* cane guida
guilt (ghilt) *n* colpa *f*
guilty (*ghil*-ti) *adj* colpevole
guinea-pig (*ghi*-ni-pigh) *n* porcellino d'India
guitar (ghi-*taa*) *n* chitarra *f*
gulf (ghalf) *n* golfo *m*
gull (ghal) *n* gabbiano *m*
gum (gham) *n* gengiva *f*; gomma *f*; colla *f*
gun (ghan) *n* fucile *m*, rivoltella *f*; cannone *m*
gunpowder (*ghan*-pau-dö) *n* polvere da sparo
gust (ghasst) *n* raffica *f*
gusty (*gha*-ssti) *adj* ventoso
gut (ghat) *n* intestino *m*; **guts** coraggio *m*
gutter (*gha*-tö) *n* cunetta *f*
guy (ghai) *n* tipo *m*
gymnasium (dʒim-*nei*-si-öm) *n* (pl ~s, -sia) palestra *f*
gymnast (*dʒim*-næsst) *n* ginnasta *m*
gymnastics (dʒim-*næ*-sstikss) *pl* ginnastica *f*
gynaecologist (ghai-nö-*ko*-lö-dʒisst) *n* ginecologo *m*

H

haberdashery (*hæ*-bö-dæ-ʃö-ri) *n* merceria *f*
habit (*hæ*-bit) *n* abitudine *f*
habitable (*hæ*-bi-tö-böl) *adj* abitabile
habitual (hö-*bi*-tʃu-öl) *adj* consueto
had (hæd) *v* (p, pp have)
haddock (*hæ*-dök) *n* (pl ~) merluzzo *m*
haemorrhage (*hê*-mö-ridʒ) *n* emorragia *f*
haemorrhoids (*hê*-mö-roids) *pl* emorroidi *fpl*
hail (heil) *n* grandine *f*
hair (hêö) *n* capello *m*; ~ **cream** brillantina *f*; ~ **piece** toupet *m*; ~ **rollers** bigodini *mpl*; ~ **tonic** tonico per capelli
hairbrush (*hêö*-braʃ) *n* spazzola per capelli
haircut (*hêö*-kat) *n* taglio di capelli
hair-do (*hêö*-duu) *n* capigliatura *f*, acconciatura *f*
hairdresser (*hêö*-drê-ssö) *n* parrucchiere *m*
hair-dryer (*hêö*-drai-ö) *n* asciugacapelli *m*
hair-grip (*hêö*-ghrip) *n* forcina *f*
hair-net (*hêö*-nêt) *n* reticella *f*
hair-oil (*hêö*-roil) *n* olio per capelli
hairpin (*hêö*-pin) *n* forcina *f*
hair-spray (*hêö*-ssprei) *n* lacca per capelli
hairy (*hêö*-ri) *adj* peloso
half[1] (haaf) *adj* mezzo; *adv* a metà
half[2] (haaf) *n* (pl halves) metà *f*
half-time (haaf-*taim*) *n* intervallo *m*
halfway (haaf-*uei*) *adv* a mezza strada
halibut (*hæ*-li-böt) *n* (pl ~) ippoglosso *m*
hall (hool) *n* vestibolo *m*; sala *f*
halt (hoolt) *v* fermarsi
halve (haav) *v* dimezzare
ham (hæm) *n* prosciutto *m*
hamlet (*hæm*-löt) *n* frazione *f*
hammer (*hæ*-mö) *n* martello *m*
hammock (*hæ*-mök) *n* amaca *f*
hamper (*hæm*-pö) *n* paniere *m*
hand (hænd) *n* mano *f*; *v* *porgere; ~ **cream** crema per le mani
handbag (*hænd*-bægh) *n* borsetta *f*
handbook (*hænd*-buk) *n* manuale *m*
hand-brake (*hænd*-breik) *n* freno a mano
handcuffs (*hænd*-kafss) *pl* manette *fpl*
handful (*hænd*-ful) *n* manciata *f*

handicraft (*hæn*-di-kraaft) *n* lavoro manuale; artigianato *m*
handkerchief (*hæng*-kö-tʃif) *n* fazzoletto *m*
handle (*hæn*-döl) *n* manico *m*, impugnatura *f*; *v* maneggiare; trattare
hand-made (hænd-*meid*) *adj* fatto a mano
handshake (*hænd*-ʃeik) *n* stretta di mano
handsome (*hæn*-ssöm) *adj* avvenente
handwork (*hænd*-ᵘöök) *n* lavoro fatto a mano
handwriting (*hænd*-rai-ting) *n* scrittura *f*
handy (*hæn*-di) *adj* maneggevole
***hang** (hæng) *v* *appendere; pendere
hanger (*hæng*-ö) *n* attaccapanni *m*
hangover (*hæng*-ou-vö) *n* malessere *m*
happen (*hæ*-pön) *v* *accadere, *succedere
happening (*hæ*-pö-ning) *n* evento *m*
happiness (*hæ*-pi-nöss) *n* felicità *f*
happy (*hæ*-pi) *adj* contento, felice
harbour (*haa*-bö) *n* porto *m*
hard (haad) *adj* duro; difficile; **hardly** appena
hardware (*haad*-ᵘêᵒ) *n* ferramenta *fpl*; ~ **store** negozio di ferramenta
hare (hêᵒ) *n* lepre *f*
harm (haam) *n* danno *m*; male *m*; *v* *nuocere
harmful (*haam*-föl) *adj* dannoso, nocivo
harmless (*haam*-löss) *adj* innocuo
harmony (*haa*-mö-ni) *n* armonia *f*
harp (haap) *n* arpa *f*
harpsichord (*haap*-ssi-kood) *n* clavicembalo *m*
harsh (haaʃ) *adj* aspro; severo; crudele
harvest (*haa*-visst) *n* raccolto *m*
has (hæs) *v* (pr have)
haste (heisst) *n* premura *f*, fretta *f*
hasten (*hei*-ssön) *v* affrettarsi
hasty (*hei*-ssti) *adj* frettoloso
hat (hæt) *n* cappello *m*; ~ **rack** attaccapanni *m*
hatch (hætʃ) *n* botola *f*
hate (heit) *v* detestare; odiare; *n* odio *m*
hatred (*hei*-trid) *n* odio *m*
haughty (*hoo*-ti) *adj* altezzoso
haul (hool) *v* trainare
***have** (hæv) *v* *avere; *fare; ~ **to** *dovere
haversack (*hæ*-vö-ssæk) *n* bisaccia *f*
hawk (hook) *n* astore *m*; falcone *m*
hay (hei) *n* fieno *m*; ~ **fever** febbre del fieno
hazard (*hæ*-söd) *n* rischio *m*
haze (heis) *n* foschia *f*
hazelnut (*hei*-söl-nat) *n* nocciola *f*
hazy (*hei*-si) *adj* fosco; nebbioso
he (hii) *pron* egli
head (hêd) *n* testa *f*; capo *m*; *v* *dirigere; ~ **of state** capo di stato; ~ **teacher** direttore di scuola, preside *m*
headache (*hê*-deik) *n* mal di testa
heading (*hê*-ding) *n* titolo *m*
headlamp (*hêd*-læmp) *n* fanale *m*
headland (*hêd*-lönd) *n* promontorio *m*
headlight (*hêd*-lait) *n* faro *m*
headline (*hêd*-lain) *n* titolo *m*
headmaster (hêd-*maa*-sstö) *n* direttore di scuola; preside *m*
headquarters (hêd-*kᵘoo*-tös) *pl* quartiere generale
head-strong (*hêd*-sstrong) *adj* testardo
head-waiter (hêd-*ᵘei*-tö) *n* capocameriere *m*
heal (hiil) *v* guarire
health (hêlθ) *n* salute *f*; ~ **centre** centro sanitario; ~ **certificate** certi-

ficato di sanità
healthy (*hêl*-θi) *adj* sano
heap (hiip) *n* cumulo *m*, mucchio *m*
***hear** (hi^{ö}) *v* *udire
hearing (*hi^{ö}*-ring) *n* udito *m*
heart (haat) *n* cuore *m*; nocciolo *m*; **by** ~ a memoria; ~ **attack** attacco cardiaco
heartburn (*haat*-böön) *n* bruciore di stomaco
hearth (haaθ) *n* focolare *m*
heartless (*haat*-löss) *adj* spietato
hearty (*haa*-ti) *adj* cordiale
heat (hiit) *n* calore *m*, caldo *m*; *v* scaldare; **heating pad** cuscino elettrico
heater (*hii*-tö) *n* riscaldatore *m*; **immersion** ~ scaldacqua ad immersione
heath (hiiθ) *n* landa *f*
heathen (*hii*-ðön) *n* pagano *m*
heather (*hê*-ðö) *n* erica *f*
heating (*hii*-ting) *n* riscaldamento *m*
heaven (*hê*-vön) *n* cielo *m*
heavy (*hê*-vi) *adj* pesante
Hebrew (*hii*-bruu) *n* ebraico *m*
hedge (hêdʒ) *n* siepe *f*
hedgehog (*hêdʒ*-hogh) *n* riccio *m*
heel (hiil) *n* tallone *m*; tacco *m*
height (hait) *n* altezza *f*; colmo *m*, culmine *m*
hell (hêl) *n* inferno *m*
hello! (hê-*lou*) ciao!
helm (hêlm) *n* timone *m*
helmet (*hêl*-mit) *n* casco *m*
helmsman (*hêlms*-mön) *n* timoniere *m*
help (hêlp) *v* aiutare; *n* aiuto *m*
helper (*hêl*-pö) *n* aiutante *m*
helpful (*hêlp*-föl) *adj* servizievole
helping (*hêl*-ping) *n* porzione *f*
hem (hêm) *n* orlo *m*
hemp (hêmp) *n* canapa *f*
hen (hên) *n* gallina *f*
henceforth (hênss-*fooθ*) *adv* d'ora innanzi
her (höö) *pron* la, le; *adj* suo
herb (hööb) *n* erba *f*
herd (hööd) *n* gregge *m*
here (hi^{ö}) *adv* qui; ~ **you are** ecco
hereditary (hi-*rê*-di-tö-ri) *adj* ereditario
hernia (*höö*-ni-ö) *n* ernia *f*
hero (*hi^{ö}*-rou) *n* (pl ~es) eroe *m*
heron (*hê*-rön) *n* airone *m*
herring (*hê*-ring) *n* (pl ~, ~s) aringa *f*
herself (höö-*ssêlf*) *pron* si; essa stessa
hesitate (*hê*-si-teit) *v* esitare
heterosexual (hê-tö-rö-*ssêk*-ʃu-öl) *adj* eterosessuale
hiccup (*hi*-kap) *n* singhiozzo *m*
hide (haid) *n* pelle *f*
***hide** (haid) *v* *nascondere; celare
hideous (*hi*-di-öss) *adj* orrendo
hierarchy (*hai^{ö}*-raa-ki) *n* gerarchia *f*
high (hai) *adj* alto
highway (*hai*-^{u}ei) *n* via maestra; *nAm* autostrada *f*
hijack (*hai*-dʒæk) *v* dirottare
hijacker (*hai*-dʒæ-kö) *n* dirottatore *m*
hike (haik) *v* camminare
hill (hil) *n* collina *f*
hillside (*hil*-ssaid) *n* pendio *m*
hilltop (*hil*-top) *n* vetta *f*
hilly (*hi*-li) *adj* collinoso
him (him) *pron* lo, gli
himself (him-*ssêlf*) *pron* si; egli stesso
hinder (*hin*-dö) *v* ostacolare
hinge (hindʒ) *n* cardine *m*
hip (hip) *n* fianco *m*
hire (hai^{ö}) *v* noleggiare; **for** ~ a nolo
hire-purchase (hai^{ö}-*pöö*-tʃöss) *n* vendita a rate
his (his) *adj* suo
historian (hi-*sstoo*-ri-ön) *n* storico *m*
historic (hi-*ssto*-rik) *adj* storico
historical (hi-*ssto*-ri-köl) *adj* storico
history (*hi*-sstö-ri) *n* storia *f*

hit (hit) *n* successo *m*
***hit** (hit) *v* colpire; toccare
hitchhike (*hitʃ*-haik) *v* *fare l'autostop
hitchhiker (*hitʃ*-hai-kö) *n* autostoppista *m*
hoarse (hooss) *adj* roco, rauco
hobby (*ho*-bi) *n* passatempo *m*, hobby *m*
hobby-horse (*ho*-bi-hooss) *n* pallino *m*
hockey (*ho*-ki) *n* hockey *m*
hoist (hoisst) *v* issare
hold (hould) *n* stiva *f*
***hold** (hould) *v* *tenere; conservare; ~ **on** *reggersi; ~ **up** *sostenere
hold-up (*houl*-dap) *n* rapina *f*
hole (houl) *n* buca *f*, buco *m*
holiday (*ho*-lö-di) *n* ferie *fpl*; festa *f*; ~ **camp** colonia di vacanze; ~ **resort** luogo di villeggiatura; **on** ~ in ferie
Holland (*ho*-lönd) Olanda *f*
hollow (*ho*-lou) *adj* vuoto
holy (*hou*-li) *adj* santo
homage (*ho*-midʒ) *n* omaggio *m*
home (houm) *n* casa *f*; ospizio *m*, abitazione *f*; *adv* a casa; **at** ~ in casa
home-made (houm-*meid*) *adj* casalingo
homesickness (*houm*-ssik-nöss) *n* nostalgia *f*
homosexual (hou-mö-*ssêk*-ʃu-öl) *adj* omosessuale
honest (*o*-nisst) *adj* onesto; sincero
honesty (*o*-ni-ssti) *n* onestà *f*
honey (*ha*-ni) *n* miele *m*
honeymoon (*ha*-ni-muun) *n* luna di miele
honk (hangk) *vAm* suonare il clacson
honour (*o*-nö) *n* onore *m*; *v* onorare, *rendere omaggio
honourable (*o*-nö-rö-böl) *adj* onorevole; onesto
hood (hud) *n* cappuccio *m*; *nAm* cofano *m*
hoof (huuf) *n* zoccolo *m*
hook (huk) *n* uncino *m*
hoot (huut) *v* suonare il clacson
hooter (*huu*-tö) *n* clacson *m*
hoover (*huu*-vö) *v* pulire con l'aspirapolvere
hop[1] (hop) *v* saltellare; *n* saltello *m*
hop[2] (hop) *n* luppolo *m*
hope (houp) *n* speranza *f*; *v* sperare
hopeful (*houp*-föl) *adj* speranzoso
hopeless (*houp*-löss) *adj* disperato
horizon (hö-*rai*-sön) *n* orizzonte *m*
horizontal (ho-ri-*son*-töl) *adj* orizzontale
horn (hoon) *n* corno *m*; clacson *m*
horrible (*ho*-ri-böl) *adj* orribile; spaventevole, atroce
horror (*ho*-rö) *n* raccapriccio *m*, orrore *m*
hors-d'œuvre (oo-*döövr*) *n* antipasto *m*
horse (hooss) *n* cavallo *m*
horseman (*hooss*-mön) *n* (pl -men) cavallerizzo *m*
horsepower (*hooss*-pauö) *n* cavallo vapore
horserace (*hooss*-reiss) *n* corsa di cavalli
horseradish (*hooss*-ræ-diʃ) *n* rafano *m*
horseshoe (*hooss*-ʃuu) *n* ferro di cavallo
horticulture (*hoo*-ti-kal-tʃö) *n* orticoltura *f*
hosiery (*hou*-ʒö-ri) *n* maglieria *f*
hospitable (*ho*-sspi-tö-böl) *adj* ospitale
hospital (*ho*-sspi-töl) *n* ospedale *m*
hospitality (ho-sspi-*tæ*-lö-ti) *n* ospitalità *f*
host (housst) *n* ospite *m*
hostage (*ho*-sstidʒ) *n* ostaggio *m*

hostel (*ho*-sstöl) *n* ostello *m*
hostess (*hou*-sstiss) *n* ospite *f*
hostile (*ho*-sstail) *adj* ostile
hot (hot) *adj* caldo
hotel (hou-*têl*) *n* albergo *m*
hot-tempered (hot-*têm*-pöd) *adj* irascibile
hour (au^ö) *n* ora *f*
hourly (*au^ö*-li) *adj* ogni ora
house (hauss) *n* casa *f*; abitazione *f*; immobile *m*; ~ **agent** agente immobiliare; ~ **block** *Am* isolato *m*; **public** ~ caffè *m*
houseboat (*hauss*-bout) *n* casa galleggiante
household (*hauss*-hould) *n* ménage *m*
housekeeper (*hauss*-kii-pö) *n* governante *f*
housekeeping (*hauss*-kii-ping) *n* faccende domestiche, faccende di casa
housemaid (*hauss*-meid) *n* domestica *f*
housewife (*hauss*-^uaif) *n* casalinga *f*
housework (*hauss*-^uöök) *n* lavori domestici
how (hau) *adv* come; che; ~ **many** quanto; ~ **much** quanto
however (hau-*ê*-vö) *conj* tuttavia, eppure
hug (hagh) *v* abbracciare; *n* abbraccio *m*
huge (h^iuudʒ) *adj* immenso, enorme
hum (ham) *v* canticchiare
human (*h^iuu*-mön) *adj* umano; ~ **being** essere umano
humanity (h^iu-*mæ*-nö-ti) *n* umanità *f*
humble (*ham*-böl) *adj* umile
humid (*h^iuu*-mid) *adj* umido
humidity (h^iu-*mi*-dö-ti) *n* umidità *f*
humorous (*h^iuu*-mö-röss) *adj* comico, spiritoso
humour (*h^iuu*-mö) *n* spirito *m*
hundred (*han*-dröd) *n* cento
Hungarian (hang-*ghê^ö*-ri-ön) *adj* ungherese
Hungary (*hang*-ghö-ri) Ungheria *f*
hunger (*hang*-ghö) *n* fame *f*
hungry (*hang*-ghri) *adj* affamato
hunt (hant) *v* cacciare; *n* caccia *f*; ~ **for** cercare
hunter (*han*-tö) *n* cacciatore *m*
hurricane (*ha*-ri-kön) *n* uragano *m*; ~ **lamp** lanterna vento
hurry (*ha*-ri) *v* spicciarsi, affrettarsi; *n* fretta *f*; **in a** ~ in fretta
***hurt** (hööt) *v* *dolere, ferire; *offendere
hurtful (*hööt*-föl) *adj* nocivo
husband (*has*-bönd) *n* marito *m*
hut (hat) *n* capanna *f*
hydrogen (*hai*-drö-dʒön) *n* idrogeno *m*
hygiene (*hai*-dʒiin) *n* igiene *f*
hygienic (hai-*dʒii*-nik) *adj* igienico
hymn (him) *n* inno *m*
hyphen (*hai*-fön) *n* lineetta *f*
hypocrisy (hi-*po*-krö-ssi) *n* ipocrisia *f*
hypocrite (*hi*-pö-krit) *n* ipocrita *m*
hypocritical (hi-pö-*kri*-ti-köl) *adj* ipocrita
hysterical (hi-*sstê*-ri-köl) *adj* isterico

I

I (ai) *pron* io
ice (aiss) *n* ghiaccio *m*
ice-bag (*aiss*-bægh) *n* borsa da ghiaccio
ice-cream (*aiss*-kriim) *n* gelato *m*
Iceland (*aiss*-lönd) Islanda *f*
Icelander (*aiss*-lön-dö) *n* islandese *m*
Icelandic (aiss-*læn*-dik) *adj* islandese
icon (*ai*-kon) *n* icona *f*
idea (ai-*di^ö*) *n* idea *f*; trovata *f*, pensiero *m*; nozione *f*, concetto *m*
ideal (ai-*di^öl*) *adj* ideale; *n* ideale *m*

identical (ai-*dên*-ti-köl) *adj* identico
identification (ai-dên-ti-fi-*kei*-ʃön) *n* identificazione *f*
identify (ai-*dên*-ti-fai) *v* identificare
identity (ai-*dên*-tö-ti) *n* identità *f*; ~ **card** carta d'identità
idiom (*i*-di-öm) *n* idioma *m*
idiomatic (i-di-ö-*mæ*-tik) *adj* idiomatico
idiot (*i*-di-öt) *n* idiota *m*
idiotic (i-di-*o*-tik) *adj* idiota
idle (*ai*-döl) *adj* ozioso; pigro; vano
idol (*ai*-döl) *n* idolo *m*
if (if) *conj* se
ignition (igh-*ni*-ʃön) *n* accensione *f*; ~ **coil** bobina di accensione
ignorant (*igh*-nö-rönt) *adj* ignorante
ignore (igh-*noo*) *v* ignorare
ill (il) *adj* ammalato; cattivo; malvagio
illegal (i-*lii*-ghöl) *adj* illegale
illegible (i-*lê*-dʒö-böl) *adj* illeggibile
illiterate (i-*li*-tö-röt) *n* analfabeta *m*
illness (*il*-nöss) *n* malattia *f*
illuminate (i-*luu*-mi-neit) *v* illuminare
illumination (i-luu-mi-*nei*-ʃön) *n* illuminazione *f*
illusion (i-*luu*-ʒön) *n* illusione *f*; inganno *m*
illustrate (*i*-lö-sstreit) *v* illustrare
illustration (i-lö-*sstrei*-ʃön) *n* illustrazione *f*
image (*i*-midʒ) *n* immagine *f*
imaginary (i-*mæ*-dʒi-nö-ri) *adj* immaginario
imagination (i-mæ-dʒi-*nei*-ʃön) *n* immaginazione *f*
imagine (i-*mæ*-dʒin) *v* immaginare; figurarsi
imitate (*i*-mi-teit) *v* imitare
imitation (i-mi-*tei*-ʃön) *n* imitazione *f*
immediate (i-*mii*-dʲöt) *adj* immediato
immediately (i-*mii*-dʲöt-li) *adv* subito, immediatamente
immense (i-*mênss*) *adj* smisurato, enorme, immenso
immigrant (*i*-mi-ghrönt) *n* immigrante *m*
immigrate (*i*-mi-ghreit) *v* immigrare
immigration (i-mi-*ghrei*-ʃön) *n* immigrazione *f*
immodest (i-*mo*-disst) *adj* immodesto
immunity (i-*mʲuu*-nö-ti) *n* immunità *f*
immunize (*i*-mʲu-nais) *v* immunizzare
impartial (im-*paa*-ʃöl) *adj* imparziale
impassable (im-*paa*-ssö-böl) *adj* impraticabile
impatient (im-*pei*-ʃönt) *adj* impaziente
impede (im-*piid*) *v* impedire
impediment (im-*pê*-di-mönt) *n* impedimento *m*
imperfect (im-*pöö*-fikt) *adj* imperfetto
imperial (im-*piö*-ri-öl) *adj* imperiale
impersonal (im-*pöö*-ssö-nöl) *adj* impersonale
impertinence (im-*pöö*-ti-nönss) *n* impertinenza *f*
impertinent (im-*pöö*-ti-nönt) *adj* impertinente, insolente
implement[1] (*im*-pli-mönt) *n* utensile *m*, strumento *m*
implement[2] (*im*-pli-mênt) *v* effettuare
imply (im-*plai*) *v* implicare; comportare
impolite (im-pö-*lait*) *adj* scortese
import[1] (im-*poot*) *v* importare
import[2] (*im*-poot) *n* importazione *f*; ~ **duty** dazio *m*
importance (im-*poo*-tönss) *n* rilievo *m*, importanza *f*
important (im-*poo*-tönt) *adj* rilevante, importante
importer (im-*poo*-tö) *n* importatore *m*
imposing (im-*pou*-sing) *adj* imponente
impossible (im-*po*-ssö-böl) *adj* impossibile
impotence (*im*-pö-tönss) *n* impotenza *f*

impotent (*im*-pö-tönt) *adj* impotente
impound (im-*paund*) *v* sequestrare
impress (im-*prêss*) *v* impressionare
impression (im-*prê*-ʃön) *n* impressione *f*
impressive (im-*prê*-ssiv) *adj* impressionante
imprison (im-*pri*-sön) *v* imprigionare
imprisonment (im-*pri*-sön-mönt) *n* imprigionamento *m*
improbable (im-*pro*-bö-böl) *adj* improbabile
improper (im-*pro*-pö) *adj* improprio
improve (im-*pruuv*) *v* migliorare
improvement (im-*pruuv*-mönt) *n* miglioramento *m*
improvise (*im*-prö-vais) *v* improvvisare
impudent (*im*-pⁱu-dönt) *adj* impudente
impulse (*im*-palss) *n* impulso *m*; stimolo *m*
impulsive (im-*pal*-ssiv) *adj* impulsivo
in (in) *prep* in; entro, su; *adv* dentro
inaccessible (i-næk-*ssê*-ssö-böl) *adj* inaccessibile
inaccurate (i-*næ*-kⁱu-röt) *adj* inesatto
inadequate (i-*næ*-di-kᵘöt) *adj* inadeguato
incapable (ing-*kei*-pö-böl) *adj* incapace
incense (*in*-ssênss) *n* incenso *m*
incident (*in*-ssi-dönt) *n* incidente *m*
incidental (in-ssi-*dên*-töl) *adj* incidentale
incite (in-*ssait*) *v* incitare
inclination (ing-kli-*nei*-ʃön) *n* inclinazione *f*
incline (ing-*klain*) *n* pendio *m*
inclined (ing-*klaind*) *adj* propenso, tendente; ***be ~ to** *v* *tendere
include (ing-*kluud*) *v* *comprendere, *includere
inclusive (ing-*kluu*-ssiv) *adj* compreso
income (*ing*-köm) *n* reddito *m*
income-tax (*ing*-köm-tækss) *n* imposta sul reddito
incompetent (ing-*kom*-pö-tönt) *adj* incompetente
incomplete (in-köm-*pliit*) *adj* incompleto
inconceivable (ing-kön-*ssii*-vö-böl) *adj* inconcepibile
inconspicuous (ing-kön-*sspi*-kⁱu-öss) *adj* insignificante
inconvenience (ing-kön-*vii*-nⁱönss) *n* scomodità *f*, inconveniente *m*
inconvenient (ing-kön-*vii*-nⁱönt) *adj* inconveniente; fastidioso
incorrect (ing-kö-*rêkt*) *adj* inesatto, scorretto
increase[1] (ing-*kriiss*) *v* aumentare; *salire, *accrescersi
increase[2] (*ing*-kriiss) *n* aumento *m*; incremento *m*
incredible (ing-*krê*-dö-böl) *adj* incredibile
incurable (ing-*kⁱuö*-rö-böl) *adj* incurabile
indecent (in-*dii*-ssönt) *adj* indecente
indeed (in-*diid*) *adv* effettivamente
indefinite (in-*dê*-fi-nit) *adj* indefinito
indemnity (in-*dêm*-nö-ti) *n* risarcimento *m*, indennità *f*
independence (in-di-*pên*-dönss) *n* indipendenza *f*
independent (in-di-*pên*-dönt) *adj* indipendente; autonomo
index (*in*-dêkss) *n* indice *m*; ~ **finger** indice *m*
India (*in*-di-ö) India *f*
Indian (*in*-di-ön) *adj* indiano; *n* indiano *m*
indicate (*in*-di-keit) *v* segnalare, indicare
indication (in-di-*kei*-ʃön) *n* indizio *m*, indicazione *f*
indicator (*in*-di-kei-tö) *n* freccia *f*

indifferent (in-*di*-fö-rönt) *adj* indifferente
indigestion (in-di-*dʒêss*-tʃön) *n* indigestione *f*
indignation (in-digh-*nei*-ʃön) *n* indignazione *f*
indirect (in-di-*rêkt*) *adj* indiretto
individual (in-di-*vi*-dʒu-öl) *adj* singolo, individuale; *n* singolo *m*, individuo *m*
Indonesia (in-dö-*nii*-si-ö) Indonesia *f*
Indonesian (in-dö-*nii*-si-ön) *adj* indonesiano
indoor (*in*-doo) *adj* in casa
indoors (in-*doos*) *adv* in casa
indulge (in-*daldʒ*) *v* cedere
industrial (in-*da*-sstri-öl) *adj* industriale; ~ **area** zona industriale
industrious (in-*da*-sstri-öss) *adj* laborioso
industry (*in*-dö-sstri) *n* industria *f*
inedible (i-*nê*-di-böl) *adj* immangiabile
inefficient (i-ni-*fi*-ʃönt) *adj* inefficace
inevitable (i-*nê*-vi-tö-böl) *adj* inevitabile
inexpensive (i-nik-*sspên*-ssiv) *adj* economico
inexperienced (i-nik-*sspi*ö-ri-önsst) *adj* inesperto
infant (*in*-fönt) *n* neonato *m*
infantry (*in*-fön-tri) *n* fanteria *f*
infect (in-*fêkt*) *v* infettare
infection (in-*fêk*-ʃön) *n* infezione *f*
infectious (in-*fêk*-ʃöss) *adj* contagioso
infer (in-*föö*) *v* *dedurre
inferior (in-*fi*ö-ri-ö) *adj* inferiore
infinite (*in*-fi-nöt) *adj* infinito
infinitive (in-*fi*-ni-tiv) *n* infinito *m*
infirmary (in-*föö*-mö-ri) *n* infermeria *f*
inflammable (in-*flæ*-mö-böl) *adj* infiammabile
inflammation (in-flö-*mei*-ʃön) *n* infiammazione *f*
inflatable (in-*flei*-tö-böl) *adj* gonfiabile
inflate (in-*fleit*) *v* gonfiare
inflation (in-*flei*-ʃön) *n* inflazione *f*
influence (*in*-flu-önss) *n* influenza *f*; *v* influire
influential (in-flu-*ên*-ʃöl) *adj* influente
influenza (in-flu-*ên*-sö) *n* influenza *f*
inform (in-*foom*) *v* informare; *mettere al corrente, comunicare
informal (in-*foo*-möl) *adj* informale
information (in-fö-*mei*-ʃön) *n* informazione *f*; ragguaglio *m*, comunicazione *f*; ~ **bureau** ufficio informazioni
infra-red (in-frö-*rêd*) *adj* infrarosso
infrequent (in-*frii*-kuönt) *adj* infrequente
ingredient (ing-*ghrii*-di-önt) *n* ingrediente *m*
inhabit (in-*hæ*-bit) *v* abitare
inhabitable (in-*hæ*-bi-tö-böl) *adj* abitabile
inhabitant (in-*hæ*-bi-tönt) *n* abitante *m*
inhale (in-*heil*) *v* aspirare
inherit (in-*hê*-rit) *v* ereditare
inheritance (in-*hê*-ri-tönss) *n* eredità *f*
initial (i-*ni*-ʃöl) *adj* iniziale; *n* iniziale *f*; *v* *apporre le iniziali
initiative (i-*ni*-ʃö-tiv) *n* iniziativa *f*
inject (in-*dʒêkt*) *v* iniettare
injection (in-*dʒêk*-ʃön) *n* iniezione *f*
injure (*in*-dʒö) *v* ferire; *offendere
injury (*in*-dʒö-ri) *n* ferita *f*; lesione *f*
injustice (in-*dʒa*-sstiss) *n* ingiustizia *f*
ink (ingk) *n* inchiostro *m*
inlet (*in*-lêt) *n* insenatura *f*
inn (in) *n* locanda *f*
inner (*i*-nö) *adj* interno; ~ **tube** camera d'aria
inn-keeper (*in*-kii-pö) *n* albergatore *m*
innocence (*i*-nö-ssönss) *n* innocenza *f*
innocent (*i*-nö-ssönt) *adj* innocente

inoculate (i-*no*-kʲu-leit) *v* inoculare
inoculation (i-no-kʲu-*lei*-ʃön) *n* inoculazione *f*
inquire (ing-*kᵘaiö*) *v* informarsi, indagare
inquiry (ing-*kᵘaiö*-ri) *n* domanda *f*, indagine *f*; inchiesta *f*; ~ **office** ufficio informazioni
inquisitive (ing-*kᵘi*-sö-tiv) *adj* inquisitivo
insane (in-*ssein*) *adj* insano
inscription (in-*sskrip*-ʃön) *n* iscrizione *f*
insect (*in*-ssêkt) *n* insetto *m*; ~ **repellent** insettifugo *m*
insecticide (in-*ssêk*-ti-ssaid) *n* insetticida *m*
insensitive (in-*ssên*-ssö-tiv) *adj* insensibile
insert (in-*ssööt*) *v* inserire
inside (in-*ssaid*) *n* interno *m*; *adj* interno; *adv* dentro; *prep* dentro, dentro a; ~ **out** alla rovescia; **insides** interiora *fpl*
insight (*in*-ssait) *n* penetrazione *f*
insignificant (in-ssigh-*ni*-fi-könt) *adj* insignificante; irrilevante; futile
insist (in-*ssisst*) *v* insistere; persistere
insolence (*in*-ssö-lönss) *n* insolenza *f*
insolent (*in*-ssö-lönt) *adj* impertinente, insolente
insomnia (in-*ssom*-ni-ö) *n* insonnia *f*
inspect (in-*sspêkt*) *v* ispezionare
inspection (in-*sspêk*-ʃön) *n* ispezione *f*; controllo *m*
inspector (in-*sspêk*-tö) *n* ispettore *m*
inspire (in-*sspaiö*) *v* ispirare
install (in-*sstool*) *v* installare
installation (in-sstö-*lei*-ʃön) *n* installazione *f*
instalment (in-*sstool*-mönt) *n* rata *f*
instance (*in*-sstönss) *n* esempio *m*; caso *m*; **for** ~ per esempio
instant (*in*-sstönt) *n* istante *m*
instantly (*in*-sstönt-li) *adv* all'istante, subito, immediatamente
instead of (in-*sstêd* ov) invece di
instinct (*in*-sstingkt) *n* istinto *m*
institute (*in*-ssti-tʲuut) *n* istituto *m*; istituzione *f*; *v* istituire
institution (in-ssti-*tʲuu*-ʃön) *n* istituto *m*, istituzione *f*
instruct (in-*sstrakt*) *v* istruire
instruction (in-*sstrak*-ʃön) *n* istruzione *f*
instructive (in-*sstrak*-tiv) *adj* istruttivo
instructor (in-*sstrak*-tö) *n* istruttore *m*
instrument (in-ssö-*fi*-ʃönt) *n* strumento *m*; **musical** ~ strumento musicale
insufficient (*in*-ssö-*fi*-ʃönt) *adj* insufficiente
insulate (*in*-ssʲu-leit) *v* isolare
insulation (in-ssʲu-*lei*-ʃön) *n* isolamento *m*
insulator (*in*-ssʲu-lei-tö) *n* isolatore *m*
insult[1] (in-*ssalt*) *v* insultare
insult[2] (*in*-ssalt) *n* insulto *m*
insurance (in-*ʃuö*-rönss) *n* assicurazione *f*; ~ **policy** polizza di assicurazione
insure (in-*ʃuö*) *v* assicurare
intact (in-*tækt*) *adj* intatto
intellect (*in*-tö-lêkt) *n* intelletto *m*
intellectual (in-tö-*lêk*-tʃu-öl) *adj* intellettuale
intelligence (in-*tê*-li-dʒönss) *n* intelligenza *f*
intelligent (in-*tê*-li-dʒönt) *adj* intelligente
intend (in-*tênd*) *v* *intendere
intense (in-*tênss*) *adj* intenso; veemente
intention (in-*tên*-ʃön) *n* intenzione *f*
intentional (in-*tên*-ʃö-nöl) *adj* intenzionale
intercourse (*in*-tö-kooss) *n* rapporto *m*

interest (*in*-trösst) *n* interesse *m*, interessamento *m*; *v* interessare
interesting (*in*-trö-ssting) *adj* interessante
interfere (in-tö-*fiö*) *v* interferire; ~ **with** intromettersi in
interference (in-tö-*fiö*-rönss) *n* interferenza *f*
interim (*in*-tö-rim) *n* interim *m*
interior (in-*tiö*-ri-ö) *n* interiore *m*
interlude (*in*-tö-luud) *n* intermezzo *m*
intermediary (in-tö-*mii*-dʲö-ri) *n* intermediario *m*
intermission (in-tö-*mi*-ʃön) *n* intervallo *m*
internal (in-*töö*-nöl) *adj* interno
international (in-tö-*næ*-ʃö-nöl) *adj* internazionale
interpret (in-*töö*-prit) *v* *fare da interprete; interpretare
interpreter (in-*töö*-pri-tö) *n* interprete *m*
interrogate (in-*tê*-rö-gheit) *v* interrogare
interrogation (in-tê-rö-*ghei*-ʃön) *n* interrogatorio *m*
interrogative (in-tö-*ro*-ghö-tiv) *adj* interrogativo
interrupt (in-tö-*rapt*) *v* *interrompere
interruption (in-tö-*rap*-ʃön) *n* interruzione *f*
intersection (in-tö-*ssêk*-ʃön) *n* intersezione *f*
interval (*in*-tö-völ) *n* intervallo *m*
intervene (in-tö-*viin*) *v* *intervenire
interview (*in*-tö-vʲuu) *n* intervista *f*
intestine (in-*tê*-sstin) *n* intestino *m*
intimate (*in*-ti-möt) *adj* intimo
into (*in*-tu) *prep* in
intolerable (in-*to*-lö-rö-böl) *adj* intollerabile
intoxicated (in-*tok*-ssi-kei-tid) *adj* ubriaco
intrigue (in-*triigh*) *n* intrigo *m*
introduce (in-trö-*dʲuuss*) *v* presentare; *introdurre
introduction (in-trö-*dak*-ʃön) *n* presentazione *f*; introduzione *f*
invade (in-*veid*) *v* *invadere
invalid[1] (*in*-vö-liid) *n* invalido *m*; *adj* invalido
invalid[2] (in-*væ*-lid) *adj* nullo
invasion (in-*vei*-ʒön) *n* irruzione *f*, invasione *f*
invent (in-*vênt*) *v* inventare
invention (in-*vên*-ʃön) *n* invenzione *f*
inventive (in-*vên*-tiv) *adj* inventivo
inventor (in-*vên*-tö) *n* inventore *m*
inventory (*in*-vön-tri) *n* inventario *m*
invert (in-*vööt*) *v* invertire
invest (in-*vêsst*) *v* investire
investigate (in-*vê*-ssti-gheit) *v* investigare
investigation (in-vê-ssti-*ghei*-ʃön) *n* investigazione *f*
investment (in-*vêsst*-mönt) *n* investimento *m*
investor (in-*vê*-sstö) *n* finanziatore *m*
invisible (in-*vi*-sö-böl) *adj* invisibile
invitation (in-vi-*tei*-ʃön) *n* invito *m*
invite (in-*vait*) *v* invitare
invoice (*in*-voiss) *n* fattura *f*
involve (in-*volv*) *v* *coinvolgere
inwards (*in*-ᵘöds) *adv* verso l'interno
iodine (*ai*-ö-diin) *n* iodio *m*
Iran (i-*raan*) Iran *m*
Iranian (i-*rei*-ni-ön) *adj* iraniano
Iraq (i-*raak*) Iraq *m*
Iraqi (i-*raa*-ki) *adj* iracheno
irascible (i-*ræ*-ssi-böl) *adj* irascibile
Ireland (*aiö*-lönd) Irlanda *f*
Irish (*aiö*-riʃ) *adj* irlandese
Irishman (*aiö*-riʃ-mön) *n* (pl -men) irlandese *m*
iron (*ai*-ön) *n* ferro *m*; ferro da stiro; di ferro; *v* stirare
ironical (ai-*ro*-ni-köl) *adj* ironico
ironworks (*ai*-ön-ᵘöökss) *n* ferriera *f*

irony (*ai*ö-rö-ni) *n* ironia *f*
irregular (i-*rê*-ghⁱu-lö) *adj* irregolare
irreparable (i-*rê*-pö-rö-böl) *adj* irreparabile
irrevocable (i-*rê*-vö-kö-böl) *adj* irrevocabile
irritable (*i*-ri-tö-böl) *adj* irritabile
irritate (*i*-ri-teit) *v* irritare
is (is) *v* (pr be)
island (*ai*-lönd) *n* isola *f*
isolate (*ai*-ssö-leit) *v* isolare
isolation (ai-ssö-*lei*-ʃön) *n* isolamento *m*
Israel (*is*-reil) Israele *m*
Israeli (is-*rei*-li) *adj* israeliano
issue (*i*-ʃuu) *v* distribuire; *n* emissione *f*, tiratura *f*, edizione *f*; questione *f*, punto *m*; conseguenza *f*, risultato *m*, conclusione *f*, esito *m*; uscita *f*
isthmus (*iss*-möss) *n* istmo *m*
Italian (i-*tæl*-ˈön) *adj* italiano
italics (i-*tæ*-likss) *pl* caratteri corsivi
Italy (*i*-tö-li) Italia *f*
itch (itʃ) *n* prurito *m*; *v* prudere
item (*ai*-töm) *n* articolo *m*; punto *m*
itinerant (ai-*ti*-nö-rönt) *adj* ambulante
itinerary (ai-*ti*-nö-rö-ri) *n* itinerario *m*
ivory (*ai*-vö-ri) *n* avorio *m*
ivy (*ai*-vi) *n* edera *f*

J

jack (dʒæk) *n* cricco *m*
jacket (*dʒæ*-kit) *n* giacchetta *f*, giacca *f*; copertina *f*
jade (dʒeid) *n* giada *f*
jail (dʒeil) *n* prigione *m*
jailer (*dʒei*-lö) *n* carceriere *m*
jam (dʒæm) *n* marmellata *f*; ingorgo *m*
janitor (*dʒæ*-ni-tö) *n* portinaio *m*
January (*dʒæ*-nˈu-ö-ri) gennaio
Japan (dʒö-*pæn*) Giappone *m*
Japanese (dʒæ-pö-*niis*) *adj* giapponese
jar (dʒaa) *n* giara *f*
jaundice (*dʒoon*-diss) *n* itterizia *f*
jaw (dʒoo) *n* mascella *f*
jealous (*dʒê*-löss) *adj* geloso
jealousy (*dʒê*-lö-ssi) *n* gelosia *f*
jeans (dʒiins) *pl* jeans *mpl*
jelly (*dʒê*-li) *n* gelatina *f*
jelly-fish (*dʒê*-li-fiʃ) *n* medusa *f*
jersey (*dʒöö*-si) *n* jersey *m*; maglione *m*
jet (dʒêt) *n* getto *m*; aviogetto *m*
jetty (*dʒê*-ti) *n* molo *m*
Jew (dʒuu) *n* ebreo *m*
jewel (*dʒuu*-öl) *n* gioiello *m*
jeweller (*dʒuu*-ö-lö) *n* gioielliere *m*
jewellery (*dʒuu*-öl-ri) *n* gioie; gioielli
Jewish (*dʒuu*-iʃ) *adj* ebraico
job (dʒob) *n* lavoro *m*; impiego *m*
jockey (*dʒo*-ki) *n* fantino *m*
join (dʒoin) *v* unire; unirsi a, associarsi; riunire
joint (dʒoint) *n* articolazione *f*; saldatura *f*; *adj* unito, congiunto
jointly (*dʒoint*-li) *adv* insieme
joke (dʒouk) *n* scherzo *m*
jolly (*dʒo*-li) *adj* allegro
Jordan (*dʒoo*-dön) Giordania *f*
Jordanian (dʒoo-*dei*-ni-ön) *adj* giordano
journal (*dʒöö*-nöl) *n* giornale *m*
journalism (*dʒöö*-nö-li-söm) *n* giornalismo *m*
journalist (*dʒöö*-nö-lisst) *n* giornalista *m*
journey (*dʒöö*-ni) *n* viaggio *m*
joy (dʒoi) *n* delizia *f*, gioia *f*
joyful (*dʒoi*-föl) *adj* allegro, gioioso
jubilee (*dʒuu*-bi-lii) *n* anniversario *m*
judge (dʒadʒ) *n* giudice *m*; *v* giudicare

judgment (*dʒadʒ*-mönt) *n* giudizio *m*
jug (dʒagh) *n* brocca *f*
Jugoslav (ⁱuu-ghö-*sslaav*) *adj* iugoslavo
Jugoslavia (ⁱuu-ghö-*sslaa*-vi-ö) Iugoslavia *f*
juice (dʒuuss) *n* succo *m*
juicy (*dʒuu*-ssi) *adj* succoso
July (dʒu-*lai*) luglio
jump (dʒamp) *v* saltare; *n* salto *m*
jumper (*dʒam*-pö) *n* golf *m*
junction (*dʒangk*-ʃön) *n* incrocio *m*; crocevia *m*
June (dʒuun) giugno
jungle (*dʒang*-ghöl) *n* giungla *f*
junior (*dʒuu*-nⁱö) *adj* minore
junk (dʒangk) *n* spazzatura *f*
jury (*dʒu*ᵒ-ri) *n* giuria *f*
just (dʒasst) *adj* giusto; esatto; *adv* appena; esattamente
justice (*dʒa*-sstiss) *n* giustizia *f*
juvenile (*dʒuu*-vö-nail) *adj* giovanile

K

kangaroo (kæng-ghö-*ruu*) *n* canguro *m*
keel (kiil) *n* chiglia *f*
keen (kiin) *adj* appassionato; aguzzo
***keep** (kiip) *v* *tenere; *mantenere; continuare; ~ **away from** *tenersi lontano da; ~ **off** lasciar *stare; ~ **on** continuare; ~ **quiet** *tacere; ~ **up** perseverare; ~ **up with** *stare al passo con
keg (kêgh) *n* bariletto *m*
kennel (*kê*-nöl) *n* canile *m*
Kenya (*kê*-nⁱö) Kenia *m*
kerosene (*kê*-rö-ssiin) *n* petrolio *m*
kettle (*kê*-töl) *n* bollitore *m*
key (kii) *n* chiave *f*
keyhole (*kii*-houl) *n* buco della serratura
khaki (*kaa*-ki) *n* kaki *m*
kick (kik) *v* tirare calci, *prendere a calci; *n* calcio *m*, pedata *f*
kick-off (ki-*kof*) *n* calcio d'inizio
kid (kid) *n* bambino *m*; capretto *m*; *v* stuzzicare
kidney (*kid*-ni) *n* rene *m*
kill (kil) *v* ammazzare, *uccidere
kilogram (*ki*-lö-ghræm) *n* chilo *m*
kilometre (*ki*-lö-mii-tö) *n* chilometro *m*
kind (kaind) *adj* gentile, benevolo; buono; *n* genere *m*
kindergarten (*kin*-dö-ghaa-tön) *n* giardino d'infanzia, asilo infantile
king (king) *n* re *m*
kingdom (*king*-döm) *n* regno *m*
kiosk (*kii*-ossk) *n* chiosco *m*
kiss (kiss) *n* bacio *m*; *v* baciare
kit (kit) *n* corredo *m*
kitchen (*ki*-tʃin) *n* cucina *f*; ~ **garden** orto *m*
kleenex (*klii*-nêkss) *n* fazzoletto di carta
knapsack (*næp*-ssæk) *n* zaino *m*
knave (neiv) *n* fante *m*
knee (nii) *n* ginocchio *m*
kneecap (*nii*-kæp) *n* rotula *f*
***kneel** (niil) *v* inginocchiarsi
knew (nⁱuu) *v* (p know)
knickers (*ni*-kös) *pl* mutandine *fpl*
knife (naif) *n* (pl knives) coltello *m*
knight (nait) *n* cavaliere *m*
***knit** (nit) *v* lavorare a maglia
knob (nob) *n* manopola *f*
knock (nok) *v* bussare; *n* colpo *m*; ~ **against** urtare contro; ~ **down** atterrare
knot (not) *n* nodo *m*; *v* annodare
***know** (nou) *v* *sapere, *conoscere
knowledge (*no*-lidʒ) *n* conoscenza *f*
knuckle (*na*-köl) *n* nocca *f*

L

label (*lei*-böl) *n* etichetta *f*; *v* etichettare
laboratory (lö-*bo*-rö-tö-ri) *n* laboratorio *m*
labour (*lei*-bö) *n* lavoro *m*; doglie *fpl*; *v* lavorare sodo, faticare; **labor permit** *Am* permesso di lavoro
labourer (*lei*-bö-rö) *n* operaio *m*
labour-saving (*lei*-bö-ssei-ving) *adj* che risparmia lavoro
labyrinth (*læ*-bö-rinθ) *n* labirinto *m*
lace (leiss) *n* merletto *m*; laccio *m*
lack (læk) *n* mancanza *f*; *v* mancare
lacquer (*læ*-kö) *n* lacca *f*
lad (læd) *n* giovane *m*, ragazzo *m*
ladder (*læ*-dö) *n* scala *f*
lady (*lei*-di) *n* signora *f*; **ladies' room** gabinetto per signore
lagoon (lö-*ghuun*) *n* laguna *f*
lake (leik) *n* lago *m*
lamb (læm) *n* agnello *m*
lame (leim) *adj* paralitico, zoppicante, zoppo
lamentable (*læ*-mön-tö-böl) *adj* lamentevole
lamp (læmp) *n* lampada *f*
lamp-post (*læmp*-pousst) *n* lampione *m*
lampshade (*læmp*-ʃeid) *n* paralume *m*
land (lænd) *n* paese *m*, terra *f*; *v* atterrare; sbarcare
landlady (*lænd*-lei-di) *n* affittacamere *f*
landlord (*lænd*-lood) *n* padrone di casa, proprietario *m*; affittacamere *m*
landmark (*lænd*-maak) *n* punto di riferimento; pietra miliare
landscape (*lænd*-sskeip) *n* paesaggio *m*
lane (lein) *n* vicolo *m*, sentiero *m*; corsia *f*
language (*læng*-ghᵘidʒ) *n* lingua *f*; ~ **laboratory** laboratorio linguistico
lantern (*læn*-tön) *n* lanterna *f*
lapel (lö-*pêl*) *n* risvolta *f*
larder (*laa*-dö) *n* dispensa *f*
large (laadʒ) *adj* grande; spazioso
lark (laak) *n* allodola *f*
laryngitis (læ-rin-*dʒai*-tiss) *n* laringite *f*
last (laasst) *adj* ultimo; scorso; *v* durare; **at** ~ finalmente
lasting (*laa*-ssting) *adj* duraturo, durevole
latchkey (*lætʃ*-kii) *n* chiave di casa
late (leit) *adj* tardivo; in ritardo
lately (*leit*-li) *adv* ultimamente, recentemente
lather (*laa*-ðö) *n* schiuma *f*
Latin America (*læ*-tin ö-*mê*-ri-kö) America Latina
Latin-American (læ-tin-ö-*mê*-ri-kön) *adj* latino americano
latitude (*læ*-ti-tⁱuud) *n* latitudine *f*
laugh (laaf) *v* *ridere; *n* riso *m*
laughter (*laaf*-tö) *n* risata *f*
launch (loontʃ) *v* lanciare; *n* motonave *f*
launching (*loon*-tʃing) *n* varo *m*
launderette (loon-dö-*rêt*) *n* lavanderia automatica
laundry (*loon*-dri) *n* lavanderia *f*; bucato *m*
lavatory (*læ*-vö-tö-ri) *n* gabinetto *m*
lavish (*læ*-viʃ) *adj* prodigo
law (loo) *n* legge *f*; ~ **court** tribunale *m*
lawful (*loo*-föl) *adj* legale
lawn (loon) *n* prato *m*
lawsuit (*loo*-ssuut) *n* processo *m*, causa *f*
lawyer (*loo*-ⁱö) *n* avvocato *m*; giurista *m*
laxative (*læk*-ssö-tiv) *n* lassativo *m*

***lay** (lei) *v* collocare, *mettere, posare; ~ **bricks** murare

layer (lei^{ö}) *n* strato *m*

layman (*lei*-mön) *n* profano *m*

lazy (*lei*-si) *adj* pigro

lead[1] (liid) *n* vantaggio *m*; guida *f*; guinzaglio *m*

lead[2] (lêd) *n* piombo *m*

***lead** (liid) *v* *dirigere

leader (*lii*-dö) *n* leader *m*, dirigente *m*

leadership (*lii*-dö-ʃip) *n* comando *m*

leading (*lii*-ding) *adj* dominante, principale

leaf (liif) *n* (pl leaves) foglia *f*

league (liigh) *n* lega *f*

leak (liik) *n* sgocciolamento *m*

leaky (*lii*-ki) *adj* perdente

lean (liin) *adj* magro

***lean** (liin) *v* appoggiarsi

leap (liip) *n* salto *m*

***leap** (liip) *v* balzare

leap-year (*liip*-^{i}i^{ö}) *n* anno bisestile

***learn** (löön) *v* imparare

learner (*löö*-nö) *n* principiante *m*

lease (liiss) *n* contratto di affitto; locazione *f*; *v* *dare in locazione, *dare in affitto; *prendere in affitto

leash (liiʃ) *n* guinzaglio *m*

least (liisst) *adj* minimo; **at** ~ almeno

leather (*lê*-ðö) *n* pelle *f*; di pelle

leave (liiv) *n* congedo *m*

***leave** (liiv) *v* partire, lasciare; ~ **out** *omettere

Lebanese (lê-bö-*niis*) *adj* libanese

Lebanon (*lê*-bö-nön) Libano *m*

lecture (*lêk*-tʃö) *n* lezione *f*, conferenza *f*

left[1] (lêft) *adj* sinistro

left[2] (lêft) *v* (p, pp leave)

left-hand (*lêft*-hænd) *adj* sinistro, a sinistra

left-handed (lêft-*hæn*-did) *adj* mancino

leg (lêgh) *n* piede *m*, gamba *f*

legacy (*lê*-ghö-ssi) *n* legato *m*

legal (*lii*-ghöl) *adj* legittimo, legale; giuridico

legalization (lii-ghö-lai-*sei*-ʃön) *n* legalizzazione *f*

legation (li-*ghei*-ʃön) *n* legazione *f*

legible (*lê*-dʒi-böl) *adj* leggibile

legitimate (li-*dʒi*-ti-möt) *adj* legittimo

leisure (*lê*-ʒö) *n* comodo *m*

lemon (*lê*-mön) *n* limone *m*

lemonade (lê-mö-*neid*) *n* limonata *f*

***lend** (lênd) *v* prestare

length (lêngθ) *n* lunghezza *f*

lengthen (*lêng*-θön) *v* allungare

lengthways (*lêngθ*-^{u}eis) *adv* per il lungo

lens (lêns) *n* lente *f*; **telephoto** ~ teleobbiettivo *m*; **zoom** ~ zoom *m*

leprosy (*lê*-prö-ssi) *n* lebbra *f*

less (lêss) *adv* meno

lessen (*lê*-ssön) *v* diminuire

lesson (*lê*-ssön) *n* lezione *f*

***let** (lêt) *v* lasciare; affittare; ~ **down** *deludere

letter (*lê*-tö) *n* lettera *f*; ~ **of credit** lettera di credito; ~ **of recommendation** lettera di raccomandazione

letter-box (*lê*-tö-bokss) *n* cassetta postale

lettuce (*lê*-tiss) *n* lattuga *f*

level (*lê*-völ) *adj* piano; piatto, spianato; *n* livello *m*; livella *f*; *v* pareggiare, livellare; ~ **crossing** passaggio a livello

lever (*lii*-vö) *n* leva *f*

Levis (*lii*-vais) *pl* jeans *mpl*

liability (lai-ö-*bi*-lö-ti) *n* responsabilità *f*

liable (*lai*-ö-böl) *adj* responsabile; ~ **to** soggetto a

liberal (*li*-bö-röl) *adj* liberale; generoso, prodigo

liberation (li-bö-*rei*-ʃön) *n* liberazione *f*

Liberia (lai-*bi*ö-ri-ö) Liberia *f*
Liberian (lai-*bi*ö-ri-ön) *adj* liberiano
liberty (*li*-bö-ti) *n* libertà *f*
library (*lai*-brö-ri) *n* biblioteca *f*
licence (*lai*-ssönss) *n* licenza *f*; **driving** ~ patente di guida; ~ **number** *Am* numero di targa; ~ **plate** *Am* targa automobilistica
license (*lai*-ssönss) *v* autorizzare
lick (lik) *v* leccare
lid (lid) *n* coperchio *m*
lie (lai) *v* mentire; *n* menzogna *f*
***lie** (lai) *v* *star disteso; ~ **down** sdraiarsi
life (laif) *n* (pl lives) vita *f*; ~ **insurance** assicurazione sulla vita
lifebelt (*laif*-bêlt) *n* cintura di salvataggio
lifetime (*laif*-taim) *n* vita *f*
lift (lift) *v* alzare, sollevare; *n* ascensore *m*
light (lait) *n* luce *f*; *adj* leggero; chiaro; ~ **bulb** bulbo *m*
***light** (lait) *v* *accendere
lighter (*lai*-tö) *n* accendino *m*
lighthouse (*lait*-hauss) *n* faro *m*
lighting (*lai*-ting) *n* illuminazione *f*
lightning (*lait*-ning) *n* lampo *m*
like (laik) *v* *voler bene; gradire; *adj* simile; *conj* come
likely (*lai*-kli) *adj* probabile
like-minded (laik-*main*-did) *adj* unanime
likewise (*laik*-ᵘais) *adv* nello stesso modo, inoltre
lily (*li*-li) *n* giglio *m*
limb (lim) *n* membro *m*
lime (laim) *n* calce *f*; tiglio *m*; cedro *m*
limetree (*laim*-trii) *n* tiglio *m*
limit (*li*-mit) *n* limite *m*; *v* limitare
limp (limp) *v* zoppicare; *adj* floscio
line (lain) *n* riga *f*; tratto *m*; cordicella *f*; linea *f*; fila *f*; **stand in** ~ *Am* *fare la coda
linen (*li*-nin) *n* lino *m*; biancheria *f*
liner (*lai*-nö) *n* nave di linea
lingerie (*long*-ʒö-rii) *n* biancheria *f*
lining (*lai*-ning) *n* fodera *f*
link (lingk) *v* collegare; *n* legame *m*; maglia *f*
lion (*lai*-ön) *n* leone *m*
lip (lip) *n* labbro *m*
lipsalve (*lip*-ssaav) *n* pomata per le labbra
lipstick (*lip*-sstik) *n* rossetto *m*
liqueur (li-*k*ⁱ*u*ö) *n* liquore *m*
liquid (*li*-kᵘid) *adj* liquido; *n* liquido *m*
liquor (*li*-kö) *n* bevande alcooliche
liquorice (*li*-kö-riss) *n* liquirizia *f*
list (lisst) *n* elenco *m*; *v* elencare
listen (*li*-ssön) *v* sentire, ascoltare
listener (*liss*-nö) *n* ascoltatore *m*
literary (*li*-trö-ri) *adj* letterario
literature (*li*-trö-tʃö) *n* letteratura *f*
litre (*lii*-tö) *n* litro *m*
litter (*li*-tö) *n* rifiuti; figliata *f*
little (*li*-töl) *adj* piccolo; poco
live[1] (liv) *v* *vivere; abitare
live[2] (laiv) *adj* vivo
livelihood (*laiv*-li-hud) *n* sussistenza *f*
lively (*laiv*-li) *adj* vivace
liver (*li*-vö) *n* fegato *m*
living-room (*li*-ving-ruum) *n* soggiorno *m*, salotto *m*
load (loud) *n* carico *m*; peso *m*; *v* caricare
loaf (louf) *n* (pl loaves) pagnotta *f*
loan (loun) *n* prestito *m*
lobby (*lo*-bi) *n* atrio *m*; ridotto *m*
lobster (*lob*-sstö) *n* aragosta *f*
local (*lou*-köl) *adj* locale; ~ **call** chiamata locale; ~ **train** treno locale
locality (lou-*kæ*-lö-ti) *n* località *f*
locate (lou-*keit*) *v* localizzare
location (lou-*kei*-ʃön) *n* posizione *f*
lock (lok) *v* *chiudere a chiave; *n* ser-

ratura *f*; chiusa *f*; ~ **up** *chiudere a chiave
locomotive (lou-kö-*mou*-tiv) *n* locomotiva *f*
lodge (lodʒ) *v* alloggiare; *n* padiglione da caccia
lodger (*lo*-dʒö) *n* inquilino *m*
lodgings (*lo*-dʒings) *pl* alloggio *m*
log (logh) *n* ceppo *m*
logic (*lo*-dʒik) *n* logica *f*
logical (*lo*-dʒi-köl) *adj* logico
lonely (*loun*-li) *adj* solitario
long (long) *adj* lungo; ~ **for** bramare; **no longer** non... più
longing (*long*-ing) *n* bramosia *f*
longitude (*lon*-dʒi-tⁱuud) *n* longitudine *f*
look (luk) *v* guardare; sembrare, *aver l'aria; *n* occhiata *f*, sguardo *m*; aspetto *m*; ~ **after** occuparsi di, badare a; ~ **at** guardare; ~ **for** cercare; ~ **out** *stare attento, *fare attenzione; ~ **up** cercare
looking-glass (*lu*-king-ghlaass) *n* specchio *m*
loop (luup) *n* nodo scorsoio
loose (luuss) *adj* slegato
loosen (*luu*-ssön) *v* slegare
lord (lood) *n* lord *m*
lorry (*lo*-ri) *n* autocarro *m*
***lose** (luus) *v* *perdere, smarrire
loss (loss) *n* perdita *f*
lost (losst) *adj* smarrito; ~ **and found** oggetti smarriti; ~ **property office** ufficio oggetti smarriti
lot (lot) *n* fortuna *f*, sorte *f*; massa *f*, quantità *f*
lotion (*lou*-ʃön) *n* lozione *f*; **after-shave** ~ lozione dopo barba
lottery (*lo*-tö-ri) *n* lotteria *f*
loud (laud) *adj* forte, alto
loud-speaker (laud-*sspii*-kö) *n* altoparlante *m*
lounge (laundʒ) *n* salone *m*
louse (lauss) *n* (pl lice) pidocchio *m*
love (lav) *v* amare; *n* amore *m*; **in** ~ innamorato
lovely (*lav*-li) *adj* delizioso, splendido, bello
lover (*la*-vö) *n* amante *m*
love-story (*lav*-sstoo-ri) *n* storia d'amore
low (lou) *adj* basso; abbattuto; ~ **tide** bassa marea
lower (*lou*-ö) *v* abbassare; ribassare; calare; *adj* inferiore
lowlands (*lou*-lönds) *pl* bassopiano *m*
loyal (*loi*-öl) *adj* leale
lubricate (*luu*-bri-keit) *v* lubrificare
lubrication (luu-bri-*kei*-ʃön) *n* lubrificazione *f*; ~ **oil** lubrificante *m*; ~ **system** sistema lubrificante
luck (lak) *n* successo *m*, fortuna *f*; caso *m*; **bad** ~ sfortuna *f*
lucky (*la*-ki) *adj* fortunato; ~ **charm** portafortuna *m*
ludicrous (*luu*-di-kröss) *adj* irrisorio, ridicolo
luggage (*la*-ghidʒ) *n* bagaglio *m*; **hand** ~ bagaglio a mano; **left** ~ **office** deposito bagagli; ~ **rack** portabagagli *m*; ~ **van** bagagliaio *m*
lukewarm (*luuk*-^uoom) *adj* tiepido
lumbago (lam-*bei*-ghou) *n* lombaggine *f*
luminous (*luu*-mi-nöss) *adj* luminoso
lump (lamp) *n* nodo *m*, grumo *m*, pezzo *m*; protuberanza *f*; ~ **of sugar** zolletta di zucchero; ~ **sum** somma globale
lumpy (*lam*-pi) *adj* grumoso
lunacy (*luu*-nö-ssi) *n* pazzia *f*
lunatic (*luu*-nö-tik) *adj* pazzo; *n* pazzo *m*
lunch (lantʃ) *n* pranzo *m*, seconda colazione, colazione *f*
luncheon (*lan*-tʃön) *n* colazione *f*
lung (lang) *n* polmone *m*

lust (lasst) *n* concupiscenza *f*
luxurious (lagh-*ʒuö*-ri-öss) *adj* lussuoso
luxury (*lak*-ʃö-ri) *n* lusso *m*

M

machine (mö-*ʃiin*) *n* apparecchio *m*, macchina *f*
machinery (mö-*ʃii*-nö-ri) *n* macchinario *m*; meccanismo *m*
mackerel (*mæ*-kröl) *n* (pl ~) sgombro *m*
mackintosh (*mæ*-kin-toʃ) *n* impermeabile *m*
mad (mæd) *adj* matto, pazzo, folle; rabbioso
madam (*mæ*-döm) *n* signora *f*
madness (*mæd*-nöss) *n* pazzia *f*
magazine (mæ-ghö-*siin*) *n* rivista *f*
magic (*mæ*-dʒik) *n* magia *f*; *adj* magico
magician (mö-*dʒi*-ʃön) *n* prestigiatore *m*
magistrate (*mæ*-dʒi-sstreit) *n* magistrato *m*
magnetic (mægh-*nê*-tik) *adj* magnetico
magneto (mægh-*nii*-tou) *n* (pl ~s) magnete *m*
magnificent (mægh-*ni*-fi-ssönt) *adj* magnifico; grandioso, splendido
magpie (*mægh*-pai) *n* gazza *f*
maid (meid) *n* cameriera *f*
maiden name (*mei*-dön neim) cognome da nubile
mail (meil) *n* posta *f*; *v* impostare; ~ **order** *Am* vaglia postale
mailbox (*meil*-bokss) *nAm* cassetta postale
main (mein) *adj* principale; maggiore; ~ **deck** ponte di coperta; ~ **line** linea principale; ~ **road** strada principale; ~ **street** via principale
mainland (*mein*-lönd) *n* terraferma *f*
mainly (*mein*-li) *adv* principalmente
mains (meins) *pl* linea elettrica principale
maintain (mein-*tein*) *v* *mantenere
maintenance (*mein*-tö-nönss) *n* manutenzione *f*
maize (meis) *n* granturco *m*
major (*mei*-dʒö) *adj* grande; maggiore; *n* maggiore *m*
majority (mö-*dʒo*-rö-ti) *n* maggioranza *f*
***make** (meik) *v* *fare; guadagnare; *riuscire; ~ **do with** arrangiarsi con; ~ **good** compensare; ~ **up** compilare
make-up (*mei*-kap) *n* trucco *m*
malaria (mö-*lêö*-ri-ö) *n* malaria *f*
Malay (mö-*lei*) *n* malese *m*
Malaysia (mö-*lei*-si-ö) Malesia *f*
Malaysian (mö-*lei*-si-ön) *adj* malese
male (meil) *adj* maschio
malicious (mö-*li*-ʃöss) *adj* malevolo
malignant (mö-*ligh*-nönt) *adj* maligno
mallet (*mæ*-lit) *n* maglio *m*
malnutrition (mæl-n'u-*tri*-ʃön) *n* denutrizione *f*
mammal (*mæ*-möl) *n* mammifero *m*
mammoth (*mæ*-möθ) *n* mammut *m*
man (mæn) *n* (pl men) uomo *m*; **men's room** gabinetto per signori
manage (*mæ*-nidʒ) *v* *dirigere; *riuscire
manageable (*mæ*-ni-dʒö-böl) *adj* maneggiabile
management (*mæ*-nidʒ-mönt) *n* direzione *f*; gestione *f*
manager (*mæ*-ni-dʒö) *n* capo *m*, direttore *m*
mandarin (*mæn*-dö-rin) *n* mandarino *m*
mandate (*mæn*-deit) *n* mandato *m*

manger (*mein*-dʒö) *n* mangiatoia *f*
manicure (*mæ*-ni-kⁱuᵒ) *n* manicure *f*; *v* curare le unghie
mankind (mæn-*kaind*) *n* umanità *f*
mannequin (*mæ*-nö-kin) *n* indossatrice *f*
manner (*mæ*-nö) *n* modo *m*, maniera *f*; **manners** *pl* maniere
man-of-war (mæ-növ-ᵘ*oo*) *n* nave da guerra
manor-house (*mæ*-nö-hauss) *n* casa padronale
mansion (*mæn*-ʃön) *n* palazzo *m*
manual (*mæ*-nⁱu-öl) *adj* manuale
manufacture (mæ-nⁱu-*fæk*-tʃö) *v* confezionare, fabbricare
manufacturer (mæ-nⁱu-*fæk*-tʃö-rö) *n* fabbricante *m*
manure (mö-*nⁱuᵒ*) *n* concime *m*
manuscript (*mæ*-nⁱu-sskript) *n* manoscritto *m*
many (*mê*-ni) *adj* molti
map (mæp) *n* carta *f*; mappa *f*; pianta *f*
maple (*mei*-pöl) *n* acero *m*
marble (*maa*-böl) *n* marmo *m*; pallina *f*
March (maatʃ) marzo
march (maatʃ) *v* marciare; *n* marcia *f*
mare (mêᵒ) *n* cavalla *f*
margarine (maa-dʒö-*riin*) *n* margarina *f*
margin (*maa*-dʒin) *n* margine *m*
maritime (*mæ*-ri-taim) *adj* marittimo
mark (maak) *v* marcare; segnare; caratterizzare; *n* segno *m*; voto *m*; bersaglio *m*
market (*maa*-kit) *n* mercato *m*
market-place (*maa*-kit-pleiss) *n* piazza del mercato
marmalade (*maa*-mö-leid) *n* marmellata *f*
marriage (*mæ*-ridʒ) *n* matrimonio *m*
marrow (*mæ*-rou) *n* midollo *m*
marry (*mæ*-ri) *v* sposare; **married couple** coniugi *mpl*
marsh (maaʃ) *n* palude *f*
marshy (*maa*-ʃi) *adj* paludoso
martyr (*maa*-tö) *n* martire *m*
marvel (*maa*-völ) *n* meraviglia *f*; *v* meravigliarsi
marvellous (*maa*-vö-löss) *adj* meraviglioso
mascara (mæ-*sskaa*-rö) *n* mascara *m*
masculine (*mæ*-sskⁱu-lin) *adj* maschile
mash (mæʃ) *v* schiacciare
mask (maassk) *n* maschera *f*
Mass (mæss) *n* messa *f*
mass (mæss) *n* massa *f*; ~ **production** produzione in serie
massage (*mæ*-ssaaʒ) *n* massaggio *m*; *v* massaggiare
masseur (mæ-*ssöö*) *n* massaggiatore *m*
massive (*mæ*-ssiv) *adj* massiccio
mast (maasst) *n* albero *m*
master (*maa*-sstö) *n* maestro *m*; padrone *m*; professore *m*, insegnante *m*; *v* dominare
masterpiece (*maa*-sstö-piiss) *n* capolavoro *m*
mat (mæt) *n* stuoia *f*; *adj* pallido, opaco
match (mætʃ) *n* fiammifero *m*; partita *f*; *v* intonarsi con
match-box (*mætʃ*-bokss) *n* scatola di fiammiferi
material (mö-*tiᵒ*-ri-öl) *n* materiale *m*; stoffa *f*; *adj* materiale
mathematical (mæ-θö-*mæ*-ti-köl) *adj* matematico
mathematics (mæ-θö-*mæ*-tikss) *n* matematica *f*
matrimonial (mæ-tri-*mou*-ni-öl) *adj* matrimoniale
matrimony (*mæ*-tri-mö-ni) *n* matrimonio *m*
matter (*mæ*-tö) *n* materia *f*; affare

m, questione *f*, faccenda *f*; *v* *avere importanza; **as a ~ of fact** effettivamente, infatti
matter-of-fact (mæ-tö-röv-*fækt*) *adj* prosaico
mattress (*mæ*-tröss) *n* materasso *m*
mature (mö-*t'uö*) *adj* maturo
maturity (mö-*t'uö*-rö-ti) *n* maturità *f*
mausoleum (moo-ssö-*lii*-öm) *n* mausoleo *m*
mauve (mouv) *adj* lilla
May (mei) maggio
***may** (mei) *v* *potere
maybe (*mei*-bii) *adv* forse
mayor (mêö) *n* sindaco *m*
maze (meis) *n* labirinto *m*
me (mii) *pron* mi; me
meadow (*mê*-dou) *n* prato *m*
meal (miil) *n* pasto *m*
mean (miin) *adj* meschino; *n* media *f*
***mean** (miin) *v* significare; *voler dire; *intendere
meaning (*mii*-ning) *n* significato *m*
meaningless (*mii*-ning-löss) *adj* insensato
means (miins) *n* mezzo *m*; **by no ~** in nessun modo
in the meantime (in ðö *miin*-taim) intanto, nel frattempo
meanwhile (*miin*-ᵘail) *adv* frattanto
measles (*mii*-söls) *n* morbillo *m*
measure (*mê*-ʒö) *v* misurare; *n* misura *f*
meat (miit) *n* carne *f*
mechanic (mi-*kæ*-nik) *n* meccanico *m*
mechanical (mi-*kæ*-ni-köl) *adj* meccanico
mechanism (*mê*-kö-ni-söm) *n* meccanismo *m*
medal (*mê*-döl) *n* medaglia *f*
mediaeval (mê-di-*ii*-völ) *adj* medievale
mediate (*mii*-di-eit) *v* *fare da intermediario
mediator (*mii*-di-ei-tö) *n* mediatore *m*
medical (*mê*-di-köl) *adj* medico
medicine (*mêd*-ssin) *n* medicamento *m*; medicina *f*
meditate (*mê*-di-teit) *v* meditare
Mediterranean (mê-di-tö-*rei*-ni-ön) Mediterraneo *m*
medium (*mii*-di-öm) *adj* mediocre, medio
***meet** (miit) *v* incontrare
meeting (*mii*-ting) *n* assemblea *f*, riunione *f*; incontro *m*
meeting-place (*mii*-ting-pleiss) *n* luogo di riunione
melancholy (*mê*-löng-kö-li) *n* malinconia *f*
mellow (*mê*-lou) *adj* polposo
melodrama (*mê*-lö-draa-mö) *n* melodramma *m*
melody (*mê*-lö-di) *n* melodia *f*
melon (*mê*-lön) *n* melone *m*
melt (mêlt) *v* *fondere
member (*mêm*-bö) *n* membro *m*; **Member of Parliament** deputato *m*
membership (*mêm*-bö-ʃip) *n* qualità di membro
memo (*mê*-mou) *n* (pl ~s) nota *f*
memorable (*mê*-mö-rö-böl) *adj* memorabile
memorial (mö-*moo*-ri-öl) *n* monumento commemorativo
memorize (*mê*-mö-rais) *v* imparare a memoria
memory (*mê*-mö-ri) *n* memoria *f*; ricordo *m*
mend (mênd) *v* rammendare, riparare
menstruation (mên-sstru-*ei*-ʃön) *n* mestruazione *f*
mental (*mên*-töl) *adj* mentale
mention (*mên*-ʃön) *v* nominare, menzionare; *n* citazione *f*, menzione *f*
menu (*mê*-n'uu) *n* carta *f*, menu *m*
merchandise (*möö*-tʃön-dais) *n* merce *f*, mercanzia *f*

merchant (*möö*-tʃönt) *n* commerciante *m*, mercante *m*
merciful (*möö*-ssi-föl) *adj* misericordioso
mercury (*möö*-kʲu-ri) *n* mercurio *m*
mercy (*möö*-ssi) *n* misericordia *f*, clemenza *f*
mere (miᵒ) *adj* mero
merely (*miᵒ*-li) *adv* soltanto
merger (*möö*-dʒö) *n* fusione *f*
merit (*mê*-rit) *v* meritare; *n* merito *m*
mermaid (*möö*-meid) *n* sirena *f*
merry (*mê*-ri) *adj* allegro
merry-go-round (*mê*-ri-ghou-raund) *n* giostra *f*
mesh (mêʃ) *n* maglia *f*
mess (mêss) *n* disordine *m*; ~ **up** pasticciare
message (*mê*-ssidʒ) *n* commissione *f*, messaggio *m*
messenger (*mê*-ssin-dʒö) *n* messaggero *m*
metal (*mê*-töl) *n* metallo *m*; metallico
meter (*mii*-tö) *n* metro *m*
method (*mê*-θöd) *n* metodo *m*; ordine *m*
methodical (mö-*θo*-di-köl) *adj* metodico
methylated spirits (*mê*-θö-lei-tid *sspi*-ritss) alcool metilico
metre (*mii*-tö) *n* metro *m*
metric (*mê*-trik) *adj* metrico
Mexican (*mêk*-ssi-kön) *adj* messicano
Mexico (*mêk*-ssi-kou) Messico *m*
mezzanine (*mê*-sö-niin) *n* mezzanino *m*
microphone (*mai*-krö-foun) *n* microfono *m*
midday (*mid*-dei) *n* mezzogiorno *m*
middle (*mi*-döl) *n* mezzo *m*; *adj* mezzo; **Middle Ages** medioevo *m*; ~ **class** ceto medio; **middle-class** *adj* borghese
midnight (*mid*-nait) *n* mezzanotte *f*
midst (midsst) *n* mezzo *m*
midsummer (*mid*-ssa-mö) *n* piena estate
midwife (*mid*-ᵘaif) *n* (pl -wives) levatrice *f*
might (mait) *n* potenza *f*
***might** (mait) *v* *potere
mighty (*mai*-ti) *adj* poderoso
migraine (*mi*-ghrein) *n* emicrania *f*
mild (maild) *adj* mite
mildew (*mil*-dʲu) *n* muffa *f*
mile (mail) *n* miglio *m*
mileage (*mai*-lidʒ) *n* distanza in miglia
milepost (*mail*-pousst) *n* cartello indicatore
milestone (*mail*-sstoun) *n* pietra miliare
milieu (*mii*-lʲöö) *n* ambiente *m*
military (*mi*-li-tö-ri) *adj* militare; ~ **force** forze militari
milk (milk) *n* latte *m*
milkman (*milk*-mön) *n* (pl -men) lattaio *m*
milk-shake (*milk*-ʃeik) *n* frappé *m*
milky (*mil*-ki) *adj* latteo
mill (mil) *n* macinino *m*; fabbrica *f*
miller (*mi*-lö) *n* mugnaio *m*
milliner (*mi*-li-nö) *n* modista *f*
million (*mil*-ʲön) *n* milione *m*
millionaire (mil-ʲö-*nêᵒ*) *n* milionario *m*
mince (minss) *v* tritare
mind (maind) *n* mente *f*; *v* *fare obiezione a; badare a, *fare attenzione
mine (main) *n* miniera *f*
miner (*mai*-nö) *n* minatore *m*
mineral (*mi*-nö-röl) *n* minerale *m*; ~ **water** acqua minerale
miniature (*min*-ʲö-tʃö) *n* miniatura *f*
minimum (*mi*-ni-möm) *n* minimo *m*
mining (*mai*-ning) *n* industria mineraria
minister (*mi*-ni-sstö) *n* ministro *m*;

pastore *m*; **Prime Minister** primo ministro
ministry (*mi*-ni-sstri) *n* ministero *m*
mink (mingk) *n* visone *m*
minor (*mai*-nö) *adj* piccolo, esiguo, minore; subordinato; *n* minorenne *m*
minority (mai-*no*-rö-ti) *n* minoranza *f*
mint (mint) *n* menta *f*
minus (*mai*-nöss) *prep* meno
minute[1] (*mi*-nit) *n* minuto *m*; **minutes** verbale *m*
minute[2] (mai-*n*'*uut*) *adj* minuto
miracle (*mi*-rö-köl) *n* miracolo *m*
miraculous (mi-*ræ*-k'u-löss) *adj* miracoloso
mirror (*mi*-rö) *n* specchio *m*
misbehave (miss-bi-*heiv*) *v* comportarsi male
miscarriage (miss-*kæ*-ridʒ) *n* aborto *m*
miscellaneous (mi-ssö-*lei*-ni-öss) *adj* misto
mischief (*miss*-tʃif) *n* birichinata *f*; male *m*, danno *m*, malizia *f*
mischievous (*miss*-tʃi-vöss) *adj* malizioso
miserable (*mi*-sö-rö-böl) *adj* misero, miserabile
misery (*mi*-sö-ri) *n* miseria *f*; bisogno *m*
misfortune (miss-*foo*-tʃên) *n* sfortuna *f*, avversità *f*
***mislay** (miss-*lei*) *v* smarrire
misplaced (miss-*pleisst*) *adj* inopportuno; sbagliato
mispronounce (miss-prö-*naunss*) *v* pronunciar male
miss[1] (miss) signorina *f*
miss[2] (miss) *v* *rimpiangere
missing (*mi*-ssing) *adj* mancante; ~ **person** persona scomparsa
mist (misst) *n* foschia *f*, nebbia *f*
mistake (mi-*ssteik*) *n* fallo *m*, sbaglio *m*, errore *m*
***mistake** (mi-*ssteik*) *v* *confondere
mistaken (mi-*sstei*-kön) *adj* erroneo; ***be** ~ sbagliarsi
mister (*mi*-sstö) signore *m*
mistress (*mi*-sströss) *n* signora *f*; padrona *f*; amante *f*
mistrust (miss-*trasst*) *v* diffidare di
misty (*mi*-ssti) *adj* nebbioso
***misunderstand** (mi-ssan-dö-*sstænd*) *v* *fraintendere
misunderstanding (mi-ssan-dö-*sstæn*-ding) *n* malinteso *m*
misuse (miss-'*uuss*) *n* abuso *m*
mittens (*mi*-töns) *pl* muffole *fpl*
mix (mikss) *v* mescolare; ~ **with** frequentare
mixed (miksst) *adj* misto
mixer (*mik*-ssö) *n* frullatore *m*
mixture (*mikss*-tʃö) *n* miscuglio *m*
moan (moun) *v* gemere
moat (mout) *n* fossato *m*
mobile (*mou*-bail) *adj* mobile
mock (mok) *v* canzonare
mockery (*mo*-kö-ri) *n* derisione *f*
model (*mo*-döl) *n* modello *m*; indossatrice *f*; *v* modellare, plasmare
moderate (*mo*-dö-röt) *adj* moderato; mediocre
modern (*mo*-dön) *adj* moderno
modest (*mo*-disst) *adj* riservato, modesto
modesty (*mo*-di-ssti) *n* modestia *f*
modify (*mo*-di-fai) *v* modificare
mohair (*mou*-hêᵒ) *n* angora *f*
moist (moisst) *adj* bagnato, umido
moisten (*moi*-ssön) *v* inumidire
moisture (*moiss*-tʃö) *n* umidità *f*; **moisturizing cream** crema idratante
molar (*mou*-lö) *n* molare *m*
moment (*mou*-mönt) *n* attimo *m*, momento *m*
momentary (*mou*-mön-tö-ri) *adj* mo-

mentaneo
monarch (*mo*-nök) *n* monarca *m*
monarchy (*mo*-nö-ki) *n* monarchia *f*
monastery (*mo*-nö-sstri) *n* monastero *m*
Monday (*man*-di) lunedì *m*
monetary (*ma*-ni-tö-ri) *adj* monetario; ~ **unit** unità monetaria
money (*ma*-ni) *n* denaro *m*; ~ **exchange** ufficio cambio; ~ **order** vaglia *m*
monk (mangk) *n* monaco *m*
monkey (*mang*-ki) *n* scimmia *f*
monologue (*mo*-no-logh) *n* monologo *m*
monopoly (mö-*no*-pö-li) *n* monopolio *m*
monotonous (mö-*no*-tö-nöss) *adj* monotono
month (manθ) *n* mese *m*
monthly (*manθ*-li) *adj* mensile; ~ **magazine** rivista mensile
monument (*mo*-n[i]u-mönt) *n* monumento *m*
mood (muud) *n* umore *m*
moon (muun) *n* luna *f*
moonlight (*muun*-lait) *n* chiaro di luna
moor (mu[ö]) *n* brughiera *f*, landa *f*
moose (muuss) *n* (pl ~, ~s) alce *m*
moped (*mou*-pêd) *n* micromotore *m*
moral (*mo*-röl) *n* morale *f*; *adj* morale; **morals** costumi *mpl*
morality (mö-*ræ*-lö-ti) *n* moralità *f*
more (moo) *adj* più; **once** ~ ancora una volta
moreover (moo-*rou*-vö) *adv* inoltre
morning (*moo*-ning) *n* mattino *m*, mattina *f*; ~ **paper** giornale del mattino; **this** ~ stamani
Moroccan (mö-*ro*-kön) *adj* marocchino
Morocco (mö-*ro*-kou) Marocco *m*
morphia (*moo*-fi-ö) *n* morfina *f*
morphine (*moo*-fiin) *n* morfina *f*
morsel (*moo*-ssöl) *n* pezzetto *m*
mortal (*moo*-töl) *adj* letale, mortale
mortgage (*moo*-ghidʒ) *n* ipoteca *f*
mosaic (mö-*sei*-ik) *n* mosaico *m*
mosque (mossk) *n* moschea *f*
mosquito (mö-*sskii*-tou) *n* (pl ~es) zanzara *f*
mosquito-net (mö-*sskii*-tou-nêt) *n* zanzariera *f*
moss (moss) *n* muschio *m*
most (mousst) *adj* il più; **at** ~ al massimo, tutt'al più; ~ **of all** soprattutto
mostly (*mousst*-li) *adv* per lo più
motel (mou-*têl*) *n* autostello *m*
moth (moθ) *n* tarma *f*
mother (*ma*-ðö) *n* madre *f*; ~ **tongue** lingua materna
mother-in-law (*ma*-ðö-rin-loo) *n* (pl mothers-) suocera *f*
mother-of-pearl (ma-ðö-röv-*pööl*) *n* madreperla *f*
motion (*mou*-ʃön) *n* moto *m*; mozione *f*
motive (*mou*-tiv) *n* movente *m*
motor (*mou*-tö) *n* motore *m*; *v* viaggiare in automobile; ~ **body** *Am* carrozzeria *f*; **starter** ~ avviatore *m*
motorbike (*mou*-tö-baik) *nAm* motorino *m*
motor-boat (*mou*-tö-bout) *n* motoscafo *m*
motor-car (*mou*-tö-kaa) *n* automobile *f*
motor-cycle (*mou*-tö-ssai-köl) *n* motocicletta *f*
motoring (*mou*-tö-ring) *n* automobilismo *m*
motorist (*mou*-tö-risst) *n* automobilista *m*
motorway (*mou*-tö-[u]ei) *n* autostrada *f*
motto (*mo*-tou) *n* (pl ~es, ~s) motto

m
mouldy (*moul*-di) *adj* ammuffito
mound (maund) *n* elevazione *f*
mount (maunt) *v* montare; *n* monte *m*
mountain (*maun*-tin) *n* montagna *f*; ~ **pass** passo *m*; ~ **range** catena di montagne
mountaineering (maun-ti-*ni*ö-ring) *n* alpinismo *m*
mountainous (*maun*-ti-nöss) *adj* montagnoso
mourning (*moo*-ning) *n* lutto *m*
mouse (mauss) *n* (pl mice) topo *m*
moustache (mö-*sstaaʃ*) *n* baffi *mpl*
mouth (mauθ) *n* bocca *f*; fauci *fpl*; foce *f*
mouthwash (*mauθ*-uoʃ) *n* acqua dentifricia
movable (*muu*-vö-böl) *adj* mobile
move (muuv) *v* *muovere; spostare; traslocare; *commuovere; *n* mossa *f*; trasloco *m*
movement (*muuv*-mönt) *n* movimento *m*
movie (*muu*-vi) *n* film *m*; **movies** *Am* cinema *m*; ~ **theater** *Am* cinema *m*
much (matʃ) *adj* molto; **as** ~ altrettanto; tanto
muck (mak) *n* melma *f*
mud (mad) *n* fango *m*
muddle (*ma*-döl) *n* imbroglio *m*, pasticcio *m*; *v* impasticciare
muddy (*ma*-di) *adj* fangoso
mud-guard (*mad*-ghaad) *n* parafango *m*
muffler (*maf*-lö) *nAm* silenziatore *m*
mug (magh) *n* boccale *m*, tazza *f*
mulberry (*mal*-bö-ri) *n* mora *f*
mule (miuul) *n* mulo *m*
mullet (*ma*-lit) *n* triglia *f*
multiplication (mal-ti-pli-*kei*-ʃön) *n* moltiplicazione *f*
multiply (*mal*-ti-plai) *v* moltiplicare
mumps (mampss) *n* orecchioni *mpl*
municipal (miuu-*ni*-ssi-pöl) *adj* municipale
municipality (miuu-ni-ssi-*pæ*-lö-ti) *n* municipalità *f*
murder (*möö*-dö) *n* assassinio *m*; *v* assassinare
murderer (*möö*-dö-rö) *n* assassino *m*
muscle (*ma*-ssöl) *n* muscolo *m*
muscular (*ma*-sskiu-lö) *adj* muscoloso
museum (miuu-*sii*-öm) *n* museo *m*
mushroom (*maʃ*-ruum) *n* fungo mangereccio; fungo *m*
music (*miuu*-sik) *n* musica *f*; ~ **academy** conservatorio *m*
musical (*miuu*-si-köl) *adj* musicale; *n* commedia musicale
music-hall (*miuu*-sik-hool) *n* teatro di varietà
musician (miuu-*si*-ʃön) *n* musicista *m*
muslin (*mas*-lin) *n* mussolina *f*
mussel (*ma*-ssöl) *n* cozza *f*
***must** (masst) *v* *dovere
mustard (*ma*-sstöd) *n* senape *f*
mute (miuut) *adj* muto
mutiny (*miuu*-ti-ni) *n* ammutinamento *m*
mutton (*ma*-tön) *n* montone *m*
mutual (*miuu*-tʃu-öl) *adj* mutuo, reciproco
my (mai) *adj* mio
myself (mai-*ssêlf*) *pron* mi; io stesso
mysterious (mi-*ssti*ö-ri-öss) *adj* misterioso
mystery (*mi*-sstö-ri) *n* enigma *m*, mistero *m*
myth (miθ) *n* mito *m*

N

nail (neil) *n* unghia *f*; chiodo *m*
nailbrush (*neil*-braʃ) *n* spazzolino per le unghie
nail-file (*neil*-fail) *n* limetta per le unghie
nail-polish (*neil*-po-liʃ) *n* smalto per unghie
nail-scissors (*neil*-ssi-sös) *pl* forbicine per le unghie
naïve (naa-*iiv*) *adj* ingenuo
naked (*nei*-kid) *adj* nudo; spoglio
name (neim) *n* nome *m*; *v* nominare; **in the ~ of** a nome di
namely (*neim*-li) *adv* cioè
nap (næp) *n* pisolino *m*
napkin (*næp*-kin) *n* tovagliolo *m*
nappy (*næ*-pi) *n* pannolino *m*
narcosis (naa-*kou*-ssiss) *n* (pl -ses) narcosi *f*
narcotic (naa-*ko*-tik) *n* narcotico *m*
narrow (*næ*-rou) *adj* angusto, stretto
narrow-minded (næ-rou-*main*-did) *adj* meschino
nasty (*naa*-ssti) *adj* antipatico, sgradevole
nation (*nei*-ʃön) *n* nazione *f*; popolo *m*
national (*næ*-ʃö-nöl) *adj* nazionale; statale; **~ anthem** inno nazionale; **~ dress** costume nazionale; **~ park** parco nazionale
nationality (næ-ʃö-*næ*-lö-ti) *n* nazionalità *f*
nationalize (*næ*-ʃö-nö-lais) *v* nazionalizzare
native (*nei*-tiv) *n* indigeno *m*; *adj* nativo; **~ country** patria *f*, paese natio; **~ language** lingua materna
natural (*næ*-tʃö-röl) *adj* naturale; innato
naturally (*næ*-tʃö-rö-li) *adv* naturalmente
nature (*nei*-tʃö) *n* natura *f*; indole *f*
naughty (*noo*-ti) *adj* cattivo
nausea (*noo*-ssi-ö) *n* nausea *f*
naval (*nei*-völ) *adj* navale
navel (*nei*-völ) *n* ombelico *m*
navigable (*næ*-vi-ghö-böl) *adj* navigabile
navigate (*næ*-vi-gheit) *v* navigare; governare
navigation (næ-vi-*ghei*-ʃön) *n* navigazione *f*
navy (*nei*-vi) *n* marina *f*
near (niö) *prep* vicino a; *adj* vicino
nearby (*niö*-bai) *adj* vicino
nearly (*niö*-li) *adv* quasi
neat (niit) *adj* lindo, curato; puro
necessary (*nê*-ssö-ssö-ri) *adj* necessario
necessity (nö-*ssê*-ssö-ti) *n* necessità *f*
neck (nêk) *n* collo *m*; **nape of the ~** nuca *f*
necklace (*nêk*-löss) *n* collana *f*
necktie (*nêk*-tai) *n* cravatta *f*
need (niid) *v* *occorrere, *aver bisogno di, bisognare; *n* bisogno *m*, necessità *f*; **~ to** *dovere
needle (*nii*-döl) *n* ago *m*
negative (*nê*-ghö-tiv) *adj* negativo; *n* negativa *f*
neglect (ni-*ghlêkt*) *v* trascurare; *n* negligenza *f*
neglectful (ni-*ghlêkt*-föl) *adj* negligente
negligee (*nê*-ghli-ʒei) *n* vestaglia *f*
negotiate (ni-*ghou*-ʃi-eit) *v* negoziare
negotiation (ni-ghou-ʃi-*ei*-ʃön) *n* trattativa *f*
Negro (*nii*-ghrou) *n* (pl ~es) negro *m*
neighbour (*nei*-bö) *n* vicino *m*
neighbourhood (*nei*-bö-hud) *n* vicinato *m*
neighbouring (*nei*-bö-ring) *adj* conti-

guo, adiacente
neither (*nai*-ðö) *pron* né l'uno né l'altro; **neither ... nor** né ... né
neon (*nii*-on) *n* neon *m*
nephew (*nê*-f[i]uu) *n* nipote *m*
nerve (nööv) *n* nervo *m*; audacia *f*
nervous (*nöö*-vöss) *adj* nervoso
nest (nêsst) *n* nido *m*
net (nêt) *n* rete *f*; *adj* netto
the Netherlands (*nê*-ðö-lönds) Paesi Bassi
network (*nêt*-[u]öök) *n* rete *f*
neuralgia (n[i]u[ö]-*ræl*-dʒö) *n* nevralgia *f*
neurosis (n[i]u[ö]-*rou*-ssiss) *n* nevrosi *f*
neuter (*n[i]uu*-tö) *adj* neutro
neutral (*n[i]uu*-tröl) *adj* neutrale
never (*nê*-vö) *adv* non... mai
nevertheless (nê-vö-ðö-*lêss*) *adv* tuttavia
new (n[i]uu) *adj* nuovo; **New Year** anno nuovo
news (n[i]uus) *n* notiziario *m*, novità *f*; notizie
newsagent (*n[i]uu*-sei-dʒönt) *n* giornalaio *m*
newspaper (*n[i]uus*-pei-pö) *n* giornale *m*
newsreel (*n[i]uus*-riil) *n* cinegiornale *m*
newsstand (*n[i]uus*-sstænd) *n* edicola *f*
New Zealand (n[i]uu *sii*-lönd) Nuova Zelanda
next (nêksst) *adj* prossimo; ~ **to** vicino a
next-door (nêksst-*doo*) *adv* accanto
nice (naiss) *adj* carino, bellino, piacevole; buono; simpatico
nickel (*ni*-köl) *n* nichelio *m*
nickname (*nik*-neim) *n* nomignolo *m*
nicotine (*ni*-kö-tiin) *n* nicotina *f*
niece (niiss) *n* nipote *f*
Nigeria (nai-*dʒi[ö]*-ri-ö) Nigeria *f*
Nigerian (nai-*dʒi[ö]*-ri-ön) *adj* nigeriano
night (nait) *n* notte *f*; sera *f*; **by** ~ di notte; ~ **flight** volo notturno; ~ **rate** tariffa notturna; ~ **train** treno notturno
nightclub (*nait*-klab) *n* locale notturno
night-cream (*nait*-kriim) *n* crema per la notte
nightdress (*nait*-drêss) *n* camicia da notte
nightingale (*nai*-ting-gheil) *n* usignolo *m*
nightly (*nait*-li) *adj* notturno
nil (nil) niente
nine (nain) *num* nove
nineteen (nain-*tiin*) *num* diciannove
nineteenth (nain-*tiinθ*) *num* diciannovesimo
ninety (*nain*-ti) *num* novanta
ninth (nainθ) *num* nono
nitrogen (*nai*-trö-dʒön) *n* azoto *m*
no (nou) no; *adj* nessuno; ~ **one** nessuno
nobility (nou-*bi*-lö-ti) *n* nobiltà *f*
noble (*nou*-böl) *adj* nobile
nobody (*nou*-bo-di) *pron* nessuno
nod (nod) *n* cenno con la testa; *v* annuire
noise (nois) *n* rumore *m*; baccano *m*, chiasso *m*
noisy (*noi*-si) *adj* rumoroso; sonoro
nominal (*no*-mi-nöl) *adj* nominale
nominate (*no*-mi-neit) *v* nominare
nomination (no-mi-*nei*-ʃön) *n* nomina *f*
none (nan) *pron* nessuno
nonsense (*non*-ssönss) *n* sciocchezza *f*
noon (nuun) *n* mezzogiorno *m*
normal (*noo*-möl) *adj* normale
north (nooθ) *n* nord *m*; settentrione *m*; *adj* settentrionale; **North Pole** polo Nord
north-east (nooθ-*iisst*) *n* nord-est *m*
northerly (*noo*-ðö-li) *adj* settentrionale

northern (*noo*-ðön) *adj* nordico
north-west (nooθ-*ᵘêsst*) *n* nord-ovest *m*
Norway (*noo*-ᵘei) Norvegia *f*
Norwegian (noo-*ᵘii*-dʒön) *adj* norvegese
nose (nous) *n* naso *m*
nosebleed (*nous*-bliid) *n* rinorragia *f*
nostril (*no*-sstril) *n* narice *f*
not (not) *adv* non
notary (*nou*-tö-ri) *n* notaio *m*
note (nout) *n* appunto *m*, biglietto *m*; commento *m*; tono *m*; *v* annotare; osservare, notare
notebook (*nout*-buk) *n* taccuino *m*
noted (*nou*-tid) *adj* illustre
notepaper (*nout*-pei-pö) *n* carta da lettere
nothing (*na*-θing) *n* nulla *m*, niente
notice (*nou*-tiss) *v* rilevare, *accorgersi di, notare; *vedere; *n* avviso *m*, notizia *f*; attenzione *f*
noticeable (*nou*-ti-ssö-böl) *adj* percettibile; notevole
notify (*nou*-ti-fai) *v* notificare; avvisare
notion (*nou*-ʃön) *n* nozione *f*
notorious (nou-*too*-ri-öss) *adj* famigerato
nougat (*nuu*-ghaa) *n* torrone *m*
nought (noot) *n* zero *m*
noun (naun) *n* nome *m*
nourishing (*na*-ri-ʃing) *adj* nutriente
novel (*no*-völ) *n* romanzo *m*
novelist (*no*-vö-lisst) *n* romanziere *m*
November (nou-*vêm*-bö) novembre
now (nau) *adv* ora; adesso; ~ **and then** di tanto in tanto
nowadays (*nau*-ö-deis) *adv* oggigiorno
nowhere (*nou*-ᵘêᵒ) *adv* in nessun luogo
nozzle (*no*-söl) *n* becco *m*
nuance (nʲuu-*angss*) *n* sfumatura *f*
nuclear (*nʲuu*-kli-ö) *adj* nucleare; ~ **energy** energia nucleare
nucleus (*nʲuu*-kli-öss) *n* nucleo *m*
nude (nʲuud) *adj* nudo; *n* nudo *m*
nuisance (*nʲuu*-ssönss) *n* seccatura *f*
numb (nam) *adj* intorpidito; intirizzito
number (*nam*-bö) *n* numero *m*; cifra *f*; quantità *f*
numeral (*nʲuu*-mö-röl) *n* numerale *m*
numerous (*nʲuu*-mö-röss) *adj* numeroso
nun (nan) *n* monaca *f*
nunnery (*na*-nö-ri) *n* convento *m*
nurse (nööss) *n* infermiera *f*; bambinaia *f*; *v* curare; allattare
nursery (*nöö*-ssö-ri) *n* camera dei bambini; nido *m*; vivaio *m*
nut (nat) *n* noce *f*; dado *m*
nutcrackers (*nat*-kræ-kös) *pl* schiaccianoci *m*
nutmeg (*nat*-mêgh) *n* noce moscata
nutritious (nʲuu-*tri*-ʃöss) *adj* nutriente
nutshell (*nat*-ʃêl) *n* guscio di noce
nylon (*nai*-lon) *n* nailon *m*

O

oak (ouk) *n* quercia *f*
oar (oo) *n* remo *m*
oasis (ou-*ei*-ssiss) *n* (pl oases) oasi *f*
oath (ouθ) *n* giuramento *m*
oats (outss) *pl* avena *f*
obedience (ö-*bii*-di-önss) *n* ubbidienza *f*
obedient (ö-*bii*-di-önt) *adj* ubbidiente
obey (ö-*bei*) *v* ubbidire
object[1] (*ob*-dʒikt) *n* oggetto *m*; obiettivo *m*
object[2] (öb-*dʒêkt*) *v* obiettare; ~ **to** *opporsi a
objection (öb-*dʒêk*-ʃön) *n* obiezione *f*

objective (öb-*dʒêk*-tiv) *adj* oggettivo; *n* obiettivo *m*
obligatory (ö-*bli*-ghö-tö-ri) *adj* obbligatorio
oblige (ö-*blaidʒ*) *v* obbligare; ***be obliged to** *essere obbligato a; *dovere
obliging (ö-*blai*-dʒing) *adj* servizievole
oblong (*ob*-long) *adj* oblungo; *n* rettangolo *m*
obscene (öb-*ssiin*) *adj* osceno
obscure (öb-*sskⁱuö*) *adj* scuro, oscuro, buio
observation (ob-sö-*vei*-ʃön) *n* osservazione *f*
observatory (öb-*söö*-vö-tri) *n* osservatorio *m*
observe (öb-*sööv*) *v* osservare
obsession (öb-*ssê*-ʃön) *n* ossessione *f*
obstacle (*ob*-sstö-köl) *n* ostacolo *m*
obstinate (*ob*-ssti-nöt) *adj* ostinato; caparbio
obtain (öb-*tein*) *v* conseguire, *ottenere
obtainable (öb-*tei*-nö-böl) *adj* ottenibile
obvious (*ob*-vi-öss) *adj* ovvio
occasion (ö-*kei*-ʒön) *n* occasione *f*; motivo *m*
occasionally (ö-*kei*-ʒö-nö-li) *adv* ogni tanto, occasionalmente
occupant (*o*-kⁱu-pönt) *n* occupante *m*
occupation (o-kⁱu-*pei*-ʃön) *n* occupazione *f*
occupy (*o*-kⁱu-pai) *v* occupare
occur (ö-*köö*) *v* *succedere, capitare, *accadere
occurrence (ö-*ka*-rönss) *n* evento *m*
ocean (*ou*-ʃön) *n* oceano *m*
October (ok-*tou*-bö) ottobre
octopus (*ok*-tö-pöss) *n* polipo *m*
oculist (*o*-kⁱu-lisst) *n* oculista *m*
odd (od) *adj* bizzarro, strano; dispari
odour (*ou*-dö) *n* odore *m*
of (ov, öv) *prep* di
off (of) *adv* via; *prep* giù da
offence (ö-*fênss*) *n* reato *m*; offesa *f*, scandalo *m*
offend (ö-*fênd*) *v* *offendere; trasgredire
offensive (ö-*fên*-ssiv) *adj* offensivo; insultante; *n* offensiva *f*
offer (*o*-fö) *v* *offrire; presentare; *n* offerta *f*
office (*o*-fiss) *n* ufficio *m*; funzione *f*; ~ **hours** ore d'ufficio
officer (*o*-fi-ssö) *n* ufficiale *m*
official (ö-*fi*-ʃöl) *adj* ufficiale
off-licence (*of*-lai-ssönss) *n* spaccio di liquori
often (*o*-fön) *adv* spesso
oil (oil) *n* olio *m*; petrolio *m*; **fuel** ~ nafta *f*; ~ **filter** filtro dell'olio; ~ **pressure** pressione dell'olio
oil-painting (oil-*pein*-ting) *n* pittura ad olio
oil-refinery (*oil*-ri-fai-nö-ri) *n* raffineria di petrolio
oil-well (*oil*-ᵘêl) *n* pozzo di petrolio
oily (*oi*-li) *adj* oleoso
ointment (*oint*-mönt) *n* unguento *m*
okay! (ou-*kei*) d'accordo!
old (ould) *adj* vecchio; ~ **age** vecchiaia *f*
old-fashioned (ould-*fæ*-ʃönd) *adj* antiquato
olive (*o*-liv) *n* oliva *f*; ~ **oil** olio d'oliva
omelette (*om*-löt) *n* frittata *f*
ominous (*o*-mi-nöss) *adj* sinistro
omit (ö-*mit*) *v* *omettere
omnipotent (om-*ni*-pö-tönt) *adj* onnipotente
on (on) *prep* su; a
once (ᵘanss) *adv* una volta; **at** ~ subito; ~ **more** ancora una volta
oncoming (*on*-ka-ming) *adj* imminente

one (ᵘan) *num* uno; *pron* uno
oneself (ᵘan-*ssêlf*) *pron* sé stesso
onion (*a*-nⁱön) *n* cipolla *f*
only (*oun*-li) *adj* solo; *adv* solo, soltanto, solamente; *conj* però
onwards (*on*-ᵘöds) *adv* avanti
onyx (*o*-nikss) *n* onice *f*
opal (*ou*-pöl) *n* opale *m*
open (*ou*-pön) *v* *aprire; *adj* aperto; franco
opening (*ou*-pö-ning) *n* apertura *f*
opera (*o*-pö-rö) *n* opera *f*; ~ **house** teatro dell'opera
operate (*o*-pö-reit) *v* agire, funzionare; operare
operation (o-pö-*rei*-ʃön) *n* funzionamento *m*; operazione *f*
operator (*o*-pö-rei-tö) *n* centralinista *f*
operetta (o-pö-*rê*-tö) *n* operetta *f*
opinion (ö-*pi*-nⁱön) *n* parere *m*, opinione *f*
opponent (ö-*pou*-nönt) *n* avversario *m*
opportunity (o-pö-*tʲuu*-nö-ti) *n* opportunità *f*, occasione *f*
oppose (ö-*pous*) *v* *opporsi
opposite (*o*-pö-sit) *prep* di fronte a; *adj* contrario, opposto
opposition (o-pö-*si*-ʃön) *n* opposizione *f*
oppress (ö-*prêss*) *v* *opprimere
optician (op-*ti*-ʃön) *n* ottico *m*
optimism (*op*-ti-mi-söm) *n* ottimismo *m*
optimist (*op*-ti-misst) *n* ottimista *m*
optimistic (op-ti-*mi*-sstik) *adj* ottimistico
optional (*op*-ʃö-nöl) *adj* facoltativo
or (oo) *conj* o
oral (*oo*-röl) *adj* orale
orange (*o*-rindʒ) *n* arancia *f*; *adj* arancione
orchard (*oo*-tʃöd) *n* frutteto *m*
orchestra (*oo*-ki-sströ) *n* orchestra *f*; ~ **seat** *Am* poltrona d'orchestra
order (*oo*-dö) *v* comandare; ordinare; *n* ordine *m*; comando *m*; ordinazione *f*; **in** ~ in ordine; **in** ~ **to** allo scopo di; **made to** ~ fatto su misura; **out of** ~ fuori uso; **postal** ~ vaglia postale
order-form (*oo*-dö-foom) *n* modulo di ordinazione
ordinary (*oo*-dön-ri) *adj* solito, ordinario
ore (oo) *n* minerale *m*
organ (*oo*-ghön) *n* organo *m*
organic (oo-*ghæ*-nik) *adj* organico
organization (oo-ghö-nai-*sei*-ʃön) *n* organizzazione *f*
organize (*oo*-ghö-nais) *v* organizzare
Orient (*oo*-ri-önt) *n* oriente *m*
oriental (oo-ri-*ên*-töl) *adj* orientale
orientate (*oo*-ri-ön-teit) *v* orientarsi
origin (*o*-ri-dʒin) *n* origine *f*; discendenza *f*, provenienza *f*
original (ö-*ri*-dʒi-nöl) *adj* autentico, originale
originally (ö-*ri*-dʒi-nö-li) *adv* originariamente
orlon (*oo*-lon) *n* orlon *m*
ornament (*oo*-nö-mönt) *n* ornamento *m*
ornamental (oo-nö-*mên*-töl) *adj* ornamentale
orphan (*oo*-fön) *n* orfano *m*
orthodox (*oo*-θö-dokss) *adj* ortodosso
ostrich (*o*-sstritʃ) *n* struzzo *m*
other (*a*-ðö) *adj* altro
otherwise (*a*-ðö-ᵘais) *conj* altrimenti; *adv* altrimenti
***ought to** (oot) *dovere
our (auᵒ) *adj* nostro
ourselves (auᵒ-*ssêlvs*) *pron* ci; noi stessi
out (aut) *adv* fuori; ~ **of** fuori di, da
outbreak (*aut*-breik) *n* scoppio *m*
outcome (*aut*-kam) *n* risultato *m*

***outdo** (aut-*duu*) *v* superare
outdoors (aut-*doos*) *adv* all'aperto
outer (*au*-tö) *adj* esterno
outfit (*aut*-fit) *n* equipaggiamento *m*
outline (*aut*-lain) *n* contorno *m*; *v* abbozzare
outlook (*aut*-luk) *n* prospettiva *f*; punto di vista
output (*aut*-put) *n* produzione *f*
outrage (*aut*-reidʒ) *n* oltraggio *m*
outside (aut-*ssaid*) *adv* fuori; *prep* fuori di; *n* esteriore *m*, esterno *m*
outsize (*aut*-ssais) *n* taglia fuori misura
outskirts (*aut*-ssköötss) *pl* sobborgo *m*
outstanding (aut-*sstæn*-ding) *adj* eminente
outward (*aut*-ᵘöd) *adj* esterno
outwards (*aut*-ᵘöds) *adv* al di fuori
oval (*ou*-völ) *adj* ovale
oven (*a*-vön) *n* forno *m*
over (*ou*-vö) *prep* sopra; oltre; *adv* al di sopra; giù; *adj* finito; ~ **there** laggiù
overall (*ou*-vö-rool) *adj* globale
overalls (*ou*-vö-rools) *pl* tuta *f*
overcast (*ou*-vö-kaasst) *adj* coperto
overcoat (*ou*-vö-kout) *n* soprabito *m*
***overcome** (ou-vö-*kam*) *v* *vincere
overdue (ou-vö-*dʲuu*) *adj* in ritardo; arretrato
overgrown (ou-vö-*ghroun*) *adj* coperto di fogliame
overhaul (ou-vö-*hool*) *v* revisionare
overhead (ou-vö-*hêd*) *adv* in su
overlook (ou-vö-*luk*) *v* trascurare
overnight (ou-vö-*nait*) *adv* di notte
overseas (ou-vö-*ssiis*) *adj* oltremarino
oversight (*ou*-vö-ssait) *n* svista *f*
***oversleep** (ou-vö-*ssliip*) *v* dormire troppo
overstrung (ou-vö-*sstrang*) *adj* esausto
***overtake** (ou-vö-*teik*) *v* oltrepassare; **no overtaking** divieto di sorpasso
over-tired (ou-vö-*taiᵒd*) *adj* esausto
overture (*ou*-vö-tʃö) *n* ouverture *f*
overweight (*ou*-vö-ᵘeit) *n* soprappeso *m*
overwhelm (ou-vö-*ᵘêlm*) *v* *sopraffare, schiacciare
overwork (ou-vö-*ᵘöök*) *v* lavorare troppo
owe (ou) *v* *dovere; **owing to** a motivo di, a causa di
owl (aul) *n* gufo *m*
own (oun) *v* *possedere; *adj* proprio
owner (*ou*-nö) *n* proprietario *m*
ox (okss) *n* (pl oxen) bue *m*
oxygen (*ok*-ssi-dʒön) *n* ossigeno *m*
oyster (*oi*-sstö) *n* ostrica *f*

P

pace (peiss) *n* andatura *f*; passo *m*; velocità *f*
Pacific Ocean (pö-*ssi*-fik *ou*-ʃön) Oceano Pacifico
pacifism (*pæ*-ssi-fi-söm) *n* pacifismo *m*
pacifist (*pæ*-ssi-fisst) *n* pacifista *m*
pack (pæk) *v* imballare; ~ **up** imballare
package (*pæ*-kidʒ) *n* pacco *m*
packet (*pæ*-kit) *n* pacchetto *m*
packing (*pæ*-king) *n* imballaggio *m*
pad (pæd) *n* cuscinetto *m*; blocco per appunti
paddle (*pæ*-döl) *n* remo *m*
padlock (*pæd*-lok) *n* lucchetto *m*
pagan (*pei*-ghön) *adj* pagano; *n* pagano *m*
page (peidʒ) *n* pagina *f*
page-boy (*peidʒ*-boi) *n* paggio *m*
pail (peil) *n* secchio *m*
pain (pein) *n* dolore *m*; **pains** pena *f*

painful (*pein*-föl) *adj* penoso
painless (*pein*-löss) *adj* indolore
paint (peint) *n* colore *m*; *v* pitturare; verniciare
paint-box (*peint*-bokss) *n* scatola di colori
paint-brush (*peint*-braʃ) *n* pennello *m*
painter (*pein*-tö) *n* pittore *m*
painting (*pein*-ting) *n* pittura *f*
pair (pêö) *n* paio *m*
Pakistan (paa-ki-*sstaan*) Pakistan *m*
Pakistani (paa-ki-*sstaa*-ni) *adj* pachistano
palace (*pæ*-löss) *n* palazzo *m*
pale (peil) *adj* pallido; chiaro
palm (paam) *n* palma *f*
palpable (*pæl*-pö-böl) *adj* palpabile
palpitation (pæl-pi-*tei*-ʃön) *n* palpitazione *f*
pan (pæn) *n* tegame *m*
pane (pein) *n* vetro *m*
panel (*pæ*-nöl) *n* pannello *m*
panelling (*pæ*-nö-ling) *n* rivestimento a pannelli
panic (*pæ*-nik) *n* panico *m*
pant (pænt) *v* ansimare
panties (*pæn*-tis) *pl* mutandine *fpl*, mutande *fpl*
pants (pæntss) *pl* mutande *fpl*; *plAm* calzoni *mpl*
pant-suit (*pænt*-ssuut) *n* giacca e calzoni
panty-hose (*pæn*-ti-hous) *n* calzamaglia *f*
paper (*pei*-pö) *n* carta *f*; giornale *m*; di carta; **carbon** ~ carta carbone; ~ **bag** sacchetto *m*; ~ **napkin** tovagliolo di carta; **typing** ~ carta da macchina; **wrapping** ~ carta da imballaggio
paperback (*pei*-pö-bæk) *n* libro in brossura
paper-knife (*pei*-pö-naif) *n* tagliacarte *m*
parade (pö-*reid*) *n* parata *f*
paraffin (*pæ*-rö-fin) *n* petrolio *m*
paragraph (*pæ*-rö-ghraaf) *n* capoverso *m*, paragrafo *m*
parakeet (*pæ*-rö-kiit) *n* parrocchetto *m*
paralise (*pæ*-rö-lais) *v* paralizzare
parallel (*pæ*-rö-lêl) *adj* parallelo; *n* parallela *f*
parcel (*paa*-ssöl) *n* pacco *m*, pacchetto *m*
pardon (*paa*-dön) *n* perdono *m*; grazia *f*
parents (*pêö*-röntss) *pl* genitori *mpl*
parents-in-law (*pêö*-röntss-in-loo) *pl* suoceri
parish (*pæ*-riʃ) *n* parrocchia *f*
park (paak) *n* parco *m*; *v* posteggiare
parking (*paa*-king) *n* parcheggio *m*; **no** ~ divieto di sosta; ~ **fee** tariffa del parcheggio; ~ **light** luce di posizione; ~ **lot** *Am* parcheggio *m*; ~ **meter** parchimetro *m*; ~ **zone** zona di parcheggio
parliament (*paa*-lö-mönt) *n* parlamento *m*
parliamentary (paa-lö-*mên*-tö-ri) *adj* parlamentare
parrot (*pæ*-röt) *n* pappagallo *m*
parsley (*paa*-ssli) *n* prezzemolo *m*
parson (*paa*-ssön) *n* pastore *m*
parsonage (*paa*-ssö-nidʒ) *n* presbiterio *m*
part (paat) *n* parte *f*; pezzo *m*; *v* separare; **spare** ~ pezzo di ricambio
partial (*paa*-ʃöl) *adj* parziale
participant (paa-*ti*-ssi-pönt) *n* partecipante *m*
participate (paa-*ti*-ssi-peit) *v* partecipare
particular (pö-*ti*-kʲu-lö) *adj* speciale, particolare; esigente; **in** ~ in particolare
parting (*paa*-ting) *n* addio *m*; scrimi-

natura *f*
partition (paa-*ti*-ʃön) *n* divisorio *m*
partly (*paat*-li) *adv* in parte
partner (*paat*-nö) *n* compagno *m*; socio *m*
partridge (*paa*-tridʒ) *n* pernice *f*
party (*paa*-ti) *n* partito *m*; festa *f*; gruppo *m*
pass (paass) *v* *trascorrere, passare, sorpassare; *vAm* oltrepassare; **no passing** *Am* divieto di sorpasso; ~ **by** passare accanto; ~ **through** attraversare
passage (*pæ*-ssidʒ) *n* passaggio *m*; traversata *f*; brano *m*
passenger (*pæ*-ssön-dʒö) *n* passeggero *m*; ~ **car** *Am* vagone *m*; ~ **train** treno passeggeri
passer-by (paa-ssö-*bai*) *n* passante *m*
passion (*pæ*-ʃön) *n* passione *f*; collera *f*
passionate (*pæ*-ʃö-nöt) *adj* appassionato
passive (*pæ*-ssiv) *adj* passivo
passport (*paass*-poot) *n* passaporto *m*; ~ **control** controllo passaporti; ~ **photograph** foto per passaporto
password (*paass*-^{u}ööd) *n* parola d'ordine
past (paasst) *n* passato *m*; *adj* scorso, passato; *prep* lungo, al di là di
paste (peisst) *n* pasta *f*; *v* incollare
pastry (*pei*-sstri) *n* pasticceria *f*; ~ **shop** pasticceria *f*
pasture (*paass*-tʃö) *n* pascolo *m*
patch (pætʃ) *v* rappezzare
patent (*pei*-tönt) *n* brevetto *m*
path (paaθ) *n* sentiero *m*
patience (*pei*-ʃönss) *n* pazienza *f*
patient (*pei*-ʃönt) *adj* paziente; *n* paziente *m*
patriot (*pei*-tri-öt) *n* patriota *m*
patrol (pö-*troul*) *n* pattuglia *f*; *v* pattugliare; sorvegliare
pattern (*pæ*-tön) *n* disegno *m*
pause (poos) *n* pausa *f*; *v* *interrompersi
pave (peiv) *v* lastricare, pavimentare
pavement (*peiv*-mönt) *n* marciapiede *m*; pavimento *m*
pavilion (pö-*vil*-^{i}ön) *n* padiglione *m*
paw (poo) *n* zampa *f*
pawn (poon) *v* impegnare; *n* pedina *f*
pawnbroker (*poon*-brou-kö) *n* prestatore su pegno
pay (pei) *n* salario *m*, paga *f*
***pay** (pei) *v* pagare; *rendere; ~ **attention to** *stare attento a; **paying** rimunerativo; ~ **off** saldare; ~ **on account** pagare a rate
pay-desk (*pei*-dêssk) *n* cassa *f*
payee (pei-*ii*) *n* beneficiario *m*
payment (*pei*-mönt) *n* pagamento *m*
pea (pii) *n* pisello *m*
peace (piiss) *n* pace *f*
peaceful (*piiss*-föl) *adj* pacifico
peach (piitʃ) *n* pesca *f*
peacock (*pii*-kok) *n* pavone *m*
peak (piik) *n* vetta *f*; cima *f*; ~ **hour** ora di punta; ~ **season** alta stagione
peanut (*pii*-nat) *n* arachide *f*
pear (pê^{ö}) *n* pera *f*
pearl (pööl) *n* perla *f*
peasant (*pê*-sönt) *n* contadino *m*
pebble (*pê*-böl) *n* ciottolo *m*
peculiar (pi-*k^{i}uul*-^{i}ö) *adj* strano; speciale, particolare
peculiarity (pi-k^{i}uu-li-*æ*-rö-ti) *n* singolarità *f*
pedal (*pê*-döl) *n* pedale *m*
pedestrian (pi-*dê*-sstri-ön) *n* pedone *m*; **no pedestrians** vietato ai pedoni; ~ **crossing** passaggio pedonale
pedicure (*pê*-di-k^{i}u^{ö}) *n* pedicure *m*
peel (piil) *v* sbucciare; *n* buccia *f*
peep (piip) *v* spiare
peg (pêgh) *n* gancio *m*

pelican (*pê*-li-kön) *n* pellicano *m*
pelvis (*pêl*-viss) *n* bacino *m*
pen (pên) *n* penna *f*
penalty (*pê*-nöl-ti) *n* penalità *f*; pena *f*; ~ **kick** calcio di rigore
pencil (*pên*-ssöl) *n* matita *f*
pencil-sharpener (*pên*-ssöl-ʃaap-nö) *n* temperamatite *m*
pendant (*pên*-dönt) *n* pendente *m*
penetrate (*pê*-ni-treit) *v* penetrare
penguin (*pêng*-ghᵘin) *n* pinguino *m*
penicillin (pê-ni-*ssi*-lin) *n* penicillina *f*
peninsula (pö-*nin*-ssⁱu-lö) *n* penisola *f*
penknife (*pên*-naif) *n* (pl -knives) temperino *m*
pension[1] (*pang*-ssi-ong) *n* pensione *f*
pension[2] (*pên*-ʃön) *n* pensione *f*
people (*pii*-pöl) *pl* gente *f*; *n* popolo *m*
pepper (*pê*-pö) *n* pepe *m*
peppermint (*pê*-pö-mint) *n* menta peperina
perceive (pö-*ssiiv*) *v* percepire
percent (pö-*ssênt*) *n* percento *m*
percentage (pö-*ssên*-tidʒ) *n* percentuale *f*
perceptible (pö-*ssêp*-ti-böl) *adj* percettibile
perception (pö-*ssêp*-ʃön) *n* percezione *f*
perch (pöötʃ) (pl ~) pesce persico
percolator (*pöö*-kö-lei-tö) *n* filtro *m*
perfect (*pöö*-fikt) *adj* perfetto
perfection (pö-*fêk*-ʃön) *n* perfezione *f*
perform (pö-*foom*) *v* compiere, eseguire
performance (pö-*foo*-mönss) *n* rappresentazione *f*
perfume (*pöö*-fⁱuum) *n* profumo *m*
perhaps (pö-*hæpss*) *adv* forse
peril (*pê*-ril) *n* pericolo *m*
perilous (*pê*-ri-löss) *adj* pericoloso
period (*piᵒ*-ri-öd) *n* epoca *f*, periodo *m*; punto *m*
periodical (piᵒ-ri-*o*-di-köl) *n* periodico *m*; *adj* periodico
perish (*pê*-riʃ) *v* perire
perishable (*pê*-ri-ʃö-böl) *adj* deperibile
perjury (*pöö*-dʒö-ri) *n* spergiuro *m*
permanent (*pöö*-mö-nönt) *adj* duraturo, permanente; stabile, fisso; ~ **press** stiratura permanente; ~ **wave** permanente *f*
permission (pö-*mi*-ʃön) *n* permesso *m*, autorizzazione *f*; licenza *f*
permit[1] (pö-*mit*) *v* *permettere
permit[2] (*pöö*-mit) *n* permesso *m*
peroxide (pö-*rok*-ssaid) *n* acqua ossigenata *m*
perpendicular (pöö-pön-*di*-kⁱu-lö) *adj* perpendicolare
Persia (*pöö*-ʃö) Persia *f*
Persian (*pöö*-ʃön) *adj* persiano
person (*pöö*-ssön) *n* persona *f*; **per** ~ per persona
personal (*pöö*-ssö-nöl) *adj* personale
personality (pöö-ssö-*næ*-lö-ti) *n* personalità *f*
personnel (pöö-ssö-*nêl*) *n* personale *m*
perspective (pö-*sspêk*-tiv) *n* prospettiva *f*
perspiration (pöö-sspö-*rei*-ʃön) *n* traspirazione *f*, sudore *m*
perspire (pö-*sspaiᵒ*) *v* traspirare, sudare
persuade (pö-*ssᵘeid*) *v* *persuadere; *convincere
persuasion (pö-*ssᵘei*-ʒön) *n* convinzione *f*
pessimism (*pê*-ssi-mi-söm) *n* pessimismo *m*
pessimist (*pê*-ssi-misst) *n* pessimista *m*
pessimistic (pê-ssi-*mi*-sstik) *adj* pessimistico
pet (pêt) *n* animale domestico; cocco

m; favorito
petal (*pê*-töl) *n* petalo *m*
petition (pi-*ti*-ʃön) *n* petizione *f*
petrol (*pê*-tröl) *n* benzina *f*; ~ **pump** pompa di benzina; ~ **station** distributore di benzina; ~ **tank** serbatoio di benzina
petroleum (pi-*trou*-li-öm) *n* petrolio *m*
petty (*pê*-ti) *adj* piccolo, futile, insignificante; ~ **cash** moneta spicciola
pewit (*pii*-ᵘit) *n* pavoncella *f*
pewter (*pʲuu*-tö) *n* peltro *m*
phantom (*fæn*-töm) *n* fantasma *m*
pharmacology (faa-mö-*ko*-lö-dʒi) *n* farmacologia *f*
pharmacy (*faa*-mö-ssi) *n* farmacia *f*
phase (feis) *n* fase *f*
pheasant (*fê*-sönt) *n* fagiano *m*
Philippine (*fi*-li-pain) *adj* filippino
Philippines (*fi*-li-piins) *pl* Isole Filippine
philosopher (fi-*lo*-ssö-fö) *n* filosofo *m*
philosophy (fi-*lo*-ssö-fi) *n* filosofia *f*
phone (foun) *n* telefono *m*; *v* telefonare
phonetic (fö-*nê*-tik) *adj* fonetico
photo (*fou*-tou) *n* (pl ~s) foto *f*
photograph (*fou*-tö-ghraaf) *n* fotografia *f*; *v* fotografare
photographer (fö-*to*-ghrö-fö) *n* fotografo *m*
photography (fö-*to*-ghrö-fi) *n* fotografia *f*
photostat (*fou*-tö-sstæt) *n* copia fotostatica
phrase (freis) *n* frase *f*
phrase-book (*freis*-buk) *n* manuale di conversazione
physical (*fi*-si-köl) *adj* fisico
physician (fi-*si*-ʃön) *n* medico *m*
physicist (*fi*-si-ssisst) *n* fisico *m*
physics (*fi*-sikss) *n* fisica *f*
physiology (fi-si-*o*-lö-dʒi) *n* fisiologia *f*

pianist (*pii*-ö-nisst) *n* pianista *m*
piano (pi-*æ*-nou) *n* pianoforte *m*; **grand** ~ pianoforte a coda
pick (pik) *v* *cogliere; *scegliere; *n* scelta *f*; ~ **up** *raccogliere; rilevare; **pick-up van** camionetta *f*
pick-axe (*pi*-kækss) *n* piccone *m*
pickles (*pi*-köls) *pl* sottaceti *mpl*
picnic (*pik*-nik) *n* picnic *m*; *v* *fare un picnic
picture (*pik*-tʃö) *n* pittura *f*; illustrazione *f*, stampa *f*; figura *f*, quadro *m*; ~ **postcard** cartolina illustrata; **pictures** cinema *m*
picturesque (pik-tʃö-*rêssk*) *adj* pittoresco
piece (piiss) *n* pezzo *m*
pier (piᵒ) *n* molo *m*
pierce (piᵒss) *v* perforare
pig (pigh) *n* maiale *m*; porco *m*
pigeon (*pi*-dʒön) *n* piccione *m*
pig-headed (pigh-*hê*-did) *adj* testardo
piglet (*pigh*-löt) *n* porcellino *m*
pigskin (*pigh*-sskin) *n* pelle di cinghiale
pike (paik) (pl ~) luccio *m*
pile (pail) *n* mucchio *m*; *v* ammucchiare; **piles** *pl* emorroidi *fpl*
pilgrim (*pil*-ghrim) *n* pellegrino *m*
pilgrimage (*pil*-ghri-midʒ) *n* pellegrinaggio *m*
pill (pil) *n* pillola *f*
pillar (*pi*-lö) *n* pilastro *m*, colonna *f*
pillar-box (*pi*-lö-bokss) *n* buca delle lettere
pillow (*pi*-lou) *n* guanciale *m*
pillow-case (*pi*-lou-keiss) *n* federa *f*
pilot (*pai*-löt) *n* pilota *m*
pimple (*pim*-pöl) *n* pustoletta *f*
pin (pin) *n* spillo *m*; *v* appuntare; **bobby** ~ *Am* fermaglio per capelli
pincers (*pin*-ssös) *pl* tenaglie *fpl*
pinch (pintʃ) *v* pizzicare
pineapple (*pai*-næ-pöl) *n* ananas *m*

ping-pong (*ping*-pong) *n* tennis da tavolo
pink (pingk) *adj* rosa
pioneer (pai-ö-*niö*) *n* pioniere *m*
pious (*pai*-öss) *adj* pio
pip (pip) *n* seme *m*
pipe (paip) *n* pipa *f*; tubatura *f*; ~ **cleaner** curapipe *m*; ~ **tobacco** tabacco da pipa
pirate (*paiö*-röt) *n* pirata *m*
pistol (*pi*-sstöl) *n* pistola *f*
piston (*pi*-sstön) *n* stantuffo *m*; ~ **ring** anello per stantuffo
piston-rod (*pi*-sstön-rod) *n* asta dello stantuffo
pit (pit) *n* buca *f*; miniera *f*
pitcher (*pi*-tʃö) *n* brocca *f*
pity (*pi*-ti) *n* pietà *f*; *v* provare compassione per, compatire; **what a pity!** peccato!
placard (*plæ*-kaad) *n* affisso *m*
place (pleiss) *n* posto *m*; *v* posare, *porre; ~ **of birth** luogo di nascita; ***take** ~ *aver luogo
plague (pleigh) *n* flagello *m*
plaice (pleiss) (pl ~) passera di mare
plain (plein) *adj* chiaro; ordinario, semplice; *n* pianura *f*
plan (plæn) *n* progetto *m*; pianta *f*; *v* progettare
plane (plein) *adj* piano; *n* aereo *m*; ~ **crash** incidente aereo
planet (*plæ*-nit) *n* pianeta *m*
planetarium (plæ-ni-*têö*-ri-öm) *n* planetario *m*
plank (plængk) *n* asse *f*
plant (plaant) *n* pianta *f*; impianto *m*; *v* piantare
plantation (plæn-*tei*-ʃön) *n* piantagione *f*
plaster (*plaa*-sstö) *n* stucco *m*, gesso *m*; cerotto *m*
plastic (*plæ*-sstik) *adj* plastico; *n* plastica *f*
plate (pleit) *n* piatto *m*; lamiera *f*
plateau (*plæ*-tou) *n* (pl ~x, ~s) altopiano *m*
platform (*plæt*-foom) *n* banchina *f*
platinum (*plæ*-ti-nöm) *n* platino *m*
play (plei) *v* giocare; sonare; *n* gioco *m*; rappresentazione teatrale; **one-act** ~ commedia in un atto; ~ **truant** marinare la scuola
player (pleiö) *n* giocatore *m*
playground (*plei*-ghraund) *n* cortile di ricreazione
playing-card (*plei*-ing-kaad) *n* carta da gioco
playwright (*plei*-rait) *n* drammaturgo *m*
plea (plii) *n* difesa *f*
plead (pliid) *v* perorare
pleasant (*plê*-sönt) *adj* gradevole, simpatico, piacevole
please (pliis) per favore; *v* *piacere; **pleased** lieto; **pleasing** gradevole
pleasure (*plê*-ʒö) *n* diletto *m*, divertimento *m*, piacere *m*
plentiful (*plên*-ti-föl) *adj* abbondante
plenty (*plên*-ti) *n* abbondanza *f*
pliers (plaiös) *pl* pinze *fpl*
plimsolls (*plim*-ssöls) *pl* scarpe da ginnastica
plot (plot) *n* congiura *f*, complotto *m*; trama *f*; appezzamento *m*
plough (plau) *n* aratro *m*; *v* arare
plucky (*pla*-ki) *adj* coraggioso
plug (plagh) *n* spina *f*; ~ **in** *connettere
plum (plam) *n* susina *f*
plumber (*pla*-mö) *n* idraulico *m*
plump (plamp) *adj* grassottello
plural (*pluö*-röl) *n* plurale *m*
plus (plass) *prep* più
pneumatic (nʲuu-*mæ*-tik) *adj* pneumatico
pneumonia (nʲuu-*mou*-ni-ö) *n* polmonite *f*

poach (poutʃ) *v* cacciare di frodo
pocket (*po*-kit) *n* tasca *f*
pocket-book (*po*-kit-buk) *n* portafoglio *m*
pocket-comb (*po*-kit-koum) *n* pettine tascabile
pocket-knife (*po*-kit-naif) *n* (pl -knives) temperino *m*
pocket-watch (*po*-kit-ᵘotʃ) *n* orologio da tasca
poem (*pou*-im) *n* poema *m*
poet (*pou*-it) *n* poeta *m*
poetry (*pou*-i-tri) *n* poesia *f*
point (point) *n* punto *m*; punta *f*; *v* additare; ~ **of view** punto di vista; ~ **out** indicare
pointed (*poin*-tid) *adj* appuntato
poison (*poi*-sön) *n* veleno *m*; *v* avvelenare
poisonous (*poi*-sö-nöss) *adj* velenoso
Poland (*pou*-lönd) Polonia *f*
Pole (poul) *n* polacco *m*
pole (poul) *n* palo *m*
police (pö-*liiss*) *pl* polizia *f*
policeman (pö-*liiss*-mön) *n* (pl -men) agente *m*, poliziotto *m*
police-station (pö-*liiss*-sstei-ʃön) *n* posto di polizia
policy (*po*-li-ssi) *n* politica *f*; polizza *f*
polio (*pou*-li-ou) *n* polio *f*, poliomielite *f*
Polish (*pou*-liʃ) *adj* polacco
polish (*po*-liʃ) *v* lucidare
polite (pö-*lait*) *adj* cortese
political (pö-*li*-ti-köl) *adj* politico
politician (po-li-*ti*-ʃön) *n* uomo politico
politics (*po*-li-tikss) *n* politica *f*
pollution (pö-*luu*-ʃön) *n* contaminazione *f*, inquinamento *m*
pond (pond) *n* stagno *m*
pony (*pou*-ni) *n* cavallino *m*
poor (puᵒ) *adj* povero; misero; scadente
pope (poup) *n* Papa *m*
poplin (*po*-plin) *n* popelina *f*
pop music (pop *mʲuu*-sik) musica pop
poppy (*po*-pi) *n* rosolaccio *m*; papavero *m*
popular (*po*-pʲu-lö) *adj* popolare
population (po-pʲu-*lei*-ʃön) *n* popolazione *f*
populous (*po*-pʲu-löss) *adj* popoloso
porcelain (*poo*-ssö-lin) *n* porcellana *f*
porcupine (*poo*-kʲu-pain) *n* porcospino *m*
pork (pook) *n* carne di maiale
port (poot) *n* porto *m*; babordo *m*
portable (*poo*-tö-böl) *adj* portatile
porter (*poo*-tö) *n* facchino *m*; portiere *m*
porthole (*poot*-houl) *n* boccaporto *m*
portion (*poo*-ʃön) *n* porzione *f*
portrait (*poo*-trit) *n* ritratto *m*
Portugal (*poo*-tʲu-ghöl) Portogallo *m*
Portuguese (poo-tʲu-*ghiis*) *adj* portoghese
position (pö-*si*-ʃön) *n* posizione *f*; situazione *f*; atteggiamento *m*
positive (*po*-sö-tiv) *adj* positivo; *n* positiva *f*
possess (pö-*sêss*) *v* *possedere; **possessed** *adj* indemoniato
possession (pö-*sê*-ʃön) *n* possesso *m*; **possessions** possedimenti *mpl*
possibility (po-ssö-*bi*-lö-ti) *n* possibilità *f*
possible (*po*-ssö-böl) *adj* possibile; eventuale
post (pousst) *n* palo *m*; impiego *m*; posta *f*; *v* impostare; **post-office** ufficio postale
postage (*pou*-sstidʒ) *n* affrancatura *f*; ~ **paid** franco di porto; ~ **stamp** francobollo *m*
postcard (*pousst*-kaad) *n* cartolina *f*; cartolina illustrata
poster (*pou*-sstö) *n* cartellone *m*,

poster *m*
poste restante (pousst rê-*sstangt*) fermo posta
postman (*pousst*-mön) *n* (pl -men) postino *m*
post-paid (pousst-*peid*) *adj* porto franco
postpone (pö-*sspoun*) *v* rimandare
pot (pot) *n* pentola *f*
potato (pö-*tei*-tou) *n* (pl ~es) patata *f*
pottery (*po*-tö-ri) *n* ceramica *f*; stoviglie *fpl*
pouch (pautʃ) *n* sacchetto *m*
poulterer (*poul*-tö-rö) *n* pollivendolo *m*
poultry (*poul*-tri) *n* pollame *m*
pound (paund) *n* libbra *f*
pour (poo) *v* versare
poverty (*po*-vö-ti) *n* povertà *f*
powder (*pau*-dö) *n* polvere *f*; ~ **compact** portacipria *m*; **talc** ~ talco *m*
powder-puff (*pau*-dö-paf) *n* piumino da cipria
powder-room (*pau*-dö-ruum) *n* gabinetto per signore
power (pau^{ö}) *n* potenza *f*, energia *f*; potere *m*
powerful (*pau*^{ö}-föl) *adj* potente, poderoso; forte
powerless (*pau*^{ö}-löss) *adj* impotente
power-station (*pau*^{ö}-sstei-ʃön) *n* centrale elettrica
practical (*præk*-ti-köl) *adj* pratico
practically (*præk*-ti-kli) *adv* praticamente
practice (*præk*-tiss) *n* pratica *f*
practise (*præk*-tiss) *v* praticare; esercitarsi
praise (preis) *v* lodare; *n* elogio *m*
pram (præm) *n* carrozzina *f*
prawn (proon) *n* gambero *m*, aragostina *f*
pray (prei) *v* pregare
prayer (prê^{ö}) *n* preghiera *f*
preach (priitʃ) *v* predicare
precarious (pri-*kê*^{ö}-ri-öss) *adj* precario
precaution (pri-*koo*-ʃön) *n* precauzione *f*
precede (pri-*ssiid*) *v* precedere
preceding (pri-*ssii*-ding) *adj* precedente
precious (*prê*-ʃöss) *adj* prezioso
precipice (*prê*-ssi-piss) *n* precipizio *m*
precipitation (pri-ssi-pi-*tei*-ʃön) *n* precipitazione *f*
precise (pri-*ssaiss*) *adj* preciso, esatto; meticoloso
predecessor (*prii*-di-ssê-ssö) *n* predecessore *m*
predict (pri-*dikt*) *v* *predire
prefer (pri-*föö*) *v* preferire
preferable (*prê*-fö-rö-böl) *adj* preferibile
preference (*prê*-fö-rönss) *n* preferenza *f*
prefix (*prii*-fikss) *n* prefisso *m*
pregnant (*prêgh*-nönt) *adj* incinta
prejudice (*prê*-dʒö-diss) *n* pregiudizio *m*
preliminary (pri-*li*-mi-nö-ri) *adj* preliminare
premature (*prê*-mö-tʃu^{ö}) *adj* prematuro
premier (*prêm*-i^{ö}) *n* primo ministro
premises (*prê*-mi-ssis) *pl* stabile *m*
premium (*prii*-mi-öm) *n* premio *m*
prepaid (prii-*peid*) *adj* pagato in anticipo
preparation (prê-pö-*rei*-ʃön) *n* preparazione *f*
prepare (pri-*pê*^{ö}) *v* preparare
preposition (prê-pö-*si*-ʃön) *n* preposizione *f*
prescribe (pri-*sskraib*) *v* *prescrivere
prescription (pri-*sskrip*-ʃön) *n* ricetta *f*
presence (*prê*-sönss) *n* presenza *f*
present[1] (*prê*-sönt) *n* regalo *m*, dono

m; presente *m*; *adj* attuale; presente
present² (pri-*sênt*) *v* presentare
presently (*prê*-sönt-li) *adv* a momenti, subito
preservation (prê-sö-*vei*-ʃön) *n* preservazione *f*
preserve (pri-*söov*) *v* conservare; *mettere in conserva
president (*prê*-si-dönt) *n* presidente *m*
press (prêss) *n* stampa *f*; *v* schiacciare, premere; stirare; ~ **conference** conferenza stampa
pressing (*prê*-ssing) *adj* pressante, urgente
pressure (*prê*-ʃö) *n* pressione *f*; tensione *f*; **atmospheric** ~ pressione atmosferica
pressure-cooker (*prê*-ʃö-ku-kö) *n* pentola a pressione
prestige (prê-*sstiiʒ*) *n* prestigio *m*
presumable (pri-*sʲuu*-mö-böl) *adj* presumibile
presumptuous (pri-*samp*-ʃöss) *adj* presuntuoso
pretence (pri-*tênss*) *n* pretesa *f*
pretend (pri-*tênd*) *v* *fingere, *pretendere
pretext (*prii*-têksst) *n* pretesto *m*
pretty (*pri*-ti) *adj* bello, carino; *adv* alquanto, piuttosto, abbastanza
prevent (pri-*vênt*) *v* impedire; *prevenire
preventive (pri-*vên*-tiv) *adj* preventivo
previous (*prii*-vi-öss) *adj* precedente, anteriore, previo
pre-war (prii-*ᵘoo*) *adj* d'anteguerra
price (praiss) *v* prezzare; ~ **list** listino prezzi
priceless (*praiss*-löss) *adj* inestimabile
price-list (*praiss*-lisst) *n* prezzo *m*
prick (prik) *v* *pungere
pride (praid) *n* fierezza *f*
priest (priisst) *n* prete *m*
primary (*prai*-mö-ri) *adj* primario; primo, principale; elementare
prince (prinss) *n* principe *m*
princess (prin-*ssêss*) *n* principessa *f*
principal (*prin*-ssö-pöl) *adj* principale; *n* preside *m*, direttore *m*
principle (*prin*-ssö-pöl) *n* principio *m*
print (print) *v* stampare; *n* positiva *f*; stampa *f*; **printed matter** stampe
prior (praiᵒ) *adj* anteriore
priority (prai-*o*-rö-ti) *n* precedenza *f*, priorità *f*
prison (*pri*-sön) *n* prigione *f*
prisoner (*pri*-sö-nö) *n* detenuto *m*, prigioniero *m*; ~ **of war** prigioniero di guerra
privacy (*prai*-vö-ssi) *n* intimità *f*
private (*prai*-vit) *adj* privato; personale
privilege (*pri*-vi-lidʒ) *n* privilegio *m*
prize (prais) *n* premio *m*; ricompensa *f*
probable (*pro*-bö-böl) *adj* probabile
probably (*pro*-bö-bli) *adv* probabilmente
problem (*pro*-blöm) *n* problema *m*
procedure (prö-*ssii*-dʒö) *n* procedimento *m*
proceed (prö-*ssiid*) *v* procedere
process (*prou*-ssêss) *n* procedimento *m*, processo *m*
procession (prö-*ssê*-ʃön) *n* processione *f*, corteo *m*
proclaim (prö-*kleim*) *v* proclamare
produce¹ (prö-*dʲuuss*) *v* *produrre
produce² (*prod*-ʲuuss) *n* prodotto *m*
producer (prö-*dʲuu*-ssö) *n* produttore *m*
product (*pro*-dakt) *n* prodotto *m*
production (prö-*dak*-ʃön) *n* produzione *f*
profession (prö-*fê*-ʃön) *n* professione *f*
professional (prö-*fê*-ʃö-nöl) *adj* pro-

fessionale
professor (prö-*fê*-ssö) *n* professore *m*
profit (*pro*-fit) *n* profitto *m*, guadagno *m*; vantaggio *m*; *v* approfittare
profitable (*pro*-fi-tö-böl) *adj* fruttuoso
profound (prö-*faund*) *adj* profondo
programme (*prou*-ghræm) *n* programma *m*
progress[1] (*prou*-ghrêss) *n* progresso *m*
progress[2] (prö-*ghrêss*) *v* progredire
progressive (prö-*ghrê*-ssiv) *adj* progressista; progressivo
prohibit (prö-*hi*-bit) *v* proibire
prohibition (prou-i-*bi*-ʃön) *n* divieto *m*
prohibitive (prö-*hi*-bi-tiv) *adj* proibitivo
project (*pro*-dʒêkt) *n* piano *m*, progetto *m*
promenade (pro-mö-*naad*) *n* corso *m*
promise (*pro*-miss) *n* promessa *f*; *v* *promettere
promote (prö-*mout*) *v* *promuovere
promotion (prö-*mou*-ʃön) *n* promozione *f*
prompt (prompt) *adj* sollecito, pronto
pronoun (*prou*-naun) *n* pronome *m*
pronounce (prö-*naunss*) *v* pronunciare
pronunciation (prö-nan-ssi-*ei*-ʃön) *n* pronuncia *f*
proof (pruuf) *n* prova *f*
propaganda (pro-pö-*ghæn*-dö) *n* propaganda *f*
propel (prö-*pêl*) *v* propulsare
propeller (prö-*pê*-lö) *n* elica *f*
proper (*pro* pö) *adj* giusto; decente, conveniente, adatto, appropriato
property (*pro*-pö-ti) *n* proprietà *f*
prophet (*pro*-fit) *n* profeta *m*
proportion (prö-*poo*-ʃön) *n* proporzione *f*
proportional (prö-*poo*-ʃö-nöl) *adj* proporzionale
proposal (prö *pou*-söl) *n* proposta *f*
propose (prö-*pous*) *v* *proporre
proposition (pro-pö-*si*-ʃön) *n* proposta *f*
proprietor (prö-*prai*-ö-tö) *n* proprietario *m*
prospect (*pro*-sspêkt) *n* prospettiva *f*
prospectus (prö-*sspêk*-töss) *n* prospetto *m*
prosperity (pro-*sspê*-rö-ti) *n* prosperità *f*
prosperous (*pro*-sspö-röss) *adj* fiorente
prostitute (*pro*-ssti-tʲuut) *n* prostituta *f*
protect (prö-*têkt*) *v* *proteggere
protection (prö-*têk*-ʃön) *n* protezione *f*
protein (*prou*-tiin) *n* proteina *f*
protest[1] (*prou*-têsst) *n* protesta *f*
protest[2] (prö-*têsst*) *v* protestare
Protestant (*pro*-ti-sstönt) *adj* protestante
proud (praud) *adj* fiero; orgoglioso
prove (pruuv) *v* dimostrare, provare; mostrarsi
proverb (*pro*-vööb) *n* proverbio *m*
provide (prö-*vaid*) *v* fornire, *provvedere; **provided that** purché
province (*pro*-vinss) *n* provincia *f*
provincial (prö-*vin*-ʃöl) *adj* provinciale
provisional (prö-*vi*-ʒö-nöl) *adj* provvisorio
provisions (prö-*vi*-ʒöns) *pl* provvisioni *fpl*
prune (pruun) *n* prugna secca
psychiatrist (ssai-*kai*-ö-trisst) *n* psichiatra *m*
psychic (*ssai*-kik) *adj* psichico
psychoanalyst (ssai-kou-*æ*-nö-lisst) *n* psicoanalista *m*
psychological (ssai-ko-*lo*-dʒi-köl) *adj* psicologico
psychologist (ssai-*ko*-lö-dʒisst) *n* psi-

cologo *m*
psychology (ssai-*ko*-lö-dʒi) *n* psicologia *f*
pub (pab) *n* taverna *f*; bar *m*
public (*pa*-blik) *adj* pubblico; generale; *n* pubblico *m*; ~ **garden** giardino pubblico; ~ **house** taverna *f*
publication (pa-bli-*kei*-ʃön) *n* pubblicazione *f*
publicity (pa-*bli*-ssö-ti) *n* pubblicità *f*
publish (*pa*-bliʃ) *v* pubblicare
publisher (*pa*-bli-ʃö) *n* editore *m*
puddle (*pa*-döl) *n* pozzanghera *f*
pull (pul) *v* tirare; ~ **out** partire; ~ **up** fermarsi
pulley (*pu*-li) *n* (pl ~s) carrucola *f*
Pullman (*pul*-mön) *n* vettura pullman
pullover (*pu*-lou-vö) *n* maglione *m*
pulpit (*pul*-pit) *n* cattedra *f*, pulpito *m*
pulse (palss) *n* polso *m*
pump (pamp) *n* pompa *f*; *v* pompare
punch (pantʃ) *v* sferrare pugni; *n* pugno *m*
punctual (*pangk*-tʃu-öl) *adj* puntuale
puncture (*pangk*-tʃö) *n* foratura *f*, bucatura *f*
punctured (*pangk*-tʃöd) *adj* bucato
punish (*pa*-niʃ) *v* punire
punishment (*pa*-niʃ-mönt) *n* punizione *f*
pupil (*p^i^uu*-pöl) *n* scolaro *m*
puppet-show (*pa*-pit-ʃou) *n* rappresentazione di marionette
purchase (*pöö*-tʃöss) *v* comprare; *n* compera *f*, acquisto *m*; ~ **price** prezzo d'acquisto; ~ **tax** tassa di scambio
purchaser (*pöö*-tʃö-ssö) *n* compratore *m*
pure (p^i^u^ö^) *adj* casto, puro
purple (*pöö*-pöl) *adj* porporino
purpose (*pöö*-pöss) *n* proposito *m*, fine *m*, intenzione *f*; **on** ~ apposta
purse (pööss) *n* borsellino *m*
pursue (pö-*ss^i^uu*) *v* perseguire
pus (pass) *n* pus *m*
push (puʃ) *n* urto *m*, spinta *f*; *v* *spingere; *farsi largo
push-button (*puʃ*-ba-tön) *n* pulsante *m*
***put** (put) *v* collocare, posare, *mettere; *porre; ~ **away** *mettere a posto; ~ **off** rinviare; ~ **on** indossare; ~ **out** *spegnere
puzzle (*pa*-söl) *n* rompicapo *m*; enigma *m*; *v* imbarazzare; **jigsaw** ~ puzzle
puzzling (*pas*-ling) *adj* imbarazzante
pyjamas (pö-*dʒaa*-mös) *pl* pigiama *m*

Q

quack (k^u^æk) *n* medicone *m*, ciarlatano *m*
quail (k^u^eil) *n* (pl ~, ~s) quaglia *f*
quaint (k^u^eint) *adj* bizzarro; antiquato
qualification (k^u^o-li-fi-*kei*-ʃön) *n* qualifica *f*; riserva *f*, restrizione *f*
qualified (*k^u^o*-li-faid) *adj* qualificato; competente
qualify (*k^u^o*-li-fai) *v* *addirsi
quality (*k^u^o*-lö-ti) *n* qualità *f*; caratteristica *f*
quantity (*k^u^on*-tö-ti) *n* quantità *f*; numero *m*
quarantine (*k^u^o*-rön-tiin) *n* quarantena *f*
quarrel (*k^u^o*-röl) *v* litigare; *n* litigio *m*, lite *f*
quarry (*k^u^o*-ri) *n* cava *f*
quarter (*k^u^oo*-tö) *n* quarto *m*; trimestre *m*; quartiere *m*; ~ **of an hour** quarto d'ora
quarterly (*k^u^oo*-tö-li) *adj* trimestrale

quay (kii) *n* molo *m*
queen (k^{u}iin) *n* regina *f*
queer (k^{u}i^{ö}) *adj* singolare, strano; bizzarro
query (*k^{u}i^{ö}*-ri) *n* domanda *f*; *v* domandare; *mettere in dubbio
question (*k^{u}êss*-tʃön) *n* questione *f*; problema *m*; *v* interrogare; *mettere in dubbio; ~ **mark** punto interrogativo
queue (k^{j}uu) *n* coda *f*; *v* *fare la coda
quick (k^{u}ik) *adj* svelto
quick-tempered (k^{u}ik-*têm*-pöd) *adj* irascibile
quiet (*k^{u}ai*-öt) *adj* quieto, calmo, tranquillo; *n* quiete *f*, tranquillità *f*
quilt (k^{u}ilt) *n* coperta *f*
quinine (k^{u}i-*niin*) *n* chinino *m*
quit (k^{u}it) *v* cessare, *smettere
quite (k^{u}ait) *adv* interamente, completamente; alquanto, abbastanza, piuttosto; assai, molto
quiz (k^{u}is) *n* (pl ~zes) quiz *m*
quota (*k^{u}ou*-tö) *n* quota *f*
quotation (k^{u}ou-*tei*-ʃön) *n* citazione *f*; ~ **marks** virgolette *fpl*
quote (k^{u}out) *v* citare

R

rabbit (*ræ*-bit) *n* coniglio *m*
rabies (*rei*-bis) *n* rabbia *f*
race (reiss) *n* gara *f*, corsa *f*; razza *f*
race-course (*reiss*-kooss) *n* pista da corsa, ippodromo *m*
race-horse (*reiss*-hooss) *n* cavallo da corsa
race-track (*reiss*-træk) *n* pista da corsa
racial (*rei*-ʃöl) *adj* razziale
racket (*ræ*-kit) *n* chiasso *m*
racquet (*ræ*-kit) *n* racchetta *f*
radiator (*rei*-di-ei-tö) *n* radiatore *m*
radical (*ræ*-di-köl) *adj* radicale
radio (*rei*-di-ou) *n* radio *f*
radish (*ræ*-diʃ) *n* ravanello *m*
radius (*rei*-di-öss) *n* (pl radii) raggio *m*
raft (raaft) *n* zattera *f*
rag (rægh) *n* straccio *m*
rage (reidʒ) *n* furore *m*, rabbia *f*; *v* infierire
raid (reid) *n* irruzione *f*
rail (reil) *n* ringhiera *f*, sbarra *f*
railing (*rei*-ling) *n* inferriata *f*
railroad (*reil*-roud) *nAm* strada ferrata, ferrovia *f*
railway (*reil*-^{u}ei) *n* ferrovia *f*
rain (rein) *n* pioggia *f*; *v* *piovere
rainbow (*rein*-bou) *n* arcobaleno *m*
raincoat (*rein*-kout) *n* impermeabile *m*
rainproof (*rein*-pruuf) *adj* impermeabile
rainy (*rei*-ni) *adj* piovoso
raise (reis) *v* sollevare; aumentare; allevare, coltivare; *riscuotere; *nAm* aumento *m*
raisin (*rei*-sön) *n* uvetta *f*
rake (reik) *n* rastrello *m*
rally (*ræ*-li) *n* raduno *m*
ramp (ræmp) *n* rampa *f*
ramshackle (*ræm*-ʃæ-köl) *adj* sgangerato
rancid (*ræn*-ssid) *adj* rancido
rang (ræng) *v* (p ring)
range (reindʒ) *n* portata *f*
range-finder (*reindʒ*-fain-dö) *n* telemetro *m*
rank (rængk) *n* ceto *m*; fila *f*
ransom (*ræn*-ssöm) *n* riscatto *m*
rape (reip) *v* violentare
rapid (*ræ*-pid) *adj* veloce, rapido
rapids (*ræ*-pids) *pl* rapida *f*
rare (rê^{ö}) *adj* raro

rarely (*rêö*-li) *adv* raramente
rascal (*raa*-ssköl) *n* birbante *m*, monello *m*
rash (ræʃ) *n* esantema *m*, eruzione *f*; *adj* avventato, sconsiderato
raspberry (*raas*-bö-ri) *n* lampone *m*
rat (ræt) *n* ratto *m*
rate (reit) *n* prezzo *m*, tariffa *f*; velocità *f*; **at any** ~ ad ogni modo, comunque; ~ **of exchange** corso del cambio
rather (*raa*-ðö) *adv* abbastanza, alquanto; piuttosto
ration (*ræ*-ʃön) *n* razione *f*
rattan (ræ-*tæn*) *n* malacca *f*
raven (*rei*-vön) *n* corvo *m*
raw (roo) *adj* crudo; ~ **material** materia prima
ray (rei) *n* raggio *m*
rayon (*rei*-on) *n* raion *m*
razor (*rei*-sö) *n* rasoio *m*
razor-blade (*rei*-sö-bleid) *n* lama di rasoio
reach (riitʃ) *v* *raggiungere; *n* portata *f*
reaction (ri-*æk*-ʃön) *n* reazione *f*
***read** (riid) *v* *leggere
reading (*rii*-ding) *n* lettura *f*
reading-lamp (*rii*-ding-læmp) *n* lampada da tavolo
reading-room (*rii*-ding-ruum) *n* sala di lettura
ready (*rê*-di) *adj* pronto
ready-made (rê-di-*meid*) *adj* confezionato
real (riöl) *adj* reale
reality (ri-*æ*-lö-ti) *n* realtà *f*
realizable (*riö*-lai-sö-böl) *adj* realizzabile
realize (*riö*-lais) *v* realizzare; attuare
really (*riö*-li) *adv* davvero, veramente; in realtà
rear (riö) *n* parte posteriore; *v* allevare
rear-light (riö-*lait*) *n* fanalino posteriore
reason (*rii*-sön) *n* causa *f*, ragione *f*; senso *m*; *v* ragionare
reasonable (*rii*-sö-nö-böl) *adj* ragionevole
reassure (rii-ö-*ʃuö*) *v* tranquillizzare
rebate (*rii*-beit) *n* riduzione *f*, sconto *m*
rebellion (ri-*bêl*-iön) *n* rivolta *f*, ribellione *f*
recall (ri-*kool*) *v* ricordarsi; richiamare; revocare
receipt (ri-*ssiit*) *n* ricevuta *f*; ricevimento *m*
receive (ri-*ssiiv*) *v* ricevere
receiver (ri-*ssii*-vö) *n* ricevitore *m*
recent (*rii*-ssönt) *adj* recente
recently (*rii*-ssönt-li) *adv* di recente, recentemente
reception (ri-*ssêp*-ʃön) *n* ricevimento *m*; accoglienza *f*; ~ **office** ufficio ricevimento
receptionist (ri-*ssêp*-ʃö-nisst) *n* capo ufficio ricevimento
recession (ri-*ssê*-ʃön) *n* recessione *f*
recipe (*rê*-ssi-pi) *n* ricetta *f*
recital (ri-*ssai*-töl) *n* recital *m*
reckon (*rê*-kön) *v* *fare i calcoli; considerare; credere
recognition (rê-kögh-*ni*-ʃön) *n* riconoscimento *m*
recognize (*rê*-kögh-nais) *v* *riconoscere
recollect (rê-kö-*lêkt*) *v* ricordarsi
recommence (rii-kö-*mênss*) *v* ricominciare
recommend (rê-kö-*mênd*) *v* raccomandare; consigliare
recommendation (rê-kö-mên-*dei*-ʃön) *n* raccomandazione *f*
reconciliation (rê-kön-ssi-li-*ei*-ʃön) *n* riconciliazione *f*
record[1] (*rê*-kood) *n* disco *m*; primato

m; registrazione *f*; **long-playing** ~ microsolco *m*
record[2] (ri-*kood*) *v* registrare
recorder (ri-*koo*-dö) *n* magnetofono *m*
recording (ri-*koo*-ding) *n* registrazione *f*
record-player (*rê*-kood-pleiö) *n* giradischi *m*
recover (ri-*ka*-vö) *v* ricuperare; guarire
recovery (ri-*ka*-vö-ri) *n* guarigione *f*
recreation (rê-kri-*ei*-ʃön) *n* ricreazione *f*, svago *m*; ~ **centre** centro di ricreazione; ~ **ground** campo di gioco
recruit (ri-*kruut*) *n* recluta *f*
rectangle (*rêk*-tæng-ghöl) *n* rettangolo *m*
rectangular (rêk-*tæng*-ghiu-lö) *adj* rettangolare
rector (*rêk*-tö) *n* pastore *m*
rectory (*rêk*-tö-ri) *n* presbiterio *m*
rectum (*rêk*-töm) *n* retto *m*
red (rêd) *adj* rosso
redeem (ri-*diim*) *v* *redimere
reduce (ri-*diuuss*) *v* *ridurre, diminuire
reduction (ri-*dak*-ʃön) *n* ribasso *m*, riduzione *f*
redundant (ri-*dan*-dönt) *adj* ridondante
reed (riid) *n* giunco *m*
reef (riif) *n* banco *m*
reference (*rêf*-rönss) *n* referenza *f*, riferimento *m*; relazione *f*; **with ~ to** riguardo a
refer to (ri-*föö*) rimandare a
refill (*rii*-fil) *n* ricambio *m*
refinery (ri-*fai*-nö-ri) *n* raffineria *f*
reflect (ri-*flêkt*) *v* *riflettere
reflection (ri-*flêk*-ʃön) *n* riflesso *m*; immagine riflessa
reflector (ri-*flêk*-tö) *n* riflettore *m*
reformation (rê-fö-*mei*-ʃön) *n* riforma *f*
refresh (ri-*frêʃ*) *v* rinfrescare
refreshment (ri-*frêʃ*-mönt) *n* rinfresco *m*
refrigerator (ri-*fri*-dʒö-rei-tö) *n* frigorifero *m*
refund[1] (ri-*fand*) *v* rimborsare
refund[2] (*rii*-fand) *n* rimborso *m*
refusal (ri-*fiuu*-söl) *n* rifiuto *m*
refuse[1] (ri-*fiuus*) *v* rifiutare
refuse[2] (*rê*-fiuuss) *n* immondizia *f*
regard (ri-*ghaad*) *v* considerare; osservare; *n* riguardo *m*; **as regards** per quanto riguarda
regarding (ri-*ghaa*-ding) *prep* riguardo a; in relazione a
regatta (ri-*ghæ*-tö) *n* regata *f*
régime (rei-*ʒiim*) *n* regime *m*
region (*rii*-dʒön) *n* regione *f*
regional (*rii*-dʒö-nöl) *adj* regionale
register (*rê*-dʒi-sstö) *v* registrarsi; raccomandare; **registered letter** raccomandata *f*
registration (rê-dʒi-*sstrei*-ʃön) *n* registrazione *f*; ~ **form** foglio di registrazione; ~ **number** numero di targa; ~ **plate** targa automobilistica
regret (ri-*ghrêt*) *v* *rimpiangere; *n* rimpianto *m*
regular (*rê*-ghiu-lö) *adj* regolato, regolare; normale
regulate (*rê*-ghiu-leit) *v* regolare
regulation (rê-ghiu-*lei*-ʃön) *n* regolamento *m*; regolamentazione *f*
rehabilitation (rii-hö-bi-li-*tei*-ʃön) *n* rieducazione *f*
rehearsal (ri-*höö*-ssöl) *n* prova *f*
rehearse (ri-*hööss*) *v* *fare le prove
reign (rein) *n* regno *m*; *v* regnare
reimburse (rii-im-*bööss*) *v* *rendere, rimborsare
reindeer (*rein*-diö) *n* (pl ~) renna *f*
reject (ri-*dʒêkt*) *v* rifiutare, *respinge-

re; rigettare
relate (ri-*leit*) *v* raccontare
related (ri-*lei*-tid) *adj* congiunto
relation (ri-*lei*-ʃön) *n* relazione *f*, attinenza *f*; parente *m*
relative (*rê*-lö-tiv) *n* parente *m*; *adj* relativo
relax (ri-*lækss*) *v* rilassarsi
relaxation (ri-læk-*ssei*-ʃön) *n* rilassamento *m*
reliable (ri-*lai*-ö-böl) *adj* fidato
relic (*rê*-lik) *n* reliquia *f*
relief (ri-*liif*) *n* sollievo *m*; aiuto *m*; rilievo *m*
relieve (ri-*liiv*) *v* mitigare; *dare il cambio
religion (ri-*li*-dʒön) *n* religione *f*
religious (ri-*li*-dʒöss) *adj* religioso
rely on (ri-*lai*) contare su
remain (ri-*mein*) *v* *rimanere; restare
remainder (ri-*mein*-dö) *n* avanzo *m*, resto *m*, residuo *m*
remaining (ri-*mei*-ning) *adj* rimanente
remark (ri-*maak*) *n* osservazione *f*; *v* osservare
remarkable (ri-*maa*-kö-böl) *adj* notevole
remedy (*rê*-mö-di) *n* rimedio *m*
remember (ri-*mêm*-bö) *v* ricordarsi
remembrance (ri-*mêm*-brönss) *n* ricordo *m*
remind (ri-*maind*) *v* *far ricordare
remit (ri-*mit*) *v* *rimettere
remittance (ri-*mi*-tönss) *n* rimessa *f*
remnant (*rêm*-nönt) *n* resto *m*, rimanenza *f*, residuo *m*
remote (ri-*mout*) *adj* distante, remoto
removal (ri-*muu*-völ) *n* spostamento *m*
remove (ri-*muuv*) *v* spostare
remunerate (ri-*m*ⁱ*uu*-nö-reit) *v* rimunerare
remuneration (ri-mⁱuu-nö-*rei*-ʃön) *n* rimunerazione *f*
renew (ri-*n*ⁱ*uu*) *v* rinnovare
rent (rênt) *v* affittare; *n* affitto *m*
repair (ri-*pê*ᵒ̈) *v* riparare; *n* restauro *m*
reparation (rê-pö-*rei*-ʃön) *n* riparazione *f*
***repay** (ri-*pei*) *v* rimborsare
repayment (ri-*pei*-mönt) *n* rimborso *m*
repeat (ri-*piit*) *v* ripetere
repellent (ri-*pê*-lönt) *adj* ripugnante, repellente
repentance (ri-*pên*-tönss) *n* pentimento *m*
repertory (*rê*-pö-tö-ri) *n* repertorio *m*
repetition (rê-pö-*ti*-ʃön) *n* ripetizione *f*
replace (ri-*pleiss*) *v* sostituire
reply (ri-*plai*) *v* *rispondere; *n* risposta *f*; **in ~** in risposta
report (ri-*poot*) *v* riferire; presentarsi; *n* relazione *f*, rapporto *m*
reporter (ri-*poo*-tö) *n* corrispondente *m*
represent (rê-pri-*sênt*) *v* rappresentare; raffigurare
representation (rê-pri-sên-*tei*-ʃön) *n* rappresentanza *f*
representative (rê-pri-*sên*-tö-tiv) *adj* rappresentativo
reprimand (*rê*-pri-maand) *v* rimproverare
reproach (ri-*proutʃ*) *n* rimprovero *m*; *v* rimproverare
reproduce (rii-prö-*d*ⁱ*uuss*) *v* *riprodurre
reproduction (rii-prö-*dak*-ʃön) *n* riproduzione *f*
reptile (*rêp*-tail) *n* rettile *m*
republic (ri-*pa*-blik) *n* repubblica *f*
republican (ri-*pa*-bli-kön) *adj* repubblicano
repulsive (ri-*pal*-ssiv) *adj* ributtante
reputation (rê-pⁱu-*tei*-ʃön) *n* reputa-

zione *f*; fama *f*
request (ri-*kᵘêsst*) *n* richiesta *f*; domanda *f*; *v* *richiedere
require (ri-*kᵘaiö*) *v* *esigere
requirement (ri-*kᵘaiö*-mönt) *n* esigenza *f*
requisite (*rê*-kᵘi-sit) *adj* richiesto
rescue (*rê*-sskʲuu) *v* salvare; *n* salvataggio *m*
research (ri-*ssöötʃ*) *n* ricerca *f*
resemblance (ri-*sêm*-blönss) *n* somiglianza *f*
resemble (ri-*sêm*-böl) *v* assomigliare a
resent (ri-*sênt*) *v* risentirsi per
reservation (rê-sö-*vei*-ʃön) *n* prenotazione *f*
reserve (ri-*sööv*) *v* riservare; prenotare; *n* riserva *f*
reserved (ri-*söövd*) *adj* riservato
reservoir (*rê*-sö-vᵘaa) *n* serbatoio *m*
reside (ri-*said*) *v* abitare
residence (*rê*-si-dönss) *n* residenza *f*; ~ **permit** permesso di soggiorno
resident (*rê*-si-dönt) *n* residente *m*; *adj* residente; interno
resign (ri-*sain*) *v* *dimettersi
resignation (rê-sigh-*nei*-ʃön) *n* dimissioni *fpl*
resin (*rê*-sin) *n* resina *f*
resist (ri-*sisst*) *v* resistere
resistance (ri-*si*-sstönss) *n* resistenza *f*
resolute (*rê*-sö-luut) *adj* risoluto, deciso
respect (ri-*sspêkt*) *n* rispetto *m*; stima *f*, deferenza *f*; *v* rispettare
respectable (ri-*sspêk*-tö-böl) *adj* rispettabile
respectful (ri-*sspêkt*-föl) *adj* rispettoso
respective (ri-*sspêk*-tiv) *adj* rispettivo
respiration (rê-sspö-*rei*-ʃön) *n* respirazione *f*
respite (*rê*-sspait) *n* dilazione *f*
responsibility (ri-sspon-ssö-*bi*-lö-ti) *n* responsabilità *f*
responsible (ri-*sspon*-ssö-böl) *adj* responsabile
rest (rêsst) *n* riposo *m*; resto *m*; *v* riposarsi
restaurant (*rê*-sstö-rong) *n* ristorante *m*
restful (*rêsst*-föl) *adj* riposante
rest-home (*rêsst*-houm) *n* casa di riposo
restless (*rêsst*-löss) *adj* inquieto; irrequieto
restrain (ri-*sstrein*) *v* *contenere, *trattenere
restriction (ri-*sstrik*-ʃön) *n* restrizione *f*
result (ri-*salt*) *n* risultato *m*; conseguenza *f*; esito *m*; *v* risultare
resume (ri-*sʲuum*) *v* *riprendere
résumé (*rê*-sʲu-mei) *n* riassunto *m*
retail (*rii*-teil) *v* vendere al minuto; ~ **trade** commercio al minuto, vendita al minuto
retailer (*rii*-tei-lö) *n* dettagliante *m*; rivenditore *m*
retina (*rê*-ti-nö) *n* retina *f*
retired (ri-*taiöd*) *adj* pensionato
return (ri-*töön*) *v* ritornare; *n* ritorno *m*; ~ **flight** volo di ritorno; ~ **journey** viaggio di ritorno
reunite (rii-ʲuu-*nait*) *v* riunire
reveal (ri-*viil*) *v* svelare, rivelare
revelation (rê-vö-*lei*-ʃön) *n* rivelazione *f*
revenge (ri-*vêndʒ*) *n* vendetta *f*
revenue (*rê*-vö-nʲuu) *n* entrate, reddito *m*
reverse (ri-*vööss*) *n* contrario *m*; rovescio *m*; marcia indietro; rivolgimento *m*; *adj* inverso; *v* *far marcia indietro
review (ri-*vʲuu*) *n* recensione *f*; rivista *f*
revise (ri-*vais*) *v* revisionare
revision (ri-*vi*-ʒön) *n* revisione *f*

revival (ri-*vai*-völ) *n* ripristino *m*
revolt (ri-*voult*) *v* rivoltarsi; *n* ribellione *f*, rivolta *f*
revolting (ri-*voul*-ting) *adj* stomachevole, rivoltante, disgustoso
revolution (rê-vö-*luu*-ʃön) *n* rivoluzione *f*
revolutionary (rê-vö-*luu*-ʃö-nö-ri) *adj* rivoluzionario
revolver (ri-*vol*-vö) *n* rivoltella *f*
revue (ri-*vⁱuu*) *n* rivista *f*
reward (ri-*ᵘood*) *n* ricompensa *f*; *v* ricompensare
rheumatism (*ruu*-mö-ti-söm) *n* reumatismo *m*
rhinoceros (rai-*no*-ssö-röss) *n* (pl ~, ~es) rinoceronte *m*
rhubarb (*ruu*-baab) *n* rabarbaro *m*
rhyme (raim) *n* rima *f*
rhythm (*ri*-ðöm) *n* ritmo *m*
rib (rib) *n* costola *f*
ribbon (*ri*-bön) *n* nastro *m*
rice (raiss) *n* riso *m*
rich (ritʃ) *adj* ricco
riches (*ri*-tʃis) *pl* ricchezza *f*
riddle (*ri*-döl) *n* indovinello *m*
ride (raid) *n* corsa *f*
***ride** (raid) *v* *andare in macchina; cavalcare
rider (*rai*-dö) *n* cavallerizzo *m*
ridge (ridʒ) *n* cresta *f*
ridicule (*ri*-di-kⁱuul) *v* ridicolizzare
ridiculous (ri-*di*-kⁱu-löss) *adj* ridicolo
riding (*rai*-ding) *n* equitazione *f*
riding-school (*rai*-ding-sskuul) *n* scuola di equitazione
rifle (*rai*-föl) *v* fucile *m*
right (rait) *n* diritto *m*; *adj* corretto, giusto; retto; destro; equo; **all right!** va bene!; * **be** ~ *avere ragione; ~ **of way** precedenza *f*
righteous (*rai*-tʃöss) *adj* giusto
right-hand (*rait*-hænd) *adj* destro
rightly (*rait*-li) *adv* giustamente

rim (rim) *n* cerchione *m*; orlo *m*
ring (ring) *n* anello *m*; cerchio *m*; pista *f*
***ring** (ring) *v* suonare; ~ **up** telefonare
rinse (rinss) *v* sciacquare; *n* sciacquata *f*
riot (*rai*-öt) *n* sommossa *f*
rip (rip) *v* strappare
ripe (raip) *adj* maturo
rise (rais) *n* aumento *m*; altura *f*; rialzo *m*; ascesa *f*
***rise** (rais) *v* alzarsi; *sorgere; *salire
rising (*rai*-sing) *n* insurrezione *f*
risk (rissk) *n* rischio *m*; pericolo *m*; *v* rischiare
risky (*ri*-sski) *adj* rischioso
rival (*rai*-völ) *n* rivale *m*; concorrente *m*; *v* rivaleggiare
rivalry (*rai*-völ-ri) *n* rivalità *f*; concorrenza *f*
river (*ri*-vö) *n* fiume *m*; ~ **bank** argine *m*
riverside (*ri*-vö-ssaid) *n* lungofiume *m*
roach (routʃ) *n* (pl ~) lasca *f*
road (roud) *n* strada *f*; ~ **fork** *n* bivio *m*; ~ **map** carta stradale; ~ **system** rete stradale; ~ **up** strada in riparazione
roadhouse (*roud*-hauss) *n* locanda *f*
roadside (*roud*-ssaid) *n* margine della strada; ~ **restaurant** locanda *f*
roadway (*roud*-ᵘei) *nAm* rotabile *f*
roam (roum) *v* vagabondare
roar (roo) *v* mugghiare, ruggire; *n* ruggito *m*, rombo *m*
roast (rousst) *v* *cuocere arrosto, arrostire
rob (rob) *v* rubare
robber (*ro*-bö) *n* ladro *m*
robbery (*ro*-bö-ri) *n* rapina *f*, furto *m*
robe (roub) *n* abito femminile; veste *f*
robin (*ro*-bin) *n* pettirosso *m*
robust (rou-*basst*) *adj* robusto

rock (rok) *n* roccia *f*; *v* dondolare
rocket (*ro*-kit) *n* razzo *m*
rocky (*ro*-ki) *adj* roccioso
rod (rod) *n* barra *f*, stecca *f*
roe (rou) *n* uova di pesce
roll (roul) *v* rotolare; *n* rotolo *m*; panino *m*
roller-skating (*rou*-lö-sskei-ting) *n* pattinaggio a rotelle
Roman Catholic (*rou*-mön *kæ*-θö-lik) cattolico
romance (rö-*mænss*) *n* idillio *m*
romantic (rö-*mæn*-tik) *adj* romantico
roof (ruuf) *n* tetto *m*; **thatched ~** tetto di paglia
room (ruum) *n* camera *f*, stanza *f*; spazio *m*, vano *m*; **~ and board** vitto e alloggio; **~ service** servizio in camera; **~ temperature** temperatura ambientale
roomy (*ruu*-mi) *adj* spazioso
root (ruut) *n* radice *f*
rope (roup) *n* corda *f*
rosary (*rou*-sö-ri) *n* rosario *m*
rose (rous) *n* rosa *f*; *adj* rosa
rotten (*ro*-tön) *adj* marcio
rouge (ruuʒ) *n* rossetto *m*
rough (raf) *adj* malagevole
roulette (ruu-*lêt*) *n* roulette *f*
round (raund) *adj* rotondo; *prep* attorno a, intorno a; *n* ripresa *f*; **~ trip** *Am* andata e ritorno
roundabout (*raun*-dö-baut) *n* rotonda *f*
rounded (*raun*-did) *adj* arrotondato
route (ruut) *n* rotta *f*
routine (ruu-*tiin*) *n* abitudine *f*
row[1] (rou) *n* fila *f*; *v* remare
row[2] (rau) *n* lite *f*
rowdy (*rau*-di) *adj* turbolento
rowing-boat (*rou*-ing-bout) *n* barca a remi
royal (*roi*-öl) *adj* reale
rub (rab) *v* strofinare
rubber (*ra*-bö) *n* caucciù *m*; gomma per cancellare; **~ band** elastico *m*
rubbish (*ra*-biʃ) *n* immondizia *f*; sciocchezza *f*, stupidaggini *fpl*; **talk ~** *dire stupidaggini
rubbish-bin (*ra*-biʃ-bin) *n* pattumiera *f*
ruby (*ruu*-bi) *n* rubino *m*
rucksack (*rak*-ssæk) *n* zaino *m*
rudder (*ra*-dö) *n* timone *m*
rude (ruud) *adj* grossolano
rug (ragh) *n* tappeto *m*
ruin (*ruu*-in) *v* rovinare; *n* rovina *f*
ruination (ruu-i-*nei*-ʃön) *n* rovina *f*
rule (ruul) *n* regola *f*; regime *m*, governo *m*, dominio *m*; *v* dominare, governare; **as a ~** generalmente, di norma
ruler (*ruu*-lö) *n* monarca *m*, sovrano *m*; riga *f*
Rumania (ruu-*mei*-ni-ö) Romania *f*
Rumanian (ruu-*mei*-ni-ön) *adj* romeno
rumour (*ruu*-mö) *n* diceria *f*
***run** (ran) *v* *correre; **~ into** incontrare
runaway (*ra*-nö-ᵘei) *n* fuggitivo *m*
rung (ran) *v* (pp ring)
runway (*ran*-ᵘei) *n* pista di decollo
rural (*ruᵒ*-röl) *adj* rurale
ruse (ruus) *n* astuzia *f*
rush (raʃ) *v* affrettarsi; *n* giunco *m*
rush-hour (*raʃ*-auᵒ) *n* ora di punta
Russia (*ra*-ʃö) Russia *f*
Russian (*ra*-ʃön) *adj* russo
rust (rasst) *n* ruggine *f*
rustic (*ra*-sstik) *adj* rustico
rusty (*ra*-ssti) *adj* arrugginito

S

saccharin (*ssæ*-kö-rin) *n* saccarina *f*
sack (ssæk) *n* sacco *m*

sacred (*ssei*-krid) *adj* sacro
sacrifice (*ssæ*-kri-faiss) *n* sacrificio *m*; *v* sacrificare
sacrilege (*ssæ*-kri-lidʒ) *n* sacrilegio *m*
sad (ssæd) *adj* triste; mesto, afflitto, malinconico
saddle (*ssæ*-döl) *n* sella *f*
sadness (*ssæd*-nöss) *n* tristezza *f*
safe (sseif) *adj* sicuro; *n* cassaforte *f*
safety (*sseif*-ti) *n* sicurezza *f*
safety-belt (*sseif*-ti-bêlt) *n* cintura di sicurezza
safety-pin (*sseif*-ti-pin) *n* spillo di sicurezza
safety-razor (*sseif*-ti-rei-sö) *n* rasoio *m*
sail (sseil) *v* navigare; *n* vela *f*
sailing-boat (*ssei*-ling-bout) *n* barca a vela
sailor (*ssei*-lö) *n* marinaio *m*
saint (sseint) *n* santo *m*
salad (*ssæ*-löd) *n* insalata *f*
salad-oil (*ssæ*-löd-oil) *n* olio da tavola
salary (*ssæ*-lö-ri) *n* stipendio *m*, salario *m*
sale (sseil) *n* vendita *f*; **clearance ~** svendita *f*; **for ~** in vendita; **sales** saldi; **sales tax** tassa di scambio
saleable (*ssei*-lö-böl) *adj* vendibile
salesgirl (*sseils*-ghööl) *n* commessa *f*
salesman (*sseils*-mön) *n* (pl -men) commesso *m*
salmon (*ssæ*-mön) *n* (pl ~) salmone *m*
salon (*ssæ*-long) *n* salone *m*
saloon (ssö-*luun*) *n* bar *m*
salt (ssoolt) *n* sale *m*
salt-cellar (*ssoolt*-ssê-lö) *n* saliera *f*
salty (*ssool*-ti) *adj* salato
salute (ssö-*luut*) *v* salutare
salve (ssaav) *n* unguento *m*
same (sseim) *adj* stesso
sample (*ssaam*-pöl) *n* campione *m*
sanatorium (ssæ-nö-*too*-ri-öm) *n* (pl ~s, -ria) sanatorio *m*
sand (ssænd) *n* sabbia *f*
sandal (*ssæn*-döl) *n* sandalo *m*
sandpaper (*ssænd*-pei-pö) *n* carta vetrata
sandwich (*ssæn*-ᵘidʒ) *n* tramezzino *m*
sandy (*ssæn*-di) *adj* sabbioso
sanitary (*ssæ*-ni-tö-ri) *adj* sanitario; **~ towel** pannolino igienico
sapphire (*ssæ*-faiᵒ) *n* zaffiro *m*
sardine (ssaa-*diin*) *n* sardina *f*
satchel (*ssæ*-tʃöl) *n* cartella *f*
satellite (*ssæ*-tö-lait) *n* satellite *m*
satin (*ssæ*-tin) *n* raso *m*
satisfaction (ssæ-tiss-*fæk*-ʃön) *n* appagamento *m*, soddisfazione *f*
satisfy (*ssæ*-tiss-fai) *v* *soddisfare; **satisfied** accontentato, soddisfatto
Saturday (*ssæ*-tö-di) sabato *m*
sauce (ssooss) *n* salsa *f*
saucepan (*ssooss*-pön) *n* casseruola *f*
saucer (*ssoo*-ssö) *n* piattino *m*
Saudi Arabia (ssau-di-ö-*rei*-bi-ö) Arabia Saudita
Saudi Arabian (ssau-di-ö-*rei*-bi-ön) *adj* saudita
sauna (*ssoo*-nö) *n* sauna *f*
sausage (*sso*-ssidʒ) *n* salsiccia *f*
savage (*ssæ*-vidʒ) *adj* selvaggio
save (sseiv) *v* salvare; risparmiare
savings (*ssei*-vings) *pl* risparmi *mpl*; **~ bank** cassa di risparmio
saviour (*ssei*-vⁱö) *n* salvatore *m*
savoury (*ssei*-vö-ri) *adj* saporito; piccante
saw[1] (ssoo) *v* (p see)
saw[2] (ssoo) *n* sega *f*
sawdust (*ssoo*-dasst) *n* segatura *f*
saw-mill (*ssoo*-mil) *n* segheria *f*
***say** (ssei) *v* *dire
scaffolding (*sskæ*-föl-ding) *n* impalcatura *f*
scale (sskeil) *n* scala *f*; scala musicale; squama *f*; **scales** *pl* bilancia *f*

scandal (*sskæn*-döl) *n* scandalo *m*
Scandinavia (sskæn-di-*nei*-vi-ö) Scandinavia *f*
Scandinavian (sskæn-di-*nei*-vi-ön) *adj* scandinavo
scapegoat (*sskeip*-ghout) *n* capro espiatorio
scar (sskaa) *n* cicatrice *f*
scarce (sskê^{ö}ss) *adj* scarso
scarcely (*sskê^{ö}*-ssli) *adv* scarsamente
scarcity (*sskê^{ö}*-ssö-ti) *n* penuria *f*
scare (sskê^{ö}) *v* spaventare; *n* spavento *m*
scarf (sskaaf) *n* (pl ~s, scarves) sciarpa *f*, scialle *m*
scarlet (*sskaa*-löt) *adj* scarlatto
scary (*sskê^{ö}*-ri) *adj* allarmante
scatter (*sskæ*-tö) *v* sparpagliare
scene (ssiin) *n* scena *f*
scenery (*ssii*-nö-ri) *n* paesaggio *m*
scenic (*ssii*-nik) *adj* pittoresco
scent (ssênt) *n* profumo *m*
schedule (*ʃê*-d^{i}uul) *n* orario *m*
scheme (sskiim) *n* schema *m*; progetto *m*
scholar (*ssko*-lö) *n* erudito *m*; allievo *m*
scholarship (*ssko*-lö-ʃip) *n* borsa di studio
school (sskuul) *n* scuola *f*
schoolboy (*sskuul*-boi) *n* scolaro *m*
schoolgirl (*sskuul*-ghööl) *n* scolara *f*
schoolmaster (*sskuul*-maa-sstö) *n* insegnante *m*, maestro *m*
schoolteacher (*sskuul*-tii-tʃö) *n* insegnante *m*
science (*ssai*-önss) *n* scienza *f*
scientific (ssai-ön-*ti*-fik) *adj* scientifico
scientist (*ssai*-ön-tisst) *n* scienziato *m*
scissors (*ssi*-sös) *pl* forbici *fpl*
scold (sskould) *v* riprovare; inveire
scooter (*sskuu*-tö) *n* scooter *m*; monopattino *m*
score (sskoo) *n* punteggio *m*; *v* marcare
scorn (sskoon) *n* scherno *m*, disprezzo *m*; *v* disprezzare
Scot (sskot) *n* scozzese *m*
Scotch (sskotʃ) *adj* scozzese; **scotch tape** nastro gommato
Scotland (*sskot*-lönd) Scozia *f*
Scottish (*ssko*-tiʃ) *adj* scozzese
scout (sskaut) *n* boy-scout *m*
scrap (sskræp) *n* pezzetto *m*
scrap-book (*sskræp*-buk) *n* album per ritagli
scrape (sskreip) *v* raschiare
scrap-iron (*sskræ*-pai^{ö}n) *n* rottame di ferro
scratch (sskrætʃ) *v* scalfire, graffiare; *n* scalfittura *f*, graffio *m*
scream (sskriim) *v* urlare, strillare; *n* strillo *m*, grido *m*
screen (sskriin) *n* riparo *m*; video *m*, schermo *m*
screw (sskruu) *n* vite *f*; *v* avvitare
screw-driver (*sskruu*-drai-vö) *n* cacciavite *m*
scrub (sskrab) *v* strofinare; *n* cespuglio *m*
sculptor (*sskalp*-tö) *n* scultore *m*
sculpture (*sskalp*-tʃö) *n* scultura *f*
sea (ssii) *n* mare *m*
sea-bird (*ssii*-bööd) *n* uccello marino
sea-coast (*ssii*-kousst) *n* litorale *m*
seagull (*ssii*-ghal) *n* gabbiano *m*
seal (ssiil) *n* sigillo *m*; foca *f*
seam (ssiim) *n* cucitura *f*
seaman (*ssii*-mön) *n* (pl -men) marinaio *m*
seamless (*ssiim*-löss) *adj* senza cucitura
seaport (*ssii*-poot) *n* porto di mare
search (ssöötʃ) *v* cercare; perquisire, perlustrare; *n* ricerca *f*
searchlight (*ssöötʃ*-lait) *n* riflettore *m*
seascape (*ssii*-sskeip) *n* marina *f*
sea-shell (*ssii*-ʃêl) *n* conchiglia *f*

seashore (*ssii*-ʃoo) *n* riva del mare
seasick (*ssii*-ssik) *adj* sofferente di mal di mare
seasickness (*ssii*-ssik-nöss) *n* mal di mare
seaside (*ssii*-ssaid) *n* riva del mare; ~ **resort** stazione balneare
season (*ssii*-sön) *n* stagione *f*; **high** ~ alta stagione; **low** ~ bassa stagione; **off** ~ fuori stagione
season-ticket (*ssii*-sön-ti-kit) *n* abbonamento *m*
seat (ssiit) *n* sedia *f*; posto *m*; sede *f*
seat-belt (*ssiit*-bêlt) *n* cintura di sicurezza
sea-urchin (*ssii*-öö-tʃin) *n* riccio di mare
sea-water (*ssii*-ᵘoo-tö) *n* acqua di mare
second (*ssê*-könd) *num* secondo; *n* secondo *m*; istante *m*
secondary (*ssê*-kön-dö-ri) *adj* secondario; ~ **school** scuola media
second-hand (ssê-könd-*hænd*) *adj* d'occasione
secret (*ssii*-kröt) *n* segreto *m*; *adj* segreto
secretary (*ssê*-krö-tri) *n* segretaria *f*; segretario *m*
section (*ssêk*-ʃön) *n* sezione *f*; scomparto *m*, reparto *m*
secure (ssi-*kⁱuᵒ̈*) *adj* sicuro; *v* assicurarsi
security (ssi-*kⁱuᵒ̈*-rö-ti) *n* sicurezza *f*; cauzione *f*
sedate (ssi-*deit*) *adj* composto
sedative (*ssê*-dö-tiv) *n* sedativo *m*
seduce (ssi-*dⁱuuss*) *v* *sedurre
***see** (ssii) *v* *vedere; capire, *rendersi conto; ~ **to** occuparsi di
seed (ssiid) *n* semenza *f*
***seek** (ssiik) *v* cercare
seem (ssiim) *v* sembrare, *parere
seen (ssiin) *v* (pp see)
seesaw (*ssii*-ssoo) *n* altalena *f*
seize (ssiis) *v* afferrare
seldom (*ssêl*-döm) *adv* raramente
select (ssi-*lêkt*) *v* selezionare, *scegliere; *adj* selezionato, scelto
selection (ssi-*lêk*-ʃön) *n* scelta *f*, selezione *f*
self-centred (ssêlf-*ssên*-töd) *adj* egocentrico
self-employed (ssêl-fim-*ploid*) *adj* indipendente
self-evident (ssêl-*fê*-vi-dönt) *adj* lampante
self-government (ssêlf-*gha*-vö-mönt) *n* autogoverno *m*
selfish (*ssêl*-fiʃ) *adj* egoista
selfishness (*ssêl*-fiʃ-nöss) *n* egoismo *m*
self-service (ssêlf-*ssöö*-viss) *n* self-service *m*
***sell** (ssêl) *v* vendere
semblance (*ssêm*-blönss) *n* apparenza *f*
semi- (*ssê*-mi) semi-
semicircle (*ssê*-mi-ssöö-köl) *n* semicerchio *m*
semi-colon (ssê-mi-*kou*-lön) *n* punto e virgola
senate (*ssê*-nöt) *n* senato *m*
senator (*ssê*-nö-tö) *n* senatore *m*
***send** (ssênd) *v* mandare, spedire; ~ **back** rinviare, rispedire; ~ **for** *far venire; ~ **off** spedire
senile (*ssii*-nail) *adj* senile
sensation (ssên-*ssei*-ʃön) *n* sensazione *f*
sensational (ssên-*ssei*-ʃö-nöl) *adj* sensazionale
sense (ssênss) *n* senso *m*; discernimento *m*, ragione *f*; significato *m*; *v* percepire; ~ **of honour** sentimento dell'onore
senseless (*ssênss*-löss) *adj* insensato
sensible (*ssên*-ssö-böl) *adj* ragionevo-

le
sensitive (*ssên*-ssi-tiv) *adj* sensibile
sentence (*ssên*-tönss) *n* frase *f*; sentenza *f*; *v* condannare
sentimental (ssên-ti-*mên*-töl) *adj* sentimentale
separate[1] (*ssê*-pö-reit) *v* separare
separate[2] (*ssê*-pö-röt) *adj* distinto, separato
separately (*ssê*-pö-röt-li) *adv* a parte
September (ssêp-*têm*-bö) settembre
septic (*ssêp*-tik) *adj* settico; ***become** ~ infiammarsi
sequel (*ssii*-kuöl) *n* continuazione *f*
sequence (*ssii*-kuönss) *n* successione *f*; serie *f*
serene (ssö-*riin*) *adj* calmo; sereno
serial (*ssi*ö-ri-öl) *n* romanzo a puntate
series (*ssi*ö-riis) *n* (pl ~) serie *f*
serious (*ssi*ö-ri-öss) *adj* serio
seriousness (*ssi*ö-ri-öss-nöss) *n* serietà *f*
sermon (*ssöö*-mön) *n* sermone *m*
serum (*ssi*ö-röm) *n* siero *m*
servant (*ssöö*-vönt) *n* servitore *m*
serve (ssööv) *v* servire
service (*ssöö*-viss) *n* servizio *m*; ~ **charge** servizio *m*; ~ **station** distributore di benzina
serviette (ssöö-vi-*êt*) *n* tovagliolo *m*
session (*ssê*-ʃön) *n* sessione *f*
set (ssêt) *n* assieme *m*, gruppo *m*
***set** (ssêt) *v* *mettere; ~ **menu** pranzo a prezzo fisso; ~ **out** partire
setting (*ssê*-ting) *n* scenario *m*; ~ **lotion** fissatore per capelli
settle (*ssê*-töl) *v* sistemare, fissare; ~ **down** sistemarsi
settlement (*ssê*-töl-mönt) *n* accomodamento *m*, aggiustamento *m*, accordo *m*
seven (*ssê*-vön) *num* sette
seventeen (ssê-vön-*tiin*) *num* diciassette
seventeenth (ssê-vön-*tiinθ*) *num* diciassettesimo
seventh (*ssê*-vönθ) *num* settimo
seventy (*ssê*-vön-ti) *num* settanta
several (*ssê*-vö-röl) *adj* diversi, parecchi
severe (ssi-*vi*ö) *adj* violento, rigoroso, severo
sew (ssou) *v* cucire; ~ **up** suturare
sewer (*ssuu*-ö) *n* fogna *f*
sewing-machine (*ssou*-ing-mö-ʃiin) *n* macchina da cucire
sex (ssêkss) *n* sesso *m*
sexton (*ssêk*-sstön) *n* sagrestano *m*
sexual (*ssêk*-ʃu-öl) *adj* sessuale
sexuality (ssêk-ʃu-*æ*-lö-ti) *n* sessualità *f*
shade (ʃeid) *n* ombra *f*; tinta *f*
shadow (*ʃæ*-dou) *n* ombra *f*
shady (*ʃei*-di) *adj* ombreggiato
***shake** (ʃeik) *v* agitare
shaky (*ʃei*-ki) *adj* vacillante
***shall** (ʃæl) *v* *dovere
shallow (*ʃæ*-lou) *adj* poco profondo
shame (ʃeim) *n* vergogna *f*; disonore *m*; **shame!** vergogna!
shampoo (ʃæm-*puu*) *n* shampoo *m*
shamrock (*ʃæm*-rok) *n* trifoglio *m*
shape (ʃeip) *n* forma *f*; *v* formare
share (ʃêö) *v* *condividere; *n* parte *f*; azione *f*
shark (ʃaak) *n* pescecane *m*
sharp (ʃaap) *adj* affilato
sharpen (*ʃaa*-pön) *v* affilare
shave (ʃeiv) *v* *radere
shaver (*ʃei*-vö) *n* rasoio elettrico
shaving-brush (*ʃei*-ving-braʃ) *n* pennello da barba
shaving-cream (*ʃei*-ving-kriim) *n* crema da barba
shaving-soap (*ʃei*-ving-ssoup) *n* sapone da barba
shawl (ʃool) *n* scialle *m*
she (ʃii) *pron* essa

shed (ʃêd) *n* baracca *f*
* **shed** (ʃêd) *v* versare; *diffondere
sheep (ʃiip) *n* (pl ~) pecora *f*
sheer (ʃiö) *adj* assoluto, puro; fino, trasparente, sottile
sheet (ʃiit) *n* lenzuolo *m*; foglio *m*; lamina *f*
shelf (ʃêlf) *n* (pl shelves) scaffale *m*
shell (ʃêl) *n* conchiglia *f*; guscio *m*
shellfish (*ʃêl*-fiʃ) *n* crostaceo *m*
shelter (*ʃêl*-tö) *n* riparo *m*, rifugio *m*; *v* riparare
shepherd (*ʃê*-pöd) *n* pastore *m*
shift (ʃift) *n* squadra *f*
* **shine** (ʃain) *v* brillare; scintillare, risplendere
ship (ʃip) *n* nave *f*; *v* spedire; **shipping line** linea di navigazione
shipowner (*ʃi*-pou-nö) *n* armatore *m*
shipyard (*ʃip*-ⁱaad) *n* cantiere navale
shirt (ʃööt) *n* camicia *f*
shiver (*ʃi*-vö) *v* tremare, rabbrividire; *n* brivido *m*
shivery (*ʃi*-vö-ri) *adj* infreddolito
shock (ʃok) *n* scossa *f*; *v* *scuotere; ~ **absorber** ammortizzatore *m*
shocking (*ʃo*-king) *adj* urtante
shoe (ʃuu) *n* scarpa *f*; **gym shoes** scarpe da ginnastica; ~ **polish** lucido per scarpe
shoe-lace (*ʃuu*-leiss) *n* stringa per scarpe
shoemaker (*ʃuu*-mei-kö) *n* calzolaio *m*
shoe-shop (*ʃuu*-ʃop) *n* calzoleria *f*
shook (ʃuk) *v* (p shake)
* **shoot** (ʃuut) *v* sparare
shop (ʃop) *n* negozio *m*; *v* *fare la spesa; ~ **assistant** commesso *m*; **shopping bag** borsa per la spesa; **shopping centre** centro commerciale
shopkeeper (*ʃop*-kii-pö) *n* negoziante *m*
shop-window (ʃop-ᵘ*in*-dou) *n* vetrina *f*
shore (ʃoo) *n* riva *f*, sponda *f*
short (ʃoot) *adj* corto; basso; ~ **circuit** corto circuito
shortage (*ʃoo*-tidʒ) *n* carenza *f*, mancanza *f*
shortcoming (*ʃoot*-ka-ming) *n* deficienza *f*
shorten (*ʃoo*-tön) *v* raccorciare
shorthand (*ʃoot*-hænd) *n* stenografia *f*
shortly (*ʃoot*-li) *adv* presto, tra breve, prossimamente
shorts (ʃootss) *pl* calzoncini *mpl*; *plAm* mutande *fpl*
short-sighted (ʃoot-*ssai*-tid) *adj* miope
shot (ʃot) *n* sparo *m*; iniezione *f*; sequenza *f*
* **should** (ʃud) *v* *dovere
shoulder (*ʃoul*-dö) *n* spalla *f*
shout (ʃaut) *v* urlare, gridare; *n* grido *m*
shovel (*ʃa*-völ) *n* pala *f*
show (ʃou) *n* rappresentazione *f*, spettacolo *m*; esposizione *f*
* **show** (ʃou) *v* mostrare; *far vedere, esibire; dimostrare
show-case (*ʃou*-keiss) *n* bacheca *f*
shower (ʃauö) *n* doccia *f*; acquazzone *m*, precipitazione *f*
showroom (*ʃou*-ruum) *n* sala di esposizione
shriek (ʃriik) *v* strillare; *n* strillo *m*
shrimp (ʃrimp) *n* gamberetto *m*
shrine (ʃrain) *n* santuario *m*
* **shrink** (ʃringk) *v* *restringersi
shrinkproof (*ʃringk*-pruuf) *adj* irrestringibile
shrub (ʃrab) *n* arbusto *m*
shudder (*ʃa*-dö) *n* brivido *m*
shuffle (*ʃa*-föl) *v* mescolare
* **shut** (ʃat) *v* *chiudere; ~ **in** *rinchiudere
shutter (*ʃa*-tö) *n* imposta *f*, persiana *f*

shy (ʃai) *adj* schivo, timido
shyness (*ʃai*-nöss) *n* timidezza *f*
Siam (ssai-*æm*) Siam *m*
Siamese (ssai-ö-*miis*) *adj* siamese
sick (ssik) *adj* ammalato; nauseato
sickness (*ssik*-nöss) *n* male *m*; nausea *f*
side (ssaid) *n* lato *m*; parte *f*; **one-sided** *adj* unilaterale
sideburns (*ssaid*-bööns) *pl* basette *fpl*
sidelight (*ssaid*-lait) *n* luce laterale
side-street (*ssaid*-sstriit) *n* traversa *f*
sidewalk (*ssaid*-ᵘook) *nAm* marciapiede *m*
sideways (*ssaid*-ᵘeis) *adv* lateralmente
siege (ssiidʒ) *n* assedio *m*
sieve (ssiv) *n* setaccio *m*; *v* setacciare
sift (ssift) *v* vagliare
sight (ssait) *n* vista *f*; veduta *f*, spettacolo *m*; curiosità *f*
sign (ssain) *n* segno *m*; gesto *m*, cenno *m*; *v* *sottoscrivere, firmare
signal (*ssigh*-nöl) *n* segnale *m*; segno *m*; *v* segnalare
signature (*ssigh*-nö-tʃö) *n* firma *f*
significant (ssigh-*ni*-fi-könt) *adj* significativo
signpost (*ssain*-pousst) *n* cartello indicatore
silence (*ssai*-lönss) *n* silenzio *m*; *v* *far tacere
silencer (*ssai*-lön-ssö) *n* silenziatore *m*
silent (*ssai*-lönt) *adj* silenzioso; ***be** ~ *tacere
silk (ssilk) *n* seta *f*
silken (*ssil*-kön) *adj* di seta
silly (*ssi*-li) *adj* grullo, sciocco
silver (*ssil*-vö) *n* argento *m*; d'argento
silversmith (*ssil*-vö-ssmiθ) *n* argentiere *m*
silverware (*ssil*-vö-ᵘêᵒ) *n* argenteria *f*
similar (*ssi*-mi-lö) *adj* analogo, simile
similarity (ssi-mi-*læ*-rö-ti) *n* rassomiglianza *f*
simple (*ssim*-pöl) *adj* ingenuo, semplice; ordinario
simply (*ssim*-pli) *adv* semplicemente
simulate (*ssi*-mʲu-leit) *v* simulare
simultaneous (ssi-möl-*tei*-ni-öss) *adj* simultaneo
sin (ssin) *n* peccato *m*
since (ssinss) *prep* da; *adv* da allora; *conj* dacché; poiché
sincere (ssin-*ssiᵒ*) *adj* sincero
sinew (*ssi*-nʲuu) *n* tendine *m*
***sing** (ssing) *v* cantare
singer (*ssing*-ö) *n* cantante *m*
single (*ssing*-ghöl) *adj* singolo; celibe
singular (*ssing*-ghʲu-lö) *n* singolare *m*; *adj* strano
sinister (*ssi*-ni-sstö) *adj* sinistro
sink (ssingk) *n* lavello *m*
***sink** (ssingk) *v* affondare
sip (ssip) *n* sorsetto *m*
siphon (*ssai*-fön) *n* sifone *m*
sir (ssöö) signore *m*
siren (*ssaiᵒ*-rön) *n* sirena *f*
sister (*ssi*-sstö) *n* sorella *f*
sister-in-law (*ssi*-sstö-rin-loo) *n* (pl sisters-) cognata *f*
***sit** (ssit) *v* *sedere; ~ **down** *sedersi
site (ssait) *n* sito *m*; posizione *f*
sitting-room (*ssi*-ting-ruum) *n* soggiorno *m*
situated (*ssi*-tʃu-ei-tid) *adj* situato
situation (ssi-tʃu-*ei*-ʃön) *n* situazione *f*; ubicazione *f*
six (ssikss) *num* sei
sixteen (ssikss-*tiin*) *num* sedici
sixteenth (ssikss-*tiinθ*) *num* sedicesimo
sixth (ssikssθ) *num* sesto
sixty (*ssikss*-ti) *num* sessanta
size (ssais) *n* grandezza *f*, misura *f*; dimensione *f*; formato *m*
skate (sskeit) *v* pattinare; *n* pattino *m*

skating (*sskei*-ting) *n* pattinaggio *m*
skating-rink (*sskei*-ting-ringk) *n* pista di pattinaggio
skeleton (*sskê*-li-tön) *n* scheletro *m*
sketch (sskêtʃ) *n* disegno *m*, schizzo *m*; *v* disegnare, abbozzare
sketch-book (*sskêtʃ*-buk) *n* album da disegno
ski[1] (sskii) *v* sciare
ski[2] (sskii) *n* (pl ~, ~s) sci *m*; ~ **boots** scarponi da sci; ~ **pants** calzoni da sci; ~ **poles** *Am* bastoni da sci; ~ **sticks** bastoni da sci
skid (sskid) *v* scivolare
skier (*sskii*-ö) *n* sciatore *m*
skiing (*sskii*-ing) *n* sci *m*
ski-jump (*sskii*-dʒamp) *n* salto con gli sci
skilful (*sskil*-föl) *adj* esperto, destro, abile
ski-lift (*sskii*-lift) *n* teleferica per sciatori
skill (sskil) *n* abilità *f*
skilled (sskild) *adj* abile; esperto
skin (sskin) *n* pelle *f*; buccia *f*; ~ **cream** crema per la pelle
skip (sskip) *v* saltellare; *omettere
skirt (ssköötˌ) *n* gonna *f*
skull (sskal) *n* cranio *m*
sky (sskai) *n* cielo *m*; aria *f*
skyscraper (*sskai*-sskrei-pö) *n* grattacielo *m*
slack (sslæk) *adj* lento
slacks (sslækss) *pl* calzoni *mpl*
slam (sslæm) *v* sbattere
slander (*sslaan*-dö) *n* calunnia *f*
slant (sslaant) *v* inclinare
slanting (*sslaan*-ting) *adj* obliquo, pendente, inclinato
slap (sslæp) *v* schiaffeggiare; *n* schiaffo *m*
slate (ssleit) *n* ardesia *f*
slave (ssleiv) *n* schiavo *m*
sledge (sslêdʒ) *n* slitta *f*
sleep (ssliip) *n* sonno *m*
***sleep** (ssliip) *v* dormire
sleeping-bag (*sslii*-ping-bægh) *n* sacco a pelo
sleeping-car (*sslii*-ping-kaa) *n* vagone letto
sleeping-pill (*sslii*-ping-pil) *n* sonnifero *m*
sleepless (*ssliip*-löss) *adj* insonne
sleepy (*sslii*-pi) *adj* assonnato
sleeve (ssliiv) *n* manica *f*; busta *f*
sleigh (sslei) *n* slitta *f*
slender (*sslên*-dö) *adj* snello
slice (sslaiss) *n* fetta *f*
slide (sslaid) *n* scivolata *f*; scivolo *m*; diapositiva *f*
***slide** (sslaid) *v* slittare
slight (sslait) *adj* leggero; scarso
slim (sslim) *adj* snello; *v* dimagrire
slip (sslip) *v* scivolare; scappare; *n* svista *f*; sottoveste *f*
slipper (*ssli*-pö) *n* ciabatta *f*, pantofola *f*
slippery (*ssli*-pö-ri) *adj* viscido, sdrucciolevole
slogan (*sslou*-ghön) *n* motto *m*, slogan *m*
slope (ssloup) *n* pendio *m*; *v* pendere
sloping (*sslou*-ping) *adj* inclinato
sloppy (*sslo*-pi) *adj* disordinato
slot (sslot) *n* fessura *f*
slot-machine (*sslot*-mö-ʃiin) *n* distributore automatico
slovenly (*ssla*-vön-li) *adj* sciatto
slow (sslou) *adj* ottuso, lento; ~ **down** rallentare
sluice (ssluuss) *n* chiusa *f*
slum (sslam) *n* quartiere povero
slump (sslamp) *n* calo di prezzo
slush (sslaʃ) *n* neve fangosa
sly (sslai) *adj* astuto
smack (ssmæk) *v* picchiare; *n* ceffone *m*
small (ssmool) *adj* piccolo; scarso

smallpox (*ssmool*-pokss) *n* vaiolo *m*
smart (ssmaat) *adj* elegante; sveglio, intelligente
smell (ssmêl) *n* odore *m*
***smell** (ssmêl) *v* odorare; puzzare
smelly (*ssmê*-li) *adj* puzzolente
smile (ssmail) *v* *sorridere; *n* sorriso *m*
smith (ssmiθ) *n* fabbro *m*
smoke (ssmouk) *v* fumare; *n* fumo *m*; **no smoking** vietato fumare
smoker (*ssmou*-kö) *n* fumatore *m*; scompartimento per fumatori
smoking-compartment (*ssmou*-king-köm-paat-mönt) *n* compartimento per fumatori
smoking-room (*ssmou*-king-ruum) *n* sala per fumatori
smooth (ssmuuð) *adj* levigato, piano, liscio; morbido
smuggle (*ssma*-ghöl) *v* contrabbandare
snack (ssnæk) *n* spuntino *m*
snack-bar (*ssnæk*-baa) *n* tavola calda
snail (ssneil) *n* lumaca *f*
snake (ssneik) *n* serpente *m*
snapshot (*ssnæp*-ʃot) *n* istantanea *f*
sneakers (*ssnii*-kös) *plAm* scarpe da ginnastica
sneeze (ssniis) *v* starnutire
sniper (*ssnai*-pö) *n* franco tiratore
snooty (*ssnuu*-ti) *adj* arrogante
snore (ssnoo) *v* russare
snorkel (*ssnoo*-köl) *n* respiratore *m*
snout (ssnaut) *n* muso *m*
snow (ssnou) *n* neve *f*; *v* nevicare
snowstorm (*ssnou*-sstoom) *n* tormenta *f*
snowy (*ssnou*-i) *adj* nevoso
so (ssou) *conj* dunque; *adv* così; talmente; **and ~ on** e così via; **~ far** finora; **~ that** così che, affinché
soak (ssouk) *v* ammollare, inzuppare
soap (ssoup) *n* sapone *m*; **~ powder** sapone in polvere
sober (*ssou*-bö) *adj* sobrio; assennato
so-called (ssou-*koold*) *adj* cosiddetto
soccer (*sso*-kö) *n* calcio *m*; **~ team** squadra *f*
social (*ssou*-ʃöl) *adj* sociale
socialism (*ssou*-ʃö-li-söm) *n* socialismo *m*
socialist (*ssou*-ʃö-lisst) *adj* socialista; *n* socialista *m*
society (ssö-*ssai*-ö-ti) *n* società *f*; associazione *f*; compagnia *f*
sock (ssok) *n* calza *f*
socket (*sso*-kit) *n* portalampada *m*
soda-water (*ssou*-dö-ᵘoo-tö) *n* acqua di seltz
sofa (*ssou*-fö) *n* sofà *m*
soft (ssoft) *adj* morbido; **~ drink** bibita analcoolica
soften (*sso*-fön) *v* ammorbidire
soil (ssoil) *n* suolo *m*; terreno *m*, terra *f*
soiled (ssoild) *adj* sudicio
sold (ssould) *v* (p, pp sell); **~ out** esaurito
solder (*ssol*-dö) *v* saldare
soldering-iron (*ssol*-dö-ring-aiᵒn) *n* saldatore *m*
soldier (*ssoul*-dʒö) *n* militare *m*, soldato *m*
sole[1] (ssoul) *adj* unico
sole[2] (ssoul) *n* suola *f*; sogliola *f*
solely (*ssoul*-li) *adv* esclusivamente
solemn (*sso*-löm) *adj* solenne
solicitor (ssö-*li*-ssi-tö) *n* procuratore legale, avvocato *m*
solid (*sso*-lid) *adj* robusto, solido; massiccio; *n* solido *m*
soluble (*sso*-lⁱu-böl) *adj* solubile
solution (ssö-*luu*-ʃön) *n* soluzione *f*
solve (ssolv) *v* *risolvere
sombre (*ssom*-bö) *adj* tetro
some (ssam) *adj* alcuni, qualche; *pron* alcuni, taluni; una parte; ~

day un giorno o l'altro; ~ **more** ancora; ~ **time** un giorno
somebody (*ssam*-bö-di) *pron* qualcuno
somehow (*ssam*-hau) *adv* in un modo o nell'altro
someone (*ssam*-ᵘan) *pron* qualcuno
something (*ssam*-θing) *pron* qualcosa
sometimes (*ssam*-taims) *adv* qualche volta
somewhat (*ssam*-ᵘot) *adv* alquanto
somewhere (*ssam*-ᵘêᵒ) *adv* in qualche posto
son (ssan) *n* figlio *m*
song (ssong) *n* canzone *f*
son-in-law (*ssa*-nin-loo) *n* (pl sons-) genero *m*
soon (ssuun) *adv* presto, tra poco; **as** ~ **as** non appena
sooner (*ssuu*-nö) *adv* piuttosto
sore (ssoo) *adj* indolenzito; *n* piaga *f*; ulcera *f*; ~ **throat** mal di gola
sorrow (*sso*-rou) *n* tristezza *f*, dolore *m*, dispiacere *m*
sorry (*sso*-ri) *adj* spiacente; **sorry!** scusa!, scusate!, scusi!
sort (ssoot) *v* classificare, assortire; *n* genere *m*, specie *f*; **all sorts of** ogni sorta di
soul (ssoul) *n* anima *f*; spirito *m*
sound (ssaund) *n* suono *m*; *v* suonare; *adj* solido
soundproof (*ssaund*-pruuf) *adj* insonorizzato
soup (ssuup) *n* minestra *f*
soup-plate (*ssuup*-pleit) *n* scodella *f*
soup-spoon (*ssuup*-sspuun) *n* cucchiaio da minestra
sour (ssauᵒ) *adj* agro
source (ssooss) *n* sorgente *f*
south (ssauθ) *n* sud *m*; **South Pole** polo Sud
South Africa (ssauθ *æ*-fri-kö) Africa del Sud
south-east (ssauθ-*iisst*) *n* sud-est *m*
southerly (*ssa*-ðö-li) *adj* meridionale
southern (*ssa*-ðön) *adj* meridionale
south-west (ssauθ-ᵘ*êsst*) *n* sud-ovest *m*
souvenir (*ssuu*-vö-niᵒ) *n* ricordo *m*
sovereign (*ssov*-rin) *n* sovrano *m*
Soviet (*ssou*-vi-öt) *adj* sovietico
Soviet Union (*ssou*-vi-öt ⁱ*uu*-nⁱön) Unione Sovietica
***sow** (ssou) *v* seminare
spa (sspaa) *n* stazione termale
space (sspeiss) *n* spazio *m*; distanza *f*; *v* spaziare
spacious (*sspei*-ʃöss) *adj* spazioso
spade (sspeid) *n* zappa *f*, vanga *f*
Spain (sspein) Spagna *f*
Spaniard (*sspæ*-nⁱöd) *n* spagnolo *m*
Spanish (*sspæ*-niʃ) *adj* spagnolo
spanking (*sspæng*-king) *n* sculacciata *f*
spanner (*sspæ*-nö) *n* chiave fissa
spare (sspêᵒ) *adj* di riserva, disponibile; *v* *fare a meno di; ~ **part** pezzo di ricambio; ~ **room** camera degli ospiti; ~ **time** tempo libero; ~ **tyre** pneumatico di ricambio; ~ **wheel** ruota di ricambio
spark (sspaak) *n* scintilla *f*
sparking-plug (*sspaa*-king-plagh) *n* candela d'accensione
sparkling (*sspaa*-kling) *adj* scintillante; spumante
sparrow (*sspæ*-rou) *n* passero *m*
***speak** (sspiik) *v* parlare
spear (sspiᵒ) *n* lancia *f*
special (*sspê*-ʃöl) *adj* particolare, speciale; ~ **delivery** per espresso
specialist (*sspê*-ʃö-lisst) *n* specialista *m*
speciality (sspê-ʃi-*æ*-lö-ti) *n* specialità *f*
specialize (*sspê*-ʃö-lais) *v* specializzarsi

specially (*sspê*-ʃö-li) *adv* particolarmente
species (*sspii*-ʃiis) *n* (pl ~) specie *f*
specific (sspö-*ssi*-fik) *adj* specifico
specimen (*sspê*-ssi-mön) *n* esemplare *m*
speck (sspêk) *n* macchiolina *f*
spectacle (*sspêk*-tö-köl) *n* spettacolo *m*; **spectacles** occhiali *mpl*
spectator (sspêk-*tei*-tö) *n* spettatore *m*
speculate (*sspê*-kʲu-leit) *v* speculare
speech (sspiitʃ) *n* parola *f*; discorso *m*; linguaggio *m*
speechless (*sspiitʃ*-löss) *adj* muto
speed (sspiid) *n* velocità *f*; rapidità *f*, fretta *f*; **cruising** ~ velocità di crociera; ~ **limit** limite di velocità; ~ **up** *v* accelerare
***speed** (sspiid) *v* *correre; *correre troppo
speeding (*sspii*-ding) *n* eccesso di velocità
speedometer (sspii-*do*-mi-tö) *n* tachimetro *m*
spell (sspêl) *n* incanto *m*
***spell** (sspêl) *v* compitare
spelling (*sspê*-ling) *n* ortografia *f*
***spend** (sspênd) *v* *spendere; impiegare
sphere (ssfiö) *n* sfera *f*
spiced (sspaisst) *adj* condito
spicy (*sspai*-ssi) *adj* piccante
spider (*sspai*-dö) *n* ragno *m*; **spider's web** ragnatela *f*
***spill** (sspil) *v* *spandere
***spin** (sspin) *v* filare; *far girare
spinach (*sspi*-nidʒ) *n* spinaci *mpl*
spine (sspain) *n* spina dorsale
spinster (*sspin*-sstö) *n* zitella *f*
spire (sspaiö) *n* guglia *f*
spirit (*sspi*-rit) *n* spirito *m*; fantasma *m*; umore *m*; **spirits** bevande alcooliche; morale *m*; ~ **stove** fornello a spirito
spiritual (*sspi*-ri-tʃu-öl) *adj* spirituale
spit (sspit) *n* sputo *m*, saliva *f*; spiedo *m*
***spit** (sspit) *v* sputare
in spite of (in sspait ov) nonostante, malgrado
spiteful (*sspait*-föl) *adj* malevolo
splash (ssplæʃ) *v* schizzare
splendid (*ssplên*-did) *adj* magnifico, splendido
splendour (*ssplên*-dö) *n* splendore *m*
splint (ssplint) *n* stecca *f*
splinter (*ssplin*-tö) *n* scheggia *f*
***split** (ssplit) *v* *fendere
***spoil** (sspoil) *v* guastare; viziare
spoke[1] (sspouk) *v* (p speak)
spoke[2] (sspouk) *n* raggio *m*
sponge (sspandʒ) *n* spugna *f*
spook (sspuuk) *n* spettro *m*
spool (sspuul) *n* rocchetto *m*
spoon (sspuun) *n* cucchiaio *m*
spoonful (*sspuun*-ful) *n* cucchiaiata *f*
sport (sspoot) *n* sport *m*
sports-car (*sspootss*-kaa) *n* macchina sportiva
sports-jacket (*sspootss*-dʒæ-kit) *n* giacchetta sportiva
sportsman (*sspootss*-mön) *n* (pl -men) sportivo *m*
sportswear (*sspootss*-ᵘêö) *n* abbigliamento sportivo
spot (sspot) *n* chiazza *f*, macchia *f*; località *f*, luogo *m*
spotless (*sspot*-löss) *adj* immacolato
spotlight (*sspot*-lait) *n* proiettore *m*
spotted (*sspo*-tid) *adj* chiazzato
spout (sspaut) *n* getto *m*
sprain (ssprein) *v* *storcere; *n* distorsione *f*
***spread** (ssprêd) *v* *stendere
spring (sspring) *n* primavera *f*; molla *f*; sorgente *f*
springtime (*sspring*-taim) *n* primavera

f
sprouts (ssprautss) *pl* cavolini *mpl*
spy (sspai) *n* spia *f*
squadron (*sskᵘo*-drön) *n* squadriglia *f*
square (sskᵘêᵒ) *adj* quadrato; *n* quadrato *m*; piazza *f*
squash (sskᵘoʃ) *n* succo di frutta
squirrel (*sskᵘi*-röl) *n* scoiattolo *m*
squirt (sskᵘööt) *n* zampillo *m*
stable (*sstei*-böl) *adj* stabile; *n* stalla *f*
stack (sstæk) *n* pila *f*
stadium (*sstei*-di-öm) *n* stadio *m*
staff (sstaaf) *n* personale *m*
stage (ssteidʒ) *n* scena *f*; stadio *m*, fase *f*; tappa *f*
stain (sstein) *v* macchiare; *n* macchia *f*; **stained glass** vetro colorato; ~ **remover** smacchiatore *m*
stainless (*sstein*-löss) *adj* immacolato; ~ **steel** acciaio inossidabile
staircase (*sstêᵒ*-keiss) *n* scala *f*
stairs (sstêᵒs) *pl* scala *f*
stale (ssteil) *adj* raffermo
stall (sstool) *n* bancarella *f*; poltrona d'orchestra
stamina (*sstæ*-mi-nö) *n* vigore *m*
stamp (sstæmp) *n* francobollo *m*; timbro *m*; *v* affrancare; pestare; ~ **machine** distributore automatico di francobolli
stand (sstænd) *n* banco *m*; tribuna *f*
***stand** (sstænd) *v* *stare in piedi
standard (*sstæn*-död) *n* norma *f*; normale; ~ **of living** livello di vita
stanza (*sstæn*-sö) *n* strofa *f*
staple (*sstei*-pöl) *n* graffetta *f*
star (sstaa) *n* stella *f*
starboard (*sstaa*-böd) *n* tribordo *m*
starch (sstaatʃ) *n* amido *m*; *v* inamidare
stare (sstêᵒ) *v* fissare
starling (*sstaa*-ling) *n* stornello *m*
start (sstaat) *v* cominciare; *n* inizio *m*; **starter motor** avviatore *m*
starting-point (*sstaa*-ting-point) *n* punto di partenza
state (ssteit) *n* stato *m*; *v* affermare
the States Stati Uniti
statement (*ssteit*-mönt) *n* dichiarazione *f*
statesman (*ssteitss*-mön) *n* (pl -men) uomo di stato
station (*sstei*-ʃön) *n* stazione *f*; posto *m*
stationary (*sstei*-ʃö-nö-ri) *adj* stazionario
stationer's (*sstei*-ʃö-nös) *n* cartoleria *f*
stationery (*sstei*-ʃö-nö-ri) *n* cartoleria *f*
station-master (*sstei*-ʃön-maa-sstö) *n* capostazione *m*
statistics (sstö-*ti*-sstikss) *pl* statistica *f*
statue (*sstæ*-tʃuu) *n* statua *f*
stay (sstei) *v* *rimanere, *stare; soggiornare, *trattenersi; *n* soggiorno *m*
steadfast (*sstêd*-faasst) *adj* fermo
steady (*sstê*-di) *adj* stabile
steak (ssteik) *n* bistecca *f*
***steal** (sstiil) *v* rubare
steam (sstiim) *n* vapore *m*
steamer (*sstii*-mö) *n* piroscafo *m*
steel (sstiil) *n* acciaio *m*
steep (sstiip) *adj* ripido
steeple (*sstii*-pöl) *n* campanile *m*
steering-column (*sstiᵒ*-ring-ko-löm) *n* piantone di guida
steering-wheel (*sstiᵒ*-ring-ᵘiil) *n* volante *m*
steersman (*sstiᵒs*-mön) *n* (pl -men) timoniere *m*
stem (sstêm) *n* gambo *m*
stenographer (sstê-*no*-ghrö-fö) *n* stenografo *m*
step (sstêp) *n* passo *m*; scalino *m*; *v* camminare
stepchild (*sstêp*-tʃaild) *n* (pl -children) figliastro *m*

stepfather (*sstêp*-faa-ðö) *n* patrigno *m*
stepmother (*sstêp*-ma-ðö) *n* matrigna *f*
sterile (*sstê*-rail) *adj* sterile
sterilize (*sstê*-ri-lais) *v* sterilizzare
steward (*sst*ʲ*uu*-öd) *n* steward *m*
stewardess (*sst*ʲ*uu*-ö-dêss) *n* hostess *f*
stick (sstik) *n* bastone *m*
***stick** (sstik) *v* appiccicare, incollare
sticky (*ssti*-ki) *adj* appiccicaticcio
stiff (sstif) *adj* rigido
still (sstil) *adv* ancora; comunque; *adj* tranquillo
stillness (*sstil*-nöss) *n* quiete *f*
stimulant (*ssti*-mʲu-lönt) *n* stimolante *m*
stimulate (*ssti*-mʲu-leit) *v* stimolare
sting (ssting) *n* puntura *f*
***sting** (ssting) *v* *pungere
stingy (*sstin*-dʒi) *adj* taccagno
***stink** (sstingk) *v* puzzare
stipulate (*ssti*-pʲu-leit) *v* stipulare
stipulation (ssti-pʲu-*lei*-ʃön) *n* stipulazione *f*
stir (sstöö) *v* *muovere; mescolare
stirrup (*ssti*-röp) *n* staffa *f*
stitch (sstitʃ) *n* punto *m*, fitta *f*
stock (sstok) *n* scorta *f*; *v* *tenere in magazzino; ~ **exchange** borsa valori, borsa *f*; ~ **market** borsa *f*; **stocks and shares** titoli
stocking (*ssto*-king) *n* calza *f*
stole[1] (sstoul) *v* (p steal)
stole[2] (sstoul) *n* stola *f*
stomach (*ssta*-mök) *n* stomaco *m*
stomach-ache (*ssta*-mö-keik) *n* mal di pancia, mal di stomaco
stone (sstoun) *n* sasso *m*, pietra *f*; pietra preziosa; nocciolo *m*; di pietra; **pumice** ~ pietra pomice
stood (sstud) *v* (p, pp stand)
stop (sstop) *v* *smettere; terminare, cessare; *n* fermata *f*; **stop**! alt!
stopper (*ssto*-pö) *n* tappo *m*
storage (*sstoo*-ridʒ) *n* magazzinaggio *m*
store (sstoo) *n* riserva *f*; bottega *f*; *v* immagazzinare
store-house (*sstoo*-hauss) *n* magazzino *m*
storey (*sstoo*-ri) *n* piano *m*
stork (sstook) *n* cicogna *f*
storm (sstoom) *n* tempesta *f*
stormy (*sstoo*-mi) *adj* tempestoso
story (*sstoo*-ri) *n* racconto *m*
stout (sstaut) *adj* grosso, obeso, corpulento
stove (sstouv) *n* stufa *f*; cucina *f*
straight (sstreit) *adj* dritto; onesto; *adv* dritto; ~ **ahead** sempre diritto; ~ **away** direttamente, subito; ~ **on** avanti dritto
strain (sstrein) *n* fatica *f*; sforzo *m*; *v* forzare; filtrare
strainer (*sstrei*-nö) *n* colapasta *m*
strange (sstreindʒ) *adj* strano; bizzarro
stranger (*sstrein*-dʒö) *n* straniero *m*; estraneo *m*
strangle (*sstræng*-ghöl) *v* strangolare
strap (sstræp) *n* cinghia *f*
straw (sstroo) *n* paglia *f*
strawberry (*sstroo*-bö-ri) *n* fragola *f*
stream (sstriim) *n* ruscello *m*; corrente *f*; *v* *scorrere
street (sstriit) *n* strada *f*
streetcar (*sstriit*-kaa) *nAm* tram *m*
street-organ (*sstrii*-too-ghön) *n* organetto di Barberia
strength (sstrêngθ) *n* resistenza *f*, forza *f*
stress (sstrêss) *n* tensione *f*; accento *m*; *v* sottolineare
stretch (sstrêtʃ) *v* *tendere; *n* segmento *m*
strict (sstrikt) *adj* severo; rigido
strife (sstraif) *n* lotta *f*

strike (sstraik) *n* sciopero *m*
***strike** (sstraik) *v* picchiare; colpire; scioperare; ammainare
striking (*sstrai*-king) *adj* impressionante, notevole, vistoso
string (sstring) *n* spago *m*; corda *f*
strip (sstrip) *n* striscia *f*
stripe (sstraip) *n* stria *f*
striped (sstraipt) *adj* striato
stroke (sstrouk) *n* colpo *m*
stroll (sstroul) *v* passeggiare; *n* passeggiata *f*
strong (sstrong) *adj* forte; robusto
stronghold (*sstrong*-hould) *n* roccaforte *f*
structure (*sstrak*-tʃö) *n* struttura *f*
struggle (*sstra*-ghöl) *n* combattimento *m*, lotta *f*; *v* lottare
stub (sstab) *n* matrice *f*
stubborn (*ssta*-bön) *adj* cocciuto
student (*sstʲuu*-dönt) *n* studente *m*; studentessa *f*
study (*ssta*-di) *v* studiare; *n* studio *m*
stuff (sstaf) *n* sostanza *f*; roba *f*
stuffed (sstaft) *adj* ripieno
stuffing (*ssta*-fing) *n* ripieno *m*
stuffy (*ssta*-fi) *adj* stantio
stumble (*sstam*-böl) *v* inciampare
stung (sstang) *v* (p, pp sting)
stupid (*sstʲuu*-pid) *adj* stupido
style (sstail) *n* stile *m*
subject[1] (*ssab*-dʒikt) *n* soggetto *m*; suddito *m*; ~ **to** soggetto a
subject[2] (ssöb-*dʒêkt*) *v* *sottomettere
submit (ssöb-*mit*) *v* *sottomettersi
subordinate (ssö-*boo*-di-nöt) *adj* subalterno; secondario
subscriber (ssöb-*sskrai*-bö) *n* abbonato *m*
subscription (ssöb-*sskrip*-ʃön) *n* abbonamento *m*
subsequent (*ssab*-ssi-kᵘönt) *adj* successivo
subsidy (*ssab*-ssi-di) *n* sovvenzione *f*
substance (*ssab*-sstönss) *n* sostanza *f*
substantial (ssöb-*sstæn*-ʃöl) *adj* materiale; reale; sostanziale
substitute (*ssab*-ssti-tʲuut) *v* sostituire; *n* sostituto *m*
subtitle (*ssab*-tai-töl) *n* sottotitolo *m*
subtle (*ssa*-töl) *adj* sottile
subtract (ssöb-*trækt*) *v* *sottrarre
suburb (*ssa*-bööb) *n* sobborgo *m*
suburban (ssö-*böö*-bön) *adj* suburbano
subway (*ssab*-ᵘei) *nAm* metropolitana *f*
succeed (ssök-*ssiid*) *v* *riuscire; *succedere
success (ssök-*ssêss*) *n* successo *m*
successful (ssök-*ssêss*-föl) *adj* riuscito
succumb (ssö-*kam*) *v* soccombere
such (ssatʃ) *adj* simile, tale; *adv* così; ~ **as** come
suck (ssak) *v* succhiare
sudden (*ssa*-dön) *adj* improvviso
suddenly (*ssa*-dön-li) *adv* improvvisamente
suede (ssᵘeid) *n* pelle scamosciata
suffer (*ssa*-fö) *v* *soffrire; subire
suffering (*ssa*-fö-ring) *n* sofferenza *f*
suffice (ssö-*faiss*) *v* bastare
sufficient (ssö-*fi*-ʃönt) *adj* bastante, sufficiente
suffrage (*ssa*-fridʒ) *n* suffragio *m*
sugar (*ʃu*-ghö) *n* zucchero *m*
suggest (ssö-*dʒêsst*) *v* suggerire
suggestion (ssö-*dʒêss*-tʃön) *n* suggerimento *m*
suicide (*ssuu*-i-ssaid) *n* suicidio *m*
suit (ssuut) *v* *convenire; adattare; *addirsi; *n* vestito da uomo *m*
suitable (*ssuu*-tö-böl) *adj* adeguato, adatto
suitcase (*ssuut*-keiss) *n* valigia *f*
suite (ssᵘiit) *n* appartamento *m*
sum (ssam) *n* somma *f*
summary (*ssa*-mö-ri) *n* sommario *m*,

sunto *m*
summer (*ssa*-mö) *n* estate *f*; ~ **time** orario estivo
summit (*ssa*-mit) *n* vetta *f*
summons (*ssa*-möns) *n* (pl ~es) citazione *f*
sun (ssan) *n* sole *m*
sunbathe (*ssan*-beið) *v* *fare il bagno di sole
sunburn (*ssan*-böön) *n* abbronzatura *f*
Sunday (*ssan*-di) domenica *f*
sun-glasses (*ssan*-ghlaa-ssis) *pl* occhiali da sole
sunlight (*ssan*-lait) *n* luce del sole
sunny (*ssa*-ni) *adj* soleggiato
sunrise (*ssan*-rais) *n* aurora *f*
sunset (*ssan*-ssêt) *n* tramonto *m*
sunshade (*ssan*-ʃeid) *n* ombrellino *m*
sunshine (*ssan*-ʃain) *n* luce del sole
sunstroke (*ssan*-sstrouk) *n* colpo di sole
suntan oil (*ssan*-tæn-oil) olio abbronzante
superb (ssu-*pööb*) *adj* grandioso, superbo
superficial (ssuu-pö-*fi*-ʃöl) *adj* superficiale
superfluous (ssu-*pöö*-flu-öss) *adj* superfluo
superior (ssu-*piö*-ri-ö) *adj* migliore, maggiore, superiore
superlative (ssu-*pöö*-lö-tiv) *adj* superlativo; *n* superlativo *m*
supermarket (*ssuu*-pö-maa-kit) *n* supermercato *m*
superstition (ssuu-pö-*ssti*-ʃön) *n* superstizione *f*
supervise (*ssuu*-pö-vais) *v* *soprintendere
supervision (ssuu-pö-*vi*-ʒön) *n* soprintendenza *f*, sorveglianza *f*
supervisor (*ssuu*-pö-vai-sö) *n* ispettore *m*
supper (*ssa*-pö) *n* cena *f*
supple (*ssa*-pöl) *adj* pieghevole, flessibile, agile
supplement (*ssa*-pli-mönt) *n* supplemento *m*
supply (ssö-*plai*) *n* rifornimento *m*, fornitura *f*; provvista *f*; offerta *f*; *v* fornire
support (ssö-*poot*) *v* appoggiare, *sostenere; *n* sostegno *m*; ~ **hose** calze elastiche
supporter (ssö-*poo*-tö) *n* tifoso *m*
suppose (ssö-*pous*) *v* *supporre; **supposing that** supposto che
suppository (ssö-*po*-si-tö-ri) *n* supposta *f*
suppress (ssö-*prêss*) *v* *reprimere
surcharge (*ssöö*-tʃaadʒ) *n* supplemento *m*
sure (ʃuö) *adj* sicuro
surely (*ʃuö*-li) *adv* certamente
surface (*ssöö*-fiss) *n* superficie *f*
surf-board (*ssööf*-bood) *n* acquaplano *m*
surgeon (*ssöö*-dʒön) *n* chirurgo *m*; **veterinary** ~ veterinario *m*
surgery (*ssöö*-dʒö-ri) *n* operazione *f*; consultorio *m*
surname (*ssöö*-neim) *n* cognome *m*
surplus (*ssöö*-plöss) *n* eccedenza *f*
surprise (ssö-*prais*) *n* sorpresa *f*; meraviglia *f*; *v* *sorprendere; stupire
surrender (ssö-*rên* dö) *v* *arrendersi; *n* resa *f*
surround (ssö-*raund*) *v* circondare
surrounding (ssö-*raun*-ding) *adj* circostante
surroundings (ssö-*raun*-dings) *pl* dintorni *mpl*
survey (*ssöö*-vei) *n* rassegna *f*
survival (ssö-*vai*-völ) *n* sopravvivenza *f*
survive (ssö-*vaiv*) *v* *sopravvivere
suspect[1] (ssö-*sspêkt*) *v* sospettare;

*supporre
suspect² (*ssa*-sspêkt) *n* indiziato *m*
suspend (ssö-*sspênd*) *v* *sospendere
suspenders (ssö-*sspên*-dös) *plAm* bretelle *fpl*; **suspender belt** reggicalze *m*
suspension (ssö-*sspên*-ʃön) *n* molleggio *m*, sospensione *f*; ~ **bridge** ponte sospeso
suspicion (ssö-*sspi*-ʃön) *n* sospetto *m*
suspicious (ssö-*sspi*-ʃöss) *adj* sospetto; sospettoso
sustain (ssö-*sstein*) *v* sopportare
Swahili (ssᵘö-*hii*-li) *n* swahili *m*
swallow (*ssᵘo*-lou) *v* ingoiare, inghiottire; *n* rondine *f*
swam (ssᵘæm) *v* (p swim)
swamp (ssᵘomp) *n* palude *f*
swan (ssᵘon) *n* cigno *m*
swap (ssᵘop) *v* barattare
***swear** (ssᵘêᵒ) *v* giurare; bestemmiare
sweat (ssᵘêt) *n* sudore *m*; *v* sudare
sweater (*ssᵘê*-tö) *n* maglione *m*
Swede (ssᵘiid) *n* svedese *m*
Sweden (*ssᵘii*-dön) Svezia *f*
Swedish (*ssᵘii*-diʃ) *adj* svedese
***sweep** (ssᵘiip) *v* scopare
sweet (ssᵘiit) *adj* dolce; *n* caramella *f*; dolce *m*; **sweets** dolciumi *mpl*
sweeten (*ssᵘii*-tön) *v* zuccherare
sweetheart (*ssᵘiit*-haat) *n* amore *m*
sweetshop (*ssᵘiit*-ʃop) *n* pasticceria *f*
swell (ssᵘêl) *adj* magnifico
***swell** (ssᵘêl) *v* gonfiare
swelling (*ssᵘê*-ling) *n* gonfiore *m*
swift (ssᵘift) *adj* rapido
***swim** (ssᵘim) *v* nuotare
swimmer (*ssᵘi*-mö) *n* nuotatore *m*
swimming (*ssᵘi*-ming) *n* nuoto *m*; ~ **pool** piscina *f*
swimming-trunks (*ssᵘi*-ming-trangkss) *n* mutandine da bagno
swim-suit (*ssᵘim*-ssuut) *n* costume da bagno
swindle (*ssᵘin*-döl) *v* truffare; *n* truffa *f*
swindler (*ssᵘin*-dlö) *n* truffatore *m*
swing (ssᵘing) *n* altalena *f*
***swing** (ssᵘing) *v* dondolare
Swiss (ssᵘiss) *adj* svizzero
switch (ssᵘitʃ) *n* interruttore *m*; *v* cambiare; ~ **off** *spegnere; ~ **on** *accendere
switchboard (*ssᵘitʃ*-bood) *n* quadro di distribuzione
Switzerland (*ssᵘit*-ssö-lönd) Svizzera *f*
sword (ssood) *n* spada *f*
swum (ssᵘam) *v* (pp swim)
syllable (*ssi*-lö-böl) *n* sillaba *f*
symbol (*ssim*-böl) *n* simbolo *m*
sympathetic (ssim-pö-*θê*-tik) *adj* cordiale, comprensivo
sympathy (*ssim*-pö-θi) *n* simpatia *f*; compassione *f*
symphony (*ssim*-fö-ni) *n* sinfonia *f*
symptom (*ssim*-töm) *n* sintomo *m*
synagogue (*ssi*-nö-ghogh) *n* sinagoga *f*
synonym (*ssi*-nö-nim) *n* sinonimo *m*
synthetic (ssin-*θê*-tik) *adj* sintetico
syphon (*ssai*-fön) *n* sifone *m*
Syria (*ssi*-ri-ö) Siria *f*
Syrian (*ssi*-ri-ön) *adj* siriano
syringe (ssi-*rindʒ*) *n* siringa *f*
syrup (*ssi*-röp) *n* sciroppo *m*
system (*ssi*-sstöm) *n* sistema *m*; **decimal** ~ sistema decimale
systematic (ssi-sstö-*mæ*-tik) *adj* sistematico

T

table (*tei*-böl) *n* tavola *f*; tabella *f*; ~ **of contents** indice *m*; ~ **tennis** ping-pong *m*

table-cloth (*tei*-böl-kloθ) *n* tovaglia *f*
tablespoon (*tei*-böl-sspuun) *n* cucchiaio *m*
tablet (*tæ*-blit) *n* pasticca *f*
taboo (tö-*buu*) *n* tabù *m*
tactics (*tæk*-tikss) *pl* tattica *f*
tag (tægh) *n* etichetta *f*
tail (teil) *n* coda *f*
tail-light (*teil*-lait) *n* luce posteriore
tailor (*tei*-lö) *n* sarto *m*
tailor-made (*tei*-lö-meid) *adj* fatto su misura
***take** (teik) *v* *prendere; accompagnare; capire, afferrare; ~ **away** portar via; *togliere, levare; ~ **off** decollare; ~ **out** *togliere; ~ **over** rilevare; ~ **place** *aver luogo; ~ **up** occupare
take-off (*tei*-kof) *n* decollo *m*
tale (teil) *n* storia *f*, racconto *m*
talent (*tæ*-lönt) *n* attitudine *f*, talento *m*
talented (*tæ*-lön-tid) *adj* dotato
talk (took) *v* parlare; *n* conversazione *f*
talkative (*too*-kö-tiv) *adj* loquace
tall (tool) *adj* alto; lungo
tame (teim) *adj* mansueto, addomesticato; *v* addomesticare
tampon (*tæm*-pön) *n* tampone *m*
tangerine (tæn-dʒö-*riin*) *n* mandarino *m*
tangible (*tæn*-dʒi-böl) *adj* tangibile
tank (tængk) *n* serbatoio *m*
tanker (*tæng*-kö) *n* petroliera *f*
tanned (tænd) *adj* abbronzato
tap (tæp) *n* rubinetto *m*; colpetto *m*; *v* bussare
tape (teip) *n* nastro *m*; **adhesive** ~ nastro adesivo; cerotto *m*
tape-measure (*teip*-mê-ʒö) *n* centimetro *m*, metro a nastro
tape-recorder (*teip*-ri-koo-dö) *n* magnetofono *m*
tapestry (*tæ*-pi-sstri) *n* arazzo *m*, tappezzeria *f*
tar (taa) *n* catrame *m*
target (*taa*-ghit) *n* bersaglio *m*
tariff (*tæ*-rif) *n* tariffa *f*
tarpaulin (taa-*poo*-lin) *n* tela cerata
task (taassk) *n* compito *m*
taste (teisst) *n* gusto *m*; *v* *sapere; assaggiare
tasteless (*teisst*-löss) *adj* insipido
tasty (*tei*-ssti) *adj* gustoso, saporito
taught (toot) *v* (p, pp teach)
tavern (*tæ*-vön) *n* taverna *f*
tax (tækss) *n* tassa *f*; *v* tassare
taxation (tæk-*ssei*-ʃön) *n* imposta *f*
tax-free (*tækss*-frii) *adj* esente da tassa
taxi (*tæk*-ssi) *n* tassì *m*; ~ **rank** posteggio di autopubbliche; ~ **stand** *Am* posteggio di autopubbliche
taxi-driver (*tæk*-ssi-drai-vö) *n* tassista *m*
taxi-meter (*tæk*-ssi-mii-tö) *n* tassametro *m*
tea (tii) *n* tè *m*; merenda *f*
***teach** (tiitʃ) *v* insegnare
teacher (*tii*-tʃö) *n* docente *m*, insegnante *m*; professoressa *f*; maestro *m*
teachings (*tii*-tʃings) *pl* insegnamento *m*
tea-cloth (*tii*-kloθ) *n* canovaccio per stoviglie
teacup (*tii*-kap) *n* tazzina da tè
team (tiim) *n* squadra *f*
teapot (*tii*-pot) *n* teiera *f*
tear[1] (tiö) *n* lacrima *f*
tear[2] (têö) *n* strappo *m*; ***tear** *v* strappare
tear-jerker (*tiö*-dʒöö-kö) *n* sdolcinatura *f*
tease (tiis) *v* stuzzicare
tea-set (*tii*-ssêt) *n* servizio da tè
tea-shop (*tii*-ʃop) *n* sala da tè
teaspoon (*tii*-sspuun) *n* cucchiaino *m*

teaspoonful (*tii*-sspuun-ful) *n* cucchiaino *m*
technical (*têk*-ni-köl) *adj* tecnico
technician (têk-*ni*-ʃön) *n* tecnico *m*
technique (têk-*niik*) *n* tecnica *f*
technology (têk-*no*-lö-dʒi) *n* tecnologia *f*
teenager (*tii*-nei-dʒö) *n* adolescente *m*
teetotaller (tii-*tou*-tö-lö) *n* astemio *m*
telegram (*tê*-li-ghræm) *n* telegramma *m*
telegraph (*tê*-li-ghraaf) *v* telegrafare
telepathy (ti-*lê*-pö-θi) *n* telepatia *f*
telephone (*tê*-li-foun) *n* telefono *m*; ~ **book** *Am* elenco telefonico; ~ **booth** cabina telefonica; ~ **call** chiamata *f*; ~ **directory** elenco telefonico; ~ **exchange** centralino *m*; ~ **operator** telefonista *f*
telephonist (ti-*lê*-fö-nisst) *n* telefonista *f*
television (*tê*-li-vi-ʒön) *n* televisione *f*; ~ **set** televisore *m*
telex (*tê*-lêkss) *n* telex *m*
***tell** (têl) *v* *dire; raccontare
temper (*têm*-pö) *n* stizza *f*
temperature (*têm*-prö-tʃö) *n* temperatura *f*
tempest (*têm*-pisst) *n* tempesta *f*
temple (*têm*-pöl) *n* tempio *m*; tempia *f*
temporary (*têm*-pö-rö-ri) *adj* provvisorio, temporaneo
tempt (têmpt) *v* tentare
temptation (têmp-*tei*-ʃön) *n* tentazione *f*
ten (tên) *num* dieci
tenant (*tê*-nönt) *n* inquilino *m*
tend (tênd) *v* *tendere a; badare a; ~ **to** *tendere a
tendency (*tên*-dön-ssi) *n* inclinazione *f*, tendenza *f*
tender (*tên*-dö) *adj* delicato, dolce; tenero
tendon (*tên*-dön) *n* tendine *m*
tennis (*tê*-niss) *n* tennis *m*; ~ **shoes** scarpe da tennis
tennis-court (*tê*-niss-koot) *n* campo di tennis
tense (tênss) *adj* teso
tension (*tên*-ʃön) *n* tensione *f*
tent (tênt) *n* tenda *f*
tenth (tênθ) *num* decimo
tepid (*tê*-pid) *adj* tiepido
term (tööm) *n* termine *m*; periodo *m*; condizione *f*
terminal (*töö*-mi-nöl) *n* termine *m*
terrace (*tê*-röss) *n* terrazza *f*
terrain (tê-*rein*) *n* terreno *m*
terrible (*tê*-ri-böl) *adj* tremendo, spaventoso, terribile
terrific (tö-*ri*-fik) *adj* formidabile
terrify (*tê*-ri-fai) *v* sgomentare; **terrifying** spaventevole
territory (*tê*-ri-tö-ri) *n* territorio *m*
terror (*tê*-rö) *n* terrore *m*
terrorism (*tê*-rö-ri-söm) *n* terrorismo *m*
terrorist (*tê*-rö-risst) *n* terrorista *m*
terylene (*tê*-rö-liin) *n* terital *m*
test (têsst) *n* prova *f*, esame *m*; *v* provare, saggiare
testify (*tê*-ssti-fai) *v* testimoniare
text (têksst) *n* testo *m*
textbook (*têkss*-buk) *n* manuale *m*
textile (*têk*-sstail) *n* tessuto *m*
texture (*têkss*-tʃö) *n* struttura *f*
Thai (tai) *adj* tailandese
Thailand (*tai*-lænd) Tailandia *f*
than (ðæn) *conj* che
thank (θængk) *v* ringraziare; ~ **you** grazie
thankful (*θængk*-föl) *adj* riconoscente
that (ðæt) *adj* quello; *pron* quello; che; *conj* che
thaw (θoo) *v* disgelarsi; *n* disgelo *m*
the (ðö,ði) *art* il *art*; **the ... the** più ... più

theatre (*θiö*-tö) *n* teatro *m*
theft (θêft) *n* furto *m*
their (ðêö) *adj* loro
them (ðêm) *pron* li; loro
theme (θiim) *n* tema *m*, argomento *m*
themselves (ðöm-*ssêlvs*) *pron* si; essi stessi
then (ðên) *adv* allora; in seguito, poi; dunque
theology (θi-*o*-lö-dʒi) *n* teologia *f*
theoretical (θiö-*rê*-ti-köl) *adj* teorico
theory (*θiö*-ri) *n* teoria *f*
therapy (*θê*-rö-pi) *n* terapia *f*
there (ðêö) *adv* là; di là
therefore (*ðêö*-foo) *conj* quindi
thermometer (θö-*mo*-mi-tö) *n* termometro *m*
thermostat (*θöö*-mö-sstæt) *n* termostato *m*
these (ðiis) *adj* questi
thesis (*θii*-ssiss) *n* (pl theses) tesi *f*
they (ðei) *pron* essi
thick (θik) *adj* spesso; denso
thicken (*θi*-kön) *v* ispessire
thickness (*θik*-nöss) *n* spessore *m*
thief (θiif) *n* (pl thieves) ladro *m*
thigh (θai) *n* coscia *f*
thimble (*θim*-böl) *n* ditale *m*
thin (θin) *adj* sottile; magro
thing (θing) *n* cosa *f*
***think** (θingk) *v* pensare; *riflettere; ~ **of** pensare a; ricordare; ~ **over** ripensare
thinker (*θing*-kö) *n* pensatore *m*
third (θööd) *num* terzo
thirst (θöösst) *n* sete *f*
thirsty (*θöö*-ssti) *adj* assetato
thirteen (θöö-*tiin*) *num* tredici
thirteenth (θöö-*tiinθ*) *num* tredicesimo
thirtieth (*θöö*-ti-öθ) *num* trentesimo
thirty (*θöö*-ti) *num* trenta
this (ðiss) *adj* questo; *pron* questo
thistle (*θi*-ssöl) *n* cardo *m*
thorn (θoon) *n* spina *f*
thorough (*θa*-rö) *adj* minuzioso, accurato
thoroughbred (*θa*-rö-brêd) *adj* purosangue
thoroughfare (*θa*-rö-fêö) *n* strada maestra, arteria *f*
those (ðous) *adj* quei; *pron* quelli
though (ðou) *conj* sebbene, quantunque, benché; *adv* comunque
thought[1] (θoot) *v* (p, pp think)
thought[2] (θoot) *n* pensiero *m*
thoughtful (*θoot*-föl) *adj* pensieroso; premuroso
thousand (*θau*-sönd) *num* mille
thread (θrêd) *n* filo *m*; refe *m*; *v* infilare
threadbare (*θrêd*-bêö) *adj* liso
threat (θrêt) *n* minaccia *f*
threaten (*θrê*-tön) *v* minacciare; **threatening** minaccioso
three (θrii) *num* tre
three-quarter (θrii-*kuoo*-tö) *adj* tre quarti
threshold (*θrê*-ʃould) *n* soglia *f*
threw (θruu) *v* (p throw)
thrifty (*θrif*-ti) *adj* parsimonioso
throat (θrout) *n* gola *f*; collo *m*
throne (θroun) *n* trono *m*
through (θruu) *prep* attraverso
throughout (θruu-*aut*) *adv* dappertutto
throw (θrou) *n* tiro *m*
***throw** (θrou) *v* lanciare, gettare, buttare
thrush (θraʃ) *n* tordo *m*
thumb (θam) *n* pollice *m*
thumbtack (*θam*-tæk) *nAm* puntina da disegno
thump (θamp) *v* *percuotere
thunder (*θan*-dö) *n* tuono *m*; *v* tuonare
thunderstorm (*θan*-dö-sstoom) *n* tem-

porale *m*
thundery (*θan*-dö-ri) *adj* temporalesco
Thursday (*θöös*-di) giovedì *m*
thus (ðass) *adv* così
thyme (taim) *n* timo *m*
tick (tik) *n* segno *m*; ~ **off** segnare
ticket (*ti*-kit) *n* biglietto *m*; contravvenzione *f*; ~ **collector** controllore *m*; ~ **machine** biglietteria automatica
tickle (*ti*-köl) *v* solleticare
tide (taid) *n* marea *f*; **high** ~ alta marea; **low** ~ bassa marea
tidings (*tai*-dings) *pl* notizie
tidy (*tai*-di) *adj* ordinato; ~ **up** riordinare
tie (tai) *v* annodare, legare; *n* cravatta *f*
tiger (*tai*-ghö) *n* tigre *f*
tight (tait) *adj* stretto; attillato; *adv* strettamente
tighten (*tai*-tön) *v* serrare; *stringere; *restringersi
tights (taitss) *pl* calzamaglia *f*
tile (tail) *n* mattonella *f*; tegola *f*
till (til) *prep* fino a; *conj* finché non, finché
timber (*tim*-bö) *n* legname *m*
time (taim) *n* tempo *m*; volta *f*; **all the** ~ continuamente; **in** ~ in tempo; ~ **of arrival** ora di arrivo; ~ **of departure** ora di partenza
time-saving (*taim*-ssei-ving) *adj* che fa risparmiare tempo
timetable (*taim*-tei-böl) *n* orario *m*
timid (*ti*-mid) *adj* timido
timidity (ti-*mi*-dö-ti) *n* timidezza *f*
tin (tin) *n* stagno *m*; barattolo *m*, latta *f*; **tinned food** conserve *fpl*
tinfoil (*tin*-foil) *n* stagnola *f*
tin-opener (*ti*-nou-pö-nö) *n* apriscatole *m*
tiny (*tai*-ni) *adj* minuscolo
tip (tip) *n* punta *f*; mancia *f*
tire[1] (taiö) *n* pneumatico *m*
tire[2] (taiö) *v* stancare
tired (taiöd) *adj* affaticato, stanco; ~ **of** stufo di
tiring (*taiö*-ring) *adj* faticoso
tissue (*ti*-ʃuu) *n* tessuto *m*; fazzoletto di carta
title (*tai*-töl) *n* titolo *m*
to (tuu) *prep* fino a; a, per, da, verso; allo scopo di
toad (toud) *n* rospo *m*
toadstool (*toud*-sstuul) *n* fungo *m*
toast (tousst) *n* crostino *m*; brindisi *m*
tobacco (tö-*bæ*-kou) *n* (pl ~s) tabacco *m*; ~ **pouch** astuccio per tabacco
tobacconist (tö-*bæ*-kö-nisst) *n* tabaccaio *m*; **tobacconist's** tabaccheria *f*
today (tö-*dei*) *adv* oggi
toddler (*tod*-lö) *n* bimbo *m*
toe (tou) *n* dito del piede
toffee (*to*-fi) *n* caramella *f*
together (tö-*ghê*-ðö) *adv* insieme
toilet (*toi*-löt) *n* gabinetto *m*; ~ **case** astuccio di toeletta
toilet-paper (*toi*-löt-pei-pö) *n* carta igienica
toiletry (*toi*-lö-tri) *n* articoli da toeletta
token (*tou*-kön) *n* segno *m*; prova *f*; gettone *m*
told (tould) *v* (p, pp tell)
tolerable (*to*-lö-rö-böl) *adj* tollerabile
toll (toul) *n* pedaggio *m*
tomato (tö-*maa*-tou) *n* (pl ~es) pomodoro *m*
tomb (tuum) *n* tomba *f*
tombstone (*tuum*-sstoun) *n* pietra sepolcrale
tomorrow (tö-*mo*-rou) *adv* domani
ton (tan) *n* tonnellata *f*
tone (toun) *n* tono *m*; timbro *m*

tongs (tongs) *pl* pinze *fpl*
tongue (tang) *n* lingua *f*
tonic (*to*-nik) *n* tonico *m*
tonight (tö-*nait*) *adv* stanotte, stasera
tonsilitis (ton-ssö-*lai*-tiss) *n* tonsillite *f*
tonsils (*ton*-ssöls) *pl* tonsille *fpl*
too (tuu) *adv* troppo; anche
took (tuk) *v* (p take)
tool (tuul) *n* attrezzo *m*, arnese *m*; ~ **kit** cassetta degli arnesi
toot (tuut) *vAm* suonare il clacson
tooth (tuuθ) *n* (pl teeth) dente *m*
toothache (*tuu*-θeik) *n* mal di denti
toothbrush (*tuuθ*-braʃ) *n* spazzolino da denti
toothpaste (*tuuθ*-peisst) *n* dentifricio *m*
toothpick (*tuuθ*-pik) *n* stuzzicadenti *m*
toothpowder (*tuuθ*-pau-dö) *n* polvere dentifricia
top (top) *n* cima *f*; parte superiore; coperchio *m*; sommo; **on ~ of** in cima a; ~ **side** lato superiore
topcoat (*top*-kout) *n* soprabito *m*
topic (*to*-pik) *n* soggetto *m*
topical (*to*-pi-köl) *adj* attuale
torch (tootʃ) *n* torcia *f*; lampadina tascabile
torment[1] (too-*mênt*) *v* tormentare
torment[2] (*too*-mênt) *n* tormento *m*
torture (*too*-tʃö) *n* tortura *f*; *v* torturare
toss (toss) *v* gettare
tot (tot) *n* bimbetto *m*
total (*tou*-töl) *adj* totale; completo, assoluto; *n* totale *m*
totalitarian (tou-tæ-li-*têö*-ri-ön) *adj* totalitario
totalizator (*tou*-tö-lai-sei-tö) *n* totalizzatore *m*
touch (tatʃ) *v* toccare; colpire; *n* contatto *m*, tocco *m*; tatto *m*
touching (*ta*-tʃing) *adj* commovente
tough (taf) *adj* duro
tour (tuö) *n* gita turistica
tourism (*tuö*-ri-söm) *n* turismo *m*
tourist (*tuö*-risst) *n* turista *m*; ~ **class** classe turistica; ~ **office** ufficio turistico
tournament (*tuö*-nö-mönt) *n* torneo *m*
tow (tou) *v* trainare
towards (tö-*uoods*) *prep* verso
towel (tauöl) *n* asciugamano *m*
towelling (*tauö*-ling) *n* spugna *f*
tower (tauö) *n* torre *f*
town (taun) *n* città *f*; ~ **centre** centro della città; ~ **hall** municipio *m*
townspeople (*tauns*-pii-pöl) *pl* cittadinanza *f*
toxic (*tok*-ssik) *adj* tossico
toy (toi) *n* giocattolo *m*
toyshop (*toi*-ʃop) *n* negozio di giocattoli
trace (treiss) *n* traccia *f*; *v* rintracciare
track (træk) *n* binario *m*; pista *f*
tractor (*træk*-tö) *n* trattore *m*
trade (treid) *n* commercio *m*; mestiere *m*; *v* commerciare
trademark (*treid*-maak) *n* marchio di fabbrica
trader (*trei*-dö) *n* mercante *m*
tradesman (*treids*-mön) *n* (pl -men) commerciante *m*
trade-union (treid-*iuu*-niön) *n* sindacato *m*
tradition (trö-*di*-ʃön) *n* tradizione *f*
traditional (trö-*di*-ʃö-nöl) *adj* tradizionale
traffic (*træ*-fik) *n* traffico *m*; ~ **jam** ingorgo *m*; ~ **light** semaforo *m*
trafficator (*træ*-fi-kei-tö) *n* indicatore di direzione
tragedy (*træ*-dʒö-di) *n* tragedia *f*
tragic (*træ*-dʒik) *adj* tragico
trail (treil) *n* traccia *f*, sentiero *m*

trailer (*trei*-lö) *n* rimorchio *m*; *nAm* roulotte *f*
train (trein) *n* treno *m*; *v* ammaestrare, addestrare; **stopping** ~ accelerato *m*; **through** ~ treno diretto
training (*trei*-ning) *n* addestramento *m*
trait (treit) *n* tratto *m*
traitor (*trei*-tö) *n* traditore *m*
tram (træm) *n* tram *m*
tramp (træmp) *n* vagabondo *m*, barbone *m*; *v* vagabondare
tranquil (*træng*-kᵘil) *adj* tranquillo
tranquillizer (*træng*-kᵘi-lai-sö) *n* tranquillante *m*
transaction (træn-*sæk*-ʃön) *n* transazione *f*
transatlantic (træn-söt-*læn*-tik) *adj* transatlantico
transfer (trænss-*föö*) *v* trasferire
transform (trænss-*foom*) *v* trasformare
transformer (trænss-*foo*-mö) *n* trasformatore *m*
transition (træn-*ssi*-ʃön) *n* transizione *f*
translate (trænss-*leit*) *v* *tradurre
translation (trænss-*lei*-ʃön) *n* traduzione *f*
translator (trænss-*lei*-tö) *n* traduttore *m*
transmission (træns-*mi*-ʃön) *n* trasmissione *f*
transmit (træns-*mit*) *v* *trasmettere
transmitter (træns-*mi*-tö) *n* trasmettitore *m*
transparent (træn-*sspêᵒ*-rönt) *adj* trasparente
transport[1] (*træn*-sspoot) *n* trasporto *m*
transport[2] (træn-*sspoot*) *v* trasportare
transportation (træn-sspoo-*tei*-ʃön) *n* trasporto *m*
trap (træp) *n* trappola *f*
trash (træʃ) *n* robaccia *f*; ~ **can** *Am* pattumiera *f*
travel (*træ*-völ) *v* viaggiare; ~ **agency** agenzia viaggi; ~ **agent** agente di viaggio; ~ **insurance** assicurazione viaggi; **travelling expenses** spese di viaggio
traveller (*træ*-vö-lö) *n* viaggiatore *m*; **traveller's cheque** assegno turistico
tray (trei) *n* vassoio *m*
treason (*trii*-sön) *n* tradimento *m*
treasure (*trê*-ʒö) *n* tesoro *m*
treasurer (*trê*-ʒö-rö) *n* tesoriere *m*
treasury (*trê*-ʒö-ri) *n* Tesoro *m*
treat (triit) *v* trattare
treatment (*triit*-mönt) *n* trattamento *m*
treaty (*trii*-ti) *n* trattato *m*
tree (trii) *n* albero *m*
tremble (*trêm*-böl) *v* tremare; vibrare
tremendous (tri-*mên*-döss) *adj* enorme
trespass (*trêss*-pöss) *v* trasgredire
trespasser (*trêss*-pö-ssö) *n* trasgressore *m*
trial (traiᵒl) *n* processo *m*; prova *f*
triangle (*trai*-æng-ghöl) *n* triangolo *m*
triangular (trai-*æng*-ghʲu-lö) *adj* triangolare
tribe (traib) *n* tribù *f*
tributary (*tri*-bʲu-tö-ri) *n* braccio *m*
tribute (*tri*-bʲuut) *n* omaggio *m*
trick (trik) *n* tiro *m*; trucco *m*
trigger (*tri*-ghö) *n* grilletto *m*
trim (trim) *v* raccorciare
trip (trip) *n* gita *f*, viaggio *m*
triumph (*trai*-ömf) *n* trionfo *m*; *v* trionfare
triumphant (trai-*am*-fönt) *adj* trionfante
trolley-bus (*tro*-li-bass) *n* filobus *m*
troops (truupss) *pl* truppe *fpl*
tropical (*tro*-pi-köl) *adj* tropicale
tropics (*tro*-pikss) *pl* tropici *mpl*

trouble (*tra*-böl) *n* preoccupazione *f*, pena *f*, guaio *m*; *v* disturbare
troublesome (*tra*-böl-ssöm) *adj* molesto
trousers (*trau*-sös) *pl* pantaloni *mpl*
trout (traut) *n* (pl ~) trota *f*
truck (trak) *nAm* autocarro *m*
true (truu) *adj* vero; reale, autentico; leale, fedele
trumpet (*tram*-pit) *n* tromba *f*
trunk (trangk) *n* baule *m*; tronco *m*; *nAm* bagagliaio *m*; **trunks** *pl* calzoncini *mpl*
trunk-call (*trangk*-kool) *n* interurbana *f*
trust (trasst) *v* fidarsi; *n* fiducia *f*
trustworthy (*trasst*-^{u}öö-ði) *adj* fidato
truth (truuθ) *n* verità *f*
truthful (*truuθ*-föl) *adj* veritiero
try (trai) *v* tentare; sforzarsi; *n* tentativo *m*; ~ **on** provare
tube (t^{i}uub) *n* tubo *m*; tubetto *m*
tuberculosis (t^{i}uu-böö-k^{i}u-*lou*-ssiss) *n* tubercolosi *f*
Tuesday (*t^{i}uus*-di) martedì *m*
tug (tagh) *v* rimorchiare; *n* rimorchiatore *m*; strattone *m*
tuition (t^{i}uu-*i*-ʃön) *n* insegnamento *m*
tulip (*t^{i}uu*-lip) *n* tulipano *m*
tumbler (*tam*-blö) *n* bicchiere *m*
tumour (*t^{i}uu*-mö) *n* tumore *m*
tuna (*t^{i}uu*-nö) *n* (pl ~, ~s) tonno *m*
tune (t^{i}uun) *n* aria *f*, melodia *f*; ~ **in** sintonizzare
tuneful (*t^{i}uun*-föl) *adj* melodioso
tunic (*t^{i}uu*-nik) *n* tunica *f*
Tunisia (t^{i}uu-*ni*-si-ö) Tunisia *f*
Tunisian (t^{i}uu-*ni*-si-ön) *adj* tunisino
tunnel (*ta*-nöl) *n* galleria *f*
turbine (*töö*-bain) *n* turbina *f*
turbojet (töö-bou-*dʒêt*) *n* aereo a reazione
Turk (töök) *n* turco *m*
Turkey (*töö*-ki) Turchia *f*
turkey (*töö*-ki) *n* tacchino *m*
Turkish (*töö*-kiʃ) *adj* turco; ~ **bath** bagno turco
turn (töön) *v* voltare; *volgere, girare; *n* cambiamento *m*, giro *m*; tornante *m*; turno *m*; ~ **back** ritornare; ~ **down** *respingere; ~ **into** trasformarsi in; ~ **off** *chiudere; ~ **on** *accendere; *aprire; ~ **over** *capovolgere; ~ **round** voltare; rigirarsi
turning (*töö*-ning) *n* svolta *f*
turning-point (*töö*-ning-point) *n* punto decisivo
turnover (*töö*-nou-vö) *n* giro d'affari; ~ **tax** tassa sugli affari
turnpike (*töön*-paik) *nAm* strada a pedaggio
turpentine (*töö*-pön-tain) *n* trementina *f*
turtle (*töö*-töl) *n* tartaruga *f*
tutor (*t^{i}uu*-tö) *n* precettore *m*; tutore *m*
tuxedo (tak-*ssii*-dou) *nAm* (pl ~s, ~es) smoking *m*
tweed (t^{u}iid) *n* tweed *m*
tweezers (*t^{u}ii*-sös) *pl* pinzette *fpl*
twelfth (t^{u}êlfθ) *num* dodicesimo
twelve (t^{u}êlv) *num* dodici
twentieth (*t^{u}ên*-ti-öθ) *num* ventesimo
twenty (*t^{u}ên*-ti) *num* venti
twice (t^{u}aiss) *adv* due volte
twig (t^{u}igh) *n* ramoscello *m*
twilight (*t^{u}ai*-lait) *n* crepuscolo *m*
twine (t^{u}ain) *n* spago *m*
twins (t^{u}ins) *pl* gemelli *mpl*; **twin beds** letti gemelli
twist (t^{u}isst) *v* *torcere; *n* torsione *f*
two (tuu) *num* due
two-piece (tuu-*piiss*) *adj* in due pezzi
type (taip) *v* dattilografare; *n* tipo *m*
typewriter (*taip*-rai-tö) *n* macchina da scrivere
typewritten (*taip*-ri-tön) dattiloscritto

typhoid (*tai*-foid) *n* tifoidea *f*
typical (*ti*-pi-köl) *adj* caratteristico, tipico
typist (*tai*-pisst) *n* dattilografa *f*
tyrant (*taiö*-rönt) *n* tiranno *m*
tyre (taiö) *n* copertone *m*; ~ **pressure** pressione gomme

U

ugly (*a*-ghli) *adj* brutto
ulcer (*al*-ssö) *n* ulcera *f*
ultimate (*al*-ti-möt) *adj* ultimo
ultraviolet (al-trö-*vaiö*-löt) *adj* ultravioletto
umbrella (am-*brê*-lö) *n* ombrello *m*
umpire (*am*-paiö) *n* arbitro *m*
unable (a-*nei*-böl) *adj* incapace
unacceptable (a-nök-*ssêp*-tö-böl) *adj* inaccettabile
unaccountable (a-nö-*kaun*-tö-böl) *adj* inesplicabile
unaccustomed (a-nö-*ka*-sstömd) *adj* non abituato
unanimous (ⁱuu-*næ*-ni-möss) *adj* unanime
unanswered (a-*naan*-ssöd) *adj* senza riposta
unauthorized (a-*noo*-θö-raisd) *adj* illecito
unavoidable (a-nö-*voi*-dö-böl) *adj* inevitabile
unaware (a-nö-*ᵘêö*) *adj* incosciente
unbearable (an-*bêö*-rö-böl) *adj* insopportabile
unbreakable (an-*brei*-kö-böl) *adj* infrangibile
unbroken (an-*brou*-kön) *adj* intatto
unbutton (an-*ba*-tön) *v* sbottonare
uncertain (an-*ssöö*-tön) *adj* incerto
uncle (*ang*-köl) *n* zio *m*
unclean (an-*kliin*) *adj* sudicio
uncomfortable (an-*kam*-fö-tö-böl) *adj* scomodo
uncommon (an-*ko*-mön) *adj* insolito, raro
unconditional (an-kön-*di*-ʃö-nöl) *adj* incondizionato
unconscious (an-*kon*-ʃöss) *adj* inconscio
uncork (an-*kook*) *v* stappare
uncover (an-*ka*-vö) *v* *scoprire
uncultivated (an-*kal*-ti-vei-tid) *adj* incolto
under (*an*-dö) *prep* sotto
underestimate (an-dö-*rê*-ssti-meit) *v* sottovalutare
underground (*an*-dö-ghraund) *adj* sotterraneo; *n* metropolitana *f*
underline (an-dö-*lain*) *v* sottolineare
underneath (an-dö-*niiθ*) *adv* sotto
underpants (*an*-dö-pæntss) *plAm* mutandine *fpl*
undershirt (*an*-dö-ʃööt) *n* maglietta *f*
undersigned (*an*-dö-ssaind) *n* sottoscritto *m*
***understand** (an-dö-*sstænd*) *v* *comprendere, capire
understanding (an-dö-*sstæn*-ding) *n* comprensione *f*
***undertake** (an-dö-*teik*) *v* *intraprendere
undertaking (an-dö-*tei*-king) *n* impresa *f*
underwater (*an*-dö-ᵘoo-tö) *adj* subacqueo
underwear (*an*-dö-ᵘêö) *n* biancheria personale
undesirable (an-di-*saiö*-rö-böl) *adj* indesiderabile
***undo** (an-*duu*) *v* *disfare
undoubtedly (an-*dau*-tid-li) *adv* indubbiamente
undress (an-*drêss*) *v* spogliarsi
undulating (*an*-dⁱu-lei-ting) *adj* ondulato

unearned (a-*nöönd*) *adj* non meritato
uneasy (a-*nii*-si) *adj* inquieto
uneducated (a-*nê*-d'u-kei-tid) *adj* incolto
unemployed (a-nim-*ploid*) *adj* disoccupato
unemployment (a-nim-*ploi*-mönt) *n* disoccupazione *f*
unequal (a-*nii*-kᵘöl) *adj* ineguale
uneven (a-*nii*-vön) *adj* ineguale, ruvido; irregolare
unexpected (a-nik-*sspêk*-tid) *adj* inatteso, inaspettato
unfair (an-*fêö*) *adj* disonesto, ingiusto
unfaithful (an-*feiθ*-föl) *adj* infedele
unfamiliar (an-fö-*mil*-'ö) *adj* sconosciuto
unfasten (an-*faa*-ssön) *v* slacciare
unfavourable (an-*fei*-vö-rö-böl) *adj* sfavorevole
unfit (an-*fit*) *adj* disadatto
unfold (an-*fould*) *v* spiegare
unfortunate (an-*foo*-tʃö-nöt) *adj* sfortunato
unfortunately (an-*foo*-tʃö-nöt-li) *adv* disgraziatamente, sfortunatamente
unfriendly (an-*frênd*-li) *adj* poco gentile
unfurnished (an-*föö*-niʃt) *adj* non ammobiliato
ungrateful (an-*ghreit*-föl) *adj* ingrato
unhappy (an-*hæ*-pi) *adj* infelice
unhealthy (an-*hêl*-θi) *adj* malsano
unhurt (an-*hööt*) *adj* incolume
uniform (*'uu*-ni-foom) *n* uniforme *f*; *adj* uniforme
unimportant (a-nim-*poo*-tönt) *adj* insignificante
uninhabitable (a-nin-*hæ*-bi-tö-böl) *adj* inabitabile
uninhabited (a-nin-*hæ*-bi-tid) *adj* disabitato
unintentional (a-nin-*tên*-ʃö-nöl) *adj* involontario
union (*'uu*-n'ön) *n* unione *f*; lega *f*, confederazione *f*
unique ('uu-*niik*) *adj* unico
unit (*'uu*-nit) *n* unità *f*
unite ('uu-*nait*) *v* unire
United States ('uu-*nai*-tid ssteitss) Stati Uniti
unity (*'uu*-nö-ti) *n* unità *f*
universal ('uu-ni-*vöö*-ssöl) *adj* generale, universale
universe (*'uu*-ni-vööss) *n* universo *m*
university ('uu-ni-*vöö*-ssö-ti) *n* università *f*
unjust (an-*dʒasst*) *adj* ingiusto
unkind (an-*kaind*) *adj* sgarbato, scortese
unknown (an-*noun*) *adj* ignoto
unlawful (an-*loo*-föl) *adj* illegale
unlearn (an-*löön*) *v* disimparare
unless (ön-*lêss*) *conj* a meno che
unlike (an-*laik*) *adj* dissimile
unlikely (an-*lai*-kli) *adj* improbabile
unlimited (an-*li*-mi-tid) *adj* sconfinato, illimitato
unload (an-*loud*) *v* scaricare
unlock (an-*lok*) *v* *aprire
unlucky (an-*la*-ki) *adj* sfortunato
unnecessary (an-*nê*-ssö-ssö-ri) *adj* superfluo
unoccupied (a-*no*-k'u-paid) *adj* vacante
unofficial (a-nö-*fi*-ʃöl) *adj* ufficioso
unpack (an-*pæk*) *v* *disfare
unpleasant (an-*plê*-sönt) *adj* increscioso, spiacevole; sgradevole, antipatico
unpopular (an-*po*-p'u-lö) *adj* impopolare
unprotected (an-prö-*têk*-tid) *adj* indifeso
unqualified (an-*kᵘo*-li-faid) *adj* incompetente
unreal (an-*riöl*) *adj* irreale
unreasonable (an-*rii*-sö-nö-böl) *adj* ir-

ragionevole
unreliable (an-ri-*lai*-ö-böl) *adj* non fidato
unrest (an-*rêsst*) *n* agitazione *f*; inquietudine *f*
unsafe (an-*sseif*) *adj* malsicuro
unsatisfactory (an-ssæ-tiss-*fæk*-tö-ri) *adj* insoddisfacente
unscrew (an-*sskruu*) *v* svitare
unselfish (an-*ssêl*-fiʃ) *adj* disinteressato
unskilled (an-*sskild*) *adj* non qualificato
unsound (an-*ssaund*) *adj* malsano
unstable (an-*sstei*-böl) *adj* instabile
unsteady (an-*sstê*-di) *adj* barcollante, malfermo; vacillante
unsuccessful (an-ssök-*ssêss*-föl) *adj* infruttuoso
unsuitable (an-*ssuu*-tö-böl) *adj* inadatto
unsurpassed (an-ssö-*paasst*) *adj* insuperato
untidy (an-*tai*-di) *adj* disordinato
untie (an-*tai*) *v* slacciare
until (ön-*til*) *prep* fino a, finché
untrue (an-*truu*) *adj* falso
untrustworthy (an-*trasst*-ᵘöö-ði) *adj* malfido
unusual (an-*ⁱuu*-ʒu-öl) *adj* inconsueto, insolito
unwell (an-*ᵘêl*) *adj* indisposto
unwilling (an-*ᵘi*-ling) *adj* restio
unwise (an-*ᵘais*) *adj* incauto
unwrap (an-*ræp*) *v* *disfare
up (ap) *adv* verso l'alto, in su, su
upholster (ap-*houl*-sstö) *v* tappezzare
upkeep (*ap*-kiip) *n* mantenimento *m*
uplands (*ap*-lönds) *pl* altopiano *m*
upon (ö-*pon*) *prep* su
upper (*a*-pö) *adj* superiore
upright (*ap*-rait) *adj* diritto; *adv* in piedi
upset (ap-*ssêt*) *v* turbare; *adj* costernato
upside-down (ap-ssaid-*daun*) *adv* sottosopra
upstairs (ap-*sstêᵒs*) *adv* di sopra; su
upstream (ap-*sstriim*) *adv* contro corrente
upwards (*ap*-ᵘöds) *adv* in su
urban (*öö*-bön) *adj* urbano
urge (öödʒ) *v* stimolare; *n* impulso *m*
urgency (*öö*-dʒön-ssi) *n* urgenza *f*
urgent (*öö*-dʒönt) *adj* urgente
urine (*ⁱuᵒ*-rin) *n* urina *f*
Uruguay (*ⁱuᵒ*-rö-ghᵘai) Uruguay *m*
Uruguayan (ⁱuᵒ-rö-*ghᵘai*-ön) *adj* uruguaiano
us (ass) *pron* ci
usable (*ⁱuu*-sö-böl) *adj* usabile
usage (*ⁱuu*-sidʒ) *n* usanza *f*
use¹ (ⁱuus) *v* usare; ***be used to** *essere abituato a; ~ **up** consumare
use² (ⁱuuss) *n* uso *m*; utilità *f*; ***be of** ~ giovare
useful (*ⁱuuss*-föl) *adj* utile
useless (*ⁱuuss*-löss) *adj* inutile
user (*ⁱuu*-sö) *n* utente *m*
usher (*a*-ʃö) *n* usciere *m*
usherette (a-ʃö-*rêt*) *n* maschera *f*
usual (*ⁱuu*-ʒu-öl) *adj* solito
usually (*ⁱuu*-ʒu-ö-li) *adv* abitualmente
utensil (ⁱuu-*tên*-ssöl) *n* arnese *m*, utensile *m*
utility (ⁱuu-*ti*-lö-ti) *n* utilità *f*
utilize (*ⁱuu*-ti-lais) *v* utilizzare
utmost (*at*-mousst) *adj* estremo
utter (*a*-tö) *adj* completo, totale; *v* *emettere

V

vacancy (*vei*-kön-ssi) *n* posto libero
vacant (*vei*-könt) *adj* vacante
vacate (vö-*keit*) *v* sgombrare

vacation (vö-*kei*-ʃön) *n* vacanza *f*
vaccinate (*væk*-ssi-neit) *v* vaccinare
vaccination (væk-ssi-*nei*-ʃön) *n* vaccinazione *f*
vacuum (*væ*-k'u-öm) *n* vuoto *m*; *vAm* pulire con l'aspirapolvere; ~ **cleaner** aspirapolvere *m*; ~ **flask** termos *m*
vagrancy (*vei*-ghrön-ssi) *n* vagabondaggio *m*
vague (veigh) *adj* vago
vain (vein) *adj* vano; inutile; **in** ~ inutilmente, invano
valet (*væ*-lit) *n* cameriere *m*, valletto *m*
valid (*væ*-lid) *adj* valido
valley (*væ*-li) *n* valle *f*
valuable (*væ*-l'u-böl) *adj* prezioso; **valuables** *pl* valori
value (*væ*-l'uu) *n* valore *m*; *v* valutare
valve (vælv) *n* valvola *f*
van (væn) *n* furgone *m*
vanilla (vö-*ni*-lö) *n* vaniglia *f*
vanish (*væ*-niʃ) *v* sparire
vapour (*vei*-pö) *n* vapore *m*
variable (*vê*ö-ri-ö-böl) *adj* variabile
variation (vêö-ri-*ei*-ʃön) *n* variazione *f*; mutamento *m*
varied (*vê*ö-rid) *adj* assortito
variety (vö-*rai*-ö-ti) *n* varietà *f*; ~ **show** spettacollo di varietà; ~ **theatre** teatro di varietà
various (*vê*ö-ri-öss) *adj* vari, parecchi
varnish (*vaa*-niʃ) *n* lacca *f*, vernice *f*; *v* verniciare
vary (*vê*ö-ri) *v* differire, variare; cambiare
vase (vaas) *n* vaso *m*
vaseline (*væ*-ssö-liin) *n* vasellina *f*
vast (vaasst) *adj* immenso, vasto
vault (voolt) *n* volta *f*; camera blindata
veal (viil) *n* vitello *m*
vegetable (*vê*-dʒö-tö-böl) *n* verdura *f*; ~ **merchant** fruttivendolo *m*
vegetarian (vê-dʒi-*tê*ö-ri-ön) *n* vegetariano *m*
vegetation (vê-dʒi-*tei*-ʃön) *n* vegetazione *f*
vehicle (*vii*-ö-köl) *n* veicolo *m*
veil (veil) *n* velo *m*
vein (vein) *n* vena *f*; **varicose** ~ vena varicosa
velvet (*vêl*-vit) *n* velluto *m*
velveteen (vêl-vi-*tiin*) *n* velluto di cotone
venerable (*vê*-nö-rö-böl) *adj* venerabile
venereal disease (vi-*ni*ö-ri-öl di-*siis*) malattia venerea
Venezuela (vê-ni-*s*u*ei*-lö) Venezuela *m*
Venezuelan (vê-ni-*s*u*ei*-lön) *adj* venezolano
ventilate (*vên*-ti-leit) *v* ventilare; aerare
ventilation (vên-ti-*lei*-ʃön) *n* ventilazione *f*; aerazione *f*
ventilator (*vên*-ti-lei-tö) *n* ventilatore *m*
venture (*vên*-tʃö) *v* arrischiare
veranda (vö-*ræn*-dö) *n* veranda *f*
verb (vööb) *n* verbo *m*
verbal (*vöö*-böl) *adj* verbale
verdict (*vöö*-dikt) *n* sentenza *f*, verdetto *m*
verge (vöödʒ) *n* bordo *m*
verify (*vê*-ri-fai) *v* verificare
verse (vööss) *n* verso *m*
version (*vöö*-ʃön) *n* versione *f*; traduzione *f*
versus (*vöö*-ssöss) *prep* contro
vertical (*vöö*-ti-köl) *adj* verticale
vertigo (*vöö*-ti-ghou) *n* vertigine *f*
very (*vê*-ri) *adv* assai, molto; *adj* vero, preciso; estremo
vessel (*vê*-ssöl) *n* nave *f*, vascello *m*; recipiente *m*

vest (vêsst) *n* maglia *f*; *nAm* panciotto *m*
veterinary surgeon (*vê*-tri-nö-ri *ssöö*-dʒön) veterinario *m*
via (vai[ö]) *prep* via
viaduct (*vai[ö]*-dakt) *n* viadotto *m*
vibrate (vai-*breit*) *v* vibrare
vibration (vai-*brei*-ʃön) *n* vibrazione *f*
vicar (*vi*-kö) *n* vicario *m*
vicarage (*vi*-kö-ridʒ) *n* presbiterio *m*
vice-president (vaiss-*prê*-si-dönt) *n* vicepresidente *m*
vicinity (vi-*ssi*-nö-ti) *n* prossimità *f*, vicinanza *f*
vicious (*vi*-ʃöss) *adj* corrotto
victim (*vik*-tim) *n* vittima *f*
victory (*vik*-tö-ri) *n* vittoria *f*
view (v[i]uu) *n* vista *f*; parere *m*, opinione *f*; *v* guardare
view-finder (*v[i]uu*-fain-dö) *n* mirino *m*
vigilant (*vi*-dʒi-lönt) *adj* vigilante
villa (*vi*-lö) *n* villa *f*
village (*vi*-lidʒ) *n* villaggio *m*
villain (*vi*-lön) *n* furfante *m*
vine (vain) *n* vite *f*
vinegar (*vi*-ni-ghö) *n* aceto *m*
vineyard (*vin*-[i]öd) *n* vigna *f*
vintage (*vin*-tidʒ) *n* vendemmia *f*
violation (vai[ö]-*lei*-ʃön) *n* violazione *f*
violence (*vai[ö]*-lönss) *n* violenza *f*
violent (*vai[ö]*-lönt) *adj* violento; intenso, impetuoso
violet (*vai[ö]*-löt) *n* violetta *f*; *adj* violetto
violin (vai[ö]-*lin*) *n* violino *m*
virgin (*vöö*-dʒin) *n* vergine *f*
virtue (*vöö*-tʃuu) *n* virtù *f*
visa (*vii*-sö) *n* visto *m*
visibility (vi-sö-*bi*-lö-ti) *n* visibilità *f*
visible (*vi*-sö-böl) *adj* visibile
vision (*vi*-ʒön) *n* visione *f*
visit (*vi*-sit) *v* visitare; *n* visita *f*; **visiting hours** ore di visita
visiting-card (*vi*-si-ting-kaad) *n* biglietto da visita
visitor (*vi*-si-tö) *n* visitatore *m*
vital (*vai*-töl) *adj* vitale
vitamin (*vi*-tö-min) *n* vitamina *f*
vivid (*vi*-vid) *adj* vivido
vocabulary (vö-*kæ*-b[i]u-lö-ri) *n* vocabolario *m*; glossario *m*
vocal (*vou*-köl) *adj* vocale
vocalist (*vou*-kö-lisst) *n* cantante *m*
voice (voiss) *n* voce *f*
void (void) *adj* nullo
volcano (vol-*kei*-nou) *n* (pl ~es, ~s) vulcano *m*
volt (voult) *n* volt *m*
voltage (*voul*-tidʒ) *n* voltaggio *m*
volume (*vo*-l[i]um) *n* volume *m*
voluntary (*vo*-lön-tö-ri) *adj* volontario
volunteer (vo-lön-*ti[ö]*) *n* volontario *m*
vomit (*vo*-mit) *v* rigettare, vomitare
vote (vout) *v* votare; *n* voto *m*; votazione *f*
voucher (*vau*-tʃö) *n* buono *m*, ricevuta *f*
vow (vau) *n* promessa *f*, giuramento *m*; *v* giurare
vowel (vau[ö]l) *n* vocale *f*
voyage (*voi*-idʒ) *n* viaggio *m*
vulgar (*val*-ghö) *adj* volgare; popolano, triviale
vulnerable (*val*-nö-rö-böl) *adj* vulnerabile
vulture (*val*-tʃö) *n* avvoltoio *m*

W

wade ([u]eid) *v* guadare
wafer (*[u]ei*-fö) *n* ostia *f*
waffle (*[u]o*-föl) *n* cialda *f*
wages (*[u]ei*-dʒis) *pl* stipendio *m*
waggon (*[u]æ*-ghön) *n* vagone *m*
waist ([u]eisst) *n* vita *f*
waistcoat (*[u]eiss*-kout) *n* panciotto *m*

wait (ᵘeit) *v* aspettare ; ~ **on** servire
waiter (ᵘ*ei*-tö) *n* cameriere *m*
waiting (ᵘ*ei*-ting) *n* attesa *f*
waiting-list (ᵘ*ei*-ting-lisst) *n* lista di attesa
waiting-room (ᵘ*ei*-ting-ruum) *n* sala d'aspetto
waitress (ᵘ*ei*-triss) *n* cameriera *f*
***wake** (ᵘeik) *v* svegliare ; ~ **up** destarsi, svegliarsi
walk (ᵘook) *v* camminare ; passeggiare ; *n* passeggiata *f* ; andatura *f* ; **walking** a piedi
walker (ᵘ*oo*-kö) *n* camminatore *m*
walking-stick (ᵘ*oo*-king-sstik) *n* bastone da passeggio
wall (ᵘool) *n* muro *m* ; parete *f*
wallet (ᵘ*o*-lit) *n* portafoglio *m*
wallpaper (ᵘ*ool*-pei-pö) *n* carta da parati
walnut (ᵘ*ool*-nat) *n* noce *f*
waltz (ᵘoolss) *n* valzer *m*
wander (ᵘ*on*-dö) *v* errare, vagare
want (ᵘont) *v* *volere ; desiderare ; *n* bisogno *m* ; scarsezza *f*, mancanza *f*
war (ᵘoo) *n* guerra *f*
warden (ᵘ*oo*-dön) *n* custode *m*, guardiano *m*
wardrobe (ᵘ*oo*-droub) *n* guardaroba *m*
warehouse (ᵘ*êö*-hauss) *n* magazzino *m*, deposito *m*
wares (ᵘêös) *pl* merci
warm (ᵘoom) *adj* caldo ; *v* scaldare
warmth (ᵘoomθ) *n* calore *m*
warn (ᵘoon) *v* avvisare
warning (ᵘ*oo*-ning) *n* avvertimento *m*
wary (ᵘ*êö*-ri) *adj* prudente
was (ᵘos) *v* (p be)
wash (ᵘoʃ) *v* lavare ; ~ **and wear** non si stira ; ~ **up** lavare i piatti
washable (ᵘ*o*-ʃö-böl) *adj* lavabile
wash-basin (ᵘ*oʃ*-bei-ssön) *n* lavandino *m*
washing (ᵘ*o*-ʃing) *n* lavaggio *m* ; bucato *m*
washing-machine (ᵘ*o*-ʃing-mö-ʃiin) *n* lavatrice *f*
washing-powder (ᵘ*o*-ʃing-pau-dö) *n* detersivo *m*
washroom (ᵘ*oʃ*-ruum) *nAm* toletta *f*
wash-stand (ᵘ*oʃ*-sstænd) *n* lavandino *m*
wasp (ᵘossp) *n* vespa *f*
waste (ᵘeisst) *v* sprecare ; *n* spreco *m* ; *adj* incolto
wasteful (ᵘ*eisst*-föl) *adj* spendereccio
wastepaper-basket (ᵘeisst-*pei*-pö-baa-sskit) *n* cestino *m*
watch (ᵘotʃ) *v* guardare, osservare ; *tenere d'occhio ; *n* orologio *m* ; ~ **out** *stare in guardia
watch-maker (ᵘ*otʃ*-mei-kö) *n* orologiaio *m*
watch-strap (ᵘ*otʃ*-sstræp) *n* cinturino da orologio
water (ᵘ*oo*-tö) *n* acqua *f* ; **iced** ~ acqua ghiacciata ; **running** ~ acqua corrente ; ~ **pump** pompa ad acqua ; ~ **ski** sci d'acqua
water-colour (ᵘ*oo*-tö-ka-lö) *n* acquerello *m*
watercress (ᵘ*oo*-tö-krêss) *n* crescione *m*
waterfall (ᵘ*oo*-tö-fool) *n* cascata *f*
watermelon (ᵘ*oo*-tö-mê-lön) *n* anguria *f*
waterproof (ᵘ*oo*-tö-pruuf) *adj* impermeabile
water-softener (ᵘoo-tö-ssof-nö) *n* addolcitore *m*
waterway (ᵘ*oo*-tö-ᵘei) *n* via d'acqua
watt (ᵘot) *n* watt *m*
wave (ᵘeiv) *n* ricciolo *m*, onda *f* ; *v* sventolare
wave-length (ᵘ*eiv*-lêngθ) *n* lunghezza d'onda
wavy (ᵘ*ei*-vi) *adj* ondulato

wax (ᵘækss) *n* cera *f*
waxworks (*ᵘækss*-ᵘöökss) *pl* museo delle cere
way (ᵘei) *n* maniera *f*, modo *m*; via *f*; lato *m*, direzione *f*; distanza *f*; **any ~** comunque; **by the ~** a proposito; **one-way traffic** senso unico; **out of the ~** remoto; **the other ~ round** alla rovescia; **~ back** ritorno *m*; **~ in** entrata *f*; **~ out** uscita *f*
wayside (*ᵘei*-ssaid) *n* margine della strada
we (ᵘii) *pron* noi
weak (ᵘiik) *adj* debole; diluito
weakness (*ᵘiik*-nöss) *n* debolezza *f*
wealth (ᵘêlθ) *n* ricchezza *f*
wealthy (*ᵘêl*-θi) *adj* ricco
weapon (*ᵘê*-pön) *n* arma *f*
***wear** (ᵘêᵒ) *v* indossare, vestire; **~ out** logorare
weary (*ᵘiᵒ*-ri) *adj* affaticato, stanco
weather (*ᵘê*-ðö) *n* tempo *m*; **~ forecast** bollettino meteorologico
***weave** (ᵘiiv) *v* tessere
weaver (*ᵘii*-vö) *n* tessitore *m*
wedding (*ᵘê*-ding) *n* sposalizio *m*, matrimonio *m*
wedding-ring (*ᵘê*-ding-ring) *n* fede *f*
wedge (ᵘêdʒ) *n* cuneo *m*
Wednesday (*ᵘêns*-di) mercoledì *m*
weed (ᵘiid) *n* erbaccia *f*
week (ᵘiik) *n* settimana *f*
weekday (*ᵘiik*-dei) *n* giorno feriale
weekend (*ᵘii*-kênd) *n* fine-settimana
weekly (*ᵘii*-kli) *adj* settimanale
***weep** (ᵘiip) *v* *piangere
weigh (ᵘei) *v* pesare
weighing-machine (*ᵘei*-ing-mö-ʃiin) *n* bilancia *f*
weight (ᵘeit) *n* peso *m*
welcome (*ᵘêl*-köm) *adj* benvenuto; *n* accoglienza *f*; *v* *accogliere
weld (ᵘêld) *v* saldare
welfare (*ᵘêl*-fêᵒ) *n* benessere *m*
well[1] (ᵘêl) *adv* bene; *adj* sano; **as ~** pure, come pure; **as ~ as** come pure; **well!** ebbene!
well[2] (ᵘêl) *n* pozzo *m*
well-founded (ᵘêl-*faun*-did) *adj* fondato
well-known (*ᵘêl*-noun) *adj* noto
well-to-do (ᵘêl-tö-*duu*) *adj* agiato
went (ᵘênt) *v* (p go)
were (ᵘöö) *v* (p be)
west (ᵘêsst) *n* occidente *m*, ovest *m*
westerly (*ᵘê*-sstö-li) *adj* occidentale
western (*ᵘê*-sstön) *adj* occidentale
wet (ᵘêt) *adj* bagnato; umido
whale (ᵘeil) *n* balena *f*
wharf (ᵘoof) *n* (pl ~s, wharves) molo *m*
what (ᵘot) *pron* che cosa; quello che; **~ for** perché
whatever (ᵘo-*tê*-vö) *pron* qualsiasi
wheat (ᵘiit) *n* frumento *m*
wheel (ᵘiil) *n* ruota *f*
wheelbarrow (*ᵘiil*-bæ-rou) *n* carriola *f*
wheelchair (*ᵘiil*-tʃêᵒ) *n* sedia a rotelle
when (ᵘên) *adv* quando; *conj* qualora, quando
whenever (ᵘê-*nê*-vö) *conj* ogniqualvolta
where (ᵘêᵒ) *adv* dove; *conj* dove
wherever (ᵘêᵒ-*rê*-vö) *conj* dovunque
whether (*ᵘê*-ðö) *conj* se; **whether ... or** se ... o
which (ᵘitʃ) *pron* quale; che
whichever (ᵘi-*tʃê*-vö) *adj* qualsiasi
while (ᵘail) *conj* mentre; *n* istante *m*
whilst (ᵘailsst) *conj* mentre
whim (ᵘim) *n* ghiribizzo *m*, capriccio *m*
whip (ᵘip) *n* frusta *f*; *v* sbattere
whiskers (*ᵘi*-ssksös) *pl* basette *fpl*
whisper (*ᵘi*-sspö) *v* mormorare; *n* sussurro *m*

whistle (*ᵘi*-ssöl) *v* fischiare; *n* fischio *m*
white (ᵘait) *adj* bianco
whitebait (*ᵘait*-beit) *n* pesciolino *m*
whiting (*ᵘai*-ting) *n* (pl ~) merlano *m*
Whitsun (*ᵘit*-ssön) Pentecoste *f*
who (huu) *pron* chi; che
whoever (huu-*ê*-vö) *pron* chiunque
whole (houl) *adj* completo, intero; intatto; *n* totale *m*
wholesale (*houl*-sseil) *n* ingrosso *m*; ~ **dealer** grossista *m*
wholesome (*houl*-ssöm) *adj* salubre
wholly (*houl*-li) *adv* completamente
whom (huum) *pron* a chi
whore (hoo) *n* puttana *f*
whose (huus) *pron* il cui; di chi
why (ᵘai) *adv* perché
wicked (*ᵘi*-kid) *adj* scellerato
wide (ᵘaid) *adj* vasto, largo
widen (*ᵘai*-dön) *v* allargare
widow (*ᵘi*-dou) *n* vedova *f*
widower (*ᵘi*-dou-ö) *n* vedovo *m*
width (ᵘidθ) *n* larghezza *f*
wife (ᵘaif) *n* (pl wives) consorte *f*, moglie *f*
wig (ᵘigh) *n* parrucca *f*
wild (ᵘaild) *adj* selvatico; feroce
will (ᵘil) *n* volontà *f*; testamento *m*
***will** (ᵘil) *v* *volere
willing (*ᵘi*-ling) *adj* compiacente
willingly (*ᵘi*-ling-li) *adv* volentieri
will-power (*ᵘil*-pauᵒ) *n* forza di volontà
***win** (ᵘin) *v* *vincere
wind (ᵘind) *n* vento *m*
***wind** (ᵘaind) *v* zigzagare; caricare, *avvolgere
winding (*ᵘain*-ding) *adj* serpeggiante
windmill (*ᵘind*-mil) *n* mulino a vento
window (*ᵘin*-dou) *n* finestra *f*
window-sill (*ᵘin*-dou-ssil) *n* davanzale *m*
windscreen (*ᵘind*-sskriin) *n* parabrezza *m*; ~ **wiper** tergicristallo *m*
windshield (*ᵘind*-ʃiild) *nAm* parabrezza *m*; ~ **wiper** *Am* tergicristallo *m*
windy (*ᵘin*-di) *adj* ventoso
wine (ᵘain) *n* vino *m*
wine-cellar (*ᵘain*-ssê-lö) *n* cantina *f*
wine-list (*ᵘain*-lisst) *n* lista dei vini
wine-merchant (*ᵘain*-möö-tʃönt) *n* mercante di vini
wine-waiter (*ᵘain*-ᵘei-tö) *n* cantiniere *m*
wing (ᵘing) *n* ala *f*
winkle (*ᵘing*-köl) *n* chiocciola di mare
winner (*ᵘi*-nö) *n* vincitore *m*
winning (*ᵘi*-ning) *adj* vincente; **winnings** *pl* vincita *f*
winter (*ᵘin*-tö) *n* inverno *m*; ~ **sports** sport invernali
wipe (ᵘaip) *v* strofinare, asciugare; spazzare
wire (ᵘaiᵒ) *n* filo *m*; filo di ferro
wireless (*ᵘaiᵒ*-löss) *n* radio *f*
wisdom (*ᵘis*-döm) *n* saggezza *f*
wise (ᵘais) *adj* saggio
wish (ᵘiʃ) *v* desiderare; *n* desiderio *m*
witch (ᵘitʃ) *n* strega *f*
with (ᵘið) *prep* con; presso; per
***withdraw** (ᵘið-*droo*) *v* ritirare
within (ᵘi-*ðin*) *prep* dentro; *adv* all'interno
without (ᵘi-*ðaut*) *prep* senza
witness (*ᵘit*-nöss) *n* testimone *m*
wits (ᵘitss) *pl* ragione *f*
witty (*ᵘi*-ti) *adj* spiritoso
wolf (ᵘulf) *n* (pl wolves) lupo *m*
woman (*ᵘu*-mön) *n* (pl women) donna *f*
womb (ᵘuum) *n* utero *m*
won (ᵘan) *v* (p, pp win)
wonder (*ᵘan*-dö) *n* miracolo *m*; stupore *m*; *v* *chiedersi
wonderful (*ᵘan*-dö-föl) *adj* stupendo, meraviglioso; delizioso

wood (uud) *n* legno *m*; bosco *m*
wood-carving (*uud*-kaa-ving) *n* scultura in legno
wooded (*uu*-did) *adj* boscoso
wooden (*uu*-dön) *adj* di legno; ~ **shoe** zoccolo *m*
woodland (*uud*-lönd) *n* terreno boscoso
wool (uul) *n* lana *f*; **darning** ~ lana da rammendo
woollen (*uu*-lön) *adj* di lana
word (uööd) *n* parola *f*
wore (uoo) *v* (p wear)
work (uöök) *n* lavoro *m*; attività *f*; *v* lavorare; funzionare; **working day** giorno lavorativo; ~ **of art** opera d'arte; ~ **permit** permesso di lavoro
worker (*uöö*-kö) *n* lavoratore *m*
working (*uöö*-king) *n* funzionamento *m*
workman (*uöök*-mön) *n* (pl -men) operaio *m*
works (uöökss) *pl* fabbrica *f*
workshop (*uöök*-ʃop) *n* officina *f*
world (uööld) *n* mondo *m*; ~ **war** guerra mondiale
world-famous (uööld-*fei*-möss) *adj* di fama mondiale
world-wide (*uööld*-uaid) *adj* mondiale
worm (uööm) *n* verme *m*
worn (uoon) *adj* (pp wear) consumato
worn-out (uoon-*aut*) *adj* usato
worried (*ua*-rid) *adj* preoccupato
worry (*ua*-ri) *v* preoccuparsi; *n* ansia *f*, preoccupazione *f*
worse (uööss) *adj* peggiore; *adv* peggio
worship (*uöö*-ʃip) *v* venerare; *n* culto *m*
worst (uöösst) *adj* pessimo; *adv* peggio
worsted (*uu*-sstid) *n* lana pettinata
worth (uööθ) *n* valore *m*; ***be** ~ *valere; ***be worth-while** *valer la pena
worthless (*uööθ*-löss) *adj* senza valore
worthy of (*uöö*-ði öv) degno di
would (uud) *v* (p will) *solere
wound[1] (uuund) *n* ferita *f*; *v* *offendere, ferire
wound[2] (uaund) *v* (p, pp wind)
wrap (ræp) *v* *avvolgere
wreck (rêk) *n* relitto *m*; *v* *distruggere
wrench (rêntʃ) *n* chiave *f*; storta *f*; *v* *storcere
wrinkle (*ring*-köl) *n* ruga *f*
wrist (risst) *n* polso *m*
wrist-watch (*risst*-uotʃ) *n* orologio da polso
***write** (rait) *v* *scrivere; **in writing** per iscritto; ~ **down** annotare
writer (*rai*-tö) *n* scrittore *m*
writing-pad (*rai*-ting-pæd) *n* blocco per appunti, blocco di carta da lettere
writing-paper (*rai*-ting-pei-pö) *n* carta da lettere
written (*ri*-tön) *adj* (pp write) per iscritto
wrong (rong) *adj* erroneo, sbagliato; *n* torto *m*; *v* *fare un torto; ***be** ~ *avere torto
wrote (rout) *v* (p write)

Xmas (*kriss*-möss) Natale
X-ray (*êkss*-rei) *n* radiografia *f*; *v* radiografare

Y

yacht (ˈot) *n* panfilo *m*
yacht-club (ˈ*ot*-klab) *n* circolo nautico
yachting (ˈ*o*-ting) *n* sport velico
yard (ˈaad) *n* cortile *m*
yarn (ˈaan) *n* filo *m*
yawn (ˈoon) *v* sbadigliare
year (ˈiö) *n* anno *m*
yearly (ˈ*iö*-li) *adj* annuale
yeast (ˈiisst) *n* lievito *m*
yell (ˈêl) *v* strillare; *n* strillo *m*
yellow (ˈ*ê*-lou) *adj* giallo
yes (ˈêss) sì
yesterday (ˈ*ê*-sstö-di) *adv* ieri
yet (ˈêt) *adv* ancora; *conj* eppure, però, ma
yield (ˈiild) *v* *rendere; cedere
yoke (ˈouk) *n* giogo *m*
yolk (ˈouk) *n* tuorlo *m*
you (ˈuu) *pron* tu; ti; Lei; Le; voi; vi
young (ˈang) *adj* giovane
your (ˈoo) *adj* Suo; tuo; vostro, vostri
yourself (ˈoo-*ssêlf*) *pron* ti; tu stesso; Lei stesso
yourselves (ˈoo-*ssêlvs*) *pron* vi; voi stessi
youth (ˈuuθ) *n* gioventù *f*; ~ **hostel** ostello della gioventù
Yugoslav (ˈuu-ghö-*sslaav*) *n* iugoslavo *m*
Yugoslavia (ˈuu-ghö-*sslaa*-vi-ö) Iugoslavia *f*

Z

zeal (siil) *n* zelo *m*
zealous (*sê*-löss) *adj* zelante
zebra (*sii*-brö) *n* zebra *f*
zenith (*sê*-niθ) *n* zenit *m*; apice *m*
zero (*siö*-rou) *n* (pl ~s) zero *m*
zest (sêsst) *n* gusto *m*
zinc (singk) *n* zinco *m*
zip (sip) *n* chiusura lampo; ~ **code** *Am* codice postale
zipper (*si*-pö) *n* chiusura lampo
zodiac (*sou*-di-æk) *n* zodiaco *m*
zone (soun) *n* zona *f*
zoo (suu) *n* (pl ~s) giardino zoologico
zoology (sou-*o*-lö-dʒi) *n* zoologia *f*

Lessico gastronomico

Cibi

à la carte secondo la lista delle vivande
almond mandorla
anchovy acciuga
angel food cake dolce a base di albumi
angels on horseback ostriche avvolte in fettine di pancetta, cotte alla griglia e servite su pane tostato
appetizer stuzzichino
apple mela
~ **charlotte** torta di mele coperta con fette di pane
~ **dumpling** mela ricoperta di pasta e cotta nel forno
~ **sauce** salsa di mele
apricot albicocca
Arbroath smoky eglefino affumicato
artichoke carciofo
asparagus asparago
~ **tip** punta d'asparago
aspic gelantina
assorted assortito
aubergine melanzana
bacon pancetta
~ **and eggs** uova con pancetta
bagel panino a forma di corona
baked al forno
~ **Alaska** omelette alla norvegese; dessert con gelato alla vaniglia e meringhe
~ **beans** fagioli bianchi con salsa di pomodoro
~ **potato** patate cotte al forno con la buccia
Bakewell tart crostata con mandorle e marmellata di lamponi
baloney varietà di mortadella
banana banana
~ **split** banana tagliata a metà e servita con gelato, noci, sciroppo o cioccolata
barbecue 1) carne di manzo tritata, servita in un panino con salsa di pomodoro piccante 2) pasto all'aperto a base di carne ai ferri fatta al momento
~ **sauce** salsa di pomodoro molto piccante
barbecued ai ferri
basil basilico
bass branzino
bean fagiolo
beef manzo
~ **olive** involtino di manzo
beefburger medaglione di carne di manzo ai ferri, servito in un panino
beet, beetroot barbabietola
bilberry mirtillo
bill conto
~ **of fare** menù, lista delle vi-

vande
biscuit 1) biscotto, pasticcino (GB) 2) panino (US)
black pudding sanguinaccio
blackberry mora
blackcurrant ribes nero
bloater aringa salata e affumicata
blood sausage sanguinaccio
blueberry mirtillo
boiled bollito
Bologna (sausage) mortadella
bone osso
boned disossato
Boston baked beans piatto di fagioli bianchi, cotti con pancetta e zucchero grezzo
Boston cream pie torta a strati, ripiena di crema e con glassa al cioccolato
brains cervella
braised brasato
bramble pudding budino di more a cui possono essere aggiunte mele tagliate a pezzetti
braunschweiger specie di paté di fegato
bread pane
breaded impanato
breakfast prima colazione
bream pagello
breast petto
brisket punta di petto
broad bean grossa fava
broth brodo
brown Betty torta di mele con spezie, coperta di uno strato di pasta frolla
brunch pasto abbondante, preso in tarda mattinata, che riunisce la colazione e il pranzo
brussels sprout cavolino di Bruxelles
bubble and squeak frittelle di purea di patate e di cavolo, a volte con pezzetti di manzo
bun 1) panino al latte con frutta secca (GB) 2) varietà di panino (US)
butter burro
buttered imburrato
cabbage cavolo
Caesar salad insalata con crostini all'aroma d'aglio, acciughe e formaggio grattugiato
cake torta, dolce
cakes pasticcini, biscotti
calf vitello
Canadian bacon filetto di maiale affumicato, tagliato a fette sottili
canapé panino imbottito
cantaloupe melone
caper cappero
capercaillie, capercailzie gallo cedrone
caramel caramello
carp carpa
carrot carota
cashew noce di acagiù
casserole casseruola; stufato
catfish pesce gatto
catsup ketchup, salsa di pomodoro con aceto e spezie
cauliflower cavolfiore
celery sedano
cereal fiocchi di mais, avena o altri cereali, serviti con latte freddo e zucchero
  hot ~ pappa di cereali calda
chateaubriand filetto di manzo di prima scelta cotto ai ferri
check il conto
Cheddar (cheese) formaggio di pasta dura, grasso e di gusto leggermente acido
cheese formaggio
  ~ board piatto di formaggio
  ~ cake dolce al formaggio doppia panna

cheeseburger amburghese con una fetta di formaggio fuso, servito in un panino
chef's salad insalata di prosciutto, pollo, uova sode, pomodoro, lattuga e formaggio
cherry ciliegia
chestnut castagna
chicken pollo
chicory 1) indivia (GB) 2) cicoria (US)
chili con carne piatto a base di manzo tritato, fagioli borlotti e pepe di Caienna
chili pepper pepe di Caienna
chips 1) patate fritte (GB) 2) patatine (US)
chitt(er)lings trippa di maiale
chive erba cipollina
chocolate cioccolato
~ **pudding** 1) budino al cioccolato (GB) 2) spuma al cioccolato (US)
choice scelta
chop cotoletta, braciola
~ **suey** piatto a base di carne o di pollo, verdure e riso
chopped sminuzzato, tritato
chowder zuppa densa di pesce, di frutti di mare o di carne
Christmas pudding budino a base di frutta candita, scorza di limone, cedro; a volte alla fiamma
cinnamon cannella
chutney salsa indiana molto piccante
clam vongola, tellina
club sandwich panino imbottito con pancetta, pollo, pomodoro, lattuga e maionese; a diversi strati
cobbler crostata di frutta, ricoperta di pasta frolla
cock-a-leekie soup minestra di pollo e di porri
coconut noce di cocco
cod merluzzo
Colchester oyster la più pregiata ostrica inglese
cold cuts/meat affettati
coleslaw insalata di cavolo
compote composta, conserva
condiment condimento
consommé brodo ristretto
cooked cotto
cookie biscotto
corn 1) grano (GB) 2) granturco (US)
~ **on the cob** pannocchia di granturco
cornflakes fiocchi di granturco
corned beef carne di manzo in scatola
cottage cheese formaggio bianco, fresco
cottage pie carne tritata ricoperta di cipolle e purea di patate, il tutto passato al forno
course portata
cover charge coperto
crab granchio
cranberry varietà di mirtillo
~ **sauce** marmellata di mirtilli rossi, servita con carne e selvaggina
crawfish, crayfish 1) gambero di fiume 2) aragosta (GB) 3) scampo (US)
cream 1) crema, panna 2) dessert 3) zuppa densa
~ **cheese** formaggio doppia panna
~**puff** bignè
creamed potatoes patate tagliate a dadi, in besciamella
creole alla creola; piatto preparato con salsa di pomodoro molto

piccante, peperoni, cipolle e servito con riso
cress crescione
crisps patatine
croquette polpetta
crumpet panino leggero di forma rotonda, tostato e imburrato
cucumber cetriolo
Cumberland ham prosciutto inglese molto rinomato
Cumberland sauce gelatina di ribes, con vino, succo d'arancia e spezie
cupcake varietà di pasticcino
cured salato, affumicato, marinato (pesce o carne)
currant 1) uva sultanina 2) ribes
curried con curry
custard crema, sformato
cutlet cotoletta, scaloppina
dab genere di pesce, simile alla sogliola
Danish pastry pasticceria danese
date dattero
Derby cheese tipo di formaggio piccante
devilled alla diavola; condimento molto piccante
devil's food cake torta al cioccolato, molto sostanziosa
devils on horseback prugne secche cotte nel vino rosso e ripiene di mandorle e di acciughe, avvolte nella pancetta, passate alla griglia e servite su pane tostato
Devonshire cream crema cagliata
diced tagliato a dadi
diet food cibo dietetico
dill aneto
dinner cena
dish piatto
donut, doughnut frittella a forma di ciambella
double cream doppia panna, panna intera
Dover sole sogliola di Dover, molto rinomata
dressing 1) condimento per insalata 2) ripieno per tacchino (US)
Dublin Bay prawn scampo
duck anitra
duckling anatroccolo
dumpling gnocchetto di pasta, bollito
Dutch apple pie torta di mele, ricoperta da un impasto di burro e zucchero grezzo
éclair pasticcino glassato ripieno di crema
eel anguilla
egg uovo
  boiled ~ alla coque
  fried ~ al tegame
  hard-boiled ~ sodo
  poached ~ in camicia
  scrambled ~ strapazzato
  soft-boiled ~ molle
eggplant melanzana
endive 1) cicoria, insalata riccia (GB) 2) indivia (US)
entrecôte costata
entrée 1) antipasto (GB) 2) piatto principale (US)
escalope scaloppina
fennel finocchio
fig fico
fillet filetto di carne o di pesce
finnan haddock eglefino affumicato
fish pesce
  ~ **and chips** pesce fritto con contorno di patatine fritte
  ~ **cake** polpette di pesce
flan crostata alla frutta
flapjack frittella dolce e spessa
flounder passerino
forcemeat ripieno, farcia

fowl pollame
frankfurter wurstel
French bean fagiolino verde
French bread sfilatino (pane)
French dressing 1) condimento per insalata a base di olio e aceto (GB) 2) condimento per insalata un po' denso, con ketchup (US)
french fries patatine fritte
French toast fette di pane imbevute di uova battute e fritte in padella, servite con marmellata o zucchero
fresh fresco
fricassée fricassea
fried fritto
fritter frittella
frogs' legs cosce di rana
frosting glassa
fruit frutto
fry frittura
galantine galantina
game cacciagione
gammon prosciutto affumicato
garfish aguglia di mare, luccio
garlic aglio
garnish contorno
gherkin cetriolino
giblets rigaglie
ginger zenzero
goose oca
~**berry** uva spina
grape uva
~**fruit** pompelmo
grated grattugiato
gravy sugo a base di carne
grayling temolo
green bean fagiolino verde
green pepper peperone verde
green salad insalata verde
greens verdura
grilled alla griglia, ai ferri
grilse salmone giovane
grouse starna
gumbo 1) legume di origine africana 2) piatto creolo a base di *okra* con pomodori e carne o pesce
haddock eglefino
haggis frattaglie di pecora (o di vitello) tagliate a pezzetti e mescolate con fiocchi d'avena
hake baccalà
half mezzo, metà
halibut passera, pianuzza
ham prosciutto
~ **and eggs** uova con prosciutto
hamburger polpetta di carne di manzo tritata e cipolla, servita in un panino
hare lepre
haricot bean fagiolo
hash carne tritata o sminuzzata; piatto di carne sminuzzata, con patate e verdure
hazelnut nocciola
heart cuore
herb erbe, odori
herring aringa
home-made fatto in casa
hominy grits specie di polenta
honey miele
~**dew melon** melone molto dolce dalla polpa verde-gialla
hors-d'œuvre antipasto
horse-radish rafano
hot 1) caldo 2) piccante
~ **cross bun** brioche a forma di croce, con uvetta e ricoperta di una glassa (per la Quaresima)
~ **dog** wurstel caldo in un panino
huckleberry mirtillo
hush puppy frittella di farina di mais e di cipolle
ice-cream gelato
iced glassato, gelato

icing glassa
Idaho baked potato qualità di patata specialmente adatta per essere cotta al forno
Irish stew stufato di montone con cipolle e patate
Italian dressing condimento per insalata a base di olio e aceto
jam marmellata
jellied in gelatina
Jell-O dolce di gelatina
jelly gelatina
Jerusalem artichoke topinamburo
John Dory orata
jugged hare lepre in salmì
juice succo
juniper berry bacca di ginepro
junket latte cagliato zuccherato
kale cavolo ricciuto
kedgeree pesce sminuzzato, accompagnato da riso, uova e burro
kidney rognone
kipper aringa affumicata
lamb agnello
Lancashire hot pot stufato di cotolette e rognoni d'agnello, con patate e cipolle
larded lardellato
lean magro
leek porro
leg cosciotto, coscia
lemon limone
~ **sole** sogliola
lentil lenticchia
lettuce lattuga, lattuga cappuccina
lima bean specie di grossa fava
lime limoncino verde
liver fegato
loaf pagnotta
lobster astice
loin lombata
Long Island duck anitra di Long Island, molto rinomata
low-calorie povero in calorie
lox salmone affumicato
lunch pranzo
macaroon amaretto
macaroni maccheroni
mackerel sgombro
maize granturco, mais
mandarin mandarino
maple syrup sciroppo d'acero
marinade salsa di aceto e spezie
marinated marinato
marjoram maggiorana
marmalade marmellata d'arance
marrow midollo
~ **bone** osso con midollo
marshmallow caramella gelatinosa e gommosa
marzipan pasta di mandorle
mashed potatoes purea di patate
mayonnaise maionese
meal pasto
meat carne
~ **ball** polpetta di carne
~ **loaf** polpettone cotto al forno e servito a fette
~ **pâté** pasticcio di carne
medium (done) cotto a puntino
melon melone
melted fuso
Melton Mowbray pie pasticcio a base di carne
meringue meringa
milk latte
mince trito
~ **pie** dolce ripieno di frutta
minced tritato
~ **meat** carne tritata
mint menta
minute steak bistecca cotta velocemente a fuoco vivo da ambo le parti
mixed misto
~ **grill** spiedini con salsicce, fegatini, rognoni, cotolette e pan-

cetta, passati alla griglia
molasses melassa
morel spugnolo (fungo)
mousse 1) dolce o dessert a base di panna o albumi battuti 2) spuma leggera di carne o di pesce
mulberry mora
mullet triglia, muggine
mulligatawny soup minestra di pollo, molto piccante, di origine indiana
mushroom fungo
muskmelon varietà di melone
mussel mitilo, cozza
mustard mostarda, senape
mutton montone
noodle taglierini
nut noce
oatmeal (porridge) pappa d'avena
oil olio
okra baccelli di *gumbo* utilizzati per rendere dense zuppe, minestre e stufati
olive oliva
omelet frittata
onion cipolla
orange arancia
ox tongue lingua di bue
oxtail coda di bue
oyster ostrica
pancake frittella
paprika paprica
Parmesan (cheese) parmigiano
parsley prezzemolo
parsnip pastinaca
partridge pernice
pastry pasta, pasticcino
pasty polpetta, pasticcio
pea pisello
peach pesca
peanut arachide
~ **butter** burro di arachidi
pear pera
pearl barley orzo perlato
pepper pepe
~ **mint** menta piperita
perch pesce persico
persimmon kaki
pheasant fagiano
pickerel piccolo luccio
pickle 1) sottaceto 2) negli US si riferisce solo al cetriolino
pickled sott'aceto
pie pasticcio o torta, spesso ricoperta da uno strato di pasta, ripiena di carne, verdura, frutta o crema alla vaniglia
pig maiale
pigeon piccione
pike luccio
pineapple ananas
plaice passerino, pianuzza
plain liscio, al naturale
plate piatto
plum susina, prugna
~ **pudding** budino a base di frutta candita, scorza di limone, cedro; a volte alla fiamma
poached in camicia, affogato
popover piccolo dolce di pasta farcito alla frutta
pork maiale
porridge pappa di fiocchi d'avena o preparata con farina di altri cereali
porterhouse steak equivalente di bistecca alla fiorentina
pot roast arrosto brasato
potato patata
~ **chips** 1) patatine fritte (GB) 2) patatine (US)
~ **in its jacket** patata cotta con la buccia
potted shrimps gamberetti serviti in piccoli stampi con burro fuso aromatizzato
poultry pollame
prawn gambero

prune prugna secca
ptarmigan pernice delle nevi
pudding budino, sformato
pumpernickel pane di segale integrale
pumpkin zucca
quail quaglia
quince mela cotogna
rabbit coniglio
radish ravanello
rainbow trout trota fario
raisin uva passa
rare poco cotto, al sangue
raspberry lampone
raw crudo
red mullet triglia
red (sweet) pepper peperone rosso
redcurrant ribes rosso
relish condimento a base di verdura sott'aceto sminuzzata
rhubarb rabarbaro
rib (of beef) costola di manzo
rib-eye-steak grossa bistecca
rice riso
rissole polpetta di carne o di pesce avvolta in pasta frolla
river trout trota di torrente
roast(ed) arrosto
Rock Cornish hen galletto specialmente adatto per essere preparato arrosto
roe uova di pesce
roll panino
rollmop herring filetto di aringa, arrotolato attorno a un cetriolo, marinato nel vino bianco
round steak girello di manzo
Rubens sandwich carne tritata su toast, con crauti, emmental, condimento per insalata; servita calda
rump steak bistecca di girello
rusk pane biscottato
rye bread pane di segale
saddle la parte del dorso di un animale macellato
saffron zafferano
sage salvia
salad insalata
~ **bar** vasta scelta di insalate
~ **cream** condimento per insalata a base di panna, leggermente dolce
~ **dressing** condimento per insalata
salami salame
salmon salmone
~ **trout** trota salmonata
salt sale
salted salato
sardine sardina
sauce salsa, sugo
sauerkraut crauti
sausage salsiccia
sauté(ed) rosolato, fritto in padella
scallop 1) conchiglia S. Giacomo 2) scaloppina di vitello
scone focaccia di pasta leggera a base di farina d'avena o d'orzo
Scotch broth brodo di manzo o di agnello con verdure sminuzzate
Scotch woodcock crostino coperto di uova strapazzate e acciughe
sea bass spigola
sea kale cavolo di mare
seafood frutti di mare, pesce
(in) season (di) stagione
seasoning condimento
service servizio
~ **charge** prezzo del servizio
~ **(not) included** servizio (non) compreso
set menu menù a prezzo fisso
shad alosa, salacca (genere di sardina)
shallot scalogno
shellfish crostaceo
sherbet sorbetto

shoulder spalla
shredded wheat fiocchi d'avena serviti a colazione
shrimp gamberetto
silverside (of beef) controgirello
sirloin steak bistecca di lombo di manzo
skewer spiedino
slice fetta
sliced a fette
sloppy Joe carne di manzo tritata con salsa di pomodoro piccante, servita in un panino
smelt eperlano
smoked affumicato
snack spuntino
sole sogliola
soup minestra, zuppa
sour agro, acido
soused herring aringa marinata in aceto e spezie
spare rib costola di maiale o manzo
spice spezia
spinach spinacio
spiny lobster aragosta
(on a) spit (allo) spiedo
sponge cake pan di Spagna
sprat spratto (piccola aringa)
squash zucca
starter antipasto
steak and kidney pie stufato di manzo e rognoni, coperto di pasta
steamed cotto a vapore
stew stufato, in umido
Stilton (cheese) uno dei più rinomati formaggi inglesi a venatura blu
strawberry fragola
string bean fagiolino
stuffed ripieno, farcito
stuffing ripieno, farcia
suck(l)ing pig maialino da latte
sugar zucchero
sugarless senza zucchero
sundae varietà di cassata con noci, crema e talora sciroppo
supper cena
swede specie di rapa
sweet dolce, torta
~ **corn** granturco bianco
~ **potato** patata dolce
sweetbread animella
Swiss cheese emmental
Swiss roll brioche alla crema o marmellata
Swiss steak fetta di manzo brasata con legumi e spezie
T-bone steak bistecca di manzo formata dal filetto e dal controfiletto separati da un'osso a forma di T
table d'hôte menù a prezzo fisso
tangerine specie di mandarino
tarragon dragoncello, estragone
tart torta di frutta
tenderloin filetto di carne
Thousand Island dressing condimento per insalata a base di maionese, peperoni, olive e uova sode
thyme timo
toad-in-the-hole carne di manzo o salsiccia avvolta in pasta e cotta al forno
toasted tostato
~ **cheese** crostino spalmato di formaggio fuso
tomato pomodoro
tongue lingua
tournedos medaglione di filetto
treacle melassa
trifle genere di zuppa inglese; charlotte allo sherry o al brandy con mandorle, marmellata e panna montata
tripe trippa

trout trota
truffle tartufo
tuna, tunny tonno
turbot rombo
turkey tacchino
turnip rapa
turnover calzone ripieno
turtle tartaruga
underdone poco cotto, al sangue
vanilla vaniglia
veal vitello
~ **bird** involtino di vitello
~ **escalope** scaloppina di vitello
vegetable verdura
~ **marrow** zucchino
venison cacciagione, capriolo
vichyssoise zuppa fredda a base di panna, patate e porri
vinegar aceto
Virginia baked ham prosciutto americano, steccato con chiodi di garofano, cotto al forno e decorato con fette di ananas, ciliege e glassato con lo sciroppo di questi frutti
vol-au-vent pasticcino di pasta sfoglia ripieno di carne o altro intingolo
wafer cialda
waffle sorta di cialda calda
walnut noce
water ice sorbetto
watercress crescione
watermelon cocomero, anguria
well-done ben cotto
Welsh rabbit/rarebit formaggio fuso su un toast
whelk buccina (mollusco)
whipped cream panna montata
whitebait bianchetti
Wiener schnitzel scaloppina impanata
wine list lista dei vini
woodcock beccaccia
Worcestershire sauce salsa piccante a base di aceto e soia
York ham uno dei più rinomati prosciutti inglesi, servito a fette sottili
Yorkshire pudding sformato a base di farina, latte e uova cotto con sugo di manzo; si mangia col rosbif
zwieback fettine di pane biscottato

Bevande

ale birra scura, leggermente dolce, fermentata ad alta temperatura
bitter ~ scura, amara e forte
brown ~ scura in bottiglia, leggermente dolce
light ~ chiara in bottiglia
mild ~ scura alla spina, dal gusto spiccato
pale ~ chiara in bottiglia
applejack acquavite di mele
Athol Brose bevanda scozzese composta da whisky, mele e talora fiocchi di avena
Bacardi cocktail cocktail al rum e

al gin, con sciroppo di melagrana e succo di limone verde
barley water bibita rinfrescante a base di orzo e aromatizzata con limone
barley wine birra scura a forte gradazione alcoolica
beer birra
bottled ~ in bottiglia
draft, draught ~ alla spina
black velvet champagne con *stout* (servito spesso con le ostriche)
bloody Mary vodka con succo di pomodoro e spezie
bourbon whisky americano, distillato soprattutto dal granturco
brandy 1) appellazione generica dell'acquavite distillata dall'uva o da altra frutta 2) cognac
~ Alexander acquavite, crema di cacao e panna
British wines vini fatti con uva (o succo d'uva) importata in Gran Bretagna
cherry brandy liquore di ciliege
chocolate latte al cacao
cider sidro
~ cup miscuglio di sidro, spezie, zucchero e ghiaccio
claret vino rosso di Bordeaux
cobbler *long drink* ghiacciato, a base di frutta, al quale si aggiunge vino o altra bevanda alcoolica
coffee caffè
~ with cream con panna
black ~ nero
caffeine-free ~ decaffeinato
white ~ con latte
cordial cordiale
cream panna
cup bevanda rinfrescante composta da vino molto freddo, seltz, liquore, e guarnita con una fetta di limone, di arancia o di cetriolo
daiquiri bevanda composta da rum, succo di limone verde e di ananasso
double doppia quantità
Drambuie liquore fatto da whisky e miele
dry martini 1) vermuth secco (GB) 2) cocktail al gin con un po' di vermuth secco (US)
egg-nog bevanda preparata con rum e altro liquore forte, tuorli battuti e zucchero
gin and it gin e vermut italiano
gin-fizz bevanda composta da gin, zucchero, succo di limone e soda
ginger ale bevanda non alcoolica allo zenzero
ginger beer bevanda leggermente alcoolica a base di zenzero e zucchero
grasshopper bevanda composta da crema di menta, crema di cacao e panna
Guinness (stout) birra molto scura e dal gusto dolciastro, ad alta gradazione di malto e luppolo
half pint misura di capacità: circa 0,3 litri
highball whisky o altri superalcoolici con acqua gasata o con *ginger ale*
iced ghiacciato
Irish coffee caffè con zucchero, un po' di whisky irlandese e ricoperto di panna montata
Irish Mist liquore irlandese a base di whisky e miele
Irish whiskey whisky irlandese, più secco dello *scotch*, fatto non solo da orzo ma anche da segale, avena e grano

juice succo
lager birra chiara e leggera, servita molto fredda
lemon squash succo di limone
lemonade limonata
lime juice succo di limoncini verdi
liqueur liquore
liquor bevanda molto alcoolica
long drink bevanda alcoolica allungata con acqua o acqua tonica e ghiaccio
madeira madera
Manhattan bevanda a base di whisky americano, vermut secco e angostura
milk latte
  ~ **shake** frappè
mineral water acqua minerale
mulled wine vin brûlé; vino caldo con spezie
neat liscio
old-fashioned bevanda a base di whisky, zucchero, angostura e ciliege al maraschino
on the rocks con cubetti di ghiaccio
Ovaltine Ovomaltina
Pimm's cup(s) bevanda alcoolica con aggiunta di succo di frutta e talvolta seltz
  ~ **No. 1** a base di gin
  ~ **No. 2** a base di whisky
  ~ **No. 3** a base di rum
  ~ **No. 4** a base di acquavite
pink champagne champagne rosé
pink lady cocktail composto da albumi, calvados, succo di limone, succo di melagrana e gin
pint misura di capacità: circa 0,6 litri
port (wine) porto
porter birra scura e amara
quart misura di capacità: 1,14 litri (US 0,95 litri)
root beer bevanda gasata e analcoolica dolce, ricavata da erbe e radici varie
rye (whiskey) whisky di segale, più forte e più aspro del *bourbon*
scotch (whisky) miscuglio di whisky di grano e d'orzo
screwdriver vodka e succo d'arancia
shandy *bitter ale* con l'aggiunta di limonata o di *ginger beer*
sherry xeres
short drink bevanda alcoolica liscia
shot piccola dose di whisky o di altro liquore
sloe gin-fizz liquore di prugnola con soda e succo di limone
soda water acqua gasata, seltz
soft drink bevanda analcoolica
spirits bevande molto alcooliche
stinger cognac e crema di menta
stout birra scura, aromatizzata fortemente con il luppolo
straight liscio
tea tè
toddy grog, ponce
Tom Collins bevanda a base di gin, succo di limone, acqua di seltz e zucchero
tonic (water) acqua brillante, acqua tonica
water acqua
whisky sour bevanda a base di whisky, succo di limone, zucchero e soda
wine vino
  dry ~ secco
  red ~ rosso
  rosé ~ rosato, rosatello
  sparkling ~ spumante
  sweet ~ dolce
  white ~ bianco

Verbi irregolari inglesi

Vi elenchiamo qui di seguito i verbi irregolari inglesi. I verbi composti o quelli con prefisso si coniugano come i verbi semplici, es. *mistake* e *overdrive* si coniugano come *take* e *drive*.

Infinito	*Passato remoto*	*Participio passato*	
arise	arose	arisen	*alzare*
awake	awoke	awoken	*svegliare*
be	was	been	*essere*
bear	bore	borne	*portare*
beat	beat	beaten	*battere*
become	became	become	*diventare*
begin	began	begun	*cominciare*
bend	bent	bent	*curvare*
bet	bet	bet	*scommettere*
bid	bade/bid	bidden/bid	*comandare*
bind	bound	bound	*legare*
bite	bit	bitten	*mordere*
bleed	bled	bled	*sanguinare*
blow	blew	blown	*soffiare*
break	broke	broken	*rompere*
breed	bred	bred	*allevare*
bring	brought	brought	*portare*
build	built	built	*costruire*
burn	burnt/burned	burnt/burned	*bruciare*
burst	burst	burst	*scoppiare*
buy	bought	bought	*comprare*
can*	could	—	*potere*
cast	cast	cast	*gettare*
catch	caught	caught	*afferrare*
choose	chose	chosen	*scegliere*
cling	clung	clung	*aderire*
clothe	clothed/clad	clothed/clad	*vestire*
come	came	come	*venire*
cost	cost	cost	*costare*
creep	crept	crept	*strisciare*
cut	cut	cut	*tagliare*
deal	dealt	dealt	*trattare*
dig	dug	dug	*scavare*
do (he does)	did	done	*fare*
draw	drew	drawn	*tirare*
dream	dreamt/dreamed	dreamt/dreamed	*sognare*
drink	drank	drunk	*bere*
drive	drove	driven	*guidare*
dwell	dwelt	dwelt	*abitare*
eat	ate	eaten	*mangiare*
fall	fell	fallen	*cadere*

* indicativo presente

feed	fed	fed	*nutrire*
feel	felt	felt	*sentire*
fight	fought	fought	*combattere*
find	found	found	*trovare*
flee	fled	fled	*fuggire*
fling	flung	flung	*gettare*
fly	flew	flown	*volare*
forsake	forsook	forsaken	*abbandonare*
freeze	froze	frozen	*gelare*
get	got	got	*ottenere*
give	gave	given	*dare*
go	went	gone	*andare*
grind	ground	ground	*macinare*
grow	grew	grown	*crescere*
hang	hung	hung	*appendere*
have	had	had	*avere*
hear	heard	heard	*udire*
hew	hewed	hewed/hewn	*spaccare*
hide	hid	hidden	*nascondere*
hit	hit	hit	*colpire*
hold	held	held	*tenere*
hurt	hurt	hurt	*dolere*
keep	kept	kept	*tenere*
kneel	knelt	knelt	*inginocchiarsi*
knit	knitted/knit	knitted/knit	*congiungere*
know	knew	known	*conoscere*
lay	laid	laid	*posare*
lead	led	led	*dirigere*
lean	leant/leaned	leant/leaned	*inclinare*
leap	leapt/leaped	leapt/leaped	*balzare*
learn	learnt/learned	learnt/learned	*imparare*
leave	left	left	*lasciare*
lend	lent	lent	*prestare*
let	let	let	*permettere*
lie	lay	lain	*giacere*
light	lit/lighted	lit/lighted	*accendere*
lose	lost	lost	*perdere*
make	made	made	*fare*
may*	might	—	*potere*
mean	meant	meant	*significare*
meet	met	met	*incontrare*
mow	mowed	mowed/mown	*falciare*
must*	—	—	*dovere*
ought (to)*	—	—	*dovere*
pay	paid	paid	*pagare*
put	put	put	*mettere*
read	read	read	*leggere*
rid	rid	rid	*sbarazzare*
ride	rode	ridden	*cavalcare*

* indicativo presente

ring	rang	rung	*suonare*
rise	rose	risen	*sorgere*
run	ran	run	*correre*
saw	sawed	sawn	*segare*
say	said	said	*dire*
see	saw	seen	*vedere*
seek	sought	sought	*cercare*
sell	sold	sold	*vendere*
send	sent	sent	*mandare*
set	set	set	*mettere*
sew	sewed	sewed/sewn	*cucire*
shake	shook	shaken	*scuotere*
shall*	should	—	*dovere*
shed	shed	shed	*spandere*
shine	shone	shone	*splendere*
shoot	shot	shot	*sparare*
show	showed	shown	*mostrare*
shrink	shrank	shrunk	*restringere*
shut	shut	shut	*chiudere*
sing	sang	sung	*cantare*
sink	sank	sunk	*affondare*
sit	sat	sat	*sedere*
sleep	slept	slept	*dormire*
slide	slid	slid	*scivolare*
sling	slung	slung	*scagliare*
slink	slunk	slunk	*sgattaiolare*
slit	slit	slit	*fendere*
smell	smelled/smelt	smelled/smelt	*fiutare*
sow	sowed	sown/sowed	*seminare*
speak	spoke	spoken	*parlare*
speed	sped/speeded	sped/speeded	*affrettarsi*
spell	spelt/spelled	spelt/spelled	*compitare*
spend	spent	spent	*spendere*
spill	spilt/spilled	spilt/spilled	*versare*
spin	spun	spun	*(far) girare*
spit	spat	spat	*sputare*
split	split	split	*spaccare*
spoil	spoilt/spoiled	spoilt/spoiled	*viziare*
spread	spread	spread	*spargere*
spring	sprang	sprung	*scattare*
stand	stood	stood	*stare in piedi*
steal	stole	stolen	*rubare*
stick	stuck	stuck	*ficcare*
sting	stung	stung	*pungere*
stink	stank/stunk	stunk	*puzzare*
strew	strewed	strewed/strewn	*spargere*
stride	strode	stridden	*camminare a grandi passi*
strike	struck	struck/stricken	*percuotere*

* indicativo presente

string	strung	strung	*legare*
strive	strove	striven	*sforzarsi*
swear	swore	sworn	*giurare*
sweep	swept	swept	*scopare*
swell	swelled	swollen	*gonfiare*
swim	swam	swum	*nuotare*
swing	swung	swung	*dondolare*
take	took	taken	*prendere*
teach	taught	taught	*insegnare*
tear	tore	torn	*stracciare*
tell	told	told	*dire*
think	thought	thought	*pensare*
throw	threw	thrown	*gettare*
thrust	thrust	thrust	*spingere*
tread	trod	trodden	*calpestare*
wake	woke/waked	woken/waked	*svegliare*
wear	wore	worn	*indossare*
weave	wove	woven	*tessere*
weep	wept	wept	*piangere*
will*	would	—	*volere*
win	won	won	*vincere*
wind	wound	wound	*avvolgere*
wring	wrung	wrung	*torcere*
write	wrote	written	*scrivere*

* indicativo presente

Abbreviazioni inglesi

AA	*Automobile Association*	Automobile Club Britannico
AAA	*American Automobile Association*	Automobile Club Americano
ABC	*American Broadcasting Company*	società privata radiotelevisiva americana
A.D.	*anno Domini*	A.D.
Am.	*America; American*	America; americano
a.m.	*ante meridiem (before noon)*	di mattina (00.00–12.00)
Amtrak	*American railroad corporation*	società di ferrovie americana
AT & T	*American Telephone and Telegraph Company*	società americana dei telefoni e telegrafi
Ave.	*avenue*	viale
BBC	*British Broadcasting Corporation*	Radio-Televisione Britannica
B.C.	*before Christ*	a.C.
bldg.	*building*	edificio
Blvd.	*boulevard*	viale
B.R.	*British Rail*	ferrovie britanniche
Brit.	*Britain; British*	Gran Bretagna; britannico
Bros.	*brothers*	fratelli
¢	*cent*	1/100 di dollaro
Can.	*Canada; Canadian*	Canada; canadese
CBS	*Columbia Broadcasting System*	società privata radiotelevisiva americana
CID	*Criminal Investigation Department*	polizia giudiziaria britannica
CNR	*Canadian National Railway*	ferrovie nazionali canadesi
c/o	*(in) care of*	presso (negli indirizzi)
Co.	*company*	compagnia
Corp.	*corporation*	tipo di società
CPR	*Canadian Pacific Railways*	società di ferrovie canadesi
D.C.	*District of Columbia*	Distretto Federale della Columbia (Washington, D.C.)
DDS	*Doctor of Dental Science*	dentista
dept.	*department*	reparto, sezione
EEC	*European Economic Community*	C.E.E., Comunità Economica Europea
e.g.	*for instance*	per esempio

Eng.	*England; English*	Inghilterra; inglese
excl.	*excluding; exclusive*	esclusivo, non compreso
ft.	*foot/feet*	piede/piedi
GB	*Great Britain*	Gran Bretagna
H.E.	*His/Her Excellency; His Eminence*	Sua Eccellenza; Sua Eminenza
H.H.	*His Holiness*	Sua Santità
H.M.	*His/Her Majesty*	Sua Maestà
H.M.S.	*Her Majesty's ship*	nave della marina reale inglese
hp	*horsepower*	cavallo (vapore)
Hwy	*highway*	strada a grande scorrimento
i.e.	*that is to say*	cioè
in.	*inch*	pollice (2,54 cm)
Inc.	*incorporated*	tipo di società anonima americana
incl.	*including, inclusive*	inclusivo, compreso
£	*pound sterling*	lira sterlina
L.A.	*Los Angeles*	Los Angeles
Ltd.	*limited*	società anonima
M.D.	*Doctor of Medicine*	Dottore in Medicina
M.P.	*Member of Parliament*	deputato
mph	*miles per hour*	miglia all'ora
Mr.	*Mister*	Signor
Mrs.	*Missis*	Signora
Ms.	*Missis/Miss*	Signora/Signorina
nat.	*national*	nazionale
NBC	*National Broadcasting Company*	società privata radio-televisiva americana
No.	*number*	numero
N.Y.C.	*New York City*	città di New York
O.B.E.	*Officer (of the Order) of the British Empire*	Ufficiale (dell'Ordine) dell'Impero Britannico
p.	*page; penny/pence*	pagina; 1/100 di lira sterlina
p.a.	*per annum*	per anno
Ph.D.	*Doctor of Philosophy*	Dottore in Filosofia
p.m.	*post meridiem (after noon)*	del pomeriggio o della sera (12.00–24.00)
PO	*Post Office*	ufficio postale
POO	*post office order*	mandato postale
pop.	*population*	abitanti
P.T.O.	*please turn over*	vedi retro
RAC	*Royal Automobile Club*	Real Automobile Club Inglese

RCMP	*Royal Canadian Mounted Police*	polizia reale canadese a cavallo
Rd.	*road*	strada
ref.	*reference*	riferimento
Rev.	*reverend*	reverendo della chiesa anglicana
RFD	*rural free delivery*	distribuzione della posta in campagna
RR	*railroad*	ferrovia
RSVP	*please reply*	si prega rispondere
$	*dollar*	dollaro
Soc.	*society*	società
St.	*saint ; street*	santo; strada
STD	*Subscriber Trunk Dialling*	telefono automatico
UN	*United Nations*	N.U., Nazioni Unite
UPS	*United Parcel Service*	servizio spedizione pacchi americano
US	*United States*	Stati Uniti
USS	*United States Ship*	nave della marina americana
VAT	*value added tax*	I.V.A.
VIP	*very important person*	V.I.P., persona molto importante
Xmas	*Christmas*	Natale
yd.	*yard*	iarda (91,44 cm)
YMCA	*Young Men's Christian Association*	A.C.D.G.
YWCA	*Young Women's Christian Association*	U.C.D.G.
ZIP	*ZIP code*	codice di avviamento postale

Numeri

Numeri cardinali

0 zero
1 one
2 two
3 three
4 four
5 five
6 six
7 seven
8 eight
9 nine
10 ten
11 eleven
12 twelve
13 thirteen
14 fourteen
15 fifteen
16 sixteen
17 seventeen
18 eighteen
19 nineteen
20 twenty
21 twenty-one
22 twenty-two
23 twenty-three
24 twenty-four
25 twenty-five
30 thirty
40 forty
50 fifty
60 sixty
70 seventy
80 eighty
90 ninety
100 a/one hundred
230 two hundred and thirty
1,000 a/one thousand
10,000 ten thousand
100,000 a/one hundred thousand
1,000,000 a/one million

Numeri ordinali

1st first
2nd second
3rd third
4th fourth
5th fifth
6th sixth
7th seventh
8th eighth
9th ninth
10th tenth
11th eleventh
12th twelfth
13th thirteenth
14th fourteenth
15th fifteenth
16th sixteenth
17th seventeenth
18th eighteenth
19th nineteenth
20th twentieth
21st twenty-first
22nd twenty-second
23rd twenty-third
24th twenty-fourth
25th twenty-fifth
26th twenty-sixth
27th twenty-seventh
28th twenty-eighth
29th twenty-ninth
30th thirtieth
40th fortieth
50th fiftieth
60th sixtieth
70th seventieth
80th eightieth
90th ninetieth
100th hundredth
230th two hundred and thirtieth
1,000th thousandth

L'ora

I Britannici e gli Americani usano il sistema di dodici ore. L'espressione *a.m. (ante meridiem)* indica le ore che precedono mezzogiorno e *p.m. (post meridiem)* quelle fino a mezzanotte. Tuttavia in Inghilterra gli orari sono di più in più indicati alla maniera continentale.

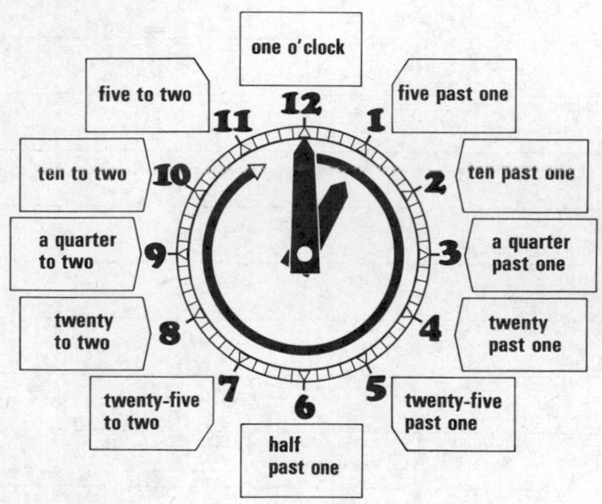

I'll come at seven a.m.	Verrò alle 7 (del mattino).
I'll come at two p.m.	Verrò alle 2 (del pomeriggio).
I'll come at eight p.m.	Verrò alle 8 (di sera).

I giorni della settimana

Sunday	domenica	*Thursday*	giovedi
Monday	lunedì	*Friday*	venerdì
Tuesday	martedì	*Saturday*	sabato
Wednesday	mercoledì		

Notes

Notes

Notes

Appunti

Appunti

Appunti